The Dark Side of Paradise

Asia East by South

A series published under the auspices of
the Southeast Asia Program, Cornell University

A list of titles in the series appears at the end of the book.

THE DARK SIDE
OF PARADISE

Political Violence in Bali

GEOFFREY ROBINSON

Cornell University Press

ITHACA AND LONDON

Publication of this book has been supported by a grant from the National Endowment for the Humanities, an independent federal agency.

First published 1995 by Cornell University Press.

Printed in the United States of America

♾ The paper in this book meets the minimum requirements of the American National Standard for Information Sciences—Permanence of Paper for Printed Library Materials, ANSI X39.48-1984.

Library of Congress Cataloging-in-Publication Data

Robinson, Geoffrey, 1957–
   The dark side of paradise : political violence in Bali / Geoffrey Robinson.
      p.   cm. — (Asia, east by south)
   Includes bibliographical references and index.
   ISBN 0-8014-2965-X
   1. Bali Island (Indonesia)—Politics and government.   2. Violence—Indonesia—Bali Island.   I. Title.   II. Series.
DS647.B2R63   1995
959.8′6—dc20   95-9754

1000845489 T

For Lovisa

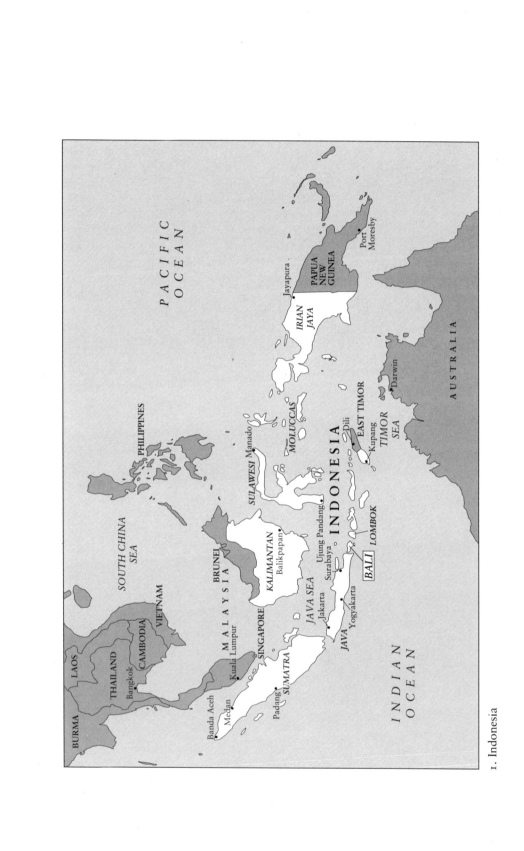

1. Indonesia

Contents

Illustrations

TABLES

MAPS

Preface

W HEN I FIRST VISITED BALI IN 1978 I was, like most outsiders, deeply impressed by its physical beauty and by the richness of its culture. Unaware of how many others had had the same thought, I also imagined that the Balinese had discovered a uniquely peaceful and harmonious way of life; and I held to this belief even when I saw and recorded evidence to the contrary. On 18 April 1978 I wrote in my diary:

> As we walked through Ubud we were overwhelmed by the number of armed men who hovered about. Apparently six or seven people have been murdered by these local paramilitaries. These have all occurred in Kuta, but there is a real fear that the trouble-makers (Javanese according to the Balinese) will soon be in Ubud to terrorize residents and tourists alike. There is nothing light-hearted about it at all. Even Ketut, who's about 14, was out most of the night with a large club. Other men carry sickles, axes, spears etc. Something very serious may be in the offing. There is a sense of excitement on the part of the men of the night-squads. A certain gruesome glee which they derive from the involvement (or potential involvement) in violence.

This event should have told me that everything was not as beautiful and harmonious as it seemed. But I was under Bali's spell. In the following days I made no further reference in my diary to violence or paramilitaries. Despite the evidence, I managed to preserve my image of Bali and to forget what I had seen. So complete was my amnesia that when, in 1985, I set out to research political violence in Indonesia in the 1950s, I decided to focus on the rebellions in Sulawesi and Sumatra, and to look at Bali only as a place that for some reason had escaped such political troubles. I hoped to discover why rebel movements had emerged in some parts of Indonesia but not in others.

At the outset I was confronted by two perplexing problems. The first was that I could not find a single book or article that set out clearly what had actually happened in Bali in the previous century or so. Frustration gave way to puzzlement. Why, I wondered, had no one bothered to write a political history of this extraordinary place? The second problem was that the available sources made it clear that Bali had suffered an unusually turbulent and bloody history. It was a picture that fitted very poorly with the pleasing and romantic image of Bali with which I was familiar.

After spending some time examining the colonial archives in the Netherlands and conducting field work in Bali, I shifted my focus to the political history of modern Bali, paying particular attention to the periods and issues that I had found so conspicuously absent in the available literature. At the same time I hoped to trace the origins of the romantic image of Bali and to examine its political implications.

Those aims have, to a great extent, determined this book's shape. Whenever I have had to choose, I have opted for historical richness and accuracy over theoretical elegance, for so little is known about what actually happened in Bali, who the principal characters were, and so on. Still, I have also addressed broader questions and have allowed myself to be guided by analytical approaches that I thought might be helpful in doing so. Earlier investigators have either ignored the periods of political violence in Bali or portrayed them as historical aberrations from an ostensible norm of social and political harmony. In contrast, I show that violence and conflict are integral parts of Balinese history. I have also provided an extended historiographical critique of prevailing scholarly, popular, and government discourse about Balinese history and politics. I have paid particular attention to the tradition that views Balinese society as essentially harmonious and apolitical and explains Bali's politics and history principally in terms of presumed features of its culture and religion.

Owing to the scarcity of secondary sources on the modern political history of Bali, this book is based primarily on archival sources, interviews, unpublished theses—mostly in Indonesian—and accounts from Indonesian-language national and local media. The materials available on the colonial and revolutionary periods are plentiful, but sources on the Japanese period are extremely limited, in part because much was destroyed in advance of the arrival of Allied forces in 1946. The disappearance of vast quantities of documents in the aftermath of 1965 and the tragic deaths of tens of thousands of suspected communists make the period 1950–65 especially difficult to document. The problem is compounded by the fact that it is still a serious crime in Indonesia to have any link with the Communist party, so that few people wish to discuss the period openly, still less to admit any deep knowledge of the party.

I was fortunate in gaining access to a substantial number of official Dutch and Indonesian archives—some of them only recently opened to the public—both from the period of the Revolution and from the prewar years. These archives contain detailed political, military, and economic reports from Bali, as well as documents captured from the Balinese resistance in 1946–49. In Indonesia and in the Netherlands, I was also given generous access to private collections containing materials from the colonial, Japanese, and revolutionary eras. Interviews conducted in Bali, Java, and the Netherlands over the course of two years contributed substantially to my understanding of events and were indispensable in the interpretation of the archival evidence. The people interviewed included dozens of Balinese and many former Dutch colonial officials and military officers who had served in Bali. All interviews cited were conducted by me unless I indicate otherwise. I have supplemented the information obtained from interviews and archives with accounts from national Indonesian newspapers and local Balinese papers and magazines published between the 1920s and the 1960s.

In writing this book I have accumulated substantial debts of gratitude. I first thank George Kahin, Benedict Anderson, and Vivienne Shue of Cornell University for their rigorous criticism. Ben Anderson has taught me a good deal of what I know about Indonesia, but his greatest contribution has been in reminding me of what I did not know or had too readily forgotten. Vivienne Shue provided valuable comparative comment on earlier drafts of this book and encouraged me to make it more accessible to a wider audience. A very special debt of gratitude is due to George Kahin, who from the day of our first meeting in 1980 has been a source of inspiration and personal support. Without his encouragement and his example of scholarly excellence and intellectual integrity, this book would not have seen the light of day. Through their friendship and their generosity, he and Audrey Kahin have helped me over many hurdles along the way. I also owe a great intellectual debt to many teachers and friends, including Daniel Lev, Ruth McVey, the late Milton Barnett, John Wolff, Alexander Woodside, David Marr, Diane Mauzy, Stephen Milne, and the late John Holmes. In their own ways they have helped to shape and to enrich my appreciation not only of Southeast Asia but also of history and politics generally.

Though I disagree with much that has been written about modern Balinese history and politics, my own work could scarcely have begun had it not been for the rich body of scholarship about Bali. I was fortunate to meet several students of Balinese history and culture in the Netherlands in 1985. In the early days, Henk Schulte Nordholt, Tessel Pollman, and Margaret Wiener helped me to navigate the waters of popular and scholarly discourse about Bali, and later they generously shared their ideas and their notes on subjects of mutual interest. To the former Dutch colonial officials who found time to speak to me about their experiences, I offer my sincere thanks and my hope that the history I have written does not diverge too dramatically from the events they remember.

The politically sensitive subject matter of this work makes it inadvisable for me to mention by name the people in Bali and other parts of Indonesia who have helped me in so many ways over the years. I trust that they will accept this general expression of my deepest thanks for their generosity of spirit and for tolerating yet another foreign researcher in their midst. I hope, too, that they will not feel that I have done much injustice to their history.

I also express my appreciation to the organizations and institutions that have assisted me in this research. Financial support from the Social Sciences and Humanities Research Council of Canada and from Cornell University's Southeast Asia Program, Department of Government, and Graduate School sustained me in both hemispheres. A Killam Postdoctoral Fellowship at the University of British Columbia allowed me to make crucial final changes to this book, and a grant from the National Endowment for the Humanities helped to cover the publication costs.

A version of Chapter 5 appeared as "State, Society, and Political Conflict in Bali, 1945–1946" in *Indonesia* 45 (April 1988): 1–48. A version of Chapter 10 appeared as "The Economic Foundations of Political Conflict in Bali, 1950–1965" in *Indonesia* 54 (October 1992): 59–93. I thank Cornell University's Southeast Asia Program Publications for permission to use this material here.

In the Netherlands, the professionalism and courtesy of the archivists and staff at the Algemeen Rijksarchief, the Centraal Archievendepot of the Ministerie van Defensie, the Sectie Militaire Geschiedenis, the Rijksinstituut voor Oorlogs Documentatie, the Hendrik Kraemer Instituut, and the Koninklijk Instituut voor Taal-, Land-, en Volkenkunde made the use of their vast archival sources both rewarding and enjoyable. In Indonesia, special thanks are due to the helpful staff members at the National Library (Perpustakaan Nasional), the National Archives (Arsip Nasional), the Center for Military History (Pusat Sejarah ABRI), the archives of the *Bali Post* in Denpasar, the Gedung Kirtya-Liefrinck in Singaraja, the office of the Governor of Bali, and a variety of other government offices at the subprovincial level. Without their help, it is unlikely that this project could ever have been properly completed. I also thank the Indonesian Academy of Sciences (LIPI) and other official bodies in Indonesia for permission to pursue this research in Indonesia from 1985 to 1987.

To my colleagues at the Research Department of Amnesty International in London I offer my sincere thanks, and also an apology for the times when, because of my preoccupation with finishing this book, they were saddled with an unfair share of the burden. For their friendship and for more than the odd cup of coffee over the years, I thank Carol Grumbach, Michael Cohen, Kamala Soedjatmoko, William Sunderlin, Thaveeporn Vasavakul, David Baldwin, Donna Amoroso, Jojo Abinales, Vincent Boudreau, Myo Myint, Saya Shiraishi, Ben Abel, Dolina Millar, and other members of the

102 West Avenue and 640 Stewart Avenue gangs. Special thanks are also due to friends who made me feel at home in the Netherlands, including Mevrouw Dubois-Raupp, Doris Classen, Steven Tabor, and Anneke De-Lorm.

I am most deeply indebted to my parents, to my family, and to my wife, Lovisa, for reasons that are too obvious to mention.

GEOFFREY ROBINSON

London

A Note on Spelling
and Translation

IN GRAPPLING WITH THE PROBLEM of variation and change in Indonesian spellings I have opted for simplicity and consistency, while trying to maintain historical accuracy. I have spelled the names of people and institutions consistently throughout the book, generally using the simpler modern spellings rather than the older ones: *u*, not *oe*; *j*, not *dj*; *y*, not *j*; and *c*, not *tj*. The only exceptions to this rule are quotations from other sources and citations of authors and titles that use the old spellings. I have also retained the old spellings of the names of people who are best known by, or continue to use, those spellings.

The arcane vocabulary of Indonesian politics presents special translation problems, for the literal meanings of the terms are often either uninformative or misleading. To minimize confusion I have sometimes provided a gloss as well as a literal translation. All of the translations from Indonesian and Dutch sources are my own unless I have indicated otherwise.

Abbreviations and Foreign Terms

abangan	nominal Muslim, Java
ABRI	Angkatan Bersenjata Republik Indonesia (Armed Forces of the Republic of Indonesia)
adat	customary law
AFNEI	Allied Forces, Netherlands East Indies
aksi sepihak	"unilateral actions" by PKI and affiliated organizations to implement land-reform legislation
Amacab	Allied Military Administration, Civil Affairs Branch
Ansor	NU-affiliated youth organization
APRIS	Angkatan Perang Republik Indonesia Serikat (Armed Forces of the United States of Indonesia)
Baliseering	"Balinization"
banjar	hamlet, Bali
Baperki	Badan Permusyawaratan Kewarganegaraan Indonesia (Deliberative Association for Indonesian Citizenship)
BKD	Badan Keamanan Desa (Village Security Body)
BKN	Badan Keamanan Negara (Body for the Defense of the Realm)
BKR	Badan Keamanan Rakyat (People's Security Organization)
BPH	Badan Pemerintahan Harian (Executive Council)
BPI	Badan Pusat Intelijen (Central Intelligence Agency)
BPP	Badan Pemberantas Pengacau (Body of Fighters against Terrorists)
BTI	Barisan Tani Indonesia (Indonesian Peasants' League)
bupati	administrative head of a kabupaten, a subprovincial administrative unit
CIA	[United States] Central Intelligence Agency
daidan, daidanco	[Japanese] battalion, battalion commander
desa	village, a territorial unit
Dewan Raja-Raja	Council of Rajas, Bali
DPD	Dewan Pemerintah Daerah (Regional Government Council)

DPR	Dewan Perwakilan Rakyat (People's Representative Assembly)
DPRD	Dewan Perwakilan Rakyat Daerah (Regional People's Representative Assembly)
DPRD-GR	Dewan Perwakilan Rakyat Daerah, Gotong Royong (Gotong Royong Regional People's Representative Assembly)
DPR-GR	Dewan Perwakilan Rakyat, Gotong Royong (Gotong Royong People's Representative Assembly)
Dwikora	Dwikomando Rakyat (the people's two mandates: to crush Malaysia and defend the Revolution)
Gerpindo	Gerakan Pemuda Indonesia (Indonesian Youth Movement)
Gerwani	Gerakan Wanita Indonesia (Indonesian Women's Movement)
Gestapu	Gerakan September Tiga-puluh (Thirtieth September Movement)
GMNI	Gerakan Mahasiswa Nasional Indonesia (National Students' Movement of Indonesia)
GNI	Gerakan Nasionalis Indonesia (Indonesian Nationalist Movement)
GSNI	Gerakan Siswa Nasional Indonesia (Indonesian National School Pupils' Movement)
G-30-S	Gerakan Tiga-puluh September (Thirtieth September Movement)
Hansip	Pertahanan Sipil (Civil Defense Force)
HIS	Hollandsch-Inlandsche School (Dutch Native School)
"Indonesia Raya"	"Great Indonesia" (national anthem)
IRMI	Ikatan Rakyat Murba Indonesia (Indonesian Murba People's Union)
ITI	Ikatan Tani Indonesia (Indonesian Farmers' League)
jero	noble house, Bali
kabupaten	regency, administrative district
Kaigun Heiho	[Japanese] Land-Based Navy Auxiliary
Kenpeitai	[Japanese] Military Police
kepala daerah	regional head
kerajaan	kingdom or principality
KNI	Komite Nasional Indonesia (Indonesian National Committee)
KNIL	Koninklijk Nederlands Indisch Leger (Royal Netherlands Indies Army)
KODAM	Komando Daerah Militer (Regional Military Command)
KODIM	Komando District Militer (District Military Command)
Kopkamtib	Komando Operasi Pemulihan Keamanan dan Ketertiban (Operational Command for the Restoration of Security and Order)
KOSTRAD	Komando Cadangan Strategis Angkatan Darat (Army Strategic Reserve Command)
KPDI	Kesatuan Pamong Desa Indonesia (Indonesian Union of Village Officials)

KPNI	Kesatuan Pemuda Nasionalis Indonesia (Indonesian Union of Nationalist Youth)
Lekra	Lembaga Kebudayaan Rakyat (Institute for People's Culture)
LOGIS	Lanjutan Organisasi Gerilya Indonesia Seluruhnya (Continuation of the All-Indonesia Guerrilla Organization)
Masyumi	Majelis Syuro Muslimin Indonesia (Consultative Council of Indonesian Muslims)
MBI	Markas Besar Istimewah (Special Headquarters)
MBU-DPRI-SK	Markas Besar Umum, Dewan Perjuangan Republik Indonesia, Sunda Kecil (General Headquarters, Resistance Council of the Republic of Indonesia, Sunda Kecil)
merdeka	freedom, liberation
MPRS	Majelis Permusyawaratan Rakyat Sementara (Provisional People's Consultative Assembly)
Nasakom	Nasionalisme, agama, komunisme (nationalism, religion, communism)
Nefis	Netherlands Forces Intelligence Service
negara	principality or state
negara-bestuurder	ruler of a principality
NICA	Netherlands Indies Civil Administration
NIT	Negara Indonesia Timor (State of East Indonesia)
NU	Nahdatul Ulama (Council of Muslim Scholars)
OKD	Organisasi Keamanan Desa (Village Security Organization)
ormas	organisasi massa (mass organization)
padi	unhusked rice
PADI	Partai Demokrat Indonesia (Indonesian Democratic Party)
Pancasila	Five Principles (national philosophy)
Pangdam	Panglima Daerah Militer (Regional Military Commander)
Paras	Partai Rakyat Sosialis (Socialist People's party)
Parindra	Partij Indonesia Raya (Greater Indonesia party)
Parrindo	Partai Rakyat Indonesia (Indonesian People's party)
Partai Buruh Indonesia	Indonesian Workers' party
Partindo	Partai Indonesia (Indonesia party)
Paruman Agung	Legislative Council of Bali
Paruman Negara	Legislative council of each kingdom or negara in Bali
PDRI	Pemerintah Darurat Republik Indonesia (Emergency Government of the Republic of Indonesia)
pedanda	Brahmana priest, Bali
pemuda	youth
Pemuda Rakyat	People's Youth (PKI-affiliated youth organization)
pencak silat	traditional martial art
Pepelrada	Penguasa Pelaksanaan Dwikora Daerah (Regional [Military] Authority to Implement Dwikora)
Peperda	Penguasa Perang Daerah (Regional War Authority)
Peperpu	Penguasa Perang Pusat (Central War Authority)
Peperti	Penguasa Perang Tinggi (Supreme War Authority)
perbekel	subdistrict head, Bali
Permesta	Perjuangan Semesta (Sulawesi-based rebel movement)

Pesindo	Pemuda Sosialis Indonesia (Socialist Youth of Indonesia)
Peta	Pembela Tanah Air (Defenders of the Fatherland)
Petani	Petani Nasionalis Indonesia (Indonesian Nationalist Farmers)
PGSI	Pasukan Gerilya Seluruh Indonesia (All Indonesia Guerrilla Force)
PKD	Pembantu Keamanan Desa (Village Security Auxiliary)
PKI	Partai Komunis Indonesia (Indonesian Communist party)
PNI	Partai Nasionalis Indonesia (Indonesian Nationalist party)
PPN	Pemuda Pembela Negara (Youth for the Defense of the Kingdom)
PPP	Pemuda Pembela Pancasila (Youth for the Defense of Pancasila)
Prayoda Corps	Balinese military auxiliary corps
PRI	Pemuda Republik Indonesia (Youth of the Republic of Indonesia)
PRN	Partai Rakyat Nasional (National People's party)
PRRI	Pemerintah Revolusioner Republik Indonesia (Revolutionary Government of the Republic of Indonesia)
PSI	Partai Sosialis Indonesia (Indonesian Socialist party)
punggawa	district head, Bali
puri	noble house, Bali
Raad van Kerta	Judicial Council for Native Law, Bali
Resident	Dutch administrator, beneath governor
RIS	Republik Indonesia Serikat (United States of Indonesia)
romusha	[Japanese] forced labor
RPKAD	Resimen Para Komando Angkatan Darat (Army Paracommando Regiment)
Rukun Tani	farmers' cooperative organization
santri	committed Muslim, Java
sawah	irrigated rice field
SEAC	South East Asia Command
sedahan	irrigation and tax officer, Bali
sedahan agung	chief irrigation and tax officer, Bali
Seinendan	[Japanese] Young Men's Association
Sendenbu	[Japanese] Department of Propaganda
SOB	Staat van Oorlong en Beleg (State of War and Siege)
sudra	commoners, Bali
Taman Siswa	Garden of Pupils (Indonesian nationalist school system)
Tameng Marhaenis	Marhaenist Shield (PNI-affiliated vigilante network)
TKR	Tentara Keamanan Rakyat (People's Security Army)
TOM	Team Penerangan Operasi Mental (Operation Mental Information Teams)
triwangsa	three highest castes or orders: Brahmana, Satria, and Wesia
wayang kulit	traditional Balinese and Javanese puppet drama
zelfbestuur	self-government
zelfbestuurder	ruler of a self-governing territory

A Brief Chronology

1846	First Dutch military expedition to Bali
1848	Second Dutch military expedition to Bali
1849	Third Dutch military expedition to Bali; Buleleng and Jembrana defeated, brought under indirect rule
1882	Jembrana and Buleleng brought under direct rule
1896	Karangasem brought under indirect rule
1901	Gianyar brought under indirect rule
1906	Badung defeated, brought under direct rule
1906	Tabanan defeated, brought under direct rule
1908	Klungkung defeated, brought under direct rule
1909	Bangli brought under indirect rule
1917	Earthquake in Bali destroys temples and villages
1917	Bangli and Gianyar brought under direct rule
1921	Karangasem brought under direct rule
1922	New land-tax ordinance in Bali
1929	Former rajas granted royal titles and privileges
1938	Restoration of *zelfbestuur* in Bali
18 Feb. 1942	Japanese forces occupy Bali
9 March 1942	Netherlands Indies authorities surrender to Japanese
24 May 1945	Sukarno visits Bali
14 Aug. 1945	Japanese capitulate
17 Aug. 1945	Indonesian independence proclaimed
8 Oct. 1945	Japanese transfer civil administration in Bali to local Indonesian National Committee (KNI-Bali)
November 1945	Pemuda groups PRI and Pesindo established in Bali
13 Dec. 1945	Republicans attack Japanese installations in Denpasar
29 Jan. 1946	KNI-Bali transfers authority to rajas and Paruman Agung
2 March 1946	Netherlands Indies (KNIL) troops land at Sanur Beach State of War and Siege (SOB) declared in Bali
11 March 1946	Governor I Gusti Ketut Puja and other KNI-Bali members arrested by KNIL forces in Singaraja
July 1946	Malino Conference to discuss formation of federal states

November 1946	Linggajati Accord between Netherlands and Republic of Indonesia drafted
20 Nov. 1946	Battle at Marga; 96 Republican troops killed in one day
6 Dec. 1946	Partai Rakyat Indonesia (Parrindo) formed in Bali
December 1946	Denpasar Conference to establish federal states
	State of East Indonesia (NIT) established
25 March 1947	Linggajati Accord ratified by Netherlands
April 1947	Balinese resistance organization (MBU-DPRI) frames "Minimum Program" in response to Linggajati Accord
April 1947	Elections for Paruman Agung; results annulled in Badung and Buleleng
June 1947	Parrindo banned
21 July 1947	First Dutch military action begins on Java
July 1947	MBU-DPRI issues "New Struggle Program" in response to Dutch military action
15 Jan. 1948	Renville Agreement signed
17 Jan. 1948	Republic of Indonesia recognizes NIT
24 May 1948	MBU-DPRI issues "special instruction" leading to "surrender" of at least 1,000 resistance fighters
September 1948	New elections for Paruman Agung
19 Dec. 1948	Second Dutch military action begins on Java
3 Mar. 1949	Civil authority transferred to chair of Council of Rajas
7 May 1949	Roem–van Royen Agreement signed
Mid-1949	SOB lifted in Bali
August 1949	Festival of Jayaprana at Kalianget, Buleleng
17 Aug. 1949	Gerakan Nasionalis Indonesia (GNI) formed in Bali
5 Sept. 1949	Gerakan Pemuda Indonesia (Gerpindo) formed in Bali
December 1949	Transfer of sovereignty to Indonesia
January 1950	SOB declared in Bali
August 1950	Unitary Republic formed
	Suteja selected as kepala daerah of Bali
September 1950	Paruman Agung dissolved, replaced by DPRD-Bali
15 May 1951	SOB lifted in Bali
December 1951	Thirteen Balinese pemuda to Jakarta to meet Sukarno
29 July 1955	National parliamentary elections
15 Dec. 1955	National elections for Constituent Assembly
14 May 1957	Declaration of martial law (national)
14 Aug. 1958	Bali gains provincial status
	Suteja selected as governor of Bali
July 1959	1945 constitution restored
1960	Sukarno assumes role of Supreme War Authority
1960	National land-reform laws enacted
17 March 1963	First eruption of Gunung Agung
1 May 1963	Martial law lifted
16 May 1963	Second eruption of Gunung Agung
1 Oct. 1965	Untung coup (G-30-S) and Suharto countercoup
7 Dec. 1965	RPKAD and Brawijaya troops land on Bali from Java, massacre begins

The Dark Side of Paradise

I   Political Conflict and Violence in Modern Bali: An Overview

In the wake of an Indonesian military coup in October 1965, the island of Bali erupted in political violence in which an estimated 80,000 people, or roughly 5 percent of the population, died.[1] In its intensity and in the proportion of the population killed, the violence on Bali probably exceeded that witnessed on Java in the same period.[2] The populations of whole villages were executed, the victims either shot with automatic weapons or hacked to death with knives and machetes. Some of the killers were said to have drunk the blood of their victims or to have gloated over the numbers of people they had put to death.

One might have expected that these events would stimulate some serious discussion about Balinese society and politics. After all, a massacre did not fit well with the widely accepted view that Bali was an earthly paradise, whose artistic and deeply religious people lived in harmony with nature and with one another. Yet, far from provoking a reconsideration of the prevailing images of Bali or a debate about its politics, the massacre has been treated either as proof of Bali's presumed exoticism or as an unpleasant anomaly that would be better forgotten.

The best-known references to the killings draw attention to the calm and dignified manner in which suspected communists allegedly allowed themselves to be executed, as if to suggest that a massacre was just another of the many mysteries of exotic Bali, or that if the Balinese were able to treat death with such resigned indifference, so might we. The authors of a *National Geographic* article written a few years after the massacre had few qualms about reiterating the familiar lore about Balinese culture and society:

[1] The coup and the massacre are discussed in detail in chapter 11.
[2] On the postcoup violence in Java, see Robert Cribb, ed., *The Indonesian Killings of 1965–1966: Studies from Java and Bali,* Monash Papers on Southeast Asia, no. 21 (Clayton, Victoria, 1990).

Hiking through peaceful villages in central Bali, we found it difficult to envision the fires of retribution that lit the island's skyline just four years ago. Nowhere does the Balinese instinct for beauty and creativity find more fluent expression than in the clusters of palm-shaded islands that float unobtrusively amidst a convoluted sea of thirsty paddy. Here man has not intruded upon nature but has enhanced the original design, blending his own patterns and hues into the harmony of greens, grays, and ochers. Even the bronze bodies match the tone of the rich soil. But flaming hibiscus interrupts the awning of green foliage that shades the villages, and flashes of brightly colored sarongs accent the landscape.[3]

Within the community of Bali scholars, the events of 1965–66 have been treated as a kind of academic no-man's-land. No doubt they too have found it "difficult to envision" the gruesome reality of those years. To the extent that it has been discussed at all by academics, the postcoup violence has generally been portrayed as a historical aberration, caused by the lamentable meddling of outsiders—communists, Sukarnoists, Javanese—thereby casting no doubt on prevailing views of a harmonious, apolitical Bali.[4] Some accounts have drawn, though only in the most cursory way, on other elements of the standard discourse about Bali, such as the deep religiosity of the people and the exotic wild side of their culture, to explain the violence. The massacre has often been described, for example, as the consequence of a religiously rooted "Balinese" desire to rid the island of evil and restore a cosmic balance. The "frenzy" with which it was carried out has been attributed to schizophrenic tendencies in the "Balinese character" and to a cultural predilection for going into a trance.[5] Analyses of the violent conflict of 1965–66 as a political problem with historical origins have been conspicuously absent.

This lacuna is all the more striking in view of the fact that the twenty years before the 1965 coup were marked by chronic political violence among Balinese, as were the years before the final imposition of Dutch colonial rule at the turn of the twentieth century. In the precolonial period Bali existed in a more or less constant state of political rivalry and war among petty princes (rajas) and lords. The Netherlands' final subjugation of the last three of Bali's kingdoms, between 1906 and 1908, was accomplished amid considerable bloodshed and only after several Dutch military campaigns against

---

[3] Donna K. Grosvenor and Gilbert Grosvenor, "Bali by the Back Roads," *National Geographic*, November 1969, pp. 667–70.

[4] See, for example, Willard Hanna, *Bali Profile: People, Events, Circumstances (1001–1976)* (New York: American Universities Field Staff, 1976).

[5] Such references allude to the classic anthropological studies of Balinese "temper" and "character" from earlier periods. See, for example, Jane Belo, *Trance in Bali* (New York: Columbia University Press, 1960); Gregory Bateson and Margaret Mead, *Balinese Character: A Photographic Analysis* (New York: Special Publication of the New York Academy of Sciences, 1942).

other kingdoms on the island commencing in 1846. Even during the period of Dutch rule, the apparent "peace and order" (*rust en orde*) masked serious conflicts over caste, as well as political and economic issues. During the National Revolution (1945–49), which was ostensibly a conflict between "Indonesians" and "Dutch," roughly 2,000 Balinese died, about a third of whom had been fighting on the Dutch side. In 1950–51, immediately after independence, a spate of politically motivated beatings and killings left hundreds dead, and from 1953 to 1956 armed gangs roamed the interior with impunity, engaging in extortion and acts of political intimidation and murder, many of them related to the national elections of 1955. In the early 1960s, antagonism between the two major political parties—the Communist party (PKI) and the Nationalist party (PNI)—and bitter conflict over land reform led to violent mass confrontations, arson, beatings, and killings.

The urge to write the conflict and violence out of Balinese history is part of a much larger problem in the field of Bali studies: the tendency to leave history itself, and particularly modern political history, out of the picture altogether.[6] Perhaps uniquely among societies that have experienced two decades of violent political conflict, modern Bali has not been the subject of any serious political historical study. A thorough history of the Japanese occupation has yet to be written. The only substantial history of the National Revolution in Bali, written by a Balinese freedom fighter and published in 1954, has not yet been translated into English.[7] The situation is not much better for the years 1950–65, for which only a handful of works address political and economic issues in any detail.[8] Compared to the depth and breadth of historical studies for this period on Java and many other parts of Indonesia, this is a most extraordinary gap.

Other themes are also missing from the literature on Bali. Writers on the colonial period seldom squarely address the impact of colonial policy and practice on Balinese social relations, class formation, and political development. They tell us little about the heavy tax burden in Bali, the system of corvée labor, how these burdens were experienced by various groups and classes, and what the political implications were. Likewise, though it is generally accepted that economic conditions had badly deteriorated by 1965, we still have no detailed analysis of Bali's economy between 1950 and

[6] Studies of Balinese religion, dance, music, art, architecture, and so on we have in abundance, but, with very few exceptions, they have been written with only scant attention to the broader historical and political context.

[7] Nyoman S. Pendit, *Bali Berjuang*, 2d ed. (Jakarta: Gunung Agung, 1979).

[8] The exceptions include Jef Last, *Bali in de Kentering* (Amsterdam: De Bezige Bij, 1955), and Max Lane, "Wedastera Suyasa in Balinese Politics, 1962–1972; From Charismatic Politics to Socio-Educational Activities," B.A. thesis, Sydney University, 1972. In his recent cultural history of Bali, Adrian Vickers has gone further than most in trying to elucidate this period. See Vickers, *Bali: A Paradise Created* (Victoria: Penguin, 1989). Several students in the History Department at Bali's Udayana University have written theses about various aspects of this period, to which I refer where appropriate.

1965.[9] And despite their obvious significance for the political violence before and after the coup, we do not yet have a single study of changing rural relations in Bali's countryside, or of the land reform of the early 1960s. Under the circumstances, it is scarcely surprising that the violence of 1965–66 appeared to come out of nowhere and that its causes have remained a mystery.

This book is an effort to fill the gap in historical scholarship on modern Bali from the imposition of Dutch rule at the end of the nineteenth century to the massacre of 1965–66. I shall describe and attempt to explain the political conflicts and violence that have gripped the island repeatedly over this period. The transformation of political, economic, and social conflicts in Bali through the colonial period (1882–1942), the Japanese occupation (1942–45), the National Revolution (1945–49), and the postindependence years culminating in the massacre of 1965–66 are examined, with special attention to the years 1945–66.

Bali in Historical Perspective

In addition to providing a political history of Bali, this work also offers an extended historiographical critique of academic, popular, and official government discourse about Balinese society and politics. This critique runs parallel to the narrative of the text, so that prevailing perceptions and views may be contrasted with the historical evidence. Of particular interest is the elaborate myth in which Bali appears as a fertile land of material abundance and social harmony, whose peaceable, artistic people have little interest in things "political." Although there have been some signs of change in recent years, this image still lies at the heart of much that is written about Bali. The historical analysis presented in subsequent chapters will demonstrate, I think, that it is seriously misleading. More important, I hope that this book will point the way toward a more comprehensive and satisfactory debate about Bali's political history, based in part on some of the general arguments outlined below. What follows here is a brief introduction to the genesis of the prevailing discourse on Balinese politics, viewed against the background of Bali's modern political history.[10]

[9] Virtually the only work on the subject of any value is the economic survey of Bali by I Gusti Gde Raka, *Monografi Pulau Bali* (Jakarta: Jawatan Pertanian Rakyat, 1955).

[10] For works that consider the origins and development of the image of Bali, see, for example, James A. Boon, "The Birth of the Idea of Bali," in Benedict R. O'G. Anderson and Audrey Kahin, eds., *Interpreting Indonesian Politics: Thirteen Contributions to the Debate*, Interim Report Series, no. 62 (Ithaca: Cornell Modern Indonesia Project, 1982), pp. 1–12; James Boon, *The Anthropological Romance of Bali, 1597–1972: Dynamic Perspectives in Marriage and Caste, Politics and Religion* (Cambridge: Cambridge University Press, 1977); Vickers, *Bali, A Paradise Created;* and Tessel Pollmann, "Margaret Mead's Balinese: Fitting Symbols of the American Dream," *Indonesia* 49 (April 1990): 1–36.

1. A Balinese beauty, about 1910. Photographs of bare-breasted Balinese women, encapsulating and reinforcing the image of Bali as an erotic paradise, were common fare in the travel literature, art books, and tourist brochures of the 1920s and 1930s, and helped to obscure the political and economic realities of Dutch colonial rule. (*Photo and print collection of the Koninklijk Instituut voor Taal-, Land- en Volkenkunde, Leiden*)

The image of a harmonious, exotic, and apolitical Bali gained wide acceptance in the late 1920s, when Dutch colonial power in Bali was at its height and the restoration of Balinese "tradition" had become a central feature of a conservative Dutch colonial strategy of indirect rule. By the 1930s, the bureaucratic memoranda of Dutch colonial officials had, with a tedious uniformity, begun to describe the people of Bali as more interested by nature, in art, culture, and religion—dance, music, painting, carving, ceremonies, festivals, and so on—than in "politics." The generally unspoken assumption in colonial circles (and in the foreign anthropological and artistic community in Bali) was that "culture" and "politics" were mutually exclusive categories, and that a "cultural" people could not at the same time be a "political" one. So long as Balinese "culture" remained strong, the reasoning went, "political" influence would be weak. This perception powerfully influenced colonial policy in Bali from about 1920 to the collapse of Dutch power in 1942.

It was within this historical and political setting of late Dutch colonialism that the still dominant scholarly tradition of "Baliology" emerged. Dutch scholars and colonial officials—notably F. A. Liefrinck and V. E. Korn[11]— had laid the foundations of scholarship on Bali through a series of ethnographic, philological, and legal studies conducted from the late nineteenth century to the 1920s, but it was through a handful of American anthropologists and their circle of friends that knowledge of Balinese culture and society reached a wider academic audience, both in North America and in Europe.[12]

While their portrayals of Balinese society were by no means uniformly romanticized, they carried in them sufficient raw material from which such an image could easily be developed. Even the most sophisticated anthropological analyses of the period, for example, suggested that "balance," "harmony," "order," and "happiness" were inherent in Balinese culture and social organization. Signs of tension or disharmony—the "frenzy" of trance dancers or the phenomenon of "running amok"—were understood essentially as the functionally integrative mechanisms of a "well-ordered" "traditional" society.[13] These themes became the cornerstones of the exotic image of Bali.

Observing Balinese behavior and "character" within the narrow, and historically atypical, confines of the colonial order, Margaret Mead, Gregory Bateson, Jane Belo, and others took the "harmony and stability" of Balinese society as an ethnographic given. They appear not to have reflected seriously

[11] Dr. V. E. Korn, *Het Adatrecht van Bali*, 2d ed. (The Hague: G. Naeff, 1932); F. A. Liefrinck, *Bali en Lombok* (Amsterdam: J. H. de Bussy, 1927). The contributions of these and other authors are discussed in greater detail in chapters 2 and 3.

[12] The core group of anthropologists who lived and worked in Bali in the 1930s were Margaret Mead, Gregory Bateson, and Jane Belo. Also part of the circle, and influential in developing the prewar discourse about Bali in the 1930s, were the artist Walter Spies, the musician Colin McPhee, the dancer Katherine Mershon, and the Mexican illustrator Miguel Covarrubias.

[13] See, for example, Jane Belo, "The Balinese Temper," in *Traditional Balinese Culture* (New York: Columbia University Press, 1970); Bateson and Mead, *Balinese Character*; and Gregory Bateson, "Bali: The Value System of a Steady State," in Belo, ed., *Traditional Balinese Culture*, pp. 384–401.

on the political and historical conditions within which they were making their observations, nor did they consider how changes in those conditions might influence the way Balinese "character" might manifest itself. Indeed, little attention was paid in any of the prewar ethnographic studies of Bali to the larger political environment—Dutch colonial power in particular—within which Balinese society existed. The assumption appeared to be that "politics" could somehow be factored out of the ethnographic picture, that there was an essential Balinese character which transcended politics and history.

The ahistorical and apolitical quality that marked the original corpus of prewar discourse continued to be distinguishing features of scholarly works, official perceptions, and received wisdom about Bali after the war. Indeed, as we shall see, the highly romanticized notions that Dutch military and civilian officials brought with them as they prepared to reoccupy the island in 1946 had an important effect on their strategy and on the course of politics during the National Revolution.

The idea of a harmonious and apolitical Bali, however, was not just an obsession of Dutch government and military officials. It was still widely accepted in "intellectual" circles as well. In his account of the Indonesian Revolution, published in 1948, the British author David Wehl wrote: "Indonesian Republicans from Java made a determined effort to set up the Republic in Bali, but in that beautiful land of beautiful, dreamy and artistic people, the call to battle sounded strangely and was little heeded."[14] Wehl's description was highly inaccurate, but it was representative of the view held by most people with knowledge of Indonesia and Bali at that time. In 1949—that is, four years into the Revolution—Gregory Bateson published an article, based on his prewar field research, in which he continued to claim that Balinese culture and personality were characterized by balance and stability. He argued, moreover, that the distinguishing feature of Balinese society was its avoidance of "climax," competition, rivalry, and competitiveness.[15] He made no mention of the war or the Revolution.

The image of a Bali aloof from politics also survived the fifteen-year period of chronic political conflict from 1950 to 1965. Following in the footsteps of the prewar anthropologists, Clifford Geertz and Hildred Geertz established the terms of discourse for postwar Bali studies through a series of publications based on field work conducted in the late 1950s.[16] Important

---

14 David Wehl, *The Birth of Indonesia* (London: Allen & Unwin, 1948), p. 8.

15 Borrowing a term from communications engineering, Bateson characterized Balinese society as a "steady state," and said that individual Balinese were principally concerned with maintaining that condition: "Bali: The Value System of a Steady State," p. 398.

16 Among the more important works from this period are Hildred Geertz, "The Balinese Village," in G. William Skinner, ed., *Local, Ethnic, and National Loyalties in Village Indonesia: A Symposium*, pp. 24–33 (New Haven: Yale University Cultural Report Series, 1959). Hildred Geertz and Clifford Geertz, *Kinship in Bali* (Chicago: University of Chicago Press, 1975); Clifford Geertz, *Peddlers and Princes: Social Development and Economic Change in*

as they were as anthropological studies, to a political historian these early postwar works are remarkable for their lack of attention to time, place, or historical and political context beyond the village level.

Only a few years before the Geertzes arrived in Bali, Indonesia had experienced its first general elections, in which the Socialist party (PSI) had come second only to the Nationalist party (PNI) in Bali, and the Communist party (PKI) had come a convincing third. Moreover, by the late 1950s, when the Geertzes were conducting their field work, the PKI was growing steadily more powerful. Yet, in their studies based on this field work, the Geertzes made only the most fleeting reference to the realm of political parties, the national state, or political conflict. In his study comparing entrepreneurs in Tabanan (Bali) and Modjokuto (Java) in the 1950s, for example, Clifford Geertz referred casually to political party affiliation as a "reflection" of "traditional" groupings, but otherwise offered no analysis of politics.[17] Indeed, there is little indication in these works that Bali had been through decades of colonial rule, more than three years of Japanese occupation, and a bitter war of independence. There is no hint that, through all of this, Bali's social structure had continued to change and that Balinese were political actors in their own right within the national political arena.

The violent clashes over land reform, which began in 1963, and the massacre of 1965–66 produced no appreciable impact on academic discourse about Bali. In her introduction to a collection of (largely prewar) anthropological works published in 1970, Jane Belo reiterated the familiar themes of harmony, balance, and prosperity, avoiding any mention whatsoever of the grisly events just four years past, which contrasted so dramatically with all that she and others had written.[18] Three years later, in *The Interpretation of Cultures,* a collection of his own works which became a classic in the field of anthropology—and which contained at least three articles specifically about Bali—Clifford Geertz devoted one sentence to the events of 1965–66 in Bali: "[After the 1965 coup] there followed several months of extraordinary popular savagery—mainly in Java and Bali, but also sporadically in Sumatra—directed against individuals considered to be followers of the Indonesian Communist Party."[19] His highly acclaimed work *Negara,* published in 1980, was one of the first works to address explicitly the question of the state in Bali. Notably, however, the discussion was framed so that it stopped abruptly with the imposition of Dutch colonial rule over the southern part of the island. After that date, he seemed to imply, the discussion of Balinese politics would take one beyond the realm of the

---

Two Indonesian Towns (Chicago: University of Chicago Press, 1963); and Clifford Geertz, "Deep Play: Notes on the Balinese Cockfight," in *The Interpretation of Cultures* (New York: Basic Books, 1973).

[17] Geertz, *Peddlers and Princes,* p. 22.
[18] Belo, *Traditional Balinese Culture.*
[19] Geertz, "The Integrative Revolution," in *Interpretation of Cultures,* p. 282.

"authentic" or original Bali, and into the sordid modern world of auto-mobiles, tax officials, poverty, and political conflict. Though Geertz clearly intended his analysis to have some relevance to debates on the state, he conspicuously avoided even the faintest allusion to the transformation of the state in Bali after 1906.

In recent years, somewhat greater attention has been paid to historical context and political issues in works about Bali.[20] Yet despite these signs of change, the scholarly study of Bali remains very much the preserve of an-thropologists, ethnomusicologists, and art historians, and continues to re-flect the particular preoccupations and limitations of those disciplines. There is, of course, much to appreciate in these works; yet one consequence of the continued dominance of these disciplines and traditions has been that certain questions, analytical approaches, and methods have scarcely begun to be explored. It is my hope that, in addition to providing a more compre-hensive political history of modern Bali, this book will provoke more of that sort of exploration. Toward that end, I shall here outline briefly the broader analytical issues that have arisen in the course of writing this history and explain how I have tried to deal with them.

States, Society, and Political Conflict

A political history of modern Bali must provide plausible explanations for at least two major historical problems. First, it must be able to explain the considerable variation in the patterns of Balinese politics from one period to the next. For while it is important to draw attention to the conflict and violence in Balinese history, one must also address analytically the periods of apparent harmony and political calm. Second, it must account for the character of Balinese politics and, in particular, for the ways in which it differed from politics in other parts of Indonesia. Why, for example, has Balinese politics in this century principally come to express conflicts among Balinese—based on caste, class, familial ties, and the like—and not between Balinese and some other ethnic group, or between Bali and the central government? In other words, we must account for the historical absence of strong ethnically based or regionalist political movements in Bali, and simul-taneously for the strength of intra-Balinese political conflict.

In grappling with these problems of variation and difference, I have found it useful to think in terms of the external parameters shaping Balinese poli-

[20] See, for example, Boon, *Anthropological Romance of Bali;* C. Fasseur, "De weg naar het paradijs: Nederland en Bali," *Spiegel Historiael* 20 (December 1987): 535–42; Henk Schulte Nordholt, "Een Balische Dynastie: Hierarchie en Conflict in de Negara Mengwi, 1700–1940," Ph.D. diss., Vrij Universiteit te Amsterdam, 1988; Vickers, *Bali: A Paradise Created;* and Hildred Geertz, ed., *State and Society in Bali: Historical, Textual and Anthropological Ap-proaches* (Leiden: KITLV Press, 1991).

tics, which have changed rather strikingly during the twentieth century, rather than look exclusively at the cultural and psychological makeup of "Balinese," which is more notable for its continuity. Just as the recurring political violence suggests that there is nothing inherently peaceable or harmonious about Balinese society, so the long periods of apparent political quiescence under Dutch rule (and again under President Suharto's New Order) lead one to doubt that there is anything inherent in Balinese culture or society which alone can account for the periods of open political violence. Furthermore, because intense political conflict and civil war were not unique to Bali during this period of Indonesian history, efforts to understand Balinese politics by reference to culture or personality alone seem likely to miss the mark or to provide only partial explanations.

On the other hand, dramatic changes have occurred over the last century in Bali's political environment. Particularly noteworthy, I think, have been the shifts in the character and the policies of the various states under whose authority Bali has fallen: the Netherlands Indies colonial regime, the Japanese military administration, the revolutionary Republican government on Java, the State of East Indonesia (NIT), and the Old Order regime of President Sukarno. These changes at the center have coincided, more or less, with broad shifts in the pattern of Balinese politics, suggesting that there is a connection between the two. For example, the thirty-five years of apparent peace and order before World War II coincided with the imposition of a single, overarching colonial state authority throughout the island. In contrast, violent political conflict among Balinese broke out—notably in 1945–49 and 1965–66—when there was a sudden collapse of or acute division in central state power. At the most basic level, this suggests that political turmoil and violence did not emerge simply because of a certain configuration of societal forces—although it was partly that—but that they were structured and conditioned by the character of the state.[21]

The term "state" is used here *not* in the sense of a single, autonomous actor with its own particular interests, nor does it denote a mere "arena" within which social groups "make demands and engage in political struggles or compromises."[22] I use the term to mean a set of potentially powerful political structures and institutions whose precise historical significance varies depending on their relationship with societal forces. These include systems of administration, justice, and coercion; mechanisms of surplus extraction; and institutions that both reflect and sustain the ideological

---

[21] Skocpol labels this approach "Tocquevillian," in that it focuses on the structural "impact of states on the content and working of politics." "In this perspective," she explains, ". . . states matter not simply because of the goal-oriented activities of state officials. They matter because their organizational configurations, along with their overall patterns of activity, affect political culture, encourage some kinds of group formation and collective political actions (but not others) and make possible the raising of certain political issues (but not others)": Theda Skocpol et al., *Bringing the State Back In* (New York: Cambridge University Press, 1985), pp. 8, 21.

[22] Ibid., p. 8.

preoccupations and cultural norms of those in power. This does not mean that the state apparatus is necessarily a tool of a particular class, although in some historical circumstances it might be.

From the considerable body of literature on the nature of the state, I have found several arguments especially useful in making sense of the historical evidence from Bali. The first is that divisions within a state may create opportunities for the emergence of political protest, resistance, or conflict.[23] In states that are incohesive or divided, it is argued, there is a greater tendency for open political conflict.[24] The reason lies not simply in the absence or weakness of state authority but in the active participation of elements of the state apparatus in the process of political protest or conflict. This argument offers a valuable insight into the pattern of politics in Bali. It suggests, for example, that the roots of the political conflict and violence from 1945 to 1966 may be located in the actual participation of elements of the state—or the use of state institutions—on either or both sides of various political struggles.

A variation on this argument is that the existence of more than one state claiming authority within a given territory, or competing for the allegiance of a single community, is likely to increase the incidence of political conflict and violence.[25] In the Southeast Asian context, the claims of national or central states have often overlapped or conflicted with those of "local states."[26] The term "local state" is coined here to denote a range of statelike

[23] A large body of literature within the general field of social movement theory deals with the way states and political systems may structure the "opportunities" of social movements. One of the formative works on this subject was Eisinger, "The Conditions of Protest in American Cities," *American Political Science Review (APSR)* 67 (March 1973): 11–28. Other important studies include Charles Tilly, *From Mobilization to Revolution* (Reading, Mass.: Addison-Wesley, 1978), chap. 4; Frances Fox Piven and Richard A. Cloward, *Poor People's Movements* (New York: Random House, 1979), Introduction and chap. 1. Sidney Tarrow, "Struggling to Reform," paper no. 15 (Ithaca: Cornell Western Societies Program, 1984), chap. 3, provides a crisp synthesis of major theoretical contributions to this field of study.

[24] This is hardly a new idea; Aristotle and Plato both understood it quite well.

[25] The existence of discrete but overlapping levels and types of statelike authority is most evident during periods of political transformation or confrontation, but even in times of peace and stability such overlapping authorities are not unusual. Wars of independence or secession, for example, may be understood as conflicts between at least two rival claimants to state authority over a territory and population. In times of peace, challengers at the center may try either to seize control of the old state apparatus, or they may attempt to establish an independent state apparatus including militia, judicial structures, systems of taxation, ideological norms, etc. In peripheral areas of a country, political challengers more often attempt the latter; that is, to set up an alternative state apparatus.

[26] In thinking about this problem I have found Ruth McVey's discussion of the integral relationship between the "center" and the "locality" very useful. What colonialism did, writes McVey, was to "destroy the autonomy of the small communities, transform the position of local elites and cause spheres of action to be reshaped or rendered irrelevant until all meaningful power relationships followed the pattern of the state": "Local Voices, Central Power," in *Southeast Asian Transitions: Approaches Through Social History* (New Haven: Yale University Press, 1978). Although she uses different terminology, Audrey Kahin's edited volume on the regional dynamics of the National Revolution has also been most helpful: *Regional Dynamics of the Indonesian Revolution: Unity from Diversity* (Honolulu: University of Hawaii Press, 1985).

structures at the subnational level that vary in their degree of independence of the central state. I do not mean to imply a simple dichotomy between "central" and "local" states. On the contrary, state systems that vary in kind and in geographical extent may develop and compete for the loyalty of populations at the subnational level, and may be founded on very different ideological or cultural principles and institutions. These variations, in themselves, are important factors in the patterns of political conflict that develop.

Despite these variations, however, the basic argument about the political significance of central and local states remains more or less the same. When the central state is not strong or unified and a local state is, the conditions exist for political conflict between the two, in the form of either a civil war or a local rebellion. A local state that is relatively weak or divided and lacks autonomy is much less likely to form a focus of local solidarity or opposition to the center or any other group. It is far more likely to be easily penetrated by or to reflect the movements and conflicts emanating from the center.

In twentieth-century Bali, there have been at least two types of state authority beneath the various central states: those with their locus in the island's individual kingdoms and those encompassing the entire island of Bali. Both types have been arenas of political contention, and both have been potential loci of political allegiance for Balinese. I think it can be shown that the historical weakness of local states encompassing the whole of Bali has contributed significantly to the pattern of recurrent political conflict among Balinese and the absence of strong regionalist or ethnic-based movements there. This pattern has been accentuated by the existence of relatively well established state systems at the kingdom level.

It goes without saying that it is not only the relative strength or cohesiveness of central and local states that shapes political relations within a given community. Equally significant are the unique structures, styles, and policies of those states and the cultural forms in which they are embedded. Moreover, to focus on the character of states is not to dismiss the role of cultural and societal forces in political conflict. On the contrary, it requires us to examine the historical relationship between political structures and influences emanating from the center and the political, economic, and cultural forces at the local level. Because, while the character and policies of the center inevitably shape politics locally, the particular course of politics depends on the configuration of such local forces. The task of the political historian is to show how a state—its administrative and judicial structures, its coercive apparatus, its means of surplus extraction, and its policies, ideological preoccupations, and cultural forms—intersect with specific social and economic forces, such as class structure, ethnic identity, and cultural institutions, to influence the formation of politically relevant categories, patterns of political relations, and the detailed course of historical change. In this book I have tried to provide a plausible explanation for the historical variation in Bali's modern politics and for the particular salience of conflict

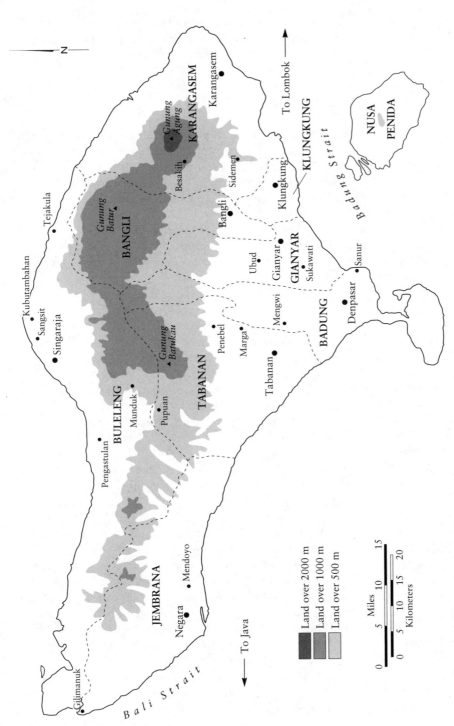

2. Kingdoms and major towns in Bali, c. 1945

N

To Lombok →

NUSA
PENIDA

Badung Strait

Karangasem

KARANGASEM

Gunung
Agung ▲

Besakih

Sidemen

KLUNGKUNG

Tejakula

Gunung
Batur ▲

BANGLI

Bangli

Klungkung

Kubutambahan

Ubud

Gianyar

GIANYAR

Sukawati

Sanur

Sangsit

Denpasar

Singaraja

Mengwi

BADUNG

Penebel

Marga

TABANAN

Pengastulan

BULELENG

Munduk

Gunung
Batukau ▲

Pupuan

Tabanan

JEMBRANA

Mendoyo

Negara

← To Java

Gilimanuk

Bali Strait

Land over 2000 m
Land over 1000 m
Land over 500 m

Miles
0   5   10   15

Kilometers
0   5   10   15   20

among Balinese, rather than between Balinese and outsiders. To give a more concrete sense of what this means, let me very briefly summarize the main historical arguments presented in later chapters.

Bali's Political History in Brief

Beneath the apparent *rust en orde* of the colonial period (1908–42), Dutch policy exacerbated old social and economic tensions and gave rise to new ones. The colonial regime, made nervous by what was seen as evidence of emerging "communism" and "nationalism" in the 1920s, embarked on a policy of restoring Balinese "tradition." This project required the revival— in some cases the creation—of "traditional" cultural, religious, and legal practices. It also entailed the restoration of Bali's old ruling families, whose leading members, once regarded by the Dutch as despots and sent into exile, were now viewed as the indispensable guarantors of a harmonious "traditional" order.

The structure of the colonial state—in particular its overwhelming strength—and its system of indirect rule served to limit the likelihood of open political opposition. Indeed, it encouraged political and social conflict among Balinese—notably along caste and class lines and among noble houses—rather than giving rise to Balinese solidarity against the Dutch state. In the 1920s, for example, Bali experienced an acrimonious public debate over caste prerogatives, which pitted educated commoners (*sudra*) against conservative representatives of the three highest castes (*triwangsa*). Though the debate was cut short by the Dutch, caste tensions continued beneath the surface and reemerged again during the National Revolution and in the postindependence period.

A similar dynamic was evident in the economic sphere. Even before the Depression had brought economic problems to a head, Balinese already suffered under one of the heaviest tax burdens in the Netherlands Indies, and were still required to perform an average of twenty-five days per year in corvée labor for the government or its indigenous agents. When the effects of the Depression began to be fully felt about 1932, poverty, hunger, and landlessness became acute. Because Balinese rather than Dutch officials were responsible for the system of tax and corvée extraction at the local level, resentment and anger tended to be directed against Balinese officials rather than the Dutch colonial state.

The collapse of the Dutch colonial regime and the imposition of an equally powerful Japanese military administration in March 1942 marked the beginning of a period of profound change in Balinese politics. The continued use of indirect rule by the Japanese, coupled with an increasingly harsh system of surplus extraction, heightened existing conflicts among Balinese and generated new ones. While the overwhelming power of the Japanese state—like the Dutch state before it—prevented any open opposition or political conflict, its various efforts to mobilize the Balinese population behind the war effort provided unprecedented experience for many young Balinese in political and military organization. It also gave rise to significant changes in the terms of political discourse in Bali.

The political significance of these developments became evident with the collapse of Japanese state power and the proclamation of Indonesian independence by the Republican leader, Sukarno, in August 1945. Balinese began immediately to mobilize politically and militarily for and against the newly declared Indonesian Republic, and to settle old scores with alleged collaborators. The delay of more than six months before Dutch forces arrived in Bali to take the place of the Japanese administration provided a unique opportunity for continuing political mobilization and conflict among Balinese. This opportunity was created almost entirely by the discord between the British military administration on Java, which did not wish to become overextended in the Netherlands Indies, and Dutch military and civilian authorities, who sought the earliest possible reoccupation of Bali.

The opportunity created by the collapse of central state power produced varied results in different parts of Bali. Local differences in class structure, access to education, rural relations of production, and the pattern of rivalry between noble houses (*puri*) affected the social and geographic distribution of support for Indonesian republicanism in 1945–46. The main base areas of Republican support were the central kingdoms of Buleleng, Badung, Tabanan, and for a time Jembrana, where the old ruling families and feudal traditions were relatively weak. The eastern kingdoms of Karangasem, Bangli, Gianyar, and Klungkung, where the ruling puri remained powerful, formed the backbone of antirepublicanism.

In their eagerness to return to the Indies, Dutch strategists failed to take account of the changes Bali had undergone since 1942. Still believing that Balinese had "no interest in politics" and that the society was likely to be "well ordered" and harmonious, they concluded that there would be little or no opposition to the reimposition of Dutch rule in 1946. They were mistaken. When Dutch Indies troops landed at Sanur Beach in March 1946, they stepped onto an island already divided between the supporters and opponents of Indonesian independence. Stiff military resistance by Balinese Republican forces lasted into 1948, and the political struggle continued after that date. In response to this resistance, Dutch strategists set about using the "well-intentioned" Balinese and their feudal rulers to spy upon, report, and kill Republicans, whom they designated as "terrorists." In this way, Dutch strategy encouraged enmity and open fighting among Balinese. By late 1949, roughly 2,000 Balinese had died—about 700 on the Dutch side of the question—compared to only a handful of Dutch soldiers.

External political developments continued to influence local conflicts during the revolutionary period. After 1946 several states—Republican, Dutch colonial, and the indirectly Dutch-ruled State of East Indonesia (NIT)—competed for supremacy in Bali. Balinese did not look uniformly to any one of these political centers but to all of them in different measure and at different times. The directives and impulses emanating from the shifting centers helped to shape the political and military strategies of different groups in Bali, often in a very detailed way. More important, they intersected with and reinforced existing tensions.

By 1949, there was a deep division between Balinese who had fought for Indonesian independence and those who had collaborated with the Dutch and its puppet state, the NIT. This political divide also had a powerful cultural dimension. Republicans spoke of the need to do away with "feudal" and caste privilege, while their opponents spoke of the need to preserve Balinese "tradition" and culture. The dynamic of national and international politics also helped to accentuate splits within the Republican camp. Particularly important was the rift between the main body of freedom fighters who came down from the mountains in early 1948, after the signing of the truce between the Netherlands and the Republic (the Renville Agreement), and those who continued the armed struggle until January 1950.

The achievement of Indonesian independence in late 1949 did not bring an end to political conflict among Balinese. On the contrary, divisions between collaborators (actual or alleged) and Republicans and splits within the Republican camp itself continued to be expressed through open political violence and through a protracted struggle to control the local state apparatus. Though the social and political makeup of the protagonists changed over the next fifteen years, the struggle remained substantially unresolved. In 1965, on the eve of the October coup, groupings with diametrically opposed political, economic, and class interests controlled different elements of the state apparatus, such as the military, the police, the bureaucracy, and the executive. The coup provided the pretext and the opportunity for the consolidation of the political power of one grouping, led by the PNI, at the expense of the other, the PKI and its allies.

From 1950 to 1965, political conflict was transformed by seriously deteriorating economic conditions, government economic policies, and concomitant changes in Bali's class structure. The aggressive implementation of land reform in Bali—led by the PKI and its peasant organization and assisted by key elements in the local state—contributed to an increasing political polarization along class lines after 1963. The struggles over land set the stage for a powerful and violent reaction by landowners and their allies in the PNI after the coup and the anticommunist countercoup of October 1965.

Political conflict among Balinese was further reinforced by the financial dependence of the local state on the center and by the emergence of a new Balinese bourgeoisie with close ties to the local state. Lacking any significant financial autonomy, the local state had neither the means nor the motivation to support the regional rebellions against the center in the late 1950s. Rather, it came to act as a local dispenser of patronage, with the indigenous bourgeoisie as a major beneficiary. This system gave rise to allegations of political bias and cronyism, and contributed to the dynamic of local political conflict. As the local state shifted increasingly to the left in the 1960s, with the Sukarnoist Governor Suteja at the helm, many who felt excluded from the flow of patronage rallied behind the PNI, thereby strengthening the political reaction against the PKI and Suteja after October 1965.

The weakness and lack of autonomy of the local state apparatus meant that political impulses emanating from the center tended to reinforce and to transform political divisions in Bali. Particularly important in this process were the national-level political parties and the system of political competition and mobilization under Sukarno's system of Guided Democracy after 1959. By the early 1960s, the struggle for local state power in Bali had come to be expressed through increasingly combative mass rallies and confrontations between the supporters of the PNI and PKI. In this way, thousands of ordinary people came to share powerful bonds of solidarity with other

2. Gunung Agung erupting in early 1963 behind Pura Besakih, Bali's "mother temple." After showing signs of activity in February 1963, the first major eruption, on 17 March, coincided with the *Eka Dasa Rudra* ceremony at the temple. It also coincided with a wave of pestilence and crop failure, and with an aggressive land-reform campaign backed by the PKI and Bali's Governor Suteja. Many Balinese apparently saw the eruption as a sign of cosmic imbalance and as a portent of further disaster. (*Indonesia, Department of Information, Denpasar*)

members of their political organization and deep antagonism toward those in the opposing camp.

Together with seriously deteriorating economic conditions, a cluster of natural disasters and pest plagues in the early 1960s fueled speculation that Bali was in a state of cosmic imbalance. The eruption of the volcano Gunung Agung in 1963, during the course of an elaborate religious ceremony intended to restore that balance, was seen as a portent of further disaster. The coincidence of these events with the rising militancy of the PKI, and in particular with its aggressive land-reform campaign, gave rise to allegations that the PKI was in some way responsible for the imbalance. Such suggestions were consciously encouraged by the PNI, and by others who for other reasons felt threatened by or antagonistic to the PKI. Echoing the accusations of the Dutch and of conservative Balinese against the Republicans during the Revolution, they labeled the PKI-Bali antireligious and an enemy of Balinese culture. This accusation undoubtedly accentuated the intensity of the conflict in the 1960s and provided a powerful motivation and pretext for violent retribution after the 1965 coup.

Also significant was the relatively weak position of the military in Bali. Unlike units elsewhere in Indonesia, which had gained access to large tracts of land and other assets with the nationalization of foreign enterprises in the late 1950s, the military in Bali lacked any strong, independent economic base. As a consequence, it tended to move opportunistically with the leftward political tide in Bali. When the tide turned convincingly in late 1965, however, the military in Bali was quick to change its orientation. Though some officers were arrested and tried for their alleged support for the PKI and the coup, most escaped by taking a lead in the assault on alleged communists. Up until October 1965, violent political conflict had to some extent been contained by the roughly equal access of both sides to key state institutions at the local level. With the coup, however, that tenuous balance was ruptured, and the way was open for violent retribution by the PNI and its followers, with the hearty assistance of the national and local military.

To someone unfamiliar with the discourse on modern Balinese history and politics, these observations about the importance of economic forces, the state, class relations, political parties, and the military in shaping Bali's history might appear unexceptional, even commonplace. Indeed, if they were made in relation to another society with a similarly volatile and bloody history, they probably would be. But to advance such claims or interpretations about Balinese history is to run against a heavy tide of scholarly and popular opinion. It is only fair to say at the outset, then, that this book is explicitly intended to run against that tide. It aims to demystify Bali, to take the romance out, and to restore to their rightful place the conflict and the violence that have characterized the island's politics on and off throughout the twentieth century.

2 Colonial Policy and
Political Relations in Bali

THE IMPOSITION OF DUTCH RULE over the whole of Bali at the turn of this century—though itself attended by great violence—began a thirty-five-year period of apparent political calm and social harmony unprecedented in recorded Balinese history. It was during these years of the *Pax Neerlandica,* as some colonial officials liked to call it, that the image of Bali became firmly entrenched both in popular descriptions and in scholarly works. The 1920s and 1930s in particular were years in which a variety of experts in the fields of anthropology, linguistics, archaeology, and religion came to work in Bali and developed an elaborate and respectable portrait of the island as a sort of "Last Paradise," even when they saw evidence to the contrary.[1]

To a considerable extent, discussion of Bali's twentieth-century history and politics continues to be shaped by the notion that the "harmony" and apparent political calm of the prewar years represented the authentic or normal Bali, and that the years of violence and civil war from 1945 to 1966 were an unfortunate aberration.[2] It is much more plausible, I believe, to view the years of *rust en orde* (1908–42) as atypical in Bali's modern history, and to see in the turbulence of 1945–66 at least a partial return to an earlier pattern in Balinese politics: a pattern of chronic and violent political con-

[1] The genesis of the romantic image of Bali has been the subject of many studies. In "The Birth of the Idea of Bali," James Boon describes the tendency of a generation of scholars to view evidence contrary to their idealized image of Bali simply as an aberration rather than the norm. A recent work on this theme, Vickers' *Bali,* traces the development of European conceptions of Bali from the earliest European contact to the present day, but also discusses Balinese images of Bali. Also see Mark Hobart, "Thinker, Thespian, Soldier, Slave? Assumptions about Human Nature in the Study of Balinese Society," in Mark Hobart and Robert H. Taylor, eds., *Context, Meaning, and Power in Southeast Asia* (Ithaca: Cornell SEAP Studies on Southeast Asia, 1986).

[2] Referring to an earlier period, Hobart has noted that "western commentators seem to have great difficulty with the role of violence in Balinese society. The editors of *Siwaratrikalpa,* an Old Javanese text found in Bali, felt it necessary to excuse 'the gruesome methods of warfare which the poet's imagination conjures up'": "Thinker, Thespian, Soldier, Slave?" p. 145.

flict. One of the aims of this chapter is to offer an explanation of the apparent political serenity of colonial Bali, which can also account for the open political conflict that preceded and followed it.

What distinguished the Dutch interregnum of the early twentieth century was the existence of a single, powerful state encompassing the entire island. No such state apparatus had existed before full Dutch rule; certainly not in the nineteenth century. As Henk Schulte Nordholt has argued, "the Balinese *negara* [state] had not even the vaguest signs of things like a bureaucracy, uniformity in regulations or government, nor a monopoly of power in the center."[3] Similarly, the renowned Dutch scholar of Balinese history and law V. E. Korn identified "the lack of a powerful government over the whole realm" as "the great failing" of the island's rulers.[4] It was only the imposition of an unusually strong state—replete with regularized systems of taxation, administration, coercion, and customary law (*adat*)—which temporarily put an end to the overt manifestations of political rivalry among the kingdoms and the noble houses (puri), and to the social conflict between members of different castes and social groups.

Yet at the same time—and this is the second major theme of this chapter—the structure and the policies of the colonial state served to heighten latent social and political tensions and create new ones. The discussion here and in chapter 3 of a number of aspects of Dutch policy in Bali and of the response to Dutch policy and practice reveals rather strikingly, I think, that even in the years of rust en orde the harmony of Balinese life was superficial. For most Balinese, Bali was no paradise.

The manner in which Dutch colonial policy shaped or inspired particular forms of political consciousness and organization in Bali is the third major focus of this chapter. The primacy of disputes over issues of caste, feudal privilege, religion, and culture in Bali's political discourse and the relative weakness of either an all-Bali ethnic consciousness, an anti-Dutch Indonesian nationalist awareness, or a discourse based on class have been alluded to by other scholars, but none adequately explain why this should have been the case.[5] The "cultural" focus of Balinese politics appears to be taken as a given.

I argue instead that there was a structural, not to say causal, link between the nature of Dutch colonial policy and practice and the character of politi-

---

[3] Henk Schulte Nordholt, *Bali: Colonial Conceptions and Political Change 1700–1940, From Shifting Hierarchies to "Fixed Order,"* paper no. 15 (Rotterdam: Comparative Asian Studies Program, 1986), p. 20.

[4] Korn, *Adatrecht van Bali,* p. 307. Korn also served as a Controleur in Badung (1919–21) and as Assistant Resident of South Bali (1929–30).

[5] In his work on nineteenth-century Bali, for example, Clifford Geertz maintains that disputes over prestige and status were the essence of political life, while Vickers writes that "Balinese" responses to colonial rule "centred on ideas of Balinese culture and identity": Geertz, *Negara: The Theater State in Nineteenth-Century Bali* (Princeton: Princeton University Press, 1980); Vickers, *Bali,* p. 131.

cal and social conflict and discourse that emerged in Bali. That is to say, the configuration of political conflict and the nature of political discourse were not in any sense the "natural" or necessary outcomes of specific cultural or sociological givens in Bali, but were shaped, sometimes unconsciously but often deliberately, by the policy and practice of the colonial state. An important corollary of this argument is the claim, which I will also advance here, that the Balinese "tradition" so admired by foreign observers until this day was essentially an artifact of Dutch colonial policy, and that Dutch "respect" for Balinese culture was frequently motivated by highly conservative political calculations. This is not a wholly new claim, but it warrants more detailed and rigorous treatment than it has thus far received.[6]

Precolonial Bali

Early Dutch accounts of Bali from the late sixteenth century portray it, in James Boon's words, as "a stable realm of an unchallenged divine monarch" and as a land of abundance, natural beauty, and social harmony.[7] Many elements of this image reemerged in the scholarly and official colonial literature of the 1920s and 1930s. In the intervening years, however, the descriptions of foreign travelers suggested a rather different scene, one in which political intrigue within aristocratic families, perennial war between kingdoms, slavery, and other "barbaric" social practices such as "widowburning" were the norm.[8]

Examples of political intrigue and civil war are legion and occur without significant interruption up to the beginning of the twentieth century.[9] In the latter half of the nineteenth century, for example, Klungkung was in a nearly constant state of war with either Karangasem or Gianyar; the kingdoms of Buleleng and Bangli waged continuous disputes, and in 1849 Bangli assisted the Dutch in their military expedition against Buleleng; in the same year, the raja of Karangasem was murdered by Balinese troops of the kingdom of Mataram on Lombok; between 1849 and 1872 the kingdoms of Jembrana

[6] Vickers has described the emergence of the romantic image of Bali during the 1930s in considerable detail, but he has paid relatively little attention to the unique role of the colonial state in shaping it. Rather, he has described the changing image of Bali as a product of the free interaction of the impressions of a series of politically disinterested visitors. Thus he writes: "Along the way the views of the various visitors met to produce the image of Bali which persists today": *Bali*, p. 78.

[7] Boon, "Birth of the Idea of Bali," p. 5. Also see Vickers, *Bali*, p. 12, for a summary of the account of Cornelis de Houtman, who visited Bali in 1597.

[8] See, for example, [Dr. Medhurst], *Journal of a Tour along the Coast of Java and Bali and with a Short Account of the Island of Bali Particularly Bali Baliling* (Singapore: Mission Press, 1830). Also see Fritz Dubois, "Huit jours dans l'île de Bali," *Revue des Deux Mondes*, [1890], pp. 571–601.

[9] Henk Schulte Nordholt writes that in the second half of the nineteenth century "not a decade passed without fierce war": *Bali*, p. 20.

and Buleleng were rocked by domestic insurrections and coups d'état; Mengwi was defeated in 1891 and partitioned among the three victorious kingdoms, Gianyar, Badung, and Tabanan; between 1886 and 1893, a district head, Dewa Manggis, led a violent rebellion to free Gianyar from the authority of Klungkung; after 1893 Badung allied with Bangli and Karangasem to harass Gianyar; and in 1904, Bangli attacked Karangasem and destroyed irrigation works in neighboring Gianyar.

Earlier claims of social harmony are similarly contradicted by evidence that, from the seventeenth to the early nineteenth century, Bali's chief export was Balinese slaves, with as many as 2,000 exported each year during the seventeenth century.[10] Although it was generally Chinese who were involved in the final stage of the transaction, Balinese rajas and district heads were responsible for the harvesting of this, Bali's most lucrative cash crop, and they were also its chief beneficiaries. Those who might, by convention, be legitimately sold into slavery included prisoners captured in battle, widows without heirs, debtors, and other criminals. However, strong demand from private traders and the Dutch colonial government probably stimulated the practice of taking slaves and encouraged abuses. According to an English missionary who visited Bali in the early nineteenth century,

> the subjects may not always be culprits . . . but happening to be without friends to take their part have been apprehended and sold perhaps for a very trifling fault, or even on false or frivolous pretenses. At any rate, the circumstances of a certain price being offered per head, for stout young men, would induce the rajahs more readily to condemn such [men] in order to sell them, or prompt them to make war on their more defenseless neighbour, just on purpose that they may have subjects to supply the Dutch market with.[11]

Balinese slaves were sold in Batavia, in the West Indies, in southern Africa, and throughout the islands of the Pacific and Indian oceans. In mid-seventeenth-century Batavia, where the total slave population was about 18,000, approximately half were Balinese.[12] The formal abolition of slave trafficking during the English interregnum (1811–17) dealt a serious economic blow to the Balinese rajas, but the sale of slaves continued into the 1860s.[13]

[10] Anak Agung Gde Putra Agung, "Masalah Perdagangan Budak Bali (Abad 17–19)," *Basis*, November 1971, pp. 38–48; Alfons van der Kraan, "Bali: Slavery and the Slave Trade," in Anthony Reid, ed., *Slavery, Bondage, and Dependency in Southeast Asia*, St. Lucia (Brisbane: University of Queensland Press, 1983), pp. 315–40.
[11] Medhurst, *Journal*, pp. 31–32.
[12] Vickers, *Bali*, pp. 8–15.
[13] W. F. van der Kaaden, "Geschiedenis van de Bestuursvoering over Bali en Lombok van 1898–1938," *Tropische Nederland* 11 (1938–39): 203–4. The English missionary Dr. Medhurst referred in 1830 to a Dutch contract to purchase 1,000 men at a price of $20 a head. He also mentioned the arrival of French slave traders from Mauritius who purchased about 500 Balinese women, paying 150 rupees for young, plump ones and 50 rupees for the middle-aged: Medhurst, *Journal*, pp. 31–32.

It is worth noting here, too, that far from being regarded as playful, artistic, happy, and peace loving, the Balinese were often described in nineteenth-century accounts as "surly," warlike, quick to lose their tempers, and untrustworthy. A Dutch traveler who visited the island in 1800 described the Balinese as "a fierce, savage, perfidious, and bellicose people,"[14] and a French visitor in 1890 wrote of the "evil instincts of the Balinese people."[15]

Balinese men, moreover, had a reputation for being formidable soldiers, one of the reasons they were so eagerly sought by the Dutch to fill the ranks of the colonial army. Dutch military officers learned at firsthand the quality of Balinese fighting men during three military expeditions (1846, 1848, 1849). After suffering defeat in 1846 and 1848, the Dutch attacked Buleleng in 1849 with some 15,000 troops and several warships, and even then managed a tenuous victory only after securing the assistance of Balinese collaborators from the village of Sangsit, the neighboring kingdom of Bangli, and the kingdom of Mataram on Lombok. A subsequent attack on Klungkung in 1849 proved unsuccessful, resulting in the death of the Dutch military commander. A contemporary account of the 1849 expedition described the Balinese as the most formidable military opponents ever encountered by the Dutch colonial forces in the Indies.[16]

Recent scholarly studies suggest that these less complimentary portraits come closer to the mark in describing precolonial Balinese politics and society than the earliest and now dominant images of harmony and peace. They have also demonstrated rather convincingly that, at least since the demise of the kingdom of Gelgel in the mid-seventeenth century, the Balinese polity had been not centralized but rent by internal divisions, not stable but in a state of perpetual crisis and flux.[17] They have shown, too, that Balinese were not innately peaceable, but as capable of violence as any other people.[18]

[14] Dirk van Hogendorp, *Bericht van den Tegenwoordigen Toestand der Bataafsche Bezittingen in Oost-Indie en den Handel op Dezelve,* 2d ed. (Delft: Roeloffwaert, 1800), p. 191, quoted in Vickers, *Bali,* p. 2.

[15] Dubois, "Huit jours dans l'ile de Bali."

[16] Kapt. A. W. P. Weitzel, *De derde militaire expeditie naar het eiland Bali in 1849* (Gorinchem: J. Noorduyn en Zoon, 1859), p. 5.

[17] For a time the Gelgel dynasty ruled in a fashion over all of Bali and parts of East Java, Lombok, and Sumbawa. Yet even during the Golden Age of Gelgel, the political power of the center was limited. Swellengrebel writes that from 1500 to 1900 "Buleleng, Karangasem, and the central Balinese mountain areas stayed outside the reach of the system; even more so did Jembrana. The power of the rulers was uncertain in those regions": in W. F. Wertheim, ed., *Bali: Studies in Life, Thought, and Ritual* (Dordrecht: Foris, 1984), p. 31. Perhaps the foremost scholar on Bali's legal and political history, V. E. Korn, argued that the language of the royal decrees of Bali's kings—the *paswara* and *titiswara*—gave a very misleading sense of the power of those kings, which in reality must have been very limited: *Adatrecht van Bali,* pp. 50–51.

[18] These are notable themes in Geertz's *Negara.* He argues that while Bali's kings aspired to the establishment of an "exemplary center" that would both represent and serve as paradigm for a political and social order in harmony with the cosmos, the reality on the ground was very different. There was, he writes, "no unitary government, weak or powerful, over the whole

The "Ethical" State

Bali was colonized piecemeal over more than half a century, so that it was not until 1908 that the Dutch established a colonial state apparatus over the whole island and the period of apparent peace and order began.[19] In the preceding decades, Dutch intervention had anything but a stabilizing effect on Balinese politics. Indeed, the instability of the nineteenth-century Balinese polity must be attributed, at least in part, to the pestering military, political, and economic interference of the Dutch from about 1830. Intermittently, the Dutch intervened on behalf of one kingdom or another, playing the role of contender and ally, and effectively encouraging rivalries and disputes. Only in the first decade of the twentieth century did the Dutch establish anything like a hegemonic state in Bali.

Although Bali's royal families later earned a reputation for collaboration with the Dutch, five of the island's kingdoms—Buleleng, Jembrana, Badung, Tabanan, and Klungkung—came under Dutch control only after military resistance at various times between 1846 and 1908; many of the rajas and members of their families actually died in the process.[20] Surviving members of these royal families were sent into exile in Lombok, Java, Madura, and Sumatra, much of their landed wealth was confiscated, and their former territories and subjects were brought under direct colonial rule. Three kingdoms—Bangli, Gianyar, and Karangasem—came under Dutch authority without military resistance around the turn of the century.[21] Though they had not always taken a conciliatory posture toward the Dutch, the royal

---

realm at all" (p. 68). Rather, the Balinese polity was partitioned into "a set of rivalrous factions of varying size, strength, and structural complexity" (p. 28). Rivalry was manifested in, among other things, "the steady hum of political violence which plagued the Balinese state all through the nineteenth century and . . . probably through the whole course of its history" (p. 85). These themes are also central to Schulte Nordholt's work on the kingdom of Mengwi, in which he characterizes the political systems of Bali as fragmented, offering "numerous opportunities for rebellion and fission," and fraught with "internal strife" and "war" with neighboring kingdoms: "Een Balische Dynastie," p. 352.

[19] For an outline of the colonization process in Bali, see van der Kaaden, "Geschiedenis," pp. 203–8, 219–24, 234–40, 253–56, 265–72; and Korn, *Adatrecht van Bali*, pp. 112–13, 309, 315, 317.

[20] Buleleng and Jembrana succumbed to Dutch military force in 1849, after surviving two expeditions in 1846 and 1848. In 1855 the Dutch appointed new rajas in both kingdoms, but when they were judged to be insufficiently loyal they were exiled. The two kingdoms were finally brought under direct rule in 1882. Badung and Tabanan were conquered in 1906 and brought under direct rule the same year; and Klungkung suffered the same fate in 1908. The raja of Badung and several hundreds of his followers died in the now famous *puputan* (a heroic last stand cum mass suicide) of 1906. Shortly after the defeat of the kingdom of Tabanan, the raja and his son took their own lives. The raja of Klungkung was killed leading a puputan in 1908, in the face of insuperable Dutch military might.

[21] Karangasem was brought under indirect rule in 1896 but remained a self-governing territory until 1921. Gianyar and Bangli came under indirect rule in 1901 and 1909, respectively, and both were brought under direct rule in 1917. In return for recognizing Dutch sovereignty, the three rajas were first designated as *stedehouders* (representatives of the Dutch colonial government) and, after 1913, as *regents* within their kingdoms.

families in these three kingdoms were allowed to retain their wealth and much of their royal status; and their kingdoms were, in practice if not always in name, governed as indirect-ruled territories.[22]

In 1929 the Dutch authorities permitted a designated descendant of the former raja in each kingdom to assume the old royal title (Anak Agung, Cokorda, Dewa Agung). The appointees were officially called *negara-bestuurders* (rulers) within their ancestors' former kingdoms, now called *negara*. In 1938 the negara-bestuurders were given the status of raja or *zelfbestuurders* (self-rulers) with a measure of real authority within their respective realms. The establishment of the eight *zelfbesturend landschappen* (self-ruling territories) in 1938 officially marked the end of direct Dutch rule in Bali. However, the Dutch colonial state remained in place there until 1942, when most Dutch civil servants and soldiers fled to Java before the advancing Japanese forces.

The push to extend the colonial administrative apparatus over the whole of Bali was consistent with a pattern of Dutch colonial expansion throughout the Outlying Territories in the late nineteenth and early twentieth centuries.[23] The shifting political objectives of the Dutch colonial state can be detected in the official accounts of Balinese politics and culture at this time. The frequency of war, the alleged cruelty of Bali's opium-smoking despots,[24] and the barbarity of its social practices were evoked by turn-of-the-century officials to justify, usually after the fact, military intervention and direct colonial administration. Shortly after the 1906 military actions in which the rajas of Badung and Tabanan and many of their relatives and retainers died, one Dutch commentator remarked that "the people are greatly relieved that their tyrannical kings have been removed."[25] A lecture given in 1909 by G. F. de Bruyn Kops, the Resident of Bali and Lombok (1905–9), catalogued the "intolerable" conditions in South Bali which had necessitated Dutch military intervention between 1906 and 1908 in Badung, Tabanan, and Klungkung, in the name of order and civilization.

[22] The terms used to describe Bali's "kingdoms" and its "kings" have varied a good deal. The Dutch referred to them at various times as *landschappen, gouvernements landschappen, zelfbesturend landschappen,* and *negara.* The Indonesian term most commonly used is *kerajaan,* which can be translated as "kingdom" or "principality." Though their small scale might lead one to prefer "principality," I believe that "kingdom" better conveys the complexity and sophistication of the eight "royal" courts. Depending on his administrative status under the Dutch, the ruler of a kingdom was known as raja, *negara-bestuurder, stedehouder, regent, bestuurder,* or *zelfbestuurder,* and also by his royal title—Cokorda, Dewa Agung, Anak Agung. The term "raja" is used here.

[23] The islands of Nusa Tenggara (Sumbawa, Flores, Sumba, Savu, Roti, and Timor) were, for example, brought under formal Dutch administration in the 1900s; the final conquest of the Bugis and Makassarese states occurred in 1905–6.

[24] On the opium addiction of Bali's rajas and the "motherly" efforts of the colonial administration to wean them from the drug, see Dr. Julius Jacobs, *Eenigen tijd onder de Baliers: Eene reisbeschrijving met aanteekeningen betreffende Hygiene, Land en Volkenkunde van de eilanden Bali en Lombok* (Batavia: G. Kolff, 1883).

[25] M. van Geunsz, "Een en ander over Bali en zijne bewoners," reprinted from *Soerabajasch Handelsblad,* 24, 27, and 29 November and 1, 4, 6, 11, 14, and 17 December 1906, p. 16.

One found in those kingdoms conditions which could no longer be tolerated by a civilized state which had sovereignty over the area: a condition of chronic war, extreme arbitrariness on the part of those in power, a total absence of legal security for the ordinary man, widow-burning, slavery, usury, extensive smuggling with Java, and so on. All revenues, such as taxes, lease payments and fines, flowed into the pocket of the king, who literally spent none of it for the good of the country and the people but instead used it all for his personal benefit. If someone died without leaving a son, then not only did his property go to the king, but also his widow and daughters became the king's slaves or concubines. If a dispute between two subjects, over a piece of land, remained unresolved, then the land in question simply went to the king. The death penalty was a very common punishment and was often applied without any semblance of an investigation.[26]

Without a more general shift in Dutch policy, these objections to Bali's kings would scarcely have led to an extension, by force, of Dutch state authority over the whole of Bali. Barbara Harvey has argued that Dutch expansionism in this period was part of the Liberal Policy of the late nineteenth century to expand free trade and markets and to preempt foreign control. Terance Bigalke has similarly suggested that the Dutch drive into south and central Sulawesi was a part of the "drive of imperialism."[27] I am suggesting that the move, into South Bali at least, was also strongly influenced by the so-called Ethical Policy that emerged about the turn of the century, with all that it implied regarding the activist and interventionist role of the colonial state. Resident de Bruyn Kops's list of the "intolerable" conditions in Bali and his explanation of the reasons for expanding power into the outer islands provide a clear picture of the new conception of the responsibilities and the prerogatives of the colonial state, which developed together with that policy: the state should guarantee the legal security of persons and property, ensure peace and order, have monopolistic control of revenue collection, and use such revenues for the "public good." Because Balinese kings did not appear to do these things, colonial intervention was justified.[28]

By the second decade of this century, there was a significant degree of uniformity in Dutch colonial policy and practice toward the so-called direct- and indirect-ruled territories in Bali. First, in both sorts of territories a

[26] G. F. de Bruyn Kops, "Het evolutie tijdperk op Bali, 1906–1909," *Koloniaal Tijdschrift* 4 (1915): 459–79. The lecture was given to the "Vereeniging van Ambtenaren bij het Binnenlands-Bestuur in Nederlandsch-Indie," 13 March 1915.

[27] Barbara S. Harvey, "Tradition, Islam, and Rebellion: South Sulawesi, 1950–1965," Ph.D. diss., Cornell University, 1974, chap. 2; Terance W. Bigalke, "Social History of Tanah Toraja, 1870–1965," Ph.D. diss., Cornell University, 1981, chap. 4.

[28] In the words of de Bruyn Kops, the guiding principle of the colonial administration was "to make clear to the Native chiefs that what was expected was full cooperation in bringing about the reforms which the [Dutch] government regarded as necessary; and if efforts to secure such cooperation were stymied by the ill-will of the chiefs, to take forceful action against them. Such an approach was, in the end, also necessary in Bali": "Evolutie tijdperk op Bali," pp. 464–65.

handful of Dutch officials controlled and directed the key administrative, economic, and judicial structures. Dutch officials devised, imposed, and presided over a new administrative setup, a new tax regime (which included the lucrative state opium monopoly), new regulations on the use of corvée labor, a new judicial system, and a new police force.[29] In short, while keeping some royal families intact and permitting them relative autonomy in certain functions, the Dutch brought the whole of Bali under a single, over-arching colonial state.

Next, Balinese aristocrats and notables, as well as Chinese traders, were effectively employed as agents of the new colonial state. In this respect, even Bali's direct-ruled territories shared features of the system of indirect rule practiced by the Dutch in Java. As in Java, the aristocracy and the Chinese effectively served as buffers between the colonial state and the peasantry, allowing more to be exacted from the latter, for example in taxation and corvée labor, while preserving a superficial *rust en orde*.[30] This was the case even where particular royal families had been toppled and direct rule imposed, because the demise of these *puri*, far from undermining other aristocrats and notables, actually provided new opportunities for them to increase their wealth and influence. The tendency for conflict to be focused against other Balinese and Chinese, rather than against the colonial state, was accentuated by the relatively low profile of European officialdom. For all their influence, the number of European officials in Bali through most of the colonial period was minuscule, never totaling more than a few hundred men and women, so that the Dutch colonial apparatus was virtually invisible to most Balinese, even in the direct-ruled territories.[31]

Kings, Caste, and Colonial Power

From the turn of the century there was a difference of opinion within the colonial leadership over the substance of the "ethical" administrative policy

[29] In an address before the Indisch Genootschap, the Resident of Bali and Lombok (1920–23), Damsté, noted that "the regulations that obtained in the [indirect-ruled kingdoms] with respect to criminal investigation, the opium monopoly, justice, corvée labor, and taxation were the same as those elsewhere in the territory": Indisch Genootschap, minutes of the Annual Meeting, 28 May 1923, p. 114.

[30] For Java, see D. H. Burger, *De ontsluiting van Java's binnenland voor het wereldverkeer* (Wageningen: H. Veenmen, 1939). For the Netherlands Indies as a whole, see J. S. Furnivall, *Netherlands India: A Study of Plural Economy* (Cambridge: Cambridge University Press, 1944).

[31] According to official census figures, the total "European" population in Bali was 243 in 1920 (of a total population of 947,233) and 403 in 1930 (of a total population of 1,101,037); these figures included many who were not colonial officials, such as artists, scholars, and businessmen. The figures are cited by J. L. Swellengrebel, Introduction to Wertheim, *Bali*, p. 6. This was a smaller percentage of "Europeans" than most Residencies in the Netherlands Indies. In Aceh, where the total population in 1930 was slightly smaller than that in Bali (980,166), the number of "Europeans" was 21,656. See Mailrapport 514/1938, Ministerie von Kolonie na 1900 (hereafter MvK), Algemeen Rijksarchief, The Hague (hereafter ARA).

to be pursued in Bali. Whereas F. A. Liefrinck, the Resident of Bali and Lombok from 1896 to 1901, appeared to favor a policy of leaving Balinese institutions "intact"[32] while encouraging the rulers gradually to accept Dutch tutelage and authority, Governor General J. B. van Heutz wanted to see sweeping administrative reforms and modernization.[33] This difference in administrative philosophy was reflected in the shifting trajectory of much government rhetoric and action over the next few decades.

Yet, even as the conflict developed between those who would see Bali's "traditions" preserved and those who wanted them swept away, the effects of the two currents on Bali's political life were, paradoxically, rather similar. The preservationists were at least as responsible for profound changes in Balinese society and politics as were the modernizers, and perhaps more so. The case of administrative reform in the early part of this century provides a first glimpse both of the internal contradictions in Dutch policy and of the ways in which the impulse to preserve could give rise to profound changes. The paradox that conservatism brings change lies at the heart of Bali's political history in this century, and helps to explain how the outward peace and order of the colonial era could lead to civil war.

Based on the premise that the political essence of traditional Bali was the autonomous village republic (*dorps-republiek*)[34] and that the rajas and their courtly institutions were later, inauthentic accretions, an effort was made in the early years of this century to "simplify the village administration and return it to its original state" and to "purge village administration of royal impositions and intrusions."[35] A good deal of effort was expended in forming new, more uniformly sized territorial administrative units from the existing potpourri of administrative arrangements. Villages and districts considered "too large" were broken up into smaller entities, and those considered "too small" were recombined into larger units, in the hope of achieving greater administrative efficiency. The irrigation societies (*subak*) underwent similar restructuring, so that their boundaries would be isomorphic with the newly created districts, and their numbers were reduced in the interest of efficiency.[36]

[32] Dubois, "Huit jours dans l'ile de Bali," pp. 600–601.

[33] Schulte Nordholt, *Bali,* p. 27.

[34] Originally articulated by Sir Thomas Stamford Raffles, who visited Bali in the early nineteenth century, the dorps-republiek concept was elaborated by the Dutch scholar and colonial civil servant F. A. Liefrinck toward the end of the century. According to this model, the removal of Bali's kings did away with the unnatural and the corrupt; with freedom from this encumbrance and the assistance of the Dutch colonial state, Bali's authentic "native" institutions would once more flourish.

[35] From the "Memorie van Overgave" of H. J. E. F. Schwartz, the Assistant Resident for South Bali, 1909, quoted in Schulte Nordholt, *Bali,* p. 32.

[36] Immediately after the military defeat of Tabanan, for example, Dutch authorities reorganized the kingdom into thirteen districts, and the number was further reduced to six in 1913: Regerings Commissaris voor de Bestuurshervorming in de Groote Oost, "Nota van Toelichtingen van het in te stellen Zelfbesturend Landschap Tabanan," by H. J. Hoekstra (1938?), typescript, Gedung Kirtya Liefrinck, Singaraja, pp. 58–59.

With the imposition of a territorially based system of political authority, control over people and control over land became enmeshed, and differences in landed wealth became an increasingly salient aspect of political and social power. Control of formal political office became similarly important. One consequence was that the focus of rivalry within and among noble houses expanded to encompass not simply the claims to status and deference which Geertz argues were central in late-nineteenth-century Bali but also control over political office, land, and labor. The major political offices, as they were understood in the 1940s, were raja, *punggawa* or district head, of which there were several in each kingdom, and *sedahan agung,* the chief irrigation and tax officer in each kingdom. In addition to these posts were others that were coveted: *manca,* an assistant punggawa; *perbekel,* a subdistrict officer; *sedahan,* a tax and irrigation officer for an entire watershed; and member of the Raad van Kerta, the Judicial Council for Native Law in each kingdom.[37]

Against this background, Dutch policy with respect to the landed wealth and access to office of the royal families had strong political consequences. In the five direct-ruled kingdoms—Badung, Tabanan, Klungkung, Buleleng, and Jembrana—the colonial authorities had taken early steps to limit the landed wealth of the ruling families and remove them from political office. In 1855 the Dutch had appointed new rajas in Buleleng and Jembrana, and when even these new appointees turned out to be insufficiently loyal, they were exiled. Surviving members of the royal families of Tabanan, Badung, and Klungkung were also sent into exile; and the bulk of the landed wealth, of the first two at least, was expropriated.[38] Land and populations that had once been under the authority of the royal families of Tabanan and Badung were distributed among new Dutch-appointed punggawa and perbekel.[39] Paradoxically, while undermining the royal families in the direct-ruled kingdoms, the government's policy of administrative reform tended to enhance the power of other aristocratic families and particularly those who secured official positions.

In the three indirect-ruled kingdoms of Bangli, Gianyar, and Karangasem, the wealth and status of the royal families were not significantly disrupted. In fact, the Dutch made efforts to protect them against other influential

[37] For a description of these offices in precolonial Bali, see Geertz, *Negara,* pp. 63–67.

[38] Precise information on the landed wealth of the royal families in the colonial period is notoriously difficult to come by. One of the very few references I have come across is in a letter from the Resident of Bali and Lombok (H. J. E. Moll) to the Governor General, dated 25 April 1938, in Mailrapport 636 geh./1938, Box AA160, MvK, ARA. Resident Moll wrote that three of the eight royal families still had substantial income from land, while the others had very little. He did not identify the three kingdoms by name, but there is reason to believe he was referring to the indirect-ruled kingdoms Gianyar, Bangli, and Karangasem. For information about the landed wealth of the royal families in later periods, see chaps. 5 and 10.

[39] See Regerings Commissaris, "Nota van Toelichtingen van het in te stellen Zelfbesturend Landschap Badoeng," by H. J. Hoekstra, Gedung Kirtya Liefrinck, Singaraja, p. 77. On Tabanan, see Regerings Commissaris, "Nota van Toelichtingen van . . . Tabanan," by Hoekstra, ibid., pp. 58–59.

families in their domains. Thus, for example, the Dutch parliamentarian H. H. van Kol, who visited Bali in 1902, spoke approvingly of the efforts of the Controleur H. J. E. F. Schwartz in Gianyar to shore up the position of the raja vis-à-vis one of his punggawa: "The position of the once powerful punggawa is now reduced, as it should be, to that of a servant of the radja under our watchful supervision."[40]

While it is true that some new administrative positions were available to members of the lowest or commoner caste on account of their administrative ability or education, there was on the whole a tendency to favor the "well-born." Thus, in spite of the evident concern for administrative rationality and modernization and the policy of undermining some of the old royal families, Dutch policy had a strong elitist element or, more precisely, a caste bias. However much Dutch administrators disparaged the recalcitrant rulers whom they wished to subdue and displace, their strategy was to seek alliance with the "natural" or traditional leaders in Balinese society, and to make use of what they conceived to be the traditional forms of Balinese political authority. Even after the imposition of direct rule in North Bali, the Resident and his staff were at pains to show their respect for "local custom." This invariably meant working closely with men of high caste, particularly Brahmana priests (*pedanda*) and "native chiefs" of the Satria caste. Thus the French traveler Fritz Dubois, who visited Buleleng in 1890, wrote that

> the Dutch are for them more like allies than masters. One can say that in Boeleleng . . . the colonial authorities have become the friends of the priests and are treated with deference by the princes [rajas] and lesser chiefs. It is true that the colonial authorities display all possible respect for the religious customs of the country. . . . This friendly alliance [*entente amicale*] with the priests and the chiefs, in many cases, allows the Dutch to convert them to ideas of humanity and justice.[41]

The first Dutch colonial officials in Bali were heavily influenced by the work and thought of a handful of early-nineteenth-century visitors and scholars who viewed Bali principally as an example of a Hindu society, or as a living museum of old Java, before its "corruption" by Islam. The most influential of these commentators were J. Crawfurd, who visited Buleleng in 1814; Sir Thomas Stamford Raffles, who visited in 1815; and the German sanskritist Rudolf Friederich, who visited the island in the 1840s.[42] All three were well

---

[40] Quoted in Hanna, *Bali Profile*, p. 89.

[41] Dubois, "Huit jours dans l'ile de Bali," p. 599. According to Korn, turn-of-the-century Residents habitually issued government orders in the form of ancient Balinese royal edicts (paswara) to give them the ring of royal credibility: *Adatrecht van Bali*, p. 50.

[42] See J. Crawfurd, "On the Existence of the Hindu Religion in the Island of Bali," *Asiatick Researches* (1820): 128–70; Thomas Stamford Raffles, *The History of Java*, 2 vols. (London: Black, Parbury & Allen, 1817); and Rudolf Th. A. Friederich, *The Civilization and Culture of Bali* (Calcutta: Susil Gupta, 1959).

3. The raja of Buleleng with his daughter and two retainers in 1865. Buleleng was formally brought under direct colonial rule in 1882 but strong Dutch political influence dated at least from 1849, when the kingdom succumbed to Dutch military force. Appointed by Dutch colonial authorities in 1855, the raja pictured here was the third Balinese designated to rule the territory in six years. He was exiled to Sumatra in 1872 for abuse of authority. The kingdom was then ruled for a time by a Dutch Controleur and a council of district heads. (*Photo and print collection of the Koninklijk Instituut voor Taal-, Land- en Volkenkunde, Leiden*)

acquainted with classical Hinduism, and all based their analysis on surviving Hindu texts in Bali and on conversations with Brahmana priests and members of the ruling families. J. L. Swellengrebel writes: "What they saw on Bali, in their contact with Brahmins and rulers, reminded them of it [Hinduism]. True, they also saw many things that struck them as being anything but Hindu, but they saw such things through Hindu spectacles, and so had a distorted view."[43]

[43] Swellengrebel, Introduction to Wertheim, *Bali,* p. 25.

According to two internal critics of government policy, V. E. Korn and C. Lekkerkerker, Dutch officials accepted too readily the aristocratic and the Hindu view of Balinese society. In their judgment, nineteenth-century commentators had mistaken the Hinducentric ideology of the highest castes—the centrality of an immutable four-tiered caste system in which the highest three (the Brahmana, Satria, and Wesia) held an automatic political and social superiority—for the social reality of Balinese life, which was considerably more flexible.[44] Given their own limited knowledge of Bali, it was scarcely surprising that the first colonial officials sent there were so open to the ideas of these "experts" and that they came to view Bali in a similar light. Moreover, like them, virtually all colonial officials went first to the royal courts and priestly houses, so that their understanding of Balinese society, like the experts', was necessarily mediated by members of the highest castes.

Thus, in spite of the harsh official criticism of Bali's kings around the turn of the century, there persisted an appreciation, even a reverence for Bali's aristocratic "culture," which eventually became part of the collective, institutional knowledge of the Dutch civil service. In 1923 Lekkerkerker complained that "among the European civil servants there are those who are 'plus royalistes que le roi,' that is to say more inclined to show deference and respect to members of the highest castes than the Balinese themselves."[45] One consequence was that the Dutch disproportionately appointed members of the three highest castes to high political, judicial, and religious office. As Korn pointed out, there had been far more sudras (commoners) in positions of political authority—punggawa, sedahan, perbekel, and so on—before the imposition of Dutch colonial rule than there were after it.[46]

Native Justice

The Dutch bias was especially noticeable and had far-reaching political and social consequences in the administration of justice. Not only did Dutch policy and practice help to strengthen the caste character of Balinese society, it also ensured that Balinese social and political discourse came to focus heavily on matters of interpretation of tradition, religion, caste, and culture.

[44] James Boon discusses the transformation of caste as a set of fluid social conventions into a rigid set of rules during the colonial period in *Anthropological Romance of Bali*, pp. 52–54.

[45] According to Lekkerkerker, "in the time of the kings . . . powerful soedra [commoner] personalities effectively ruled small kingdoms and districts for years at a time": "De tegenwoordige economische toestand van het geweest Bali en Lombok," *Koloniaal Tijdschrift* 12 (1923): 162.

[46] Korn wrote: "Owing to the fact that the European government was so convinced of the idea that the three highest castes constitute the most important foundation of Balinese society, it was almost exclusively members of these castes who were being appointed to high positions": *Adatrecht van Bali*, p. 41. In mid-nineteenth-century Buleleng, by contrast, sixteen of the twenty-six punggawa were *not* of the three highest castes (pp. 41, 176). Korn also noted that many commoners had held high positions as tax officials and judges in precolonial times, and cited several examples (p. 288).

Courts of customary law, the Raad van Kerta, were established in 1882 in Buleleng and Jembrana, and in the other kingdoms as they were brought under Dutch control. From the outset, the regulations dictated that members of these courts must be ordained Hindu priests.[47] And even after 1901, when the general rules on administration stipulated that no such limitations should apply, priests continued to dominate the Raad van Kerta established in the eight kingdoms.[48] The creation of a priest-dominated court system tended to strengthen the Hindu character of Balinese society and introduced a high degree of legal rigidity into the caste system.

The strongly elitist tendency in the state-sponsored native judicial system was typified and reinforced by the Dutch insistence on the use of certain ancient Balinese legal and religious texts—such as the *Agama Adigama,* the *Purwa Agama,* and the *Kutara Agama*—as the basis of a Balinese code of "customary" law. One problem with this approach, they soon discovered, was that even the pedanda on the courts were seldom able to read the texts, which were written in Old Javanese. Deeply concerned at this apparent "decay" in legal understanding and seeing an urgent need to bring customary practice back into line with the "true" law as written in the texts, Dutch experts set about preparing translations into Balinese and Malay for use by the members of the Raad van Kerta.[49] There is perhaps no more striking example of the way in which Balinese "tradition" was manufactured by the Dutch colonial state.

In 1910 an official decision was taken "to uphold the caste concept, being the principal foundation of Balinese society."[50] In so doing, the colonial state legalized and entrenched a caste hierarchy and a set of rules regarding caste relations and prerogatives which in practice had never before existed. In Korn's words: "Not only were the triwangsa given too prominent a place, but also the caste system itself . . . was protected through a series of provisions, which . . . went very much farther than many of the former kings and legal texts."[51] In short, what was construed as a Dutch attempt to work within Balinese "tradition" was in effect the creation of a new fixed hierarchical order, in which the power of the highest castes was greater than ever, and which was, moreover, sanctioned by the legal, ideological, and coercive structures of the colonial state. By the mid-1920s, this new order had begun to give rise to visible signs of frustration on the part of the more educated of Bali's sudra.

One such sign was the public polemic over caste privilege which raged in the local Malay-language newspapers *Surya Kanta* and *Bali Adnyana* in the 1920s. These papers had grown out of an earlier publication whose editorial

[47] The relevant pieces of legislation were Staatsbald [Stbl.] 1882 no. 143 and Stbl. 1888 no. 2.

[48] The relevant legislation was Stbl. 1901 no. 306, art. 7: Korn, *Adatrecht van Bali,* p. 55.

[49] Korn, *Adatrecht van Bali,* pp. 53–54.

[50] Minutes of an administrative conference, 15–17 September 1910, Collectie Korn, no. 166, Koninklijk Instituut voor Taal-, Land-, en Volkenkunde (KITLV).

[51] Korn, *Adatrecht van Bali,* p. 55.

staff had split along caste lines—triwangsa against sudra.[52] *Surya Kanta,* edited by educated sudra, was openly critical of existing caste distinctions and prerogatives, and criticized the colonial government for backing that system.[53] It called upon the colonial government to base the selection of government officials on criteria of education and merit rather than caste.[54] It also urged a simplification of religious ceremonies to reduce the economic burden on ordinary Balinese, and demanded a demystification of religious knowledge to weaken the excessive social and religious power of the pedanda.[55] Finally, it called for a relaxation in social relations, particularly in language, dress, and the rules governing cross-caste marriage.[56]

Bali Adnyana, edited by triwangsa and called by Korn "a newspaper exclusively for the aristocracy,"[57] responded with indignation to the criticisms of *Surya Kanta.*[58] In society and in language, argued the editors, hierarchy is a natural principle, which ought not to be disrupted by mere humans.[59] Rather like Dutch colonial officials, the editors of *Bali Adnyana* also sounded the alarm against the "Red Peril" which they claimed the *Surya Kanta,* with its "communistic" philosophy, represented.[60] And in an article titled "The Island of Bali Will Become Bali Again" the editors praised Dutch moves toward the retraditionalization of Bali in 1929.[61]

In response to this debate in North Bali, new organizations and newspapers emerged throughout the island. In 1926 the Tjwadega Hindu Bali,

[52] The earlier publication was *Santi Adnyana.* The debate that led to the split centered on the use of the term "Hindu-Bali" to describe the local religion. Sudra members argued that the term placed too great an emphasis on the Hindu, and therefore also the caste, elements in Balinese culture and religion. They preferred the term "Bali-Hindu": Korn, *Adatrecht van Bali,* pp. 46–47.

[53] See, for example, "Damai? Damai?" *Surya Kanta* 9/10 (September/October 1926): 132–134; "Pengadilan," *Surya Kanta* 3/4 (March/April 1927): 26.

[54] On the educational question, see, for example, "Pemoeda-pemoeda Bali jang akan mendjadi bibit di tanah itoe dengan Osvia," *Surya Kanta* 3/4 (March/April 1927): 33–34; and "Keperloean Onderwijs," *Surya Kanta* 5 (May 1926): 68–69.

[55] See, for example, "Ngaben di Bali," *Surya Kanta* 9/10 (September/October 1926): 141–42.

[56] According to Balinese adat, as it was then enforced, a man was not permitted to marry "up" or above his caste. Thus, when the commoner HIS (Dutch Native School) teacher I Nengah Metra married a Brahmana woman in 1924, the Raad van Kerta ruled that he must be exiled to Lombok for this offense against adat. This continued to be a cause célèbre among educated commoners through the 1930s. See Ni Ketut Putri Adnyani, "Perkumpulan Bali Dharma Laksana di Bali, Th. 1936 sampai Th. 1942," thesis, Universitas Udayana, Denpasar, 1982.

[57] Korn, *Adatrecht van Bali,* p. 47.

[58] See, for example, "Surya Kanta Pengroesak Keamanan Tjatoerwangsa," *Bali Adnyana* 7 (March 1928): 1; "Bahasa," *Bali Adnyana* 16 (June 1926): 1–2; "Perhatikanlah," *Bali Adnyana* 16 (June 1926): 5–6.

[59] Strangely, the editors did not question the use of the Malay language as the medium for articulating this debate: their own paper was written entirely in Malay. It was the Dutch who, some years later, struck upon the idea of shifting the language of discourse to Balinese.

[60] "Akan meradja lelahkah bahaja merah di poelau Bali dan Lombok?" *Bali Adnyana* 16 (June 1926): 4–5.

[61] "Poelau Bali Akan Kombali Mendjadi Bali," *Bali Adnyana* 19 (August 1929): 1–2.

for example, was set up in Klungkung by a triwangsa, with the explicit aim of averting the spread of caste conflict to South Bali. In the same year the raja of Karangasem authored a booklet, *Darmasoesila,* in which he defended the caste system and sharply criticized the "semi-intellectuals" who wished to destroy it.[62] And in 1931 the periodical *Bhawanagara*—"a monthly magazine of Balinese cultural concerns"—began publication. These publications received the enthusiastic endorsement of the colonial government, which had an obvious interest in promoting a consciousness of Balinese cultural identity, rather than an identity based on caste difference or national Indonesian/Indies unity.[63] Indeed, *Bhawanagara* actually was conceived by the Dutch administration with the intention of calming the caste debate.[64] Its arid style and consciously apolitical tone bore witness to its origins. Korn described the thinking behind the paper's creation:

> Like the Balinese themselves, the writing style of these papers [i.e., *Surya Kanta* and *Bali Adnyana*] is inflammatory and bold. The Dutch administration anticipated the often overweening commentary with regard to the aristocracy, and it is through the monthly *Bhawanagara*, which is open to contributors from both sides, that it hopes to provide a more becoming expression of opinion.[65]

By the end of 1927, *Surya Kanta,* the only paper to have challenged the ideology of caste harmony, had ceased publication, and by 1929 it was followed by *Bali Adnyana,* which had been perhaps too virulent in its defense of triwangsa prerogatives. Yet even after the public polemic had died away, conflict over caste privilege remained a pervasive undercurrent of Balinese social and political life. Decisions about duties at religious ceremonies, rights to exemption from certain corvée and tax obligations, regulations regarding virtually every aspect of social life, all were contingent on caste, and more important, on how one interpreted the criteria for caste membership and the rules regarding caste prerogatives. Caste disputes, though scarcely mentioned in the precolonial anthropological literature, were endemic in those years. The evidence to that effect comes both from the published decisions of the Raad van Kerta, which dealt with an endless stream of caste claims and violations,[66] and from commoner survivors of the

---

[62] Korn, *Adatrecht van Bali,* p. 46.

[63] In the early 1920s Couvreur had seen caste differences on Bali as a dangerous opening for the nationalist movement: R. C. Kwantes, ed., *De ontwikkeling van de nationalistische beweging in Nederlandsche-Indie (1923–1928),* vol. 2 (Groningen: Wolters-Noordhoff, 1978), p. 126.

[64] It was handsomely published under the auspices of the prestigious institute of Balinese culture, the Kirtija Liefrinck van der Tuuk, with the noted Bali expert Dr. Goris as editor until mid-1933, and thereafter as one of two members of the Commissie van Advies.

[65] Korn, *Adatrecht van Bali,* p. 47.

[66] Scores of the decisions of the Raad van Kerta in Bali can be found in the *Adatrechtbundels,* ser. U, *Bali en Lombok:* Bundel XV, no. 30, Adatvonissen (1894, 1914); Bundel XVIII, no. 31, Adatvonissen (1917); Bundel XXIII, no. 35, Adatvonissen (1915–22); Bundel XXXVII, no. 75, Adatvonissen (1915–21).

colonial period, who affirm without malicious intent that tension between castes was a given of Balinese social life.

The polemic between *Surya Kanta* and *Bali Adnyana,* as the Dutch surely knew, was only a symptom of more fundamental problems in Bali and throughout the Netherlands Indies. The communist uprisings of the late 1920s in other parts of the Indies, the emergence of organized labor and political activism in areas that had undergone rapid economic change, and the spread of secular Indonesian nationalist ideology were warnings to the Dutch authorities that times were changing. The emergence in the 1920s of an articulate, Malay-speaking commoner opposition seems to have spurred Dutch efforts to ensure that the rot would not spread and to seek a return to the ostensible harmony and order of "traditional" Bali. Such considerations were at the heart of the Dutch move to restore royal authority in the late 1920s.

Restoring Tradition: Stage 1

By the mid-1920s, the early policies of administrative reform had come to be regarded as ill-informed. The reformers, it was said, had failed to recognize the spiritual significance of the old system of governance and the religious functions of village and other leaders. As a result of the reforms, which had made district and village heads into agents of a bureaucratic state, they had "lost a great deal of their religious aspect."[67] A reaction to these policies within the Dutch bureaucracy took the form of a move to return to "traditional" Balinese institutions and to restore "traditional" Balinese leaders to positions of political and religious authority. What had been implicit now became official. If, as I have argued, the conservative and elitist strain in Dutch administrative policy contributed to the turmoil of the 1920s, then the entrenchment of that approach in colonial law and administrative policy was bound to have serious political consequences for Bali. In the event, the hegemony of the ideology of tradition made political and social conflicts at once less visible and more serious.

In 1929 the decision was taken to change the administrative status of the former kingdoms to negara and to designate their Balinese heads as negara-bestuurders.[68] Although it was claimed that the reforms of 1929 were simply "administrative" and not "constitutional" changes—the negara-bestuurders were still under direct Dutch rule—they marked the beginning of a conscious policy of enhancing the real and symbolic authority of the former Balinese rajas, which culminated in the restoration of "self-rule" (*zelfbestuur*) in 1938.

Many Balinese, perhaps encouraged by the negara-bestuurders, took the

---

[67] "Herstel van zelfbesturen op Bali," report prepared by the Algemene Secretarie te Batavia Eerste Zending (Cabinet to the Governor General in Batavia), June 1935, in Mailrapport 655 geh./35 (Verbaal, 16 June 1937, no. 4), Box 3703, MvK, ARA, p. 31.

[68] Stbl. 1924 no. 226.

4. The raja of Karangasem, I Gusti Bagus Djelantik, in 1925, four years before the Dutch allowed Bali's rajas to resume their royal titles and "traditional" prerogatives. Here the raja is dressed in accordance with his status as *stedehouder* of the Netherlands Indies government, a position inherited from his uncle in 1908 with Dutch approval. Notwithstanding four decades of official backing, an internal Dutch memo of 1946 described him as "a big-size schemer and exceedingly vain." (*Photo and print collection of the Koninklijk Instituut voor Taal-, Land- en Volkenkunde, Leiden*)

1929 change in status to mean that the rajas had in fact already been restored, and they began to use once again the old forms of royal address (Anak Agung, Cokorda, and Dewa Agung). Dutch authorities did nothing to discourage this trend, and in fact officially legalized the use of royal titles in 1930 with an amendment to the original law.[69] Very soon the negara-bestuurders began to assume many of their old "adat functions," some of

[69] The amendment was Bijblad 12499. See "Herstel van zelfbesturen op Bali," in Mailrapport, 655 geh./1935 (Verbaal, 16 June 1937, no. 4), Box 3703, MvK, ARA.

which implied the resumption of various responsibilities and financial contributions on the part of their subjects.[70] A Dutch report disingenuously claimed that the reemergence of the old "functions" had occurred "naturally, on account of the fact that the people again expected this of [the negara-bestuurders]."[71] No measures were taken to bring an end to these practices.[72] In 1932 the negara were given a measure of control of their local finances; the former *onderafdelingskassen* were now called *negarakassen*.[73] In the same year the negara-bestuurders were given increased responsibility for the native judicial system within their territory.[74]

These moves were clearly aimed at regaining the loyalty of the old royal and aristocratic families, to ease the burden of administration and maintain (or restore) the desired state of rust en orde. But there were additional reasons for restoring self-rule in Bali. Chief among them was a perceived need to protect or insulate Balinese society from the decadent influences emanating from Java and beyond. In part, this view was based on a genuine concern among Bali experts that the beauty and uniqueness of Balinese culture might be destroyed by indiscriminate contact with outside and essentially "modern" forces. Traditional Bali, it was felt, ought not to be allowed to perish under the weight of crass modernity, Islamic penetration, and "politics." But it was also part of a political calculation aimed at weakening and isolating the forces of political opposition (in particular nationalism and communism) which had emerged in Java and Sumatra with such alarming speed in the first few decades of the century. Bali was important not only in itself but also as a force to be employed in the larger colonial effort to staunch the flow of political change in the Indies.

As early as 1922, some colonial officials had come to regard Bali as the cornerstone of the Dutch effort to contain the spread of Islamic radicalism and the movement for national independence. At a government conference in that year, the Resident of Bali and Lombok, H. T. Damsté, presented a report with the intriguingly sexual title "Java Courts Bali," in which he

[70] In addition to "normal" contributions to courtly religious events or building projects, subjects became responsible for an increasing number of grand ceremonial affairs, such as the all-Bali land purification ceremony, sponsored by the new negara-bestuurders in 1930. This was the first ceremony of its kind in several decades and undoubtedly required substantial contributions of labor, food, cash, and materials from ordinary Balinese.

[71] "Herstel van zelfbesturen op Bali," Mailrapport 655 geh./1935 (Verbaal, 16 June 1937, no. 4), Box 3703, MvK, ARA.

[72] Interview with J. van Baal, former Assistant Resident, South Bali, 9 May 1987, Doorn. Also see Schulte Nordholt, *Bali.*

[73] They were given control of the negarakassen under Stbl. 1932 no. 520, which became effective 1 January 1932: Mailrapport 655 geh./1935 (Verbaal, 16 June 1937, no. 4), Box 3703, MvK, ARA.

[74] Letter from F. A. E. Drossaers, Directeur van Binnenlands-Bestuur, to Governor General, 7 December 1937, in Mailrapport no. 1219/1937 (Verbaal, 15 July 1938, no. 14), Box 3779, MvK, ARA. The decision on legal affairs was Stbl. 1932 no. 520.

made an explicit plea to keep Bali free from the influence of Java.[75] In the following year, a debate that began in the Raad van Indie over the proposal that the Residencies of Bali/Lombok and Timor be joined to form one large *Gouvernement* very quickly came to focus on the appropriate administrative policy to be pursued in Bali. The protagonists in the debate—A. J. L. Couvreur, a former Assistant Resident of South Bali (1917–20) and then Resident of Timor, and H. T. Damsté—represented differing viewpoints on the wisdom of protecting Balinese culture as opposed to stage-managing its demise through evangelization. The position that Bali ought to be insulated from destructive outside influences was taken up by Damsté, while Couvreur proposed that the island be Christianized by Roman Catholic missionaries.

Despite rather different premises, the arguments on both sides revealed that concern about the spread of Islam and nationalism were at the heart of the issue. Both sides wished to ensure that Islam would not spread its influence over Bali, and both wanted to prevent the seepage of nationalist and other subversive ideas into Bali and from there into the territories farther to the east. The arguments are worth outlining here in some detail because they indicate clearly the primacy of conservative political motivations—as opposed to benevolent cultural, religious, or sociological concerns—at the heart of the arguments of both the preservationists and the modernizers. Let us begin with Couvreur's argument, which is the more unusual.

The culture and religion of Bali, Couvreur argued, would inevitably succumb to the powerful influence of either Islam or Christianity; Dutch colonial efforts to stay this process were neither desirable nor likely to be effective.[76] Given the choice between Islam and Christianity, it would clearly make better sense to encourage the rapid Christianization of Bali by promoting Catholic missionary activity there.[77] Christianization would bear obvious political advantages. Balinese would be less susceptible, for example, to what were seen as Islamic-based political movements in Java.[78] Moreover, a

[75] Cited in "Herstel van zelfbesturen op Bali," Mailrapport 655 geh./35 (Verbaal, 16 June 1937, no. 4), Box 3703, MvK, ARA. *Surya Kanta* joined the debate using similar imagery some years later. See, for example, "Dengan siapakah Bali akan dikawinkan?" ("To whom will Bali be married off?"), *Surya Kanta* 5 (May 1927): 49–54, which argues in favor of an administrative and cultural link with Java.

[76] The following summary of Couvreur's argument is based on selected documents in Kwantes, *De ontwikkeling*, 2:118–32. Couvreur's views are also summarized in the report "Herstel van zelfbesturen op Bali," in Mailrapport 655 geh./1935 (Verbaal, 16 June 1937, no. 4), Box 3703, MvK, ARA.

[77] Missionary activity had been prohibited in Bali since the late nineteenth century, after a Dutch missionary was murdered by his predecessor's only Balinese convert. Nonetheless, Couvreur argued that the transformation would likely be smooth because of the numerous points of similarity between Bali-Hinduism and Catholicism: both, he said, were hierarchical, placed great emphasis on ceremony and art, and were flexible in adapting to local circumstances.

[78] In the years before the communist uprisings of the late 1920s, most Dutch officials held that Indonesian nationalism was essentially an Islamic movement. This view persisted for rather

Christian Bali would serve to cut off "Islamic" Lombok, Sumbawa, South Celebes, and Bima from Java, thereby isolating the latter, and limiting the likelihood of the spread of Islamic radicalism to the eastern islands.[79] If Bali were included in a much larger administrative territory, with the capital in Makassar—a proposal Couvreur favored—these eastern Islamic areas would be effectively "encircled" and would become a weak minority grouping among a Christian majority. The choice of Makassar as capital was not without importance. Its milieu, according to Couvreur, was not Islamic but "cosmopolitan," a fact that he believed would weaken the nationalist movement both in Bali and within the entire area under Makassar's authority.

Lying so close to Java, with clear historical and economic links, Bali was, in Couvreur's judgment, the most "vulnerable" to nationalist tendencies of all the eastern territories. "Still, under present circumstances, that block [the Great East] has an extremely vulnerable side. That is Bali, which at present is secure, but unless we take timely action will not long remain that way."[80] The inclusion of Bali within a large eastern administrative region would consolidate, it was hoped, a solid antinationalist bloc that would act as a political counterweight to nationalist Java.[81] "Once Bali is consolidated," wrote Couvreur, ". . . then truly will the Great East also be secured."[82]

Damsté denied the inevitability of the demise of Balinese culture and religion and argued strongly in favor of its "preservation" through active government intervention. He favored the existing religious policy, which prohibited missionary activity in Bali, on the grounds that Christian proselytizing would disrupt the delicate relationship between religious belief and political order which alone could guarantee the preservation of *rust en orde*.[83] The debate over religious policy in Bali came to a head in the 1930s. While Christian leaders, such as H. Kraemer, appealed to the principle of freedom of religion, Damsté and other colonial officials resisted, claiming that such freedom could be permitted only if it did not endanger peace and order.[84] The position against missionary activity was also taken up by Korn, who argued that Christian propaganda would give rise to something that

---

a long time in some circles. The former Controleur in Tabanan (1930–33) and Buleleng (1933–35) F. W. T. Hunger wrote in a personal communication, June 1988, "All those nationalist leaders were no Hindus. It was a major Islamitic movement and done via religious gatherings and papers."

[79] Kwantes, *De ontwikkeling*, 2:127.

[80] Ibid., p. 125.

[81] Couvreur put this argument in a letter to the Governor General, dated 26 January 1925, cited in ibid., p. 131.

[82] Ibid., p. 128.

[83] Damsté expressed his views at some length in an address to the annual meeting of the Indisch Genootschap, 28 May 1923. See Indisch Genootschap, minutes of the annual meeting, 1923, pp. 112–42.

[84] See Hendrik Kraemer, *De strijd over Bali en de zending* (Amsterdam: H. J. Paris, 1933); and a reply by R. Goris, *"De strijd over Bali en de zending": De waarde van Dr. Kraemer's boek* (Batavia: Minerva, 1933).

until then was unknown in Bali—"hatred of Europeans and mistrust of the colonial government."[85]

Damsté also rejected the plan to group Bali together with the "Christian" territories to the east on the grounds that Bali's culture and religion shared nothing with those societies. Bali was unique—had an *apart character*—he maintained, and it should therefore remain as an autonomous Residency. In this argument, Damsté placed himself in the company of many Bali experts and Baliphiles who could not bear the prospect of Bali's cultural disintegration; and like many colonial officials who succeeded him, he made good use of "expert" opinion. In a 1924 article on the missions question, for example, Damsté approvingly cited Korn and G. P. Rouffaer. Rouffaer, a former director of the Bali Instituut, which was part of the Koloniaal Instituut, provided the classic statement of the preservationist position:

> Let the Balinese live their own beautiful native life as undisturbed as possible! Their agriculture, their village life, their own forms of worship, their religious art, their own literature—all bear witness to an autonomous native civilization of rare versatility and richness. No railroads on Bali; no Western coffee plantations; and especially no sugar factories! But also no proselytizing, neither Mohammedan (by zealous natives from other parts of the Indies) nor Protestant nor Roman Catholic. Let the colonial administration, with the strong backing of the Netherlands government, treat the island of Bali as a rare jewel that we must protect and whose virginity must remain intact.[86]

Though the arguments of Couvreur and Damsté were in some respects diametrically opposed, then, both favored the administrative and political separation of Bali from Java. For Couvreur, the isolation from Java was to place Bali together with an antinationalist and anti-Islamic eastern bloc of "Christian" societies. For Damsté, Bali ought to remain isolated both from Java and from the eastern islands. By 1936, with the creation of the Government of the Great East (*Gouvernement van de Groote Oost*), it was clear that Couvreur's arguments in favor of a large eastern bloc that included Bali, though without the element of Christianization, had won acceptance.[87] It was Damsté's position on the preservation of Balinese culture, however, that had come to set the tone of government policy toward Bali itself. Bali's cultural uniqueness had become a question no longer subject to debate and the need to preserve it a point of faith within the colonial administration. It was only too clear, however, that the underlying and continuing concern of the government was the maintenance of a conservative

---

[85] Cited in Damsté, "Balische Splinters—Zending," *Koloniaal Tijdschrift* 13 (1924): 538.
[86] Ibid.
[87] See, for example, G. A. W. Ch. de Haze Winkelman, Resident of Bali and Lombok (1933–1937), to Governor General, 20 July 1936, in which he argued that Bali and Lombok should be made a part of the Groote Oost, and not an administrative part of Java: Mailrapport 739 geh./1936 (Verbaal, 15 July 1938, no. 14), Box 3779, MvK, ARA.

"peace and order," both in Bali and in the Indies as a whole. A similar preoccupation was evident in the debate over the full restoration of self-rule in 1938.

Restoring Tradition: Stage 2

As we have seen, Bali's cultural and geographical proximity to Java had long been a major concern. The serious effects of the economic depression in Bali—including rising poverty and declining tax payment—opened Dutch eyes to the seriousness of the problem, so that by 1935 the discussion of a full restoration of self-rule in Bali was well under way. The complete resurrection of "traditional" political institutions and power relations, it was argued, would provide the surest guarantee that disruptive outside influences would be held at bay. According to an internal report on the issue prepared in 1935, restoration would ensure that "Bali would not be defenselessly exposed to the influences from outside, which in these times of rapid communications have such free play."[88]

The need to batten down the political hatches was all the more urgent in view of the fact that the forces of nationalism and communism were, in Dutch eyes, no longer being expressed in an Islamic idiom, but increasingly in the symbology of "old" Java, which they judged to "have great influence on Bali." An example of the danger was the Hindu-Javanese movement of the Javanese Atmodjo Koesoemo, which, according to a Dutch report, had "a large number of followers among the Balinese chiefs," and which, "behind the guise of Hindu-Javanese ideas, insidiously disseminates communist propaganda."[89]

The argument that restoration would help in the fight against nationalism and communism was based on the premise that the return of Balinese royalty would win the favor of all Balinese, who would then look favorably upon the Dutch government for bringing it about. The 1935 report argued that "recognition of the existing organizations offers the advantage that it will increase the gratitude and appreciation of the Balinese for the government, and in that way will yield political profit, which is of great importance in the face of the nationalist currents that are also exercising some influence in Bali."[90] It was true that most of the negara-bestuurders themselves—as well as the sole Balinese member of the Raad van Indie, the nobleman Cokorda Gde Raka Sukawati—favored the idea of self-rule, and they made a formal request to that effect as early as 1935. The language they used was remarkably

[88] "Herstel van zelfbesturen op Bali," in Mailrapport 655 geh./1935 (Verbaal, 16 June 1937, no. 4), Box 3703, MvK, ARA, p. 32.

[89] Ibid., p. 33.

[90] Ibid., pp. 27–28.

similar in tone and content to that of the Dutch authorities.[91] It revealed the extent to which the Balinese elite had learned to engage in the discourse of the colonial state in order to be effectively heard. This was a lesson of no small importance in the shaping of Bali's own internal political discourse.

Despite the appeal of the negara-bestuurders' reasoning to Dutch ears, it was far from obvious that all Balinese were enthusiastic about a restoration. The relationship between royalty and ordinary Balinese was not purely a "symbolic" one. It also entailed work and payments on the part of the subject, and broad prerogatives and customary entitlements for royalty. The claim that royal excesses would be held in check by Dutch supervision was pure fantasy, and most Dutch officials knew it.[92]

On at least one occasion, the Directeur van Binnenlands-Bestuur, F. A. E. Drossaers, suggested that the interests of the Balinese were not the same as those of their kings. In a letter to the Governor General in October 1936 he wrote: "To suggest that the ordinary people of Bali expressly asked for the restoration of self-rule would be incorrect. The great mass of the Balinese people live their own lives in the village and the subak, and would like nothing more than to be left alone in peace."[93] This was an unusually solid bit of advice, but finally a voice in the wind. The habit of conflating the wills of the Balinese and their "traditional" rulers was becoming well entrenched, and it was justified with the rather simplistic proposition that the "magical bond" between rulers and ruled in Bali made all "traditional" rulers ipso facto legitimate in the eyes of their subjects. Accordingly, a certain amount of effort was devoted to proving that, even after the years of direct rule, such a magical bond still existed. One report explained soberly that the negara-bestuurders still provided "magical cures" to afflicted subjects who requested them, and from that evidence drew the conclusion that "the magical significance of the kings, which is the major precondition for the restoration of self-rule, lives on undiminished among the people."[94]

Signs of social unrest, caste conflict, decay in certain areas of religious and cultural practice, the emergence of a group of antifeudal commoner intellectuals—all were seen as the consequence of ill-advised policies of

---

[91] Part of the request read as follows: "Luckily Bali has not yet been contaminated by the evil of provocation that results from the excessive influence and examples from other regions. . . . If the government introduces self-rule in each of the negara, then in our opinion, such evil influence will have more difficulty in reaching Bali": "Verzoekschrift" (n.d.), Mailrapport 655 geh./1935 (Verbaal, 15 July 1938, no. 14), Box 3779, MvK, ARA.

[92] In a letter to the Governor General, 20 July 1936, G. A. W. de Haze Winkelman, Resident of Bali and Lombok, indicated that the loss of European control over the rajas would be one of the major problems of the restoration: Mailrapport 739 geh./1936 (Verbaal, 15 July 1938, no. 14), Box 3779, MvK, ARA.

[93] Drossaers to Governor General, 31 October 1936, in Mailrapport 1089 geh./1936 (Verbaal, 15 July 1938, no. 14), Box 3779, MvK, ARA, p. 12.

[94] "Herstel van zelfbesturen op Bali," in Mailrapport 655 geh./35 (Verbaal, 16 June 1937, no. 4), Box 3703, MvK, ARA, p. 42.

weakening the authority of the original rajas and removing a number of traditional district and village heads from office.[95] A report on Tabanan prepared in the mid-1930s, for example, argued that the "menacing dislocation" of native institutions there had been the consequence of the earlier Dutch policy of administrative reform, and in particular the removal of the raja.[96]

The obvious solution, therefore, was to restore the rajas and the traditional ruling families to their former positions of power. It is worth stressing that what the Dutch had in mind was not simply a superficial or symbolic resurrection—that had been achieved in 1929—but a move to strengthen the rulers both materially and institutionally, in the interest of political order. According to a 1936 report, "recognition of the old forms of native rule will have the effect of strengthening, preserving and making more resilient the powers present there, and there is perhaps no area in the Netherlands Indies where this is more necessary than Bali."[97]

Evidence of the government's interest in perpetuating the economic power of the rajas can be found in various reports on the issue of restoration. These reports state clearly that every effort would have to be taken to ensure that the financial position of the rajas was maintained. The rajas were to be given authority over the disposal of all locally generated revenue, hitherto controlled by Dutch officials, while at the same time continuing to receive the regular monthly salaries that had been introduced as compensation with the imposition of direct rule. In addition, all of the rajas would continue to receive children's allowances of an unspecified amount, which were aimed at encouraging them to send their children to school, so that Bali's future leaders would be "qualified" aristocrats.[98]

Though the eight rajas were, in principle, to be treated as equals from a financial viewpoint, some clearly did better than others. The rajas of the last kingdoms to have been brought under direct rule—Bangli, Gianyar, and Karangasem—received, in addition to their monthly salaries of between f. 700 and f. 850 per month, compensation for the abolition of the "palace service" (*ayahan kadalem*). Moreover, according to the Resident of Bali and Lombok, H. J. E. Moll, in 1938 "three of the eight prospective zelfbestuurders

[95] Ibid., p. 29.

[96] Regerings Commissaris, "Nota van Toelichtingen van . . . Tabanan," pp. 58–67. This was one of a series of reports on the eight kingdoms in Bali, prepared under the auspices of the Regerings Commissaris voor de Bestuurshervorming in de Groote Oost (Government Commission for Government Reform in the Great East), in anticipation of the transition to self-rule.

[97] "Herstel van zelfbesturen op Bali," in Mailrapport 655 geh./35 (Verbaal, 16 June 1937, no. 4), Box 3703, MvK, ARA, p. 28.

[98] In a letter to the Governor General, 25 April 1938, the Resident commented on the children's allowance: "In this regulation, in my opinion, there is a pedagogical stimulus for the chiefs and government officials, to provide their sons and daughters with a decent education and thereby to protect the children from these families from a dependent and empty existence, in which only their high-birth would place them above the ordinary people": Mailrapport 636 geh./1938, Box AA160, MvK, ARA.

. . . also receive a substantial personal income from land and goods."[99]
Moll did not identify the kingdoms by name but it is reasonable to assume
that they were those that had not had their properties confiscated at the time
of incorporation under colonial rule: Bangli, Gianyar, and Karangasem.

Currents of Change

The decision to restore "traditional" elites to power, and indeed the general trend in this direction before 1938, gave rise to a number of political
problems. First, it brought into political focus rivalries among noble houses
(*puri* and *jero*).[100] The prospect of a royal restoration led to renewed (and
open) claims to royal legitimacy among rivals as early as 1929. The situation
was complicated by the fact that over the preceding years, particularly in the
kingdoms longest under direct rule, newly influential puri had emerged to
challenge the puri of the old "legitimate" line. After a tour of Bali in October
1936, Drossaers noted that such rivalries seemed to exist in every kingdom,
though they appeared to be most acute in Buleleng and Jembrana and least
serious in Bangli, Gianyar, and Karangasem.[101]

By 1929 Buleleng and Jembrana had experienced several decades of direct
Dutch rule and nearly a century of colonial political control, during which
time the position of the royal families had dramatically declined.[102] In Badung and Tabanan the duration of direct Dutch rule had been shorter, but the
impact on the old royal families, through deaths, exile, and the confiscation
of property, had been similarly dramatic. In these kingdoms the "restoration" entailed the reimposition of the symbols and many of the material
benefits of royal power after a lapse of several decades. Given the gap in
royal rule in these kingdoms, it was not a simple matter to choose the royal
heir to be designated as zelfbestuurder and there was no guarantee that the

[99] H. J. E. Moll to Governor General, 25 April 1938, in Mailrapport 636 geh./1938, Box
AA160, MvK, ARA.

[100] The terms *puri* and *jero* describe extended households of Satria caste with a genealogical
claim to noble status. In theory, relative status is based on the principle of proximity to a core or
royal lineage. The houses of those most closely related to a "reigning" raja may legitimately be
referred to as *puri gde,* while those more distantly related are designated, in declining order, as
puri, jero gde, and *jero.* Historically, however, there has been a more or less continuous debate
over status claims. See Geertz, *Negara,* pp. 26–34, 60; Geertz and Geertz, *Kinship in Bali,*
pp. 117–52.

[101] Drossaers to Governor General, 31 October 1936, in Mailrapport 1089 geh./1936
(Verbaal, 15 July 1938, no. 14), Box 3779, MvK, ARA.

[102] In a letter to the Governor General in July 1936, the Resident of Bali and Lombok drew
attention to the differences in the status of the prospective zelfbestuurders in the various
kingdoms. In particular he contrasted Buleleng and Jembrana, on the one hand, where "until
1929 the descendants of the former kings were . . . serving in subordinate positions with the
government," with Karangasem, on the other, "where the current negara-bestuurder was until
1921 the Viceroy in his territory": G. A. W. de Haze Winkelman to Governor General, 20 July
1936, in Mailrapport 739 geh./1936 (Verbaal, 15 July 1938, no. 14), MvK, ARA.

5. The raja of Gianyar, Anak Agung Ngurah Agung, at his puri in 1930. The restoration of Bali's rajas and the return to "tradition," evident in the style of dress worn here, was part of a Dutch strategy for maintaining political stability, but did not always reflect a genuine respect for the rajas themselves. An official memo of 1946 described the raja of Gianyar as "an Oriental schemer and extortioner. His conduct under the Japanese occupation was so bad that even the Japs would not maintain him in his position, so that he was exiled." (*Photo and print collection of the Koninklijk Instituut voor Taal-, Land- en Volkenkunde, Leiden*)

appointee would be regarded as legitimate by his new subjects. In Bangli, Gianyar, and Karangasem, by contrast, the royal families had endured a relatively brief period of direct Dutch rule and their landed wealth had not been confiscated. For them the restoration meant a continuation of royal power, but with the added prestige of royal title and prerogatives. With the backing of the colonial state, the royal families in these territories became increasingly powerful.

In the territories where the royal families had been deposed, restoration of "traditional" rulers inevitably meant that choices had to be made between contending puri, and that formal, hereditary criteria had to be weighed against the criteria of political influence and merit. The government came down firmly on the side of the former. Thus some of the new zelfbestuurders ultimately lacked political credibility and social status, and those denied access to political position were prey to frustration and bitterness. The details of puri rivalry in Bali and their articulation in the early years of the National Revolution are dealt with in chapter 5. Here it is enough to note that the Dutch decision to return to a "traditional" system of royal hereditary rule ensured that puri rivalry would remain at the heart of Bali's political life through the colonial period and well beyond.

A second major difficulty with the return to self-rule along "traditional" lines was the fact that Bali had already begun to change, socially, economically, and politically. Consequently, significant elements—not numerous but certainly significant in the challenge they posed to colonial orthodoxy— were not at all enthusiastic to see a return to what they now termed "feudalism." Dutch authorities were aware that there were opponents of their policy among Bali's educated youth and teachers in particular, but they were reasonably confident that in the new traditional Bali, the "strange" or "foreign" ideas of these troublemakers would not take root. In a condescending style that became familiar over the next decade, government reports dismissed these opponents of Balinese feudalism as "a small group of Balinese youth who are filled with foreign theories, and who see salvation only in the complete dismantling of Balinese society as it now exists."[103]

Whereas the commoner intellectuals of the 1920s had been preoccupied with the evils of the caste system, by the late 1930s the current of nationalist Indonesian thought had grown stronger.[104] The spread of nationalist consciousness in Bali was largely the consequence of contact with Java, both through education and through a small but important group of Javanese civil servants posted in Bali. As such, the prewar nationalist movement in Bali—with the possible exception of Tabanan—remained largely an urban "middle-class" phenomenon.

The first and only prewar nationalist political party to establish a branch in Bali was Parindra (Partij Indonesia Raya, Greater Indonesia party) and it was a Javanese medical doctor, Murjani, who took the initiative in doing so, shortly after his transfer from Java to Jembrana in 1939.[105] Budi Welas Asih (BWA), a nationalist organization active in the fields of education, mutual aid, and farmers' cooperatives, had been established in Tabanan in 1937.

[103] "Herstel van zelfbesturen op Bali," in Mailrapport 655 geh./1935 (Verbaal, 16 June 1937, no. 4), Box 3703, MvK, ARA, p. 49.
[104] A reasonably good summary of early nationalist trends in Bali can be found in Nyoman S. Pendit, *Bali Berjuang*, 2d ed. (Jakarta: Gunung Agung, 1979), Introduction and chap. 1.
[105] The first Parindra branches in Bali were established in Jembrana, where Murjani lived, and then in Singaraja, Denpasar, and Tabanan: Pendit, *Bali Berjuang*, pp. 7–14.

The BWA had contact with Parindra before Murjani's arrival, so it was natural that he set up a subbranch of the party in Tabanan and that it soon became the most active Parindra section in Bali. To a considerable extent, the strength of the nationalist movement in Tabanan was a result of the early development of grass-roots organizations outside of the main town. Indeed, there is some indication that Parindra targeted Tabanan as a promising base area precisely because of the existence there of self-help groups, village cooperatives, and local study clubs.

Although the BWA played no formal role in Balinese "politics," it was active in the dissemination of nationalist ideas both through the distribution of newspapers and literature—such as the *Suara Parindra, Mustika, Suara Teosofie, Takbir Mahabarata,* the writings of Sutomo, Sun Yat-sen, and Wahidin Sudiro Husudo—and through the organization of seminars and public meetings.[106] The BWA was as much concerned with spiritual renewal as with the struggle for simple political independence, and it looked especially to the Javanese spiritual traditions and to the works of Mohandas Gandhi for inspiration. Instruction in the art of self-defense (*pencak silat*), which had both spiritual and physical aspects, also became an important part of the BWA's program. Another organization with nationalist inclinations, Bali Dharma Laksana, was formed out of two smaller school groups: Eka Laksana, a student organization ostensibly concerned with "the advancement of Balinese culture," and Balische Studie Fonds, which raised money to help Balinese attend school. In 1936 Bali Dharma Laksana began publication of a magazine called *Djatajoe* (1936–41), which, though moderately nationalist in orientation, had a similar focus on educational and cultural issues.

The preoccupation of prewar Balinese nationalists with spiritual renewal, education, literacy, and self-reliance owed a great deal to the Parindra philosophy, but it was stimulated by the particular conditions prevailing in colonial Bali. To Bali's young nationalists, one of the most obnoxious features of the Dutch regime was its systematic efforts to keep Bali locked in the "dark ages," as expressed in the cultural cum educational policy of *Baliseering* (Balinization), which began in the 1920s.[107] The Dutch, they argued, wanted to maintain Bali as a "living museum" and to reshape Balinese culture according to a romantic image that appealed to outsiders but not to Balinese interested in controlling their own destiny. Balinese calls for a degree of democratization and reform in the system of adat law were met with an extraordinary arrogance. The young teachers and intellectuals,

---

[106] Junianti, "Peranan Budi Welas Asih Dalam Merintis Ide Nasionalisme di Tabanan, 1937–42," thesis, Universitas Udayana, Denpasar, 1982, chap. 4.

[107] Interviews with I Made Wija Kusuma, 23 March 1986, Denpasar; I Made Kaler, 2 June 1986, Denpasar; Ibu Jasmin Oka, 2 June 1986, Denpasar. One of the earliest proponents of this policy was Resident Damsté. He received the support of such renowned Bali experts as Korn, Roelof Goris, and the artist Walter Spies.

wrote Drossaers in 1936, displayed "a great overestimation of Western democratic forms and a serious underestimation and misunderstanding of eastern institutions and practices."[108]

As cultural policy, Baliseering entailed the reintroduction of "traditional" styles of dress, architectural forms, dance, and rules of speech. According to the Dutch authorities, Balinese ought to wear "Balinese" clothes; modern construction techniques, no matter how practical or desirable to those who used them, were determined to be aesthetically "bad," and therefore to be avoided; Balinese (*not* Malay) language was to be encouraged and the strict observance of its status-marking code enforced as adat law. In the context of this state-sponsored "renaissance" of Balinese culture, the wearing of pants by men or the *kebaya* (Javanese blouse) by women became a subversive act. The use of the inappropriate level of Balinese language or the use of Malay was seen by government authorities as a brazen act of resistance, and was punishable in the Raad van Kerta.

As educational policy, Baliseering meant instruction in traditional Balinese dance, sculpture, music, language, and script, and the near absence of such subjects as world history, mathematics, and "foreign" languages, whether Malay, Dutch, or English. To educated Balinese, these policies were patronizing and obnoxious, and they helped to make educational and cultural issues a chief focus of Balinese nationalist discourse, through the Revolution and into the Sukarno era. Their significance was heightened by the peculiarly limited educational opportunities available in Bali. Balinese who wanted to attend advanced high school or teacher's school had to travel to Java to do so.[109] The situation was particularly difficult for low-caste Balinese with no connection to the colonial civil service because Dutch educational policy gave preference to triwangsa and to civil servants.[110] Balinese students in Malang, Probolinggo, Surabaya, and Yogyakarta quickly set up political and social organizations and began to take part for the first time in the debates on national independence both as Balinese and as Indonesians. When they returned to Bali in the late 1930s and early 1940s, many of them joined branches of moderate nationalist organizations such as Parindra and BWA, or became teachers in the growing network of independent Taman Siswa schools.[111]

[108] Drossaers also scoffed at the teachers' criticism of the system of adat law and their proposals to introduce elections: Drossaers to Governor General, 31 October 1936, in Mailrapport 1089 geh./1936 (Verbaal, 15 July 1938, no. 14), Box 3779, MvK, ARA.

[109] In 1923 Bali had only one Europeesche School, two Hollandsch-Inlandsche School (HIS), twenty-five Gouvernements Inlandsche School, and sixty-eight Volksschool. According to one report, in 1920 a mere 6% of the population in Buleleng could read, whereas in 1850 it was estimated that at least 50% could do so. See Damsté, "Balische splinters," p. 532.

[110] Anak Agung Gde Putra Agung, "Lahirnya Idee-idee Pembaharuan Dalam Organisasi Sosial di Bali," *Basis* 21 (March 1972): 183–89.

[111] On the Taman Siswa schools in Bali, see I Gusti Putu Wirata, "Pergerakan Taman Siswa di Bali: Tahun 1933 Sampai 1943," thesis, Universitas Udayana, Denpasar, 1979.

With the establishment of a Taman Siswa school system in Bali after 1933, young people who were unable to travel to Java had access to a nongovernment, nationalist-oriented education.[112] As we shall see in later chapters, the Taman Siswa network also forged links between the nationalist movements on Java and Bali through the National Revolution and beyond. The central figure in this network was the Javanese nationalist Wiyono Suryokusumo, who lived and taught in Bali for several years before the Japanese occupation. Balinese Taman Siswa graduates almost uniformly point to Suryokusumo (as he was known in Bali) as the inspiration for their later nationalist activism. More concretely, it was through Suryokusumo that they were brought in touch with such nationalist leaders as Sjahrir and Djohan Sjahroezah and were encouraged to organize an anti-Japanese underground beginning in mid-1944, and later a branch of the Indonesian Socialist party (Partai Sosialis Indonesia, or PSI).[113] Personal friendships and networks developed through other schools as well. At the Dutch Native School (HIS) in Singaraja, the Balinese teacher Nengah Metra inspired some of the most prominent pemuda leaders.[114] In short, the schools, particularly the high schools, formed a strong basis for the development of nationalist consciousness in Bali.

The imposition of a hegemonic Dutch state over the whole of Bali in the first decades of this century produced profound changes in Balinese society and generated new kinds of political and social conflicts, even while it appeared to preserve "traditional" native rule and a high degree of outward political and social harmony. The element of state paternalism—sometimes in the name of preservation, sometimes in the name of change—was particularly significant. Beginning in the 1920s, fears of political disruption and social decay, aided by the pretense of Bali's unique character, reinforced tendencies in the direction of preservation, so that Bali ultimately became something of a showpiece of the Ethical Policy. It was conservative political motivations that prompted the moves to restore "tradition" in Bali, yet these moves led to significant changes in Balinese social and political relations.

The prior and paramount authority of the colonial state in Bali shaped

[112] A Taman Siswa committee was set up in 1933 on the initiative of a leading member of the Puri Pemecutan in Denpasar, I Gusti Ngurah Pemecutan. The earliest members of the committee included several non-Balinese civil servants, then posted in Denpasar, and a number of low-caste Balinese: interview with I Nyoman Pegeg, 21 July 1986, Denpasar.

[113] Interview with I Nyoman Pegeg, 16 September 1986, Denpasar. Djohan Sjahroezah was a leading prewar nationalist and a central figure in the anti-Japanese underground in Java. Together with Sjahrir he founded Paras (Partai Rakyat Sosialis, or Socialist People's party), which fused with Amir Sjarifuddin's Parsi (Partai Sosialis Indonesia, or Indonesian Socialist party) to form the PS (Partai Sosialis, or Socialist party). On 12 February 1948, Sjahrir and Djohan led the split from the PS and established the PSI.

[114] Interviews with Ketut Wijana, 29 September 1986, Singaraja; I Nengah Wirta Tamu, 19 December 1986, Denpasar; and Ida Bagus Indera, 30 September 1986, Singaraja.

political, social, and economic relations and structured Balinese political discourse. Colonial rule reinforced and to some extent created a pattern of political affiliation and consciousness that divided Balinese over essentially internal issues, rather than one in which they were united behind some broader cross-class consciousness of Balinese ethnicity, regional identity, or Indonesian nationalism. These divisions were reflected in Balinese political and social discourse, which tended to focus on issues of caste, feudalism, education, and culture even within the nascent nationalist movement of the late 1930s. Apart from the rather obvious point that this pattern reflected the legal limits imposed by a colonial state concerned about peace and order, the somewhat narrow focus of Balinese political discourse emerged precisely because of the structure of the colonial state. These were the real issues raised by the particular system of colonial rule established in Bali, and they reflected, as it were, the abiding concerns of the people who were required to live within it.

3 Paupers in Paradise: Bali's Colonial Economy

DEEP CAPITALIST PENETRATION, large foreign-owned plantation agriculture, and the forced production of cash crops for export, which so profoundly affected rural Java in the late nineteenth and early twentieth centuries, were almost wholly absent in Bali.[1] Drawing a connection between the
rise of capitalist agriculture and the emergence of political consciousness in
Java, colonial officials argued for the maintenance of a "pure and unadulte-
rated agrarian Bali."[2] To the extent that large estates and industry could be
kept out of Bali and the agricultural economy maintained in its "traditional" state, they argued, clashes between capital and labor, as well as the
resulting nationalist awareness, would be kept to a minimum and the conditions for continued Dutch rule more favorable.[3]

Yet if Bali escaped the harsh imprint of the "Cultivation System" and if its
smallholder agricultural system appeared to carry on in the traditional pattern, still by the early 1930s the problems of rural landlessness and pauperization were as marked there as in much of Java.[4] A 1935 government report
noted that Bali's smallholders "could scarcely make ends meet" and that the

---

[1] In the kingdoms of Jembrana and Buleleng, some tracts of land were leased on a long-term
basis (*erfpachten*) to foreign capitalists as early as 1860. The tract known as Tjandikoesoema,
in Jembrana, later became the object of a contentious debate over the wisdom of permitting
such leasing arrangements in Bali. Most of the land leased in the early years, however, was of
inferior quality and lay in undesirable sparsely populated areas, so that the practice did not
significantly affect the economic situation for Balinese. See Lekkerkerker, "De tegenwoordige
economische toestand," pp. 197–202. According to J. L. Swellengrebel, 6,800 acres of land on
Bali were still foreign-owned in 1954: Introduction to Wertheim, *Bali*, p. 9.

[2] Memo from Dr. Korn, noted in the "Memorie van Overgave" of H. T. Damsté, Box
AA191, MvK, ARA.

[3] Kwantes, *De ontwikkeling*, 2:124–25.

[4] For a stimulating reexamination of the "Cultivation System" in Java, see Cornelis Fasseur,
The Politics of Colonial Exploitation: Java, the Dutch, and the Cultivation System, trans. R. E.
Elson and Ary Kral (Ithaca: Cornell Studies on Southeast Asia, 1992).

general state of health on the island was poor, with high levels of malnutrition, tuberculosis, and venereal disease.[5] Nearly fifteen years after the disastrous earthquake of 1917—in which roughly 1,400 died, tens of thousands of houses and temples were destroyed, and thousands of hectares of land ruined—the economy had not recovered.[6] Korn, writing *before* the full effects of the Depression of the early 1930s were evident, wrote what few wanted to hear: "Whoever gets to know more fully the living conditions of the ordinary man in Bali quickly discovers what a gray and impoverished mass of humanity populates this beautiful island . . . in Gianjar, Badung, and Karangasem the people live for the most part in bitter poverty . . . and this poverty is growing worse."[7]

It was the Depression, however, that revealed the severity of the problem in Bali, and the extent to which Balinese agriculture and economy had already been drawn into the capitalist sphere. Those convinced that Bali was an island of economic bounty made studious efforts to ignore the facts. Gregory Bateson, for example, wrote that "the Balinese, especially in the plains, are not hungry or poverty stricken. They are wasteful of food,"[8] and G. A. W. de Haze Winkelman—Resident of Bali and Lombok (1933–37)—claimed that "the people of Bali are amongst the best fed in the Netherlands Indies."[9] The Dutch state, after all, had intervened to save the common people from the harsh extractions of despotic kings and had worked to protect the traditional Balinese agricultural economy from unscrupulous foreign investors; landlessness, poverty, and hunger could not possibly have been the result. Yet these denials obscured the central fact. Pauperization in

[5] "Herstel van zelfbesturen op Bali," Mailrapport 655 geh./1935 (Verbaal, 16 June 1937, no. 4), Box 3703, MvK, ARA. As early as 1920, P. de Kat Angelino had warned of serious health problems in Bali, including in his list the high rate of infant mortality and high incidence of opium addiction and suicide. See "De hygiene, de ziekten en de geneeskunst der Baliers," *Tijdschrift Bataafsche Genootschap* 59 (1920): 209–48. In 1923 Lekkerkerker reported a similar state of ill health: "De tegenwoordige economische toestand," pp. 177–80.

[6] According to a 1935 report, "Long before his colleagues, who all came to the [government] conference with favorable reports, the Resident of Bali and Lombok, as early as the beginning of 1931, had to report that the economic situation in Bali was unfavorable": "Herstel van zelfbesturen op Bali," Mailrapport 655 geh./1935 (Verbaal, 16 June 1937, no. 4), Box 3703, MvK, ARA, p. 46.

[7] Korn, *Adatrecht van Bali*, pp. 336–37. Ch. J. Grader, a colonial civil servant in Bali in the 1930s, wrote that on a tour of the Mengwi district of Badung in 1932 he found that "a great many people consider themselves lucky if they manage to eat one decent meal per day": quoted in Schulte Nordholt, "Een Balische Dynastie," p. 270.

[8] Gregory Bateson, "The Value System of a Steady State," in Belo, *Traditional Balinese Culture*, p. 391. Bateson's article, originally published in 1949, was based on observations made in the 1930s, when he and Margaret Mead were in Bali. These views have since been reiterated in popular and scholarly studies of the island. Willard Hanna, for instance, writes that "life in Bali in the 1930s was agreeable not only for the affluent foreigners but also for the Balinese . . . the ordinary people had on the whole plenty of rice and relatively few complaints" *Bali Profile*, pp. 106–7.

[9] G. A. W. Ch. de Haze Winkelman to Governor General, 20 July 1936, in Mailrapport 739 geh./1936 (Verbaal, 15 July 1938, no. 14), Box 3779, MvK, ARA.

Bali was the consequence not of unbridled penetration by foreign capital but rather of the system of revenue extraction of the Dutch state itself.

The political significance of the systems of taxation and corvée labor lay not only in the absolute levels of rural poverty to which they contributed but also in the way they structured class relations in the countryside. Who paid tax or contributed labor, to whom and according to what rules: these were, politically speaking, the key questions. At the local level, tax and corvée labor relied on a network of Balinese officials and local notables, many of whom were aristocrats. One result was that tension over tax and corvée labor tended to be focused against Balinese aristocrats, not against the colonial state or individual Dutch officials.[10] Incidents of overt resistance to taxation and corvée labor, which occurred with surprising frequency in the first two decades of this century, appeared to diminish as the colonial state was consolidated through the 1920s and 1930s.

The Tax Regime

The generation of revenue was a central concern of the Dutch administration in Bali as early as 1855, when the first Controleur, P. L. van Bloemen Waanders, was sent to Singaraja. Through the second half of the nineteenth century, Dutch administrators set about to make the tax system more efficient with a view to increasing state revenues. By the turn of the century, according to one source, the rate of taxation on wet rice land (*sawah*) in Buleleng increased from an average of 4 percent of the yield to about 12 percent. Over the same period, annual land-tax revenues, now accruing to the Dutch state rather than the raja, increased from about f. 6,000 to about f. 150,000.[11]

Opium provided another source of revenue for the colonial state in Bali. The Dutch, like the rajas they had deposed, sold licenses for the trade in opium to individual Chinese businessmen known as *pachter*. The value of opium imports grew steadily after 1855, and so did Dutch revenues. In 1875 the Dutch administration in North Bali earned f. 217,000 through its control of the opium trade.[12] And in 1910, two years after it had established a state opium monopoly throughout the island, the figure was f. 1,000,000, a substantial proportion of the Residency's total administrative budget.[13]

[10] To the extent that the heavy tax burden necessitated borrowing, Chinese money lenders may have become an additional target of antagonism, though I have not come across any clear evidence to this effect.

[11] Hanna, *Bali Profile*, pp. 65, 69, and 90. These figures must be treated with some caution, as Hanna does not clearly indicate their source.

[12] In 1859 opium imports into Buleleng were worth f. 450,000, or more than 80 percent of the value of all imports in that year, and by 1873, opium imports had grown to f. 2,250,000: ibid., pp. 64–65.

[13] The official opium monopoly (*opium regie*) was established on 1 January 1908: ibid., pp. 96–99.

Calculations of potential state income preoccupied the colonial authorities. For the colonial enterprise to be viable, especially in the era of the Ethical Policy, it was important that it be able to pay its own way. A successful Resident, therefore, was one who could secure a revenue surplus without endangering "peace and order." A 1935 internal report on the restoration of self-rule in Bali summarized the situation: "After the incorporation of the kingdoms of Bali, the entire administrative structure was revised principally in the interest of the mobilization of corvée labor and the collection of taxes, particularly the land tax."[14]

In the brief half-century of Dutch rule over the whole of Bali, tax assessments and actual tax revenues increased several times. In 1917 the state extracted f. 3,794,353 from the Residency of Bali and Lombok; by 1930 the figure had more than doubled to f. 8,235,000. Overall, it was estimated that in those years the government obtained in revenues roughly f. 37,000,000 more than it spent in the Residency.[15] During the 1920s, which were relatively prosperous years, Balinese gained a reputation for being good taxpayers. However, this apparent willingness to pay taxes could not long disguise the fact that, in the words of the author of the 1935 report, "the surplus from Bali has been obtained through the imposition of an extremely heavy tax burden on the people."[16]

Balinese were subjected to a bewildering array of taxes, including a much-resented slaughter tax, an income tax, a personal wealth tax, export and import duties, street-light tax, firearms tax, bicycle tax, and the corvée labor (*heerendienst*) exemption fee, to say nothing of the local taxes, fines, and religious obligations levied by the irrigation society (*subak*), the hamlet (*banjar*), and the village community (*desa*).[17] The chief source of government revenue in Bali, however, was the land tax (*landrente*). In the early years of Dutch rule, an interim land tax had been assessed according to a complex of often ill-understood regulations.[18] Beginning in 1922, a more

[14] "Herstel van zelfbesturen op Bali," Mailrapport 655 geh./1935 (Verbaal, 16 June 1937, no. 4), Box 3703, MvK, ARA, p. 31.
[15] Ibid., p. 47.
[16] Ibid.
[17] Studies of the locally levied "village and adat" taxes suggested that they were heavier in Bali than in any other part of the Netherlands Indies. See, for example, *Verslag van den belastingdruk op de Inlandsche bevolking in de buitengewesten* (Weltevreden: Landsdrukkerij, 1929), pp. 182–229. A 1935 government report concluded that in the area of "village and adat" taxes the people of Bali "are obliged to make alarmingly high expenditures": in "Herstel van zelfbesturen op Bali," Mailrapport 655 geh./1935 (Verbaal, 16 June 1937, no. 4), Box 3703, MvK, ARA, p. 49.
[18] Agrarian relations in the precolonial period varied widely from one kingdom, even one district, to the next. Lekkerkerker admitted in 1923 that "we knew very little at all about agrarian relations in Bali": "De tegenwoordige economische toestand," p. 187. There were at least two distinct forms of "private" land: (1) *sawah kasoegian* was sawah unconditionally owned by an individual or family; (2) *sawah pengayah* was sawah held on long lease from a king, which bore with it certain obligations in labor and produce.

regularized land-tax system was introduced in accordance with the Bali Landrente Ordonnantie of that year.[19]

Based on modern topographical survey techniques and a scientific estimate of the potential productivity of each plot of land, the new tax regime brought with it an immediate and dramatic increase both in the rates of taxation and in the taxable area.[20] In some areas, tax rates increased by more than 100 percent on sawah and 200 percent on drylands,[21] and in certain areas the average was even higher.[22] Moreover, the highest rate on sawah—found in Buleleng, Bangli, and Klungkung—were roughly two and one-half times as high as the heaviest average rate in the territories outside Java and Madura.[23] On drylands, the situation was much the same; the average tax rate in Bali was the highest anywhere in the Netherlands Indies, Java included.[24] Finally, calculated as a percentage of the value of gross agricultural production, the combined sawah and dryland tax burden in Bali was the highest in the colony. A 1929 government report on taxation concluded that the new land-tax regime in Bali had brought about a "sudden and very important increase in the tax burden."[25] In 1927 the revenue from land tax in Bali constituted nearly two-thirds of all land-tax revenues collected in all territories outside Java and Madura.[26]

These figures provide convincing evidence that Bali was no economic paradise for the ordinary Balinese peasant or tenant farmer, and that the chief source of the problem was the tax system of the colonial state. As a result, taxes were commonly evaded even in the prosperous 1920s, at least where one could evade them without detection. It was only after 1931 however—when the Depression began to bite and it became increasingly

[19] The full name of the law was the Bali Landrente Ordonnantie: Regeling nopens den aanslag en de inning van landrente in genoemde geweest, Stbl. 1922, no. 812. For a discussion of the new system see ibid., pp. 186–92.

[20] In Buleleng, for instance, the area of drylands subject to taxation increased by 245%. The corresponding figures for increases in other kingdoms were Badung, 307%; Gianyar, 197%; Klungkung, 191%; Karangasem, 91%; Jembrana, 65%; and the district of Nusa Penida, an extraordinary 704%. See *Verslag van den belastingdruk,* p. 85.

[21] The tax rates in Buleleng increased by 101.25% on sawah and 205% on dryland. The corresponding figures in four other kingdoms were, respectively, Badung, 50.38% and 173.39%; Gianyar, 99.30% and 27.30%; Klungkung, 94.26% and 92.66%; and Tabanan, 25.29% and 178.72%. Compiled from "Herstel van zelfbesturen op Bali," Mailrapport 655 geh./1935 (Verbaal, 16 June 1937, no. 4), Box 3703, MvK, ARA; and *Verslag van den belastingdruk.*

[22] In Buleleng it was f. 18.76/hectare, in Badung f. 17.71/hectare, in Klungkung f. 15.71/hectare, and in Jembrana f. 16.71/hectare: *Verslag van den belastingdruk,* p. 71.

[23] The average tax rate on sawah in Bali, after 1927, was f. 10.87/hectare, which was higher than in many parts of Java. In Madiun and Semarang, for example, the rates were f. 4.20 and f. 4.42/hectare, respectively: *Verslag van den belastingdruk,* p. 73.

[24] The average figure for Bali was f. 27/pikul of padi. Corresponding figures from Java and the outlying territories were Madiun, f. 19; Semarang, f. 19; Banyumas, f. 20; Surabaya, f. 26; Borneo, f. 22; Celebes, f. 19; and Timor, f. 20: ibid., pp. 80–81.

[25] Ibid., p. 86.

[26] The revenue from all outlying territories was f. 3,155,243 of which the amount from Bali was f. 1,946,811: ibid., pp. 67–68.

difficult to get the Balinese to pay their taxes—that the severity of the problem was brought home to colonial officials in Bali and Batavia. The case of Tabanan is instructive. After reviewing the land tax in 1932, the Dutch authorities had to reduce the assessment by up to 10 percent to make up for "the sharp deterioration in the general standard of living" there, and were forced to grant further exemptions of between 10 and 25 percent per year over the next five years.[27] Yet in spite of these adjustments, the rate of nonpayment of land tax between 1931 and 1935 in Tabanan still averaged 42 percent on dryland and 31 percent on sawah.[28] In 1933, in Bali as a whole, more than 50 percent of the assessed land tax remained unpaid.

The root of the problem lay in the fact that after 1919 all taxes in Bali and Lombok had to be paid in Netherlands Indies cash.[29] In the 1920s Balinese peasants had responded to the need for cash by expanding their household production of exports such as copra, coffee, pigs, cattle, and rice. So long as the prices for these products remained buoyant, as they did through most of the 1920s, most people were able to pay their taxes.[30] Dependence on these export products as the main source of cash, however, led to serious difficulties after 1931, when their value dropped dramatically. In desperate need of cash, Balinese producers more than doubled the volume of their exports between 1930 and 1932, but the total value of those exports still declined in absolute terms (see Table 1). And whereas in 1928 more than 90 percent of those required to do corvée labor had instead paid the average f. 10 exemption fee, in 1932 fewer than 10 percent could manage to do so.[31]

One of the lasting consequences of the Depression in Bali was a high incidence of landlessness. Precise figures do not exist, in part because the vast majority of land transfers were handled either informally or by the irrigation and tax officials (sedahan and sedahan agung) without the knowledge of the Dutch bureaucracy, and also because the colonial authorities made no serious effort to look into the issue. Scattered evidence, however, suggests that landlessness had reached serious proportions in the early

[27] Regerings Commissaris, "Nota van Toelichtingen betreffende . . . Tabanan," p. 41.

[28] These figures are based on data provided in ibid., pp. 40–42.

[29] This was a decision of the Resident of Bali and Lombok, Residentiebesluit No. 1205, which came into effect on 31 December 1919.

[30] According to one report, the prices of Bali's major exports were three to five times higher during the 1920s than they were even in 1936, after the worst of the Depression was over. See de Haze Winkelman to Governor General, 20 July 1936, Mailrapport 739 geh./1936 (Verbaal, 15 July 1938, no. 4), Box 3779, MvK, ARA.

[31] In Bali and Lombok as a whole, the percentage paying the fee had jumped from a minuscule 0.11 in 1926 to 51.6 in 1917. In South Bali, the figure for 1928 was 99%, while in North Bali it was only marginally lower at 87%: *Verslag van den belastingdruk*, pp. 87–92. In Badung, the number of people paying the exemption fee—which was reduced in 1932 to f. 3 per year—dropped from 25,791 in 1931 to just 945 in 1934: Schulte Nordholt, "Een Balische dynastie," p. 275. Similarly, the number who paid the exemption fee in Tabanan dropped from 17,003 in 1932 to only 1,945 in 1934, or a decline from about 56% to just over 6% of those required to do corvée labor. These figures are derived from data in Regerings Commissaris, "Nota van Toelichtingen van . . . Tabanan," p. 43.

Table 1. Volume and value of imports and exports, Residency of Bali and Lombok, 1927–1934

Year	Volume of exports (kgs)	Value of exports (guilders)	Volume of imports (kgs)	Value of imports (guilders)
1927	19,604	6,778,341	—	3,205,407
1930	17,086	5,872,446	6,057	3,007,931
1931	17,647	4,629,000	2,041	1,098,000
1932	34,772	4,556,000	1,403	650,000
1933	35,132	3,701,000	1,359	534,000
1934	32,327	2,720,000	1,435	440,000

Sources: Compiled from Department van Economische Zaken, *Jaaroverzicht van den in- en uitvoer van Nederlandsch-Indie gedurende het jaar* [various], *Deel II, Buitengewesten; Mede-deeling van het Centraal Kantoor voor de Statistiek,* nos. 67/1927, 98/1930, 105/1931, 114/1932, 121/1933, 129/1934.

1920s, and that it grew much worse during the Depression. C. Lekkerkerker wrote in 1923 that "the number of landless [farmers] is large, in some areas comprising as much as half of the adult population."[32]

In Tabanan, for example, the Depression accelerated a process of large-scale land transfers from small farmers to larger landowners, which had been triggered by the new land-tax system, creating in effect a new landed elite.[33] A government report on Tabanan noted that the severe difficulties experienced by peasants in paying the land tax during the Depression left many with large debts at the end of each year "which could be met only through numerous foreclosures—far below the real value of the land."[34] The Controleur for Gianyar, H. K. Jacobs, reported in 1934 that there, too, the incidence of landlessness was extremely high.[35]

It was not simply the increase in the absolute levels of exploitation and landlessness, however, that gave the colonial tax regime its political signifi-cance. What mattered, politically, was who paid the tax, in what form, and to whom. From this perspective, the structure of the tax system implied much more than a simple exploitation of the "the Balinese" by "the Dutch." It meant as well the exploitation, both apparent and real, of some Balinese by others, and it engendered a consciousness of inequality that focused resentment toward powerful Balinese.

There were two elements in this dynamic. First, although Dutch officials of the land-tax office determined the rates of taxation and established the legal boundaries and productive capacities of Bali's landholdings, it was Balinese officials—particularly the sedahan agung, sedahan, and local tax

[32] Lekkerkerker, "De tegenwoordige economische toestand."
[33] The puri Kaba-Kaba in eastern Tabanan, for example, is said to have amassed consider-able landed wealth during these years: Schulte Nordholt, "Een Balische dynastie," p. 273.
[34] Regerings Commissaris, "Nota van Toelichtingen van . . . Tabanan," p. 41.
[35] Cited in Schulte Nordholt, "Een Balische dynastie," p. 269.

officials—who were responsible for the actual collection of the tax. The incentive to enforce a strict (and perhaps excessive) rate of extraction was powerful because these officials received a healthy percentage of the collected revenue; the sedahan agung, for instance, received as much as 10 percent. In addition, their de facto power to determine boundaries, recategorize tracts of land, and even alter rates of taxation provided these officials with unequaled opportunities to accumulate personal landed wealth.[36]

Second, the land-tax regulations did not specify whether owner or tenant was responsible for the payment of the tax. This was a matter of convention and negotiation between the landlord and the tenant. Generally speaking, where land was most scarce, the burden was borne primarily by the tenant, in addition to the payment of a percentage of the yield, as part of the fee for using the land.[37] In cases where previously untaxed lands had become taxable, the owner frequently attempted to place the responsibility for payment entirely on the tenant.[38] The land tax then, was often paid by those farmers and tenants in the weakest economic position. Under these circumstances, the "willingness" of Balinese tenants to pay the land tax may have been evidence of their fear of losing access to the land, rather than their loyalty to traditional leaders or the colonial government.

Apart from indications of tax evasion, there is little evidence of open protest against these heavy extractions on the part of Bali's peasantry after about 1920. It would be wrong to conclude, however, that Bali's peasants had few complaints. Rather, I think it is clear that the colonial economy—and particularly the tax system—both in the absolute burden it placed on the rural sector and in the way that burden was distributed, placed Bali's peasants in a peculiarly powerless position, making open rebellion less likely.

Corvée Labor

One of the clearest examples of significant change occurring behind the rationale of traditional practice was the transformation of the system of corvée labor under Dutch rule. Corvée labor of various kinds—including *heerendienst* and *desa-dienst*—existed in precolonial Bali, but the conditions and terms of work varied considerably from one region to the next and seem to have been enforced with some flexibility.[39] Where the prestige and power

---

[36] Schulte Nordholt writes: "All the evidence suggests that this category of officials had considerable autonomy in conducting their work, . . . in addition, countless informal transactions occurred which remained off the record": ibid., p. 269.

[37] By the early 1920s the terms of tenancy were already extremely unfavorable for the tenant, who was often able to keep as little as one-third of the crop he or she produced: Lekkerkerker, "De tegenwoordige economische toestand," p. 194.

[38] Ibid., p. 266.

[39] At the turn of the century, Dutch observers understood *heerendienst* (in Balinese, *ayahan kadalem*) to mean service or labor for one's lord or patron. It could encompass "the mainte-

of the raja and lesser nobles or patrons were measured in the number of their followers, a situation that prevailed in most of Bali in the nineteenth century, and where ordinary people were able to change patrons, the latter naturally tried to avoid alienating followers by imposing too heavy a burden on them. Taken together, heerendienst and desa-dienst, according to late nineteenth-century accounts, were not an onerous burden. In late-nineteenth-century Tabanan, for example, it was not uncommon for villagers unhappy with their patron simply to leave and take up with a more lenient or helpful patron.

> Every subject has the right to withdraw his obedience from a patron, and to request from the king that he be placed under a different lord whenever his [the subject's] interests are not being looked after to his satisfaction, or if the rule of his lord is in some respect not to his liking. . . . This right is currently being claimed by the dependents of Jero Denbatas because they had suffered a great deal from the lord's arrogance and arbitrariness.[40]

At the turn of the century, the total number of workdays required in Tabanan seldom amounted to more than twenty per year, and in Karangasem the total was less than ten.[41]

Colonial rule did not lead to the abolition of existing forms of unremunerated labor. Rather, the legal right to use such labor was channeled through the administrative and legal structures of the colonial state to the punggawa and rajas who now derived their authority from it.[42] Moreover, the substantial public works projects—roads, bridges, harbors, dams, and irrigation canals—implied by the Ethical Policy made the burden of corvée labor far

---

nance, restoration, and guarding of puris and jeros, the upkeep of the main roads, a service that is very seldom required, the performance of guard duty where tolls are levied, and coolie work": J. H. Liefrinck and H. J. E. F. Schwartz, "Dagverhaal van eene reis van den Resident van Bali en Lombok vergezeld van den Controleur voor de Politieke Aanrakingen en de Poenggawa's Ida Bagoes Gelgel en Goesti Ktoet Djlantik naar Tabanan en Badoeng van 17 Juli t/m 5 Augustus 1899," *Tijdschrift voor Indische Taal-, Land-, en Volkenkunde* 43 (1901): 146. *Desa-dienst* (in Balinese *ayahan banjar*), or neighborhood service, included "the construction and maintenance of roads, temples, cockfighting arenas, and village bathing places": H. J. E. F. Schwartz, "Dagverhaal van eene reis van den Resident van Bali en Lombok vergezeld van den Controleur voor de Politieke Aangelegenheden en de Poenggawa's Ida Njoman Bandjar en Goesti Njoman Raka naar Karangasem en Kloengkoeng van 11 t/m 26 April 1898," ibid., p. 117.

40 Liefrinck and Schwartz, "Dagverhaal van eene reis van den Resident van Bali en Lombok . . . naar Tabanan en Badoeng van 17 Juli t/m 5 Augustus 1899," p. 143.

41 Schwartz, "Dagverhaal," p. 117.

42 In the kingdoms of Gianyar, Bangli, and Karangasem, the ayahan kadalem was abolished in 1917 (Stbl. 1916 no. 162), and the rajas and punggawa received monetary compensation thereafter. The rajas originally received f. 100/month, while the punggawa received between f. 15 and f. 50/month. The total cost to the colonial administration was f. 710/month or f. 8,520/year. In the five remaining kingdoms, the right of the rajas and punggawa to claim ayahan kadalem was abolished at the time of their incorporation under direct Dutch rule. See Moll to Governor General, 25 April 1938, on the subject "Civiele lijsten der zelfbestuurders op Bali," in Mailrapport 636 geh./1938, Box AA160, MvK, ARA.

6. Corvée laborers building a road in Bali, about 1920. Under Dutch colonial rule Balinese of low caste were required to perform an average of thirty days of unremunerated manual labor each year, reduced to twenty-five in 1931 and to twenty in 1938. Here the Balinese overseer of a road-building project, holding a surveyor's rod and pith helmet, is flanked by his assistants. (*Photo and print collection of the Koninklijk Instituut voor Taal-, Land- en Volkenkunde, Leiden*)

greater in the colonial period than it had been before.[43] Within each Residency, bureaucratic regulations were established regarding the number of workdays required, eligibility for exemption, and so on, with the result that the system became, in some respects, more "efficient" and uniform. Sustained now by legal sanctions, it therefore also became more onerous and more unforgiving than it had been as recently as the late nineteenth century.

The corvée rules underwent a series of changes under Dutch rule, ostensibly in the direction of reducing the labor burden. In 1931 a decision was taken to reduce the number of workdays required throughout the Outlying Territories. In Bali the new figure was twenty-five days per man per year, which was still at least five days more than were required at the turn of the century in Tabanan, and fifteen more than were required in Karangasem.[44]

[43] For examples of the use of Balinese corvée labor in the major colonial public works projects, such as the Oongan Dam, Benoa harbor, and the hundreds of miles of new roads, see Lekkerkerker, "De tegenwoordige economische toestand," pp. 153–210.

[44] Only two Residencies in the Outlying Territories had higher figures—Benkoelen and Manado, where the average number of workdays/man/year were 30 and 28, respectively.

Two years later, in 1933, the rules were again amended to bring them into line with international regulations on forced labor. The total number of workdays required, however, remained at twenty-five until 1938, when they were reduced to twenty.[45] Any further reduction, it was argued, would interfere with government operations, particularly in public works.[46]

The true political and social significance of the corvée system, however, lay not solely in the absolute number of workdays required but in the regulations on the use of labor and the terms of exemption. Although the forced labor system was legally regulated by the colonial state, the rules and norms of its implementation left Balinese punggawa responsible for the mobilization of labor and, in many cases, for the determination of the projects undertaken, with little or no direct Dutch supervision. The result was a system that worked to the personal benefit of the noble families of district heads or rajas. In the district of Mengwi, Henk Schulte Nordholt writes that "the punggawa could easily employ large groups of corvée laborers for his own purpose. The institution of corvée labor thus solved one of the biggest troubles the Balinese elite had to cope with in the precolonial period: how to mobilize enough manpower. Paradoxically, it was the colonial state which provided the labor system with which Gusti Putu Mayun [the punggawa] could articulate his own royal ambitions."[47] In 1926, years after personal service and labor obligations to rajas and lords had been officially abolished, the drafters of a new agrarian law for Bali and Lombok felt it necessary to state explicitly that such obligations were no longer required by law; this was a clear indication that, in practice, the unauthorized levy of such labor was still common.[48]

Responding to criticism of this state of affairs, the colonial government enacted new regulations as late as 1933 to control abuses of the corvée system.[49] Even the new law, however, left substantial room for maneuver by Balinese notables. The maintenance of all bridges, dikes, canals, and roads, for example, were to be "so far as possible the responsibility of the local authorities."[50] And since control of the labor system by local elites was ensconced with an elaborate set of formal rules and procedures, they could

[45] See "Herziening Heerendienst Ordonnantie," in Mailrapport 26/1938, Box 415, MvK, ARA.

[46] In Tabanan, the average number of workdays/man/year required actually increased marginally between 1934 and 1937, from 20.92 to 22.77. See Regerings Commissaris, "Nota van Toelichtingen van . . . Tabanan," p. 43.

[47] Henk Schulte Nordholt, "Temple and Authority in South Bali," paper presented at the Sixth European Colloquium on Indonesian and Malay Studies, Passau, June 1987, p. 17.

[48] The legislation was Agrarische Aangelegenheden Bali en Lombok, Stbl. 1926 no. 396. Art. 1 stated: "Those lands to which was attached responsibility for service to the former lords [the *petjatoe ayahan dalem*] and those who till such lands in the sub-Residency of South Bali . . . are now released from all obligation in respect to those former lords."

[49] The legislation was Stbl. 1933 no. 261. Art. 4 required the approval of the Resident before any major new work project could be undertaken.

[50] See, for example, art. 12, sect. II, of Stbl. 1933 no. 261.

rely on the colonial state to intervene on their behalf in the case of local recalcitrance.

Colonial regulations governing exemption from corvée labor in Bali discriminated in favor of triwangsa at the expense of the sudra.[51] On the rare occasion that triwangsa were called upon to perform some service, the Dutch rules stipulated that they were to be "burdened only with those kinds of work that are permissible according to local institutions and custom."[52] The tasks permitted under this ruling were the delivery of government documents and mail when the postal service was unavailable, and escorting prisoners when no police were available. All manual labor was ruled out. In effect, the triwangsa got off scot-free, and the burden of hard labor fell entirely on the sudra. Moreover, the determination of "eligibility" for service and the mobilization of labor were tasks left to the district or locality, which left much room for manipulation by local elites.[53]

Owing to the administrative rigor with which matters of obligation and exemption could now be enforced and the legalistic rigidity of the caste hierarchy imposed by colonial law, numerous Balinese now scrambled to lay legal claim to triwangsa status.[54] At the same time, many of the respected but "nonaristocratic" groups or clan networks, such as the Pande, Pasek, and Sengguhuh, were unceremoniously dumped into the large and undifferentiated residual sudra category, thereby losing substantial political rights and prestige.[55] Not surprisingly, the creation of legal social categories and the attachment of differential privileges and obligations to them led to a storm of litigation and to the existence, in Balinese social discourse, of a

[51] Bali en Lombok Heerendienst Ordonnantie, arts. 3 and 12(v). The precise list of those exempted from service changed periodically. The 1938 regulations, for example, listed eleven categories for exemption, including judges of the Raad van Kerta, local heads, government servants, teachers, medical doctors, house servants, public school pupils, and recently arrived Javanese or Madurese migrants. This list supplemented earlier rulings: Stbl. 1923 no. 113, Stbl. 1926 no. 500, and Stbl. 1925 no. 169. For a discussion of the 1938 ordinance see "Herziening Heerendienst Ordonnantie," in Mailrapport 26/1938, Box 415, MvK, ARA.

[52] In fact, the exemption of all triwangsa was not in keeping with precolonial practice throughout the island. In Tabanan, for example, only Brahmana had been exempt from such labor obligations; members of the Satria and Wesia groups had not been: Regerings Commissaris, "Nota van Toelichtingen van . . . Tabanan," p. 49.

[53] Art. 14 of the Bali en Lombok Heerendienst Ordonnantie read: "With regard to the mobilization of corvée labor, this should be done as far as possible in consultation with the authorities of the Native community concerned." Art. 13(2) left it to the "village community" to determine "who would be considered liable . . . for corvée labor, and who not."

[54] Schulte Nordholt writes: "Many families on the fringes of the nobility did their best to have dormant claims to titles recognized as quickly as possible because the demarcation between aristocrat and nonaristocrat was no longer fluid but had become rigid. Those who missed the boat were to be excluded for a long time": *Bali,* pp. 30–31.

[55] Pande, which literally means "smith," is the name of the closely knit clan of metalsmiths. Pasek, the largest single clan of commoners, traces its roots to Java's Brahmana caste. Sengguhu is the name of a group of non-Brahmana priests. For further information on the Pande, see Roelof Goris, "The Position of the Pande Wesi (1929)," in Wertheim, ed., *Bali,* pp. 289–99. For information on all three clans, see Fred B. Eiseman, Jr., *Bali: Sekala and Niskala,* vol. 1: *Essays on Religion, Ritual, and Art* (Berkeley: Periplus, 1989), chaps. 3, 7, and 8.

category of "paper Satria" (*Satria kertas*). It also led to considerable bitterness on the part of unsuccessful litigants and the mass of Balinese sudra, who accounted for roughly 90 percent of the population.

Rural Resistance

Political reports from Bali in the first two decades of the twentieth century recount a surprising number of acts of rural protest for an island with a reputation for peace and harmony. The available evidence suggests that much of it was resistance to excessive taxation or corvée labor.[56] Yet, paradoxically, as the burden of taxation and corvée grew weightier through the 1920s and 1930s, the incidence of open protest appears to have diminished. The apparent harmony and peace in rural Bali during these years was, I think, principally the result of the consolidation of colonial state power and the structure of the colonial economy.

The relationship between state power and the decline of open protest had at least three dimensions. In the first place, the Dutch were both willing and able to use force to still any overt sign of resistance, thereby increasing the costs of protest. Second, by gradually co-opting a large part of the Balinese aristocracy, the Dutch diminished the pool of influential and powerful Balinese in rural areas who might mobilize some resistance to the colonial state. Finally, through the ideology of "tradition," colonial officials managed to obscure the extent and the political significance of less overt resistance. By consolidating the state in these ways the Dutch managed to establish in Bali both an appearance and a mythology of harmony, peace, and order.

The Dutch authorities generally responded to acts of protest with a swift show of force, and they did so with the enthusiastic support of the rajas and punggawa. Colonial troops were deployed at least as often in response to disturbances in the indirect-ruled kingdoms as in those under direct colonial rule.[57] Thus, even in the areas that were, in a formal sense, least directly under the control of the colonial state apparatus, the balance of power

[56] Resistance included, for example, the movement led by a messianic healer named Nang Moekanis, in Jembrana. For details, see Damsté to Governor General, 16 May 1921, in Mailrapport 514/1921, MvK, ARA; and H. T. Damsté, "Balische Splinters—Nang Moekanis, de wonderdokter," *Koloniaal Tijdschrift* 13 (1924): 650–55. Another case was a plot to kill the punggawa of Tojapakeh, Nusa Penida, led by the village head of Koetampi, in alliance with hamlet heads from the area. The plot is detailed in "Dagboek van den Controleur van Klungkung over het tijdvak tot en met 9 Feb. 1916," in Mailrapport 1071/1916, MvK, ARA. there were several cases of refusal to pay taxes, some of which are discussed later in this chapter. There were also cases of resistance to the sentences handed down by the Raad van Kerta and protests against corvée labor.

[57] In 1916 nineteen platoon-sized "brigades" of armed police were stationed in the Residency of Bali and Lombok. They were joined by four "independent brigades." See report on South Bali, 1 September 1916, to the Directeur van Binnenlands-Bestuur from the Adviseur voor Bestuurszaken der Buitenbezittingen, in Mailrapport 2430/1916, Mvk, ARA.

within the Balinese polity had begun to shift in favor of Balinese aristocrats as a consequence of the backing they now received from that state. The case of resistance by an entire village (Sukawati, Gianyar) to the demands for corvée labor in May 1917 is instructive, and gives a flavor of the political climate in Bali at the time.[58]

Sentenced to six days of hard labor as punishment for refusing to carry out their heerendienst for the raja of Gianyar, 136 men from Sukawati, followed by several hundred supporters, marched to the town of Gianyar to protest the verdict of the Raad van Kerta. In a showdown with armed police in Gianyar, five of the protesters were killed, eleven seriously wounded, and twenty-six taken prisoner. With all the "ringleaders" either dead or in jail, the Resident announced one month later that both the heerendienst and the hard-labor punishment had been carried out without further incident.

Subsequent investigations revealed that the rebels in Sukawati had vowed in a temple not to perform the heerendienst and not to submit to punishment for their refusal. Before their departure for Gianyar, moreover, they had sworn not to obey any orders from outside of their own group, and to observe strict solidarity throughout. One of those arrested was reported to have said to the police: "If the others work, I will too. If not, then I also refuse. Work alone I will not."[59] Over 500 strong, they collectively refused to march to the jail in Gianyar as ordered by the raja, the police, and the punggawa. Instead they walked to the central marketplace, where they sat in protest and refused all orders to move. The raja, acting with the approval of the Controleur (who stood at a safe distance), threatened them with still harsher punishments if they refused to comply with his orders. The threats were ignored and the crowd began to hurl abuse at the raja, saying that the men charged were not guilty of any crime and that the heerendienst imposed an unfairly heavy burden.

With the arrival of a "brigade" of armed police—about the size of a platoon—the protesters were compelled to stand and march toward the prison. A few yards outside the market, however, they stopped, sat down, and began to talk among themselves in unusually loud voices. Once again, with the help of the armed police, they were made to stand and walk, only to

---

[58] The following account is drawn from several reports of the event, including telegrams from the Resident, L. van Stenis, to the Governor General (28 May 1917) and the Minister of Colonies (29 May 1917), in Mailrapport 1104/1917; "Rapport omtrent het verzet in Gianjar door een 136 tal veroordeelden op Zondag, den 27sten Mei 1917," with a covering letter from Resident van Stenis to the Governor General, 9 June 1917, in Mailrapport 1281/1917; a report by the Controleur of Gianyar, J. F. Mirandolle, "Vervolg op het rapport omtrent het verzet in Gianjar op Zondag, 27 Mei 1917," 3 June 1917, in Mailrapport 1201/1917; and a report by Hove Kamp, "Kort verslag der Residentie Bali en Lombok over Mei 1917," 3 July 1917, in Mailrapport 1451/1917, MvK, ARA.

[59] J. F. Mirandolle, "Vervolg op het rapport omtrent het verzet in Gianjar op Zondag, 27 Mei 1917," 3 June 1917, in Mailrapport, 1201/1917, MvK, ARA.

stop yet again at the gate to the raja's puri. Here they remained for some time, saying they would rather die than move. Soon shouting began, and when the Controleur ordered that those responsible be detained, the crowd gathered round to protect them and swept them down the road amid loud chanting. Shortly thereafter one of the original "shouters" returned, dressed in white and supported by a group of men now armed with daggers (krises) and spears. At this point, allegedly in self-defense, the police began to fire on the crowd.

The political meaning of this protest, and others like it, is worth consider-ing. First, it is evident that this was not a demonstration against "the Dutch," the "state," or even the Controleur. Indeed, a spokesman of the group was reported to have said explicitly, while seated at the puri gate, that they were not opposed to the Controleur or to the Gouvernement, but to the raja of Gianyar. The Controleur replied that the refusal to obey the raja was the same as disobedience to the Gouvernement. From the Dutch viewpoint, of course, this was true, even in the indirect-ruled kingdoms. Yet the struc-ture of Dutch rule in Bali—the near invisibility of the Dutch hand—was such that the focus of the protesters' anger was not the colonial state but the raja.

Second, the source of irritation in Sukawati seems clearly to have been the various forms of corvée labor and other extractions demanded by or through the raja. In the preceding year, the people of Sukawati had on three occa-sions performed their labor service only after being forced to do so by armed police, and they had similarly refused to pay a new trade tax introduced in 1914 until threatened with arrest and the seizure of their property.[60] While these were in one sense clearly economic issues, the refusal to obey the orders or answer the demands of the raja of Gianyar was essentially an act of political resistance that in the past, with the support of a perbekel or pung-gawa, might have been expected to bring positive results. The manner in which these acts of resistance were put down, however, pointed to significant changes in the extent and the nature of the rajas' power under colonial rule.

A tax revolt in the village of Lodjeh, Karangasem, in 1916 bears interest-ing similarities to the Gianyar protest.[61] On the night of 20 June 1916 the villagers of Lodjeh gathered in a temple and swore a collective oath not to pay the tax on drylands (*oepeti*) or to perform the required heerendienst, and to resist with force any attempt to make them do either. Later that evening, the perbekel of the neighboring village of Sidemen reported to the raja of Karangasem that the people of Lodjeh were "behaving in a hostile fashion." This news was in turn conveyed to the Controleur of Karangasem, A. M. Ballot, who, after consultation with the police commander for South

<hr>

[60] "Rapport omtrent het verzet in Gianjar" in Mailrapport, 1281/1917, MvK, ARA.
[61] The following account is based on "Kort verslag der Residentie Bali en Lombok over Juni 1916," in Mailrapport 1655/1916, and "Politieke Verslag," a report by the Controleur of Karangasem, A. M. Ballot, 24 June 1916, in Mailrapport 1703/1916, MvK, ARA.

Bali, dispatched a force of forty armed police to the village. Confronting villagers who were clad in white and armed with krises and spears, the police advanced and fired, killing one, wounding one, and taking eighty-five people into custody before the revolt was brought under control. Controleur Ballot described the scene as follows:

> On the terraced . . . sawahs, with their village in the background, stood a crowd armed with krises and lances, almost all dressed in white, who at our approach adopted a defiant attitude and began to shout while a number of them with lances began to advance, and in the village a particular rhythm was beaten furiously on the *tong-tong*—according to the raja, a war song.[62]

Among those arrested were three suspected "agitators" whose alleged crimes give a sense of the character of the uprising. The first was said to have told the people of Lodjeh that the gods had exempted them from the payment of the oepeti and the performance of the heerendienst. He was also said to have told them to buy white cloth in preparation for ritual death. A second was accused of pronouncing mantras intended to ensure that the police guns would not fire. The third, it was alleged, had written a threatening letter to the perbekel of Telibang, who had official jurisdiction over Lodjeh. The letter indicated that the incident was not simply a "tax revolt" but a direct challenge to the legitimacy of the perbekel of the subdistrict. "Perbekel," the letter read, "recently you became angry with our subdistrict, you scolded us, you must remember; you told us then that we could not have our own chief, but take note that we have now chosen our own pung-gawa."[63]

Dutch officials were determined to find no "political importance" in statements and acts of resistance of this kind. Resident L. van Stenis wrote in his summary report that the uprising in Lodjeh "had no political significance, rather it was all the result of the easily inflamed character of the Balinese in that area."[64] The denial of true political content in these protest movements served to reassure the bureaucracy—or at least one's superiors in it—that the colonial apparatus was working as it ought. Unless one was interested in arguing for a change in policy, or in shooting one's own foot, there was no sense in drawing attention to "political" difficulties. To the extent that an uprising or disturbance could be attributed to the psychological idiosyncrasies of a small group of people, the need to consider its general political implications seriously could be avoided.

For a variety of reasons, it was also preferable to view these incidents as

---

[62] "Politieke Verslag," a report by the Controleur of Karangasem, A. M. Ballot, 24 June 1916.

[63] Ibid.

[64] Note by Resident van Stenis appended to "Politieke Verslag," a report by the Controleur of Karangasem, A. M. Ballot, 24 June 1916, in Mailrapport 1703/1916, Afschrift 5418/1, MvK, ARA.

7. Dutch colonial officials and their wives gather with members of the Balinese elite, about 1925. Seated in the center are the Resident of Bali and Lombok and the raja of Karangasem, flanked by their wives. The royal children, dressed in velvet suits and bowler hats, stand in the foreground. To their left, dressed in white, are four priests (pedanda), possibly members of the Raad van Kerta; and to their right, the district head (punggawa) of Karangasem. The Bali expert and then Controleur of Badung, V. E. Korn, is also visible. (*Photo and print collection of the Koninklijk Instituut voor Taal-, Land- en Volkenkunde, Leiden*)

offenses against customary law, and so in both cases the agitators were tried before the Raad van Kerta, accused of breaches of social obligations to their lord or raja. The use of the Raad van Kerta not only ensured that a stiff warning would be sent to others who would resist their superiors, it also preserved the near invisibility of the colonial state, an attribute which was central to the maintenance of Dutch power in Bali. The decision to try these cases in the Raad van Kerta, moreover, effectively defined the protests as something within the realm of "custom," and therefore ostensibly not political. The fact was, of course, that "customary" issues could be intensely political. However, the "adat-ification" of Balinese politics—the renaming of political acts as breaches of custom—allowed those in power to maintain the fiction that Bali was an apolitical place, that Balinese society was essentially harmonious, and that the status quo was acceptable to all Balinese.[65]

[65] The conscious depoliticization of Balinese life found an interesting parallel in the changing format of the weekly and monthly political reports ("Politiek Verslag") of the Controleurs and

Unlike much of Java, which had suffered nearly three centuries of mercantilist extraction and later capitalist penetration, Bali's experience within the colonial economy was, by and large, limited to its penetration by an activist revenue-seeking state. The colonial state imposed a heavy burden on Bali's rural population, through both taxation and corvée labor, which contributed to serious poverty and increasing landlessness in the 1930s. Colonial rule also shifted the political relationship between Balinese officials and ordinary people to the advantage of the officials. One reason for this change was the unprecedented availability of armed force, provided by the Dutch state, which could put a swift end to incipient uprisings. Also important was the way in which the tax and labor systems structured class relations in the countryside, directing the antagonism of the peasantry against other Balinese.

While it was the Dutch who managed the means of force, it was the Balinese rajas and punggawa who were seen to call for and benefit from its use. In both the Sukawati and the Lodjeh incidents, the rebels protested the impositions of their Balinese lords, appealed to the gods to justify their refusal to pay tax to or perform labor service for Balinese authorities, shouted insults at the native police force in low Balinese, and were ultimately tried according to "Balinese" law. The Dutch state was scarcely visible in these incidents, though it was at the heart of the changing political relations among Balinese. It is hardly surprising, then, that there was little or no evidence of anti-Dutch sentiment in these acts of resistance. Bali's rural rebels, at least at this stage, were simply not anti-Dutch.

In late-nineteenth- and early-twentieth-century Bali there was still some opportunity for open protest involving alliances between peasants and more powerful figures in the community. After about 1920, however, the structure of the colonial economy, particularly the tax and corvée systems, increasingly limited the likelihood of any such broad cross-class alliance against the colonial state. And, as the incidents at Sukawati and Lodjeh suggest, the consolidation of the colonial state made open protest an increasingly risky and fruitless business.

---

the Resident. Until about 1919, these reports had included a good deal of commentary on puri rivalries, tax revolts, and the domestic squabbles of the aristocracy. In the 1920s and 1930s they became quite empty, reporting only occasionally on formal political organizations, which were rather scarce. What had once been known as "politics" was now carefully hidden away in reports on "administration" and "adat."

4   *The Japanese Occupation*

JAPANESE FORCES LANDED AT SANUR BEACH ON 18 FEBRUARY 1942, bringing an abrupt end to Dutch colonial rule in Bali.[1] The three-and-a-half-year
period of Japanese rule marked a turning point in the island's political
history. By August 1945 Bali was straining under grinding poverty, its villages were mobilized into quasi-military organizations, and its youth were
fired with a militant nationalism. Perhaps most important, deep hostility
had developed toward Balinese who had worked too closely with the Japanese and, before them, with the Dutch. With Japan's surrender in August
1945 the stage was set for the revolutionary upheaval of 1945–49.[2]
    When one assesses the dramatic changes in Bali during the brief Japanese
interregnum and their political significance, certain themes become evident.
First, the administrative structures that the Japanese inherited from the
Dutch—particularly the system of indirect rule—were easily adapted to the
aims of the Japanese state. As in Java and other areas under Japanese control,
these aims included the forced production of food and other agricultural
products necessary for the war; corvée labor on an unprecedented scale; and
the mobilization of the general population for both political and military
ends. Further, while the Japanese system of surplus extraction caused great
suffering in Bali, the structure of Japanese rule, like the Dutch system before
it, tended to generate social and political conflict among Balinese, rather
than simply cause a uniform antagonism toward the Japanese. Finally, the
Japanese did not share the Dutch obsession with preserving Balinese culture

---

[1] The Japanese landed in Manado, Tarakan, and Kalimantan in the first half of January
1942; in South Sumatra on 14 February; and in Java on 1 March 1942. Dutch authorities,
acting unilaterally on behalf of Allied Forces, surrendered unconditionally to the Japanese on 9
March 1942.
[2] For an overview of the period of Japanese rule in Indonesia, see George McT. Kahin,
Nationalism and Revolution in Indonesia (Ithaca: Cornell University Press, 1970), chap. 4.

70

and protecting it from "modern" influences. On the contrary, they consciously mobilized and cultivated the political and military ambitions of the Balinese. As in Java, therefore, Japanese rule had a profound impact on the political consciousness, the degree of political organization, and the quasi-military experience of Balinese, and particularly of the youth.

Indirect Rule

Apart from the inexperienced all-Balinese Prayoda Corps,[3] commanded by a few Dutch officers, in 1942 the Dutch had no troops stationed in Bali, and the total European population probably numbered fewer than one hundred.[4] Perhaps realizing the utter inadequacy of their defenses, the Dutch offered no resistance when the Japanese landed at Sanur. A few days before the landing, officers of the Royal Netherlands Indies Army (Koninklijk Nederlands Indische Leger, or KNIL) had ordered the disabling of all military vehicles and the destruction of oil and gas reserves stored at depots near Denpasar and Singaraja.[5] And when it appeared certain that the Japanese would land, KNIL officers commanded the Prayoda Corps troops to retreat inland from their positions along the south coast, Denpasar, and the airport at Tuban. At Penebel in northern Tabanan, the KNIL commander reportedly ordered them to lay down their weapons and other equipment, remove their uniforms, and go home.[6] Without further explanation, the Prayoda Corps, established in 1938 ostensibly to allow Balinese to assist in the defense of their country, was disbanded.

Precisely what the KNIL officers and Dutch civil servants did next is unclear. Some at least were arrested by arriving Japanese forces and sent to camps in Java.[7] Others are said to have fled to a region of Java that had not yet been occupied, and from there to Australia.[8] Whatever happened to them, it was clear to most Balinese that the Dutch regime, which had once appeared so permanent, had completely disappeared. To educated Balinese and to those of a nationalist inclination, the decision to declare war on the Japanese without first consulting Indonesians, followed by failure to put up

---

[3] The Prayoda Corps was a native military auxiliary force set up by the Dutch in 1938. It had its equivalents in Java, Madura, and other parts of Indonesia. The idea was to enlist the support of the local population in defense of the Netherlands Indies. Interview with Meganda, 18 September 1986, Singaraja.

[4] According to Dutch statistics, there were only 63 Europeans on Bali in 1941, in a total population of 1,100,396. See "Statistics on Bali and Lombok," Nishijima Collection, Materials on the Japanese Military Administration in Indonesia, Institute of Social Sciences, Waseda University, Tokyo.

[5] Pendit, *Bali Berjuang*, p. 18.

[6] Ibid., pp. 19–20.

[7] Ibid., p. 23. No Allied prisoners of war were held in Bali.

[8] I Gusti Ngurah Putra, "Masa Pendudukan Jepang di Bali," thesis, Universitas Udayana, Denpasar, 1977, p. 11.

any sort of resistance to the invading Japanese army, seriously diminished the prestige of the Dutch and removed any lingering claim to legitimacy they may have had. As a result, the move toward support of Japan's "Greater East Asia Co-Prosperity Sphere" was much easier.

Overwhelmed by the swiftness of the Japanese victory, Balinese themselves offered no resistance whatever.[9] Some, in particular intellectuals and nationalists, openly welcomed the Japanese as liberators and helped them to bring a swift end to the Dutch regime. As in other parts of Indonesia, the initial enthusiasm of this group was reinforced by Japanese moves to place educated Indonesians in many of the upper administrative posts once occupied by the Dutch. Others fled from the towns to villages farther inland to escape the looting and other crimes that accompanied the collapse of Dutch power.[10] Yet within a matter of months, the Japanese had persuaded most to return to the towns.

To a remarkable extent, life appears to have returned to normal, at least temporarily. A Japanese radio broadcast of 27 March 1942 provided the following description of life in Bali:

> The Indonesian residents of Bali Island are enjoying a peaceful life under the control of the Japanese forces. . . . Buses are running as before and highways destroyed by the Dutch have been repaired by the Indonesian Voluntary Labor Corps. The 3,000 Chinese residents who control business activities have returned to their homes and are fully cooperating with the Japanese military authorities.[11]

The temporary return to a relatively normal existence may be attributed to the fact that, unlike Java and Madura, Bali did not remain long under Japanese Army occupation. In May 1942, Army troops, which had earned a reputation for brutality, were replaced by Japanese Navy forces, whose behavior was noticeably better. Nyoman Pendit writes, for example, that the

[9] When they first arrived, the Japanese played Indonesian "national" songs such as "Indonesia Raya" over the radio, and permitted the flying of the Indonesian flag alongside the Japanese. These indulgences ended after the Japanese had established themselves in power. See Putra, "Masa Pendudukan Jepang di Bali," pp. 2, 11.

[10] Pendit, *Bali Berjuang*, p. 25; Putra, "Masa Pendudukan Jepang di Bali," p. 17. In the first quarter of 1942, forty-three criminal incidents were reported in the District of Sukasada, Buleleng. In the second quarter the number of crimes reported dropped to twenty-seven. See "Lapoeran kwartalan tentang economi rajat II 2602," by I Goesti Gde Djlantik, Poenggawa Sukasada [3 July 1942], in Archive Anak Agung Nyoman Panji Tisna, Singaraja (hereafter Archive Tisna). These are the papers of the late raja Anak Agung Nyoman Panji Tisna of Buleleng, which his family kindly made available to me in 1986–87.

[11] O.S.S. Research and Analysis Branch, *Programs of the Japanese Government in Java and Bali* (Honolulu, 1945), p. 35. While perhaps too rosy, this description does not differ markedly from those provided by educated Balinese. According to Nyoman Pendit, a young man living in Denpasar at the time, by early 1943 "people were busily assisting the efforts of the Japanese in every field. Public security was guaranteed, the schools ran efficiently, civil servants worked with a new and fresh spirit. The economy was running smoothly and disobedience toward emergency laws and regulations was practically non-existent": *Bali Berjuang*, p. 28.

Navy troops "appeared cleaner, more polite and friendly than the soldiers of the Japanese Army."[12]

By June 1942 the Japanese had established a civilian administration that, despite changes in terminology, did not differ markedly in its structure from that of the Dutch.[13] Bali and Lombok were, as before, grouped together as a Residency (*Syo Sunda Minseibu*) under the authority of a Japanese Resident (*Cokan*), based in Singaraja.[14] An official from the governor's office served as the administrative head of Bali, performing a function similar to that of the prewar Dutch Assistant Resident. He was assisted by an advisory board of eleven Indonesians, whose function remains obscure.[15] Bali itself was divided administratively into two areas, each headed by a Balinese: North Bali covered the kingdoms of Buleleng and Jembrana; South Bali covered the other six kingdoms.[16] The authority of the rajas (*syuco*) within their king-doms was recognized from the outset, and each was eventually assigned a Japanese adviser (*bunken kanrinkan*), whose function was similar to that of a Dutch Controleur.[17] The Bali-wide consultative assembly (Paruman

[12] Pendit, *Bali Berjuang,* p. 23. The differences in the behavior and policies of the Japanese Navy and Army forces probably deserve more attention than they have, to my knowledge, received. It would be interesting to know, for example, whether the efforts of Vice Admiral Maeda (chief of intelligence at Navy headquarters in Makassar) in establishing schools for training young nationalists in Java were replicated by Navy officers elsewhere. On Maeda's initiatives in Java, see Kahin, *Nationalism and Revolution,* pp. 115–18.

[13] This outline of the Japanese civilian administration is compiled from several sources: Pindha, "Masa Pendudukan Jepang di Bali"; Pendit, *Bali Berjuang;* and an anonymous report, "Bestuur over Bali en Lombok tijdens de Japanse bezetting en daarna" [1946], in Archive Resident Dr. M. Boon (hereafter Archive Boon). This is a collection of the papers of M. Boon, Resident of Bali and Lombok from 1946 to 1949. I am grateful to the Boon family and to Henk Schulte Nordholt for permitting me to consult this collection.

[14] From early 1943 to April 1944, Singaraja was also the seat of the government of Ceram, which had previously been based in Ambon. During this period the Moluccas and the Lesser Sundas (covering Bali and Lombok) were brought under a single government. In April 1944, a separate government of Lesser Sundas was established, still based in Singaraja. The new *Cokan,* formally known as *Paduka Tuan Besar Syo Sunda Minseibu Cokan,* was a Japanese named Kosino, who arrived in Singaraja in March 1944. He replaced Sjimizu, who left Singaraja on 24 January 1944. See "Tjatatan harian dari Sjutjo Boeleleng dalam boelan San-Gatsu 2604" [3 April 1944], Archive Tisna.

[15] It is conceivable that this was a local version of the Central Advisory Board established by the Japanese in Java in September 1943. That body was an appointed representative council of which Sukarno was named president. See Kahin, *Nationalism and Revolution,* p. 106.

[16] The head of North Bali was I Gusti Ketut Puja, who was appointed Republican governor of Sunda Kecil in August 1945; South Bali was headed by Putu Serangan: Putra, "Masa Pendudukan Jepang di Bali," pp. 33–34. The titles by which Puja was sometimes referred to, *Wakil Pembesar Bali* and *Rejikan-deri,* suggest that at some stage he may have been appointed as Assistant Resident with responsibility for the whole of Bali. Such a move would probably have come in late 1944 or early 1945, at the time the Japanese appointed Indonesians as Assistant Residents in Java and Madura. See ibid., p. 121.

[17] The title zelfbestuurder was formally changed to *Syuco* on 22 June 1942, by order of the Japanese naval authorities. See "Lapoeran kwartalan tentang economi rajat II 2602," Archive Tisna. Initially the Japanese assigned only three "Controleurs," one each to Jembrana, Den-pasar, and Klungkung. After April 1944 a "Controleur" was placed in each kingdom except Buleleng, where a member of the governor's staff performed the function.

Agung) continued to meet, though infrequently, and served as the formal link between the rajas and the Japanese government.[18] Beneath the rajas, the hierarchy of state officials remained virtually unchanged, from the punggawa to the perbekel down to the klian banjar; the offices of sedahan agung and sedahan were also maintained.

In essence the Japanese adopted the structure and the strategy of indirect rule which the Dutch had used so skillfully and to such profitable effect.[19] The element of continuity was reinforced by the new regime's reliance on the Dutch legal apparatus. According to a report from 1946, "Insofar as they were not in conflict with Japanese political objectives, existing Netherlands Indies laws and regulations were maintained [by the Japanese]."[20] If there was a difference in the Japanese approach, it was that, primarily for reasons of expediency, more educated Balinese were incorporated into upper levels of the civilian administrative apparatus than had been the case under the Dutch. By co-opting both the traditional aristocracy and older educated Balinese into the system, the Japanese initially secured a breadth of elite support at least equal to, and perhaps greater than, that obtained by the Dutch.[21]

Yet if the structure of Japanese civilian administration followed the basic outline established by the Dutch colonial state, the content and the style of Japanese rule in Bali were fundamentally different. Japanese policy and practice were determined principally by the wartime needs of its military, entailing a highly authoritarian system that had important consequences for Balinese politics. Whereas the Dutch system of revenue and labor extraction had been embedded in a policy of respect for and preservation of "tradition," the Japanese showed little subtlety in their system of surplus extraction, unabashedly using Balinese officials as tools of state policy, and not infrequently expressing contempt for the very "traditional" structures of which they made use. Whereas the Dutch had aimed to control and to limit political activity, the Japanese sought deliberately to politicize the Balinese and to mobilize them behind the war. And whereas the Dutch had tried to "protect" and "preserve" Balinese culture from the corrupting influence of Java—and in particular from nationalism—the Japanese actively encouraged such interaction in the interest of more effective mobilization.

[18] The Paruman Agung seems to have met only once yearly to discuss the annual budget for the whole island. One such meeting was held in March 1944 in Singaraja. In his notes on that meeting the raja of Buleleng referred to a previous meeting on 23 February 1943. See "Tjatatan harian dari Sjutjo Boeleleng dalam boelan San-Gatsu," 3 February 1944, Archive Tisna.

[19] Though the administrative structure did not change significantly, in June 1942 the Japanese reduced by 30% all salaries over f. 50 per month. See "Lapoeran kwartalan economi rajat II 2602," Archive Tisna.

[20] See "Bestuur over Bali en Lombok tijdens de Japanse bezetting en daarna" Archive Boon.

[21] Describing a similar phenomenon in Java, Kahin writes: "Of great importance in winning the initial acceptance by the majority of educated Indonesians of the Japanese occupation was the tremendous upward rise in socio-economic status of such people which expediency alone forced the new rulers to bring about": *Nationalism and Revolution*, p. 102.

These features of Japanese rule, present in some measure from the outset, became increasingly evident in the second half of 1944, after Japanese forces began to suffer serious setbacks in the Pacific war.[22] As the Japanese began to require more and more in the way of food and other materials, the burden on the local population increased dramatically and the role of Balinese officials working within the system became increasingly problematic. Unless they made clear efforts to protect their community from such extractions, which some appear to have done, they came to be viewed increasingly as agents of a predatory and brutal state. Yet they knew that if they failed to comply with the demands of the Japanese, they could easily be replaced, exiled, or worse. Every official knew, for example, that the Japanese had summarily dismissed the raja of Gianyar and exiled him to Lombok.[23]

Forced Production and Labor

Perhaps the most onerous burden borne by Balinese during the Japanese occupation was that imposed by the system of forced production of agricultural products. Documents from the kingdom of Buleleng in 1944–45 provide a sense of the actual mechanisms of the Japanese system, and how Balinese officials, among others, must have come to be resented for their role in that system.

Decisions about agricultural production were made by the Japanese authorities in Singaraja and then conveyed as instructions to villagers through the hierarchy of the raja, punggawa, sedahan, perbekel, klian, and mandur (foreman). At monthly meetings the raja gave instructions to the punggawa and other officials for their districts and communities regarding, for example, the amount of rice that had to be collected for the government, the number of bamboo poles required from each district, the targets for the area cultivated, and the yields for cotton and rice.[24] The punggawa then conveyed these instructions to the perbekel and other local officials at monthly meetings in the district capitals. On occasion these meetings were also attended by the raja, who took the opportunity to issue "instructions" to the perbekel. No doubt punggawa and perbekel varied in the degree to which they were prepared to act solely as agents of the Japanese, and their popularity probably depended to a considerable extent on their willingness or ability to resist the excessive demands of their Balinese and Japanese superiors.

As early as 1942 Bali's economy was being organized primarily for Japan's

[22] The Japanese lost Guam and Saipan to U.S. forces in mid-1944; General MacArthur's forces landed at Leyte on 20 October 1944; U.S. forces took Iwojima on 17 February 1945; and the Japanese Navy was all but destroyed by April 1945. Okinawa fell on 26 June 1945 and heavy bombing of Tokyo began in the same month.

[23] His son, Anak Agung Gde Agung, assumed the post.

[24] The proceedings of several of these meetings in Buleleng are recorded in monthly reports usually titled "Tjatatan dari Pembitjaraan Waktoe Sangkepan Para Poenggawa," Archive Tisna.

war needs, and as the fighting in the Pacific wore on, Japanese authorities made clear their intention of intensifying agricultural production. A radio broadcast of 30 April 1944 announced that

> the military administration began to strengthen its structure in accordance with the war situation at the beginning of this year. That is to say, the . . . food production drive placed its objective in promoting self-sufficiency in the various areas. The areas including southern Celebes, Bali, Lombok . . . and northern Celebes, southern and western Borneo are engaged in striving to attain increased production.[25]

A central feature of the Japanese system was a network of government-backed "companies" with monopoly control over various economic sectors.[26] These companies served effectively as agencies of the Japanese state, and some became integral parts of the system of compulsory production and surplus extraction.

Rice and other basic foodstuffs were requisitioned according to a system of quotas, or purchased at artificially low prices, through the Mitsui Bussan Kaisha.[27] In Buleleng, the only kingdom for which we have any precise figures, the total amount delivered annually was roughly 5,000 tons.[28] The low fixed purchase price for rice imposed a heavy burden on producers, particularly as the costs of labor and tools rose with inflation. In June 1945, for example, the punggawa of Kubutambahan suggested that the price paid for rice needed to be raised by at least 50 percent in order to cover the costs of production.[29] One consequence of the low official purchase price appears to have been an absolute decline in rice production during the Japanese occupation.

The precise methods used to fulfill government rice quotas varied from one kingdom to the next. According to a contemporary report from October 1944, Balinese officials in one kingdom extracted a uniform 30 percent of the total yield from every producing household, "regardless of whether they are considered to have too little."[30] The rice was then sold at a fixed price to the Mitsui Bussan Kaisha, as required. The various punggawa of Buleleng met in October 1944 to discuss the issue of rice deliveries, and the minutes of their meeting record that they "decided not to use this system in Buleleng

---

[25] O.S.S., *Programs of the Japanese Government*, 30 April 1944, p. 135.

[26] These organizations included Mitsui Bussan Kaisha, for purchasing, milling, and distributing rice; Mitsui Norin Suisanka, for the cultivation of various agricultural products, including cotton, rice, and vegetable crops; Barri Chusan Kai, for purchasing livestock as well as meat canning and drying; Tubuno, for coconut oil processing; Ibnomaru, for fish purchasing and fishing-related industries such as boat building; and Hakiai Kumiai, for cloth rationing and distribution. See Pendit, *Bali Berjuang*, p. 23.

[27] Ibid., p. 37.

[28] "Tjatatan dari Pembitjaraan" [15 August 1945], Archive Tisna.

[29] "Tjatatan dari Pembitjaraan" [5 June 1945], ibid.

[30] "Tjatatan dari Pembitjaraan" [October 1944], ibid.

because to take the *padi* of *those who already suffer a shortage of it* would cause considerable distress and anger."[31]

In principle the state was to redistribute sufficient rice to each household after the collections, but in practice many peasant households suffered serious privation.[32] In 1944 the average allocation in Buleleng was set at 400 grams of milled rice per person.[33] By 1945 the daily allocation for residents of "minus" areas had dropped to a meager 200 grams.[34] And as supplies of rice declined, even this amount could not be guaranteed. Government officials, most of them Balinese, advised a hungry population not to expect assistance from the "plus" areas and instead to practice self-reliance.[35] Commenting on his visit to various districts to look into the matter of food supplies in September 1944, the raja of Buleleng wrote: "To the punggawa whose areas are suffering shortages I advised that they act on the assumption that there will be no assistance coming from the 'plus' areas. So far as possible, the punggawa in these areas must try to meet the food needs of the population on their own."[36] In July 1945 the sedahan agung recommended to a meeting of punggawa in Buleleng that the distribution of food be further limited, as it was now clear that a great deal of rice had been destroyed by drought.[37]

There were already reports of food shortages in parts of Buleleng in early 1944, before the worst of the requisitioning began, and the shortages grew more acute through the year.[38] In September 1944 the raja met various Japanese officials "to discuss the extreme food shortage in Boeleleng."[39] In early 1945, after a year of unprecedented food shortages for rural people throughout the island, the Japanese authorities proudly announced that "the system of rice collection is virtually perfected. The collections for the year 1944 have reached 80% of the estimated amount, and this has been greatly due to the efforts of the [Balinese?] members of the Japanese firms who have been explaining the significance of the war to the farmers."[40]

Partly in response to signs of severe shortfalls in rice, the government laid down plans and quotas for the production of cassava, corn, potatoes, and

---

[31] Ibid. (emphasis in original).

[32] Putra, "Masa Pendudukan Jepang di Bali," p. 39.

[33] "Tjatatan dari Pembitjaraan" [August 1944], Archive Tisna.

[34] "Tjatatan dari Pembitjaraan" [5 June 1945], ibid.

[35] This was the advice delivered by the raja of Buleleng and Balinese officials from the Agricultural Service on a visit to Galungan village, Sawan District, in August 1944. See "Tjatatan dari Pembitjaraan" [17 August 1944], ibid. The raja gave similar advice on visits to Kubutambahan and Tejakula, where there were "extreme shortages of food." See "Tjatatan dari Pembitjaraan" [October 1944], ibid.

[36] "Tjatatan dari Pembitjaraan" [September 1944], ibid.

[37] "Tjatatan Sangkepan" [7 July 1945], ibid.

[38] The districts of Kubutambahan, Banjar, and Tejakula were acknowledged to have very serious food shortages in 1944. See "Tjatatan dari Pembitjaraan" [February, September, and October 1944], ibid.

[39] "Tjatatan dari Pembitjaraan" [September 1944], ibid.

[40] O.S.S., *Programs of the Japanese Government*, 14 February 1945, p. 181.

other vegetables. The main mechanism for ensuring compliance with these plans appears to have been compulsion. At a meeting of Buleleng's sedahans in August 1944, an official of the government Agricultural Service noted that the amount of kedele planted in Buleleng exceeded the government plan. According to the minutes of that meeting, the official "ordered those concerned to see that the excess crop would be cut down and replaced with cassava and corn, which are urgently required at this time."[41] His approach was endorsed by the sedahan agung, who reportedly advised all sedahans to "warn any farmers who plant outside the regulations, and if they do not heed your warning, report them immediately, so that appropriate measures can be taken."[42]

Government regulations and instructions stipulated which crops were to be planted where, and simultaneously imposed limits on the acreage that could be cultivated according to a peasant's own wishes or needs. According to one regulation, for example, peasants were permitted to cultivate crops of their own choosing on only 10 percent of their total landholdings, up to a maximum of 10 are (100 are = 1 hectare). Such regulations were strictly, often harshly enforced by Balinese officials. In August 1944 a farmer with land in Doekoeh Lebah, Sawan District, was discovered to have planted 64 are of garlic. Balinese officials—including the sedahan agung, the punggawa of Sawan, and the raja—visited the village to investigate this infringement of the rules, and ordered the farmer to uproot 54 are of garlic immediately. According to the raja's notes, the officials "advised others [in the area] not to allow similar infractions," and told them: "There is a war going on. Food for the soldiers must be provided with an open heart. To ignore such infractions means to be the enemy of our soldiers who are standing firm on the front line. That means being a traitor to the people and to the country."[43]

In addition to rice and other food crops, the Japanese authorities sought increased production and procurement of various industrial products necessary for the war. Peasants were required to produce or deliver such products according to a plan laid down by government authorities. After 1942, for example, thousands of hectares were planted in cotton, with virtually all of the harvest then appropriated by the authorities and used for the production of thread and cloth for Japanese forces.[44] Those who failed to comply with the government plan risked strict sanctions. In a village in Sawan District, for example, an official of Mitsui Norin Suisanka reportedly uprooted the

---

[41] "Tjatatan dari Pembitjaraan" [August 1944], Archive Tisna.
[42] Ibid.
[43] Ibid.
[44] In 1943, according to Japanese statistics, 8,346 hectares were planted in cotton in Bali. The anticipated yield was 14,500 pikuls. See "Statistics on Bali and Lombok," Nishijima Collection.

cassava a farmer had planted among the cotton he had been required to cultivate.[45]

Similar orders were issued for the planting of jarak trees, the oil from which could be used for industrial purposes.[46] In some cases, these orders required peasants to destroy existing tree crops—such as coffee and fruit—which had taken years to become productive and had been a source for cash for many families. Peasants were also required to provide thousands of bamboo poles to the government or one of its "companies" on demand.[47] Similar "requests" were made for coconuts, pigs, cattle, and other products that were sources of revenue for many Balinese households. In all of these cases, the government inevitably resorted to compulsion in order to fulfill its quotas, and Balinese officials could be seen to be playing important roles in the Japanese system of surplus extraction.[48]

There is evidence that at least some of these officials were benefiting by their collaboration. Government servants and employees of Japanese "companies" were given extra allotments of or special vouchers to purchase, rice, cloth, kerosene, and other scarce commodities, while many producers of these commodities went without.[49] Moreover, punggawa were asked to prepare estimates of the amount of oil, sugar, and other scarce goods needed in their district each month, and then to oversee their distribution. These arrangements inevitably increased opportunities for corruption.

Bali's Chinese community, in a vulnerable position vis-à-vis the Japanese, nonetheless appeared to benefit economically from their cooperation with the government. Many were able to buy exemption from the most onerous labor levies imposed on the Balinese population and, because they tended to live in the urban areas, they did not suffer the same forced extractions endured by Bali's rural producers. Chinese merchants also received vouchers for and extra quotas of scarce commodities.[50] And though the practice was

[45] Officials of Mitsui Norin Suisanka were also reported to have destroyed coffee trees in Kubutambahan without the owner's permission in order to plant vegetables. See "Tjatatan Sangkepan" [7 July 1945], Archive Tisna.

[46] Putra, "Masa Pendudukan Jepang di Bali," p. 39.

[47] In July and August 1945 the punggawa of Buleleng were faced with requests for 5,000 bamboo poles and 350 lengths of *bambu tali* from various Japanese "companies," and 30,000 more bamboo poles from the "Controleur" of Buleleng. See "Tjatatan Sangkepan" [7 July 1945] and "Tjatatan dari Pembitjaraan" [15 August 1945], Archive Tisna.

[48] At the September 1944 meeting of the punggawa of Buleleng, for example, a Balinese government official, I Made Geria, said he understood that people were "reluctant to sell their livestock for various reasons" but expressed the hope that "if a head of cattle was, in fact, not needed by its owner, he should simply be forced to sell it by the punggawa concerned": quoted in "Tjatatan dari Pembitjaraan" [September 1944], ibid.

[49] For example, whereas most families were permitted to purchase a limited quantity of kerosene each month only if they had no electricity, government servants and "community leaders" were allowed to purchase 5 liters per month even if they did have electricity. See "Tjatatan dari Pembitjaraan" [August 1944], ibid.

[50] O.S.S., *Programs of the Japanese Government*, p. 214.

perhaps not widespread, enough Chinese took advantage of impoverished Balinese to obtain land to generate or aggravate feelings of antipathy toward them.[51] In short, there was cause for considerable enmity to develop among Balinese, between Balinese and Chinese, and, to a lesser extent, between Balinese and Japanese officials.

Forced labor also imposed a heavy burden on Balinese, while the system used to organize and oversee it contributed to ill feelings toward those who worked on behalf of the Japanese state. Perhaps the most notorious system of labor recruitment was the Bali Volunteer Labor Corps (Barisan Pekerja Sukarela Bali, or BPSB, also known as Romusha). Between July and November 1944 some 2,500 Balinese were recruited into the BPSB. Potential recruits were told that they would be sent to Sulawesi or Kalimantan to open up new rice production areas, and that they would receive sufficient food and clothing. In fact, most of the BPSB brigades served as gang labor—clearing forests, building roads, digging caves, and constructing fortifications—for Japanese soldiers in remote parts of the archipelago and under appalling conditions. Paid about 0.60 rupiah and 60 grams of plain rice daily, many BPSB members died of disease and starvation. When the war was over very few returned to Bali.[52]

The complicity of Balinese officials in this system was self-evident. Together, the rajas, punggawa, perbekel, and klian were responsible for recruiting three groups of 105 men in every kingdom. At least some seem to have done so with vigor, though contemporary documents suggest a certain lack of enthusiasm at the local level. In Buleleng the raja repeatedly implored his punggawa to provide more BPSB recruits in order to meet the government's quota, and traveled personally to district capitals and individual villages to drum up "volunteers."[53] On a visit to Bebetin, Sawan District, for example, the raja instructed the perbekel to work with the klian desa to provide more recruits. According to his own notes, the raja said: "This is a matter of the utmost importance to the Government, and the Perbekel must therefore focus his attention on it. The Klian Desa must help him in every way in this task."[54] As the exploitive nature of the BPSB system became clear, the anger and resentment of ordinary people must have been directed, even if not overtly, against Balinese officials who had been complicit in it.

The Japanese also used a system of corvée labor known as *kinrohosi* for

[51] In Buleleng, for example, a Chinese businessman (Tan Bun King of Banyuatis) reportedly secured twenty-five horses and twelve wagons for next to nothing from a Japanese official. See "Notulen Sangkepan Pangreh Pradja Keradjaan Boeleleng," 2 August 1947, Archive Tisna. Some Chinese also managed to purchase Balinese village land with the approval of Japanese authorities. One Chinese (Babah Manis) who purchased land in Tejakula from a Balinese (Wayan Gado) willed it to another Chinese (Wie Hok Cip), but in 1944 villagers sought the raja's intervention to return the land to the village. See "Tjatatan dari Pembitjaraan" [August 1944], ibid.

[52] Pendit, *Bali Berjuang*, pp. 35–36.

[53] See "Tjatatan dari Pembitjaraan" [November 1944], Archive Tisna.

[54] See "Tjatatan dari Pembitjaraan" [August 1944], ibid.

local public works projects, especially road building. In January 1944 an official Japanese radio broadcast announced that "thanks to the zeal of the local Japanese authorities and the collaboration of about 3,000 natives of the island," the construction of a road connecting some of the major towns in Bali had just been completed.[55] As Allied forces made advances in the Pacific through 1944 and 1945, corvée labor was used increasingly in the construction of defense fortifications. Thousands of men were employed without pay to dig caves, foxholes, tunnels, and storage depots in mountain areas and trenches along the beaches.[56] Labor was also requisitioned for use in various industries, including boat building, textile manufacturing, and oil processing.[57]

Like the BPSB, the kinrohosi labor system relied heavily on the cooperation of Balinese officials and thereby probably contributed to antagonism and conflict within the Balinese community. Labor requirements were conveyed through the raja to the punggawa, whose responsibility it became to ensure delivery of workers to the work site.[58] Wages were usually paid not directly to the laborer but to a Balinese district official or some other middleman. The opportunities for corruption were excellent.[59]

As in other parts of Indonesia, the brutality of the Japanese and the grinding poverty their rule produced left lasting impressions on Balinese and created widespread antipathy toward the Japanese. Yet the political consequences of Japanese exploitation were not clear-cut. They led not simply to antagonism between "Balinese" and "Japanese" but also to the aggravation of tensions and conflicts among Balinese and between Balinese and Chinese. Through their evident complicity in such obnoxious and clearly exploitive system, Balinese officials probably became a focus of the anger and resentment of ordinary Balinese. This anger was no doubt compounded by evidence that some Balinese and Chinese at least were benefiting economically from their collaboration.

"Reviving" Balinese Culture

Apart from its heavy extractions of labor and produce, the Japanese state became increasingly intrusive in the fields of culture and education as the

---

[55] O.S.S., *Programs of the Japanese Government*, 14 January 1944, p. 235. A separate broadcast noted that the Dutch had been unable to build this road because it traversed "a region of fierce malaria," but did not say what the Japanese had done to overcome the health danger to laborers.

[56] Pendit, *Bali Berjuang*, p. 38. Pendit also notes that toward the end of 1944 a U.S. submarine appeared in the port of Buleleng and fired a torpedo toward shore. The Japanese retaliated and claimed the next day that they had sunk the submarine. In subsequent weeks, the Japanese set up decoy artillery pieces made of wood along the north coast.

[57] See "Tjatatan dari Pembitjaraan" [August 1945], Archive Tisna.

[58] For notes of a meeting of Buleleng punggawa at which the labor requirements of Japanese companies were announced, see "Tjatatan dari Pembitjaraan" [5 June 1945], ibid.

[59] See "Tjatatan dari Pembitjaraan" [6 January 1945], ibid.

war progressed. Like the Dutch before them, the Japanese made efforts to encourage Balinese culture, awarding prizes and praise to outstanding artists in various fields. Yet, where the Dutch had ostensibly aimed to preserve Balinese culture and society from outside influences, the Japanese spoke openly of "improving" and "reviving" Balinese culture, so that it might be put to work on behalf of Greater East Asia.[60]

Japanese cultural involvement had indirect implications for Balinese politics. Balinese officials such as rajas, punggawa, and perbekel inevitably became caught up in the Japanese initiatives; and to the extent that these efforts were viewed as obnoxious or aesthetically or religiously suspect, these officials risked a loss of prestige. Japanese educational policy had more direct political implications. A sudden expansion in the number of schools, teachers, and pupils and a shift in admissions policy made education available to thousands of sudra children who would have been unlikely candidates under the Dutch because of their caste background. This expansion was accompanied by dramatic changes in the school curriculum. In addition to basic reading and writing skills, pupils began to learn military drills and political slogans that would form the basis for their later nationalist consciousness.

Toward the end of 1943 the Japanese authorities provided the following commentary on the state of Balinese culture: "On Bali Island, heretofore, the old Netherlands East Indies [government] had oppressed culture and it had been completely lifeless on the island, and now, in order to return it to the olden aspects of Asia . . . , an active revival movement has been started under the guidance of Japan."[61] Accordingly, the Japanese set up institutions aimed at promoting and improving Balinese culture, including the Bali Cultural Research Society, the Balinese Cultural Association Reference Museum, and the Bali Spirit Cultural Promotion Society.[62] The last of these, established in late 1944, was to conduct research not only into "literature, sculpture and painting" but also into "food, clothing and shelter." In January 1945 the Japanese authorities expressed "great expectations . . . for this society to contribute much towards the enhancement of the spirit of the Bali culture and Greater East Asia."[63]

[60] I Gusti Ngurah Rai, "Pengaruh Pendidikan Pada Masa Pendudukan Jepang di Singaraja Tahun 1942 Sampai Tahun 1945," thesis, Universitas Udayana, Denpasar, 1982, p. 29. There is an interesting parallel here with Japanese efforts in other parts of Indonesia to use Islam to win popular support for the Japanese war effort. For a synopsis of these efforts, see Kahin, *Nationalism and Revolution*, pp. 110–11.

[61] O.S.S., *Programs of the Japanese Government*, 15 December 1945, p. 303.

[62] Describing the objectives of the first of these institutions, a Japanese radio program said: "The Bali Cultural Research Society has been organized at Singaraja with a view to bestowing the benefit of a healthy culture upon the inhabitants of Bali Island, who have long been under the injurious habits of a special branch of Hinduism": ibid., 18 July 1943, p. 303. The museum was set up in mid-1944 for the purpose of "preserving Bali culture." Among other examples of "Balinese" culture, the museum planned to exhibit "Bali sculptures made under the direction of Torao Yazaki [a Japanese artist]": ibid., 5 March 1945, p. 303.

[63] Ibid., 9 January 1945, p. 303.

A certain clumsiness was evident in the efforts of the Japanese to make use of Balinese cultural traditions to pursue their wartime objectives. In 1944 they struck upon the idea of using Balinese theater to convey useful political messages to the population. Twenty "experienced theater folk" were assembled in Singaraja. After developing a repertoire they toured the island performing in dozens of district towns, accompanied not by a Balinese gamelan orchestra but by the Japanese military musical corps.[64] According to an official announcement, "The content of theatrical presentations will include depictions of the inhabitants who cooperate in increased production . . . and in the field of construction."[65] It is hard to imagine that such plays were met with much enthusiasm by ordinary Balinese, especially after mid-1944, when the economic situation was so dire for so many. Some idea of popular attitudes toward such productions can be glimpsed from the notes of a meeting between the raja and the punggawa of Buleleng on 3 April 1944: "The Punggawa of Bandjar was informed that there would be a Propaganda Play in Seririt on 4 and 5 April. In this connection he was asked to ensure that there would be some people there to watch it."[66] The notes also record the comment of one of the punggawa, which perhaps reflects the concern of Balinese officials at being implicated in such a palpably unpopular enterprise: "The Punggawa of Soekasada pointed out that, according to his information, people consider [the propaganda play] to be an insult to the local population."[67]

The urge to make Balinese society function more efficiently on behalf of the Japanese regime was evident in other government initiatives as well. The use of the Japanese language was at first actively promoted through the use of Japanese names, titles, and dates, but both Indonesian and Japanese were eventually spread through the radio and other media.[68] After August 1944 loudspeakers were placed in strategic locations throughout the island to broadcast radio programs in both Japanese and Indonesian.[69] Indonesian was selected as the medium for routine government business (as it was

[64] Rai, "Pengaruh Pendidikan," p. 29.
[65] O.S.S., *Programs of the Japanese Government,* 24 January 1944, p. 301.
[66] "Tjatatan dari Pembitjaraan" [April 1944], Archive Tisna. The raja's notes indicate that he attended the play in Seririt, a small coastal village ten miles west of Singaraja, on the evening of 5 April 1944. Unfortunately, he offers no commentary on the performance.
[67] Ibid.
[68] The Japanese language was taught in the schools and competitions were held in composition, reading, and conversation. A 5,000-word Japanese-Balinese dictionary was published by the Japanese authorities in July 1944. See O.S.S., *Programs of the Japanese Government,* 23 December 1943; 23 January 1944, p. 266; 28 July 1944, p. 81.
[69] One of the explicit aims of installing radio speakers was the popularization of the Japanese language. According to an August 1944 radio broadcast, "The attempt to make the Japanese language familiar among the native inhabitants through radio has proved highly successful at Singaradja, Bali Island. Encouraged by these wonderful results, the education authorities have decide to install loud-speakers throughout the island." See ibid., 7 August 1944, p. 269. Among other things, Japanese radio plays and songs with a heavy patriotic content were broadcast. See Putra, "Masa Pendudukan Jepang di Bali," p. 13.

elsewhere in Indonesia) and for the government-controlled newspaper *Bali Sinbun,* which began publication on 8 March 1944.[70] The contrast with the Dutch regime, which had so earnestly sought to "preserve" the use of Balinese and to limit the use of Indonesian and Dutch to a select group of civil servants, could not have been more dramatic.

The Japanese also initiated significant changes in education. Recognizing that education was an essential avenue for shaping ideas and mobilizing the population, they expanded the number of public schools dramatically between 1942 and 1944.[71] By 1944 some 266 schools were operating in Bali with about 50,000 students, compared to 238 schools and about 26,000 students in 1942.[72] In addition to a large number of new elementary schools, the Japanese opened several public high schools and teacher-training schools.[73] Unlike their prewar Dutch counterparts, these schools were, in principle, open to everyone regardless of caste or social position.[74] It was thus under the Japanese that education for the first time became widely available to Balinese of low caste.

The school curriculum was substantially more militaristic than it had been under the Dutch, and it became increasingly so as the war progressed. In 1942 and 1943 students were already learning to march, to salute the Japanese flag, recite an oath of allegiance to Japan, and perform simple military drills.[75] With the dramatic military reverses suffered by Japanese forces in mid-1944 the authorities explicitly revised the school curriculum to fit wartime needs. Starting in September 1944 the length of the normal course in "industrial and business schools" was reduced from four years to two, pupils were to spend more time learning such practical skills as planting trees and spinning cotton, and the quasi-military component of the curriculum was expanded.[76]

---

[70] *Bali Sinbun,* set up under the auspices of the Minseibu, was published three times a week. The Japanese authorities expressed the hope that it would "sufficiently present to the natives of Bali Island the culture of Greater East Asia": O.S.S., *Programs of the Japanese Government,* 9 March 1944, p. 81.

[71] According to one source, the Japanese did not officially close down the old Dutch schools, but they banned the use of Dutch and ordered the burning of Dutch schoolbooks. Students apparently stopped attending the old schools out of fear, so that before long they effectively stopped functioning. See Rai, "Pengaruh Pendidikan," p. 32.

[72] O.S.S., *Programs of the Japanese Government,* 21 October 1943, p. 273; 12 March 1944, p. 297; 22 May 1944, p. 297.

[73] Four basic levels of school, ranging from lowest to highest, were Fut chu ko ga ko, Ju kyu ko ga ko, Fut chu kyu ju kyu ko ga ko, and Chu ga ko. Teacher-training schools (Shian ga ko) were divided by gender, with the Dan shi bu for men and the Jo shi bu for women. See Rai, "Pengaruh Pendidikan," pp. 32–33.

[74] Ibid., p. 32.

[75] For details on the content of the curricula at the various schools, see ibid., pp. 31–36.

[76] According to an official radio broadcast in September 1944, "emphasis will be placed on practical education. Studies will be connected directly with increasing fighting power by practical education in the factories. . . . Next, in the schools [an agricultural] department will be established and [agriculture] will be taught." About the same time the authorities began to set up a Youth Corps network in elementary schools, with similar objectives. See O.S.S., *Programs of the Japanese Government,* 19 June 1944, pp. 146–47.

These changes in educational policy helped to lay the groundwork for a militant Indonesian nationalism among Bali's youth. In Japanese schools tens of thousands of Balinese children became familiar with the powerful rhetoric of militarism and anti-Westernism. The schools were also significant as centers of shared "modern" experience, bases of collective solidarity very different from that of the family, the village, or the religious community. At the same time a growing consciousness of the suffering inflicted by the regime, coupled with the harsh treatment sometimes meted out by their own teachers, caused some students to become hostile to the Japanese. As in Java, this hostility found expression first in an anti-Japanese underground movement and later in a network of armed revolutionary youth organizations.

Mobilization and Nationalism

Initiatives in the cultural and educational fields were part of a much broader Japanese effort to mobilize the population behind the regime and its wartime objectives. Mobilization strategies consciously encouraged the growth of Indonesian nationalism and, as in Java, contributed to the emergence of a revolutionary *pemuda* (youth) consciousness and a new militant political style.[77]

The new style of political expression and organization was typified by an emphasis on quasi-military ceremonies, such as flag raisings, oath taking, speech giving, and marching. There was a preoccupation with the values of self-sacrifice for the public good, physical and spiritual strength, and what George Kahin has called an "emotional anti-Westernism." For many Balinese, and especially for the young, this was their first experience with public political activity and discourse, so limited had political life been under the Dutch. It was perhaps natural, therefore, that it set a standard that would be emulated for many years to come. Even those who eventually turned against the Japanese continued to rely to a great extent on the style and the structures they had introduced.

Significantly, the Japanese authorities made no effort to protect Bali from political influences emanating from Java. On the contrary, they encouraged such influences, a fact that may help to account for the relatively greater level of nationalist consciousness evident in Bali than in other parts of East Indonesia by 1945. Japanese efforts to enlist the support of nationalist leaders in

[77] The term *pemuda* is literally the Indonesian word for youth or young person. It describes the revolutionary younger generation of Indonesians, who played a central political and military role in the period of the National Revolution of 1945–49 and after. For an analysis of the significance of the Japanese period in the formation of a pemuda consciousness in Java, see Benedict R. O'G. Anderson, *Java in a Time of Revolution: Occupation and Resistance, 1944–1946* (Ithaca: Cornell University Press, 1972), pp. 16–34. Also see Anderson, "Japan, 'The Light of Asia,'" in Josef Silverstein, ed., *Southeast Asia in World War II: Four Essays*, Yale Southeast Asia Studies, Monograph no. 7 (New Haven: Yale University Press, 1966), pp. 13–50.

Java were also felt in Bali, and with a few exceptions, branches of the nationalist organizations established in Java were eventually also set up in Bali.[78] These efforts gained additional momentum after September 1944, when Japanese Premier Koiso promised Indonesian independence "in the very near future." At a special ceremony later that month, Bali's provincial governor offered his thanks, on behalf of the Balinese people, for Japan's promise.[79] And in late June 1945 Sukarno, the Indonesian Republican leader and later president, was invited to Bali and given an opportunity to address a public gathering in Singaraja and to meet local Balinese leaders.[80]

The Japanese authorities began the process of political mobilization in Bali by disbanding all independent political and social organizations that might conceivably become the focus of anti-Japanese activity or divert resources from the war effort. A number of Tabanan's prewar nationalists were arrested in February 1944 by the Japanese Military Police (Kenpeitai), apparently on suspicion of harboring anti-Japanese nationalist aspirations.[81] The Japanese also acted to weaken older social bonds and institutions, such as obligatory community work for religious ends.[82] With the old organizations gone, the Japanese began to establish an extensive network of mass organizations, which at their height incorporated tens of thousands of young men and women in Bali alone. As in Java, these organizations brought significant changes to the structure of village life and to the mind-set of a large number of young people.

The first and largest of the mass organizations established in Bali was the Seinendan, or Young Men's Association, which was controlled by the Japanese propaganda office, the Sendenbu. Recruiting of men between the ages of twelve and thirty began in late 1943, and the first branches were set up in Denpasar, Gianyar, and Negara in November 1943.[83] Other branches soon

[78] The main exceptions were the Pusat Tenaga Rakyat, or Putera, and its successor, the Jawa Hokokai. Putera was a nationalist mass organization established on Java in March 1943. It was dissolved by the end of that year and replaced with the Jawa Hokokai, which was more tightly controlled by the Japanese. See Kahin, *Nationalism and Revolution*, pp. 106–10.

[79] O.S.S., *Programs of the Japanese Government*, 19 September 1944, p. 6.

[80] Sukarno visited Singaraja on 24 and 25 June 1945. In his daily notes, the raja of Buleleng recorded only the following details of the visit: Sukarno was received at the Residency office by Japanese and Balinese notables on 24 June. The following day, at 2:30 P.M., he attended a gathering of leading Balinese at the Sjukai building in Singaraja. At 5 P.M. the same day he addressed a public meeting in the field in front of the police station, and later that evening he joined other "distinguished guests" to watch a performance of Balinese dance. Unfortunately, the raja says nothing about the content of Sukarno's public speech. See "Tjatatan dari Pembitjaraan" [7 July 1945], Archive Tisna.

[81] Those arrested in February 1944 included Wayan Bina, Mas Suhud, Ktut Buana, Wayan Miasa, Nyoman Muka, and Made Geledig. According to Pendit, they were held by the Kenpeitai about three months, during which time they were tortured: *Bali Berjuang*, pp. 34–35.

[82] This was an unpopular move among some Balinese of the older generation: "When the Japanese attacked the temple duties, we older people knew we were lost." See "Rapport Bali," 1946, Algemeen Secretarie te Batavia, Eerste Zending (hereafter Alg. Sec. I), Kist XXII, no. 19, ARA.

[83] O.S.S., *Programs of the Japanese Government*, 8 November 1943, p. 114.

followed, and by 1944 Seinendan units had been set up in virtually all districts and villages on the island, where they functioned officially as a local security force and village watch.[84] Initiation and training were militaristic but members were not permitted to carry weapons apart from the sharpened bamboo spear (*bumbu runcing*), which would later become a romantic symbol of the pemuda struggle against the Dutch.[85]

The emphasis on physical and spiritual strength, which were so central to Japanese ideology, resonated powerfully with basic precepts of the Balinese martial arts (*pencak silat*), and resulted in a proliferation of *silat* clubs both in the towns and in rural areas. In 1945, according to one estimate, there were at least three or four silat adepts in almost every hamlet in Badung and Tabanan, and in some hamlets as many as fifty. These clubs were tolerated and even encouraged by the Japanese, and they became important bases of pemuda organization and solidarity during the Revolution. In the twilight of Japanese rule and in the heady days after Indonesia's declaration of independence, many revolutionary groups were established on the basis of these clubs.

The Japanese also established an array of quasi-military bodies, including the army auxiliary (Pembela Tanah Air, or Peta), the land-based Navy auxiliary (Kaigun Heiho), the land-based Air Force auxiliary (Kaibodan), and the suicide battalions (Bo'ei Teisin Tai, also known as Jibakutai, Kamikaze Corps, and Pasukan Berani Mati).[86] It was in these auxiliary forces that the younger generation of Bali received their first military training, an acquaintance with militant pro-Asian political thinking, and the inspiration that freedom might be achieved through violent struggle, even against great military odds. In addition these groups provided an organizational model for later military bodies in Bali, and a good part of the ideological foundation for the struggle against all colonial domination, Japanese included.

The most notable of these forces was the Peta, trained by Japanese Army instructors and designed to help Japan defend Indonesia against an Allied

---

[84] For details of the formal structure of the Seinendan, see "Tjatatan dari Pembitjaraan" [March 1944], Archive Tisna.

[85] In February 1944 the authorities published a plan for strengthening the network of youth organizations in Bali "so as to complete the defense system and strengthen the fighting power of the island." According to the plan, vocational youth associations and federations of such organizations were to be organized in villages and towns. Members of the associations were to "undergo training, including military drills, air defense drills, fire drills, as well as courses in Japanese language and etiquette. For the promotion of the labor service spirit, communal farms and workshops will also be utilized": O.S.S., *Programs of the Japanese Government*, February 1944, p. 114.

[86] The Kaigun Heiho was set up in mid-1944: ibid., 2 October 1944, p. 115. In December 1944 Japanese authorities reported that Balinese were "clamouring for a share in dealing deadly blows to the enemy" by joining the Bo'ei Teisin Tai. They noted that "intellectuals, mostly school teachers, press editors, and so forth, form the majority of the names so far registered": ibid., 15 December 1944, p. 115. The first Bo'ei Teisin Tai unit appears to have been established in March 1945, and in June 1945 a second group went from Buleleng to Gianyar for training: "Tjatatan dari Pembitjaraan" [June 1945], Archive Tisna.

88 | *The Dark Side of Paradise*

attack. Through their involvement in the Peta, more than 1,600 Balinese youths received military training and inherited an organizational structure that they would later use—albeit without much success—against the Japanese, and later in the struggle against the Dutch.[87] In the atmosphere of political uncertainty that prevailed after August 1945, the military skills learned from the Japanese were at a premium, and former Peta men felt strongly that they were uniquely qualified to lead the resistance.[88] Of equal importance was the political and spiritual awareness cultivated in Peta recruits by their Japanese Army instructors and fostered by their shared experience. Central features of this new consciousness were a rejection of the innate superiority of European peoples and a concomitant belief in the capacity of Asian peoples to govern themselves; a spirit of self-sacrifice for the good of the country; and a belief in the paramount value of spiritual strength (*semangat*) to confront the enemy. Although it was not at first explicit, this ideological training formed a solid basis for the later emergence of a militant Indonesian nationalist consciousness, independent of the Japanese.

Registration for Bali's Peta began on 2 February 1944, and on 6 April the first Balinese officers and soldiers were formally enlisted. A radio broadcast summarizing the enlistment ceremony suggests the atmosphere of the times:

Dressed in military uniform, these [Peta recruits] received inspection by local Navy and Army commanders. Following this inspection they listened to an address by the Army commander who stressed the high responsibility resting upon them as leaders of the Volunteer Army, and encouraged them to undergo strenuous military training with unshakable confidence in victory, and to realize that they are people of Greater East Asia.[89]

Japanese authorities announced that registration for Peta in Bali had exceeded requirements by fifteen times, and the military instructors expressed admiration for the "ferocity" and "fighting spirit" of the Balinese recruits.[90] Even when the possibility of exaggeration for propaganda purposes is taken into account, there appears to have been considerable enthusiasm for joining

[87] In addition to the more familiar military training techniques of drills and physical exercise, Bali's Peta recruits and soldiers were often shown Japanese war films depicting heroic military campaigns as well as the techniques of martial arts. See Rai, "Pengaruh Pendidikan," p. 30.

[88] In the words of a former Peta captain: "In all honesty, from the point of view of fighting spirit [*semangat*], we Peta soldiers were among the best soldiers in the world, while the Dutch were not in the same league": I Gusti Ngurah Pindha, *Kirikumi Besar2an Terhadap Kota Denpasar*, Serie Gempilan Perjuangan Physic di Bali, no. 1 [Denpasar], 1973.

[89] O.S.S., *Programs of the Japanese Government*, 19 April 1944, p. 103.

[90] According to a Japanese radio broadcast, "Balinese youths now under training to become officers to the island's defense corps have favorably impressed the Japanese commander. [The commander said] they have distinguished themselves by their strong fighting spirit, and he was amazed by the ferocity with which they carry out their military exercises": ibid., 17 June 1944, p. 115.

the Peta among Balinese youth. Part of the attraction was undoubtedly economic; Peta soldiers received food, clothing, wages, and other facilities at a time of considerable economic hardship.[91] An opportunity to learn military skills and take up arms on behalf of one's country also had undeniable appeal.[92] Perhaps equally significant, Japanese military doctrine resonated strongly with indigenous Balinese traditions of self-sacrifice and the spiritual bases of power.[93]

Recruits underwent a three-month training course under Japanese Army instructors at the old Prayoda Corps camp at Banyumala in Singaraja. The following description of Peta training, provided by Japanese authorities, gives an idea of the combination of military and political cum spiritual training encountered by Peta recruits.

> Daily routine starts with the flag raising at 7 a.m., when the cadets bow in the direction of the Imperial Palace and recite the Imperial oath, following which they solemnly voice the pledge "trust implicitly Japanese soldiers and cultivate self-confidence." Bayonet practice follows flag raising, then at 9 a.m., they study the Japanese language, military [and] scientific subjects. Three hours every afternoon are devoted to military manoeuvers, followed by [a] two hour study period.[94]

After training, recruits were assigned to one of the three Peta battalions (*daidan*) based in Jembrana, Kediri (Tabanan), and Gunaksa (Klungkung).[95] According to Japanese Army sources, when the Peta was officially disbanded in August 1945, it had 1,625 soldiers and officers in Bali, armed with 1,121 weapons, most of them rifles and pistols.[96]

The organization provided an unusual opportunity for young men who were not part of the prewar aristocratic elite to assume positions of some importance. The caste bias that had been so central to Dutch policy in Bali

[91] Members of the Seinendan received similar privileges, including road-tax exemptions, free medical treatment, and traveling expenses. See "Tjatatan dari Pembitjaraan" [February 1944], Archive Tisna.

[92] For example, a Peta officer, Anak Agoeng Ktoet Karang, was quoted in May 1944 as saying that he had "learned the fighting spirit motivating the Japanese," and that he was "thrilled with true joy and pride in being able to defend my own fatherland against any and all enemies": O.S.S., *Programs of the Japanese Government*, 9 May 1944, p. 62.

[93] On the spiritual bases of power in Bali, see Linda H. Connor, "In Darkness and Light: A Study of Peasant Intellectuals in Bali," Ph.D. diss., University of Sydney, 1982.

[94] O.S.S., *Programs of the Japanese Government*, 9 May 1944, p. 62. For additional details and the names of some of the Japanese instructors, see Pendit, *Bali Berjuang*, pp. 31–33.

[95] According to Japanese Army sources, each *daidan* comprised 522 officers and men. See Headquarters of the 16th Army, Java, "Explanations Regarding All Kinds of Armed Bodies," Nishijima Collection, no. JV.45, pp. 1–2. According to Balinese sources, however, there were about 700 men in some *daidan*. Each *daidan* comprised four *codan* (companies), each made up of four *sodan* (platoons), which in turn comprised four *budan* (sections). These units were commanded by Balinese officers respectively called *daidanco* (major), *codanco* (captain), *sodanco* (lieutenant), and *budanco* (sergeant).

[96] By comparison, Java's sixty-six Peta daidan held some 20,500 weapons. See Headquarters of the 16th Army, "Explanations," pp. 1–2.

was less conspicuous in such military auxiliary bodies as Peta. It is true that the three most senior Peta officers—the battalion commanders—were exclusively men of high caste and members of the royal families. Yet among company, platoon, and section commanders, with the ranks of captain, lieutenant, and sergeant, respectively, there were a significant number of sudra. Although no figures are available, it seems likely that a large number of ordinary Peta soldiers were also of the lowest caste.[97] In short, Peta appears to have provided significant new opportunities for young Balinese, regardless of their caste origins. It is perhaps partly for this reason that many of them were attracted to the antifeudal nationalism of Bali's pemuda, to the anti-Japanese underground movement that they formed in 1944, and later to the revolutionary struggle against the Dutch.[98]

The Anti-Japanese Underground

The development of the anti-Japanese underground in Bali depended, in the early stages, on personal contacts between a handful of Balinese youth and key members of the underground in Java.[99] In mid-1944 a young man named Nyoman Mantik traveled to Yogyakarta to contact a former Taman Siswa teacher, Wiyono Suryokusumo. Others, including Made Wija Kusuma, who later became an important resistance leader, traveled frequently to Java through 1944 and 1945, gathering and disseminating information on developments there. Working together with pemuda in other organizations and with high school students, they helped to establish secret networks through which they shared information about political developments abroad and discussed plans for overthrowing the Japanese.[100] As in

[97] The predominance of men of high caste in the most senior positions appears to have resulted not from deliberate Japanese discrimination on the basis of caste but from a policy favoring men with experience as Prayoda Corps officers and a certain level of education. See Putra, "Masa Pendudukan Jepang di Bali," pp. 51–53.

[98] Particularly active in the anti-Japanese underground were Peta officers of the rank of codanco (captain). Some fifteen codanco were among those who gathered in the village of Bangsal Gaji on 16 August 1945 for a ceremonial raising of the Indonesian flag. Interview with Meganda, 18 September 1986, Denpasar. The former daidanco were the principal organizers of the TKR (Tentara Keamanan Rakyat—People's Security Army), 1 November 1945. See Pendit, *Bali Berjuang*, p. 99. The military men who gathered to plan the 8 April 1946 attack on Denpasar included no fewer than nineteen former Peta officers: Pindha, *Kirikumi Besar2an Terhadap Kota Denpasar*, p. 7; interview with I Nengah Wirta Tamu (Cilik), former Peta captain, 19 December 1986, Denpasar.

[99] On the anti-Japanese underground in Java, see Kahin, *Nationalism and Revolution*, pp. 104–6, 111–14.

[100] Pendit names the key figures in the underground as follows: in Badung, Gusti Ngurah Rai, Made Wija Kusuma, Made Regog, Anom Gangga, and Nyoman Pegeg; in Tabanan, Wayan Bina; in Jembrana, Anak Agung Bagus Suteja, Nengah Tamu, and Gede Muka; in Buleleng, Gede Puger; in Karangasem, Gusti Lanang Rai and Ktut Gebun; in Klungkung, Ngurah Anom and Gusti Bagus Sugianjar; and in Gianyar, Anom Dada. On the emergence, structure, and activities of the anti-Japanese underground, see Pendit, *Bali Berjuang*, pp. 43–52.

Java, they worked with some success to indoctrinate Peta soldiers and officers with Indonesian nationalism. According to some informants, they also
infiltrated such bodies as the Kenpeitai and even the Japanese intelligence
organization Yama Butai.[101]

Bali's pemuda activists developed a variety of organizations, both legal
and illegal, through which to work. In Denpasar they established a group
called ESTTI, with a view to spreading the message of anti-Japanese resistance to pemuda in surrounding villages. Overtly an organization of youths
interested in learning and practicing pencak silat, it was ultimately aimed at
military and political objectives.[102] About the same time, high school students in Denpasar set up the ISSM, a legal organization with secret links to
the underground.[103] Students in the high school at Singaraja linked up with
Gede Puger, a pemuda who worked at the Japanese radio station across the
street.[104] Through Puger's monitoring of radio transmissions, the Balinese
underground was able to learn of Allied advances in the Pacific and of the
weakening position of the Japanese. The students shared this information
with friends in Peta and with pemuda in the Singaraja area, who in turn
spread the word to others within their communities.[105]

In spite of efforts to maintain secrecy, some members of the underground
movement were eventually discovered by the Kenpeitai. One of them, a
former Parindra activist and teacher from Tabanan named Made Gelgel, was
reportedly arrested at the beginning of 1945 and never seen again. The
movement managed to survive such setbacks, but its leadership became
increasingly divided over whether direct military action ought to be taken
against the Japanese. Plans were formulated for a coordinated military assault on Japanese installations in Denpasar, to be led by three Peta officers
with support from the pemuda and students.[106] With the passage of time
and continuing disagreement, however, the opportunity for a successful attack steadily diminished.

In March 1945 the Japanese substantially reduced the weapons and ammunition at the disposal of Bali's Peta battalions and removed the confiscated matériel to a military base at the Tuban airport, outside Denpasar.[107]

[101] Interviews with Wayan Rana, 21 September 1986, and I Made Wija Kusuma, 22 March
1986, Denpasar.

[102] ESSTI (Eka Sentosa Stiti) was established in Badung and later spread to Tabanan, Gianyar, and Karangasem. The founder was Made Regog, who worked with the Yama Butai.
Interviews with Meganda, 18 September 1986, Singaraja, and Wayan Rana (general secretary
of ESSTI), 21 September 1986, Denpasar. Also see Pendit, *Bali Berjuang,* p. 45.

[103] ISSM = Ikatan Siswa Sekolah Menengah (Union of Secondary School Pupils).

[104] Interview with Dewa Made Dhana, 7 October 1986, Singaraja. Also see Rai, "Pengaruh
Pendidikan," p. 39.

[105] They established links with pemuda in Banjar Jawa, Liligundi, Paketan, Beraban, and
Penataran, among others: Pendit, *Bali Berjuang,* p. 45.

[106] For details of the plans, see ibid., pp. 49–50. At this time the underground movements in
Java and Sumatra were organizing for an uprising against the Japanese to coincide with the
anticipated Allied attack. See Kahin, *Nationalism and Revolution,* p. 127.

[107] Pendit, *Bali Berjuang,* p. 38.

8. Officers of the Royal Netherlands Indies Army (KNIL) accepting the Japanese surrender on Sanur Beach, Bali, March 1946. Japanese forces had landed on the same beach four years earlier, and they remained in Bali for more than six months after their defeat and the proclamation of Indonesian independence in August 1945. On Allied orders, Japanese troops established a beachhead to facilitate the KNIL landing. (*Rijksinstituut voor Oorlogsdocumentatie, Amsterdam*)

Then on 16 August 1945, before news of the Japanese surrender had filtered through to Bali, the Peta battalions were disarmed and summarily disbanded. Although we have little precise information on this score, some smaller Peta units apparently did manage to retain weapons and ammunition with assistance from their Japanese instructors. Nevertheless, with the Peta disbanded, plans for a direct assault on the 3,000 well-armed Japanese troops were set aside. For the time being Bali's pemuda, together with a group of older nationalists, focused instead on the task of political mobilization to give substance to Sukarno's 17 August declaration of independence.

On 23 August 1945 I Gusti Ketut Puja returned to Bali from Java, having been appointed Republican governor of Sunda Kecil by Sukarno.[108] Before long a local branch of the Indonesian National Committee had been formed, and with it a local unit of the Republican army, the BKR.[109] These groups

---

[108] In Java, Puja had been serving on the Committee for the Preparation of Indonesian Independence (Panitia Persiapan Kemerdekaan Indonesia, or PPKI), which the Japanese set up in early August 1945 to prepare for a transfer of power to the Indonesians. See Kahin, *Nationalism and Revolution*, p. 127.

[109] The BKR (Badan Keamanan Rakyat—People's Security Organization) was formed on 31 August 1945; it was replaced by the TKR on 1 November 1945.

were followed shortly by more militant pemuda organizations, such as Pesindo and PRI.[110] Under pressure from the pemuda groups, Governor Puja put a series of demands to the Japanese authorities, most of which were initially refused.[111] In time, however, the Japanese agreed to certain limited demands and acknowledged Puja's nominal authority as civilian administrator. The majority of Japanese troops were then moved to a base, probably in Kediri, where they awaited the arrival of Allied forces.

Political developments in Bali after August 1945 were strongly influenced by the direct links established earlier between the Balinese underground and like-minded activists in Java. Indeed, some Balinese pemuda were still in Java when the Japanese surrendered, and were able to witness how the pemuda there responded to the new situation. As we shall see in later chapters, they returned to Bali in October and November 1945, inspired by the resistance that had begun to develop in Java's major towns. Their ideas were enthusiastically welcomed by Bali's youth, who were not far behind in appreciating the political opportunities created by Japan's defeat.

The state established by the Japanese in Bali in 1942 was similar to the Dutch colonial apparatus in many respects, especially the system of indirect rule. The Japanese state, however, penetrated far more deeply and more disruptively into the economic and political life of the average Balinese than the Dutch state had ever done. The burden of Japanese rule was felt most heavily through corvée labor and forced delivery of agricultural produce. By August 1945 these policies had left many hundreds and possibly thousands dead and had impoverished most of the rural population. Moreover, Japanese policy stressed the propaganda value of cultural endeavors in a way that was often arrogant and heavy-handed. As in Java, the experience of Japanese rule in Bali "aroused a consciousness of common suffering and humiliation and a common resentment against the Japanese."[112]

While this suffering stimulated anti-Japanese feeling and an unprecedented nationalist consciousness, it also led to conflicts among Balinese. The sheer harshness of life under the Japanese occupation, compounded by the vicissitudes of a wartime economy, gave rise to even greater resentment within the Balinese community than had been the case during the Dutch colonial period. What kept this conflict in check was the Japanese state, bolstered by a significant military presence and the cultivated mystique of Japanese invincibility.

Tensions within Balinese society were accentuated by significant changes

---

[110] The Bali branches of Pesindo (Pemuda Sosialis Indonesia—Socialist Youth of Indonesia) and the PRI (Pemuda Republik Indonesia—Youth of the Republic of Indonesia) were both founded in mid-November 1945.

[111] See "Bestuur over Bali en Lombok tijdens de Japanse bezetting en daarna" [1946], Archive Boon, p. 2.

[112] Kahin, *Nationalism and Revolution*, p. 128.

in political style and rhetoric introduced during the occupation. The deliberate political and quasi-military mobilization that was a central feature of Japanese rule contrasted sharply with Dutch efforts to protect "traditional" Bali from "modern" political influences. The growth of a new militant political style among young Balinese found expression in an anti-Japanese underground movement from which emerged organizations that were to play central roles in the revolutionary movement after August 1945. As in Java, these groups were monopolized by the pemuda, who would become the real revolutionary vanguard.

5   *"Anarchy Prevails"*

T HE SURRENDER OF THE JAPANESE was known in Bali as early as 23 August 1945, but it was not until 2 March 1946 that KNIL troops landed to restore Dutch political authority there. The period after the Japanese defeat and before the Dutch return was a time of intense and sometimes violent political activity in Bali. During these six months the terms of Balinese political discourse were fundamentally and irrevocably changed, as mass political and military mobilization occurred on an unprecedented scale, and new political and social conflicts emerged while old rivalries became more visible and often more acute.

When the Dutch returned, Bali was in a state of turmoil, and the lines of social and political division had been drawn. Although some 2,000 KNIL troops managed to land at Sanur Beach and Benoa without firing a shot, within one week they were facing fierce guerrilla resistance. A secret Netherlands Forces Intelligence Service (Nefis) overview of the week 22–28 March 1946 reported that "everywhere anarchy prevails and terror is taking on serious proportions."[1] And in early April, Dutch officials wrote: "This once so peaceful island is now bowed down by a terror of revolutionary youths, principally in the kingdoms of Tabanan and Badung, which threatens to cause a total dislocation of the so well ordered Balinese social system. . . . So long as this evil is not combated, normal government administration on Bali cannot be expected."[2]

From late 1945 through 1948 political conflict on Bali was chronic and frequently violent. With the exception of one large-scale battle, in which

---

[1] "Geheim Militaire Overzicht—Nefis," no. 5, 22 March 1945, in Rapportage Indonesie, no. 151, ARA.

[2] Report from the Secretary of the Cabinet, Sanders, early April 1946, in S. L. van der Wal, ed., *Officiële Bescheiden Betreffende de Nederlands-Indonesische Betrekkingen, 1945–1950* (hereafter *Officiële Bescheiden*), vol. 4, doc. no. 33, p. 84.

9. Dutch (KNIL) troops landing at Sanur Beach on 2 March 1946. The landing of some 2,000 troops was unopposed, but serious fighting soon erupted between KNIL and Balinese Republican forces, resulting in hundreds of casualties within a few months. The National Revolution (1945–49) also led to fighting and disagreement among Balinese, which shaped political relations in the postindependence period. (*Rijksinstituut voor Oorlogsdocumentatie, Amsterdam*)

ninety-six died in one day, all of the casualties fell in close guerrilla combat, in ones and twos, some stabbed, others beheaded or burned in their houses, the lucky ones shot.[3] After December 1945 the fighting took place primarily in the villages and rural areas. There were no forward lines of combat, no safe areas or impenetrable mountain sanctuaries. It was a war in which nobody could choose to remain neutral.

[3] In the first few months after the Dutch return to Bali, several hundred Balinese were killed by KNIL troops and their Balinese auxiliaries, and thousands were taken as "prisoners of war." Over the course of the Revolution (1945–49) roughly 1,400 Balinese died on the Republican side alone, and 700 more died fighting on the side of the Dutch. Pendit lists the names of 1,371 casualties on the Republican side in *Bali Berjuang,* pp. 368–90. The figure of 700 Balinese is my own estimate of those who died fighting on the side of the Dutch or their allies and those who were the unrecorded victims of terror on both sides, and is based on the weekly and monthly casualty statistics from Dutch military and political reports. The relevant archives are (1) "Overzicht en Ontwikkeling van de Toestand Troepenco Bali/Lombok" (hereafter OOT/BL) in Rapportage Indonesie, nos. 740–41, ARA; (2) "Wekelijksch (Militaire) In-lichtingenrapport" (hereafter WIR), in Rapportage Indonesie, no. 737, ARA; (3) "Politiek Verslag" (title varies), in Alg. Sec. I, ARA. Additional copies of the OOT/BLs are held in the Ministerie van Defensie Centraal Archievendepot, The Hague (hereafter MvD/CAD), "Hoofd-kwartier van de Generale Staf van het Leger in Indonesie" (hereafter HKGS), Inv. no. 32/1, GG 2, 35. Additional copies of the WIR can be found in the MvD/CAD, Inv. no. 32/1, GG 5, 1407.

The extent and degree of political conflict, however, varied significantly. The base areas of resistance and the major centers of open fighting were in the kingdoms of Tabanan, Badung, and Buleleng (see Map 3). Jembrana was an early center of Republicanism in 1945, but it did not remain a base area for long. The four kingdoms in the eastern part of the island—Bangli, Gianyar, Karangasem, and Klungkung—were not areas of widespread Republican sympathy. The latter two were, in fact, notoriously pro-Dutch; the former were more divided. Even within the base areas of Republican resistance, significant numbers of Balinese were prepared to cooperate, politically and militarily, with the arriving Dutch forces.

It simply made no sense, therefore, when the Dutch spoke of "the Balinese" as a single entity, because the people of Bali were sharply divided, and on both sides of the issue they were prepared to fight. The six months before the return of the Dutch, then, suggest some of the reasons why the Revolution was experienced as a war among Balinese and not directly as a fight between "the Balinese" and "the Dutch." If the Revolution in Bali is understood as a local civil war rather than a regional manifestation of a national war of liberation, the conflictual politics of the Sukarno era and especially the violence of 1965–66 make a good deal more sense.

But how had a society with a reputation for order and harmony fallen into chaos and political conflict? What had moved the ostensibly apolitical and peaceable Balinese to become involved in violent "terrorist" pemuda organizations? Why did the strength of the resistance vary as it did? Open political conflict and widespread resistance occurred where a particular configuration of social forces and economic relations combined with a collapse or sudden weakening of state authority. The variation in socioeconomic formations in Bali—in the nature of the rivalry among the puri, in caste relations and social mobility, and in relations of production—strongly influenced both the geographical and the social distribution of conflict in 1945–46 and thereafter.

Political conflict was not merely a playing out of perceived social or economic injustices, however, but the consequence of variations in the nature of state power in Bali, and of the struggles to establish or to dominate state structures at the regional (Bali-wide) and local (kingdom) levels which took place in the power vacuum left by the Japanese defeat. Thus, for example, the initial concentration of violence in Tabanan and the apparent peacefulness of Klungkung were the result not simply of the somewhat different socioeconomic conditions prevailing in these regions—though it was partly that—but also of the differing capacities of the local states to exert their authority in preventing or controlling such conflict.[4]

---

[4] Anderson makes a similar argument for the case of Java in 1945–46 in *Java in a Time of Revolution*, pp. 138–66 and 332–69.

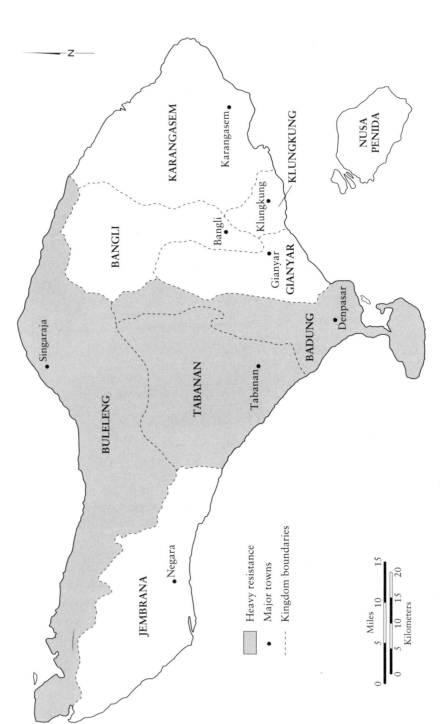

3. Areas of major Republican resistance in Bali, 1946

KARANGASEM

KLUNGKUNG

NUSA
PENIDA

Karangasem

BANGLI

Klungkung

Bangli

Gianyar GIANYAR

Denpasar

BADUNG

Singaraja

BULELENG

TABANAN

Tabanan

Negara

JEMBRANA

Heavy resistance

Major towns

Kingdom boundaries

Miles
0   5   10   15

0 5 10 15 20
Kilometers

The Sources of Conflict

We have seen how Dutch colonial rule influenced the development of economic and social tensions in Bali, and how these tensions were accentuated during the Japanese occupation. After August 1945, puri rivalries, caste issues, and economic inequality emerged as the main focal points of political conflict. Although in some respects Bali was remarkably homogeneous, internal variation influenced the pattern of political conflict. Differing socioeconomic conditions affected the kinds of problems that became politically salient in each area, the type of political alliances that were likely or feasible, and the store of political resources (organizational, ideological, military, economic) available for political mobilization.

Puri rivalries

Among the most important sources of conflict in 1945–46 were the historical rivalries among Bali's noble houses, centered on matters of social status, control of land and labor, and access to political or administrative and religious office, especially the offices of raja, punggawa, and sedahan agung. Initially, these puri rivalries often had little to do with nationalism or Indonesian independence, but after August 1945, they came increasingly to be framed in the idiom of this debate.[5] Political mobilization in the name of *merdeka* (freedom, liberation) and Indonesian Republicanism on the one hand and Balinese autonomy (independence of Java) and loyalism (to the Dutch) on the other, accentuated the conflict not simply between the noble houses but also between their respective followers. New and often intense social, political, and ideological conflicts were forged in the course of this mobilization.

In some places, such as Tabanan, the ideological question (Republicanism vs. loyalism) was already an important basis of conflict prior to 1945, largely because of the prewar development of a nationalist movement there. What happened in Tabanan in the late 1930s occurred in other parts of Bali over the course of the Revolution as the ideological debate over nationalism became a real political issue and not simply a guise for other struggles.

The political landscape was complicated by the fact that, as we have seen, Bali had been colonized piecemeal. Although after 1938 the eight kingdoms of Bali all had the status of self-governing territories, each headed by a descendant of the old hereditary rulers, five had experienced reasonably long periods of direct rule under the Dutch, while three had, with minor interruption, remained as areas of indirect rule. In the formerly direct-ruled territories—Buleleng, Jembrana, Badung, Tabanan, and Klungkung—the raja-puri often lacked their earlier material means and royal legitimacy. This

---

[5] See chapter 2 for a discussion of the term *puri*.

was especially the case with the royal families of Buleleng and Jembrana, where the memory of royal authority had seriously faded. It was also very much the case in Tabanan and Badung. The exception to the rule was Klungkung, where the raja-puri was able to reestablish its authority, wealth, and prestige with the assistance of the colonial government. The weakening of the royal tradition in the western kingdoms left the raja-puri more vulnerable to challenges in 1945–46, but, with the possible exception of Tabanan, it did not send them into the protective arms of the Dutch.

By contrast, the royal tradition in the indirect-ruled kingdoms—Bangli, Gianyar, and Karangasem—remained strong at the time of the 1938 "restoration."[6] It must be stressed, however, that the paramount position of the raja-puri in these areas had always depended to a great extent on the backing of the colonial state, and this was reflected in the general willingness of the rajas of the eastern kingdoms to cooperate with the arriving Dutch forces in 1946.

Although some noble houses maintained their paramount positions in their kingdoms under the Dutch and Japanese regimes, other houses, many of them independently wealthy and socially influential, did whatever possible to challenge the incumbents. Changes under the Dutch and Japanese were uncommon, because both regimes tended to follow a purely hereditary-based system for filling high political offices. But the collapse of state power in 1945–46 provided a unique opportunity for competing puri to act on their claims and overthrow an incumbent who had been dependent on the colonial state.[7] Where there was no higher authority to guarantee the right of a lord or puri to political title, power became a matter of evident control over a population or territory and Republican organizations became valuable political allies. The challengers for the position of raja were sometimes economically more powerful and socially more influential than the incumbents, constituting, in effect, a rising landed elite. The collapse of the old state structure was the precondition for their political rise and for the concomitant decline of the old aristocracy.

Puri rivalries existed on some scale in virtually every kingdom, district, and village on the island. Some of the larger struggles, particularly those involving raja-puri, are worth noting here, because they strongly influenced the character of political conflict in each of the eight kingdoms. Two of these

---

[6] In Gianyar and Bangli, for example, the men who were named as zelfbestuurder in 1938 had been serving as regents since 1913.

[7] It is commonly said in Bali that the Revolution was an opportune time to *membalas*, "get back at one's rivals or enemies": interview with I Nyoman Pegeg, 16 September 1986, Denpasar. In an interview in Wassenaar on 27 May 1987 the former raja of Gianyar (later prime minister of Negara Indonesia Timur, State of East Indonesia), Anak Agung Gde Agung, portrayed the revolutionary period in Bali as "a time of intrigue and calumny." These descriptions resonate rather strongly with Geertz's description of politics in late nineteenth-century Bali: *Negara*, p. 62.

kingdoms, Bangli and Karangasem, will not be discussed because reliable information is lacking.[8]

Badung: The major rivalry in Badung was between the Puri Pemecutan and the Puri Satria, both located in Denpasar. Whereas these puri had shared power (as coregents) in precolonial Badung, the Dutch had selected the patriarch of Puri Satria (then known as Puri Denpasar) to become bestuurder in 1929, and then in 1938 had restored him to the position of raja or zelfbestuurder of Badung. The post of punggawa kota had for a time been filled by members of the Puri Pemecutan, but they still resented their exclusion from the top office of raja.[9] Before the Dutch landed in early 1946 there was no substantial puri-based opposition to the Republican movement in Denpasar, but Badung was nonetheless divided politically on the basis of allegiance to different puri. After four years of Japanese rule, the Puri Satria still held power, but it was economically weak and lacked influence in large areas of the kingdom. Because two of the raja's sons were involved in the local Indonesian National Committee (KNI) and the BKR/TKR, the raja was unwilling to take any firm action against the Republican movement.[10] Members of the wealthier and more influential Puri Pemecutan (commanding a strong base of loyalty in Denpasar and the western part of the kingdom) had also been active in nationalist circles since the early 1930s.[11] In an

[8] The most important rivalries in Bangli and Karangasem appear to have been within or very close to the puri. There seems to have been some unpleasantness in Bangli, for instance, between the immediate family members of the raja and those of his brother, Anak Agung Gede Agung Anom Putera, after the latter was passed over for the position of regent in 1934. Anak Agung Gde Muditha and Anak Agung Gede Ngurah, the sons of Anom Putera and therefore also nephews of the raja of Bangli, were two of the most prominent and respected pemuda leaders in Bali. Dutch sources speculate that the young men joined the resistance out of a sense of the injustice done to their father, but that they were still close enough to the raja to be guaranteed considerable freedom of action. See R. J. F. Post, "Nopens Zelfbestuurder Bangli," 29 December 1947, Archive Boon. Two sons of the puri in Karangasem were responsible for the organization of the BKR/TKR in the kingdom. In April 1946, however, with the help of the Dutch, the raja of Karangasem set up an anti-Republican militia, AIM (Anti Indonesia Merdeka): Pendit, *Bali Berjuang,* p. 80; and interviews with I Made Wija Kusuma, 22 and 23 March 1986, Denpasar, and Dewa Made Dhana, 10 October 1986, Singaraja.

[9] Interview with I Gusti Bagus Oka (former secretary to the Paruman Agung), 19 December 1986, Denpasar. *Kota* means town. The capital of each kingdom was designated as a separate district, administered by a punggawa kota. Political rivalry between the raja and the punggawa kota was almost invariable.

[10] The sons involved in the resistance were Cokorda Ngurah Agung and Cokorda Bagus Agung. The Dutch saw the Puri Satria as a center of subversive activity in South Bali, according to a secret report on Badung by Secretary of State for Home Affairs H. van der Wal, 15 December 1948, Rapportage Indonesie, no. 737/12, ARA. Some Balinese say that the raja himself, though old and infirm, was an ardent Republican, and did not regret relinquishing the post in 1946: interview with I Made Wija Kusuma, 23 March 1986, Denpasar. Wija Kusuma also suggested that the old raja's Republicanism was based on his desire for revenge for the defeat of 1906, in which his father, the then raja, and hundreds of family and followers of the puri died.

[11] Together with five others, including two Javanese, one Ambonese, and Nyoman Pegeg, the head of the Puri Pemecutan (I Gusti Ngurah Gde Pemecutan) formed the Studi Club Ganesha in

effort to win the allegiance of the stronger Puri Pemecutan and simultaneously undercut the nationalist resistance in Badung as a whole, the Dutch dismissed the raja (from Puri Satria) in mid-1946 and bestowed the title on the patriarch of Puri Pemecutan.[12] This move succeeded in weakening the Republican movement considerably, and it also ensured that the division between the two puri continued through the Revolution and beyond.[13]

Buleleng: In Buleleng, rivalry between the raja-puri (Puri Agung Buleleng) and the Puri Sukasada had dominated the political scene at least since the imposition of indirect Dutch colonial authority in 1849.[14] As a result of the unwillingness of the Puri Sukasada to acquiesce in Dutch authority, several of its leading members were sent into exile. The Dutch acknowledged the Puri Agung Buleleng as the raja-puri until 1882, when direct rule was imposed, and then again after the nominal restoration of 1929. After a period of exile, the Puri Sukasada became the main supplier of punggawa kota and in 1945 was still voicing its claim to the throne of all Buleleng. I Gusti Ketut Puja, appointed governor of Sunda Kecil in August 1945, was from the Puri Sukasada, and many other prominent nationalists also had close relations with the puri.[15] The Puri Agung was not unsympathetic to the Republic, but

the early 1930s to discuss the works of Hatta and Sukarno. When these works were banned and the club was outlawed in 1933, the members struck on the idea of establishing a Taman Siswa school in Bali: interview with Nyoman Pegeg, 31 July 1986, Denpasar. In the early revolutionary period, the leaders of the PRI and the TKR (Wija Kusuma and Ngurah Rai, respectively) reportedly consulted with the Cokorda on matters of political and military strategy. On one occasion the Cokorda met with twelve *balian* (men and women with magical/spiritual power) to discuss their possible support for the Republican resistance: interview with I Made Wija Kusuma, 22 March 1986, Denpasar.

[12] See "Overzicht Politiek Situatie," May 1946, in Archive Boon. The old raja of Badung was eased out of his post in April 1946. For a full discussion of the rationale behind the Dutch decision, see the secret report on Badung by H. van der Wal, 15 December 1948, in Rapportage Indonesie, no. 737/12, ARA.

[13] It is sometimes said that the Puri Pemecutan betrayed the Revolution after accepting the position of raja in 1946. Others point out that the head of the puri consulted with the main Republican leader, I Gusti Ngurah Rai, before accepting the position because he feared that this move might undermine the resistance. According to this version of events, Ngurah Rai encouraged the Cokorda to accept the job so that he might help the resistance "from within": interviews with Nyoman Pegeg, 31 July 1986, Denpasar; I Made Wija Kusuma, 22 March 1986, Denpasar.

[14] The man designated by the Dutch as the raja at this time was apparently the former patih. The Puri Sukasada claimed that theirs was the lineage of the actual raja at the time of the Dutch attack and victory in 1849. A Dutch report from 1945 acknowledged that the two puri had "an equal claim to the throne": "Nota Herbezetting Bali," November 1945, Archive Boon.

[15] A Dutch report of November 1945 noted that the "influential" Puri Sukasada had a good number of strong and well-educated members apart from Puja. By comparison, among the male offspring of the Puri Agung there were "in fact no powerful, well-educated personalities." The influence of the Puri Sukasada extended well beyond Buleleng. See "Nota Herbezetting Bali," November 1945, Archive Boon. It is said that the Puri Sukasada frequently married women from Banjar Jawa in Singaraja. Banjar Jawa was later known as a center of Republican resistance and a focal point of nationalist consciousness in Buleleng: interview with I Gde Rahjasa (former pemuda leader, Buleleng), 9 October 1986, Singaraja.

the new raja (Anak Agung Nyoman Panji Tisna, appointed in 1944) was more inclined to favor peaceful, parliamentary methods than most of the pemuda would have liked. For a variety of reasons—not the least of which being that he had converted to Christianity—Panji Tisna resigned as raja in 1947 and was replaced by his brother, Mr. Jelantik.[16]

Gianyar: The Puri Agung Gianyar had a number of challengers for the status of raja-puri.[17] They were concentrated in the western border region of the kingdom, and included the leading puri of Ubud, Mas, Peliatan, Pejeng, and Sukawati. Members and followers of these puri were strong initial supporters of the Republic, and many joined the PRI and the BKR to fight against he militia of the raja of Gianyar, the PPN.[18] Yet, divided among themselves, they were unable to unseat the Puri Agung during the Revolution, and the rivalry persisted after independence.[19]

Jembrana: Two principal houses of the kingdom, Jero Pasekan and Puri Agung Negara, had been competing for the position of raja-puri for the better part of a century, but the Dutch favored the latter.[20] Nonetheless, the raja and his son (Anak Agung Bagus Suteja, later governor of Bali), had nationalist sympathies, and their puri formed the core of early KNI and pemuda organizations in the kingdom. Nearly half of the nationalist activists contacted by the Javanese Republican "propagandist" Soekardani in Oc-

[16] According to some accounts, Panji Tisna resigned because he could not reconcile his sympathy for the nationalist cause with his desire to do an honest job as raja, which included maintaining peace and order. Others suggest that he "lacked moral courage," "had no convictions," or was at heart an artist and writer, not a politician or leader. Some former pemuda claim that he was not sympathetic to the Republic at all, but was actually pro-Dutch: interviews with I Gusti Bagus Oka, 19 December 1986, Denpasar; Pak Item (I Ketut Wijana, former pemuda leader, Buleleng), 29 September 1986, Singaraja; Anak Agung Santosa (son of Anak Agung Nyoman Panji Tisna), 11 October 1986, Singaraja.

[17] For some idea of the history of these challenges, see H. J. E. F. Schwartz, "Aanteekening omtrent het Landschap Gianjar," *Tijdschrift voor het Binnenlands Bestuur* 19, no. 3 (1900): 166–89. The Puri Gianyar had lost credibility in many eyes when it surrendered to the Dutch without a fight in 1900. The raja at that time requested the status of stedehouder, and in exchange recognized the full sovereignty of the Dutch in his kingdom. Many Balinese also regarded the Puri Agung as an "upstart puri" because it was said to have been established by a commoner from Badung: interview with Nyoman Pegeg, 16 September 1986, Denpasar.

[18] The PPN (Pemuda Pembela Negara—Youth for the Defense of the Kingdom), established by the raja in late 1945, was dubbed Pemuda Pembela NICA (Youth for the Defense of NICA [Netherlands Indies Civil Administration]) by Republican pemuda. In September 1945 the raja of Gianyar, Anak Agung Gde Agung, was kidnapped twice by pemuda gangs. The kidnapping attempts were apparently initiated by the puri of Ubud and Pliatan, and possibly others, and were carried out by members of the PRI. Anak Agung Gde Agung claims that this act of "terrorism" turned him against the resistance: interviews with Anak Agung Gde Agung, 18 May 1987, Wassenaar; Nyoman Pegeg, 16 September 1986, Denpasar; I Gusti Ketut Reti, 30 July 1986, Denpasar; Dewa Made Dhana, 10 October 1986, Singaraja.

[19] In the 1950s the Puri Agung Gianyar (in particular, Anak Agung Gde Agung) became a powerful center of PSI strength, while many followers of the rival western puri favored the PNI and the PKI. See chapter 8.

[20] This summary is drawn from the collected archives and writings of the late Jembrana historian I Wayan Reken and from I Ketut Wartama, "Sedjarah Perkembangan Djembrana," thesis, Universitas Udayana, Denpasar, 1972.

tober 1945 were family members or employees of the Puri Agung.[21] Armed resistance, though strong at the outset, did not last long in Jembrana, particularly after the Dutch arrested the raja's son, Suteja. Jero Pasekan, the house of the punggawa kota, was a center of anti-Republicanism, and with the help of the Dutch it set up the BPP, an anti-Republican militia.[22]

Klungkung: The Puri Agung Klungkung had very few serious royal competitors by 1945.[23] The raja's main local rivals were the punggawa kota, who was not a triwangsa, and the sedahan agung, also of low caste and, as a native of Bangli, a "foreigner." These men lacked the social, political, and material base necessary to challenge the position of the raja, yet both attempted to do so under the banner of Republicanism, and both, together with two others, were murdered by the raja's militia, the BKN, in March 1946.[24] The raja construed Republicanism as "outside aggression" from Klungkung's old rivals, Badung and Bangli, and from Islamic Java. These claims were made more credible by the fact that bellicose armed pemuda and BKR groups from Badung did come to Klungkung in September and October 1945 to mobilize the local population.[25] Offended and threatened by the actions and demands of the pemuda groups, the Dewa Agung took an early stand against the Republic.

Tabanan: In Tabanan a large number of wealthy and influential puri and jero with strong Republican sympathies were in a position to challenge the

[21] Of thirty-seven Balinese Republican activists contacted by Soekardani, over half were from Negara. Nine persons were clearly connected with the Puri Agung; seven were family members and two were employees in the office of the raja. See "Lijst van personen, waarmede de propagandist Soekardani in aanraking is gekomen," Alg. Sec. I, Kist XXII, no. 19, ARA.

[22] The head of this house was Westra Utama, who seems to have been the driving force behind the anti-Republican movement in Jembrana. The BPP (Badan Pemberantas Pengacau—Body of Fighters against Terrorists) was known to Republicans as the Badan Penjilat Pantat Belanda (Body of Dutch Ass-Lickers).

[23] The Dewa Agung had some trouble with his own family when one of his sons, Cokorda Anom, joined the pemuda without his father's permission. When the Dewa Agung offered his resignation as raja, the same Cokorda Anom, deeply embarrassed, begged forgiveness. In Klungkung only one Brahmana household, the Griya Pidada, was an active source of Republican resistance to the Dutch, but it failed to mobilize the kind of mass following necessary for a serious political challenge. Its head, Ida Bagus Pidada, was in fact more active in Denpasar politics, becoming a member of the KNI in 1945.

[24] The BKN (Badan Keamanan Negara—Body for the Defense of the Realm) was set up by the raja of Klungkung in late 1945 to combat the rising tide of Republicanism in his kingdom. See Pendit, *Bali Berjuang*, p. 80. The responsibility of the BKN for these murders and other acts of "terror" is confirmed by Dutch intelligence reports. See, for example, "De Gebeurtenissen in Kloengkoeng op Maart 4, 1946," Archive Boon.

[25] Pendit, *Bali Berjuang*, pp. 78–79. Pemuda leaders admit that the actions of the BKR and PRI who descended on Klungkung in August and September were provocative and "too hot-headed." The Dewa Agung was the only raja who categorically refused to fly the Republican flag over government offices and the puri in late 1945. According to one account, he justified his refusal by reference to his collection of ancient manuscripts (*lontar*), which he said indicated that the day was inauspicious: interview with Dewa Made Dhana, October 10, 1986, Singaraja. For the Dewa Agung's own interpretation of events up to March 1946, see his letter to the Resident of Bali/Lombok, 6 December 1948, Archive Boon.

poverty-stricken and politically weak raja-puri, Puri Gde Tabanan.[26] The 1945–46 pattern of rivalry apparently did not parallel the major factional split of the turn of the century between the allies of Puri Gde and those of Puri Kaleran.[27] The rivalry in Tabanan, in effect, was not between the raja-puri and one major challenger (as was the case in most other kingdoms), or between "the kingdom" and "the outsiders" (as the raja construed it in Klungkung), but among several influential and wealthy puri and jero—of which Tabanan had an unusually large number—dotted about the kingdom. The vast majority of these puri had Republican sympathies, so the resistance movement soon spread beyond the town of Tabanan.[28] Moreover, in addition to the noble houses, there were a number of wealthy commoner houses with substantial landholdings and considerable political power. The weak raja-puri was forced to flow with the tide, neither leading nor resisting the Republican mobilization. The raja's "passivity" provided his challengers and the pemuda with a great deal of political room for maneuver.

In view of this evidence, it is tempting to argue that the Republican banner was taken up by political challengers or climbers, especially by the non-raja-puri. This appears to have been the case in Badung (Puri Pemecutan), in Gianyar (the puri of Ubud, Mas, Peliatan, Pejeng, and Sukawati), in Klungkung (the punggawa kota), and in Buleleng (Puri Sukasada). Yet in Jembrana it was the raja-puri that took a strong Republican stand, and in Badung the Puri Satria was a center of Republicanism even before it was displaced as raja-puri. In Tabanan and in Karangasem, too, it was the rajas who were the first to declare their support for the Republic, although they later changed their tune. It does not seem that political status alone—that is, the status as incumbent or challenger—can fully explain the political positions of the various puri.

Nor is it possible to argue that it was only the weakest or the poorest puri that supported the Republic, because several of the pro-Republican puri and jero (e.g., Subamia and Kaleran in Tabanan, Pemecutan in Badung, Sukasada in Buleleng) were both wealthy and influential. It does seem, however, that *weak* raja-puri (incumbents) took up with the side that seemed most powerful locally, whether the Republic or the Dutch. In other words, they followed the movement of social forces rather than act to influence

[26] See A. A. W. A. Ellerbeck, "Personalia—Tabanan," Archive Boon, and van Beuge, "Report on Situation in Tabanan," Inv. no. 32/1, GG 8, Bundel 1,2,3,4, d, MvD/CAD.
[27] Geertz describes the factionalism in Tabanan around 1906 in some detail. On one side were the Puri Gde, Dangin, Denpasar, Taman, Oka, Anom, Anyar, and the Jero Subamia, and on the other were the Puri Kaleran and Kediri and the Jero Gde Beng, Kompiang, and Tegeh. *Negara*, pp. 60–61.
[28] For details of the political sympathies of the various houses in Tabanan, see Ellerbeck, "Personalia."

them. *Strong* raja-puri, in contrast, took a position for or against the Republic in accordance with a prior or principled choice.

Beyond this distinction, the bases of puri political choice are difficult to unravel; they often reflected simply the personal preference of a leading family member. It is said, for example, that the raja of Klungkung had an inordinate fear that Bali would succumb to Islamic domination in the event of a Republican victory.[29] This fear of Islam colored all of his political decisions. There were, however, some broader patterns as well. The better-educated rajas and puri members, for example, tended to support the Republic. The raja of Jembrana and his son, for instance, were among the best-educated members of the royal families, whereas the raja of Tabanan was regarded as one of the most poorly educated of Bali's rajas.[30] A notable exception to the rule was the raja of Gianyar (Anak Agung Gde Agung), a highly educated opponent of the Republic.[31]

The pattern or the structure of puri rivalry in each kingdom affected the character of political conflict at this time and in later years. There were basically three structural types of puri rivalry—dispersed, polarized, and hegemonic—and these were associated with three distinct patterns of political conflict and mobilization. Resistance was strongest where both the incumbent (raja) puri and one or more challenger puri had some Republican sympathies, which gave the movement a somewhat broader base but at the same time gave rise to factionalism within the resistance. This pattern of dispersed rivalry was found in Badung, Buleleng, and Tabanan. Where strong puri divided for and against the Republic, mobilization was swift and political conflict was initially more acute, but the resistance did not last long, particularly when the Dutch arrived and supported the anti-Republican puri. This pattern of polarized conflict occurred in Jembrana and western Gianyar. Where there were no significant puri challengers, the raja-puri could establish political control and a clear ideological hegemony. Political mobilization in these kingdoms was state-initiated, and the resistance to the Dutch was by far the weakest. This hegemonic pattern existed in Klungkung and most of eastern and central Gianyar.

The relationship between the structure of puri rivalry and the nature of political resistance raises a second point of interest: the vulnerability of puri-

[29] Pendit, *Bali Berjuang*, p. 79. The Dewa Agung's fear of Islam was mentioned repeatedly in my interviews with former pemuda and older civil servants: I Gusti Bagus Oka, 18 December 1986, Denpasar; I Made Wija Kusuma, 22 March 1986, Denpasar; Professor J. van Baal, 9 May 1987, Doorn.

[30] The raja of Tabanan completed only four years (of seven) at the HIS in Denpasar. His brothers also went without education. According to a Dutch Controleur (Ellerbeck), the puri simply did not have the money to send the children to school.

[31] Anak Agung Gde Agung had studied law in Batavia. Although he now claims that he was an ardent nationalist from the start, his attitude and actions during the course of the Revolution have left some room for doubt on this score. For Agung's version of his own nationalist credentials, see his *Dari Negara Indonesia Timur ke Republik Indonesia Serikat* (Yogyakarta: UGM Press, 1986). For a different view, see chapter 7.

based political resistance to the Dutch. Where a single puri was the sole or the primary basis of political mobilization, the loss of puri leadership (through arrest or a change of heart) could mean a sudden end to or interruption of the political movement. This seems to have been the case in Jembrana. Where, on the other hand, many puri were involved on the Republican side, or where there were a variety of local bases of political mobilization (e.g., pencak silat gangs, independent military organizations, religious groups), the resistance was far more resilient. This was especially the case in Tabanan, and to some extent also in Badung and Buleleng.

These three kingdoms shared other features that may have influenced the pattern of their puri politics. First, they were the most prosperous kingdoms in Bali. Opportunities for the accumulation of wealth, and therefore the basis for the establishment of new and influential puri and commoner houses (a rising landed and entrepreneurial elite), were much greater here than in other parts of Bali.[32] The greater the number of powerful puri, the greater the number of potential centers of puri political mobilization. Second, since these were the most "cosmopolitan" of the kingdoms of Bali, new political ideologies and models for mobilization, especially those from Java, were most accessible here, and the link with the educated pemuda, as well as the older prewar nationalists and intellectuals, was more natural.[33] Finally, these were kingdoms with weak rajas, from the point of view of both their material wealth and their influence over the populations of their kingdoms.[34] The rajas were no longer a true landed aristocracy; now they were declining salaried administrators. Their weakness effectively expanded the area that was beyond the scope of the "center" in each kingdom, creating the conditions for the emergence of alternative local states under the leadership of either a local puri or an independent band of pemuda.

Caste Issues

It needs to be said that the Revolution in Bali was not primarily a movement of the lower castes against the higher. The caste character of the Revolution, however, did change over time. At the outset, men and women of all castes were found in roughly equal measure on both sides of the political debate. Men of high caste, especially Satria and Brahmana, figured prominently in the leadership of the earliest nationalist organizations, including

[32] A number of Balinese informants suggested the importance of such a new rising class in the political development of Tabanan: interview with Ida Bagus Wisnem Manuaba (early moderate nationalist leader, member KNI, later PSI leader in Bali), 10 July 1986, Tabanan. Moreover, social mobility found expression not only in the creation of new puri but also in the expanding wealth of low-caste Tabananers.

[33] In an interview on 23 March 1986, Denpasar, I Made Wija Kusuma suggested that this was a significant factor in the greater nationalist awareness of the Puri Satria in Denpasar.

[34] In Badung this was no longer true after April 1946, when the old raja (Puri Satria) was replaced by the more influential head of Puri Pemecutan.

the KNI and the BKR/TKR.[35] They were in a good position to lead because, on the one hand, by virtue of their caste they were thought to possess the "natural" ability and right to do so, and, on the other, they often had the requisite material resources and a ready-made group of followers on whom they could rely for immediate political and military support. There were historical reasons as well for the primary leadership role of the triwangsa. Among the most important of the BKR/TKR commanders were men with prewar military experience in the Balinese Prayoda Corps. The Dutch had deliberately selected the Prayoda officers from families of high birth. The BKR/TKR commanders in Bali, then, were very likely to be high-caste men.[36]

It is important to note, however, that the triwangsa did not dominate the leadership positions throughout the Revolution, nor were they equally powerful, even at the outset, in all parts of Bali. Among the prominent pemuda leaders, for example, were a number of men of low caste, including Made Wija Kusuma (leader of the PRI and later of the main resistance body, the MBU-DPRI),[37] Gede Puger (an anti-Japanese activist who became the leader of Pesindo), Nyoman Mantik (a leading figure in the PRI and later in the MBU-DPRI), and Nyoman Pegeg (leader of the BKR-Sunda Kecil and later a key figure in the Intelligence Section of the TKR). While their caste origins did not disqualify them for leadership roles, it was really their education that distinguished them as credible leaders. All were well educated by Balinese standards, and three of the four had studied in Java, something that very few Balinese of any caste had done. Indeed, as we have seen, education in Java or in one of the nationalist Taman Siswa schools in Bali was an experience shared by most of Bali's young and lower-caste Republican leaders, particularly those who were active in the urban-based movements in Denpasar and Singaraja.[38]

[35] The first commanders of the BKR in Bali were, without exception, triwangsa, and a large number of them were of the families of the rajas. Republican casualty statistics indicate that roughly 35% of all men with officer rank were triwangsa. See Yayasan Kebaktian Proklamasi [Bali], "Daftar Pahlawan Pejuang Kemerdekaan R. I. Daerah Tingkat I Propinsi Bali, Gugur Antara Tahun 1945 s/d 1950," Denpasar, n.d.

[36] In March 1946 the TKR commanders were as follows: Badung, I Gusti Putu Wisnu (former Prayoda); Buleleng, Dewa Made Swedja (former Prayoda officer); Jembrana, I Gusti Bagus Kajun (former Prayoda officer); Bangli, Anak Agung Anom Muditha (former Police officer); Gianyar, I Dewa Gde Anom Asta (former Prayoda officer); Tabanan, I Gusti Wayan Debes (former Prayoda officer); Karangasem, Anak Agung Made Karang. The commander of the TKR Resimen Sunda Kecil was I Gusti Ngurah Rai (former Prayoda officer). See Lt. Col. ter Meulen, "Nota Betreffende Bali," 16 March 1946, Archive Boon.

[37] MBU-DPRI = Markas Besar Umum [Oemoem]-Dewan Perjuangan Republik Indonesia Sunda Kecil, or General Headquarters of the Resistance Council of Indonesia for Sunda Kecil.

[38] The nationalist activists in the town of Denpasar in October 1945 were predominantly men of lower caste or non-Balinese. Most were educated men or members of the small urban middle class, including three medical doctors, at least two schoolteachers, a school head, a director of an export firm, the head of Bank Rakyat, and various government servants. See "Report on the Situation on Bali and Lombok, Compiled from the Notebooks of the Republican Propagandist Soekardani," Alg. Sec. I, Kist XXII, no. 19, ARA.

For those who could not go to Java, the independent Taman Siswa schools, established in Bali in the mid- and late 1930s, provided an appreciation of the currents of nationalist thinking there. Not every low-caste boy or girl could afford to attend the Taman Siswa (or the associated schools, Taman Dewasa and Taman Indah), it is true, but by the late 1930s there were as many as 200 pupils at the Denpasar school, and under the Japanese an estimated 600.[39] These schools encouraged the development of nationalist consciousness and solidarity. Since they were located in the major towns, this consciousness was essentially an urban phenomenon. At the same time, the fact that enthusiasm for education was generally greater among low-caste than high-caste Balinese meant that nationalism did not represent a shift in the attitudes of the aristocracy, but rather gave expression to the aspirations of a moderately affluent lower caste.

There were non-triwangsa leaders in the countryside as well. Lower-caste leaders often emerged where a powerful local lord was lacking, as was often the case in areas of cash-crop production and away from the older subsistence rice-producing settlements of the south-central region. The peripheral regions were frequently occupied by migrants, and ties to a particular lord tended to be somewhat looser there, particularly for those who owned their own land. Smallholders who produced such cash crops as coffee, cloves, vegetables, and fruit tended to be more dependent on Chinese traders, moneylenders, and the market than on a local puri or lord.[40]

In the more densely populated rice-growing regions, it was not uncommon for a lord to be unpopular with "his" people. Unpopularity had many possible sources, including excessive demands for unremunerated labor on the lord's home or public works projects or for contributions to ceremonial events, unfair terms of tenancy (where the lord was also landlord), and so on. In the absence of a higher state authority, such a lord was more vulnerable to challenge. In such situations, influential men and women of the community—experts in black and white magic, martial arts adepts, local toughs, and others with a reputation for unusual spiritual or physical powers—led the struggle against the old lord, usually in the name of merdeka.[41] This appears to have been the case with the gangs in north-central Badung and Tabanan—Beruang Hitam (Black Bear), Kucing Hitam (Black Cat), and many others.[42]

[39] During the revolutionary period the name was changed to Saraswati School, but it continued to be a center of nationalist sentiment and organization: interviews with I Nyoman Pegeg, 16 September 1986, Denpasar; and Dewa Made Dhana, 10 October 1986, Singaraja. For a discussion of the Taman Siswa schools in Bali, see I Gusti Putu Wirata, "Pergerakan Taman Siswa di Bali, Tahun 1933 Sampai Tahun 1943," thesis, Universitas Udayana, Denpasar, 1971.

[40] Interview with Dewa Made Dhana, 7 October 1986, Singaraja.

[41] In a personal communication, 3 May 1987, Hen, Schulte Nordholt suggested that this was the case in the area around Blahkiuh, central Badung.

[42] The Beruang Hitam was a band of ten or twelve well-armed men who roamed widely about northern Badung and Tabanan meting out revolutionary justice to known or suspected traitors: interview with Putu Mudera (member of the Beruang Hitam), 2 May 1986, Denpasar.

From the point of view of caste, then, there were essentially three types of Republican leaders. Men of high caste, especially from influential puri, dominated the Republican military (BKR/TKR) and political (KNI) leadership early in the Revolution. The urban educated pemuda, largely of lower caste, were prominent in the urban-based political organizations (PRI and Pesindo). After December 1945, under pressure from the Japanese, they fled the urban areas and began mobilization in the countryside. Finally, in rural areas where the state apparatus was weakest, a variety of low-caste leaders dominated the scene.

As the Revolution proceeded, the question of caste, which had surfaced in the 1920s, came increasingly to the fore. Men of lower caste became more prominent in leadership posts and, significantly, men of higher caste stopped using their caste titles. As we will see in chapter 7, the shift toward low-caste leadership was evident in the changing composition of the MBU-DPRI as early as July 1946. Another major shift in this direction came in the aftermath of the devastating battle at Marga, in November 1946, in which ninety-six men died, including many of the original leaders of the BKR/TKR. After 1945, as in the colonial period, it was primarily the educated sudra who tried to move the struggle in an antifeudal direction. This movement contributed to a radicalization of the Revolution and to fears of genuine social revolution.

Economic Inequality

Two main economic issues affected the incidence and distribution of political conflict in Bali from late 1945 to early 1946: the relative prosperity of the various regions of the island, and regional variations in landlord-tenant relations.

In the 1940s Bali could be divided roughly into regions of economic prosperity and surplus (the "plus" regions) and those of economic hardship or deficit (the "minus" regions), measured by the availability of rice for local consumption.[43] Relatively prosperous regions were those in which the population was able to eat rice virtually every day. In less prosperous regions rice had to be mixed with less desirable staples, such as corn, beans, and tubers. According to this measure, the "plus" areas included eastern Tabanan, southern Badung, parts of Buleleng, a coastal strip of Jembrana, and a small island of land around the town of Klungkung, while the "minus" areas included most of the eastern kingdoms of Klungkung, Karangasem, Bangli, and Gianyar.[44] Another measure of prosperity was the availability of a marketable surplus. Tabanan produced almost all of Bali's rice exports (about

[43] This distinction between "plus" and "minus," or "prosperous" (*makmur*) and "impoverished" (*miskin*) regions, is frequently made by Balinese and others with a knowledge of the island as a whole: interview with I Gusti Bagus Oka, 19 December 1986, Denpasar; and Hans Harten (head of the Bali Agricultural Office, 1946–50), 18 May 1987, The Hague.

[44] I Gusti Gde Raka, *Monografi Pulau Bali* (Jakarta: Jawatan Pertanian Rakyat, 1955), pp. 46–47.

15,000 tons per year) and, together with Badung and Buleleng, dominated the production of other exportable cash crops. At this level of generality, then, the relatively prosperous kingdoms of Bali appear to have formed the core are of the Republican resistance. The obvious exception was the town of Klungkung.

There are a number of possible explanations for this pattern, which can be touched on only briefly here. One is the importance of material resources in the sustenance of any political movement. In the case of a guerrilla movement, such as existed in Bali, food and shelter are prerequisites to any action; indeed, the search for them is often the primary task of a guerrilla band. Guerrilla base areas, then, must be located in regions with easy access to food surplus. Base areas established in deficit regions place an undue strain on the local economy and the local population. The guerrilla resistance in Bali was no exception. The same logic applies to other political entities, including states; they, too, require a substantial surplus to survive. Klungkung had such a surplus and, judging from the available evidence, much of it was concentrated in the hands of the raja and his relatives.

A look at the agricultural land-use map of Bali (Map 4) reveals that the first centers of resistance were located in rich rice-growing (sawah) areas: eastern Tabanan, south-central Badung, Buleleng, and coastal Jembrana. After the arrival of the Dutch in March 1946, the bases moved higher into the mountains. Yet even here it was necessary to find an area of sufficient surplus. The first base area of the MBU-DPRI at Munduk Malang, for instance, though high in the mountains, was located amid high-quality sawah, which produced two crops per year. The same was true of Bengkel Anyar in Tabanan and of the various base areas in the north, such as Bebetin, Munduk, and Panji. It was when the guerrilla groups were forced to abandon these choice productive areas that the resistance began to crumble.

Peasants in the "plus" areas of Bali differed from those in the "minus" regions in two respects. First, the percentage of peasants who owned their land was greater in the "plus" areas, and the average size of landholdings larger.[45] Second, the terms of tenancy were significantly more favorable to the tenant in the "plus" regions than in the "minus" regions. The most favorable system for the tenant was *nandu,* in which the yield was divided equally between the landlord and tenant. This system predominated in the western kingdoms of Buleleng, Jembrana, Tabanan, and Badung. The systems less advantageous to the tenant were *nelon, ngapit, nerapat,* and *melaisin,* which prevailed in the eastern part of the island.[46] The worst terms

[45] For example, the level of private ownership of sawah land in Tabanan was the highest in Bali; only about 16% of farmers who planted sawah land were tenants in 1950. See ibid., p. 34. The average size of holdings in Tabanan in the late 1930s was 0.86 hectares, significantly above the average in other kingdoms. See Regerings Commissaris, "Nota van Toelichtingen betreffende . . . Tabanan."

[46] These terms describe different systems for the division of yield between owner and tenant. Under the *nelon* system the landlord received three-fifths and the tenant two-fifths of the yield; under *ngapit,* the division was two-thirds for the landlord, one-third for the tenant; under

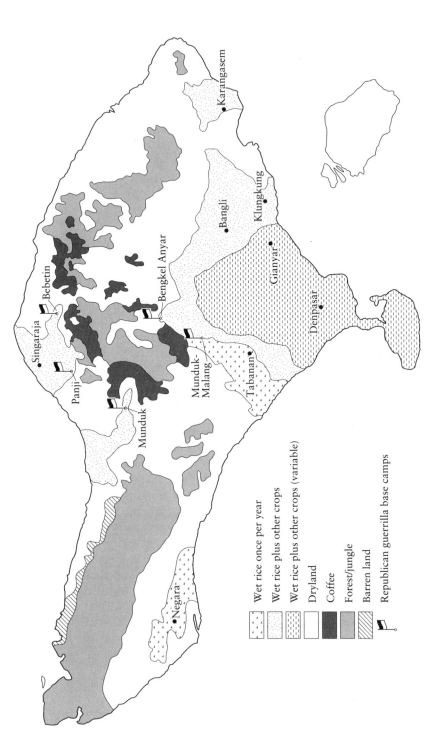

4. Agricultural land use and Republican guerrilla base camps in Bali, 1946–48

Karangasem

Klungkung

Bangli

Singaraja

Bebetin

Bengkel Anyar

Panji

Munduk

Munduk-Malang

Gianyar

Denpasar

Tabanan

Negara

Wet rice once per year
Wet rice plus other crops
Wet rice plus other crops (variable)
Dryland
Coffee
Forest/jungle
Barren land
Republican guerrilla base camps

of tenancy by far were found in Gianyar, an anti-Republican stronghold. It would appear, then, that the resistance was strongest not among peasants who were most harshly exploited but rather among those who were relatively well off.

While the peasants in the "plus" areas may have been more vulnerable to the vicissitudes of the market (as was the case in 1931–34), they also seem to have had somewhat greater economic independence from local lords. Support for the Revolution in this sector, it may be suggested, was not a defensive reaction to greater oppression but the stance of a relatively prosperous and secure peasantry. The disadvantageous terms of tenancy in the eastern kingdoms suggest that tenants in these areas were in a state of considerable dependency and vulnerability vis-à-vis the local landowning aristocracy. This condition would clearly have inhibited acts of resistance or political mobilization unless they were initiated by the lord.

The greater productive capacity of the central region may have affected the population in a negative way as well. According to Dutch sources, Japanese extractions of basic foodstuffs and forced labor were greater in these areas than in other parts of Bali.[47] By 1945, both Tabanan and Badung, the traditional areas of rice surplus, were suffering shortages. The temporary economic crisis in these kingdoms probably brought issues of water control, access to food, and control of markets and trade into much sharper focus. Indeed, judging by the nature of the first acts of violence there in 1945–46— attacks on Chinese and Chinese-controlled markets, water "robbery" and sabotage, general looting—such economic struggles were among the central issues of the early Revolution in Tabanan, in Badung, and perhaps also in Buleleng. As we have seen, however, Japanese exploitation did not have the effect of uniting the population against the Japanese, but tended to divide those Balinese who suffered for their collaboration from those who appeared to benefit from it.

It is clear that puri rivalry, caste conflict, and economic struggles between landlord and tenant existed to some extent in every kingdom. Yet there were substantial differences within Bali in the way such conflict was manifested and resolved *politically*. Political differences between western and eastern Bali can be understood, in part, as a consequence of the social and economic

---

merapat, three-fourths for the landlord, one-fourth for the tenant. The *melaisin* system required the tenant to pay the landlord money for the privilege of cultivating the land in question. It should be noted that the terms of tenancy varied slightly with the crop being cultivated (e.g., whether *padi* or *palawija*—that is, edible crops other than rice). See Raka, *Monografi Pulau Bali*, pp. 33–34.

[47] The Controleur Ellerbeck argued that the concentration of Japanese and "Japanophiles" was greatest in Tabanan because of its greater productive capacity. He also believed that the earlier development of nationalism in Tabanan had to do with the substantial economic opportunities there, which drew entrepreneurs from Java and other parts of the island: A. A. W. A. Ellerbeck, "Politiek overzicht over het Landschap Tabanan," 16 September 1946, Archive Boon.

conditions that prevailed in the various regions. In addition, the structural patterns of puri rivalries in the western region were more likely to encourage widespread political conflict and large-scale resistance than those found in the eastern kingdoms.

Taken together, these socioeconomic patterns suggest the existence of two rather different social configurations in Bali. In the western regions, we can identify essentially four social groups, which together strongly influenced patterns of political conflict and resistance: (1) an educated lower-caste urban pemuda group; (2) a declining salaried aristocracy; (3) a rising landed elite; and (4) a reasonably prosperous and independent peasantry with substantial links to urban and export markets. The moving forces in the political mobilization and the resistance of 1945–46 were the pemuda and the rising landed elite, and they were supported to some extent both by the relatively prosperous peasantry and by some among the urban middle class.

This configuration of social forces was quite inconceivable in the eastern kingdoms for the simple reason that the class or social structure here was not at all the same. The educated pemuda group was smaller and isolated from the main political currents in Java, and the salaried aristocracy was not so clearly on the decline; indeed, the small aristocracy not only dominated the local administrative structures but continued to be the major landowners. Meanwhile, no rising landed or entrepreneurial elite was in a position to challenge the old aristocracy, and the peasantry was less prosperous and more dependent on that aristocracy. In short, the social groups so central to the political mobilization and resistance in the western kingdoms simply were not present in sufficient force in the east. The old aristocracy continued to dominate the scene, and for this reason any political mobilization was from the top down.

But these socio-structural arguments tell only part of the story. Political organization, participation in political action, fighting between villages, the murder of Chinese, guerrilla warfare—these things did not spring naturally from a given social and economic situation. They occurred within a larger political environment, an environment shaped very substantially by states. Rivalries between Balinese puri had always existed, for example, but it was only in the absence of a higher political authority that they engendered open political mobilization and conflict. It is not possible to draw conclusions about the importance of, say, the pemuda, the peasantry, or the rajas without establishing the political, and particularly the state, parameters within which they were operating.

States and Political Conflict

At least three types or levels of state authority affected political relations in Bali from August 1945 to March 1946: (1) the "external" states centered on

Java, including those of the British, Dutch, Japanese, and the Indonesian Republican governments; (2) the "regional" state authorities centered on Bali, including those of the Japanese and the Balinese Republicans; and (3) the "local" states centered in the eight kingdoms of Bali.

The weakening of state authorities at the higher levels effectively increased the political centrality of those lower down, and resulted in a devolution of political authority at least to the level of the eight kingdoms, and sometimes further. This devolution created a political opening for rival state elites, such as the older Republicans and nationalists in the KNI, and the younger activist pemuda, who took advantage of the situation to set up local branches of such militant nationalist youth organizations as Pesindo and PRI. It also meant that for the first time in several decades the actual political authority of Bali's various rajas became determining factors in the maintenance of political order in their respective territories.

With the surrender of the Japanese, significant differences in the strength of the eight rajas immediately became apparent. The relative weakness of the rajas in Tabanan, Badung, and Buleleng provided early opportunities for the expression of a variety of social and political conflicts, for the emergence of new political leaders, and for the development of new political ideologies and styles. Where the rajas remained strong, as in Klungkung and Gianyar, such opportunities were limited, and political mobilization, if it occurred at all, was at the behest of the raja and the landed aristocracy.

"External" States

The British, Dutch, and Japanese states affected Balinese politics in this period primarily by their absence. The six-month delay from the time of the Japanese surrender to the Dutch reoccupation had a number of political consequences.[48] Most important, it created a political vacuum that allowed the situation in Bali to develop in a way that made a return to prewar conditions unlikely.[49]

The actions of Allied and Japanese military forces also influenced Balinese politics more directly. News of clashes between Indonesian and British Indi-

[48] For reasons that had more to do with conditions in Java, England, and India than with those in Bali, British cooperation and approval for a Bali landing were not readily forthcoming. The reoccupation, which Dutch planners hoped could take place as early as November 1945, was delayed first until January 1946, then again until 2 March 1946. The international political and military conditions that gave rise to this delay are described and analyzed in some detail in Geoffrey Robinson, "The Politics of Violence in Modern Bali, 1882–1966," Ph.D. diss., Cornell University, 1992, chap. 5.

[49] The delay had longer-term consequences as well. First, it affected the attitude of the KNIL troops and officers involved in the landing. Contemptuous of the apparent indecisiveness of their own political leaders and of the British, who were seen to be meddling in the internal affairs of their colony, they were determined to set matters straight, forcefully and quickly. As a consequence, officers were "a little trigger-happy" upon their arrival in Bali. Second, the delay caused the landing ultimately to have a more heavily military character than had been intended. The Dutch had envisioned a landing of 150 soldiers in November 1945, but the actual landing involved over 2,000 troops and a full range of modern military equipment. See ibid.

an troops in Java increased suspicion in Bali regarding the motives of Allied forces and stimulated the growth of military organizations such as the TKR. An unauthorized landing in Singaraja by a Dutch naval party in October 1945 increased Balinese hostility and gave the Revolution its first Balinese martyr.[50] Perhaps most important, after November 1945, the British, concerned by reports of increasing political unrest in Bali yet still unwilling to permit the Dutch to reoccupy the island, urged the Japanese to take more aggressive measures to maintain political order there.

By the terms of their surrender on 14 August 1945, the Japanese were delegated the task of maintaining peace and order in the territories they occupied, but the knowledge of their defeat changed irrevocably the nature of their political authority.[51] Their strength in Indonesia lay then almost entirely in their military capacity, and, as Anderson has shown, the Japanese military commanders were often disinclined to employ force of arms against the mass actions of the Republicans. Some Japanese units preferred to hand over arms and other supplies to the pemuda groups, or even to fight actively on the side of the Republic.[52] In short, the Japanese defeat weakened considerably the overarching state structures throughout Indonesia.

The Republican state, centered in Java, extended its influence to Bali in part through its delegation of legislative power to the newly established KNI.[53] Far more important, however, was the ideological or symbolic power of the Republic and its merdeka message, which passed to Bali by various routes, including radio broadcasts (especially those of the Surabaya pemuda leader Bung Tomo), written material, and the journeys of individuals between Java and Bali.[54] The founders of the main pemuda organizations in Bali had close personal contacts in the pemuda organizations of Yogya, Surabaya, and Malang, and they established the Bali branches of their organizations immediately after returning from Java in late 1945. On 1 October 1945, word was received by radio in Denpasar and Singaraja that the Re-

---

[50] The Balinese pemuda shot by the Dutch was I Ketut Merta. For an account of the "Abraham Crijnssen" incident, see Pendit, *Bali Berjuang*, pp. 87–94.

[51] See Anderson, *Java in a Time of Revolution*, particularly chap. 7.

[52] In Central Java, for example, General Nakamura began handing over arms to the Republicans in considerable quantity as early as 5 October 1945: ibid., p. 145.

[53] Bali's KNI had seventeen members, two from each of the eight kingdoms and one representing the islands of Nusa Penida and Jungul Batu. The KNI also had a working body of three: I Gusti Bagus Oka, Dr. Angsar, and Ida Bagus Putra Manuaba. Manuaba, an older moderate nationalist, was also the head of the KNIP of Sunda Kecil (of which Bali was part). He later became a prominent PNI politician in Bali and a member of Parliament. See Pendit, *Bali Berjuang*, p. 125.

[54] In October a group of seven Balinese pemuda went to East Java in search of arms and information, and made contact with Bung Tomo and Republican Navy headquarters. In November representatives of various Republican ministries, as well as officers of the TKR, came on an official mission to Bali. See Pendit, *Bali Berjuang*, p. 98. In the second half of December 1945, I Gusti Ngurah Rai led a delegation to Java, returning in April 1946 with supplies, reinforcements, and instructions from Army headquarters in Yogyakarta. See Departemen Pertahanan dan Keamanan, Pusat Sejarah ABRI, *Operasi Lintas Laut Banyuwangi-Bali* (Jakarta, 1982).

public had been recognized by China, the Soviet Union, and the United States. There was immediate rejoicing, a flurry of mass rallies, and by the end of the week a mass demonstration in Singaraja demanding that the Japanese relinquish political power.

Some movement of Republican military matériel and troops from Java to Bali took place in the months before the Dutch landing, but never on a very large scale. More telling than the actual transfer of military capacity was the symbolic recognition of the authority of the main Balinese military leaders by Java's Republican military command. Indeed, throughout the revolutionary era, the main significance of the central Republican state for Bali was not material but symbolic. To an important degree the resistance in Bali moved to the rhythm of the struggle in Java.

"Regional" States

The capitulation, of course, profoundly affected the authority of the Japanese state in Bali, all the more so as Bali lay within the command area of the Navy, which in substantial portions of East Indonesia had surrendered early on to Australian and Dutch troops. In the six months before the Dutch returned, Bali-wide state power was divided between the Japanese military and the local Republican civilian bodies.[55] They shared (though seldom cooperatively) the tasks of state, and as a consequence the authority of the regional state per se was seriously weakened. The civil administration in Bali was officially turned over to Governor Puja and the KNI on 8 October 1945, but nominal Republican authority was tightly circumscribed by Japanese military power. Japanese troop strength in early January 1946, for example, was reported to be 3,136 men.[56]

Though the Japanese were in a position to put down any major anti-Japanese uprising, they were unable to prevent political turmoil at the local level, and perhaps were unwilling to become involved in it. At first they turned a blind eye to the formation of Republican political and military organizations, and for a time they took no steps to prevent the settling of old scores—against landlords, Balinese government officials, Chinese, and so on—at the local level. Moreover, they allowed some arms and supplies to be stolen or captured by local pemuda bands, and a handful of Japanese soldiers actually joined the pemuda ranks.[57] The scale of these transfers and

[55] Pendit refers to the existence of "two governments" in Bali at this time, the Japanese and the Republican: *Bali Berjuang*, pp. 69–70, 75.
[56] For details of Japanese troop distribution in Bali, see "Nefis overzicht gegevens over Bali," Archive Boon.
[57] The famous pemuda leader Nyoman Buleleng was a Japanese soldier, and of the ninety-six men who died in the battle at Marga, at least seven were Japanese. The BKR commander from Singaraja met the Japanese Army commander in Kediri regarding the transfer of arms; and Wija Kusuma met the Japanese "sirei" in Denpasar. According to some pemuda, attacks were "staged" with the foreknowledge of the Japanese officers at Sempidi and Bela (Mengwi), in order to transfer weapons without giving the appearance that the Japanese were doing so

desertions was small in comparison with those in Java, with the effect that Bali's pemuda remained seriously short of weapons throughout the revolutionary period. Nonetheless, they were symptomatic of a certain political weakening—in spite of its military strength—of the Japanese state in Bali during this period.

Early in December 1945, however, there were clear indications of a shift in Japanese policy toward the Republic, very likely on orders from the British.[58] The Japanese presented the Republican administration of Governor Puja with an ultimatum demanding, among other things, the return of some f. 2 million that the KNI had appropriated without fuss. In response to this new get-tough policy, Bali's Republican forces decided to stage a simultaneous assault on all Japanese military installations on the night of 13 December 1945.[59] By all accounts, the attack was a dismal failure. Completely overpowered by the well-armed Japanese troops, Republican forces were forced to flee the major towns.

The Japanese attitude toward the Republicans toughened further after this attack.[60] Whereas in the immediate postcapitulation period Japanese troops had remained passively within their bases, in December 1945 they resumed full military patrols, took direct reprisals against the pemuda, and arrested the leaders of the KNI, including Governor Puja. At the same time they began to encourage the rajas to form a political counterweight to the regional Republican administration. These efforts led to the creation of a Council of Rajas (Dewan Raja-Raja) in January 1946. If the initial passivity of the Japanese provided an opportunity for Republican political mobilization, then the shift in policy had the effect of forcing the movement out of the towns and into the countryside. December 1945, then, marked the beginning of the rural guerrilla phase of the resistance in Bali. Moreover, with the arrest of the older Republican leaders, the Republican movement was quite firmly in the hands of the pemuda who had fled to the villages.[61]

The problem of state weakness in Bali was not solved by the early efforts of the older Republicans, led by Governor Puja and the KNI, to establish a

voluntarily. Interviews with Meganada, 18 September 1986, Singaraja, and I Made Wija Kusuma, 23 March 1986, Denpasar.

[58] After establishing themselves in the archipelago in October 1945, the British were able to pressure the Japanese to play a more active role in maintaining order. The shift in Japanese attitudes might also have come as news filtered in from Java about killings of Japanese by pemuda.

[59] Interviews with I Made Wija Kusuma, 22 March 1986, Denpasar, and Ida Bagus Tantra (Pak Poleng), 11 April 1986, Denpasar.

[60] Pendit, *Bali Berjuang*, pp. 101–7.

[61] They fled first to the Puri Kesiman on the outskirts of town, but, still threatened by the Japanese, they retreated to the villages of Pegayaman, Bakung, and Carangsari, and from there dispersed further to begin information and propaganda work. Carangsari was the home of the commander of the Bali TKR, I Gusti Ngurah Rai, who was of the Puri Carangsari. See Departemen Pertahanan dan Keamanan, Pusat Sejarah ABRI, *I Gusti Ngurah Rai, Pahlawan Dari Pulau Dewata* (Jakarta, 1968). Wija Kusuma went to the village of Kelating Sangging, Tabanan: Pendit, *Bali Berjuang*, pp. 108–10, 117.

regional administration. Paradoxically, one of the greatest weaknesses of the Bali-KNI leadership was its dependence on the leaders and organizations based in Java. In the absence of clear orders from Java, Puja and the older nationalists appeared overly cautious and indecisive at a time when boldness and independent thinking were clearly called for.[62] On the Dutch side as well, Puja's indecisive style drew much criticism. The Resident/CO-Amacab[63] of Bali, J. A. van Beuge, for instance, complained that Puja's indecisiveness "lends support to passive resistance and boycott campaigns."[64] In the Dutch analysis, then, the weakness of the Republican state apparatus in Bali had contributed to the condition of political turmoil in early 1946.

The establishment of a Republican administration, weak though it was, provided an unprecedented opportunity for the growth of other nationalist organizations in Bali, and through them the spread of Republican ideas, first in the towns, later in the countryside. Following the model of Java, an effort was made in November 1945 to consolidate the various groups into a single fighting and propaganda unit, the TKR (Tentara Keamanan Rakyat, or People's Security Army).[65] The TKR leaders managed to establish a Bali-wide structure and line of command, but local autonomy of the constituent units was still considerable and indiscipline was a serious problem. Moreover, as in Java, there were serious differences between the TKR and the moderate KNI leaders over questions of strategy and tactics. The KNI preferred to have nothing to do with the December assault on the Japanese, and won the displeasure of the TKR commanders by refusing to provide financial support for the action and for the armed resistance in general.

Another serious weakness was that the Republican state in Bali had no independent control over police and military forces. In late December the Japanese disarmed the Balinese police force (about 511 men, most of them armed) and called in all sport and hunting weapons. Although some police-

---

[62] In discussions with the Dutch, Dr. Made Jelantik commented that Puja could not provide general leadership for Bali, but that he (Puja) would be unwilling to see the rajas become leaders. See "Punten uit de mededeelingen van Dr. Djelantik" [n.d.], Alg. Sec. I, Kist XXII, no. 19, ARA. Balinese Republicans now say that they were also impatient with Puja: interviews with I Made Wija Kusuma, 3 April 1986, Denpasar and Nyoman Pegeg, 31 July 1986, Denpasar.

[63] CO-Amacab (Commanding Officer—Allied Military Authority, Civil Affairs Branch). Amacab was the name given to the NICA (Netherlands Indies Civil Administration) when the latter was reorganized and demilitarized at the end of October 1945. The NICA was originally established in July 1944, and its personnel accompanied the first Allied landings on Java.

[64] "Verslag betreffende de herbezetting van Bali van Commanding Officer Amacab (Van Beuge) over de period 2–15 maart 1946": van der Wal, *Officiële Bescheiden*, vol. 3, doc. no. 313, p. 385.

[65] They were assisted by two officers sent from Java, Capt. Subroto Aryo Mataram (the son of a prominent Yogya nationalist) and Capt. Sumarsudi, both of the Bagian Penyelidik (Military Intelligence), TKR, Div. IX, Yogyakarta. Subroto stayed on as the chief liaison officer for most of the Revolution. See Pendit, *Bali Berjuang*, pp. 99–100. Javanese had also been brought to Bali to assist in the Peta training in February 1944. Among the more prominent were Zulkifli Lubis and Kemal Idris: interview with I Nengah Wirta Tamu (former Peta captain), 19 December 1986, Denpasar.

men joined with the pemuda, the Republican administration did not thereby gain control of a police force, for as we have seen, Puja and his colleagues in no sense controlled the various pemuda organizations.[66] In October 1945 a British reconnaissance team in Bali reported that "there is no one at the head of the Military Organization [in Bali] and therefore any armed resistance will suffer from a lack of coordination."[67] Even when the Sunda-Kecil branch of the TKR was formed, one could not speak of autonomous Republican control over military force. For the large number of independent bands and guerrilla units that had developed so quickly after the capitulation were beyond the control of the TKR and the KNI, and remained that way throughout most of the revolutionary period. In March 1946 the estimated strength of the Bali TKR was between 500 and 1,000 men. A far greater number of people, both men and women, were actively involved in independent military and political organizations. In Tabanan, for instance, the TKR unit under the command of I Gusti Wayan Debes reportedly had only thirty-eight men, while the total number of pemuda activists was estimated to be in the tens of thousands.[68]

In short, it was not the KNI but the pemuda and, to a lesser extent, the TKR that carried the flame of Republicanism in Bali. These local organizations and military units did not contribute much to the strength of the official Republican state in Bali under the moderate KNI. Indeed, ideological differences and lack of cooperation within the Republican camp inevitably weakened it. These internal differences, moreover, were to become important sources of division among Balinese in later years and served as bases of political party affiliation after independence was achieved in 1949.

Governor Puja, of course, was acutely aware of his government's frailty. He also recognized that, though much had changed under the Japanese, some of the Balinese rajas still exerted considerable power and influence in their realms, in some cases quite independent of any higher authority. He sought, therefore, to bolster his administration by gaining their cooperation.[69] Many of the pemuda leaders, including those of the lowest caste,

---

[66] In March 1946 the commander of Dutch forces on Bali reported that the police apparatus was in a state of disorganization, while in Tabanan and Buleleng "the entire police apparatus has collapsed:" Lt. Col. F. H. ter Meulen, "Nota Betreffende Bali," 16 March 1946, Archive Boon. Some Dutch reports suggested that the police had been substantially disarmed even before the 13 December incident. Certainly other armed Balinese units, such as the Peta, were deprived of access to weapons as early as March 1945, in the aftermath of the Peta uprising in Blitar Java. See Pendit, *Bali Berjuang*, p. 39.

[67] "[British Army] Recce Report," October 1945, Archive Boon.

[68] Ter Meulen, "Nota Betreffende Bali," ibid.

[69] The Javanese "propagandist" Soekardani employed the metaphor of a horse-drawn carriage to describe the political relationship between the rajas, Governor Puja, and the mass of the Balinese people: "The driver is Mr. Poedja, the horses are the eight princes [rajas], and the passengers are the people": quoted in "Report on the Situation on Bali and Lombok Compiled from the Notebooks of the Republican Propagandist Soekardani," Alg. Sec. I, Kist XXII, no. 19, ARA.

agreed that the rajas must not be antagonized, but where possible cultivated as allies. The Revolution, at least at this early stage, was not to be anti-raja (or even antifeudal) but pro-merdeka.[70]

The clearest manifestation of the KNI's weakness and caution was the decision of 29 January 1946, through which it effectively surrendered political authority to the reconstituted Paruman Agung, the quasi-legislative body set up by the Dutch in 1938, retained by the Japanese, and in early 1946 thoroughly dominated by the rajas.[71] The KNI leaders, arrested in the aftermath of the 13 December affair, were released from prison on 21 January 1946 on the condition that they acknowledge the authority of this body, and so on 9 February 1946 the KNI decided

> to surrender the rights and the power that are in the hands of the Republic of Indonesia, which according to the 1938 regulations regarding the government of the kingdoms (Stbl., 1938, no. 529) were not yet in the hands of the kingdoms, to the Paruman Agung . . . with the stipulation that whatever is enacted by that body may not deviate from the Constitution of the Republic of Indonesia.[72]

If the act of surrendering power to the rajas and the Paruman Agung was indicative of the weakness of the regional Republican state, the legal and political terms of reference of the act suggested one reason for that weakness. While acknowledging the nominal authority of the Republican Constitution, the decision clearly treated the Dutch zelfbestuursregelen of 1938 as the relevant law regarding political authority in Bali. Moreover, by turning power over to the Paruman Agung, the KNI demonstrated an explicit institutional continuity with the Dutch era, thereby calling into question its own raison d'être and legitimacy.

As we shall see, the granting of formal governmental authority to the Paruman Agung was consistent with Dutch plans for the pacification of Bali, and it met with the enthusiastic approval of most of the rajas. The selection procedures were designed to ensure the dominance of the rajas and other reliable or "moderate" elements. Only a token effort was made to include pemuda and other new political and social organizations. Yet it was not only the inherent conservatism of the Paruman Agung that was problematic.

[70] The decision to seek the support of the rajas was taken at a meeting in Denpasar between Wija Kusuma, I Gusti Ngurah Rai, and I Gusti Ngurah Wisnu. This meeting took place shortly after a series of heated exchanges between the raja of Klungkung and the pemuda. See Pendit, *Bali Berjuang*, pp. 79–81.

[71] The Paruman Agung of January 1946 was made up of two bodies, the Dewan Raja-Raja and the Majelis Rakyat. The members of the former were the eight rajas, one of whose number was the chairman. The twenty-nine members of the Majelis Rakyat were chosen by the eight Paruman Negara, the quasi-legislative bodies chaired by the rajas of the respective kingdoms. For further details, see van der Wal, *Officiële Bescheiden*, vol. 3, doc. no. 313, pp. 581–82.

[72] This KNI declaration (Makloemat no. 01-1-20) was signed by Governor Puja and Ida Bagus Putra Manuaba. Copy in Archive Boon.

More troublesome was the question whether it could do the job of running Bali. There were reasons to doubt that it could.

The Dutch had not created the Paruman Agung to govern Bali: it had been set up as a body to discuss, intermittently, a variety of issues of general (Bali-wide) interest, such as forestry, agricultural extension, education, highways, health, and so on. Moreover, it had been intended to function under the chairmanship of a Dutch Resident. The central, authoritative power for Bali as a whole, then, had continued to be the Dutch state. In the absence of an outside executive authority, the Paruman Agung could not be expected to function properly. Finally, even in its advisory function, the Paruman Agung had an extremely brief history. The tradition of cooperation among the rajas was not well established. Executive decisions and initiatives had always come at the behest of higher authority, first the Dutch and then the Japanese. By contrast, the chairman of the 1946 Paruman Agung, the raja of Buleleng, Anak Agung Nyoman Panji Tisna, had no recognized superior authority over the other rajas.[73]

The weakness of Governor Puja's Republican administration, after its surrender of authority to the Paruman Agung, was only too clearly revealed less than two weeks after the Dutch returned. On 11 March 1946, with no opposition, Dutch troops arrested Puja and other Republican officials, reoccupied the governor's residence (the former Dutch Resident's house), and raised the Dutch flag. This action signaled the end of an important stage in the struggle for regional state power in Bali.

For over six months Puja's Republican administration had claimed sovereign political authority, but it had shared power with the defeated Japanese and finally also with the Paruman Agung. The basis of Governor Puja's power had clearly never been as solid as that of the Dutch Residents and the Japanese Cokan. The problem was in part poor local organization, ideological differences with the revolutionary pemuda, and lack of military power, and in part his administration's peripheral position within the larger Republican state on which his authority ultimately depended. The weakness of the Republican state in Bali quickly brought the rajas and the pemuda to the center of the political stage.

"Local" States

The reactions of the rajas to the transfer of civilian authority from the Japanese to Bali's Republicans on 8 October 1945 were mixed. The raja of Buleleng was thought to have Republican sympathies, but apparently he took no public position in support of the transfer. He seems to have been concerned to end the more violent actions of the pemuda and hoped that a

---

[73] The decision (Peraturan No. 43/1946) to name one of the eight rajas as chair of the Paruman Agung was taken 4 February 1946 by the Paruman Agung itself.

moderate Republican administration would do so. In Jembrana the raja was known to have been a moderate nationalist even before the war, but his stance at this juncture was not clear. It is likely that his position was influenced by the opinions of his son Suteja, a noted pemuda leader. The raja of Bangli apparently was also sympathetic to the Republic, but chose not to express this view openly. The raja of Badung did nothing to interfere with the actions of pemuda organizations in his area and appeared to welcome the transfer of sovereignty. Several rajas, then, had some sympathy for the Republic, but their approach was to wait and see.

By contrast, two rajas, Cokorda Ngurah Gde of Tabanan and Anak Agung Ngurah Putu of Karangasem, addressed large gatherings (of roughly 5,000 people) and declared themselves "to be in support of the Government of the Republic of Indonesia."[74] It soon became clear, however, that these declarations sprang from a sense of insecurity in the face of Republican mobilization rather than from a strong or principled commitment to the Republic. Clearly opposed to the transfer of authority were the raja of Klungkung, Dewa Agung Oka Geg, and the raja of Gianyar, Anak Agung Gde Agung.[75] A brief comparison of the political initiatives of the rajas of Tabanan and Klungkung and the condition of state authority in each kingdom from August 1945 to March 1946 shows how political conflict and resistance were conditioned by the character of local states.

In Tabanan there was an almost complete breakdown of normal state power.[76] In a report written less than two weeks after the return of Dutch forces, the Dutch Resident/CO-Amacab, J. A. van Beuge, said:

> The raja's government is hopelessly out of gear and has no power or perhaps not even the will to preserve order or to cooperate with our troops. It will be our duty to restore law and order with all means at our disposal and try to protect the peaceful citizens from terrorists and intimidators. Unless we do this the rot may spread to other districts where at present there is order and peace. Many of the district chiefs and village headmen have lost their former authority and have simply given up or are in a completely lethargic state, so that the very foundations of the formerly so close-knit Balinese society have crumbled and groups of young terrorists are free to do as they please.[77]

[74] "Nefis overzicht gegevens betreffende Bali," 2 January 1946, Bundel "Bezetting Bali," box 0231/4, Archief Sectie Militaire Geschiedenis, The Hague (hereafter SMG).

[75] Details of the Dewa Agung's political maneuvering in Klungkung at this time can be found in a letter he sent to the Resident on 6 December 1948, in answer to anonymous accusations that he and his anti-Republican militia, the BKN, had employed unscrupulous methods in the months before the Dutch returned. See Archive Boon. Anak Agung Gde Agung had only recently taken over the post from his father, Anak Agung Ngurah Agung, who had been dethroned by the Japanese in August 1943 and exiled to Lombok in October 1943.

[76] A good sense of the chaos that prevailed in Tabanan at this time is provided in Ellerbeck, "Personalia—Tabanan" and "Politiek Overzicht Over het Landschap Tabanan," 16 September 1946, Archive Boon.

[77] Van Beuge, "Report on Situation in Tabanan," 12 March 1946, Inv. no. 32/1, GG 8, Bundel 1.2.3.4, d, pp. 1–2, MvD/CAD.

The collapse of state power in Tabanan also entailed the decay of essential state structures, such as the taxation and judicial systems, and their replacement by systems initiated by Republican pemuda and local bands. Judicial and tax officials were either unwilling or unable to perform their duties under these conditions.

In Klungkung, on the other hand, the basic elements of state authority—administrative structures, the taxation system, the judicial and coercive apparatus—continued to function reasonably well. The Dewa Agung managed to retain a firm grip on his own officials, people, and territory, and Dutch authorities were confident of his ability to maintain order and to limit the chances for Republican mobilization: "The raja of Klungkung, Dewa Agung Oka Geg, is at present by far the most resolute of the rajas. He has the situation completely under control, and from the outset he has taken a strong stand against the Republic."[78]

The difference between Tabanan and Klungkung was perhaps most evident in the military sphere. The anti-Republican militia (BKN) established in Klungkung by the Dewa Agung in late 1945 had an estimated 5,000 recruits by January 1946, when the local BKR/TKR had managed to mobilize only about 100 for the Republican cause. By March 1946 Republicanism was an unusually weak resistance movement in Klungkung, and this situation did not change substantially throughout the revolutionary period. The local state in Klungkung, then, had a near monopoly on the means of force even before the arrival of the Dutch. This distinguished it fundamentally from Tabanan, where independent pemuda organizations, the BKR/TKR, and guerrilla bands took the military initiative, and the local state lacked any control over military or police forces.

The task of the Dewa Agung of Klungkung was facilitated by factors that set his kingdom apart from many of the others, and from Tabanan in particular: the absence of any serious royal pretender; the historical weakness of the prewar nationalist movement and of the administrative middle class in Klungkung; the comparatively small size of the kingdom, and therefore the absence of peripheral territories within it; and the persistence of "feudal" relations of production in the countryside, which implied a greater structural dependence of peasants on the landholding aristocracy.

In addition, the varied political skills, prestige, and resources of the rajas helped to determine the course of events in their respective kingdoms. Land was one potentially important resource, though the evidence of its political significance in this period is ambiguous. Rajas with substantial landed wealth tended to have large followings, and those with limited holdings often lacked political and social influence. The raja of Tabanan, who was among the poorest in Bali, was widely acknowledged to be one of the weakest. In 1942 his puri owned a mere 14 hectares of "very mediocre"

[78] Quoted in van der Wal, *Officiële Bescheiden*, vol. 3, doc. no. 313, pp. 589–90.

Table 2. Officially recorded landholdings of Bali's rajas, 1949 (hectares)

Raja	Total holdings	Sawah	Dryland
Buleleng	156	78	78
Jembrana	11	3	8
Tabanan	9	2	7
Badung	144	34	110
Gianyar	304	202	102
Klungkung	9	3	6
Karangasem	672	303	369
Bangli	240	73	16

Source: Bali Land Tax Office, April 1949.

sawah and a small amount of dryland, and by 1949 the total had been reduced to just 9 hectares (see Table 2). The total amount of sawah and dryland could not support the simplest ritual obligations or even the normal material needs of the puri.[79] According to official figures, the raja of Klungkung also owned only 9 hectares in 1949. Although these figures contradict other sources that indicate that the Puri Klungkung was among Bali's largest landowners, they appear to indicate that landed wealth alone was not a major factor in determining political authority, since the Dewa Agung was easily the most powerful and respected of the rajas in Bali.[80]

The authority of the Dewa Agung of Klungkung stemmed principally from the reputation of the puri as the first among equals and from his personal prestige as a cultural and religious leader in Klungkung and beyond. His prestige was enhanced by the reputation he had gained as protector of his people through the years of Japanese rule. Furthermore, he showed himself to be much more adept than most at using the confused legal and political situation of 1945–46 to his own advantage. Before the Dutch arrived, he had removed all potential political opponents from office and replaced them with members of his family or trusted friends.

[79] Most of the lands of Puri Gde Tabanan were confiscated by the Dutch in 1906. Indeed, the situation was so bad that in 1941 the government bought the puri a few hectares of land and assisted in paying off its accumulated debt. See Ellerbeck, "Personalia—Tabanan."

[80] There is considerable uncertainty about the precise size of the Dewa Agung's landholdings. Some Dutch sources indicate that they were considerable: interview with J. van Baal (former Assistant Resident, Bali, 1946–47), 9 May 1987, Doorn. On the other hand, the 1949 figures in Table 2 indicate that he owned less than most others rajas. One of the main reasons for thinking that the Dewa Agung's holdings were substantial is that the royal lands in Klungkung were apparently not confiscated by the Dutch at the beginning of the century. Moreover, during the land reform of 1963–65, the Dewa Agung was said to have been one of the major landowners. Like most large landowners at that time, he may have preempted redistribution by registering land in the names of wives, sons, daughters, other relatives, and loyal dependents: interview with anonymous official at the Kantor Agraria, Denpasar, November 1986.

The raja of Tabanan, by contrast, lacked both prestige and political skill. When his father died, in 1939, the Dutch considered him too young and inexperienced to be named raja. Until late 1944, when the Japanese finally appointed him raja, Tabanan was ruled by a "governing committee" of four, chaired by the punggawa kota. In 1945, then, he had scarcely one year of experience as raja, and his credibility was seriously compromised by his apparent dependence on the Japanese. Moreover, five years of rule by committee had contributed to the weakness of the royal tradition in Tabanan. In March 1946 J. A. van Beuge noted that "not much was expected of him, and unfortunately this has proved only too true. He is a figure of no authority and a weak character, and probably lost the little prestige he had in the eyes of his people by an overservile attitude toward the Japanese.[81] His weakness and unpopularity appears to have undermined the authority of other local state functionaries in Tabanan, leaving them at the mercy of a powerful "social revolution." A number of punggawa, perbekel, and other functionaries were killed, kidnapped, or otherwise swept from office in the kingdom. And, as Table 3 indicates, many punggawa and other officials elected to join the Republican side, thereby weakening still further the authority of the raja and his local state.[82]

Had the structures of administration been more clearly defined, had the rules been more widely agreed upon, and, most important, had they been enforced by a powerful higher state authority, then the personal style and prestige of the rajas would probably have been much less consequential than they were. But the period from August 1945 to March 1946 was, above all, a time of enormous uncertainty and an absence of state power. The vacuum of political authority in Bali and beyond exposed the political capacities of the various rajas and their local states, so that if political authority devolved, it did so in different measure from kingdom to kingdom. The Dewa Agung's ability in this respect did not permit Klungkung to escape the political turmoil of the postcapitulation period completely, but it did contribute to a swift resolution of open and widespread conflict and the temporary victory of anti-Republican forces there. Moreover, it permitted the political conflict and violence in Klungkung to be initiated and controlled by state forces, and not by autonomous political and military organizations. As a consequence,

[81] Van Beuge, "Report on Situation in Tabanan," Inv. no. 32/1, GG 8, Bundel 1.2.3.4, d, p. 1, MvD/CAD.
[82] A Dutch political report of April 1946 described the complete breakdown of the local administration: "The raja stays put, scared to death, in his puri, and does not dare to go out. The punggawa kota was murdered, the bendesa fled from the pemudas who wanted to kill him. The district and kingdom offices are closed. In Penebel everything is empty, the punggawa murdered, his family in refuge, the district office closed and empty, the village heads in hiding. In Krambitan the district government has disappeared, as also in Badjra and Blajoe. The old punggawa of Kediri died in 1945. His successor stayed in the town of Tabanan. The district office of Kediri is closed. Only in Baturiti is there a clerk . . . who tries to do as much of his work as possible, although he is practically in the clutches of the pemudas and dares not leave his village": "Politiek Overzicht" [April 1946], Archive Boon.

Table 3. Political orientation of punggawa and other officials in Tabanan, 1945–1946

Office or title	Puri of origin (town)	Political orientation
Punggawa kota, Tabanan	Puri Kompiang (Tabanan)	Dutch
Punggawa Marga	Puri Marga/Blayu (Marga)	Republican
Punggawa Bajra/Selemadeg	Puri Dewa-Dewa (Sam-Sam)	Republican
Punggawa Krambitan	Puri Pemecutan (Krambitan)	Republican
Punggawa Kediri	Puri Kediri (Kediri)	Republican
Punggawa Penebel	[Puri unknown] (Penebel)	Dutch
Sedahan agung	Jero Beng	Republican
Sedahan Pupuan	Jero Subamiya (Tabanan)	Republican
Police chief, Tabanan	Jero Subamiya (Tabanan)	Republican

Source: Compiled from A. W. A. A. Ellerbeck, "Personalia—Tabanan," Archive Boon.

political rivalry—between the punggawa kota and the Dewa Agung, for example—had no opportunity to develop into a mass-based political struggle or social revolution.

The raja of Tabanan, by contrast, was unable to establish a firm grip on the state apparatus in his kingdom, and political violence quickly became widespread. It is true that the social forces contributing to Republican resistance were far less formidable in Klungkung than in Tabanan, yet the particular long-term outcome in each kingdom hinged critically on the capacity of the raja to maintain the integrity of the local state in the political vacuum that followed the Japanese surrender. The processes of state decay and political mobilization went hand in hand.

The comparison of Tabanan and Klungkung suggests some general conclusions regarding the sources of political conflict and resistance in Bali during this period. It allows us to articulate more carefully the relationship between state weakness and political conflict. The weakness of the local state in Tabanan had two dimensions. First, the raja and his puri lacked any autonomous basis of political authority. Economically and politically, the Puri Gde had long been a salaried dependant of the central state; that is, a functionary of a larger state apparatus, and not in any sense the center of an autonomous local state. When the larger colonial apparatus collapsed, after August 1945, the power of the raja of Tabanan collapsed with it. Further, the condition of the raja-puri strongly affected the other elements of the local state, which rested squarely on the executive authority and legitimacy of the raja. As his authority deteriorated, so did the structures beneath him. In virtually every arena, the local state effectively ceased to exist. In both of these respects, by contrast, Klungkung was manifestly a strong local state.

The deterioration of state power in Tabanan was the primary condition for the open *political* articulation of existing social and economic conflicts and grievances. The absence of a regulating or hegemonic state, which provided a unique opportunity for political mobilization and for the expression of new political ideas without the normal constraints, distinguished Tabanan clearly from Klungkung. The opportunity was meaningful politically, however, only as long as there were people who had the organizational, economic, and ideological means to do so. In this respect, too, Tabanan was unusually well equipped, because in addition to a strong pemuda group and a substantial land-owning peasantry, it also had a large number of wealthy puri and former government officials, with the resources and the political inclination to mobilize on behalf of the Republic of Indonesia.

With the decapitation of the local state hierarchy, moreover, the conventional line between "the state" and "society" became blurred, and this was another major condition for the development of a resilient political resistance. Former state officials now became central leaders of "societal" mobilization under the banner of Republicanism. The economic, social, and political resources once harnessed for the colonial state were now the basis for the emergence of autonomous quasi-state structures throughout the kingdom of Tabanan, and much of Badung and Buleleng. A significant segment of the landed elite, as well as former officials, allied themselves with the Republican pemuda, further weakening the old regime. In this respect, the processes of state decay and societal mobilization were inseparable: the more complete the disruption of the old structures, the more resilient the resistance.

Yet the political mobilization of the puri and the pemuda was aimed not primarily at bringing down the old state but at establishing new ones. These efforts were necessarily scattered, and did not produce a fully articulated or unified state apparatus. The political ideals and the political style of the Republic, however, did gain such wide currency at this time that the old regime was beyond repair. When Dutch forces landed, they were stepping into a society already divided, already in the throes of a political struggle over regional and local state power. Under the circumstances, they could not hope to play the role of neutral guarantors of *rust en orde*. Instead, they became the new and undoubtedly the most powerful competitor for state power in Bali.

6 *The Ideology of Tradition*

THE COMFORTABLE WISDOM OF the prewar Bali experts and bureaucrats remained substantially unshaken through the period of Japanese rule and well into 1946. Bali continued to be viewed by Dutch officials and by most foreign experts as a place almost uniquely free from "political influence," by which was meant primarily nationalism and communism. A Nefis (Netherlands Forces Intelligence Service) overview of Bali in 1946 commented simply that "in general, the Balinese has little interest in politics."[1]

The idea of an apolitical, "traditional" Bali and the more complex set of images of which it was a part had a marked impact on the political and military strategies formulated and implemented by the Dutch in 1945–46, and on political conflict in Bali in subsequent years. In this chapter I examine the peculiar resilience of these perceptions in an effort to gauge their effects both on early postwar Dutch strategy and indirectly on Balinese politics through the Revolution and beyond. I argue that the Dutch view of Bali as apolitical and the strategy of restoring Balinese "tradition" and culture as a means of establishing peace and order paradoxically fueled political conflicts among Balinese and at the same time limited opportunities for the development of an indigenous state structure capable of resolving these conflicts.

Happy Natives

One might have expected the violent political struggles that began to unfold in 1945 to reveal the weakness of the view that Bali was a sort of "last paradise," but the romantic image proved to be remarkably resilient. A

---

[1] "Nefis overzicht gegevens over Bali" [1946], p. 3, Archive Boon.

striking expression of this view was contained in a brief prepared by an officer of the Bali/Lombok Brigade (Capt. J. B. T. Konig) for an incoming battalion of Dutch shock troops in July 1946. His sketch of the typical Balinese did not differ substantially from the kind found in prewar tourist brochures.

> The Balinese is a remarkable Oriental. He is very artistic, and expresses this in music, dance, wood carving, and silver work. Although he is a poor fighter, because he is cowardly, the Balinese is self-confident and therefore very free in his association with others, including Europeans, though he does this in a pleasant way. He is good-humored and likes to join in a good joke. These character traits are certainly part of the reason for the great success of tourism here.[2]

Not altogether a very daunting prospect for hardened shock troops. Political turmoil, murder, sabotage, guerrilla resistance—nothing of that sort was even implied in Konig's brief. He admitted that there had been *some* Republicanism in Bali, but claimed that it had been limited to the intellectuals and Javanese living there. Konig, who had prewar experience in Bali, was clearly unwilling to take Balinese politics and resistance seriously. In this respect he was typical of Dutch military and political planners involved in the reoccupation.

To some degree the persistence of this view was due to the relative scarcity of evidence to the contrary until early 1946. Information from within Bali during the Japanese occupation was extremely scarce, and even after the defeat of the Japanese, political intelligence was limited and of questionable reliability.[3] For the most part, it was gathered by two young men who had volunteered for the job sometime in September or October 1945. According to General A. B. Wolff (chief of staff of the Bali/Lombok Brigade), these men had some contacts with the rajas of Bali, but the intelligence they managed to gather was "almost nonexistent."[4] Officers and soldiers in the same

---

[2] Capt. J. B. T. Konig, "Mededeeling gegevens Bali—bestemd voor 8 R[egiment] S[toot-troepen] by aankomst te Singaraja op 22 Juli 1946," in Bundel "Ned. Indie 1945–1950, 1e en 2e Pol. Actie—Regiment Stoottroepen VIII, Bali, Zuid Sumatra," box 0141, SMG.

[3] One of the few Europeans to have lived on the island through the Japanese occupation, the Swiss musician Schlager had left in September 1945, before the political trouble had really begun. His reports to British and Dutch intelligence services, therefore, probably left a more favorable impression of the situation in Bali than might otherwise have been the case. See "Data about Bali [from Schlager]," 8 December 1945, memorandum from Charles O. van der Plas to Major Fisher, Alg. Sec. I, Kist XXII, no. 19, ARA.

[4] General A. B. Wolff noted in an interview that the two men, Daan Hubrecht and Daulnis de Borroville, were in their early thirties and tended to "drink a lot of Brem" (Balinese rice wine) (13 May 1946, Zeist). On the other hand, George McT. Kahin, who met Daan Hubrecht in Batavia in 1949—where Hubrecht was an official of the Government Intelligence Service—remembers him as intelligent, knowledgeable, and "not devoid of sympathy for the Republic": personal communication, July 1988.

brigade confirm that there was virtually no military or political intelligence before the landing, and that the small amount that was available was "very bad indeed."[5]

Yet these problems alone cannot explain the persistence of the romantic image, because evidence of political trouble and violence in Bali was available to the Dutch several months before the reoccupation. A Nefis report of January 1946, for example, shows that the Dutch had knowledge of fighting in Bali, of the erection of roadblocks and barricades, of weapons smuggling, and of the existence of centers of resistance throughout the island as early as October 1945. The report even concluded that "on the basis of the above some armed resistance to a landing cannot be ruled out."[6] A British intelligence report of December 1945 went even further: "Extremists predominate and have armed forces at Denpasar, Tabanan, Karangasem, Gianjar and Singaradja. Any Allied landing near these points will be opposed by force."[7] Indeed, most intelligence reports—of the Dutch, British, and Japanese—indicated trouble in Bali.

Some part of the explanation for the tenacity of the myth of a peaceful Bali appears to lie in the tendency among Dutch officers and civil servants to discount evidence that seemed inconsistent with that image.[8] Acceptance of the prevailing view was not automatic among newcomers to Bali, but the system of briefing new soldiers and civil servants before or soon after their arrival ensured a certain uniformity of opinion.

The process of socialization frequently began in Batavia, where old-timers would regale new recruits with the well-worn myths of life in Bali. Military officers and civil servants then were usually introduced to one of the "classic texts" on Bali. For military officers it was likely to be *Island of Bali,* a fanciful prewar work by the Mexican illustrator Miguel Covarrubias.[9] This book, said Colonel A. J. Treffers, head of Military Intelligence in Bali (1946–49), "was our bible."[10] Enlisted men and junior officers were given condensed versions of the classic texts, either in lecture form or in written briefs. The chief of Nefis in Bali (1946–49), Capt. L. C. van Oldenborgh, prepared

[5] Interview with Gen. G. H. de Kleijn (Bali/Lombok Brigade), 17 May 1987, The Hague.

[6] "Nefis overzicht gegevens over Bali" [1946], Archive Boon.

[7] "Report on Bali Island" [an F2 report], 7 December 1945, Bundel "Bezetting Bali (Inhoud: Operatieve instructies bezetting Bali, 1946)," box 0231/4, SMG.

[8] In contrast, news of Republicanism and anti-Dutch sentiment in Lombok was taken very seriously indeed. Sympathy for the Java-based Republic, it was argued, would surely be greater in Islamic Lombok than in Hindu Bali. In fact, quite the reverse was true. Dutch authority was easily reestablished in Lombok in less than one month, whereas in Bali significant resistance continued until late May 1948.

[9] Miguel Covarrubias, *Island of Bali* (New York: Knopf, 1938).

[10] Interview with Col. A. J. Treffers, 8 May 1987, Deventer. Other classics mentioned by Treffers as having been used by military officers posted to Bali were Vicki Baum, *Liefde en Doode op Bali,* and Johan Fabricius, *Eiland der Demonen.* Civil servants were more likely to read Korn's *Adatrecht van Bali.*

a series of lectures of this sort to be delivered to all new arrivals, military and civilian.[11]

Conspicuous in both the Covarrubias book and the condensed lectures is the near absence of references to the politics and modern history of Bali. Like so many before the war, the officers bound for Bali from 1946 to 1949 were encouraged to believe that it had an *apart karakter* (a unique character), seemingly unaffected by time and history. It was hardly surprising, then, that Dutch soldiers began their tasks with the view that Bali had no politics, and that manifestations of unrest were superficial and of no political significance.

Dutch Military Strategy in Bali

The Dutch were overoptimistic about the ease with which Bali could be reoccupied. Confidence was so great that the first plans for reoccupation were based on the expectation that it would be unopposed. A Dutch Navy report from November 1945 predicted that "if only some troops are stationed at the principal places, prewar conditions will certainly return within a very short time."[12]

The logic of Dutch military thinking was reminiscent of the prewar years. Because resistance movements were viewed essentially as the work of a handful of "extremist" troublemakers—and were therefore thought to lack any real mass base or meaningful political agenda—it was assumed that they could be easily quelled by the use of a swift show of force (*machtsvertoon*), which would "make an impression on the entire population and give them confidence in our action."[13] Without its leaders, and deeply impressed by the overwhelming power of the Dutch military, the resistance, it was assumed, would quickly melt away.

This strategy had met with considerable success in Bali in the prewar years, and Dutch confidence in the old methods was especially great because it was assumed that Balinese society was still "well rooted" and apolitical. The KNIL "Operational Instruction for the Occupation of Bali and Lombok" of early January 1946 stated that "the firmly established religious and administrative structure of the Balinese community is little influenced by Republican theories." The only possible trouble spots, it continued, were "districts where the Balinese structure is no longer firmly established, and certain

[11] The lectures were compiled in manuscript form under the title "Eenige gegevens omtrent het eiland Bali," 1946 (manuscript photocopy). I am indebted to Col. A. J. Treffers for lending me a copy of the manuscript.

[12] "Toestand op Bali op 11.11.1945," telegram from CRN to BSO tk MCA, no. 1584, received trough the Signal Office of the Royal Netherlands Navy, Bundel "Bezetting Bali," box 0231/4, SMG.

[13] Lt. Col. F. H. ter Meulen, "Aanwijzing voor het Militaire optreden op Bali," 17 January 1946, Collectie de Vries, Bundel X, no. 0518, SMG.

kampungs [i.e., villages] that have always caused trouble. Not firmly established is the structure at Denpasar and, to a lesser extent, at Buleleng."[14] The implication was clear. Pure, "traditional" Balinese would not pose any problem for the Dutch forces; only corrupted or foreign-influenced areas might cause some difficulty. As we shall see, however, the machtsvertoon approach seems to have done more to exacerbate than to soothe existing tensions, actually accelerating the process of politicization that had begun in earnest under the Japanese.

The perception that Balinese would welcome the returning Dutch went hand in hand with the belief that the Javanese were the source of political agitation on Bali.[15] This opinion was well expressed by Captain Konig, in his July 1946 brief to the Dutch shock troops. The Republican movement, he wrote, "has failed to strike a chord with the Balinese people because it was a Java import, and the Balinese people have very little sympathy for anything that comes from Java, out of fear of coming under Javanese domination in the future."[16] The view that Balinese had nothing to do with the Revolution, that the trouble had no real social base, lent credence to the machtsvertoon strategy. If the military could round up or kill the main Javanese "terrorists," they reasoned, Bali would quickly revert to its customary order and social harmony. Yet while it is true that some of the activists in Bali were of Javanese origin and that Republican ideas emanating from Java were a major inspiration for the resistance in Bali, the overwhelming majority of leaders, activists, sympathizers, and casualties were Balinese. Of an estimated 2,100 who died during the Revolution in Bali, roughly 2,000 were Balinese.

It would be wrong to suggest that support was unanimous for the machtsvertoon approach. Dutch political strategists feared that political trouble in Bali would quickly come to the attention of the world media and would damage their international reputation.[17] In this regard, Lt. Gov. Gen. Hubertus J. van Mook wrote personally to the KNIL commander, Colonel H. J. de Vries, before the March landing:

[14] "Details about Bali," Appendix 1-a to "Operational Instruction for the Occupation of Bali and Lombok," 4 January 1946, top-secret report prepared by an officer of the KNIL General Staff, Collectie de Vries, Bundel X, no. 0511, SMG.

[15] Almost without exception, the KNIL officers of the Bali/Lombok Brigade claim that the resistance in Bali was the work of Javanese and not Balinese. F. J. M. van Gessel (commander, 1st Cie, Xe Battalion, Bali/Lombok Brigade), for instance, told me in an interview (14 May 1987, Voorburg) that the Dutch troops "felt close to the normal Balinese . . . . After all, we were after the Javanese, not the Balinese." Van Gessel also claimed that KNIL soldiers were able to distinguish between Balinese and Javanese, and focused their fire on the latter. All the same, roughly 1,400 Balinese became victims of KNIL patrols.

[16] Konig, "Mededeeling gegevens Bali."

[17] The Indonesia issue was discussed for the first time in the UN in January 1946. In Lt. Gov. Gen. van Mook's judgment, there was no question that all eyes would be on the Dutch in March 1946, particularly in Bali. The absence of any mention of the Dutch operation on Bali in the *New York Times* may be taken as an indication of the impressive peacefulness of the landing, or as evidence that the world was not, in fact, watching Bali.

> If we behave in an unruly fashion, shoot at random, execute rebels without proper investigations, and violate temples, sacred forests, or other holy places out of ignorance, then we will ruin it for the Netherlands in Bali, and not only in Bali, but in the eyes of the world, on which the restoration of Dutch influence [in the Indies] now ultimately depends.[18]

Some military officers, too, opposed the use of violent methods in Bali. Among them was the first commander of the Bali/Lombok Brigade, Lt. Col. F. H. ter Meulen. Although he was not opposed to the reimposition of Dutch rule in Indonesia, he rejected explicitly the use of violence except as a last resort. In his "Force Operation Order no. 2B" (22 February 1946) he stated his intention of occupying Bali "without firing a single shot."[19] His "Commandementsorder no. 1" (8 April 1946) shows a commitment to humane military tactics.

> I know that, among civilians and military personnel alike, the idea still prevails that Orientals respect only very violent methods, and that they regard restrained and humane behavior as a sign of weakness. Indeed, the story goes around that the execution of a few murderers will lead to a strong anti-pemuda campaign. Nothing could be less true. . . . Yet the view that horrifying examples and reprisals will produce good results persists. This position is not valid, and moreover it is inconsistent with modern opinion. . . . Most important, these are precisely the Nazi methods against which the civilized world has fought in the past few years. . . . A restrained, strong, but humane approach will yield the best results in the long run. All other methods will lead to feelings of fear and hatred, which will remain for years to come. In the long run, peaceful and calm behavior will never be taken as a sign of weakness.[20]

These were prophetic words. Ter Meulen's views and his background, however, set him apart from the vast majority of the soldiers and officers under his command. Whereas most of the men of the Bali/Lombok Brigade had spent the war in Japanese prisoner of war (POW) camps in Burma and Thailand,[21] he had seen at first hand the Nazi occupation of the Nether-

---

[18] Van Mook to Hr. CLG, 22 February 1946, Alg. Sec. I, Kist XXII, no. 19, ARA.

[19] Lt. Col. F. H. ter Meulen, "Force Operation Order No. 2-B, 22 Febr. '46," Bundel "Bali/Lombok Force," box 0226/3, SMG. In an earlier operation order, Lt. Col. ter Meulen offered the following caution against the use of violent methods: "A single shot is no reason to open fire. By the deployment of sufficient strength the population will possibly refrain from offering resistance, and friendly contact with the population will be established in the quickest way possible." In Lt. Col. ter Meulen, "Summary of Landing," 15 January 1946, Bundel "Bezetting Bali," box 0231/3, SMG.

[20] Lt. Col. F. H. ter Meulen, "Commandementsorder No. 1," 8 April 1946, Rapportage Indonesie, No. 737, ARA.

[21] The battalions involved in the reoccupation were the I, II, and III Infantry Battalions of the 1st Java Echelon, which later became the X, XI, and XII Battalions of the Bali/Lombok Brigade. This brigade was also known as the Bali/Lombok Force, the Gadjah Merah Brigade, and somewhat later a part of it was renamed the Y Brigade before being transferred for service in Palembang, Sumatra, in October 1946. For further information, see "Korpsgeschiedenis van het Xe Batalyon Infanterie"; "Geschiedenis van het XI Batalyon Infanterie"; "De geschiedenis

lands. That experience had left him with an appreciation of the moral and political issues raised by a military occupation, but with very little of the "fury" that former POWs felt toward the Japanese and the Republican pemuda.[22]

In 1945–46, many of the former POWs who made up the Bali/Lombok Brigade wanted to return to the Indies to take revenge: against the pemuda, who reportedly were abusing the wives and loved ones who had been imprisoned in Java; against Republican Indonesians, who apparently had collaborated with the enemy Japanese; against all Indonesians who were presumptuously seizing control of a country they felt to be their own. As the first Dutch troops permitted to land unassisted in Indonesia, they felt strongly that the Bali/Lombok Brigade constituted a vanguard to take that revenge and to take back the Netherlands Indies from the usurpers.[23] General G. H. de Kleijn, then a company commander, later noted that the morale of the brigade had been high: "We were all anxious to fight. You must understand, we had only one flag and one queen."[24]

Under the circumstances, the cautious "pacifism" of ter Meulen and van Mook did not gain wide acceptance. The attitude of the officers and soldiers active in the field and their virtual autonomy within a particular operational area made it all but impossible to prevent excesses and to avoid the rapid escalation of violence that followed the Dutch return to Bali.[25] In the first weeks and months after the reoccupation, KNIL forces frequently behaved in an undisciplined fashion, burning entire villages, gunning down large numbers of people who had no known connection with the resistance, even strafing villages with B-25 and Piper Cub aircraft, despite explicit orders from the Supreme Allied Commander prohibiting the use of aircraft for offensive action.[26] Two weeks after the landing, ter Meulen issued "De-

---

van het XIIe Bat. Inf. v/h Terr. Tv. Tropenco Bali/Lombok"; "Overzicht omtrent VIII R.S. tot 31 December 1946"; and "Memorandum betreffende de vorming der "Y" Brigade—t/m 31 July 1946." All in Bundel "Korpsgeschiedenis," box 0110/b, SMG.

[22] Interview with F. J. M. van Gessel, 14 May 1987, Voorburg.

[23] A history of the X Infantry Battalion indicates that, while in Thailand, the troops twice received notice that they would be going into Java. In both cases, the orders were rescinded by the British authorities. This news was received with some bitterness, because the troops were anxious to return to Java to restore rust en orde. See "Korpsgeschiedenis van het Xe Batalyon Infanterie," in Bundel "Korpsgeschiedenis," box 0110/b, SMG.

[24] Interview with Gen. G. H. de Kleijn, 17 May 1987, The Hague. The high morale of the troops is also mentioned in "Korpsgeschiedenis van het Xe Batalyon Infanterie."

[25] The company commander responsible for most of Tabanan in the first months of occupation, for example, described the extent of his authority in the following terms: "I was absolute[ly] the Raja there": interview with F. J. M. van Gessel, 14 May 1987, Voorburg.

[26] Secret telegrams from the Allied Fifth Infantry Division Headquarters in Surabaya indicate that these actions in Bali not only contravened general instructions, but continued to occur after explicit orders that they be stopped: "Note that you have used B-25 for strafing village. This is contravention my orders on subject offensive action from air. . . . Policy governing use Air offensive action is that of SUPREME ALLIED COMMANDER and NOT RAF. You will confine your air action to AIR RECCE only and will take immediate steps to disarm B-25 ACK." This and related documents are compiled as "Rapport B-25 Actie, Troepencommando Bali/Lombok," 11 May 1946, Inv. no. 32/1, GG 8-D, MvD/CAD.

tachementsorde no. 22," in which he reported numerous complaints about the "unnecessarily rough and un-Netherlandish behavior of various patrols and military units."[27] In the first week of April alone, ter Meulen reported, fifty-two Balinese had been killed and many more wounded by KNIL patrols. The victims, he said, included a large number of "very unimportant pemudas, or Balinese who had been acting only under threat from members of the resistance," and even a woman and child with no connection whatsoever to the resistance.[28] Between mid-May and mid-June 1946, some 180 Balinese were killed by KNIL patrols and more than 1,500 were taken prisoner.

The presence of more than 2,000 not altogether disciplined KNIL troops scattered throughout the island made the job of the older prewar Dutch civil servants, accustomed as they were to operating with a relatively free hand, immensely frustrating. Mainly for this reason, the first months after the reoccupation were marked by tense relations between Dutch civilian and military authorities. The antipathy of the second Resident/CO-Amacab, W. G. Jacobs, toward the military command in Bali was so thinly veiled, and in the view of the military so "disruptive," that he was removed from his post before the year was out.[29] The Controleur of Tabanan, A. W. A. A. Ellerbeck, suffered a similar fate. With his prewar experience, he was inclined to view "political" strategies as more effective than simple military solutions in dealing with the resistance, and as a consequence became embroiled in a civil-military conflict that in the end involved both General Simon Spoor and the Directeur van Binnenlands-Bestuur, W. Hoven, in Batavia. Despite his expertise, Ellerbeck was gone by the end of the year. Gradually the prewar crew was replaced by a younger generation of civil servants with no experience in the Indies, let alone in Bali. On the whole, the new team cooperated more readily with the military authorities, and thereby permitted the consolidation of a highly authoritarian state apparatus in Bali.[30]

[27] Lt. Col. F. H. ter Meulen, "Detachementsorde No. 22," 17 March 1946, Archive Boon. The complaints were particularly directed at the inhumane treatment of prisoners. Lt. Col. ter Meulen noted in the order that the type of behavior which had been reported placed Netherlands troops on the same level as "the much hated and criticized Japanese." A different document reports undisciplined behavior by Ambonese troops in Bali: "It is unfortunate that the Ambonese are behaving badly here as well. There are reports, for instance, of ill-treatment for not bowing deeply enough. Also, the son of the Raja of Buleleng was beaten up by Ambonese [soldiers]." "Rapport Bali" [April 1946], Alg. Sec. I, Kist XXII, No. 19, ARA.

[28] Lt. Col. F. H. ter Meulen, "Commandementsorder No. 1," 8 April 1946.

[29] According to Controleur Lijftogt, Resident Jacobs was "desperately displeased" at having to work under the military, and in particular Captain Konig, whom he regarded as a "typical stupid military man." Jacobs also clashed with Lt. Col. ter Meulen: "To say that he and Lt. Col. ter Meulen didn't get along is a very gentle way of putting it." In the end, says Lijftogt, Jacobs "wore himself out fighting with the military." Interview with S. Lijftogt (Controleur), 20 June 1988, Deventer.

[30] There were some notable exceptions. A number of civil servants were in fact accused of being too sympathetic to the Republic. One of these was Lijftogt, Controleur in Badung. He and his wife had a reputation in Bali as *inlander liefhebbers* (roughly equivalent to "niggerlovers"). Interview with S. Lijftogt, 20 June 1988, Deventer.

This situation shaped the character of the Balinese resistance, at least for a time. Military dominance and aggressiveness in the first months after the reoccupation meant that the political strategies of co-optation, worked out in Batavia, took some time to catch on. With the moderate (KNI) Republican leadership in jail and the reoccupation taking the form of armed aggression, the Balinese resistance tended, quite naturally, to concentrate almost exclusively on the armed struggle. Through much of 1946, KNIL actions were obnoxious enough, and guerrilla resistance stiff enough, to keep all but the most obsequious Balinese either on the side of the revolutionaries or at least in an attitude of cautious indecision. For a time, then, the Revolution in Bali had the character of a military clash between "Indonesians" and the "colonial state."

Toward the end of 1946, however, the pattern of conflict began to change quite significantly. In the longer term, paradoxically, the "humane" approach of Lt. Col. ter Meulen and civilian strategists played an important part in setting Balinese to war among themselves. Like the more conventional military strategists, they accepted the necessity and the feasibility of separating the "extremist" leaders from the mass of the people.[31] The kind and sensitive treatment that Lt. Col. ter Meulen recommended was a humane strategy only insofar as the distinction between "extremists" and Balinese was valid. In fact, it was not. Kindness toward cooperative Balinese necessarily implied hostility not to a small and abstract category of "extremists" from outside but to other Balinese.

Co-optation, Collaboration, and Civil War

In addition to the use of military force, then, Dutch pacification strategy entailed cooperation with and co-optation of different elements of Balinese society. The most important were, first, the "traditional" elites, such as the rajas and members of influential aristocratic families; second, the small group of educated young Balinese; and third, the ordinary, "well-disposed" Balinese people. This strategy tended to polarize rather than to "pacify" the people of Bali, because it forced almost everyone to take sides either with the pemuda or with the forces of restoration. The wrong choice frequently had serious, even fatal consequences, and the anger and bitterness thus engendered were not easily forgotten even after 1949. It was significant, too, that Dutch strategy entailed the encouragement of a distinctly Balinese political identity and cultural consciousness, but made little provision for the development of an all-Bali state structure, controlled by Balinese.

There was general agreement among Dutch strategists that the first priority upon arrival in Bali was to make immediate and polite contact with the

[31] In January 1946 ter Meulen wrote: "It is, however, quite possible that a number of extremists from elsewhere are dwelling in Bali. It is therefore necessary quickly to isolate these people from the Balinese." Ter Meulen, "Aanwijzingen voor het Militaire optreden op Bali."

10. The raja of Klungkung greeting Lt. Col. F. H. ter Meulen, commander of KNIL forces on Bali, shortly after the Dutch landed in early 1946. The Dutch "pacification" strategy called for the establishment of friendly contact with Bali's eight rajas, and particularly with those thought to be loyal to the Dutch. Internal memos of 1946 noted that the raja of Klungkung had "displayed exemplary conduct and great loyalty." Ordinary Balinese were also encouraged to cooperate with KNIL forces in crushing the Republican movement. (*Rijksinstituut voor Oorlogsdocumentatie, Amsterdam*)

rajas.[32] It was assumed that if the rajas could be convinced of the desirability of supporting the Dutch, the rest of the population would fall into line.[33] The reliance on the rajas had little to do with Dutch estimations of their administrative abilities, intelligence, or moral worth. The calculation was that they could be used to make the task of administration easier and to limit the likelihood of popular resistance to the Dutch presence. Summarizing the expected advantages of this approach, a military blueprint of January 1946 said simply that "assistance of local chiefs saves time and blood."[34]

Lest there be any doubt about Dutch motives in seeking alliance with

[32] See Memorandum from Charles O. van der Plas to Lt. Gov. Gen. van Mook, "Herstel van het Nederlandsche gezag op Bali en Lombok," 8 November 1945, in van der Wal, ed., *Officiële Bescheiden*, vol. 1, doc. no. 323, pp. 566–70.

[33] One operational instruction for the reoccupation of Bali offered the following assessment of the political character of the Balinese: "The inhabitants of the island are simple people, very impressionable and therefore easily led." In "Appreciation of the Dutch Reoccupation of Bali," 26 January 1946, Collectie de Vries, Bundel X, box 0519, SMG.

[34] "Operational Instruction for the Occupation of Bali and Lombok," 4 January 1946.

"traditional" elites, it is worth citing some of the descriptions of the Balinese rajas in Dutch memos and reports of early 1946.

[The raja Gianyar] is an Oriental schemer and extortioner. His conduct under the Japanese occupation was so bad that even the Japs would not maintain him in his position, so that he was exiled. [The raja of Badung] is a weak figure, whose incompetence and disloyalty became apparent during and after the [Japanese] invasion. . . . A completely powerless figure . . . he is totally under the influence of his sons, who have studied in Java. [The raja of Karangasem] is a big-size schemer and exceedingly vain. He lacks the abilities of his uncle and certainly does not have his courage. [The raja of Buleleng] has always been a faithful servant of the "Kompagnie." [The raja of Klungkung] . . . , it is true, has not distinguished himself as an administrator [but nevertheless] has displayed exemplary conduct and great loyalty.[35]

Despite these uncomplimentary portraits and expressions of personal distaste—one veteran Dutch civil servant referred to the old raja of Gianyar as a "beast"—Dutch political planners accepted the need to use them to administer and pacify the island.

To some extent this was a sensible move because, in spite of social and political changes, the authority of many of the rajas was still considerable. Just the same, the Dutch appear not to have appreciated the extent to which the prewar authority of the rajas had derived from Dutch political and military power. As we have seen, without the firm backing of the colonial state, most would have been powerless or subject to serious political challenges from rival puri. Now, in 1945–46, most Dutch planners were speaking of the rajas as if their authority were intrinsic and autonomous. In fact, in the absence of an overarching state apparatus, most of Bali's rajas—with the possible exception of the raja of Klungkung—were now vulnerable to and politically dependent on the social forces beneath them, and not in any sense masters of the situation. If there was enthusiasm among the rajas for the return of the Dutch, it was because their own authority and position would be enhanced by the restoration of a strong state authority.

Among those planning the political restoration, only Charles O. van der Plas, a prewar colonial official who returned to Java in late September 1945 as Netherlands Indies government representative in Mountbatten's headquarters, seems to have appreciated the extent of the rajas' dependence on Dutch authority. With regard to their power in the prewar era, he wrote: "Two of the rajas have told me personally that, because of the enormous power of the Dutch colonial apparatus that stood behind them, their own power over the villages, the irrigation networks, . . . in short over the whole society, was far greater than before the takeover of the island by the Nether-

---

[35] These remarks are extracted from ibid. and "Nefis overzicht gegevens over Bali," p. 3.

lands."³⁶ Despite this appreciation, his conclusions did not differ from the general policy. If the rajas had been dependent for their power on the Dutch colonial state, van der Plas reasoned, then it followed that they would welcome the restoration of Dutch authority. This argument held less water in March 1946, however, than it might have six months earlier. As we have seen, the vacuum of power after the Japanese defeat had forced some of the weaker rajas to seek alternative bases of support and political legitimacy. By the time the Dutch arrived, militant pemuda organizations and the promise of a Republican state constituted plausible alternatives to the Dutch colonial guarantee. Despite these developments, the Dutch continued to stake their political future in Bali on the rajas.

Dutch planners were also confident that through the rajas they could gain the loyalty of lower officials and of the general population. The assumption was that the punggawa would not only follow the rajas but continue to be influential among Balinese lower in the political hierarchy. The "village administrators" were expected to concern themselves only with "village affairs," which were seen to be distinct from the political affairs of Bali and Indonesia.³⁷ Such judgments were based on the prewar experience, when, with the backing of the colonial state, the reliance on "traditional" leadership seemed to have worked to ensure the loyalty of ordinary Balinese. By 1946, however, political leadership was no longer the sole prerogative of "traditional" aristocrats, and there was no guarantee that the new or emerging leaders would support the goals of stability, peace, and order, or indeed a restoration of Dutch colonial authority.

The political strategists were aware, of course, that a full restoration of "feudalism" would not be acceptable to some of the population of Bali, in particular "the modern-educated young intellectuals."³⁸ If the zelfbestuur system were to be maintained in Bali, it would have to be "modernized."³⁹ The first outline of such a system—in a letter from van Mook to van der Plas, on 13 November 1945—was essentially an effort to draw Bali's intellectuals into a Dutch state apparatus as bureaucrats in the office of the Resident while leaving the powers of the rajas and local political organizations untouched.⁴⁰ This strategy was also seen as a way to undercut support

³⁶ Van der Plas to van Mook, "Herstel van het Nederlandsche gezag op Bali en Lombok," 8 November 1945.

³⁷ A top-secret KNIL report of early 1946 predicted that "the Poenggawas will mostly follow the attitude of [the rajas]. The village administrators will keep to their internal village affairs." See "Operational Instruction for the Occupation of Bali and Lombok," 4 January 1946.

³⁸ Van der Plas to van Mook, "Herstel van het Nederlandsche gezag op Bali en Lombok," 8 November 1945.

³⁹ "Nota herbezetting Bali" [November 1945], Alg. Sec. I, Kist XXII, no. 19, ARA.

⁴⁰ "Ultimately," van Mook wrote, "it will be difficult to fit educated Indonesians into a society in which hereditary princes [rajas] are invested with the highest authority": van Mook to van der Plas, 13 November 1945, Archive Boon. Also see "Instructies voor het Amacab—Detachement Bali," 1 March 1946, Archive Boon.

for the Republic, since Bali's intellectuals were understood also to be nationalists. Moves in this direction appear to have been given added impetus by the events of October and early November 1945 in Java.

The planners recognized that if reforms were introduced to appease the nationalist intellectuals, the support of the rajas would not necessarily be automatic. One of the tactics suggested for securing their loyalty was to restore the rajas' "traditional" role as military commanders. In a memorandum to van Mook, van der Plas wrote: "The eventual strengthening of the autonomy of the villages and the subak, and especially the introduction of modern democracy at the top level, can be made more palatable for the rajas by including them in the realm of military defense."[41] It is unlikely that van der Plas recognized in November 1945 that the restoration of the "traditional" military role of the rajas would lead to the escalation of violent conflict among Balinese and away from any consolidation of Balinese opinion on one side of the question or the other. Dutch support for the private armies of various rajas and acquiescence in the highly repressive anti-Republican edicts and practices of some of them were the offspring of this restoration of their "traditional" military function.

In addition to reliance on "traditional" elites and some indigenous intellectuals, the Dutch strategy called for close cooperation with the "ordinary," "well-disposed," and "loyal" Balinese people. Loyal villagers were to be enlisted to provide information to the military concerning the activities of fellow Balinese.[42] Apart from their work as spies, it was hoped that "loyal" Balinese would contribute their labor for military construction projects, and indeed would fight alongside regular KNIL troops against the "terrorists."[43] The army was to support such assistance by "organizing and arming the Balinese themselves."[44] In van der Plas's estimation, the Dutch could "count on the full support of the Balinese people" in any action to destroy "pemuda and robber gangs."[45]

The tragic ramifications of this strategy—simply put, the onset of civil war among Balinese—seem never to have been fully appreciated by Dutch military or civilian authorities. In their view the distinction between the "terrorists" and the "ordinary people" was obvious. Indeed, far from sensing the tragedy inherent in this approach, they saw it as a means of restoring

[41] Van der Plas to van Mook, "Herstel van het Nederlandsche gezag op Bali en Lombok," 8 November 1945.

[42] A military instruction of March 1946 stated: "It is the responsibility of all units to establish friendly contact with the local Balinese population and to collect information regarding extremist activity": "Instructies voor het Amacab-Detachement Bali," 1 March 1946. Another said: "The foundation of the action is a well-functioning intelligence service. . . . To this end, cooperation with the population must be pursued." See "Commandementsorder no. 1."

[43] Ter Meulen, "Commandementsorder no. 1."

[44] "Rapport Bali" [April 1946], Alg. Sec. I, Kist XXII, no. 19, ARA.

[45] Van der Plas to van Mook, "Herstel van het Nederlandsche gezag in Bali en Lombok," 8 November 1945.

a regime of "peace and order" that would be both morally satisfying and heartily appreciated by the people of Bali. "This approach will ensure that the people shall remain filled with appreciation to the army for the way in which peace and order were restored, while we will have the satisfaction of knowing that we have accomplished our task in the best possible manner."[46]

The strategy of reliance on "ordinary" Balinese was given impetus by the belief that Republican influence in Bali was primarily a consequence of contact with Java.[47] This view reinforced the tendency to view the Balinese as apolitical, loyal, and easily distinguishable from the "terrorists." Moreover, van der Plas was confident that cultural pride and anti-Javanese feeling would help to turn Bali into a powerful counterbalance to the Republican regime in Java. As a consequence, the "proper handling" of Balinese culture was one of the central concerns of Dutch civilian and military planners in 1945–46. Indeed, they appear to have devoted at least as much energy to this question as to matters of administrative reform, democratization, or even military tactics. The preoccupation with the cultural realm reflected Dutch preconceptions about the nature of Balinese society and character. "Culture" was the way to a Balinese heart; "culture" was good politics.[48]

Cultural Politics

The cultural strategy entailed both demonstration of a high degree of respect for existing religious and social practices and a program of active "restoration" of decaying norms and traditions. In the religious sphere, for example, the Dutch seemed obsessed with the need to avoid transgressing "tradition." Under no circumstances, for example, were pedanda to be touched by the KNIL troops, "because they would thereby be desanctified, and a full-blown ceremony would be necessary to purify them again."[49] Men were to be permitted to carry their krises at all times and their lances during religious ceremonies, on the grounds that these weapons formed an essential part of Balinese religion and custom. Similarly, "religious and other festivities" were to be tolerated, and under no circumstance to be treated as everyday gatherings or assemblies, which were forbidden. Drawing a hard distinction between the religious and the political spheres which few Balinese would have drawn, Lt. Col. ter Meulen wrote that "such processions

[46] Ter Meulen, "Commandementsorder no. 1."

[47] Van der Plas to van Mook, "Herstel van het Nederlandsche gezag in Bali en Lombok," 8 November 1945. According to J. van Baal—a senior civil servant who was asked to join the first NICA party on Bali as Assistant Resident in November 1945—van der Plas argued that "the time to close the gate to Java is now": interview with J. van Baal, 9 May 1987, Doorn.

[48] Van der Plas wrote, for example, that "the strength of the Balinese's attachment to his culture, together with his pride and independence, are factors that, *if properly handled,* can make of him a counterbalance against the leveling regime [on Java]": van der Plas to van Mook, "Herstel van het Nederlandsche gezag in Bali en Lombok," 8 November 1945.

[49] Konig, "Mededeeling gegevens Bali."

and gatherings must not be viewed as [political] assemblies . . . [and] they are not to be disturbed."[50] In a similar vein, Capt. Konig wrote that the colors red and white (the color of the Republican flag) were Balinese "temple colors" and therefore were not to be viewed as symbolic of Republican sympathies. Accordingly, they should not be taken down or destroyed in the way that a Republican flag or banner would be.[51]

In the Dutch view, the corruption of Balinese culture that allegedly had occurred under the Japanese might lead to political instability, but they could avert this danger by taking active steps to restore the culture to its "authentic" state. In keeping with this principle, it was suggested that the government should stimulate Balinese arts—primarily painting, carving, dance, and music—by subsidies, competitions, exhibitions, and cultural displays.[52] The government would either reward "good" works of art with prizes or buy them for resale abroad, thus stimulating greater artistic development. The stimulation of the arts would have the additional benefit of advancing tourism, which was not only vital to the Balinese economy but good for the international image of the Netherlands.

If the Dutch could quickly restore order and artistic production in Bali to prewar standards, they would impress upon the world the value and legitimacy of their claim to sovereignty in the Netherlands Indies as a whole. Indeed the exhibition and sale of Balinese works of art abroad, in van der Plas's view, would "undoubtedly have a good propaganda effect in America for the restoration of Dutch colonial rule" because it would create the impression that Dutch rule was responsible for a renaissance of Balinese culture.[53] Van Mook was especially conscious of Dutch treatment of Bali in the formation of American opinion toward the Netherlands: "In view of the generally unfavorable opinion in America toward the restoration of Dutch authority in the Netherlands Indies, the way we conduct ourselves in Bali will be of utmost importance in determining America's position."[54]

In the educational sphere, Dutch policy aimed to get rid of all Japanese and Javanese influence, and to reestablish the Baliseering-style school curriculum of the prewar years. Baliseering, with its exclusive focus on Balinese culture, language, and history, it was hoped, would shore up a decaying Balinese identity and at the same time downplay the national experience and

---

50 Ter Meulen, "Aanwijzing voor het Militaire optreden op Bali," 17 January 1946.

51 Konig, "Mededeeling gegevens Bali."

52 For detailed recommendations for encouraging the arts and promoting tourism in Bali, see van der Plas, "Verdere gegevens over Bali van Schlager," 6 December 1945, Archive Boon.

53 Ibid. A similar argument is made in "Rapport Bali" [March 1946], Alg. Sec. I, Kist XXII, no. 19, ARA.

54 Van Mook to Hr. CLG, 22 February 1946. This advice appears to have been heeded and to have created the desired impression among foreign observers. In 1948 David Wehl described the March 1946 landing operation as follows: "Everyone knew Bali, and this operation took place attended by all the glamour and publicity accorded to a film star's wedding. . . . The Dutch troops . . . were welcomed by the local population, the renowned Bali girls greeted them": Wehl, *Birth of Indonesia*, p. 106.

Indonesian identity of the Balinese. Youth organizations, such as the Boy Scouts, were similarly pegged for a thorough reorganization and Baliniza- tion. The new organizations were to be "completely adapted to Balinese social-religious life and care taken to guard against militarism."[55]

The emphasis on the restoration of Balinese culture and identity was consistent with the larger political strategy of encouraging the political au- tonomy of diverse religious and cultural communities in the Indies, as coun- terweights to the Republic in Java. Yet Dutch strategists appear not to have reflected deeply on the political implications of their "cultural" approach to pacifying Bali. Their confidence in its political benefit was rooted in the now-familiar idea that "traditional," organic Balinese society would be po- litically conservative, and would therefore reject Republicanism. They seem not to have considered how deeply the "traditional" forms and idioms of Balinese culture could be infused with conflicting political meanings or used for divergent political ends.

The somewhat exaggerated respect for Balinese religion and custom had the unexpected consequence of providing a type of cultural oasis within which the Balinese pemuda and Republicans could act with relative impuni- ty. Religious and community events such as cremations, weddings, tooth- filing ceremonies, temple anniversary festivals, dance, drama, and *wayang kulit* performances provided virtually unlimited opportunities for people to gather, sometimes from a considerable distance, and to forge bases of orga- nization and collective action. Just as important, they allowed the expression of new ideas through familiar dramatic and ritual idioms and thereby con- tributed to the formation and dissemination of new kinds of political con- sciousness and discourse. As we shall see, the blanket tolerance of all things religious in Bali, which was a hallmark of the Dutch "cultural approach" in 1946–49, provided a unique opportunity for the organization and mobiliza- tion of resistance against the colonial state and its agents.

Religious ceremonies and cultural performances, of course, were not the exclusive preserve of Bali's Republicans. Pro-Dutch Balinese also made use of such events to express and further their political aims. In Tabanan, for example, loyalists staged an elaborate dance-drama in 1946, depicting the capture and the humiliation of the Japanese and the pemuda, the burning of their allegedly ill-gotten wealth, and the return to authority of a righteous Balinese prince. The event was photographed by the Dutch Controleur, Pieter Dronkers, for inclusion in his collection documenting the restoration of Dutch rule in Bali.[56] In a village in Gianyar, in 1947, the loyalist puri staged a drama (*topeng*) performance to accompany a brutal public beating of a number of pemuda prisoners by members of the community. The topeng performance chosen was the story of Ida Bagus Batur Taskara, a Brahmana

[55] "Data about Bali [from Schlager]," 8 December 1945.
[56] Interview with Pieter and Digna Dronkers, 18 June 1988, Eindhoven.

priest beaten to death by the community because of his criminal and immoral acts. Hildred Geertz has described the deliberate juxtaposition of the beating and the topeng performance as a form of "political rhetoric." "By means of dramatic analogy," she writes, "a group of young men who were political opponents of the local royal regime [were] transformed into criminals."[57] In both instances, the familiar, "traditional" Balinese dramatic idiom served as a powerful form for the expression of the political vision and aims of loyalist forces.

Yet, if they provided useful new avenues for political expression and mobilization, the strategies employed for restoring colonial rule also served to limit the historical experience of Balinese in operating a Bali-wide state. For in spite of Dutch confidence in the support of "traditional" elites, intellectuals, and ordinary people, one basic assumption remained unquestioned: Bali, in its internal affairs and in its relations with the larger central state, was to be coordinated and supervised by an outside authority. In van der Plas's words:

> And so all three groups (princes, people, and intellectuals) will find satisfaction in the new liberated area, and the Dutch task will remain, on the one hand, to help in the coordination of these social forces into a reasonably integrated whole and on the other hand, the coordination of Bali, on a high level, with the rest of Indonesia.[58]

Bali was viewed, then, as an arena of social forces that needed to be tamed, coordinated, balanced, and rationalized. Dutch authority had once played the necessary role of coordinator, balancer, and rationalizer, and, it was supposed, would do so again. In short, the state in Bali would be Dutch. Effectively this meant that by 1949, for all the talk of Balinese autonomy, there had never been an indigenous state with authority over the whole island. The absence or weakness of a Bali-wide state tradition proved to be a key to the development of revolutionary and postrevolutionary Balinese politics.

The prewar Dutch notion of Balinese as apolitical, socially conservative, and nonviolent remained unchallenged in 1945–46. Its resilience among Dutch strategists led them to underestimate the possibility of violent resistance in Bali; they also were overly optimistic about "pacification," to be achieved by the machtsvertoon approach. As we shall see, this strategy initially inspired a degree of unity within the resistance but ultimately exacer-

[57] Hildred Geertz, "Ritual and Entertainment: An Analysis of a Topeng Performance," paper for Workshop on Balinese State and Society, KITLV, Leiden, 20–25 April 1986 (photocopy), p. 7. Geertz published a revised version of this paper as "A Theatre of Cruelty: The Contexts of a Topeng Performance," in her *State and Society in Bali*, pp. 165–98.

[58] Van der Plas to van Mook, "Herstel van het Nederlandsche gezag in Bali en Lombok," 8 November 1945.

bated incipient political conflict among Balinese, and led to an escalation of political violence. Dutch perceptions of the apolitical character of the Balinese also blinded policy makers to the serious implications of encouraging the rajas to set up anti-Republican militias. These policies, together with the decision to enlist the support of ordinary Balinese villagers in the fight against the "terrorists," plunged Bali into civil war.

7 Bali in the National Revolution

DUTCH REPORTS FROM THE REVOLUTIONARY PERIOD frequently noted the flexibility of Balinese political opinion, depending on the side that seemed likely to emerge victorious. The readiness of Balinese to change sides was not strictly a matter of political opportunism, but reflected the dependent character of Bali within the larger political arena and an awareness that the outcome of this conflict was likely to be determined elsewhere. Under the circumstances, blowing with the wind made good sense. This is not to say that changes beyond Bali determined Balinese political alignments and discourse in a linear or causal fashion. There was, rather, an interplay of impulses emanating from outside and from local political struggles.

Of particular importance was the changing configuration of political and military authority both within and among the major contenders for state power in the Indies: the Republic of Indonesia, the Netherlands Indies colonial regime, and the State of East Indonesia (Negara Indonesia Timur, or NIT), established under Dutch auspices in December 1946. Bali came under the putative authority of all three. As these states were affected by international pressures, Bali's politics were also affected.[1] The absence of a solid center accentuated political divisions in Bali, as various groupings responded to the symbolic and political authority of the competing states. Because Bali was peripheral to this struggle, shifts in the relative positions of the competing centers produced significant fluctuations in local political alignments.

This chapter examines the interaction of internal and external factors in shaping Balinese politics after the Dutch reoccupation until the transfer of sovereignty in December 1949. It analyzes the impact of the Dutch reoc-

[1] On the instrumental role of the United States in the Indonesian Revolution, see Robert J. McMahon, *Colonialism and Cold War: The United States and the Struggle for Indonesian Independence, 1945–1949* (Ithaca: Cornell University Press, 1981).

cupation on Republican links with Java, the signing of the Linggajati Accord in November 1946, the creation of the NIT in December of that year, and the initiation of the first Dutch military action in July 1947. It also examines the local implications of the signing of the Renville Agreement, the recognition of the NIT by the Indonesian Republic in January 1948, and the combination of international and domestic pressures that by mid-1949 made Indonesian independence with a strong Republican component almost inevitable. Finally it assesses the overall impact on Balinese politics of the NIT, within whose jurisdiction Bali formally lay from January 1947 to August 1950.

Republican Resistance to November 1946

The Dutch reoccupation in March 1946 prevented any major landing of Republican forces and supplies and impeded the flow of information and instructions from Java, undoubtedly weakening the resistance in Bali. Yet Bali's near isolation from Java did not lessen—indeed, it seemed to heighten—the symbolic importance of the central Republican leadership. Orders from Java were received with great reverence. It needs to be stressed, however, that it was the *interaction* between these missives from Java and the local dynamic of politics—not the missives alone—that shaped the Balinese resistance. This was very clear in the case of military organization and strategy.

On instructions from Java (Maj. Gen. Urip), conveyed by I Gusti Ngurah Rai—a former Prayoda Corps officer and commander of the TKR Sunda Kecil—on his return from Java in April 1946, the various resistance organizations had been brought under a single unified command, the MBU-DPRI.[2] For roughly two months thereafter, the bulk of Bali's Republican forces (estimated then to number 1,500 men and women) remained grouped at a base camp in the mountainous border region of Tabanan and Buleleng, at Munduk Malang. All available weapons were gathered to create a fully armed fighting unit. The logic of consolidation derived from the experience in Java, where the proliferation of independent "struggle units" outside of the command structure of the TKR had frustrated military leaders and had led to fighting among revolutionary forces.

Although Dutch KNIL forces refrained from launching a full-scale attack on the base camp, by late May 1946 it was clear that, grouped together as they were, the DPRI forces were vulnerable and ineffective. The pemuda leader, Wija Kusuma, then second in command in the MBU-DPRI, suggested a guerrilla strategy based on small mobile groups, rather than a single

---

[2] I Gusti Ngurah Rai had left for Java in December 1945, in order to secure military support and recognition for the resistance on Bali. He returned to Bali on 4 April 1946 with the rank of lieutenant colonel. See Pendit, *Bali Berjuang*, pp. 155–60.

unwieldy unit of more than 1,000.[3] On 1 June, however, I Gusti Ngurah Rai decided to move out from the base camp in a single unit and march toward the east, through Buleleng, Bangli, and Karangasem to the mountain Gunung Agung.[4] During the course of the "Long March to Gunung Agung," which continued until late July, the column of inadequately armed DPRI fighters (fewer than 50 percent had any weapons at all) were repeatedly attacked by the well-equipped KNIL troops and suffered many casualties.

Partly for this reason, disaffection arose within the MBU-DPRI leadership and among the rank and file, many of whom became convinced that under the circumstances a guerrilla strategy would make better sense. Generally speaking, it was the younger political activists from the Pesindo and the PRI, with little or no professional military training, who took this view. Wija Kusuma, for example, now regards the Long March as one of the most serious blunders of the Revolution.[5] Those with a "professional" military background, such as I Gusti Ngurah Rai, I Gusti Putu Wisnu, and I Gusti Ngurah Mataram, were less willing to disavow the more conventional military command and styles of combat.

In fact, tension between the leadership of the BKR/TKR/TNI and that of the resistance organizations dated at least from 1945. In effect, the Long March simply brought to the surface the split between "professional" soldiers turned freedom fighters and political activists–guerrillas. Under pressure from the activists, the MBU-DPRI was divided into three smaller territorial commands. One of them, commanded by I Gusti Ngurah Rai, held virtually the entire "professional" military officer corps extant on Bali, as well as the vast majority of weapons.

It was this unit that was decimated in the now-famous battle near the village of Marga on 20 November 1946—the so-called Puputan Margarana —in which ninety-six men, including I Gusti Ngurah Rai, were killed in one day.[6] Whatever the recommendations of the Army High Command in Java,

[3] Interview with Wija Kusuma, 23 March 1986, Denpasar. Also see Pendit, *Bali Berjuang*, p. 179.
[4] Ngurah Rai reportedly issued the order, saying, "Let us just begin walking. We will get new ideas as we go": Pendit, *Bali Berjuang*, p. 179. Ostensibly, the march was to draw Dutch troops away from the western part of the island to permit a major Republican landing from Java, but no major landing materialized.
[5] Interview with Wija Kusuma, 3 April 1986, Denpasar.
[6] This battle has become the centerpiece of official revolutionary history. Though it has been glorified as a *puputan*—and is the subject of at least two works in classical Balinese poetic style (*gaguritan*)—the battle at Marga could as easily be seen as the tragic result of inappropriate military strategy and tactics. For details of the battle, see Pendit, *Bali Berjuang*, pp. 212–22. Also see Dutch military reports: "Gevechtsrapport van de actie op 20-11-46" and "Bevel voor de actie op 20-11-46," by Troepen-Comandant Bali/Lombok, Capt. J. B. Th. Konig, Inv. no. 20/2, GG 28–5, MvD/CAD. Ngurah Rai, the only Balinese to be officially designated as a "hero" of the Indonesian Revolution and often compared to ancient Balinese warrior-kings, was very much the product of the prewar colonial training for "native" officers. In an interview (19 December 1986, Denpasar) I Nengah Wirta Tamu (Cilik), a Balinese pemuda who remained in the mountains until 1950, asked pointedly: "Look at the facts and ask yourself, did Ngurah Rai die a hero or did he die like a dog?" For the official view of Ngurah Rai, see Indonesia,

the loss of all but one of Bali's professional military men and a substantial proportion of available arms temporarily resolved the debate over military strategy in favor of the political activists. Immediately after Marga, on 22 November 1946, the MBU-DPRI held an emergency meeting at the village of Buahan to elect an interim leadership. Despite a challenge from the only remaining "professional" military officer, Captain I Gusti Ngurah Mataram, the pemuda activists assumed nearly all major leadership positions. After 22 November, the pemuda leader Wija Kusuma, just twenty-three years old, emerged as the leader of the central resistance organization on Bali. Like Wija Kusuma, a considerable number of the new MBU-DPRI leaders were men of low caste.

In the aftermath of Marga, struggles continued for control of the resistance movement. Some challengers, such as I Gusti Ngurah Mataram, went to Java to have their claims validated by the Republican leadership. Conflict arose even within the activist pemuda group. Nonetheless, the battle at Marga set the Revolution in Bali on a decisively new trajectory, in the sense that politically minded militant pemuda would thereafter play a dominant role. It also marked a change in the caste character of the leadership. These shifts help account for the greater openness to strategies involving political maneuver, intelligence, and diplomacy rather than sheer military force. Though some objected to this approach, there was nothing in Bali to compare to the political influence of the large-scale semiprofessional military forces in Java. The prominence of pemuda-guerrillas during the Revolution in Bali continued in the postindependence period, when pemuda assumed some of the highest political offices and became key leaders in all of the major political parties.

The Linggajati Accord and the First Dutch Military Action

Though it was paraded as political reform consistent with the aspirations of the Indonesian people, Lt. Gov. Gen. van Mook's strategy of indirect rule through the creation of federal Indonesian states was aimed primarily at undercutting the authority of the Republican government on Java by creating an impression of Indonesian political autonomy in those areas not yet under the Republic's control.[7] The federalist divide-and-rule strategy had been evident in early Dutch plans for the reoccupation of the Indies; the Malino Conference (17–20 July 1946), for example, clearly aimed at creating a

---

Departemen Pendidikan dan Kebudayaan, Proyek Biografi Pahlawan Nasional, *Kolonel TNI Anumerta I Gusti Ngurah Rai* (Jakarta, 1976); and Indonesia, Departemen Pertahanan dan Keamanan, Lembaga Sejarah, *I Gusti Ngurah Rai, Pahlawan Dari Pulau Dewata,* by Zainabun Harahap (Jakarta, 1968).

[7] On the Dutch strategy of indirect rule during this period, see Kahin, *Nationalism and Revolution,* pp. 351–54.

conservative counterweight to the Republic, through the co-optation of traditional local elites outside of Java.[8] Nowhere, perhaps, was this objective more evident, and for a time more effective, than in the NIT, which was set up at the Dutch-sponsored Denpasar Conference in December 1946.[9] A Dutch briefing on the political situation in Bali one week before that conference noted that strong support for the Republic among the pemuda and the intellectuals had put Bali's traditional elites in a difficult spot. It predicted, however, that "a successful conference that creates a state of East Indonesia, with its own interim administration and parliament, will serve as a counterweight against these tendencies."[10]

Van Mook justified the unilateral creation of the NIT, and other federal states, by reference to the Linggajati Accord between the Netherlands and the Republic, which was drafted in mid-November 1946 and finally ratified by the Netherlands on 25 March 1947. The Netherlands recognized de facto Republican authority over Java, Sumatra, and Madura, and the two sides agreed in principle to cooperate in the formation of a federal United States of Indonesia within a Netherlands-Indonesia Union under the Dutch queen.[11]

The Linggajati Accord and the creation of the NIT substantially altered the political environment in which the resistance in Bali had to operate. The changes provided new opportunities, both structural and psychological, to those, including many of the rajas, who had opposed the Republic from the outset. The new situation provided justification for the continued operation of armed anti-Republican paramilitaries.[12] Moreover, it induced many fence-sitters to side with the Dutch and work actively against the Republic as spies, informers, and so on. Linggajati and the creation of the NIT also forced the MBU-DPRI to grapple with a fundamental political problem that would plague them throughout the Revolution: their dependence, both political and military, on a leadership in Java that was only very marginally

[8] The Malino Conference was held to discuss the possibility of creating a number of "autonomous" federal states in the Indies to be run, ostensibly, by Indonesians. Bali's representatives at the conference included Cokorda Gde Raka Sukawati and I Gusti Bagus Oka. Two reports of the proceedings of the conference can be found in van der Wal, *Officiële Bescheiden*, vol. 5: "Kort verslag van de vergadering van de Malino-conferentie op 17 Juli 1946," pp. 5–15; and "Verslagen van de bijeenkomst van de Malino-conferentie met de vertegenwoordigers van Bali, Lombok en Timor op 20 Juli 1946," pp. 41–43.

[9] The Denpasar Conference was held 18–24 December 1946. The Balinese delegates to the conference were Cokorda Gde Raka Sukawati, Anak Agung Gde Agung, Gde Paneca, I Gusti Bagus Oka, Anak Agung Nyoman Panji Tisna, and Made Mendra. With the exception of Mendra and Paneca, all were men of high caste with close connections to reigning royal families. For an official Dutch account of the proceedings, see W. A. Goudoever, *Denpasar bouwt een huis* (Batavia: Regeerings Voorlichtings Dienst, 1947).

[10] "Politieke notitie nr. IV," 6–15 December 1946, Rapportage Indonesie, no. 727, ARA.

[11] Kahin, *Nationalism and Revolution*, p. 198.

[12] In addition to those organized by the rajas, some paramilitary groups were set up by local leaders. In North Badung, for example, the former punggawa of Blahkiuh established a militia force called the Nara Sadhu; and in the town of Sangsit, Buleleng, an anti-Republican militia, Anti-Pemberontak, was set up by a commoner named I Nengah Meder (Henk Schutte Nordholt, personal communication).

interested in their local struggle. Not surprisingly, there was some unhappiness in Bali with those in Java who had negotiated Linggajati. Yet because the resistance was both politically and militarily dependent on Java, Bali's Republicans had little choice but to remain loyal to the leadership at the center.

While not openly endorsing Linggajati, the MBU-DPRI sought explicitly to bring its strategy into line with the developments on Java. The principles of this new strategy were established at a meeting in early April 1947.[13] The new approach was outlined in the MBU's "Minimum Program," very likely written by Wija Kusuma, and in internal reports drawn up by his close associates. The major political principles articulated in these documents were the nonrecognition of the NIT and the demand that Bali be included with Java as a part of the Republic. Recent political and diplomatic developments (together with a serious shortage of military power after the battle at Marga), it was argued, had made a purely military strategy in Bali obsolete and counterproductive. The resistance, therefore, must now place greater emphasis on the *political* struggle, while continuing to engage in selective military resistance.

The decision to deemphasize the military aspect of the resistance was also based on the assessment that in Bali armed struggle had begun to alienate the ordinary people on whom the success of the resistance ultimately depended. A critical report (April 1947) by MBU-DPRI General Secretary Kompiang Sujana argued that "too much attention has been paid to the business of fighting, while very little thought has been devoted to the population and the task of organization. . . . In every sphere, the influence of the military has been too great." Accordingly, Sujana recommended that "military measures should be used only when they are absolutely necessary."[14]

The political struggle, as outlined in the "Minimum Program," had three related elements: (1) legal parliamentary work; (2) mass organization and propaganda; and (3) intelligence operations. In the parliamentary arena, the movement should work in Bali to influence (and if possible control) the Paruman Negara and the Paruman Agung by allying with legal political organizations such as the Parrindo (Partai Rakyat Indonesia—Indonesian People's party).[15] It should also urge Bali's NIT representatives to boycott the NIT parliament in solidarity with the demand for Bali's inclusion in the Republic, and as an expression of nonrecognition of the NIT.[16]

[13] The meeting was held in the village of Banyuning, Buleleng, 4–6 April 1947. See the MBU-DPRI internal memo from this meeting, appended to "Overzicht en ontwikkeling van de toestand, troepenco Bali/Lombok" (hereafter OOT/BL), no. 19 (11–25 September 1947), in Rapportage Indonesie, no. 740, ARA. Also see Pendit, *Bali Berjuang*, pp. 263–66, for an account of the April meeting and the genesis of the new "Minimum Program" of the MBU-DPRI.

[14] From Kompiang Sujana, "Tournee Verslag, April 17–25 1947" (Dutch translation of original), Appendix 4 to OOT/BL, no. 19, ibid.

[15] See "Minimum Program" para. II, art. 1, appendix to OOT/BL, no. 19, ibid.

[16] Ibid., art. 2.

Cooperation with Parrindo was fruitful but short-lived. Formed on 6 December 1946, the party was supported by most of Bali's urban intellectuals, particularly in Tabanan, Singaraja, and Denpasar.[17] Its ultimate objective was a unitary Indonesian state but it was not wholly opposed to a federal arrangement. While it advocated the gradual abolition of the system of feudal rule on Bali, its leaders were prepared to accept a continued role for "progressive" rajas—including the rajas of Badung, Jembrana, Buleleng, and Tabanan. In spite of its rather moderate position, Parrindo was banned in June of 1947, on the grounds that it had links to the illegal resistance.[18] The move to ban the party appears to have been instigated by Bali's rajas, who opposed Parrindo from its inception.

Propaganda work among ordinary Balinese was felt to be especially important. The earlier concentration on military struggle, without the provision of adequate information regarding the purpose and meaning of the Revolution, had produced an unstable sort of support for the resistance among the general population. Sujana's report noted that

> our earlier tactic . . . was directed only toward the pemuda, while little attention was paid to the general population, who must form the core of the resistance. Outwardly the people are willing to follow the leadership of the various struggle organizations, but inwardly they are still anxious and fear the actions of the pemuda because they do not yet understand the meaning of the Revolution. The people therefore quickly lose their spirit when they see the military power of the Dutch.[19]

The new strategy also sought to minimize random acts of terror, which had become common in some areas, on the grounds that such acts damaged the reputation of the resistance as a whole and played into the hands of the enemy, who could get good propaganda mileage from them.[20] Wija Kusuma suggested, as an alternative, the selective killing of influential collaborators. At all costs, the resistance should avoid the burning of entire villages or the punishment of innocent villagers. On the basis of captured MBU-DPRI documents, a Dutch intelligence report concluded that "the highest leader-

---

[17] The chairman of Parrindo was Gusti Putu Merta, a schoolteacher in Denpasar. The other members of the party leadership were Ida Bagus Pidada, Ktut Mandera, Gusti Bagus Oka, Gde Putra, Mahadewa, and Gde Puger. Information about Parrindo in the following paragraph is based on interviews by George McT. Kahin with Ida Bagus Pidada, Gusti Bagus Oka, and four others, 2 April 1949, Denpasar.

[18] The organizational link between the MBU-DPRI and Parrindo was the MKP (Markas Kota Pusat—Central Town Headquarters) in Denpasar, and a number of smaller MKs (Markas Kota—town headquarters) in other towns. The MKP was set up on 20 April 1947, but in June most of its leaders (including Gde Puger and Ida Bagus Mahadewa) were arrested and jailed.

[19] Sujana, "Tournee Verslag, April 17–25 1947."

[20] The results of such acts of "terror" were often turned into propaganda photo opportunities by the Dutch authorities. Groups of civil servants, journalists, and foreigners were taken to visit such sites and encouraged to photograph the carnage: interview with S. Lijftogt (Controleur), 20 June 1988, Deventer.

ship [of the MBU-DPRI] is not in favor of terrorist tactics, but because it does not have complete control of all of its armed units, it is powerless to put an end to their use."[21]

The third major component of the "Minimum Program" strategy responded to this evident lack of internal coordination and control. It involved the creation of an undercover organization, the GRRI,[22] within the MBU-DPRI, and responsible to its leader, Wija Kusuma. The GRRI had essentially two functions: "To carry out internal surveillance among pemuda-guerrillas and to conduct external espionage through the infiltration of enemy organizations."[23] The GRRI documents indicated, however, that the emphasis was on internal surveillance. The creation of the GRRI, then, allowed Wija Kusuma and his allies to consolidate their control over the movement. The effort to do so, despite its surface consistency with Republican initiatives on Java, did not put an end to conflicts within the resistance in Bali.

The most outspoken critic of the "Minimum Program" was Ida Bagus Tantra (known as Poleng), an influential guerrilla leader in the area of north Badung and east Tabanan.[24] Although he continued to hold a position within the DPRI (though not in the MBU) until January 1948, by April 1947 Poleng had already established an independent "Special Headquarters" (MBI) through which he issued orders at odds with those of the MBU.[25] According to Pendit, "a war of instructions erupted which threatened to lead to fighting among their followers."[26] In an effort to resolve their differences, Wija Kusuma met with Poleng in Banjar Puseh Kangin in north Badung. Poleng, however, refused to accept the "Minimum Program" (in particular the GRRI), and refused to disband his MBI. Wija Kusuma then declared the MBI illegal, and issued an order that the DPRI organizations of Tabanan and Badung should ignore MBI commands.

In discussing the organizational weaknesses of the MBU-DPRI, Sujana's April 1947 report had made special mention of the MBI:

> The leadership is highly unsatisfactory. The coordination among the leaders in Tabanan leaves much to be desired. In Badung the existence of the MBI has thrown the leaders of the Staff-Badung [part of the MBU-DPRI hierarchy] into confusion. Whose orders should they follow? While the objective of the MBI is

[21] OOT/BL, no. 19 (11–25 September 1947), Rapportage Indonesie, no. 740, ARA.
[22] GRRI = Gerakan Rahasia Republik Indonesia (Secret Movement of the Republic of Indonesia).
[23] Documents regarding the GRRI and its precursor, the Underground Organization (UGO), are attached as Appendix 1 to OOT/BL, no. 21 (9–23 October 1947), Rapportage Indonesie, no. 740, ARA; and Appendix 1 to OOT/BL, no. 33 (25 March–8 April 1947), ibid., no. 741.
[24] In Wija Kusuma's view, Poleng's dissatisfaction with the MBU-DPRI was a consequence of his failure to be included in the highest leadership at the time of the reorganization in April 1947: interview with Wija Kusuma, 23 March 1986, Denpasar.
[25] In an interview (11 April 1986, Denpasar) Poleng dated the establishment of the MBI (Markas Besar Istimewa—Special Headquarters) in February 1947.
[26] Pendit, *Bali Berjuang*, p. 278.

undoubtedly good, its manner of operation is causing unrest and tarnishing the name of the DPRI.[27]

Problems of precisely this sort had prompted the moves to improve internal discipline and "control" through the formation of the GRRI. Yet by some accounts, it was this internal security apparatus that pushed Poleng into his final split with Wija Kusuma's MBU. He suspected, no doubt correctly, that he would become one of the objects of its investigations. By his own account, however, Poleng set up the MBI primarily because he was concerned that the MBU had lost its commitment to the armed struggle.[28] When, in the course of their discussion in north Badung, Wija Kusuma contended that the acute shortage of weapons necessitated a controlled and cautious use of firepower, Poleng is reported to have responded: "There is more than one star that shines brightly in the heavens. If there are no guns, then we will use knives. The important thing is that we fight!"[29]

The debate between Poleng and Wija Kusuma was temporarily silenced by the first Dutch military action on 21 July 1947 and the abrogation of the Linggajati Accord which it implied.[30] On the same day, the MBU-DPRI issued its "New Struggle Program" ending for the moment the post-Linggajati strategy of passive military resistance and calling for resumption of active armed struggle:

100% Independence! As of 21 July 1947, the whole of Indonesia is at war. Linggajati is no longer in effect. For this reason, the old strategy of struggle which was drawn up after the signing of Linggajati is also no longer in effect. We are now at war with the Dutch. Smash the enemy and all collaborators with whatever strength we possess. On with the Struggle![31]

Once again the movement stepped quickly to the rhythm of events in Java, so that over the next several months the armed resistance in Bali gained new intensity. The incidence of violence inflicted by the guerrillas on suspected collaborators among the local population—killings, burnings, kidnapping, intimidation—increased significantly during this period (see Table 4) as a direct consequence of the Dutch military action and the Republican leader-

[27] Sujana, "Tournee Verslag, April 17–25 1947."

[28] Poleng claims that he heard a voice one night tell him: "There will soon be a vacuum in the resistance movement." He took the voice to be a sign that he ought to establish an alternative to the MBU: interview, 11 April 1986, Denpasar.

[29] Interviews with Poleng, 11 April 1986, Denpasar, and Wija Kusuma, 23 March 1986, Denpasar; Pendit, *Bali Berjuang*, p. 250.

[30] For a discussion of the lead-up to the first military action (Eerste Politionele Actie) and its consequences up to the signing of the Renville Agreement in January 1948, see Kahin, *Nationalism and Revolution*, pp. 147–229.

[31] This document, "The New Struggle Program," was among those seized from Kompiang Sujana after he was killed by KNIL forces in mid-1947. It is included as Appendix 6 to the military intelligence report OOT/BL, no. 19.

Table 4. Victims of government and guerrilla attacks in Bali from the first Dutch military action (21 July 1947) to May 1948

Date	Victims of government attack	Victims of guerrilla attack
1947		
August	35	54
September	14	25
October	27	16
November	35	24
December	20	22
1948		
January	18	16
February	33	23
March	35	1
April	37	9
May	13	5
Total	267	195

Sources: OOT/BL, nos. 18–26 (28 August 1947–1 January 1948); and OOT/Oost Indonesie, nos. 6–8 (24 July–4 September 1947), Inv. no. 32/2, AA37-1-1947, MvD/CAD; and "Politiek Verslag van de Residentie Bali en Lombok," January to May 1948 [title varies], Alg. Sec. I, Kist IV, no. 48, ARA.

ship's call for all-out war. A military intelligence report on Bali of September 1947 stated unequivocally: "Without any doubt, the increase in terrorist activity must be seen as a reaction to the 'Police Action' in Java."[32] Yet if for a time developments in Java submerged open objections to a strategy based primarily on armed force, it did not do away with local conflicts over strategy and power.

The Renville Agreement and the "Surrender" of May 1948

When international pressures brought the Netherlands once again to the negotiating table in December 1947, resulting in the Renville Agreement of 17 January 1948 and the official recognition of the NIT by the Republic a few days later, the earlier strains within Bali's Republican resistance surfaced once again. The cease-fire provisions of Renville—which called for the withdrawal of all Republican troops from Dutch-occupied territory—made it difficult to justify the use of violence against the Dutch to attain independence, while the recognition of the NIT as an equal partner in the struggle for Indonesian independence made continued resistance of any sort against the NIT politically problematic.[33]

[32] See OOT/BL, no. 19, p. 4. A Dutch intelligence report of early August 1947 noted that in the first two weeks after the military actions on Java "there has been a marked increase in the activity of the resistance groups": OOT/BL, no. 16 (24 July–7 August 1947), ibid.

[33] On learning of the recognition of the NIT, the leadership in Bali felt "angry and resentful," while among the rank and file, who saw the NIT as the enemy, there was widespread "confu-

These developments brought to a head the internal debate over strategy and tactics in the Republican camp in Bali.[34] On 24 May the MBU-DPRI issued a "Special Instruction" and within one week at least 1,000 guerrillas of the DPRI made their way in disciplined fashion into the major towns—principally Singaraja, Denpasar, and Tabanan—where they turned themselves over to their respective rajas.[35] The DPRI leaders maintained that the decision to come down from the mountains had been taken in recognition of the altered political situation at the national and international level after Renville and the recognition of NIT, and the excessive burden of continued armed struggle on ordinary people and guerrilla fighters, particularly in rural areas.[36] Moreover, they argued, with some justice, that the decision to come down constituted not treachery but a necessary change in strategy, from armed struggle to mass political action.

The May "surrender" was the military and political turning point of the Revolution on Bali. Not only did it effectively signify the end of the military phase of the struggle against the Dutch, it also proved to be one of the central political issues in subsequent relations among Bali's Republicans, even after independence. Politically, the "surrender"—or the "descent," as former MBU members now prefer to call it—became the focus of debate over the revolutionary credentials of the various Republican groups, those who "surrendered" (the MBU-DPRI) and those who did not.[37] The small group that remained in the mountains after May 1948 maintained underground organizations grouped around four leaders: Poleng, I Nengah Tamu (known as Cilik), Cokorda Anom Sandat (known as Sentosa), and Nyoman Buleleng, a former Japanese soldier. In anticipation of a new phase of the active armed resistance, these four joined forces in late November 1949 to form a single organization, Lanjutan Perjuangan (Continuation of the Struggle), which was renamed Pemerintah Darurat Republik Indonesia (Emergency Government of the Republic of Indonesia), or PDRI, on 4 January 1950.[38]

sion": interviews with Wija Kusuma, 23 March 1986, Denpasar, and I Gusti Bagus Teken (local guerrilla leader in West Buleleng), 10 January 1986, Jakarta.

[34] A Dutch political report noted that the recognition of the NIT and the signing of the Renville Agreement had "led to fighting within the leadership of the resistance": "Politiek Verslag Bali en Lombok over April 1948," Alg. Sec. I, Kist IV, no. 48, ARA.

[35] Estimates of the total number who came down vary from about 800 to several thousand. The number of political prisoners in Bali's jails after May 1948 (about 3,000) suggests that the figure of 800 is too low. The wife of a Controleur who was close to the pemuda claims that there were as many as 400 women among those who came down in May 1948: interview with Linde Lijftogt, 20 June 1988, Deventer. For the first official estimates, see "Overzicht politieke ontwikkeling Oost-Indonesie, Mei 1948," Alg. Sec. I, Kist V, no. 34, ARA.

[36] Interviews with Ida Bagus Indera (Markas Besar-Buleleng), 30 September 1986, Singaraja; Wija Kusuma, 3 April 1986, Denpasar; and I Ketut Wijana, 29 September 1986, Singaraja.

[37] The situation was in fact somewhat more complicated, because some of those who surrendered in May 1948 returned to the mountains after their release in 1948 and 1949.

[38] The idea of unification was suggested in a 28 October 1949 letter from the liaison officer (in Yogya), Subroto Aryo Mataram, in response to a letter by Cilik requesting instructions. See Pendit, *Bali Berjuang,* pp. 339–40.

11. Balinese Republican leaders at an Independence Day celebration, 17 August 1949, in Singaraja. Wija Kusuma (left, in sunglasses), Nurai (center, wearing khaki trousers), and Wijana (right, face obscured) were among the key leaders of Bali's main resistance organization, the MBU-DPRI. An estimated 1,400 Republicans died during the Revolution, most before May 1948, when MBU-DPRI guerrillas came down from the mountains, bringing an end to the armed phase of the resistance. (*Archive Franken, Leiden*)

Though the constituent groups of the PDRI engaged in little if any active resistance after May 1948, they did not come down from the mountains until 15 January 1950, some two weeks after the final transfer of sovereignty. On these grounds they claimed the mantle of revolutionary purity, and disparaged the DPRI as traitors, weaklings, and careerists for their surrender of May 1948. Though it would be wrong to suggest that there was complete unanimity or solidarity within the PDRI on this or on other issues, the split between the PDRI and the DPRI was easily the most significant political division within the pemuda group. After independence, a substantial number of PDRI guerrillas and sympathizers followed Poleng into the Partai Sosialis Indonesia (Indonesian Socialist party), or PSI, while a large number of DPRI fighters joined the Partai Nasionalis Indonesia (Indonesian Nationalist party), or PNI, or the Partai Komunis Indonesia (Indonesian Communist party), or PKI.[39]

---

[39] The May 1948 "surrender" remains a contentious political issue in Bali to this day. In 1987, in response to government insinuations that the May 1948 decision had been a mistake,

The MBU-DPRI had sensed immediately that the Renville Agreement and the recognition of the NIT would dramatically weaken their support among Bali's moderate nationalists and intellectuals, and eventually among the general population. Indeed, much to the satisfaction of the NIT government of Anak Agung Gde Agung, Balinese members of the "Progressive Fraction" in the NIT parliament now turned decisively against the armed resistance, "lending their support," in the words of a Dutch political report, "to the NIT and to the restoration of law and order."[40] Older nationalists in Bali began to describe Bali's young Republicans as "extreme leftists" and their objectives as "unrealistic."[41] And in Bali's Paruman Agung, the minority progressive fraction that had once supported the Republic publicly endorsed the NIT. A political report of late January 1948 noted that already "the leaders of the resistance are complaining of the sudden decline in support from the population."[42]

The Dutch and several influential Balinese exerted extra pressure on the Republican resistance at this juncture. Beginning in late January 1948, Resident Boon and the chairman of the Council of Rajas air-dropped pamphlets over guerrilla strongholds, calling on the pemuda to surrender now that the Republic had recognized the NIT and a cease-fire agreement had been reached.[43] And in February a series of letters by former pemuda, by the raja of Buleleng, and by the KNIL commander for North Bali were sent to the MBU-DPRI calling on them to surrender.[44] The Republic's endorsement of the NIT, the erstwhile enemy of Bali's Republicans, made it seem that the Indonesian government on Java had forsaken the Balinese resistance,[45] a severe blow to the morale of a movement that had placed all its trust in the Republic and that was already under considerable pressure. This blow

---

three MBU leaders were moved to prepare a report defending their actions: I Made Wija Kusuma, I Ketut Wijana, and Ida Bagus Indera, eds., "Laporan Mengenai Penurunan MBO DPRI Sunda Kecil Tanggal 24 Mei 1948," typescript, Denpasar, February 1987. And although Wija Kusuma had been named as a member of two veterans' bodies in Bali, the Dewan Paripurna Veteran Bali/Nusa Tenggara and the Dewan Paripurna Angkatan 45 Bali, in 1993 he had yet to receive full recognition of his rights as a veteran.

[40] According to the same report, the Agung cabinet had taken "a positive stand against the revolutionary ideology of violence and particularly against the criminal elements within the resistance movement." See "Overzicht politieke ontwikkeling Oost-Indonesie, Mei 1948."

[41] Interview by George McT. Kahin with Ida Bagus Pidada, 2 April 1949, Denpasar.

[42] "Politiek Verslag van de Residentie Bali en Lombok, 2e h. January 1948," Alg. Sec. I, Kist IV, no. 48, ARA.

[43] See "Politiek Verslag van de Residentie Bali en Lombok, 2e h. February 1948," ibid.

[44] The similarity of the arguments in all of these letters—all dwelled on the point that the Republic itself had called for an end to armed resistance and had recognized the NIT—suggests that this was part of one Dutch intelligence initiative. For the texts of some of these letters, see Pendit, *Bali Berjuang*, pp. 304–11.

[45] In an interview (23 March 1986, Denpasar) Wija Kusuma remarked that they felt they had been "forsaken by the Republic." He had written to the leadership in Java asking that the MBU-DPRI be recognized as part of the Tentara Nasional Indonesia (Indonesian National Army, or TNI), and that it be withdrawn into Republican territory according to the terms of Renville. He received no reply.

played a central part in the MBU-DPRI decision to come down from the mountains in late May 1948.

An internal MBU document of March 1948, "The Character of Our Struggle in Bali Now," outlined a strategic and tactical shift toward legal and what were called "passive" methods of resistance. Clearly taking its cues from the Republican leadership, the MBU document explicitly endorsed the Renville Agreement and recognition of the NIT by the Republic, and called for a combined strategy of "mass action" and intensive propaganda throughout the island to replace active armed struggle. It concluded: "Activate the Propaganda Units!!!" Yet even as the MBU-DPRI appealed for an end to the killing, it indicated that it would not disarm unilaterally or surrender, and reserved the right to defend itself against enemy aggression. Again citing a Republican leader in Java, this time General Sudirman, the MBU maintained, "We will meet aggression with aggression!"[46]

At a meeting of the MBU-DPRI and the various territorial headquarters in the same month, this somewhat ambivalent line was adopted in a series of official resolutions reflecting the fundamental dependence of the Balinese resistance on the Republican center. They appealed to the Republican government on Java to (1) pressure the NIT to recognize the MBU-DPRI as a component of the Republic; (2) put an end to the State of War and Siege (SOB) in Bali; and (3) grant a general amnesty to all freedom fighters, both those in jail and those still at large.[47]

Although initially the MBU-DPRI injunction against military aggression and acts of intimidation was obeyed—in March 1948 there was only one victim of guerrilla attack in Bali—by mid-April there were clear signs of impatience within the resistance. This was an indication that, whatever the official instructions from Java, the struggle in Bali still had its own inner logic. As Table 4 indicates, Dutch military and police activity had intensified after Renville. Several pamphlets and internal documents from the resistance reflected the anger and the defiance of the guerrillas in the face of mounting enemy aggression. Under the circumstances, a resumption of active armed resistance seemed to some both necessary and justified. An open letter to Resident Boon and the vice-chair of the Council of Rajas was characteristic in content and tone:

> The Renville cease-fire agreement is now more than two and a half months old, but you continue to go on the rampage, raging blindly, shooting at us, rounding us up, storming and thundering, making provocations, offending the honor of young Balinese girls. . . . The song you're singing here in Bali and those you

[46] The document, "Sifat Perdjuangan Kita di Bali Pada Saat Ini," called explicitly for "the voice of the bullet to be replaced by the voice of the people," and cited Sukarno approvingly. See "Politiek Verslag van de Residentie Bali en Lombok, 2e h. March 1948," Alg. Sec. I, Kist IV, no. 48, ARA.

[47] "Politieke Verslag Bali en Lombok over April 1948."

sing elsewhere in this country all come from one Dutch factory: "It's not me but the pemuda who are in the wrong . . . !!!"[48]

Among some guerrilla bands, notably those in Tabanan, the developments of January 1948 were from the outset taken as a cue to step up acts of revenge or intimidation against enemy collaborators. In mid-January, Poleng officially withdrew from the DPRI, saying that in the interests of the resistance he planned to "seek spiritual renewal."[49] Underground leaflets from Tabanan portrayed Renville as proof that the Dutch were on their last legs, and advised waverers to take the side of the Republic before it was too late. Those who did not do so would have only themselves to blame when their loved ones became victims of the Revolution. "Blood will flow in the streams and people will howl and scream, because their beloved child or spouse is dead. And thus, unhappy you will remain for the rest of your days, because you placed your trust in the Dutch and disdained the freedom fighters. . . . And by your stupidity, you killed your own wife and child."[50] In January and February 1948, killings and other acts of intimidation increased in Tabanan and especially in areas under Poleng's MBI. In one incident, Poleng organized an assault by the men of one village on another that was said to be pro-Dutch. The village wall and thatched roofs were torched, and as the inhabitants fled the fire, they were cut down by rifle and machine-gun fire.[51]

This approach produced some short-term results, at least in Tabanan. In late January 1948, for instance, several members of police auxiliary units deserted, with their weapons, to the side of the guerrillas, and Dutch intelligence reports warned that the resistance was still spreading in March 1948.[52] In the other guerrilla base areas, however, notably in Buleleng and north Badung, the resistance was placed increasingly on the defensive. Villagers who had once supported the guerrillas now began to report to the military and police authorities in unprecedented numbers, and to inform on those still in the mountains. It was with information obtained in this way that the "Dutch" were able to arrest or kill a significant number of key leaders in March and April 1948.[53]

---

[48] The open letter, signed "Perdjuangan," is among a collection of documents and photographs kindly made available to me by P. L. Dronkers, who served as Controleur in Jembrana and Tabanan during the Revolution. This collection is hereafter referred to as Archive Dronkers.

[49] The text of Poleng's letter of "resignation" from the DPRI can be found in Pendit, *Bali Berjuang*, pp. 278–79.

[50] Quoted in "Politiek Verslag van de Residentie Bali en Lombok, 2e h. January 1948."

[51] Interview with Poleng, 11 April 1986, Denpasar.

[52] A leaflet from Tabanan, titled "Pandangan Jang Tak Tersangka2," dated 31 January 1948, applauded this action. It is also mentioned in "Politiek Verslag van de Residentie Bali en Lombok, 1e h. February 1948."

[53] Between mid-February and mid-March 1948, roughly 3,500 people surrendered in the guerrilla base areas in Badung (100 in Plaga-Payangan, 1,000 in Penarukan) and Buleleng (1,733 in Banjar, 431 in Pengastulan, 212 in Banyuning). Eleven of Wija Kusuma's closest advisers and five lieutenants of the important guerrilla leader Gde Puger were arrested about the

It was in this context that I Wayan Ledang, a former Prayoda lieutenant and member of the TKR-Bali, returned to Bali on a secret mission to bring about the surrender of the DPRI. As NIT minister of the interior, Anak Agung Gde Agung played a central role in this mission; it was through him that Ledang gained approval to initiate contact with the MBU-DPRI. Ledang had left Yogya—where he had been attached to the Bali liaison office—under suspicious circumstances in 1947 and stopped for some time in Surabaya before continuing to Makassar early in 1948, where he met with Anak Agung.[54] Agung claims that Ledang worked in Makassar as head of the political branch of the police for several months, after having expressed his disenchantment with the Republic.[55] Moreover, Agung asserts that Ledang's mission to Bali to meet with the leaders of the MBU-DPRI was his own (Agung's) brainchild: "I sent him to Bali to get the guerrillas to surrender."[56] While it is possible that Agung has deliberately inflated his own role in this affair to gain credit for the restoration of "peace and order" in Bali, it is nonetheless clear that, whoever conceived it, Ledang would have had to work through and probably with Agung in order to carry out the plan. In early May 1948, Agung wrote a top-secret letter to Resident Boon of Bali/Lombok introducing Ledang and asking the Resident to provide him with any assistance he might require to carry out his task.[57]

By mid-May 1948, Ledang had managed to meet with two of the three main MBU leaders, Wijana and Nurai, in the village of Munduk, Buleleng.[58] Wijana and Nurai, who had already begun secret talks with the raja of Buleleng as early as February 1948 on the possibility of ending the armed

---

same time; and in April, four members of the best-organized band (led by I Keredek) in Tabanan were killed. See ibid., February–March 1948.

[54] It was rumored that Ledang had been accused of pilfering or misappropriating funds, and was scheduled to be court-martialed. Rather than face the music, it was said, Ledang fled to Surabaya and then to Makassar to work with the NIT. A different interpretation is that Ledang had been called to Surabaya for training as an intelligence officer, and thereafter sent to Makassar *posing* as a deserter, but in fact working for the Republic. If this version is correct, then Ledang's meetings with the MBU-DPRI were the culmination of an ingenious Republican intelligence operation. See Pendit, *Bali Berjuang*, pp. 270–71, 303, 316.

[55] Interview with Anak Agung Gde Agung, 27 May 1987, Wassenaar.

[56] Ibid.

[57] Ledang's own report of his meetings with the MBU leaders indicates that in Bali he received the full cooperation of the local military and civilian authorities. A few days before the meetings, for example, he had met with the head of the Military Intelligence Service (Militaire Inlichtingen Dienst, or MID)–Bali (Capt. A. J. Treffers), the head of Nefis-Bali (Capt. L. C. van Oldenburgh), as well as the punggawa of Singaraja, the military commander for North Bali, Capt. G. H. Gaade, and the head of the Singaraja Nefis office, Sgt. Maj. de Ruiter. See Wayan Ledang, "Lapoeran Singkat tentang peroendingan dua hari anggauta MBO-DPRI Soenda Ketjil, Sdr2: Noerai dan Widjana, pada tanggal 14 Mei 1948 di Moendoek." An unsigned copy of this report was among a collection of papers kindly given to me in 1988 by H. J. Franken, who was one of the last Dutch nationals in Bali at the end of the Revolution. These materials are hereafter referred to as Archive Franken.

[58] The date of the first meeting was 14 May 1948. Also present were two intermediaries, Wayan Pasek and I Japa, and the punggawa of Singaraja. See ibid.

resistance, gave Ledang some indication of a willingness to surrender, but they were not prepared to take a final decision in the absence of the third and leading member of the MBU, Wija Kusuma.[59] One week later (22 May 1948), Ledang met Wija Kusuma and repeated his arguments in favor of surrender. Purporting to be conveying an order from the commander of the TNI, Major General Urip, Ledang told Wija Kusuma that the surrender of the DPRI would put pressure on the Dutch to end the State of War and Siege in Bali, and would therefore permit the movement to act with relative impunity in the political sphere. He also reiterated Dutch military guarantees that DPRI members would be fairly treated if they surrendered.[60] Finally, he urged all three MBU leaders to meet with the raja of Buleleng and the local Dutch military commander in the raja's puri to work out satisfactory terms of surrender.

Within three days of this last meeting, the MBU-DPRI had issued its "Special Instruction" calling on all DPRI members to report to their respective rajas in orderly fashion.[61] The MBU leaders strenuously denied that they had made their decision on the basis of Ledang's promptings. Serious debate within the leadership over strategy and tactics, they said, predated the Ledang initiative by several months, if not years. Ledang's presence had simply brought matters to a head. Given the evidence of internal debate before May 1948, there is little reason to doubt the sincerity of this claim. Still, Ledang's initiative was extremely important in bringing about the "surrender" of May 1948. Whether he was sent by the Republic or as an agent provocateur by the NIT is very much open to speculation. In either case, however, his role in this crucial event attests to the power of external forces on Balinese politics or, what may amount to the same thing, to the susceptibility of Bali's political structure and discourse to impulses from the center.

The Shifting Center

Not long after the DPRI "surrender," Resident Boon cautioned against too much enthusiasm, noting that it might simply mark the beginning of a

[59] Nurai and Wijana to punggawa of Singaraja, dated 20 May 1948, Archive Franken. This letter, if it is authentic, indicates that Wijana and Nurai had already agreed to a surrender *before* meeting with Wija Kusuma: Part of the letter reads: ". . . with this we would like to clarify that we will begin the plan for the surrender within the month."

[60] The guarantees of the local Dutch military commander, Capt. G. H. Gaade, were contained in his letter to the MBU, dated 3 February 1948, "Djaminan keselamatan bagi pemuda2 jang menjerahkan diri." See Appendix 1 to OOT/BL, no. 36 (6–20 May 1948), Rapportage Indonesie, no. 741, ARA.

[61] The text of the instruction read: "On the basis of our meetings with His Highness the Raja of Buleleng and the Commander of the Dutch forces on 24 May 1948, the DPRI Sunda Kecil has decided to carry out a general surrender with both firearms and other weapons to the Council of Rajas of Bali." The "Instructie Istimewa," 25 May 1948, is included as Appendix 1, ibid.

new type of Republican resistance. It was not impossible, Boon argued, that Wayan Ledang had been sent by the Republic to convey a personal message from Sukarno, to shift tactics from "the bullet to the ballot."[62] The ending of armed resistance and the use of purely legal means, political reports acknowledged, would put pressure on the Dutch and NIT governments to end the State of War and Siege, which had been in force in Bali since March 1946. This was cause for worry in both civilian and military circles, because it was the SOB that had permitted the use of unorthodox military tactics, arrest procedures, military courts, heavy censorship of incoming news and information, and the almost total denial of political freedoms. A May 1948 political report from Makassar signaled the first signs of concern: "The Civil Service and the rajas are not optimistic about the political prospects in Bali. They expect that very soon the pro-Republican intellectuals will begin forming political parties with a vengeance, and that they will be helped in this by the growing stream of Republican propaganda available in Bali."[63] There was also concern that the legal Republican opposition would call for a plebiscite to determine whether Bali would come under the authority of the Republic or the NIT. Indeed, the Renville Agreement had raised hopes of such a plebiscite within the MBU-DPRI, and the argument that it could be more swiftly achieved through legal political organization had evidently contributed to the decision to give up the armed struggle in May.[64]

Finally, the tactic of mass action, spelled out explicitly in captured MBU-DPRI documents, was cause for worry among the Dutch and their conservative Balinese allies. The documents explained that in the event of military or political excesses on the part of "the enemy," "the people from around the village in question, both young and old, should come en masse to the Raja or the Punggawa to protest the behavior of the enemy, and at the same time request protection, food, and shelter from them until such time as the enemy action has genuinely stopped."[65] By placing open social and political pressure on Balinese officials, they threatened to disrupt the alliance between these figures and the Dutch state. By doing it without violence, they denied the Dutch military, in theory at least, any justification for the use of force.

Shortly after the internal MBU-DPRI memo was issued, large mass actions of precisely this kind were reported. One demonstration, which took place in Tabanan on 20 April 1948, was said to have involved over 1,000 people from various villages around Antosari. They marched together toward the town of Tabanan shouting, "Forward! Forward!" and demanded

---

[62] "Politiek Verslag, Bali/Lombok 1e h. Mei 1948," Rapportage Indonesie, no. 734, ARA.
[63] "Overzicht politieke ontwikkeling Oost-Indonesie, Mei 1948."
[64] An internal MBU-DPRI document spoke of such a plebiscite as a kind of cure-all for the Republican side in Bali: "It is now clear that the thing that will determine our fate is none other than the plebiscite; in other words, our fate rests . . . in the hands of the masses of the common people": MBU-DPRI, "Bimbingan Untuk Propaganda Rabaan Dalam Artian Naskah Renville," 20 March 1948, Archive Dronkers.
[65] Ibid.

to speak with the raja. At Megati they were intercepted by the punggawa and the local military commander, who persuaded them to return to Antosari, where they were promised an audience with the raja. In addition to meeting the raja, however, they were treated to militantly pro-Republican speeches. The author of a Dutch political report for April 1948 noted: "In this we can see clearly what a dangerous weapon the resistance movement has fashioned in its use of mass action, and what difficulty we will have in handling it, if it is successful."[66]

In spite of the surrender of the bulk of Bali's guerrilla forces in May 1948, therefore, Dutch and NIT officials chose not to end the SOB on Bali until the middle of 1949. Whereas previously it had been justified as a necessary measure to liquidate the "terrorist" elements, after May 1948 it was said to be necessary in order to protect Bali from disruptive outside (that is, Javanese) political influences. With the SOB still in effect, it was possible to keep a very large number of Bali's Republican activists in prison, to prohibit all political organizations and gatherings, and to control the flow of information and people in and out of Bali.

In March 1949 the jails in Bali were filled beyond capacity with inmates held on political charges. In addition to the 1,505 prisoners detained in conventional jails, 616 were held in military camps, bringing the total number of political prisoners to 2,121. The majority were DPRI guerrillas who had surrendered in May 1948. Of those in civilian prisons, only about 20 percent (355) had been sentenced by March 1949. Roughly 140 of this number had been sentenced to terms of more than five years and were scheduled to be exiled from Bali.[67] Included in this group were the three MBU-DPRI leaders, Wija Kusuma, Nurai, and Wijana, who received prison terms of eighteen, twelve, and ten years, respectively. It was hardly surprising, under the circumstances, that a general amnesty for political prisoners became a central demand of Republican activists in Bali in 1949.

Whereas in other parts of East Indonesia (and of course in the Republic) legal political parties had multiplied through 1947 and 1948, Bali's sole Republican party, Parrindo, had been banned in June 1947 and many of its leaders jailed.[68] In April 1949 the only legal party was the government-created anti-Republican Partai Democrat Indonesia (Indonesian Democratic party), or PADI, which Dutch officials conceded to be an empty shell. The restrictions on legal political activity through these years had forced Republican activists to work underground to establish informal networks of sympathizers throughout the island. Lesser political offenders, released from

[66] "Politiek Verslag Bali en Lombok over April 1948."

[67] These figures were compiled from a report on Bali's prisons by Controleur Hans Snelleman, 12 March 1949, Archive Boon. The report refers to the prisoners as *politieke delinquenten* and makes no mention whatsoever of ordinary criminals.

[68] For an outline of the political parties existing in the various regions of East Indonesia in mid-1948, see "Overzicht politieke ontwikkeling Oost-Indonesie, Mei 1948."

prison during 1948 and 1949, often returned to the mountains to develop such underground organizations.[69]

These organizations frequently met under the cover of religious ceremonies such as cremations, "cultural" activities including wayang kulit, dance and theatrical performances, and self-defense (pencak silat) clubs,[70] in part to avoid detection and punitive action by the military and police but also because these activities were inseparable from the fabric of Balinese political life, Republican or otherwise. Thus, in spite of the official restrictions, when the SOB was finally ended in mid-1949, underground political networks already existed to assist the development of mass-based political organizations. Yet while the lifting of the SOB provided new opportunities for political action and while underground networks were already in place, the influence of Java was still strongly felt in the timing and character of the political organization that emerged in 1949.

The second Dutch military action, which began on 19 December 1948, prompted swift criticism in the United Nations and met unexpectedly stiff military resistance and civilian noncooperation in Java. Despite a 28 January 1949 UN ceasefire resolution and U.S. pressure on the Netherlands to grant Indonesian independence amid evidence that Dutch troops were being thrown increasingly on the defensive, an ominous sense of uncertainty remained regarding the political future of the Republic. The signing of the Roem–van Royen Agreement on 7 May 1949, in which the Republic made concessions to the Dutch position, was a major diplomatic turning point but the feeling of insecurity remained. During these months the resistance in Bali remained almost invisible, concentrating more on self-preservation than on political or military action.

By late June 1949, a mounting tide of Republican military resistance in Java and the return of Republican leaders to the capital city of Yogyakarta had renewed the confidence of Republicans inside Java and out. Increasing pressure on the Netherlands government, both from its domestic critics and from the United States and the UN, began to make Indonesian independence with a strong Republican flavor appear inevitable. The changing situation influenced the position of the leaders of the federal states, leading to defections to the Republican side.[71] This shift paved the way for talks between Federal and Republican representatives beginning in mid-July 1949. The

[69] According to one weekly military intelligence summary, "reports of underground organizations, meetings of former political detainees, and pencak-silat clubs are now increasingly frequent": KNIL/KL Stafkwartier Oost-Indonesie, Wekelijkse (Militaire) Inlichtingen Rapport (hereafter WMIR/OI), no. 10 (23 June 1949), Inv. no. 32/1, GG 65, 12032, MvD/CAD.

[70] For reports of such meetings see WMIR/OI, no. 17 (11 August 1949); no. 23 (22 September 1949); no. 25 (6 October 1949); no. 27 (20 October 1949); no. 28 (27 October 1949); and no. 30 (10 November 1949), ibid.

[71] Kahin writes that "this inability of the Dutch to enforce their political decisions in Indonesia and the progressively defensive posture of their armed forces there was, undoubtedly, the most important reason for the increasing defection by Federal leaders from the Dutch camp during the late spring and early summer of 1949": *Nationalism and Revolution*, p. 429.

Inter-Indonesia Conference (held in Yogyakarta, 19–22 July, and in Batavia, 30 July–2 August) laid the groundwork for cooperation between the Federal states and the Republic in the formation of a "United Republic of Indonesia." For Balinese, it provided a rare occasion for contact with the Republican leadership in Java.[72]

Buoyed by the encouraging results of the conference and by the planned round table conference in The Hague scheduled for late August, Bali's Republicans began to mobilize almost immediately. Two older nationalist leaders and members of the NIT parliament (Ida Bagus Putra Manuaba and Made Mendra) returned from the conference and immediately formed a moderate pro-Republican party, the Gerakan Nasionalis Indonesia (Indonesian Nationalist Movement), or GNI.[73] The GNI called on the NIT government to free all political prisoners who had not committed "criminal" acts. A wide range of organizations with a Republican orientation sprang up over the next few months: youth groups; organizations of students, teachers, and women; and cooperatives, unions, and trading companies. In addition there were groups working expressly to collect funds and materials for the Republic.[74]

The most important of these new groups was Gerakan Pemuda Indonesia (Indonesian Youth Movement), or Gerpindo, established on 5 September 1949 and led by influential leftist pemuda. The key figures in Gerpindo were Suteja (who became Bali's regional head in 1950 and later governor of Bali until late November 1965), Gde Puger (an important left-wing leader after independence), and Ida Bagus Mahadewa (a left-nationalist). The Gerpindo was more active and more militant than the GNI, and through its pemuda leadership it had a much broader and more solid political base.

The strength of the nationalist and antifeudal movement was given vivid expression in the festival for Jayaprana at the village of Kalianget, Buleleng, in August 1949. This cremation ceremony for the mythical/historical folk hero Jayaprana, a loyal low-caste subject treacherously murdered by a raja who had coveted his wife, blossomed into a massive ritual display celebrating the new Republican spirit. Some aspects of the festival could be understood only as a repudiation of the old feudalism and a challenge to caste hierarchy.[75] For many of the tens of thousands of people who poured into

---

[72] Another opportunity of this sort was the Conference on Culture and Education held in Yogyakarta in October 1949. On that occasion, both Poleng and Cilik sent messages (via Ida Bagus Mahadewa and Gusti Nyoman Wirya) requesting instructions. Cilik received a letter from Subroto Aryo Mataram dated 28 October 1949, recommending that the remaining guerrilla fighters unite and prepare for the second stage of the revolution, the final victory of the unitary Republic over the federal United Republic of Indonesia: Pendit, *Bali Berjuang,* pp. 338–39.

[73] The GNI was formed in Denpasar on 17 August 1949. See "Politiek Verslag Bali/Lombok, August 1949," Rapportage Indonesie, no. 738, ARA.

[74] WMIR/OI, no. 23 (22 September 1949), Inv. no. 32/1, GG 65, 12032, MvD/CAD.

[75] H. J. Franken, who was present at the festival, writes: "At a time when the memory of the slain and missing pemudas was still very much alive, when caring for the bodies of those who

Kalianget from throughout the island, the weeks-long festival became a celebration of national Republican heroes expressed in a familiar and uniquely Balinese cultural and religious idiom. In the words of one Republican, "Jayaprana, he is we ourselves. Formerly the ruler was worshipped, but now is the time for *kemerdekaan*, for freedom; the homage is now for the people."[76]

In a matter of months the political situation in Bali had changed dramatically. Whereas a political report of May 1949 maintained that all was "peaceful," a Dutch military intelligence report of September concluded ominously: "One cannot help feeling that we are living on top of an active volcano. It might remain quiet, but it could erupt at any time."[77] Subsequent reports indicated still further increases in militant Republican activity, in villages as well as major towns. The influence of Javanese Republicanism was evident in the repeated sightings of guerrilla gangs wearing the black Islamic *peci* worn by President Sukarno and sporting long hair and red-and-white insignia.

Also noted with alarm was the increasing incidence of Republican "infiltration" from Java.[78] Rumors of an imminent TNI landing on Bali enhanced the confidence of local Republicans and prompted fence-sitters to take the Republic's side.[79] The rumors had some basis in fact. Small armed groups from Java were making successful landings on Bali during the last months of 1949. Moreover, a letter had been received through Subroto Aryo Mataram—as acting commander of the newly formed Sunda Kecil Command of the TNI—outlining clearly the plans for a TNI occupation of Bali and the Lesser Sundas.[80] The plan called for a minimum of three TNI battalions for Bali alone and the removal of all former KNIL troops.[81] In response to this news, efforts began to reestablish the Bali-TKR, so that it might be incorporated into the arriving TNI forces.[82] In the view of a Dutch intelligence analyst, the effect of these military and political developments on the political attitude of the population was profound:

---

fell in the resistance struggle was not without danger, and when it had already penetrated deeply into the popular consciousness that the revolution must be directed not only against foreign domination, but also against feudalism, it was easy to find in stories of . . . [Jayaprana] an element from which nationalism could borrow its weapons and the means to glorify itself": "The Festival of Jayaprana at Kalianget," in Wertheim, *Bali,* pp. 255–56.

[76] Ibid., p. 257.

[77] WMIR/OI, no. 23 (22 September 1949), Inv. no. 32/1 GG 65, 12032, MvD/CAD.

[78] See, for example, the reports in WMIR/OI no. 10 (23 June 1949), no. 17 (11 August 1949), no. 25 (6 October 1949), no. 34 (8 December 1949), ibid.

[79] See, for example, the reports in WMIR/OI no. 27 (20 October 1949), and no. 34 (8 December 1949), ibid.

[80] Pendit, *Bali Berjuang,* pp. 343–44.

[81] For details, see WMIR/OI, no. 32 (24 November 1949), p. 7, Inv. no. 32/1, GG 65, 12032, MvD/CAD.

[82] See ibid., no. 21 (8 September 1949), no. 35 (15 December 1949), and no. 37 (29 December 1949).

As a result of these developments, the people are turning very decisively away from Dutch authority, and especially from the military. . . . If the Round Table Conference were to fail and the troubles began here again, we could not count on the loyal support of the population. They would clearly take the side of the resistance. The longer the present situation continues, the broader will be the support for the Republic among the people.[83]

From the viewpoint of Bali's political future, however, the most ominous development was the marked increase in cases of intimidation and revenge against former Balinese and Chinese collaborators. The most common targets were suspected spies and informers, members of the police and police auxiliaries, as well as punggawa, perbekel, and lesser officials. In October 1949, for example, the punggawa of Penebel, a loyal ally of the Dutch, found a placard with the following message nailed to the door of his office: "Beware! Beware of 100% Independence. Mr. Punggawa, members of the police and the police auxiliary, and everyone else who has been working for the Dutch, prepare to die. The wheels of history are turning; the red-and-white flag of the Republic will soon be waving." In another case, during a village theatrical performance a former member of the local police auxiliary was surrounded by fifteen pemuda with long hair and black uniforms. After being publicly taunted and threatened—"Why not just kill this uppity captain from Wanagiri? What do you say we give this NICA spy a working over?"—the former policeman was released.[84]

Incidents of this kind were so common and the fear and uncertainty so pervasive that some former loyalists began to draw up lists of "collaborators" and "war criminals" in efforts to prove their "revolutionary" credentials.[85] And as KNIL troop strength gradually diminished through 1949, collaborators and revolutionaries alike began to set up secret armed groups in preparation for anticipated attacks.[86] Although there were few reports of actual killings in 1949, the stage was set—politically, organizationally, and psychologically—for the eruption of violence, which began in earnest a few months after the transfer of sovereignty.

The NIT and "Family Government" in Bali

Encompassing the same territory as the prewar "Government of the Great East," which had been created in 1938 to act as a political counterweight to nationalist Java, the NIT was inspired by similar conservative political objec-

---

[83] Ibid., no. 27 (20 October 1949).
[84] Ibid., no. 26 (13 October, 1949).
[85] Ibid., no. 23 (22 September 1949).
[86] Ibid., no. 3 (5 May 1949) and no. 37 (29 December 1949).

tives. Although the NIT was permitted greater autonomy than the other
federal states, its freedom of action was in fact heavily circumscribed by
preponderant economic, military, and legal-political Dutch strength in the
area.[87] Moreover, it was clear, at least from the time of the Malino Conference in mid-1946, that the Dutch intended to staff the NIT with the most
conservative and cooperative local leaders. The island of Bali, as it turned
out, provided two of the most influential of these leaders, the prime minister
and for a time the minister of the interior, Anak Agung Gde Agung, and the
president Cokorda Gde Raka Sukawati.

With the NIT ultimately dependent on the Netherlands Indies government, much routine administrative work could be left in the hands of these
conservative elements. Most Dutch civil servants and military men regarded
Anak Agung Gde Agung as "clever" and an effective administrator.[88] The
majority of Dutch officials in Makassar and Bali considered Cokorda Gde
Raka Sukawati to be both "charming" and "knowledgeable." And although
van Mook was said to be very sarcastic about Sukawati in private, he was
apparently not overly concerned that the president would run beyond Dutch
control.

If in Dutch eyes there was a problem with Sukawati and Agung, it was that
they were too authoritarian and "feudal" in their thinking and too cynical in
their pursuit of political power. The power of these men within the NIT, it
was feared, was permitting the rise of a type of "family government" in Bali.
Indeed, the Assistant Resident of Bali (1947–48) believed that the resurgence of feudalism in Bali "became worse than ever before during those
years."[89]

Sukawati and Agung, it will be recalled, belonged to the leading aristo-
cratic families of the kingdom of Gianyar. Sukawati was from Puri Ubud and
Anak Agung was from the raja-puri of Gianyar. Agung's younger brother,
Anak Agung Gde Oka, was the raja of Gianyar at this time, and the chair-
man of Bali's Council of Rajas; and after the dissolution of the Residency of
Bali/Lombok in March 1949, he was for a time the regional head of Bali.
Other aristocratic families also enjoyed the relative autonomy the NIT pro-
vided them, and most clearly preferred a government they could control in
Makassar over a federal or unitary government beyond their control in
Batavia.[90] In the view of many Dutch officials, the arrangement of power

[87] Kahin, *Nationalism and Revolution*, p. 355–68.
[88] Interviews with P. L. Dronkers (Controleur), 18 June 1988, Eindhoven; A. J. Treffers
(head of MID-Bali), 8 May 1987, Deventer; and Hans Harten (head of Agricultural Service,
Bali), 18 May 1987, The Hague.
[89] Interview with J. van Baal (Assistant Resident, Bali), 9 May 1987, Doorn. A political
report of January 1948 noted that "in a number of kingdoms the rajas' practice of appointing
family members to all government positions, while passing over candidates from other leading
families or other people better qualified, has led to criticism." "Politiek Verslag Bali/Lombok,
1e h. January, 1948."
[90] Interviews by George McT. Kahin with Nyoman Wirya, April 1949, Singaraja; Made
Mendra, 2 April 1949, Denpasar; Gusti Bagus Oka and four others, 2 April 1949, Denpasar. In

within the NIT had allowed these families to become too strong, and provided no effective check on their authority.[91]

As it turned out, the Dutch were right to be concerned. Sukawati displayed strongly reactionary tendencies both in his thinking and in his efforts to influence the course of Balinese politics. In the prewar years he had served as the sole Balinese representative on the Volksraad, where he had exercised a highly conservative influence in debates concerning Bali. Educated in the Netherlands, married to a French woman, and having lived much of his adult life outside of Bali, he was regarded by many people at home as arrogant and excessively westernized (*kebarat-baratan*).[92] Dutch officials stationed in Bali got some taste of his personal style on his occasional junkets to Bali. One civil servant who had occasion to deal with him described Sukawati as "corrupt down to his toes . . . a gambler and a rogue."[93]

Anak Agung Gde Agung, educated in Batavia, had briefly held the position of raja of Gianyar (1944–46) before being chosen as prime minister of the NIT. As raja in the volatile months after the Japanese defeat he had tangled with Balinese Republican pemuda and was abducted by them at least once.[94] In the view of many Balinese, he lost any claim to nationalist credentials when he reacted to pemuda activities by forming the anti-Republican armed defense organization Pemuda Pembela Negara (Youth for the Defense of the Kingdom), or PPN, in late 1945.[95] Though outwardly less obsequious toward the Dutch than Sukawati, he did his best to destroy the armed resistance in Bali in efforts to ensure that "moderate" educated aristocrats like himself would dominate whatever political system emerged from

---

his interview notes Kahin paraphrases Gusti Bagus Oka's comment: "The NIT is a state of and for the Rajahs—designed to protect their interests."

[91] Dutch officials' mistrust of Bali's feudal families was evident in their efforts to control the political agenda, despite formal restrictions. Resident Boon, Assistant Resident van Baal, and military leaders held regular meetings to discuss political developments to which the rajas were seldom invited. This slight led the chairman of the Council of Rajas, Anak Agung Gde Oka, to remark, "They do not trust us": interviews with H. Schuilwerve and P. J. van Leeuwen (secretary to the Resident), 21 June 1988, The Hague.

[92] On the Sukawati clan, see Rosemary Hilbery, *Reminiscences of a Balinese Prince, Tjokorda Gde Agung Sukawati,* Southeast Asia Series no. 14 (Honolulu: University of Hawaii, 1979). Also see Vickers, *Bali,* pp. 140–41.

[93] Interview with S. Lijftogt (Controleur), 20 June 1988, Deventer.

[94] Agung was captured by a pemuda gang on 20 September 1945 in the vicinity of Tegalalang, between Gianyar and Denpasar. He claims he was held for two days and two nights before I Gusti Ngurah Rai secured his release. According to other sources, his release was secured by the intervention of either the pemuda leader Wija Kusuma or the BKR leader Nyoman Pegeg. A few days later another kidnapping attempt was made near Batubulan, but Agung was able to flee in his car. Shortly thereafter, he set up an anti-republican paramilitary force: Interviews with Anak Agung Gde Agung, 27 May 1987, Wassenaar; Nyoman Pegeg, 16 September 1986, Denpasar; I Gusti Ketut Reti, 30 July 1986, Denpasar; and Dewa Made Dhana, 10 October 1986, Singaraja.

[95] According to one Balinese resistance leader, "Outwardly [Anak Agung Gde Agung] acted as though he was only collaborating with the Dutch in order to achieve the United States of Indonesia, but inwardly he opposed Republican elements with cruelty": personal communication from an anonymous resistance leader, 1988.

the Revolution.[96] Although Agung made a timely peace with the Republic in late 1948, both he and Sukawati gained a reputation, in Bali at least, as political opportunists and enemies of the Republic.

Indeed, in the opinion of some former resistance leaders, Anak Agung Gde Agung was personally responsible for the repressive measures—including arbitrary arrest, torture, and summary execution—taken against freedom fighters in Gianyar during the first three years of the Revolution.[97] One writes that

> all orders to arrest, torture and kill freedom fighters in Gianyar were given by Gde Agung himself, and carried out with assistance from his Pemuda Pembela Negara, which operated under a red, white, and blue [i.e., Dutch] flag. As far as Gianyar was concerned, the Dutch military didn't have to wet their hands with the blood of the freedom fighters because the job was done for them by Anak Agung Gde Agung and his paramilitary forces.[98]

One of the most notorious cases of such behavior was the arrest and execution of the punggawa of Peliatan, of the Puri Peliatan, an important resistance figure in the region.[99] The execution opened a deep rift between the Puri Peliatan and the Puri Gianyar, which lasted well beyond the revolutionary period.

In an effort to ease these strained relations, in 1948 the raja of Gianyar, Anak Agung Gde Oka (the younger brother of Anak Agung Gde Agung) married Cokorda Istri Sri Mas, the daughter of the slain resistance leader from Puri Peliatan. To the casual observer the photograph of their wedding ceremony, which shows the bride and groom clad in the ornate style of the aristocracy, may seem to confirm the resilience of "traditional" Balinese culture in spite of the revolutionary politics of the time. Yet to virtually any Balinese who was aware of it, this was self-evidently a political marriage, with its origins just as deeply embedded in modern revolutionary political struggles as in Bali's cultural traditions.

In spite of his puri's efforts in the field of marital politics, Anak Agung

---

[96] In 1988 a former pemuda leader who wishes to remain anonymous provided an unusually blunt characterization of Agung's political motivations: "He chose his political line on the basis of a personal interest in maintaining his social status as the descendant of a raja with a hereditary right to rule, and also in order to defend the Hindu caste system, which guaranteed him a place at the top. That sort of political and social position could be maintained only if Bali continued to be governed according to the system of zelfbestuur under the guardianship of the Netherlands Indies."

[97] For accounts of the arrest and killing of Republicans in Gianyar, see Legiun Veteran Republik Indonesia, Markas Cabang Gianyar, *Patah Tumbuh Hilang Berganti: Kumpulan Riwayat Hidup Pahlawan P.K.R.I. Gianyar* (Denpasar: Percetakan Bali, 1979).

[98] Personal communication from an anonymous resistance leader, 1988.

[99] According to a former pemuda leader, "he was arrested in the vicinity of Petang by Anak Agung Gde Agung and some NICA soldiers. After suffering physical torture and insults, he was taken from the police post on Agung's orders and shot dead on the grounds that he had tried to escape": ibid.

12. The marriage of the new raja of Gianyar, Anak Agung Gde Oka, and Cokorda Istri Sri Mas, daughter of the former punggawa of Peliatan, in August 1948. The punggawa had been arrested for his Republican activities and shot while in detention in 1946. The marriage was an effort to overcome differences between the pro-Republican Puri Peliatan and the loyalist Puri Gianyar. (*Douwes Dekker Collection, Division of Rare and Manuscript Collections, Carl A. Kroch Library, Cornell University*)

Gde Agung's alleged involvement in the arrest and killing of highly respected resistance leaders contributed to the alienation and the radicalization of many of Bali's Republican leaders. His eleventh-hour support for the Republic in late 1948 did little to change his reputation among Bali's more militant nationalists as an early traitor to the Republican cause. Instead, it was viewed as an act of pure opportunism. According to one interpretation, Agung had recognized by late 1948 that the tide was turning in favor of the Republic, and had realized too that he did not have the unequivocal support of the key Dutch figures van Mook and Boon. He therefore threw his weight behind the Republic and in 1950 joined the PSI, which had solid nationalist credentials. Summarizing Agung's political twists and turns during these years, a Balinese resistance leader wrote in 1988, "Gde Agung secretly stabbed the Republic with his left hand, then turned around and stabbed the Dutch in the back with his right. His knife still dripping with the blood of Bali's freedom fighters, he took cover beneath the PSI banner."[100] Thus, when he joined the PSI—which had some considerable support at that time

[100] Ibid.

among Bali's pemuda—Agung introduced a fundamental political split into the party.[101]

The presence of Balinese aristocrats of this political ilk in the highest executive offices of the NIT tipped the balance of political forces in Bali in a conservative direction. As executives of the state within which Bali lay, and with the tacit backing of the more powerful Netherlands Indies state, these men were able to exercise political influence in Bali well beyond that of local Republican forces, and certainly beyond what would have been possible for them as local aristocrats in Bali. Moreover, through their example they undoubtedly influenced the posture of other rajas and aristocrats whose positions were less prominent but still important at a local level.

The influence of Bali's feudal families was also strongly felt in the legislative bodies of the NIT and in Bali, whose structures tended to favor them. While in theory Bali's Paruman Agung shared legislative authority with the Council of Rajas, for all practical purposes it was subordinate to the council. The Paruman Agung seldom introduced legislation and rarely made more than minor amendments to laws introduced by the Council of Rajas. It also showed a marked reluctance to criticize Bali's leading aristocratic families on key issues. Elections for the Paruman Agung were held in April 1947, but the results in Badung and Buleleng, where nationalist candidates had done well, were annulled. The initiative for the cancellation of the results came from the Council of Rajas, which claimed that "extremists" had pressured people into choosing "unacceptable" candidates.[102] Even after new elections were held in September 1948, the Paruman Agung was still dominated by federalist and pro-raja forces.

A similarly antidemocratic ethos pervaded the NIT parliament, at least as far as Bali was concerned. Bali's eight parliamentary representatives were not elected but appointed jointly by the Council of Rajas and the Paruman Agung in December 1947.[103] More direct elections were scheduled for May 1949, but when they were held, Bali was still under the SOB. Political parties were still banned, as were mass meetings, and restrictions remained on the printing and circulation of printed matter. In short, the opportunities for legal political mobilization by Bali's nationalists before the NIT election were negligible.

Apart from offending the Dutch sense of administrative efficiency and order, the resurgence of Balinese feudalistic tendencies, now fueled by access to executive and legislative power beyond Bali, sparked Dutch anxiety about a backlash from ordinary Balinese. Indeed, one of the central debates after

[101] The fortunes of the PSI in Bali are discussed in greater detail in later chapters.

[102] Interview by George McT. Kahin with I Gusti Ktut Ngurah (chairman of the Paruman Agung), 1 April 1949, Denpasar.

[103] Interviews by George McT. Kahin with Nyoman Wirya, April 1949, Denpasar, and Putu Wirya (executive secretary of Paruman Agung), 2 April 1949, Denpasar.

1946 concerned the question whether the resistance in Bali constituted a "social revolution" or was simply a local manifestation of the "national revolution." On one side of the question were Anak Agung Gde Agung and Cokorda Gde Raka Sukawati, who insisted strenuously that there was no significant social revolutionary element in Bali's political troubles, and that the resistance was the work of a handful of "terrorist" youths who did not represent the general will. In their view, the Republican resistance on Bali would evaporate quickly if firm measures were taken against the trouble-makers.[104]

On the other side of the issue were Resident Boon and Assistant Resident J. van Baal. A strict Calvinist and by all accounts scrupulously even handed in his behavior toward his staff, Boon believed that Bali's hierarchical caste system was an anachronism that had fed Balinese resistance to the Dutch. He was mistrustful of Agung and reportedly clashed with him more than once on political and administrative matters.[105] Van Baal was perhaps even less sympathetic to Bali's rajas, considering most of them unfit to govern and excessively feudal in thought and behavior.[106] Lt. Gov. Gen. van Mook seems to have developed a similarly low opinion of the rajas. During a trip to Bali in late 1947 he reportedly commented to his guide, a young Dutch Controleur, that Bali's rajas were "like a bunch of expensive racing dogs—quite useless," and that resurrecting them was "really one of our greatest mistakes."[107]

Like Agung, Sukawati was in a position to influence—though not to determine—political and military strategy in Bali. On several occasions his recommendations for dealing with the resistance in Bali went beyond what the Dutch Indies military command (KNIL) considered appropriate. He repeatedly called for substantial increases in military and police power in Bali and for the use of authoritarian measures—including internment without trial and "summary justice" for troublemakers—to wipe out Bali's Republican guerrilla forces.

On 15 September 1947, less than two months after the initiation of the first Dutch military action in Java, Sukawati cabled The Hague warning that the transfer of troops out of Bali to Java, in July and August 1947, had created an opportunity for a sudden increase in "terror" and "extremism" in

---

[104] Interviews with J. van Baal, 9 May 1987, Doorn, and Anak Agung Gde Agung, 27 May 1987, Wassenaar. According to the secretary to Resident Boon, Agung was "furious" at van Baal's suggestion that there was an element of "social revolution" in the resistance: interview with C. H. Stefels, 28 June 1988, Leiden.

[105] Interviews with Lijftogt, Treffers, and Harten.

[106] The possible exception was the raja of Buleleng, Anak Agung Jelantik, an educated man well respected by most Dutch officials for his intelligence and his administrative ability: interviews with van Baal, 9 May 1987, Doorn; Schuilwerve and van Leeuwen, 21 June 1988, The Hague.

[107] Interview with Lijftogt, 20 June 1988, Deventer.

Bali, and had led to a large number of killings. The cable pleaded for military reinforcements to prevent "absolute chaos."[108] The content of the telegram was quickly made known to government and military leaders in Batavia, so that on 19 September the Netherlands Indies government wired Sukawati with the message: "Acknowledge receipt your telegram with great concern. . . . Troop reinforcements Bali planned."[109] The next day the chief of the KNIL General Staff, Maj. Gen. Buurman van Vreeden, issued orders to the KNIL Army commander to send two full companies to Bali no later than the end of September.[110]

This order brought total troop strength in Bali (not including staff, support, and regular police units) to eight companies, an increase of about one-third over August 1947. Yet Sukawati was not satisfied. In mid-October he wrote a personal letter to van Mook calling for more troops and for the use of still more draconian measures to put down the resistance in Bali. The "unrestrained terrorism" of the past few months, he claimed, was proof of the "totalitarian character of the resistance movement, and of the fanaticism, unchecked by a single humanitarian consideration, of these men and spiritually uprooted youth." Under the circumstances, he argued, what was needed was "a swift, clear, and, for the people, easily understood form of justice . . . without misplaced formalism."[111]

In February 1948, shortly after the signing of the Renville Agreement, President Sukawati was again making high-level appeals for an increase in police and military troop strength in Bali to "liquidate" the resistance. In a secret hand-delivered letter to van Mook he argued that, with the resistance running short of both supplies and public sympathy, "the time is extremely favorable for the liquidation of the resistance in the very near future, by means of increased military activity, supplemented by the suggested measures with regard to the police." His specific recommendations included an increase in troop strength of three full combat companies; a further increase in the size as well as the quality of the local police forces; and the procurement of fifteen new vehicles for the police. On this occasion Sukawati's requests were denied. Major General Buurman van Vreeden, in a marginal note to Sukawati's letter, wrote: "I do not believe that the solution is to be found in the imposition of more and more troops. Given the manner of operation of the remaining elements of the resistance, the emphasis must be placed instead on the gathering of intelligence."[112] Sukawati, it appeared,

---

[108] Cokorda Gde Raka Sukawati to The Hague, 15 September 1947, telegram, "Kabinet van de Leger Kommandant in Indonesie," Inv. no. 30/3, Doos 7, Bundel 107, MvD/CAD.

[109] Batavia to Cokorda Gde Raka Sukawati, 19 September 1947, telegram, ibid.

[110] See Maj. Gen. Buurman van Vreeden to KNIL Army Commander, 20 September 1947, and KNIL Army Commander to Lt. Gov. Gen. van Mook, 24 September 1947, ibid.

[111] Sukawati to van Mook, "Toepassing Standrecht voor Bali," 16 October 1947, memo, Archive Boon.

[112] Cokorda Gde Raka Sukawati to van Mook, 14 February 1948, "Kabinet van de Leger Kommandant in Indonesie," Inv. no. 30/3, Doos 2, Bundel 12, MvD/CAD. Van Vreeden reiterated this position in a memo of 19 April 1948 to the KNIL commander (ibid.).

was more enthusiastic about stamping out political resistance through military force than were the KNIL commanders themselves.

From the viewpoint of Dutch civil servants stationed in Bali, then, it was far from obvious that the NIT was a "puppet" state. Batavia may have regarded it as such, but to those in Bali who had to work under its authority, the NIT seemed, if anything, too powerful.[113] Assistant Resident van Baal, Controleur Lijftogt, and Resident Boon, among others, collided with high-ranking NIT officials on a number of occasions on jurisdictional and political issues.[114] As NIT minister of the interior, Anak Agung Gde Agung became a thorn in the side of several Dutch advisers and Residents, including Resident Boon, because he argued that, according to the NIT constitution, they were administratively subordinate to ministers such as himself.[115]

In March 1949, by a decision of Agung, the Residency of Bali/Lombok ceased to exist, and Bali became officially one of the thirteen regions of the NIT. On 3 March Resident Boon handed the reins of government to the chair of the Council of Rajas, Anak Agung Gde Oka, the younger brother of Agung and also the raja of Gianyar.[116] This was an important stage in a process of decreasing the Dutch presence in Bali, which began as early as December 1947. In the first few months of 1948, Dutch Controleurs had been removed from their posts in the kingdoms of Badung, Bangli, and Buleleng and replaced by Balinese political advisers. At roughly the same time, a number of prerogatives of the Resident and Assistant Resident were shifted to the Council of Rajas. By the end of 1949 only three active Dutch civil servants remained on the island.

The "Indonesianization" of the administration of Bali was offered up as evidence of the sincerity of Dutch commitment to Indonesian autonomy; and there is little doubt that some Dutch civil servants were sincere. Politically, however, these changes had rather more complicated implications. The removal of Dutch officials and their replacement by Balinese were to some extent part of a political initiative of Agung and his allies to consolidate control over Bali's postrevolutionary political system. They had the effect of deepening the dynamic of political enmity among Balinese, for two reasons.

First, with no Dutch Resident to serve as mediator between the NIT and

---

113 Interviews with J. van Baal, 9 May 1987, Doorn, and P. L. Dronkers (Controleur), 19 June 1988, Eindhoven.

114 Controleur Lijftogt was transferred out of Bali in 1947 after writing critical remarks about Anak Agung Gde Agung in a political report. According to Lijftogt, Agung wanted him transferred to a remote part of Celebes "to teach him a lesson," but Resident Boon managed to have him transferred to Lombok instead: interview with Lijftogt, 20 June 1988, Deventer.

115 See, for example, Anak Agung's letter to all Residents in NIT, 7 July 1947, in Archive Boon, citing the Gouvernement-besluit nr. 2 (9 June 1947), in which he argued that the NIT minister of the Interior was legally a higher authority than the Netherlands Indies Directeur van Binnenlands-Bestuur.

116 H. J. Franken, who was close to Resident Boon, believes that the abolition of the Residency in 1949 represented Anak Agung's final victory over Boon: interview with Franken, 28 June 1988, Leiden.

the Council of Rajas, powerful Balinese figures in the NIT could exercise more direct and unfettered influence in Bali; in this respect, the dominance of the royal family of Gianyar was an obvious concern. As we have seen, even before Resident Boon's transfer, the resurgence of a feudal "family government" came to be seen as one of Bali's central political problems. After the transfer of Resident Boon and the abolition of the post of Resident, Dutch officials expressed serious doubts about whether "the rule of law was likely to be properly guaranteed under the Council of Rajas."[117] There was also serious concern among Republicans and educated Balinese generally; indeed, the reemergence of feudalism became a focus of political debate in the postrevolutionary years.

Second, the near absence of Europeans in the civil service and in the military by the end of 1949 focused attention more clearly on the culpability of Balinese and other Indonesians who continued to work against the Republic. The willing cooperation of Balinese officials, together with the very high proportion of Balinese and other Indonesian troops involved in "Dutch" military actions, intensified enmity among Balinese. A great number of these officials were dubbed Dutch "collaborators" and a significant number were intimidated or killed during and immediately after the transfer of sovereignty in December 1949. Though it was evident as early as 1947, by late 1949 the odor of civil war grew hard to ignore, and the myth that this was simply a fight between "Indonesians" and "Dutch" became more difficult to sustain.

Balinese politics during the National Revolution were powerfully affected by the various centers of political and military power and by the shifting relations among them. The crucial centers were the Republic in Java, the Dutch colonial regime based in Batavia, and the NIT in Makassar. International pressures also had an indirect but important influence on the course of politics. Indeed, the revolutionary period demonstrates clearly that politics in Bali cannot properly be understood solely in terms of the dynamics of local culture and personalities. Unless it is viewed with reference to the broader national and international context, Balinese politics makes no sense.

For Bali's nationalists, and especially for the pemuda, the Indonesian Republic in Java was unquestionably the political center of greatest importance. They looked to it for military strategy and supplies, they sought recognition of their own roles in the struggle from its leaders, they found inspiration in its symbols, its slogans, and its philosophy, and they were ever attentive to its changing political posture toward other centers of power. Their loyalty to the Republic did not always sit well with their compatriots

---

[117] See, for example, KNIL-CMI Makassar, "14-daags Politiek Verslag over de periode 18/2 t/m 3/3, 1949," in Bundel "Hoofdkwartier van de Generale Staf van het Leger in Indonesie," Inv. no. 32/1, GG 64, 8604, MvD/CAD.

in Bali, including some older nationalists who labeled them "extreme left-ists" and believed their ideals to be "unrealistic." The lack of unanimity among the Republican leaders in Java and their evident lack of concern about the resistance in Bali contributed to these problems and helped to accentuate splits and rivalries among Bali's more militant pemuda leaders.

The Dutch colonial regime's heavy-handed military intervention in 1946 seems initially to have given momentum and unity to the nationalist movement in Bali, pushing it toward organized military resistance. The continued use of repressive tactics—typified by the perpetuation of the SOB for more than a year after armed resistance had effectively ceased—fueled the alienation of the moderate, educated nationalists and gave impetus to the underground tactics of the more militant pemuda. At the same time, the heavy Dutch reliance on Balinese collaborators and local anti-Republican paramilitary forces helped to accentuate conflict among Balinese.

The influence of the NIT was no less profound. Despite its reputation as a mere Dutch puppet state, the prominence of key Balinese aristocrats in the NIT dramatically strengthened conservative groups in Bali. By providing a psychological and political boost to Bali's reactionary forces, the NIT contributed to the dynamic of enmity between antifeudal Republicans and those who favored the retention of feudal power in some form. Emboldened by the structure of NIT authority, which provided a kind of political sanctuary from both Dutch and Republican influence, some of Bali's aristocrats revealed themselves to be more reactionary and ruthless than many Dutch colonial officials in their efforts to destroy Republican resistance. Their behavior during these years remained a political issue long after 1949.

The interaction between the various centers of state power outside Bali was also fundamental in shaping local politics during the Revolution and beyond. Paradoxically, Bali's peripheral position within the National Revolution actually intensified the effect of these external dynamics on local politics. The resistance in Bali was forced repeatedly to adjust its military and political strategies in accordance with changes in relations between the competing centers of power. The Linggajati Accord and the subsequent creation of the NIT led to a serious rethinking of military and political strategy by the MBU-DPRI and to disagreement among the pemuda. Reservations about the use of military force were waived after the first Dutch military action and the abrogation of Linggajati. The Renville Agreement and the Republican recognition of the NIT in January 1948 caused confusion and bitterness within the Republican movement in Bali, and was a key factor in the MBU-DPRI decision to come down from the mountains in May of that year. That decision, as we have seen, brought to a head longstanding differences within the armed resistance. Like the animosity between Bali's feudal and antifeudal forces, the splits among the more militant pemuda were not soon forgotten.

In short, the interplay of external and local factors contributed to the emergence of a particular pattern of political conflict in Bali. The pattern, which profoundly affected political relations on the island after December 1949, entailed basically two kinds of conflict, both *among* Balinese. First, there was the enmity between Republican resistance fighters and sympathizers, on the one hand and, on the other, those who had worked with the Dutch or the NIT state. Second, there was rivalry among the various nationalist leaders—both between older moderate nationalists and the militant pemuda and within the latter group—and among their respective followings. These divisions were transformed into open political conflict after 1949.

8 *The Struggle for the State,*
1950–1965

THE VOLATILITY AND CHRONIC VIOLENCE that characterized Balinese politics during the National Revolution continued unabated into the postindependence period. As in the revolutionary years, political conflict after 1950
was, for the most part, among Balinese—a politics of civil strife rather than
ethnic or religious solidarity. Commenting on the first two years after independence, the pemuda Nyoman Pendit wrote in 1954 that

> the situation in Bali was extremely bad, because the people of Bali were unhap-
> py with the existing system of government and asked that it be changed quickly.
> Killings, beatings, arson, theft, banditry, kidnapping, and so on were taking
> place everywhere, so that the general situation in Bali became chaotic. . . . The
> killing of former NICA collaborators occurred on a large scale.[1]

After a gradual decline, violent political conflict in Bali again increased
around the time of the first national elections, resulting in hundreds of
killings between 1954 and 1957. In the 1960s mass political confrontations
resulted in the destruction of property and many more deaths, culminating
in the widespread violence of 1965–66.

If these facts are not widely known, it is because so little has been written
about this period of Balinese history generally, and less still about the un-
comfortable and unexotic subject of political conflict.[2] This chapter seeks to

---

[1] Nyoman Pendit, *Bali Berdjuang* (Denpasar: Jajasan Kebaktian Pedjuang, 1954), p. 223. A
similar description of the violence of this period can be found in the final report of Governor
Sarimin Reksodihardjo, *Memorie Penjerahan Gubernur Kepala Daerah Propinsi Nusa Tenggara 1/4/1952—30/3/1957* ([Singaraja], 1957) pp. 204–5.

[2] Only a handful of works treat Balinese politics during these years in any detail. See Last,
Bali in de Kentering; Lane, "Wedastera Suyasa in Balinese Politics, 1962–1972"; and I Gusti
Ngurah Bagus, "Bali in the 1950s: The Role of the Pemuda Pejuang in Balinese Political
Processes," in Geertz, *State and Society in Bali.*

fill that gap in scholarly discourse and at the same time to offer an explanation of the pattern of political conflict in Bali from 1950 to 1965. As in earlier periods, Balinese politics in these years were critically shaped by the way national developments dovetailed with local political struggles. Particularly important was the struggle to control the state apparatus in Bali, which began to accelerate with the transfer of sovereignty in December 1949. This conflict had its roots in the National Revolution and even earlier, but it was given new dimensions by Bali's rapid integration into national-level Indonesian state and political party structures.[3]

The initial weakness of the state apparatus in Bali made it susceptible to political influences from without, which encouraged political clashes among Balinese and provided little basis for their final resolution until the coup of 1965. In the interests of clarity, let us begin with the broader political environment from 1950 to 1965 before we examine developments in Bali in greater detail.

National and Local States

After the creation of the unitary Republican state in August 1950, a significant number of local challengers for state power remained within the country's boundaries. It was up to the national-level political parties, the military, and such individuals as President Sukarno to extend central power to these areas. Although Republican military forces managed to put down the earliest attempts to establish independent power centers outside of Java, the state was not strong enough to remove all vestiges of old or newly emerging statelike authority in the outlying regions. Indeed, in some respects the situation in Indonesia in the 1950s was much closer to that of old Southeast Asia.

In many places local and regional power structures were not deeply penetrated or displaced by a centralized modern state, though of course the pattern varied. Local power structures mediated the relationship between the central state and the local society in a variety of ways, deeply affecting the political dynamic in each region. Strong local power structures were able to pose direct military and political challenges to the center—as in the PRRI and Permesta rebellions in Sumatra and Sulawesi in the late 1950s—or at least to develop political movements that expressed regionalist sentiments and demands vis-à-vis the central government.[4] Where local states were

---

[3] For a factual outline of the various administrative and legal changes in Bali from the Dutch period to the mid-1970s, see Panitia Penulisan Sejarah Pemerintah Daerah Bali, *Sejarah Pemerintah Daerah Bali* (Denpasar, 1977).

[4] On the Permesta rebellion, see Barbara Harvey, *Permesta: Half a Rebellion,* Monograph no. 57 (Ithaca: Cornell Modern Indonesia Project, 1977).

weak, as in Bali, politics tended to be more dependent on political movements at the center.

At least since the turn of the century, political authority in Bali had relied on and been subordinate to one or another outside state power; first the Dutch, then the Japanese, and after 1946 a combination of the Dutch and the NIT. No powerful Bali-wide political institution had existed before colonial rule, and after its demise no new structures survived with the capacity to govern the entire island. The only political structures above the level of the individual kingdoms—the Council of Rajas, the Paruman Agung, and the Residency bureaucracy —had depended ultimately on political and military support from outside colonial authorities. With the collapse of Dutch and NIT power in 1949–50, the authority of those bodies was substantially diminished, and many of their personnel were politically compromised. In 1950, then, Bali was suddenly left without a strong local state apparatus.

The relative weakness of the existing power structure in Bali in the early 1950s meant that penetration by the Republican state and by the national political parties was both swift and deep, drawing Bali rapidly into the maelstrom of national-level political debate and conflict. Political conflict in Bali, in particular the fight for local state power, intensified as it intersected and overlapped with changes in policy and power relations at the national level. In general, the dynamic of national-local interaction served to weaken tendencies toward an ethnically based Bali-wide movement expressing demands vis-à-vis the central state, and instead accentuated political conflict among Balinese.

There was one notable exception to this trend. National-level debates in the 1950s concerning religious policy and the place of religion in the constitution provoked concern among Balinese leaders, regardless of political persuasion. For a time these debates encouraged a heightened consciousness of Balinese religious and cultural distinctiveness.[5] This was the closest that Bali ever came to a "regionalist" movement like those that emerged in other parts of the country in these years. Significantly, however, the contentious religious issues were eventually resolved in Bali's favor, with the assistance of the central state, so that any emerging ethnic or regional sentiment against the center gave way again to political conflict among Balinese.

Particularly significant was the debate over whether Indonesia should become an Islamic or a secular state. Domination by an Islamic majority had long been a concern in Bali, so it was not surprising that Balinese leaders

---

[5] See the polemical series in the publication *Siasat*. The relevant articles are Muh Dimyati, "Bahaja Anarsisme dilapangan keagamaan," *Siasat* 6, no. 275 (10 August 1952), pp. 4–5; P. Shanty, "Agama, Demokrasi, Pantjasila," ibid., no. 278 (7 September 1952), p. 7; Muh. Dimyati, "Sekali Lagi Demokrasi dan Anarsi," ibid., no. 281 (28 September 1952), pp. 11, 16; [Anonymous], "Kebudajaan dan Manusia-nja," ibid., no. 284 (19 October 1952), p. 19; I Gusti Bagus Sugriwa, "Kebangsaan, Demokrasi, Agama," *Siasat* 7, no. 301 (1 March 1953), p. 10.

responded swiftly and critically to calls for the creation of an Islamic state in the early 1950s. To a minority culture and religion such as Bali's, secularism and pluralism seemed to offer a guarantee against domination by an Islamic majority. In this debate, Balinese leaders won the support of President Sukarno, for whom Bali served as an ideal rationale for a secular state.

About the same time, Bali faced a second major threat. In the early 1950s it looked very much as though Bali-Hinduism might not gain official recognition from the central state as a "religion" because it did not easily meet the government criteria: the existence of a "holy book," belief in one God and a prophet, and international recognition. Not unnaturally, Balinese leaders devoted a great deal of energy to gaining such recognition and to obtaining a separate Bali-Hindu section within the Ministry of Religious Affairs.[6] These objectives were finally achieved in 1958, again with the assistance of Sukarno.[7]

With Sukarno's support for the secular state and for the official recognition of Bali-Hinduism, Balinese no longer held a clear religious grievance against the central state. On the contrary, the president appeared as Bali's patron; and his concept of *Pancasila* (the five principles) seemed to provide a political guarantee of the state's commitment to the preservation of Balinese culture and religion.

Sukarno and Bali

As early as 1950, President Sukarno began to take an intense personal interest in the political situation in Bali. At least twice in that year he toured the island, speaking to large crowds and meeting with pemuda leaders.[8] In December 1951, responding to the worsening political violence of the previous year, the president called thirteen of Bali's leading pemuda figures to Jakarta to resolve their differences. Through the 1950s and 1960s he visited Bali several times each year, usually accompanied by important cabinet ministers, party leaders, or visiting heads of state, including Nehru, Ho Chi Minh, Tito, and Nikita Khrushchev. Each visit was an occasion of consider-

[6] A number of political/religious organizations were established as part of this effort. The PAHB (Panti Agama Hindu Bali), formed in Singaraja in 1951, appears to have been the first organization to formally request a separate and equal section for Bali-Hinduism in the Ministry of Religious Affairs. See "Ichtisar Rapat Propaganda dan Anggota PAHB Singaradja pada tanggal 11 Maart 1951," Gedong Kirtya, Singaraja. Parisada Hindu Dharma, established in 1959, has survived to become the highest body governing Bali-Hindu affairs throughout Indonesia. See Sekretariat Parisada Hindu Dharma Pusat, *Pokok-Pokok Sedjarah Perkembangan Parisada Hindu Dharma* (Denpasar, 1970).

[7] The relevant decision was the Resolution of the Ministry of Religious Affairs, no. 2, 5 September 1958. See I Gusti Ngurah Anandakusuma, *Pergolakan Hindu Dharma II* (Denpasar: Pustaka Balimas, 1966), p. 106.

[8] He visited in June and November of 1950. He is said to have addressed crowds of more than 20,000 in June. See *Penindjau*, 16 June 1950; *Sin Po*, 1 and 13 November 1950.

13. President and Mrs. Tito of Yugoslavia, with President Sukarno and Cokorda Gde Agung Sukawati of Ubud, on a visit to Bali in December 1958. Tito was one of dozens of heads of state who were invited to Bali. Sukarno had a special affection for Bali, and had a presidential palace there. (*Indonesia, Department of Information, Denpasar*)

able pomp and ceremony that provided Sukarno with an opportunity to speak at mass rallies about the most recent policy directions of the government. In spite of heavy criticism of Sukarno by the Indonesian Socialist party (PSI) in Bali, such rallies were enthusiastically attended by Balinese, many of whom now recall Sukarno's speeches with a profound sense of nostalgia. Outside of Jakarta, there were probably few places where one could feel so immediately involved in national politics as in Bali; the constant presence and attention of the president served as a symbolic bridge between the island and the center.

Sukarno's popularity in Bali had a variety of sources. As we have seen, through his opposition to the idea of an Islamic state and his advocacy of Bali-Hinduism he won the hearts of Bali's predominantly Hindu population. It did not hurt Sukarno's popularity that he claimed to be half Balinese, the son of a Javanese schoolteacher who had met and married a Balinese Brahmana woman while he was posted in Singaraja around the turn of the century.[9] Whether or not he was accepted as Balinese, Sukarno's oratorical

[9] This story is told in Cindy Adams, *Sukarno: An Autobiography* (Indianapolis: Bobbs-Merrill, 1965), pp. 18–21. Also see the discussion of Sukarno's origins in J. D. Legge, *Sukarno: A Political Biography* (Sydney: Allen & Unwin, 1990), pp. 16–17.

style, particularly his capacity to evoke powerful cultural symbols, resonated as deeply among Balinese as among Javanese. Balinese were encouraged to see themselves as sharing in the culture and tradition of ancient, pre-Islamic Java; as *wong Majapahit,* descendants of the last great Hindu kingdom in Java. Any antipathy Balinese may have felt toward Java all but disappeared under the spell of Sukarno's moving imagery of Indonesia's pre-Islamic roots. Balinese also responded well to Sukarno's frequent suggestion that to the outside world Bali *was* Indonesia. Speaking to a large crowd in Denpasar in November 1950, when the island was engulfed in political violence, Sukarno evoked both of these themes. "Bali," he said,

> has always been this country's pride and joy . . . and when Nehru visited he called it "the morning of the world." Now it is in danger of being overcome by darkness. . . . Now there are killing and burning in Bali. I ask you, did Arjuna [a satria hero from the wayang tradition] ever attack his enemy from behind? Never! A pure and noble warrior such as he always fights fairly and in the open. . . . Let us work to ensure that Bali will once again be known as the morning of the world.[10]

Between 1950 and 1965 Sukarno frequently intervened directly to change the course of Balinese politics, usually to the benefit of the more left-wing pemuda elements. Such interventions provoked angry reaction from both the local PSI and the PNI, and heightened political tensions. Perhaps the most significant of Sukarno's interventions was his selection of Suteja as governor of the newly created province of Bali in 1958.[11] Anak Agung Bagus Suteja, a highly influential pemuda leader who was the son of the raja of Jembrana, had been regarded by the Dutch as politically dangerous because he was intelligent, "ultra-left," and of high caste, a rare combination.[12]

His selection as governor and, in 1961, as Regional Military Authority (*Pepelrada*) symbolized Suteja's special relationship with the president.[13] By 1965 there was virtually no Balinese who did not know that Suteja was

[10] Quoted in *Sin Po,* 13 November 1950.

[11] In 1958 the province of Sunda Kecil was divided into three new provinces: Nusa Tenggara Timur (NTT), Nusa Tenggara Barat (NTB), and Bali. Bali officially became a province on 14 August 1958, with its capital city in Singaraja; in 1960 the capital was moved to Denpasar, where it remains.

[12] Dutch efforts to co-opt Suteja by appointing him punggawa of Mendoyo, Jembrana, in 1946 had failed miserably, as he used the prerogatives of his office to assist the armed resistance. A period of study in Makassar in 1947 and a sojourn as administrative assistant in the office of the raja of Klungkung—both intended by the Dutch to keep him out of trouble—succeeded only in making Suteja more widely known and better prepared for political office. In 1949 he had helped to establish the pemuda organization Gerpindo, and was later chosen as chairman of the umbrella pemuda organization, the KPNI.

[13] *Pepelrada: Penguasa Pelaksanaan Dwikora Daerah*—Regional (Military) Authority to Implement *Dwikora (Dwikomando Rakjat,* the people's two mandates: to crush Malaysia and defend the Revolution).

Sukarno's "favored son." This reputation enhanced his authority and, as we shall see, affected the relative strength of Bali's political parties. Like Sukarno, Suteja saw the advantage of making a formal commitment to no party, of staying "above politics." Like Sukarno, too, he nevertheless came to be seen as a sympathizer and protector of the Indonesian Communist party (PKI) and the left-nationalist Partindo. It is hardly surprising, therefore, that these parties became so popular by 1965. Nor is it entirely surprising that these two men became the target of anti-leftist forces after the October 1965 coup.

Parliamentary and Guided Democracy

The distinctive and changing style and structure of Indonesia's postindependence political system also shaped political conflict in Bali during these years. From 1950 to 1957, the system was organized according to the principles of parliamentary democracy.[14] Although national elections were not held until 1955, a large number of political parties—the most prominent were the Masyumi, PNI, PKI, PSI, and NU—were engaged well before that time in the competition for political office and particularly for cabinet positions. The system provided fertile soil for the growth of patronage and corruption, and tended to produce unstable coalition cabinets, which seldom lasted more than a year.[15] It also legitimized, especially in the campaigns for the elections of 1955, the practice of open political competition, mobilization, and conflict, not just at the center but in outlying regions as well.

In the aftermath of the inconclusive 1955 elections, the parliamentary system came increasingly under attack as the source of government inefficiency, corruption, and elitism.[16] There were those in the military who wished to stem the power of political parties (especially the PKI)[17] and to put an end to what they regarded as civilian interference in military affairs.[18]

[14] The most comprehensive work on the period of parliamentary democracy in Indonesia is Herbert Feith, *The Decline of Constitutional Democracy in Indonesia* (Ithaca: Cornell University Press, 1962).

[15] For details, see Susan Finch and Daniel Lev, *Republic of Indonesia Cabinets, 1945–1965*, Interim Report Series no. 38 (Ithaca: Cornell Modern Indonesia Project, 1965).

[16] These were only some of the criticisms launched against the parliamentary system. For a more detailed account of the attack, see Daniel Lev, *The Transition to Guided Democracy: Indonesian Politics, 1957–1959* (Ithaca: Cornell Modern Indonesia Project, 1966), pp. 11, 59.

[17] The PKI had fared rather well in the national elections and had made dramatic gains in Java by the time of the regional elections there in 1957. On the 1955 elections, see Herbert Feith, *The 1955 National Election in Indonesia* (Ithaca: Cornell Modern Indonesia Project, 1960).

[18] In 1955 the cabinet of Ali Sastroamijoyo had sought to appoint the PNI-faithful but rather junior Col. Bambang Utoyo as Army chief of staff. The Army's rejection of the appointment led to the fall of the Ali cabinet. See Harold Crouch, *The Army and Politics in Indonesia* (Ithaca: Cornell University Press, 1978), pp. 31–32.

For somewhat different reasons, in 1956 President Sukarno began his own attack on the parliamentary system and liberal democracy.[19] The PRRI and Permesta rebellions and the dispute with the Dutch over Irian Jaya had made Sukarno somewhat more dependent on the military at this time, and therefore more receptive to their suggestions regarding the appropriate constitutional setup.[20] The declaration of martial law in 1957 and the restoration of the 1945 Presidential Constitution in July 1959 marked the end of the parliamentary system and the beginning of the transition to Guided Democracy.

Guided Democracy was characterized by the "decline of the parties [except the PKI] and parliamentary institutions, the rise of the army, the growing power of the Communist Party and the apparently dominant influence of President Soekarno."[21] Although the new system was designed to place limits on open political competition and mobilization, it had the opposite effect. Political parties—with the exception of the PSI and the Masyumi, which were banned in 1960—continued to compete for power, but in the absence of elections, their efforts found no resolution. Because political posts, both legislative and executive, were now determined by executive (i.e., presidential) decision, there was room for constant lobbying, manipulation, and dispute.

The need to gain recognition from the center required an almost unceasing display of political and organizational capacity. Increasingly after 1959 it took the form of widespread political mobilization through a large number of mass organizations (*ormas*). The ormas paralleled the various "functional groups"—farmers, veterans, women, labor unions, the military, and so on—which were well represented in the new legislative bodies of Guided Democracy, the MPRS, the DPR-GR, and its regional equivalents, the DPRD-GR.[22] One consequence of this system was an unprecedented depth and breadth of political activity down to the village and neighborhood levels. The militancy and pervasiveness of ormas mobilization went far beyond anything known in the years of parliamentary democracy, and was one of the main structural causes of the political polarization and open conflict that characterized the final few years of the Old Order.

---

[19] Sukarno's critique was expressed in his "Political Manifesto" or "Manipol," and also in the "Konsepsi," which he made public on 21 February 1957. See Lev, *Transition to Guided Democracy*, pp. 11–12, 48–56.

[20] See Feith, *Decline of Constitutional Democracy*, pp. 520–48. When Indonesia achieved independence in 1949, Irian Jaya—then known as Netherlands New Guinea—remained as a Dutch possession. Under military and diplomatic pressure from Indonesia the Netherlands ceded control of the territory in 1962.

[21] Lev, *Transition to Guided Democracy*, p. 1. Also see Crouch, *Army and Politics*, pp. 43–68, for a brief characterization of Guided Democracy.

[22] MPRS (Majelis Permusyawaratan Rakyat Sementara—Provisional People's Consultative Assembly); DPR-GR (Dewan Perwakilan Rakyat-Gotong Royong—Gotong Royong People's Representative Assembly); DPRD-GR (Dewan Perwakilan Rakyat Daerah-Gotong Royong—Gotong Royong Regional People's Representative Assembly).

Bali's Unfinished Revolution

The transfer of sovereignty on 27 December 1949 did not signal the end of the political struggle in Bali; in some respects it had only just begun. During the Revolution, Dutch and NIT authorities had managed to control administrative appointments and to stymie political organizations to such an extent that "moderate" or "feudal" elements still dominated these posts at the end of 1949. Developments at the national level, however, substantially altered the balance of political forces in Bali, giving Republicans an advantage for the first time since late 1945. In 1950 as in 1945, however, no single group was able to control the local state apparatus without the intervention and assistance of a more powerful outside force.[23]

Two factors contributed to the Republican rise to power in Bali; at the same time they caused the inherent fragility of the new local state apparatus and political conflict there.[24] First, the pemuda demonstrated a capacity for mass mobilization and political organization at precisely the moment when visible mass support was the major currency of political entitlement. The Revolution had been a vital training ground for this kind of mobilization. Republican success in the fields of political mobilization and the control of the formal institutions of power, however, masked the true extent of anti-democratic sentiment in Bali and the potential for local-level resistance to change. It also contributed to conflict within the Republican camp. Second, the general movement of political forces outside of Bali from federalism toward unitarism effectively established the terms of political discourse within which Balinese struggles took place.[25] President Sukarno contributed to the emergence of this new hegemony, speaking pointedly against *bapakisme* (cronyism), *feodalisme*, and *federalisme* in a series of mass meetings and high-level discussions held in Bali in 1950.[26]

Anger arising from the revolutionary period and frustration over the delay in significant political changes in the first months after independence gave rise to isolated acts of revenge in early 1950.[27] The worst violence appears to have begun immediately after the formation of the unitary Republic in August 1950 and the concomitant demise of the federal United States of Indo-

[23] For a summary of political developments in 1950, the texts of most relevant legislation, and the composition of the first legislative and executive bodies in Bali, see Sekretariat DPRD-Bali, *Peringatan Satu Tahun Dewan Perwakilan Rakjat Daerah Bali* (Denpasar, 1951).

[24] A third factor was the arrival of military forces from Java in mid-1950. Their presence in Bali symbolized the dominance of the Republic and altered the real balance of political and coercive authority there. The political role and significance of the military in Bali are discussed in depth in chapter 9.

[25] It is striking that in the local newspapers *Penindjau* and *Berita Nusantara*, with the exception of a plea by Anak Agung Gde Agung on 16 August 1950, one cannot find a single defense of the idea of federalism. Likewise, the voice of Bali's rajas is almost wholly absent.

[26] See the report of Sukarno's trip to Bali in *Penindjau*, 16 June 1950. Significantly, Sukarno chose Gianyar, the kingdom of Anak Agung Gde Agung, to warn against "Bapakisme."

[27] Pendit, *Bali Berdjuang* (1954), p. 223.

nesia (RIS), prompting the governor of Nusa Tenggara to declare a State of War and Siege (SOB) in Bali.[28] Overshadowed by the dramatic regional-military rebellions in South Sulawesi and Maluku in the same year, the widespread killing and banditry in Bali went virtually unnoticed.[29] In October 1950 the Bali scholar Roelof Goris, then living in Singaraja, wrote to Professor J. Ph. Vogel about the events of the preceding months.

> Between August 20 and September 10, most of the murders occurred *here* (a typed list of 39 victims, among which "beheaded" is often given as the cause of death, justifies my alarm!). In addition a number of entries are listed as seriously wounded, because they [the attackers] were "pretty good with a knife!" And alas, after the development in North Bali, a revenge campaign has also begun in Jembrana and in the whole of South Bali.[30]

The number of deaths in the whole island was never officially recorded, but one estimate is that an average of 80 died each month in the second half of 1950, bringing the total to about 500 in 1950 alone.[31] Serious disturbances continued to the end of 1951.[32] The local newspaper, *Berita Nusantara,* reported only a fraction of the killings, but most of the victims who were reported were Balinese and local Chinese, not Europeans or other Indonesians.[33] Moreover, the attacks were politically motivated, targeting punggawa, perbekel, village heads, and others who allegedly had collaborated with the Dutch, including police officers, civil servants, and Chinese businessmen.

In addition to the more spontaneous acts of revenge, pemuda and other organizations began to mobilize for the purpose of removing from positions

---

[28] The SOB in Bali was officially lifted on 15 May 1951.

[29] In the early part of 1950, troops under the command of Capt. Andi Azis had resisted the landing of TNI forces in South Sulawesi. The RMS (Republik Maluku Selatan) rebellion began officially in April 1950. For the story of the rebel movements and military clashes in East Indonesia in 1950–51, see Barbara Harvey, "Tradition, Islam, and Rebellion: South Sulawesi, 1950–1965," Ph.D. diss., Cornell University, 1974, esp. chap. 5. For a brief discussion of other cases in which irregular forces refused to accept Republican authority, see Feith, *Decline of Constitutional Democracy,* pp. 54–55.

[30] Roelof Goris to J. Ph. Vogel, 3 October 1950, Collectie Korn, OR 435–59, KITLV.

[31] Last, *Bali in de Kentering,* p. 7. The official police estimates are somewhat lower; about 35 per month through the second half of 1950 and 1951. See "Bali Belum Aman," *Suara Rakjat,* 22 December 1951.

[32] A press report from December 1951, for instance, stated that in the previous month 23 killings had been officially reported. See "Bali Belum Aman," *Suara Rakjat,* 22 December 1951. Another report noted more than 100 killings in the kingdom of Tabanan alone during 1951: ibid., 6 February 1952.

[33] If coverage of the violence was scant in the local paper, it was almost nonexistent in the wider Indonesian and foreign press. Grader, writing to Korn on 7 November 1950, noted that every day there were more killings, but that "one can read nothing of all this in the newspapers": Collectie Korn, OR 435–59, KITLV. Goris, angered by comments from Holland that he was getting carried away in his reports of the chaos in Bali, wrote that "the Government in Holland simply does not *want* to know about this. . . . And even the Dutch press is now so typically unreliable!": Goris to Vogel, 3 October 1950, ibid.

of authority those who for "political and psychological reasons" were no longer "acceptable" to the local population, even if they were technically "capable."[34] The Dutch scholar Ch. J. Grader noted as early as 7 August 1950, for instance, that "there have been many changes of punggawa and similar positions because people are against feudalism."[35] A significant number of local officials of this period reveal with pride that they were installed "by the people" and only later were given official government recognition. Being chosen "by the people" generally meant that a local pemuda band or organization threatened, harassed, or if necessary killed the incumbent and replaced him with their own preference.[36] In a number of cases, direct harassment was accompanied by more formal political mobilization which included the lobbying of such state authorities as the regional head, Suteja, and President Sukarno.[37] Here again, the capacity to mobilize and to act was the sine qua non of political right.

Political mobilization, which had begun in Bali long before the transfer of sovereignty, was stimulated by the evident weakness of the RIS, the NIT, and the local state apparatus in Bali.[38] Writing to V. E. Korn from Bali in March 1950, Grader described the scene: "One can see . . . that the structure of this society is undergoing a terribly sudden transformation. There is no real state authority. Everything simply conforms to the immediate instincts and sentiments of the collectivity."[39]

Early in 1950, with only three Dutch civil servants remaining in Bali, political control rested officially in the hands of the Council of Rajas and the Paruman Agung, both of which were seriously compromised by their collaboration with the Dutch and NIT regimes. On 22 May 1950, perhaps in recognition of the imminence of a Republican victory, the Paruman Agung drew up emergency legislation that called for the creation of an Interim

---

[34] The quality of "acceptability" meant something like political correctness, while "capability" implied uncertain political credentials.

[35] Grader to Korn, 7 August 1950, Collectie Korn, OR 435–59, KITLV. Governor Sarimin Reksodihardjo also noted in his final report that "people who were regarded as unacceptable were transferred or fired": *Memorie Penjerahan Gubernur Kepala Daerah Propinsi Nusa Tenggara 1/4/1952–30/3/1957* ([Singaraja], 1957), p. 204.

[36] Interview with I Wayan Rana (former punggawa of Kuta, Badung), 21 September 1986, Denpasar. Rana was installed as punggawa in this fashion in 1950. The old punggawa was subjected to threats of various kinds—including one unsuccessful attempt on his life—until he finally fled to Denpasar, leaving the district office unoccupied. An election of sorts followed, in which Rana won sixteen of the seventeen subdistricts in Kuta. This result was sent to Suteja, the kepala daerah, who ratified the decision by telegram in December 1950.

[37] Examples of such efforts can be found in the local papers, *Penindjau* and *Berita Nusantara*. See, for example, "Menudju Demokrasi di Bali," *Penindjau*, 10 July 1950, which outlines the demand of thirty-one organizations in Pemecutan for the replacement of the old perbekel, on the grounds that he "still reeks of feudalism." Or see "Minta Perbekel Pilihan Rakjat," *Berita Nusantara*, 7 August 1950, which describes a similar demand in Mengwi.

[38] On 19 May the three remaining RIS states—the Republic of Indonesia, NIT, and East Sumatra—signed a formal agreement to establish a unitary state. See Feith, *Decline of Constitutional Democracy*, pp. 63–69.

[39] Grader to Korn, 3 March 1950, Collectie Korn, OR 435–59, KITLV.

Executive Council (Badan Pengelaksana Sementara) with broad authority to "control and direct all executive tasks of the government of the federation of [Balinese] kingdoms."[40] The members of the first Executive Council were drawn primarily from the ranks of the older nationalists, some of whom were members of the Paruman Agung, and the "moderate," educated administrative middle class.[41] Somewhat facetiously, Grader wrote to Korn: "Bali is thus now governed by a librarian, an agricultural inspector, a teacher, and a customs officer." He might have added "a prince," because the head of the Executive Council was none other than the raja of Gianyar, Anak Agung Gde Oka, the former chairman of the Council of Rajas.[42]

At least three of the four regular members of the council formed in May 1950 had well-established credentials as moderate nationalists, and two later became important leaders of the Indonesian Nationalist party (PNI). Their social and political backgrounds were typical in many ways of the men who formed the core of the PNI in Bali, and distinguished them from the pemuda. Very well educated by Balinese standards, all had worked as civil servants under the Dutch. They were genuine nationalists, but their activities before and during the Revolution had been limited to such activities as the formation of political parties, the establishment of nationalist schools, and, in one case, the development of "nationalist" literature.[43]

The effort to keep the state apparatus in the hands of these more moderate elements was made difficult by the rapid development of mass political activity in Bali in 1950. Paradoxically, Republican activism and political reform were encouraged by a piece of NIT legislation that called for the formation of more democratic institutions, in keeping with the Republican

[40] The legislation, Peraturan Darurat Daerah Bali untuk mengadakan Badan Pengelaksana Sementara, 22 Mei 1950, no. 1/Darurat, was enacted by the Paruman Agung on 8 June 1950. See Ch. J. Grader, "Bali: Tournee-Aantekeningen Juli 1950—Dewan Pemerintah Daerah Bali," Collectie Korn, OR 435–23, KITLV.

[41] The four members were I Gusti Putu Merta, I Wayan Dangin, I Gusti Gde Subamia, and I Wayan Bhadra. See ibid.

[42] Grader to Korn, 7 August 1950, Collectie Korn OR 435–59, KITLV.

[43] I Gusti Putu Merta, a schoolteacher, for example, was a founding member and chairman of the short-lived Parrindo (1946–47) and vice-chair of the GNI. In the 1950s he became the chair of the PNI's Regional Executive Council for Bali (DPD-PNI-Bali), and later the chair of the DPRD-Bali. In December 1965, in the aftermath of the coup, he replaced Suteja as governor of Bali. I Gusti Gde Subamia, an assistant punggawa under the Dutch (1940–42), and a tax and customs officer after the war, was a member of the KNI-Sunda Kecil and First Secretary of the KNI-Tabanan in 1945. He was a member of the Parrindo and was instrumental in setting up the GNI in 1949. He was imprisoned from 1947 to 1949 in connection with his nationalist activities, and after his release he became "komis" of the Council of Rajas. After independence he became a member of the DPD-PNI-Bali, but in 1956, he made the move to national politics as a member of Parliament. In 1959 he served as deputy chair of the PNI fraction in Parliament, and later was appointed to the president's Supreme Advisory Council. Wayan Bhadra was an important prewar nationalist in a slightly different mold. A student of the Balinese nationalist teacher I Nengah Metra before the war, he was a man of letters who wrote one of the first "nationalist" novels in the Balinese language, *Malangcaran ka Sasak*. He worked as the head of the Kirtya Liefrinck–van der Tuuk Library in Singaraja. According to Adrian Vickers, Wayan Bhadra "provided a kind of model of scholarship in a nationalist mode later taken up by the hero of Balinese literature, Gusti Bagus Sugriwa": personal communication, 20 October 1988.

law on regional government.[44] The fight for more genuine democratization of political structures was led by the pemuda organizations, principally the Kesatuan Pemuda Nasional Indonesia (Indonesian Union of Nationalist Youth), or KPNI. The KPNI, established in April 1950 at a Bali-wide congress of pemuda organizations,[45] represented a fairly broad spectrum of organizations and opinion and aimed to present a united pemuda front. Its head was Anak Agung Bagus Suteja, the son of the raja of Jembrana. Because he was not clearly linked to either the DPRI or PDRI, Suteja was virtually the only pemuda leader of any stature who was acceptable to all factions within the KPNI.

By the end of September 1950, both the Paruman Agung and the Dewan Raja-Raja had been abolished and replaced by a Regional People's Representative Assembly (DPRD-Bali) and a new Regional Government Council (DPD-Bali), respectively.[46] This change dealt a serious though not fatal blow to the political authority of the rajas and their closest allies. Although there were no rajas on the Regional Council and none held seats on the Regional Assembly, it was generally acknowledged that their social and political influence remained substantial. Moreover, a considerable number of former "collaborators" continued to hold positions of authority within the government bureaucracy and at the local level, as punggawa, perbekel, village heads, and so on. As we shall see, these proved to be important factors in the later development of political parties and political conflict in Bali.

The new constitutional arrangements after September 1950 left intact and perhaps enhanced the position of the older, moderate nationalists. Of the five members of the new Regional Council, three—I Gusti Gde Subamia, I Gusti Made Mudra, and I Wayan Dangin—were older men with civil service backgrounds. They were given responsibility for the portfolios of Social, Political, and Economic Affairs, respectively. Yet the constitutional changes also gave the pemuda a powerful legal voice in the political structure (see Table 5). In September 1950 Sukarno selected the twenty-seven-year-old pemuda leader Suteja (over a member of the aristocratic elite) as Regional Head of Bali.[47] Also on the Regional Council at this time was I Gusti Bagus Sugriwa, who was affiliated with the left-nationalist organization Ikatan

[44] For the text of the Undang-Undang Pemerintahan Daerah Indonesia Timoer (U.U. no. 44/June 15, 1950), see Propinsi Bali, Kantor Gubernur KDH Propinsi Bali, Biro Hukum, *Himpunan Peraturan Perundangan Mengenai Pemerintahan Daerah* (Denpasar, 1974), pp. 42–50. The relevant Republican legislation was U.U. Pokok 1948/22.

[45] A partial list of the resolutions of the congress can be found in Nyoman Pendit, *Bali Berjuang*, 2d ed. (Jakarta: Gunung Agung, 1979), p. 345. For a sense of the KPNI position, see "Badan Pengelaksana Harus Berdjuang Menguasai Djalan untuk Menudju Tjita-Tjita Kemakmuran dan Demokrasi," *Penindjau*, 5 September 1950. For a less sympathetic view of the activities of the Republican pemuda at this time, see Grader, "Bali: Tournee Aantekeningen."

[46] The Paruman Agung was dissolved on 20 September 1950 and the DPRD-Bali (Dewan Perwakilan Rakyat Daerah-Bali) was established on 25 September 1950.

[47] The other candidate was Cokorda Anom Putra, son of the raja of Klungkung. Suteja received a clear majority of votes (32), and Putra managed to beat a third contender (Anak Agung Nyoman Panji Tisna, the former raja of Buleleng) in a run-off vote. The final decision, however, was made by President Sukarno. See Pendit, *Bali Berjuang*, 2d ed., p. 358.

Table 5. Seats held in Bali's regional legislature (DPRD and DPRD-GR) by parties and functional groups, 1950, 1956, and 1960

Year	KPNI	PNI	PSI	PKI	PRI	BP	MAS	NU	PK	MUR	IRMI	FG	TOTAL
1950	11	9	–	–	–	–	6	–	–	–	3	7	36
1956	–	16	9	2	1	1	1	–	–	–	–	–	30
1960	–	7	–	1	–	1	–	1	1	1	–	13	25

Key: KPNI = Kesatuan Pemuda Republik Indonesia; PNI = Partai Nasionalis Indonesia; PSI = Partai Sosialis Indonesia; PKI = Partai Komunis Indonesia; PRI = Partai Rakyat Indonesia; BP = Biro Pancasila; MAS = Masyumi; NU = Nahdatul Ulama; PK = Partai Katolik; MUR = Partai Murba; IRMI = Ikatan Rakyat Murba Indonesia; FG = Functional Groups: in 1950, Peasants (2), Women (3), Workers (2); in 1960, Peasants (2), Women (1), Workers (2), Youth (1), Religious leaders (2), Veterans (1), Business (1), Artists (1), Military (2).

Sources: For 1950, Berataputra, "Perwakilan Rakjat di Bali," 17 February 1951; for 1956, "Bunga Rampai Pemilihan Umum 1955," Bali Post, 6 April 1977; for 1960, Suara Indonesia, 9 December 1960.

Rakyat Murba Indonesia (Indonesian Murba People's Union), or IRMI. Though he later became famous as a literary scholar, during the Revolution he had been one of the leaders of an underground organization that in November 1949 became the headquarters of the PDRI in Buleleng.[48] In mid-1950 he was a member of an emergency executive council set up in Buleleng to fill the power vacuum left by the resignation of the raja.[49] Like Suteja, Sugriwa was viewed as politically "progressive."

Pemuda groups, represented by the KPNI, also secured an unprecedented measure or representation in the new Regional People's Representative Assembly. Thus by September 1950 a group that Grader had referred to in March as "a still small number of youth who want Bali's integration into the Republic" had come to play a key role in the major executive and legislative organs of the local state apparatus. Still, they shared political power with influential older Republicans and with a variety of former collaborators and "feudal" elements.

Political conflict in Bali, however, was not simply a matter of rivalry between Republicans and former "collaborators." It was to a great extent also a struggle within the Republican camp for control of the local state. In the course of that struggle the various Republican fractions, seeking to strengthen their hold on political authority, found it expedient to form political alliances with elements with the most dubious revolutionary credentials. Partly for this reason, patterns of political party affiliation in the 1950s did not neatly reflect coherent ideological positions. Nevertheless, the rivalry among the various Republican fractions can help to explain a good deal of the political drama in Bali, including the climax in 1965.

Party Politics

Although an extraordinary number of political organizations were formed in Bali between 1949 and 1955, fewer than ten received any support in the first national elections (for the national parliament and the Constituent Assembly) held at the end of 1955.[50] Of these parties, three captured roughly 90 percent of the vote. In order of strength, they were the PNI, the PSI, and the PKI (see Table 6). The weak appeal of the major Islamic and Christian parties in predominantly Hindu Bali was hardly surprising. The prepon-

[48] The other two leaders of the organization Gerim (Gerakan Rahasia Indonesia Merdeka) were Cilik (I Nengah Tamu) and I Gusti Bagus Nyoman Panji.

[49] The other three members of the Buleleng council were Ida Bagus Indera, Bagus Brata, and Made Toya.

[50] The elections for the People's Representative Assembly (DPR) were held on 29 September 1955 and for the Constituent Assembly on 15 December 1955. The best analysis of the elections is Feith's *Indonesian Elections of 1955*. For a detailed breakdown of voting in Bali, see I Nyoman Sarwa, "Pergolakan Sosial Politik di Bali Sejak Pemilihan Umum, 1955–1965," thesis, Universitas Udayana, 1985.

Table 6. Percentage of vote and number of seats won in kabupaten-level DPRD by the three major parties in 1955 general elections

Kabupaten	Total seats	PNI %	PNI No.	PKI %	PKI No.	PSI %	PSI No.	Other[a] %	Other[a] No.
Buleleng	15	63.2%	10	6.0%	2	1.9%	0	18.9%	3
Jembrana	10	56.0	6	21.5	2	0.3	0	22.2	2
Tabanan	15	41.5	6	2.9	1	51.9	8	3.7	0
Badung	15	31.7	5	7.2	1	47.3	7	13.8	2
Gianyar	15	47.4	7	3.8	1	46.1	7	2.7	0
Bangli	12	67.2	8	0.4	0	30.0	4	2.4	0
Klungkung	11	68.8	8	8.9	1	10.8	2	11.5	0
Karangasem	15	57.7	9	6.1	1	27.6	4	8.6	1
All kabupaten	108	51.4%[b]	59	7.9%[b]	9	30.6%[b]	32	10.2%	8

[a] Other parties that received some support included Biro Pancasila, Masyumi, Partai Rakyat Indonesia, Partai Rakyat Nasional, Partai Buruh, PPPRI, NU, and Partai Murba.

[b] The voting for the Constituent Assembly, in December 1955, showed a marked drop in PSI support to about 25% of the valid vote and an increase in the percentage vote of both the PNI (to 56%) and the PKI (to 8.5%).

Sources: These figures are calculated on the basis of an unpublished list of election returns, "Daftar Hasil Pemilihan Umum Dewan Perwakilan Rakjat Nusa Tenggara Barat." Another source, "Bunga Rampai Pemilihan Umum Tahun 1955," *Bali Post*, 6 April 1977, shows slightly different vote totals—and a larger percentage for the PKI.

derance of the three Java-based national-level parties, however, clearly requires an explanation. In comparison with its showing at the national level, for example, the PSI did exceptionally well in Bali; of the five parliamentary seats it received nationally, three were from Bali. Likewise, the PKI did better in Bali than in most other parts of the country outside the party's traditional base areas in Java; and, as in Java, its influence expanded very rapidly after 1955. The PNI dominated the 1955 elections in Bali and remained a powerful though declining political force up to 1965. By contrast, the only locally based party that appealed openly to Balinese religious sentiment, the Partai Nasional Agama Hindu Bali, established in Klungkung in February 1954, received less than 1 percent of the vote in the 1955 elections.

What accounts for the overwhelming popularity of the three national parties in Bali? What explains their relative strengths and their changing political fortunes through the 1950s and 1960s? And how did party affiliation and competition influence the pattern of violent political conflict in Bali during this period? These are some of the questions to be addressed below, but first let us examine existing explanations of political affiliation and choice in Bali.

In 1963 Clifford Geertz summarized the argument that would powerfully influence all subsequent analyses of Balinese politics under the Old Order. In Bali, he wrote, political affiliation tends to follow traditional allegiances rather closely, so that rival kin-groups, villages and caste groups find themselves on opposite sides of the political fence *as a mere reflex of their position in the local social structure.* As yet, the persistence of customary social forms remains strong enough to force national political processes to realize themselves in terms of properly Balinese concerns, and rather than shaping local loyalties . . . they are able only to reflect them.[51]

In support of this claim, he referred to Hildred Geertz's assertion in 1959 that in Bali "seemingly modern [political] competition is in actuality not one of ideologies but one of traditional factions, of ancient grudges and time honored alliances."[52]

Unfortunately, the Geertzes' paradigm provides no real explanation of the process by which a particular political party may have been chosen over another as a vehicle for expressing ostensibly traditional rivalries and allegiances. Nor does it account for *changes* in the absolute and relative strength of the various parties. It cannot explain, for instance, why the PSI did so well in the 1955 elections but declined thereafter, or why the popularity of the PKI rose so dramatically in Bali in the late 1950s and early 1960s. Finally, it offers no clue to the way in which old or new rivalries were transformed into widespread political violence. If political party conflict really was simply a matter of "ancient grudges," why had they never before resulted in the murder of tens of thousands of people?

It seems clear that we must look beyond "traditional" rivalries and allegiances to examine both the historical and political dialectic through which old conflicts became new ones. We must trace the process by which the content, the character, and the significance of "traditional" cleavages in Bali changed over time. The bitterness and rivalry between groups—even "traditional" groups—did not emerge from thin air, or from an unchanging cultural or social system; they had historical, political, and economic origins. And as such rivalries came to be expressed in terms of party politics during the 1950s and 1960s, their significance continued to change. The structure, style, and rhetoric of the various political parties, as well as the system of party competition itself, necessarily altered the nature and the terms of the conflict. What might in other circumstances have been a relatively benign rivalry between neighboring villages or puri—played out through competitive cultural display—could, through the mechanism of party competition, be transformed into a violent conflict involving public disputes in abusive

---

[51] Clifford Geertz, *Peddlers and Princes: Social Development and Economic Change in Two Indonesian Towns* (Chicago: University of Chicago Press, 1963), p. 22 (emphasis added).

[52] Geertz, "Balinese Village." The Geertzes provide some—albeit rather cursory—evidence in support of these claims in a joint study based on field work conducted in the late 1950s. Discussing the hamlet of Tihingan, they note that political party affiliation overlapped almost exactly with the pattern of kin-group competition. See Geertz and Geertz, *Kinship in Bali.*

language, physical clashes over the use of temple or village land, or even the murder of one's rivals.

Anthropological and historical works written since 1965 show a greater appreciation of these historical processes, while demonstrating the importance of Balinese cultural conceptions and institutions in mediating, interpreting, and giving significance to political party membership and competition.[53] Regrettably, they still tell only part of the story. Missing is any serious treatment of the *political* sphere—the fight for political office, for political authority, and for the benefits derived from them. Indeed, there remains a strong tendency to view modern "politics" as essentially alien to Bali, and to regard Balinese as the innocent victims of a process in which they had no real interest. As one author would have it, the Balinese, who "were not much interested in national politics and not much attracted to the national parties," were subjected to a "massive and sinister politicization" conducted by a "clique of Sukarnoists."[54]

Perhaps because so much of what is written about Bali takes the hamlet, the kin group, or some other subgrouping as the basic unit of analysis, we still have only a very vague idea of what happened politically in Bali as a whole during the years 1950 to 1965. For example, we do not yet have any detailed analysis of the general characteristics and patterns—sociological, political, geographical—of the leadership and social bases of the major political parties in Bali. Nor do we have a clear picture of political processes in the legislative and executive organs at the provincial and subprovincial levels. Even less well understood are the ways in which the national political context structured such processes and affected local political choices and conflicts. It is to these questions that we may now turn.

National Parties and Local Politics

The tradition of formal political party organization was not well established in Bali at the time of independence. Most parties had taken the Java-based Republican parties as their model, both organizationally and ideo-

---

[53] Boon, for example, shows how a clan leader who had been a committed Republican during the Revolution used the extended family (ancestor-group) structure as the basis for his partisan activities in the postindependence period, with the result that the entire clan of about 500 people became politicized, and uniformly pro-PSI. See Boon, *Anthropological Romance of Bali*, pp. 71–88. Vickers, *Bali*, describes how conflicts over caste, religion, and cultural identity, dating at least since the colonial period, came to be construed during the 1950s and 1960s in terms of a split between the PNI and the PKI. He also describes the efforts of parties and political leaders to gain control of the cultural and religious agenda in Bali. Particularly useful is his treatment of the struggle to control the sacred rituals surrounding Eka Dasa Rudra in 1963. See esp. pp. 147, 161, 164–69.

[54] According to this view, "what was most disturbing of all was that Bali, the island of religion and culture, was being drenched with the most poisonous of politics. The mystical Balinese were being converted into political zealots, mouthing the Sukarno slogans about death to all demons and monsters, suddenly no mere mythical creatures but actual living persons": Hanna, *Bali Profile*, p. 111.

logically. It was natural, therefore, that with the imminent victory of the Republic, political activists in Bali looked first to the most prominent national parties, such as the PNI and the PSI, for leadership. At the same time, these parties were seeking actively to expand their influence in the former federal states immediately after the transfer of sovereignty.

The structural positions of the national political parties were enormously important in the development of support locally. A party's control over a government ministry, for example, gave it a distinct advantage over its competitors among certain sectors of the population, both because of the prestige it thus acquired and because of the real benefits—positions in the state bureaucracy, for example—that it was able to pass on to its members. At the same time, a reputation as a staunch critic of the central government clearly increased a party's appeal among a variety of dissatisfied groups. Whatever their position vis-à-vis the state bureaucracy, successful political parties offered substantial opportunities for personal advancement in their own organizations.

The timing of the first wave of party mobilization in Bali was crucial, because it determined the structural parameters within which local party competition would take place. In the early 1950s, both the PNI and the PSI had prominent positions within the central state apparatus; by late 1953 the PNI was well established as a major governing party, and the PSI had begun to develop a record of opposition to the central government. This situation influenced the pattern of party support in Bali, though not always in obvious ways. The PSI, for example, seems to have gained a part of its following as a result of its strong position within the government between 1950 and 1952, and somewhat later to have won the support of various disaffected groups.

Among the chief channels of political mobilization in Bali were the loyalty networks of former pemuda and guerrillas. The most prominent pemuda leaders commanded followings of several hundred people, who in turn could influence the political choice of family, friends, or hamlet members. Moreover, by virtue of the process of Republicanization begun in 1950, many gained positions of local political and administrative authority—for example, as punggawa, perbekel, or village head—which further enhanced their capacity to influence those in their area of authority.[55]

Initial efforts to maintain a united front among pemuda did not last long. The combination of political ambition, personal animosity, and splits from the revolutionary period sent pemuda leaders into each of the three major parties. Accordingly, former revolutionary base areas became centers of support for different political parties.[56] Splits within the pemuda group remained an important political issue through the 1960s. In Tabanan, for

---

[55] Interviews with Wayan Rana (former punggawa of Kuta and PSI member), 5 September 1986, Denpasar, and Ketut Gde Dharmayudha (former assistant punggawa [manca] of Batubulan, Gianyar, and PSI member), 28 July 1986, Desa Celuk, Gianyar.

[56] The guerrilla base of Selemadeg (west Tabanan), for instance, became a center of PNI strength, while Wongaya Gde (north Tabanan) and Panji (Buleleng) became solidly PKI.

example, where PNI-PKI confrontations had become serious by 1964, the bupati argued that "this state of chaos has emerged because there are deep conflicts among the former supporters of the Revolution, and among the former guerrilla themselves."[57] Although it is not possible to show any simple correlation between the major pemuda groupings from the revolutionary period and later party choice, some general patterns will become clear as we discuss each of the major parties.[58]

Because the pemuda were internally divided, and because they were not alone in the struggle for local-state power, they allied with a variety of other social and political forces. Among them were older prewar nationalists who had played a central role in the legal struggle during the Revolution. Many of these men and women were already affiliated with one of the national parties before 1950, or had close personal ties to party leaders in Java. Also prominent among these allies were still-powerful local officials, bureaucrats, and aristocratic elites with questionable nationalist credentials, who now sought security in one of the large nationalist parties. The PNI and the PSI, in fact, actively sought the support of such men, recognizing that they, like the pemuda leaders, constituted a good avenue for securing a wide political base.

The party groupings that resulted from such maneuvering and calculation were not particularly tight ideologically, and they were prone to factionalism and desertion. Such major policy issues as land reform and broad structural changes such as the introduction of Guided Democracy, however, produced realignments of party allegiance. Moreover, the banning of the PSI in 1960, up to that point the second most powerful party in Bali, necessarily led to major shifts in party affiliation. These factors produced increasing ideological polarization in Bali by 1965, and, as we will see, a clearer reflection of class differences in the followings of the major parties, the PNI and the PKI.

Partai Sosialis Indonesia

The PSI was strongly represented in the Natsir cabinet (September 1950–March 1951), with a PSI sympathizer in the post of deputy prime minister and others as ministers of the interior, defense, trade and industry, agriculture, and communications. Even in the PNI/Masyumi-dominated Wilopo cabinet (April 1952–June 1953), PSI men held the portfolios of Justice, Defense, and Finance. The PSI also had a strong position in the civil service, although it began to be undermined toward the end of 1953.[59] Finally, the

---

[57] "Bertekad Bulat Achiri Pertentangan2," *Suara Indonesia* (Denpasar), 9 May 1964.

[58] One of the reasons it is difficult to generalize is that the patterns of choice and of rivalry varied from region to region. In large part, this was a consequence of the dispersed character of the guerrilla struggle. Few guerrilla leaders had followings that extended beyond a single kingdom, and cooperation and contact among these leaders was limited.

[59] The weakening of the PSI position in the civil service was primarily a consequence of the personnel policies of the first Ali Sastroamijoyo cabinet (July 1953–July 1955). See Feith, *Decline of Constitutional Democracy*, pp. 366–73.

PSI had considerable influence within the Army. Thus, although the PSI did not have a broad mass base nationally, its control of strategic positions within the central state apparatus initially made it an appealing option to a variety of local groups, among them some aristocrats and civil servants with questionable nationalist credentials who sought protection within a legitimate nationalist party.

By the time of the 1955 national elections, the PSI was no longer a part of the governing coalition; in fact, it was planted quite firmly in the opposition camp. As early as 1952, for example, the PSI had joined elements of the military in criticizing Parliament for meddling in Army affairs. From 1953 to 1955 it was excluded from the Ali cabinet and was being rapidly squeezed out of important positions in the civil service. To some extent, then, the support gained by the PSI in Bali by 1955 must be seen as a local manifestation of opposition to the increasingly dominant PNI and to the central government more generally.

In Bali the PSI had four main sources of leadership: a group of older nationalist intellectuals, many with Taman Siswa backgrounds; a significant segment of former pemuda; elements in the Army; and some still-influential aristocratic families. Each group was able to mobilize, in turn, a substantial number of followers in support of the party. Although this broad coalition contributed to its unusual electoral success in Bali, the diversity of the PSI leadership and social base meant that the potential for factionalism and defection was considerable.

The early core of the PSI in Bali was a small group of older nationalists and intellectuals, many of whom had close personal ties with the Javanese Taman Siswa teacher and later PSI activist Wiyono Suryokusumo.[60] He took the initiative in organizing the PSI in Bali, though he worked through Captain Daino, a young Javanese political officer in the Ministry of Defense, who went to Bali with Republican troops in mid-1950. Before his departure, Daino met with Suryokusumo and obtained a list of about forty former friends and Taman Siswa graduates. Once in Bali, he traveled about by jeep to encourage them to establish local branches of the PSI.[61] In later years Daino continued to act as intermediary, traveling frequently to Bali to relay news of developments at the center.[62]

The personal prestige and influence of Wiyono Suryokusumo and PSI

[60] During the Revolution, Wiyono Suryokusumo had served with the national army in West Java. In 1950 he worked in the Political Department of the Ministry of Defense and was co-head of the Political Section of the central PSI leadership. See Kementerian Penerangan Republik Indonesia, *Kepartaian di Indonesia* (Jakarta, 1951).

[61] The early core of the PSI in Bali included I Nyoman Pegeg, I Gusti Ketut Reti, Ida Bagus Wisnem Manuaba, I Gusti Gde Raka, Wayan Samba, and Ida Bagus Pidada. Interview with Ida Bagus Wisnem Manuaba, 10 July 1986, Tabanan, and Ketut Gde Dharmayudha, 28 July 1986, Desa Celuk, Gianyar.

[62] Daino claims that the order to set up the PSI in Bali came from the secretary general of the party, Sitorus, but he acknowledges Wiyono Suryokusumo's role in providing the necessary information and contacts. Interviews with Daino, 2, 3 July 1986, Yogyakarta; Nyoman Pegeg, 16 September 1986, Denpasar; and I Gusti Ketut Reti, 30 July 1986, Denpasar.

leader Sutan Sjahrir were important in the further development of the PSI core in Bali. This was very much in keeping with the cadre style of the party generally. The PSI's reputation as an elitist party of westernized intellectuals, however, was only partly deserved in Bali, because it was here, arguably, that the party went furthest in consciously mobilizing a mass base before the 1955 elections. As the elections approached, awareness emerged within the party that something like the mass mobilization strategies of the PNI and the PKI might be necessary to ensure electoral success. While the PSI stuck fairly firmly to its cadre-party principles at the national level, in Bali the quiet tension between the proponents of cadre- and mass-style politics was resolved in favor of the latter.[63]

The victory of the PSI's "mass line" appears to have come at a regional party meeting in 1954. Addressing the meeting was a national PSI leader who had recently returned from Yugoslavia.[64] He argued that this was the time and Bali the place to experiment with a more popular form of party organization. The ensuing debate led to the resignation from leadership posts of at least two of the local proponents of the "cadre line" and to the election of a number of "mass line" advocates, including I Made Sugitha, who became secretary of the PSI-Sunda Kecil, and I Gusti Bonjoran.[65]

Although advocates of the cadre line remained in the party, the change in leadership marked the beginning of a conscious PSI strategy of grass-roots mobilization in Bali. Village cooperatives, many of them set up by former pemuda, were one avenue of PSI mobilization. The PSI received the bulk of its support in areas where cooperatives were already most fully developed.[66] After 1954 the party also employed a strategy of "approaching former

[63] Interviews with Nyoman Pegeg, 31 July 1986, Denpasar, and Ida Bagus Wisnem Manuaba, 10 July 1986, Tabanan. A similar policy split developed within the national PSI leadership shortly after the 1955 elections. The issue appears to have been the advisability of cooperation with Sukarno in an effort to secure a mass base. On one side of the question was Sitorus, who favored cooperation; on the other was Sjahrir, who took a more cautious view. Interview by George McT. Kahin with an anonymous PSI official, January 1971, Jakarta.

[64] Interviews with Soebadio Sastroasoetomo, 25 December 1985, Jakarta, and Nyoman Pegeg, 31 July 1986, Denpasar. Pegeg referred to the speaker as "a young PSI activist from Jakarta who had just returned from Yugoslavia." This may have been Soedjatmoko, a leading intellectual with close ties to the PSI, though never actually a party member. He visited Yugoslavia at this time on a tour through Europe, and was said to have been deeply impressed by Milovan Djilas. It may also have been Soebadio, who went to Yugoslavia at this time to attend a meeting of the Socialist International and also met Djilas.

[65] I Gusti Gde Raka, the head of PSI-Sunda Kecil, and Nyoman Pegeg, the party treasurer, resigned: interview with Nyoman Pegeg, 16 September 1986, Denpasar. Sugitha had been a schoolteacher before the war and had joined the pemuda organization PRI in 1945. His activities during the Revolution are unclear, but in 1950 he became a member of the Executive Council of the KPNI pemuda organization. He officially joined the PSI only in 1954. Bonjoran was also a former pemuda, and one of the thirteen called to Jakarta by Sukarno in 1951.

[66] The co-op movement in Tabanan, according to the PSI leader Wisnem Manuaba, "began well before anybody had heard of the PSI, but the co-ops later became the base for the party there": Interview with Ida Bagus Wisnem Manuaba, 10 July 1986, Tabanan. Co-ops were also an important base for PSI support in west Gianyar: interview with Ketut Gde Dharmayudha, 28 July 1986, Desa Celuk, Gianyar.

pemuda at the local level as a way of gaining the support of a whole hamlet or village."[67] This tactic entailed a much closer cooperation with former pemuda. In the campaigns for the 1955 elections, armed gangs also operated on behalf of the party. The shift to a grass-roots strategy and the use of such gangs accounted for the strong electoral showing of the PSI in Bali. Those changes also help to explain why PSI support was so great in the former base areas of the Revolution, Tabanan, Badung, and west Gianyar.

Support for the PSI was strongest among the PDRI pemuda (i.e., those who had not "surrendered" in May 1948) and among those of the DPRI who had returned to the mountains after their release from prison in 1949. These men and women shared a sentiment of "bitterness" (*sakit hati*) and dissatisfaction with the results of independence. In particular, they were angry that so many former "collaborators" had remained in positions of power after 1950. There was also a powerful residue of distrust toward those DPRI pemuda who had joined the PNI shortly after independence. In general, they felt that the PNI had become a haven for opportunists and former collaborators, and too strongly oriented to civil servants.[68]

There were other reasons too for PSI support among some pemuda. One of the most important was their link with the Army. Four of the top PDRI leaders—Poleng, Cilik, Tanaya, and Sandat—had joined the Army after coming down from the mountains in January 1950.[69] Through their positions in the Army, they were able to build their pemuda and family networks into a broad base of support for the PSI. Poleng, for example, commanded the loyalty of a large number of former pemuda and ordinary villagers in Tabanan and north Badung, his base area during the Revolution. Family ties with other influential figures in the area—his father, a pedanda (Brahamana priest), had been a member of the Tabanan Raad van Kerta, and the PSI leader Ida Bagus Wisnem Manuaba was a cousin—enhanced Poleng's own influence and that of the PSI. Moreover, because of his position in the military, particularly as District Military Officer for Bali between 1954 and 1956, this loyalty network, and therefore also the network of PSI support, extended a good deal further.[70] Finally, as we shall see, the PSI was able to make use of the Army link to coerce recalcitrant voters.

Through various avenues other former pemuda with PSI sympathies were also able to develop the party's mass base. Ketut Gde Dharmayudha, a comrade of Poleng, had a substantial following in the Republican base area of west Gianyar, which had led to his appointment as assistant punggawa of

[67] Interview with I Gusti Ketut Reti, 30 July 1986, Denpasar.
[68] Ibid.
[69] Interview with Poleng (Ida Bagus Tantra), 11 April 1986, Denpasar.
[70] Poleng took this post sometime at the end of 1954 and kept it until the middle of 1956, when he was promoted to captain. At the same time he was appointed to the Command Staff of Infantry Regiment 26/VII under the newly appointed commander, Lt. Col. Minggu. See Angkatan Bersenjata Republik Indonesia, Dinas Sejarah KODAM XVI/Udayana, *Komando Daerah Militer XVI/Udayana Dalam Lintasan Sejarah* (Denpasar, 1982), pp. 48–51.

Batubulan (west Gianyar) in May 1951. He was able to use his political authority there and his position in the cooperative organization Ikatan Tani Indonesia (Indonesian Farmer's League), or ITI, to develop support for the PSI.[71] A similar situation prevailed in the district of Kuta, west of Denpasar. There the former punggawa was replaced in 1950 by Wayan Rana, a PSI sympathizer, who supported the party's bid for power in 1955. Most of the perbekel in his district, moreover, were former pemuda who were personally loyal to him. They included Poleng, whose position in the local military apparatus made Rana's job as punggawa immeasurably easier: "Without a close friend in the Army, in those days a punggawa would have been in big trouble."[72]

In addition to its pemuda base, the party owed a good deal of its strength to the support of precisely those "feudal" elements against whom the pemuda had ostensibly fought. This was particularly the case in Gianyar, where the raja (Anak Agung Gde Oka) and his brother (Anak Agung Gde Agung) were known to be PSI sympathizers. The former NIT prime minister, Agung, was politically astute enough to understand the need to patch up his nationalist credentials, and he did so by joining ranks with the PSI as early as 1950. Most former PSI leaders in Bali now prefer to ignore his role during the Revolution, focusing instead on his "capability" as a justification for his acceptance into the party.[73] According to Ida Bagus Wisnem Manuaba, for instance, "The PSI did not want to join in the business of judging people for their alleged past sins; it preferred to judge them solely on the basis of their capability. Anak Agung's capability was beyond dispute."[74] Outside the party, however—and even in some quarters of the national PSI leadership—Anak Agung's leap into the arms of the PSI was, and is still, viewed as an act of pure political opportunism.[75] However, the opportunism was not only on Anak Agung's part. The PSI leaders recognized that the influence of the Puri Gianyar was still considerable, and they were more than happy to take advantage of that influence.[76]

---

[71] Interview with Ketut Gde Dharmayudha, 28 July 1986, Desa Celuk, Gianyar. Dharmayudha was a member of the Gianyar Executive Council (BPH) until October 1963, when he was dismissed in connection with the "retooling" of PSI members. See *Suara Indonesia* (Denpasar), 22 October 1963.

[72] According to Rana, the usual procedure for conducting affairs as punggawa in those days was to "first get in touch with old friends from the Revolution": interview with Wayan Rana, 21 September 1986, Denpasar.

[73] Interviews with Nyoman Pegeg, 16 November 1986, Denpasar; Daino, 3 July 1986, Yogyakarta; and Ida Bagus Wisnem Manuaba, 10 July 1986, Tabanan.

[74] Interview with Ida Bagus Wisnem Manuaba, 10 July 1986, Tabanan.

[75] Interviews with Soebadio Sastrosatomo, 25 December 1985, Jakarta; Dr. and Mrs. Made Jelantik, 4 September 1986, Denpasar; and Made Wija Kusuma, 22 March 1986. In an interview on 2 July 1986 in Yogyakarta, Daino claimed that Anak Agung explicitly sought the protection of the PSI, and in return promised to support the development of cooperatives in Gianyar.

[76] Other aristocratic houses also became centers of PSI strength, including Geria Jaksa Manuaba in Tabanan and Puri Jerokuta in Denpasar. These houses, however, had a longer association with the nationalist cause and should not therefore be grouped among the aristo-

For a time it proved advantageous to the party to have this support "from above," to complement the support from other sectors. After 1955, however, this alliance became increasingly difficult to sustain. Basic differences in ideology and in the social base of the party were brought into sharper focus by developments at the national and local levels. Splits emerged, for example, in the course of the debate over the administrative status of the former kingdoms of Bali in late 1957. Some people saw the demand for "special region" (*daerah istimewa*) status put forward by the raja of Gianyar and supported by the PSI leadership in Bali as an unblushingly "feudal" move. It led to defections by leftists and former pemuda in the PSI, and a further isolation of its conservative element.[77]

The fate of the PSI after the party was banned in 1960 gave some indication of the extent of internal ideological and social divisions at that time.[78] Supporters began to move into the PNI, the PKI, the Partindo, and a variety of smaller parties such as IPKI (the League of Upholders of Indonesian Independence).[79] The more conservative elements appear to have moved to the PNI, which by this time expressed the same anticommunist sentiments that the PSI had espoused earlier. Available evidence indicates that PSI members in some former Republican base areas moved en masse to the PKI.[80] Though the extent of such defections is difficult to gauge, it is likely that a considerable number who transferred their allegiance to the PKI after 1960 were attracted by that party's position on land reform.[81]

Partai Nasionalis Indonesia

The rapid spread of the PNI to areas outside of Java after 1949 owed a great deal to the party's ability to ride the expanding Republican bureau-

---

cratic opportunists. Anak Agung Alit Raka Made Angkasa of Puri Jerokuta and Ida Bagus Wisnem Manuaba were both Taman Siswa products with close ties to Wiyono Suryokusumo: interviews with Anak Agung Alit Raka Made Angkasa, 29 May 1986, Denpasar, and Ida Bagus Wisnem Manuaba, 10 July 1986, Tabanan.

[77] For details of the debate in Gianyar over daerah istimewa status and indications that the debate was leading to internal splits and defections, see contemporary newspaper accounts: "Resolusi Tuntut Djadi Daerah Swatantra," 12 November 1957; "Sidang Luar Biasa DPRD Swapradja Gianjar," 12, 13 November 1957; "A.A.G. Oka Takut Kehilangan Pengaruh," 21 November 1957; "Hukum Rimba di Gianjar—A.A.G. Oka Pertahankan Keras Feodalisme Kolot," 30 November 1957, all in *Suara Indonesia* (Denpasar).

[78] Interviews with Nyoman Pegeg, 16 September 1986, Denpasar, and Wedastera Suyasa, 24 February 1986, Denpasar.

[79] Many PSI leaders remained in positions of political and administrative authority through 1964, despite the banning of the party in 1960.

[80] The village of Beringkit (west Badung), for example, solidly PSI up to 1960, became more or less completely PKI by 1965: interview with Ida Bagus Mantra Manuaba (PSI leader, Tabanan), 10 July 1986, Tabanan.

[81] There is also speculation that many former pemuda chose the PKI over the PNI at this time because the head of the provincial Veterans' Affairs Office from 1950 to 1966, the Javanese Subroto Aryo Mataram, was said to be sympathetic to the party. According to unconfirmed reports, he was forced to resign in 1966 because of his alleged PKI affiliation: interview with Nyoman Pegeg, 31 July 1986, Denpasar.

cracy.[82] The first governor of Sunda Kecil, Susanto Tirtoprojo, was an avowed member of the PNI. Indeed, in 1951 he was suggested as a candidate for the prime ministership, at the time of the formation of the Sukiman cabinet. The next governor, Sarimin Reksodihardjo (1952–57), was also a PNI man. The succession of PNI governors undoubtedly influenced the political orientation of the corps of government servants who worked under their authority. The PNI's control of such key local government offices as Public Works throughout this period may well have drawn many people to the party for purely opportunistic reasons.[83]

Significant personnel changes in the civil service under the first Ali Sastroamijoyo cabinet (July 1953–July 1955) further strengthened the position of the PNI, especially in the key ministries of the Interior, Justice, and Economic affairs. This had the effect of cementing the political party loyalties of PNI members, as well as encouraging others to join.[84] The relatively long tenure of the first Ali cabinet in the years before the elections no doubt also enhanced the PNI's position in some sectors, as it gained a reputation as the governing party.[85] These structural factors had weight in the early development of a PNI base in Bali, particularly in the local civil service and among a large number of former "collaborators."

Like the PSI, the PNI-Bali also seems to have had the active support of elements of the security forces before and during the 1955 elections. But whereas the PSI had links with the Army, the PNI's backing came principally from the police, whose support may well have influenced the level of electoral support for the party in 1955. According to a leading PSI figure in Tabanan, "Maybe the PSI would have become more powerful if in 1955 before the general elections [pro-PNI] police had not entered and beaten people in the village areas."[86]

An additional factor working to the PNI's advantage was the fact that it was understood (though perhaps mistakenly) to be the party of Sukarno, who already by 1950 had a considerable following in Bali. In the early 1950s the party still had a credible nationalist reputation. Under the national leadership of Sidik Joyosukarto (until 1955), the PNI espoused a radical secular nationalist ideology that had an understandable appeal to Bali's Republicans. The fear of Islamic political domination and proselytization,

[82] On the PNI during this period, see J. Eliseo Rocamora, "Nationalism in Search of an Ideology: Indonesia's Nationalist Party 1946–1965," Ph.D. diss., Cornell University, 1974.

[83] Interview with I Gde Oki (former Public Works Department employee), 11 July 1986, Tabanan. Rocamora argues that those who joined the PNI after about 1954 were far more likely to be opportunists than those who had joined before the war or during the Revolution: *PNI 1963–1965, Menyingkap Kehidupan Sebuah Partai Politik di Indonesia* (Yogyakarta: CV Kaliwangi, 1958), p. 12.

[84] Feith, *Decline of Constitutional Democracy*, p. 371.

[85] Together with Masyumi, the PNI also formed the core of every national cabinet from April 1951 to 1955.

[86] Quoted in Boon, *Anthropological Romance of Bali*, p. 80.

which reached a peak in Bali in the early 1950s, no doubt increased the appeal of the PNI's secular (and anti-Masyumi) nationalist rhetoric.

The PNI-Bali grew from the GNI, established by Bali's moderate nationalists in August 1949. The formation of the first branches of the party, in Singaraja, Tabanan, and Jembrana, involved the absorption of the existing GNI organization and leadership into the PNI. Like the GNI before it, the PNI in Bali officially opposed the continuation of a variety of "feudal" institutions and practices. In the early 1950s, for example, it sought the abolition of certain restrictions on intercaste marriages[87] and in 1957 it campaigned actively to have the former kingdoms designated as "ordinary regions" (*daerah biasa*) rather than "special regions" (*daerah istimewa*). These positions seemed to imply opposition to "feudal" prerogatives, and to this extent they attracted many genuine Republicans to the side of the PNI.

Yet if the PNI was opposed in principle to "feudalism" like the GNI it did not object at all to influential aristocrats with "feudal" pasts and inclinations who were prepared to support it. The rajas of Klungkung and Karangasem, two of the most notorious collaborators during the Revolution, became PNI supporters; they were most welcome because the substantial personal followings they commanded could be easily transformed into mass support for the party.[88] Still, not all of the aristocrats who joined the PNI can be easily dismissed as political opportunists. As we have seen, there were noble houses with sincere Republican sympathies during the Revolution, and many of them supported the PNI after 1950. The Puri Satria of Denpasar and the former raja of Buleleng,[89] for example, were among the first to support the PNI in 1950. In fact, a PNI congress was held in the Puri Satria in September 1950.[90]

The pemuda who became active in the PNI were principally former DPRI leaders who had *not* returned to the mountains after the May 1948 "surrender." Though they had been committed Republicans, they included some of the more politically conservative within the pemuda group. Nyoman Mantik, for example, who had spent most of the Revolution in Yogyakarta at the Bali liaison office, was a staunch anticommunist. As early as 1957, he had launched a wholesale attack on the PKI and, warning of the dangers of a communist coup, had called on the president to ban the party.[91] In 1958,

---

[87] Interview with Wedastera Suyasa, 25 February 1986, Denpasar.

[88] A branch of the PNI was set up in Klungkung in June 1950: *Penindjau*, 28 June 1950. Also backing the PNI were a large number of smaller noble houses, such as Puri Mengwi, which were still influential in their own districts.

[89] It was Mr. Jelantik who became PNI; his brother, Anak Agung Nyoman Panji Tisna, was active in the PRN (Partai Rakyat Nasional—National People's party).

[90] *Berita Nusantara*, 18 September 1950.

[91] Interview with Nyoman Mantik, 5 April 1986, Tabanan. Mantik claims that he reiterated his warning in a private meeting with Sukarno in the same year, but that Sukarno remained unconvinced. After the 1965 coup, Mantik worked hard to "Golkarize" the PNI-Bali, which essentially meant purging PNI-affiliated organizations of Sukarnoist elements.

when his bid for the governorship was thwarted by Sukarno's selection of Suteja, Mantik began to accuse Suteja of communist sympathies. As a result, subsequent initiatives by the national PNI leadership to seek Governor Suteja's patronage for the PNI-Bali were stymied.

Mantik was assisted in his campaign by the virulently anticommunist Wedastera Suyasa.[92] Characterized by others as bellicose and temperamental, Wedastera has described his own attitude toward confrontations with the PKI in revealing terms: "Ida Bagus Dupem [of the PKI-Bali] once sent a messenger suggesting a cease-fire between the PNI and the PKI. I refused the offer. 'Go ahead and see if you can beat us,' I said, 'and we will do the same. That is the objective of the Revolution.'"[93] More than any other local PNI figures, it was these former pemuda—Mantik and Wedastera—who were responsible for the increasing political polarization in Bali after 1958.

Less stridently anticommunist were the former MBU-DPRI leaders Ketut Wijana and Ida Bagus Indera, who became key PNI figures in North Bali.[94] Both Indera and Wijana had been party to the negotiations leading to the May 1948 "surrender." But in late 1949 Wijana had apparently circulated a letter acknowledging that the decision had been "inappropriate" and calling on all pemuda to forget past differences and join in a united front on a nonparty basis.[95] Before long, however, Wijana had joined the PNI, thereby raising doubts about the sincerity of his united-front plan and rekindling old divisions and rivalries in the pemuda group. Particularly as the party lost its radical nationalist élan in the late 1950s, some people came to regard the pemuda who had joined it as politically ambitious. Though professing a strong Sukarnoist line throughout the 1950s and 1960s, the PNI-Bali gradually became known as a haven for opportunists and a bastion of reaction, especially on the issue of land reform. The PNI's increasingly combative stand toward "Nasakom" (Sukarno's attempt to reconcile the country's three basic political currents: nationalism, religion, and communism) and

[92] Originally from Jembrana, Wedastera earned his political wings in the student politics of Makassar during the Revolution. In the early 1950s he was active in the movement for religious reform in Bali. Later he made his way into the PNI organization, where he became one of the most active leaders throughout the Guided Democracy period. In March 1963 he was elected Third Deputy Chair of the DPD-PNI-Bali. On Wedastera Suyasa see Lane, "Wedastera Suyasa in Balinese Politics."

[93] Wedastera Suyasa, "Bung Karno Sadar, Politiknya Mengenai Bali Keliru," *Merdeka,* 12 April 1986.

[94] Indera, a former civil servant with the Health Department in Singaraja, had been active in Parindra before the war. Although he was older than the average pemuda, he fought actively with the DPRI in Buleleng. In 1950 he was one of four members on the Buleleng "Pemerintah Kolegial," and between 1950 and 1967 he served as punggawa successively in Sawan, Tejakula, and Kubutambahan, Buleleng. Wijana, a businessman-politician, was influential both in Buleleng and at the provincial level; in 1961 he was one of twenty-three members of Bali's Front Nasional. Officially he represented cooperatives, but it was clear that he also represented the PNI: interview with Ida Bagus Indera, 30 September 1986, Singaraja.

[95] Wijana to "Saudara-ku Ketjil tertjinta," 8 October 1949, Archive Cilik.

Governor Suteja contributed to its reputation for conservatism, and seems to have encouraged a number of bloc defections to the PKI and the Partindo.[96]

Partai Komunis Indonesia and Partindo

Although the PKI did not begin significant mobilization efforts in Bali until about 1953, it shared at that time some of the structural advantages of the PNI and the other parties in the governing coalition. In 1952, under the new leadership of Aidit, Nyoto, Lukman, and their colleagues, the PKI had embarked on a national united front strategy, which called for much closer cooperation with bourgeois nationalist elements, including the PNI.[97] One of the early benefits of this approach was the inclusion in the first Ali cabinet of two men sympathetic to the left—although not necessarily pro-PKI—as ministers of defense and agriculture. Gradually, too, the PKI appeared to be winning the approval of President Sukarno, who openly endorsed the party at its annual congress in March 1954.[98] These developments helped the PKI restore the nationalist credentials that in many eyes had been tarnished by its role in the Madiun uprising of 1948. Whereas it claimed a membership of less than 10,000 in 1952, by the end of 1954 it was said to have half a million members.

Of the three major parties, the PKI relied least on opportunistic alliances with former collaborators and feudal elements in Bali; this may well account for the party's relatively poor showing in 1955. Only the raja of Jembrana, Suteja's father, was said to have had any sympathy for the PKI, although it must be pointed out that he claimed to be politically neutral. The puri gained its pro-PKI reputation only in the 1960s, when there were intimations that Suteja himself was PKI. Such PNI leaders as Wedastera Suyasa then applied the PKI label rather unscrupulously in order to make it appear that the raja-puri had always had clear communist sympathies.

Though Suteja was undoubtedly a leftist, he never became a member of the PKI. In 1986 the PSI leader Ida Bagus Wisnem Manuaba had this to say about Suteja's political affiliation:

> Unofficially the PSI approached Suteja asking him to become a member, but we never did so officially as a party. Of course, Suteja never joined, and that was part of his strength—he remained at the center ensuring a fair balance of forces

[96] Interview with I Gusti Bagus Oka, 19 December 1986, Denpasar, and I Dewa Made Dhana, 7 October 1986, Singaraja.

[97] On the history of the Communist party of Indonesia, see Rex Mortimer, *Indonesian Communism under Sukarno; Ideology and Politics, 1959–1965* (Ithaca: Cornell University Press, 1974); Ruth McVey, *The Rise of Indonesian Communism* (Ithaca: Cornell University Press, 1965); and Donald Hindley, *The Communist Party of Indonesia, 1951–1963* (Berkeley and Los Angeles: University of California Press, 1964).

[98] Feith, *Decline of Constitutional Democracy*, p. 408.

in the composition of the DPRD and the DPD. . . . I do not know to this day whether he became PKI or not.[99]

When asked about his political orientation, Suteja would frequently reply: "I am a faithful student of Bung Karno [Sukarno]." And on one occasion he is reported to have said: "I say Nasakom because Bung Karno says Nasakom. If Bung Karno is a communist, then I am also a communist."[100] As Sukarno evinced a growing affinity with the PKI in the final years of the Old Order, his enemies increasingly took this leaning as evidence that Suteja was PKI. His close association with a leftist former pemuda I shall call G.P. was taken as further evidence to this effect.[101] Whether he was PKI or not, Suteja was clearly antagonistic to the growing rightist tendencies in the PNI, and for this reason he took measures to weaken the PNI. If his efforts advanced the cause of the PKI in the final years of the Old Order, the relative brevity of this alliance might help to explain the party's rather late blooming in Bali.

Suteja's "non-party" approach and eventual political trajectory were followed by a number of former pemuda with a left-nationalist orientation. Like Suteja, they originally avoided committing themselves to one of the major parties, but eventually came to be associated (often unofficially) with one of the parties of the left. Apart from Suteja and G.P., this group included many of those who had founded Gerpindo in 1949 and helped to form the KPNI in 1950.[102] Few of these pemuda leaders appeared to endorse any political party openly until well after 1955.

The exception was the Biro Pancasila, a locally based veterans' party established in 1954 by members of this pemuda group. This party aimed to put an end to the warring between the various pemuda factions that had begun to split off into the major national parties. Its candidates for the Constituent Assembly elections included I.B.S., W.K., and G.P.[103] Although it was endorsed by Suteja, the party won only one seat in Bali's Regional Assembly (DPRD-Bali). This outcome was symptomatic of the dependent character of Balinese politics at the time.[104] No party, particularly not one with only local resources, could expect to challenge the large Java-based organizations.

[99] Interview with Ida Bagus Wisnem Manuaba, 10 July 1986, Tabanan.
[100] "Andaikata Diganti, Penggantinja Pasti Veteran," *Suara Indonesia* (Denpasar), 21 August 1963.
[101] To protect their relatives and friends, only the initials of persons identified here as PKI and Partindo members or supporters are given. There were rumors that Suteja had planned to appoint G.P. as vice-governor but that in anticipation of a PNI backlash, he had simply kept him as a close personal adviser. In 1964 and 1965, Suteja referred with some frequency to the significance of Marxism for the Indonesian situation. See, for example, "Peladjari Situasi Dan Marxisme," *Suara Indonesia* (Denpasar) 14 April 1964.
[102] Pendit, *Bali Berdjuang* (1954), p. 220.
[103] See Indonesia, Kementerian Penerangan, *Daftar Tjalon Tetap Anggota Konstituante Tahun 1954* (Jakarta, 1955).
[104] Interview with Meganada (former vice-head of Yayasan Kebaktian Pejuang-Bali, 1950–65), 22 September 1986, Singaraja.

Perhaps in recognition of this fact, and perhaps following Suteja's initiative, in the early 1960s some among the pemuda group became visibly active in the PKI, while others appeared to be behind the establishment of a Bali branch of the left-nationalist party Partindo. The Partindo was formed nationally in 1958 by a PNI splinter group opposed to the conservative leadership of the party under Suwiryo. Ideologically much closer to the PKI, it was, as we shall see, highly critical of PNI foot-dragging on land reform in later years.[105] The Bali branch of the Partindo was set up in 1961.[106] In the local politics of late Guided Democracy, the PKI and Partindo were virtually indistinguishable. Both pushed hard for the "Nasakomization" of Bali's political institutions and for the implementation of land reform; and both suffered for their alleged complicity in the unsuccessful coup of 1 October 1965.[107] The pemuda leaders associated with PKI and Partindo were among the main targets of the PNI's anger in the backlash that followed.

Balinese detractors in the PSI and PNI portrayed the PKI as a party of atheists bent on "the desecration of all their cultural institutions."[108] Following a long intellectual tradition of political conservatism, outside observers have tended to sympathize uncritically with this view, lending it an aura of respectability. While there is of course some truth in the suggestion that the PKI-affiliated association known as Lekra (Lembaga Kebudayaan Rakyat, or Institute for People's Culture) was campaigning to introduce new political criteria in the judgment of artistic merit, it is not true that the PKI-Bali, broadly speaking, aimed to destroy or undermine Balinese culture. Nevertheless, these allegations—consciously generated by PNI and PSI leaders in Bali—contributed significantly to the frenzied animosity toward the PKI in the 1960s, and provided a sort of moral and cultural justification for the annihilation of its members after the October 1965 coup.

Political Conflict under Guided Democracy

Balinese politics in the 1950s and 1960s was driven principally by a struggle for control of the executive and legislative arms of the local state apparatus and articulated through political party competition. Political conflict also overlapped with disputes over religious, social, and cultural prerogatives and over access to land and other economic resources. Under Guided Democracy this competition came increasingly to be fought on the

[105] Interview with I Gusti Bagus Oka, 19 December 1986, Denpasar. Also see Rocamora, *PNI 1963–1965*, pp. 16–17.

[106] The first Partindo-Bali Congress was held 31 July–1 August 1962 in Denpasar. See *Suara Indonesia* (Denpasar), 28 July 1962.

[107] Partindo-Bali called, for example, for the ouster of those in the local government who were "anti-Nasakom, communistophobic, and cause divisions in national unity": *Suara Indonesia* (Denpasar), 22 October 1963.

[108] Hanna, *Bali Profile*, p. 111.

14. Urban women holding a banner—"Indonesia's youth are ready to liberate Irian Jaya"—at a demonstration in Denpasar, Bali, in early 1963. Encouraged by President Sukarno and by the PNI and the PKI, Balinese politics grew increasingly militant between 1960 and 1965. In the countryside, political disagreements and conflicts over land often led to violence. (*Indonesia, Department of Information, Denpasar*)

streets or in the fields, in the form of mass rallies, demonstrations, and unilateral land seizures (*aksi sepihak*). By 1965 Bali's politics had become sharply polarized between the PNI and the PKI and their respective allies at the local and national levels.

By the 1960s the PKI and Partindo controlled, or had close links with, substantial elements of the local state machinery in Bali. Governor Suteja used his executive authority to place party members and other leftists in positions of political power. In 1965 three of the eight kingdoms (by then called *kabupaten*) in Bali—Jembrana, Buleleng, and Gianyar—had pro-PKI or Partindo chief executives (*bupati*). The head of the Office of Information was a left Sukarnoist, and his wife was said to be the Gerwani representative on the Front Nasional Bali.[109] A Partindo member, I.B.K., had been appointed to head the Bali office of the state tourist agency, NITOUR. Finally, the

[109] I have been unable to confirm that his wife, Nyonya R.P., was the Gerwani representative, so this information must be treated with caution. It is clear, however, that she was one of four "vice-secretaries" of the Front Nasional. Even in 1961 the PKI and Partindo were reasonably well represented in the Front Nasional. See "Pengurus Front Nasional Bali," *Suara Indonesia* (Denpasar), 25 April 1961.

chief agricultural inspector for Bali, S., was said to be sympathetic to the PKI.

While this level of influence in the local-state apparatus was fundamental to PKI/Partindo strength, it was in fact insufficient to guarantee these parties anything like a monopoly of power locally. Suteja's support for the PKI/Partindo was of relatively recent vintage, and as a consequence, large sectors of the local civil service and the legislature were still controlled by the PNI and even the PSI. Moreover, the Executive Councils (Badan Pemerintahan Harian, or BPH) at both the kabupaten and provincial levels were dominated by the PNI until early 1965.

In spite of his position as Pepelrada, then, Suteja could not act with impunity against the PNI. His authority in Bali rested heavily on his close association with Sukarno, as the circumstances of his appointment as governor in 1958 revealed. Whereas in 1950 Suteja had been nominated by a majority in Bali's Regional Assembly, in 1958 he received fewer votes than the PNI nominee, Nyoman Mantik. The PNI-Bali had expected that Jakarta would have to choose Mantik. By 1958, however, Sukarno had already begun his campaign against parliamentary democracy, and he clearly refused to be bound by the majority opinion of the local legislature three years after the elections. With some justice, supporters of Sukarno and Suteja claimed that PNI's dominance of the Regional Assembly overrepresented its actual strength among the population in 1958. The 1957 provincial council elections in Java had indicated a dramatic increase in support for the PKI, and though regional elections were never held in Bali, there was reason to believe that the parties of the left were making similar advances there, at the expense of both the PNI and the PSI.[110] Nevertheless, Sukarno's decision exacerbated tension between the PNI and PKI, and revealed clearly the depth of Suteja's political debt to Sukarno. It was this dependence on Sukarno that ultimately made Suteja's authority in Bali so tenuous and so vulnerable to a change in the balance of forces at the center.

The strength of the PSI on Bali and the influence of Anak Agung Gde Agung ensured that Sukarno and Suteja had their detractors there. The mutual distrust between Agung and Sukarno reached a critical point in August 1961, when an unsuccessful attempt was made on Sukarno's life during a trip to Makassar. The attempt came only a few weeks after an illustrious group—including foreign diplomats, national PSI leaders, and others known to oppose Sukarno—had gathered at Agung's puri in Gianyar, ostensibly for the occasion of his father's cremation.[111] Sukarno later claimed that the PSI had used this opportunity to plot his assassination.

[110] The figures for the elections in Java can be found in Hindley, *Communist Party of Indonesia*, p. 255.

[111] The date of the cremation was 18 August 1961. The guest list included Moh. Hatta, Sutan Sjahrir, Soebadio Sastroasoetomo, Sultan Hamid, Moh. Roem, and most of the ambassadors in Jakarta.

While there is no documentary proof of a plot to kill Sukarno, there is circumstantial evidence of Agung's involvement in plans to remove him from power. According to two senior PSI leaders who attended the cremation and were subsequently imprisoned, Agung arranged the Gianyar meeting with the explicit aim of gathering anti-Sukarno elements to discuss plans for a post-Sukarno regime.[112] One of these officials has also claimed that Agung organized the gathering at the behest of former U.S. ambassador Hugh S. Cumming, with whom he had been in contact at least since 1957, when he sought Cumming's support for the Permesta rebellion in Sulawesi.[113] The same PSI official has said that Agung wished to discuss the Sukarno problem in "practical" terms, which may have included plans for Sukarno's removal. In view of evidence that the CIA supported the Permesta and PRRI rebellions in the hope of undermining Sukarno, allegations of CIA involvement in an assassination attempt on him in November 1957, and evidence of U.S. complicity in the October 1965 coup and countercoup, an assassination plot in 1961 certainly cannot be ruled out.[114]

Whether or not Agung was behind a plot to kill Sukarno, his central role in an anti-Sukarnoist cabal shortly before the Makassar assassination attempt had profound political significance. It provided a pretext for the arrest of leading PSI figures, including Sutan Sjahrir and Agung, thereby definitively weakening one of Bali's major political groupings and encouraging further polarization of the PNI and PKI. Sjahrir died while undergoing medical treatment in Switzerland; all the others remained in prison until May 1966.

Like the PKI, the PNI exerted its influence by penetrating and controlling important elements of the local-state apparatus. But whereas the PKI and Partindo managed to control a number of executive posts, principally at the provincial level, the PNI relied to a great extent on its control of administrative structures, legislative bodies, and the Executive Councils (BPH) at both the provincial and kabupaten levels. Until the 1960 "retooling" of Bali's legislative bodies, the PNI held a majority of seats in the Provincial Assembly and in six of the eight kabupaten assemblies (Badung and Tabanan had PSI majorities). The "retooling" initially threatened the PNI's position by substantially reducing the number of seats allotted to political parties and by making Governor Suteja the chairman of the new assembly (DPRD-GR). It did not, however, completely undermine the party's power.

The inclusion of functional group representation under Guided Democra-

[112] Interviews by George McT. Kahin with anonymous PSI officials, January 1971, Jakarta.

[113] At that time, Cumming was head of the State Department's Division of Intelligence and Research. In 1957 John Foster Dulles had designated him as liaison officer between the State Department and the CIA. From mid-1957 to mid-1958 he was also head of a special interdepartmental committee charged with effecting political change in Indonesia—including the removal of Sukarno, or the clipping of his wings, and the suppression of the PKI. He supported the PRRI and Permesta rebellions.

[114] The issue of U.S. complicity in the October 1965 countercoup is discussed in chapter 11.

cy was initially unfavorable to the PNI position. In the 1960 Provincial Assembly, for example, the PNI held only four of the fourteen functional group seats. As the PNI-Bali found itself increasingly cut out of positions of executive authority and frustrated in formal legislative bodies, it relied ever more heavily on a strategy of mass mobilization. This was the logic of the feverish efforts to control various "functional group" constituencies, through organizations for veterans, farmers, village heads, students, and others.[115]

Suteja's unilateral efforts to control PNI mass actions and party activity in the name of peace and order provoked bitter reaction from the local PNI, led by the combative Wedastera Suyasa. The PNI accused Suteja of gross incompetence and unfairness, and began a campaign of rallies with such themes as "Retool Suteja" and "Castrate Suteja." In 1964 a parliamentary delegation visited Bali and reported that the political situation was already seriously polarized.[116] Through 1964, party activity degenerated to a state of chronic mass confrontations between PKI and PNI ormas.[117] The troubles culminated in a dramatic showdown between the governor and Wedastera at a public rally in Denpasar on 6 March 1965, and the subsequent arrest of Wedastera on Suteja's order.[118] The PNI also took the struggle against Suteja to Jakarta, demanding the central government's intervention to restore the party's legitimate political position in the local-state apparatus.

Changes in the political composition of the Executive Councils (BPH) in May 1965—brought about principally by intervention from above—substantially enhanced the position of the PKI and Partindo at the expense of the PNI. Whereas under the old setup, the PNI had held virtually every council seat at the kabupaten level, it now held only twenty-two of the new total of forty seats, while the PKI and Partindo together controlled seventeen (see Table 7). The provincial Executive Council was expanded from three to six seats, with none of the new seats being allotted to the PNI, while the PKI, Partindo, and NU each gained one. The growing strength of the PKI was also evident in the manner of appointment of the new bupati for Gianyar and Badung. The PNI and PKI were to nominate candidates for both positions,

---

[115] The PNI-affiliated organizations included BKVM (Badan Kontak Veteran Marhaenis—Marhaenist Veterans' Contact Agency), Petani (Petani Nasionalis Indonesia—Indonesian Nationalist Farmers), KPDI (Kesatuan Pamong Desa Indonesia—Indonesian Union of Village Officials), and GMNI (Gerakan Mahasiswa Nasional Indonesia—National Students' Movement of Indonesia). For some idea of the PNI's mobilization efforts, see Lane, "Wedastera Suyasa," pp. 71–78.

[116] See "Rapat Gabungan Golongan2 Ke-7," report of a DPR-GR delegation trip to Bali/Lombok, 5–14 January 1964.

[117] See "Massa Menuntut Dihukumnja Biang Keladi Rombongan Pentjulik," *Suara Indonesia* (Denpasar), 15 April 1964; "Aksi Massa Marhaen Tabanan-Djemberana-Badung di Wongaya Gde" and "Tjeramah Umum Raksasa," ibid., 5 May 1964; "Dikerojok Ber-Ramai2," ibid., 3 September 1964.

[118] Wedastera was detained first in Denpasar and then in Jakarta until 29 January 1966. See "Bung Karno Sadar Politiknja Mengenai Bali Keliru," *Merdeka*, 12 April 1986.

Table 7. Number of seats held in Bali's kabupaten and provincial Executive Councils, 1965, by party

Kabupaten	PNI	PKI	Partindo	NU	Total
Karangasem	3	1	1	0	5
Klungkung	3	2	0	0	5
Gianyar	3	2	0	0	5
Buleleng	3	1	1	0	5
Bangli	3	1	1	0	5
Badung	2	2	1	0	5
Tabanan	3	1	1	0	5
Jembrana	2	2	0	1	5
Total	—	—	—	—	—
Kubapten	22	12	5	1	40
Province	3	1	1	1	6

Source: *Fadjar* (Denpasar), 11 May 1965.

and then the PNI was to decide which of the two kabupaten it would prefer to keep. In other words, at least one of these two important areas would have a PKI bupati. In the event, the PNI "chose" Badung and left Gianyar to the PKI. These changes provide an indication of the dramatic gains made by the PKI/Partindo in the final year of the Old Order—gains that brought them to near parity with the PNI by mid-1965.

From the Revolution there emerged deep lines of conflict both between Republicans and loyalists, and within the Republican camp. The transfer of sovereignty and the expansion of the Indonesian state apparatus and political party networks shifted the political balance in Bali, allowing Republicans to gain nominal control of many political and administrative positions in 1950. The struggle to control the local state continued, however, and was articulated primarily through political party competition. Rivalries within the Republican leadership, together with the continued strength of old aristocratic elites, initially produced amorphous cross-class patterns of party affiliation, especially within the two major parties, the PNI and the PSI.

Developments at the national and local levels in the late 1950s and early 1960s—including the transition to Guided Democracy, land reform and the banning of the PSI—transformed the nature of political competition in Bali, leading to a greater ideological and class polarization between the PNI and the PKI, the new contenders for local state power. Thus, contrary to widely accepted interpretations of Balinese politics, party affiliation and competition in this period were not mere reflections of "traditional" rivalries but the products of a dynamic interplay between national and local forces, particularly the struggle for local-state power. Though political conflict again found expression in acts of violence and open confrontation, it was constrained to some extent by a delicate balance of state power available to each side of the debate. The October 1965 coup disrupted that balance, so that in the course of a few months, local power shifted dramatically away from Suteja, the PKI, and Partindo toward the PNI (and former PSI members) and their allies. This laid the structural foundation for the violence of late 1965 and 1966.

In explaining the violent, internecine quality of Balinese politics during these years this chapter has also addressed, implicitly, two broader questions. First, how can we account for the differences in the character of Bali's politics between this and other periods of its history? Why, for example, were politics in Bali not invisible or peaceful as they had been under the Dutch before the war? Second, why did Bali's politics between 1950 and 1965 not come to express regionalist or ethnic grievances and aspirations vis-à-vis the center, as was the case in so many areas outside of Java? The answer to these questions lies principally in the changing historical interaction of national and local states and political processes.

Integration into the Indonesian national state established certain structural and ideological parameters that affected political relations and the nature of political conflict in Bali. To some extent, the political authority of the protagonists in Bali always depended on their links with the central state and national-level political parties. This was, in great part, the consequence of Bali's having been integrated into national politics before any strong local state apparatus could emerge. Balinese politics, therefore, came quickly to respond to movements and initiatives from the center. This pattern was accentuated by a profound economic and military dependence on the center.

The local state did affect the way national power and policy were articulated at the local level and the way they were experienced by ordinary citizens, yet from the outset the state in Bali was acutely divided. Broadly speaking, this lack of internal cohesion accentuated social and political conflict among Balinese and limited the chances that a politics of regional solidarity would develop. The only exception to this pattern occurred in the context of the national debate over religious policy in the mid-1950s; but this nascent Bali-wide solidarity quickly dissolved.

9 *Guns and Gangs*

THE ARMED FORCES WERE SO IMPORTANT in the National Revolution that soldiers and guerrilla fighters throughout the country expected to play a central role in politics after independence. From 1950 to 1965, however, the Indonesian military seldom spoke with a single voice. Internal divisions— cultural, political, personal, and institutional—often led to serious differences of opinion and occasionally to open fighting. Military units or services frequently took up positions on opposite sides of pressing political issues or became closely associated with one or another major political party. This pattern of fragmented politicization meant that there was always a potential for political disputes to provoke violent conflict. Throughout this period, regular military forces and semiofficial armed gangs contributed in no small measure to the pattern of political strife and to the eruption of widespread violence in late 1965.

The history, composition, and policies of the armed forces at the national, regional, and local levels shaped Balinese politics in at least three distinct ways during this period.[1] First, the central command's efforts to rationalize the armed forces immediately after independence underscored political and personal divisions that had arisen during the Revolution, both between Republican and former KNIL forces stationed there and among Bali's guerrilla fighters. Because most of the men involved still bore arms from the revolutionary period or had been incorporated into the regular army, both sorts of dispute had the potential to degenerate into violent conflict.[2]

Second, as the major political parties developed ever closer ties with

---

[1] The best works on the political role of the military during this period are Crouch, *Army and Politics in Indonesia,* and McVey, "Post-Revolutionary Transformation of the Indonesian Army."

[2] The role of the military was particularly great at this time because Sunda Kecil was officially under a State of War and Siege from mid-1950 to 15 May 1951.

15. Civilian volunteers pose with weapons after military training in September 1964. In the postindependence period, civil servants and private citizens were encouraged to undergo military training and to join the armed forces in internal security operations. As this photo suggests, the standard of training and discipline was not high. Semi-official vigilante groups, encouraged by military and political leaders, played a key role in the mass killings in Bali that followed the 1965 coup. (*Indonesia, Department of Information, Denpasar*)

branches of the military in Bali, the autonomy of the local state was compromised and the likelihood of violent political conflict increased. The problem was compounded by the growth of official and semiofficial vigilante groups, which included bands of disgruntled former guerrillas and bandits but also nonprofessional local security organizations established with the acquiescence of various political parties or elements of the state itself. The resort to civilian security bodies to restore order in the mid-1950s smoothed the way and provided a model for organized mass violence in later years, particularly after the 1965 coup.

Third, the preponderance of outside military forces deployed in Bali after 1950 permitted the political sympathies and agenda of non-Balinese military forces to exercise independent influence on local politics. Shifts in policy, personnel, and patterns of political allegiance at the center were of considerable consequence locally. Moreover, there was little basis for the development of a military-led regionalist challenge to the central government by local military commanders, as in some other parts of the country.

Demobilization and Conflict

In the first two years after independence, the central military leadership launched a drive to rationalize the Army by demobilizing large numbers of former revolutionary guerrilla fighters while at the same time incorporating units of the former colonial army, the KNIL, into the new national armed forces. These moves met with resistance and even open rebellion among the armed forces and from former guerrillas.[3] Criticism came also from civilian politicians who for various reasons sided with the nonprofessional guerrilla fighters against the "technocrats" in the Army high command. The reaction of Bali's guerrilla fighters did not differ markedly from that of guerrillas elsewhere in the country. They were not strong or united enough to mount a rebellion; instead their bitterness resulted in widespread political violence within.

Until October 1950 Bali was occupied by the Komando Pasukan Bali, a unit made up primarily of former KNIL troops, most of whom had been members of the Prayoda Corps.[4] Their presence in Bali for a full year after independence was a source of irritation to Bali's Republicans and particularly to the pemuda, who viewed the deployment of ex-KNIL forces as politically unacceptable. Resentment ran so high that it led to what the former PDRI leader Cilik has characterized as "revolutionary excess," in which "a large number of former collaborators were killed by the guerrillas."[5] Apart from the Balinese ex-Prayoda companies, the most notoriously reactionary of the forces in Bali at this time was the CPM (Corps Polisi Militer—Military Police Corps), whose members were said to be 90 percent former KNIL. The CPM was responsible for most of the mopping-up operations against the gangs of former guerrillas in 1950–51, and CPM members were the frequent victims of gang attacks.[6] There were also reports that former members of the Nefis (Netherlands Forces Intelligence Service) had gone to the interior to organize the killing of former pemuda. The former Nefis operative Joseph Lu, for example, was said to have murdered the famous pemuda leader Cokorda Anom Sandat.[7] This news motivated

---

[3] For an outline of the problems of military demobilization and reorganization in the country as a whole in 1949–50, see Feith, *Decline of Constitutional Democracy,* pp. 75–81.

[4] A newspaper report from 1950 noted that three companies of the APRIS (Angkatan Perang Republik Indonesia Serikat—Armed Forces of the United States of Indonesia) forces occupying Bali at this time were Balinese who had served in the KNIL. These companies, it said, were the first KNIL forces to be transferred to the APRIS, on 3 January 1950. See newspaper clippings in Collectie Korn, OR 435-271. An official history of the Regional Military Command says that four companies of former KNIL troops stationed in Bali were accepted into the APRIS in June (not January) 1950. See Angkatan Bersenjata Republik Indonesia, Dinas Sejarah KODAM XVI/Udayana, *Komando Daerah Militer XVI/Udayana Dalam Lintasan Sejarah* (Denpasar, 1982), p. 32.

[5] Cilik, "Kehadliran YKP di Bali," Archive Cilik.

[6] See, for example, the reports in *Sin Po,* 26 October, 30 November, and 15 December 1950.

[7] Pendit also mentions an armed group with pro-Dutch sympathies and Dutch military leadership which contributed to the political-military tension in Bali after the transfer of sovereignty: *Bali Berdjuang* (1954), p. 225.

many pemuda to return to the mountains to begin their own revenge campaign.[8]

The fluidity of the military situation in the region raised the hopes of Bali's Republicans, but it also contributed to their mounting frustration and to some violence. They had cause for hope when, in May 1950, Col. A. E. Kawilarang, commander of the Territorial Army for East Indonesia (TT/VII), established four subcommands, one of them the Sunda Kecil Command (Komando Pasukan Sunda Kecil, or KOMPAS-SK), led by a TNI officer, Lt. Col. R. A. Kosasih. During the Revolution Kosasih had been active in the BKR-Bogor and had served as chief of staff of the Sukabumi Regiment, so that his Republican credentials were not in doubt.[9] Moreover, two of the three battalions under his command in the KOMPAS-SK were TNI troops. Also encouraging to Republicans was the fact that in mid-1950 Kosasih appointed Subroto Aryo Mataram, who had been active in the Revolution in both Bali and Java, and a certain Prasmono as territorial officers in Bali.[10] It was deeply frustrating, however, that the Komando Pasukan Bali, which was part of the KOMPAS-SK, remained throughout this period under the direct command of the former KNIL officer Major Sitanala, and continued to be made up of ex-KNIL forces. Worse still, in early October Lt. Col. Kosasih was recalled to Makassar, and for a short time in October the whole of the Sunda Kecil Command (by then called KOMPAS-"C") was placed under Sitanala's command.[11] During this time the violence in Bali appears to have become very serious indeed.

Major Sitanala was finally replaced on 25 October 1950 by Major Islam Salim, son of the respected nationalist Haji Agus Salim. Islam Salim had been a staff officer in the TNI Tangerang Regiment and commander in Bangka-Belitung-Riau before his appointment as commander of KOMPAS-"C," and he was well received by Republicans and pemuda in Bali.[12] His appointment led to a decline in the violence because, in Pendit's words "as a Republican, he could be expected to understand and sympathize with the feelings of the guerrillas in Bali."[13] Under Salim, the former KNIL troops (Battalion 706) were finally transferred out of Bali and replaced by TNI troops (Battalion 711) who had just returned from Maluku.[14]

Thus, even while ex-KNIL elements remained in Bali, the restructuring of the regional military apparatus during 1950–51 changed the political equation, at the very least by providing a somewhat more congenial environment for Republican activism. A similar dynamic was evident in much of East

[8] I Nyoman Sarwa, "Pergolakan Sosial Politik di Bali Sejak Pemilihan Umum, 1955–1965," thesis, Universitas Udayana, Denpasar, 1985, p. 21.

[9] See Angkatan Bersenjata Republik Indonesia, Jarahdam XVI/Udayana, "Lembaran Sejarah; former Komandan Res. Inf. 26/VII," Edisi no. 1, 1974.

[10] *Komando Daerah Militer XVI*, p. 34.

[11] In September 1950 KOMPAS-SK became KOMPAS-"C," and in October 1950 the headquarters moved from Kupang to Denpasar.

[12] *Sin Po*, 25 October 1950.

[13] Pendit, *Bali Berdjuang* (1954), p. 228.

[14] *Komando Daerah Militer XVI*, pp. 34–40.

Indonesia. Army commanders frequently encouraged "opposition to the existing state governments and cooperated with local guerrilla groups as well as with political committees, fronts and plebiscite movements in doing this."[15] In Bali, however, it was not the presence of Republican forces per se that led to political mobilization and violence, but rather the presence of both KNIL and Republican military forces, both with some claim to authority. As these military units and commanders became enmeshed in the political struggle, the military as an institution lost any semblance of impartiality. A press report in May 1950 commented: "It appears that the Army is not simply an instrument of the government, without political aspirations, but on the contrary is the most important force in determining political developments here."[16] The coercive power the military brought to bear in these struggles inevitably worsened the conflict between Republicans on the one hand and collaborators and federalists on the other.

Developments in the military sphere also exacerbated tensions within the Republican camp in Bali. As in other parts of the country, difficulties emerged in connection with the demobilization of irregular forces. In January 1950 a TNI military commission headed by Capt. Andi Yusuf was dispatched from the RIS Territorial Command for East Indonesia in Makassar to coordinate the demobilization of Bali's Republican guerrillas. The RIS commander, Lt. Col. Mokoginta (a Republican), simultaneously issued orders for all guerrilla forces in NIT to surrender to the commission by 16 January 1950. In a rare and short-lived spirit of collegiality, pemuda leaders of the DPRI and PDRI had begun to meet in the expectation that some among both groupings would be absorbed into the national army.[17] An order dated 21 November 1949 from Lt. Col. Kahar Muzakkar, outlining plans for the formation of two full TNI battalions in Bali, had given them reason to hope that as many as might desire it could be incorporated into the regular Army.[18]

Yet on 15 January 1950 only the PDRI leaders surrendered to the commission. The immediate reason appears to have been a decision, issued on 12 January 1950 by the head of the Council of Rajas, Anak Agung Gde Oka, conferring official "freedom fighter" status only on those guerrillas who had never been arrested or jailed.[19] A significant number of DPRI men, having

[15] Feith, *Decline of Constitutional Democracy*, p. 75.
[16] *Keng Po*, 2 May 1950.
[17] When Nyoman Mantik (DPRI) met with Poleng early in January 1950, he allegedly assured Poleng that all former guerrilla forces (DPRI and PDRI) would be surrendering to the commission: interview with I Nengah Wirta Tamu (Cilik) (former PDRI leader), 11 December 1986, Denpasar.
[18] At the time, Kahar Muzakkar was still commander of the Komando Groep Seberang TNI. In July 1950 Kahar severed his ties with the national army, after the commander of TT-VII, Kawilarang, refused to accept his guerrilla forces into the regular army: Feith, *Decline of Constitutional Democracy* p. 212.
[19] The decision was issued in the form of a "fonogram" (no. J.20/1/3.) addressed to Capt. Yusuf and to local police authorities; it appears not to have been made public until several months later.

been denied access to the armed forces, turned their attention to the struggle for political and administrative office. With the establishment of the Bali Regional Council and Regional Assembly in September 1950 and the appointment of Suteja as kepala daerah, it appeared that the DPRI group had achieved something of a victory in this struggle. However, some members of the DPRI, many of whom had resumed the guerrilla struggle after release from prison, resented the a priori exclusion of the DPRI from induction into the regular armed forces. As a consequence, some of them remained in or returned to the mountains to continue their resistance and to take revenge on their former enemies.

Within the PDRI there were various reasons for anger. Apparently unaware of the decision by the Council of Rajas until several months later, they assumed that they had been duped into surrender by the DPRI, who hoped thereby to regain the lost mantle of revolutionary leadership. One of the four main PDRI leaders, Cilik, later wrote:

> Just imagine our anger when we discovered that it was only we from the PDRI who were surrendering and that the DPRI was not doing so at all, despite Nyoman Mantik's guarantee that they would. The result of this affair was that the deep-seated mistrust between the two groups—those who surrendered and those who did not—came increasingly into the open, and bore very negative consequences for later political developments.[20]

Bitterness within the body of irregular Balinese guerrilla forces seriously limited the likelihood of any united political or military activity on their part, and later affected their party choices.[21]

In retrospect, it seems somewhat surprising that a Republican military officer (Captain Yusuf) should so readily have accepted the advice of a body such as the Council of Rajas on a matter of such obvious political importance as the demobilization of guerrilla forces—unless, of course, pressure was brought to bear from other quarters. In this regard, it is worth recalling that Anak Agung Gde Oka's brother, Anak Agung Gde Agung, was then the minister of home affairs. It is not beyond the realm of possibility that Agung shifted his ministerial weight—either directly or indirectly through Defense Secretary General Ali Budiarjo, a fellow PSI man—in an effort to influence the demobilization process in Bali. It would have been advantageous to Agung to be able to weaken his erstwhile enemies, the pemuda, both by causing dissension among their leaders and by keeping over half of them out of uniform. The objective of limiting the size of Bali's military forces seems

[20] Cilik, "P.D.R.I.," manuscript, Archive Cilik.
[21] Pendit, himself a former guerrilla, wrote in 1954: "Unfortunately the actions of the TNI Military Commission under Andi Yusuf were not evenhanded, and consequently led to friction between those affiliated with the PDRI and those in the DPRI. . . . And then from the friction there developed open quarreling and fighting, particularly after Andi Yusuf left Bali": *Bali Berdjuang* (1954), p. 226.

to have been shared by Ali Budiarjo, who countermanded Kahar Muzak-kar's order to set up three TNI battalions in Bali.

The bitterness of the PDRI men intensified when, of the several hundred PDRI fighters, only about 200 were accepted into the Arjuna Battalion, which was set up to absorb them. It was November 1950—thus almost a full year—before this battalion was officially absorbed into the regular armed forces.[22] In the interim, the one-time guerrillas were required to undergo military training under the command of officers of the West Java Siliwangi Division, who did not always treat them with the respect they felt was their due.[23] Their own leader, Poleng, had been sent to Jakarta by the TT-VII commander, Alex Kawilarang, for "administrative" training.[24] During this period perhaps as many as forty PDRI guerrillas withdrew from the military and returned to the mountains.

The final insult to the PDRI came in December 1950, when the Arjuna Battalion was redesignated as the Panji Irawan Company and incorporated into a single battalion (no. 706) together with the erstwhile KNIL troops who had been occupying Bali. Resentment was compounded by what was perceived to be unfair treatment of the guerrilla company; the ranks of ex-KNIL men were raised, while those of former guerrillas were lowered. In 1951, while Battalion 706 was stationed in Kupang, the simmering anger erupted into an armed confrontation between the former guerrillas and KNIL companies.[25] Not surprisingly, many former guerrillas then withdrew from this unit and returned to the mountains in Bali. Together with a significant number of men in the PDRI group who had not been accepted into the armed forces at all, they constituted a core of military and political dissidence.

Gangs in Politics

In 1950 these PDRI men began to organize a new guerrilla network, known as PGSI (Pasukan Gerilya Seluruh Indonesia—All-Indonesia Guerrilla Force).[26] Their ostensible aim was to "mop up" former collaborators or, in other words, "to get revenge on those who had opposed them during the Revolution."[27] It is not entirely clear to what extent they had the cooperation of old friends now in the Army. However, a local Army announcement in August 1950, forbidding the unauthorized wearing of army uniforms

[22] According to a *Sin Po* report, 13 November 1950, it was officially sworn in on 10 November.
[23] Ibid.
[24] Interview with Poleng, 11 April 1986, Denpasar.
[25] Ibid.
[26] Reksodihardjo, *Memorie Penjerahan,* p. 207.
[27] Interview with Ketut Gde Dharmayudha, 28 July 1986, Desa Celuk, Gianyar. Although most of the gang members were former pemuda, there were criminal elements as well.

or insignia, refers explicitly to the problem of guerrilla groups posing as TNI.[28]

The PGSI was officially disbanded by the end of 1951, shortly after thirteen Balinese pemuda leaders were called to Jakarta by Sukarno to discuss the worsening security situation on the island.[29] According to Governor Sarimin Reksodihardjo, however, political killings and banditry continued.[30] There were 47 killings officially reported in 1952, 66 in 1953, 97 in 1954.[31] By 1955, the year of the national elections, the gangs had become increasingly active, many of them organized now under the name LOGIS (Lanjutan Organisasi Gerilya Indonesia Seluruhnya—Continuation of the All-Indonesia Guerrilla Organization).[32] As the elections approached, it became clear that LOGIS was acting in sympathy with, if not under direct orders from, the PSI.[33] In the words of a leading PSI activist, "The PSI sympathized with the political goals of LOGIS and for this reason did not act to interfere with its operations."[34] Indeed, LOGIS activity appears to have been responsible, at least in part, for the enormous electoral success of the PSI in Bali. In the elections for the Constituent Assembly, which took place in December 1955, after the police had some success against LOGIS, the PSI vote dropped substantially.[35]

The targets of LOGIS attacks were carefully selected political figures—primarily from the PNI—including punggawa, perbekel, village heads, civil servants, forestry officials, police, and police informants. Governor Sarimin Reksodihardjo pointed to the murder of the PNI punggawa of Belayu (Tabanan), Ida Bagus Gde, on 20 June 1955, as a sign that the political mur-

---

[28] See "Pengumuman Tentera," *Berita Nusantara*, 9 August 1950.

[29] The thirteen pemuda were Suteja, Subamia, Wija Kusuma, Poleng, Wijana, Ida Bagus Surya Tanaya, Nurai, Cilik, Mantik, I Gusti Bonjoran Bayupati, Mahadewa, Puger, and Sugitha. See the joint statement issued on their return to Bali, reprinted by Jawatan Penerangan Propinsi Sunda Kecil, 16 February 1952.

[30] Reksodihardjo wrote that "it was not yet possible to wipe out the PGSI organization because its leadership remained underground": *Memorie Penjerahan*, p. 207. There were even indications that the PGSI had connections with and received military supplies from Kahar Muzakkar, the rebel leader in South Sulawesi; see Sarwa, "Pergolakan Sosial Politik," p. 23.

[31] These are the official figures given by the police to a journalist in early 1956: "Apa Sebab Kekeruhan2," *Sin Po*, 26 January 1956. The actual numbers may well have been higher.

[32] For an outline of LOGIS's organization and the names of its main leaders, see Sarwa, "Pergolakan Social Politik," pp. 37–38.

[33] Arrests and raids reportedly produced evidence that this was the case. See Reksodihardjo, *Memorie Penjerahan*, p. 208. Also see, for example, the interview with Bali's police chief, Sutarto, in "Sari Berita," *Majalah Nusa Tenggara* 3 (February 1956): 23.

[34] Interview with I Gusti Ketut Reti, 30 July 1986, Denpasar. Most former PSI leaders and activists in Bali make similar statements: interviews with Ida Bagus Wisnem Manuaba, 11 July 1986, Tabanan; I Wayan Rana, 5 September 1986, Denpasar; and Poleng, 11 April 1986, Denpasar.

[35] Police Chief Sutarto claimed that behind LOGIS was a small group of intellectuals who "pulled the strings from behind the screen." See Sutarto's 1956 speech, printed as "Keamanan, Ketenteraman dan Ketertiban Umum di Daerah Bali Belum Memuaskan," in *Majalah Nusa Tenggara* 3 (July 1956): 17.

ders were about to begin in earnest. Only one week before the election, LOGIS killed a PNI member of the Gianyar Assembly, and on election day the commander of the Denpasar Mobile Brigade, Sutarjo, was shot by LOGIS elements.[36] Under the circumstances, it was not surprising that the campaign to quash LOGIS was initiated by the PNI, with some help from the PKI. According to a PNI activist in Tabanan, two former pemuda, Nyoman Mantik and Ida Bagus Mahadewa, took the lead.[37] Also active was Cokorda Bagus Sayoga of the Puri Satria, a major center of PNI activity since 1950.[38]

Equally telling was the fact that the regular army was almost completely uninvolved in the anti-LOGIS operation. There were insinuations that the Army harbored PSI sympathizers and that it was therefore unwilling to take serious action against the gangs that were acting in PSI interests.[39] There seems to have been a good deal of truth in these charges. According to one PSI figure, "Within the TNI there was a certain sympathy for LOGIS in their inner heart, though from a legal point of view they did not openly defend it. In most cases, they simply turned a blind eye to LOGIS activities."[40] The PSI influence in the Army was certainly significant at the national level in these years. The minister of defense/coordinator of security at the time of independence, Sultan Hamengku Buwono IX, was a PSI sympathizer (though not a member), and the secretary general of the Ministry of Defense, Ali Budiarjo, was an old PSI member close to Sjahrir as well as the sultan. Several of the Army officers stationed in Bali were also PSI sympathizers, including Islam Salim, the KOMPAS-"C" commander in 1950–51. The PSI sympathizer and former PDRI guerrilla leader Poleng served as special duty officer under Salim in 1950–51.

For their part, the PNI and PKI called on the politically "reliable" police in Bali and four Mobile Brigade companies from East Java to crush LOGIS. Originally from Semarang, Bali's police chief, Sutarto, had belonged to the PNI's Marhaenist Youth (Pemuda Marhaen) before joining the police, and in the early 1960s he went on to work in Subandrio's intelligence agency, Badan Pusat Intelijen, or BPI. In October 1965 he was named as a member of Lt. Col. Untung's Revolutionary Council, and was later sentenced to a long prison term as a coup conspirator. Although it is not clear that he was a PKI sympathizer while in Bali—for he may well have been PNI—it is certain

[36] Reksodihardjo, *Memorie Penjerahan*, pp. 207–8; Sutarto, "Keamanan, Ketenteraman, dan Ketertiban Umum," p. 16. The punggawa of Blahkiuh was also shot in 1955, though he did not die: interview with I Gusti Ketut Reti, 30 July 1986, Denpasar.

[37] Interview with I Gusti Putu Yasa Arimbawa (former head, Petani-Tabanan), 20 December 1986, Banjar Bongan Tengah, Tabanan. Arimbawa also claimed that the PNI had developed an ingenious plan to destroy LOGIS by setting up a rival gang.

[38] Interview with Meganada (former vice-head, Yayasan Kebaktian Pejuang–Bali, 1950–66), 22 September 1986, Singaraja.

[39] See, for example, "Apa Sebab Kekeruhan2 di Pulau Bali Ditutup?" *Sin Po*, 26 January 1956.

[40] Interview with Gusti Ketut Dharmayudha, 28 July 1986, Desa Celuk, Gianyar.

that in the opinion of the PSI, he was a political enemy.[41] Another police figure active in the anti-LOGIS campaign was the erstwhile pemuda Ida Bagus Mahadewa, who later became bupati of Buleleng.[42] Like Sutarto, Mahadewa was later thought to be sympathetic to the left; in the mid-1950s, however, he preferred the label "nonparty." In any case, this alignment of military and police forces on either side of the LOGIS question demonstrated the extent to which different political groupings had penetrated different parts of the coercive arm of the local state apparatus, and it helps to explain much of the political violence from the mid-1950s onward.

LOGIS operated primarily in the mountain regions of Tabanan, north Badung, west Gianyar, and Bangli—that is, principally in the old revolutionary base areas—and for a time established something close to an alternative state apparatus there. Governor Sarimin Reksodihardjo, who compared the LOGIS bands to dissident armed groups operating at the same time in West Java, South Sulawesi, and Aceh, wrote:

> It was as if the bands completely controlled the mountain regions of these kingdoms. Under the circumstances, the wheels of official government did not turn smoothly, because the body of officials, primarily the civil servants, were afraid to carry out their responsibilities. In addition, the local people in these regions were encouraged by the bands not to obey (that is, to pay no attention to) government rules and laws. . . . In this kind of situation, of course, the authority of the official government was much diminished.[43]

With a core of armed men numbering no more than 200, LOGIS relied to a great extent on the sympathy or passivity of local officials and villagers.[44] Former Republican base areas appear to have harbored a good deal of sympathy for the somewhat amorphous political objectives of LOGIS. Among ordinary people in these regions "there was a general feeling of dissatisfaction because they didn't see why those who had worked for the enemy were being let off easily, or even being allowed to enter the government. The natural solution was to kill them."[45] The style of operation of LOGIS was similar to that of the guerrilla bands during the Revolution. Well-armed "core" units of six to ten men moved constantly from one village to the next, meting out justice to collaborators and traitors or otherwise influencing the local political balance. In most villages these core units could rely on

[41] Most of Bali's PSI leaders view his subsequent career as evidence enough that Sutarto was pro-PKI in the mid-1950s: interviews with Ida Bagus Wisnem Manuaba, 10 July 1986, Tabanan, and I Gusti Ketut Reti, 30 July 1986, Denpasar.

[42] In the mid-1950s he was a leading member of the police officers' organization in Bali, the PPPRI (Persatuan Pegawai Polisi Republik Indonesia—Union of Police Officers of the Republic of Indonesia).

[43] Reksodihardjo, *Memorie Penjerahan*, p. 208.

[44] Interviews with Ida Bagus Tantra (Poleng), 11 April 1986, Denpasar, and I Gusti Ketut Reti, 30 July 1986, Denpasar.

[45] Interview with I Gusti Ketut Reti, 30 July 1986, Denpasar.

the assistance of local sympathizers in conducting operations. Significantly, where a village or district was solidly pro-PSI, the bands tended to cause no trouble at all.[46]

For those who were not pro-PSI, passivity was a sensible position, in view of the limited means available for protection. In the 1950s a punggawa generally had a staff of only two or three, and had no direct control over police or military forces. It was possible to call for police assistance, but it would almost invariably arrive too late to be of any use.[47] The obvious solution was to blow with the wind, in the hope of avoiding gang retaliation. State weakness, in other words, provided the gangs with considerable room to maneuver, and meant that political power was not infrequently based on manifest control over armed force. Political violence was the inevitable result.

The weakness of the local state apparatus also meant that efforts to control gang activity came to rely on the "cooperation" of ordinary Balinese citizens and a variety of village defense organizations, such as the PKD (Pembantu Keamanan Desa—Village Security Auxiliary), the PPP (Pemuda Pembela Pantjasila—Youth for the Defense of Pancasila), and the BKD (Badan Keamanan Desa—Village Security Body).[48] It is not clear who paid for the maintenance of these security bodies, but ample evidence shows that they were openly and actively supported by the official security forces. In a July 1956 speech, Police Chief Sutarto stressed that there was one central element in the success of all police operations: "the rising up of the people themselves, especially the pemuda led by the guerrilla fighters of the Revolution, to help in the government's efforts to restore order."[49] And in 1957, Iwan Stambul, then military commander for Bali, ordered the formation of the OKD (Organisasi Keamanan Desa—Village Security Organization) as an umbrella body to incorporate the PKD and other such groups.[50]

This pattern was strongly reminiscent of Dutch efforts to wipe out Republican "terrorists" during the Revolution. Ordinary Balinese citizens were once again being employed as semiofficial security forces to combat other Balinese. As in the Revolution, people were hesitant to cooperate without some assurance that they would be protected from retribution. A guarantee of sorts came in November 1956 with the arrival of four companies of Mobile Brigades from East Java.[51] In addition, the village defense organiza-

---

[46] Interview with Ketut Gde Dharmayudha, 28 July 1986, Desa Celuk, Gianyar.

[47] Interview with Ida Bagus Indera (former punggawa of Sawan, Tejakula, and Kubutambahan [Buleleng], 1950–67), 17 December 1986, Singaraja, and I Wayan Rana (former punggawa of Kuta, 1950–55), 5 September 1986, Denpasar.

[48] The PKD was established in mid-1956 in Badung and Gianyar, specifically for the purpose of assisting the police to restore order. The PPP performed the same task in Bangli and the BKD in Tabanan: Reksodihardjo, *Memorie Penjerahan*, pp. 203–4, 209.

[49] *Majalah Nusa Tenggara* 3 (July 1956): 17.

[50] On the establishment of the OKD in Bali, see "Pelaksanaan Organisasi Keamanan Desa," *Suara Indonesia* (Denpasar), 26 September 1957.

[51] For details of the military operation against LOGIS, see Sarwa, "Pergolakan Sosial Politik," pp. 32, 41.

tions were given police training relevant to the "restoration of order" in the mountain regions.

With this training, the visible presence of the well-armed Mobile Brigades in rural areas, and the removal of a few key PSI figures from office, the population gradually showed a greater inclination to assist the police. The removal of the *manca* of Tegalalang (a LOGIS base area in Gianyar), for example, had a marked effect on the behavior of the local population. Whereas earlier the villagers had not welcomed the arrival of police, wrote Governor Sarimin Rehsodihardjo, now they "not only were happy to see them, but actually joined in actively carrying out investigations and the search [for gang members]. . . . The rapid success of the village pacification movement was possible only because of the full assistance of the village *pemuda* organizations."[52]

After the elections, the reputation of LOGIS bands as ordinary bandits grew, and public sympathy waned still further. The beginning of the end for LOGIS came with the killing of one of its main leaders, Marsidi, in July 1956.[53] Originally from East Java, Marsidi had been a captain in Battalion 711 (KOMPAS-"C"). He had allegedly linked up with Balinese gangs about 1955. Over the course of the next few months many more members were killed and arrested, so that by mid-1957 the strength of LOGIS was spent.[54] For the moment, the political violence in Bali had come to an end, but there was no guarantee that it would not surface again. The state had shown a willingness to employ precisely those methods the Dutch had used during the Revolution: the establishment of village defense bodies for the restoration of "order." This was the precedent and the model for the vigilante groups that roamed the countryside and city streets in 1965–66, meting out punishment to the enemies of order, this time the PKI.

Martial Law and "Nasakom"

The political role of the military changed qualitatively with the imposition of martial law on 14 March 1957. The declaration of a national State of War and Siege came in response to the Permesta and PRRI rebellions (1956 to 1961), but it remained in effect at the national level until 1 May 1963. Under martial law, "army leaders stepped directly into the political affairs of the nation and became prime contenders for political authority."[55] In most

[52] Reksodihardjo, *Memorie Penjerahan*, p. 209.
[53] Marsidi was assumed to have PSI links: interview with Meganada, 22 September 1986 Singaraja. Also see *Komando Daerah Militer XVI*, pp. 40–44.
[54] Still, fifty-four killings were officially reported in 1956. See Reksodihardjo, *Memorie Penjerahan*, p. 179.
[55] Lev, *Transition to Guided Democracy*, p. 7. For a description of the formal powers of the military under martial law, see Crouch, *Army and Politics*, pp. 24, 60. On the involvement of the military in the economy, see Lev, *Transition to Guided Democracy*, pp. 69–70, and Crouch, *Army and Politics*, pp. 34, 38–41.

areas, Regional Military Commanders were appointed as Regional War Authorities, with extensive powers in every field.[56] Beneath them was a military administration that duplicated and often superseded the civilian political and bureaucratic apparatus. Officers also came to dominate crucial sectors of the economy and the bureaucracy, so that they quickly became "absorbed into the national political elite and gained a stake in the status quo."[57]

Partly for this reason the military became one of the staunchest opponents of the PKI and of the party system in general; the State of War and Siege suited their interests well. Yet while martial law permitted the enrichment of the Army's officer corps and provided the legal basis for some antiparty initiatives, it did not give the Army a completely free hand. It was still necessary to deal with President Sukarno, who after 1960 assumed the position of Supreme War Authority from Army Chief of Staff A. H. Nasution, who had held it since 1957.[58] Moreover, because Sukarno was conscious of the danger of excessive military power, he began to encourage the PKI. Consequently, after 1957 the Army and the PKI were locked in an increasingly vitriolic struggle for political power, a struggle in which the support of President Sukarno was fundamental. In the final years of the Old Order, Sukarno appeared to be moving progressively to the left. His conception of "Nasakom," according to which the country's three basic political currents—nationalism, religion, and communism—would be knit into a single whole, was especially worrying to the Army, for whom "Nasakomization" implied infiltration by the PKI. The PKI suggestion in 1965 that ordinary peasants and workers be armed was also deeply threatening to the Army leadership. Accordingly, some Army officers grew uneasy, and in the countercoup of October 1965 they took action against both the president and the Communist party.

For a variety of reasons, the regional rebellions that gave rise to the imposition of martial law in 1957 had little immediate impact on Balinese politics. Military officers in the TT-VII Command played a leading role in the Permesta rebellion. Because Bali lay within that territorial command, there was, in theory, a possibility that local military commanders and civilian politicians there might join the rebellion.[59] While there was some enthu-

---

[56] They were known initially as Peperda (Penguasa Perang Daerah—Regional War Authority) and later as Pepelrada (Penguasa Pelaksana Dwikora Daerah—Regional [Military] Authority to Implement Dwikora).

[57] Lev, *Transition to Guided Democracy*, p. 73.

[58] Nasution's actual title had been Peperpu (Penguasa Perang Pusat—Central War Authority); Sukarno's was Peperti (Penguasa Perang Tinggi—Supreme War Authority).

[59] In August 1952 the four subcommands of the TT-VII were designated as infantry regiments (*resimen infanteri*, or RI), so that the former KOMPAS-"C" of TT-VII became RI-26/VII. Maj. Ibnu Subroto was commander of that unit from December 1951 to March 1956. In April 1956 Subroto was replaced by Lt. Col. Minggu. With the reorganization of TT-VII in May 1957, Minggu became commander of the newly formed Regional Military Command for Nusa Tenggara (Komando Daerah Militer-Nusa Tenggara, or KDM-NT), one of the four regional commands created out of the former territorial command, TT-VII. In 1959 the KDM-NT was renamed KODAM NT/Raksabuana, and in 1960 it became KODAM XVI/Udayana. See *Komando Daerah Militer XVI*, pp. 42, 44, 50–52.

siasm for Permesta among military units posted in East Nusa Tenggara, however, support from the commanders based in Bali seems to have been very limited.[60] At the request of the TT-VII commander, Lt. Col. H. N. V. Sumual, the commander for Nusa Tenggara, Lt. Col. Minggu, selected a few delegates from each sector in his command to attend the Permesta conference in Makassar. Among those representing Bali were a number of PSI men, including Anak Agung Gde Agung, who reportedly had been approached about this time by the CIA and urged to lend his support to Permesta.[61] According to one of those who attended the conference, I Gusti Ketut Reti, the idea of regional autonomy had some support in Bali, particularly within the PSI, where there was a tendency to blame the center for local economic troubles.

But opinion was divided in Bali on whether to take an active part in the Permesta movement. Key military figures based in Bali were still very strongly pro-Sukarno and pro-center. Major Iwan Stambul, for example, the commander of Sector I of the Nusa Tenggara Command (the sector in which Bali lay), was not a Permesta sympathizer, but on the contrary a staunch PNI man, and his troops played an active role in the anti-Permesta operations in East Nusa Tenggara.[62] Lt. Col. Minggu appears to have had similar political views. Even without the influence of these officers, there were at least two other reasons why the chances of reaching unanimity on support for Permesta in Bali were slight. First, there were far fewer "native sons" in the military in Bali than in the rebel areas of Sulawesi, so it was difficult for Permesta's supporters there to portray the rebellion as an expression of "Balinese" regional or cultural sentiment. Second, the involvement of the PSI and the Army in LOGIS had led to earlier efforts to cleanse the local military apparatus, so that by late 1956 probably few soldiers or officers in Bali had much sympathy for the PSI or the Permesta cause.

The demise of PSI influence in the Army at this time was paralleled by the rise of men close to Chief of Staff Nasution, who, in the wake of the regional rebellions and after the imposition of martial law, was for a time in a relatively strong position vis-à-vis the president. Unlike the Permesta rebellion, this shift at the national level had an immediate impact on Balinese politics, tipping the balance of political forces, at least temporarily, in favor of the PNI and against Governor Suteja and the parties of the left. The appointment of Lt. Col. Supardi to the post of commander of the Nusa Tenggara Regional Military Command (KDM-NT) in August 1959, for example, was clearly Nasution's doing.[63] According to one observer, Supardi was "a staunch anticommunist . . . willing to work with the PNI in op-

---

[60] Support for Permesta was strongest in Timor and in Sumbawa. See ibid., pp. 114–20.

[61] Interview with I Gusti Ketut Reti, 30 July 1986, Denpasar.

[62] *Komando Daerah Militer XVI*, p. 116; interview with Iwan Stambul, 14 January 1987, Jakarta.

[63] A number of other high-level personnel changes were made in the KDM-NT at roughly the same time: *Komando Daerah Militer XVI*, p. 62.

posing Suteja when Suteja began to support the PKI's activities in the early sixties."[64]

But PNI domination of the military was far from complete.[65] As early as 1961 there were signs that Governor Suteja would be able to use his link with Sukarno to weaken his opponents in the local military apparatus. On 1 April 1961 Sukarno lifted martial law in Bali, explicitly curtailed Supardi's political authority as Regional Military Commander for KODAM XVI (formerly the KDM-NT), and appointed Governor Suteja as Pepelrada.[66] Presidential Decision no. 29/1961, dated 28 January 1961, stipulated that after 1 April 1961, "the Commander of KODAM XVI shall have authority that is consistent with the nature of his duties, but shall not have the power to enact legislation or to take political measures outside of the military establishment."[67]

In January 1963, no doubt again with the assistance of Sukarno, Lt. Col. Supardi was removed as military commander for Region XVI/Udayana and replaced by Brigadier General Sjafiuddin.[68] Sjafiuddin was no communist, but like Suteja he was a committed follower of Sukarno, and he was less inclined than Supardi to interfere with Suteja's plans.[69] Moreover, by 1965 he had begun to make public political statements that placed him clearly on the left. In a speech given at the May Day celebration in Denpasar, for example, he endorsed the PKI's idea of arming peasants and workers (the creation of a "fifth force").[70] His reputation as a leftist was reinforced by the fact that his wife was rumored to be active in the PKI-affiliated women's organization Gerwani.[71]

By 1965, elements sympathetic to the PKI controlled or had some influence in a number of military units and in the veterans' organization LVRI-

[64] Lane, "Wedastera Suyasa," p. 34.

[65] According to PNI-Bali leader Wedastera Suyasa, PNI sympathizers in the military included the military police commander for Region XVI, Lt. Col. Sumarsono; Lt. Col. R. S. Joyjopranoto; and Anwarsito of the police: "Bung Karno Sadar, Politiknya Mengenai Bali Keliru," *Merdeka*, 12 April 1986.

[66] See "1 April 1961 Bali Dalam Keadaan Biasa," *Suara Indonesia* (Denpasar), 1 April 1961. A few days later it was announced that Supardi would be accompanying Nasution on a trip abroad. From 1957 to 1960, the Regional War Authority, or Peperda, for all of Nusa Tenggara (including Bali) was the commander of the KDM-NT, Lt. Col. Minggu. His successor, Lt. Col. Supardi, commander of what was by then called KODAM XVI, was Peperda of Nusa Tenggara Barat and Timur, but not of Bali. See Angkatan Darat Republik Indonesia, Komando Daerah Militer Nusa Tenggara, *Himpunan Keputusan, Perintah, Instruksi, Penetapan, Peraturan, Pengumuman dari Penguasa Perang Daerah Untuk Tingkat I Bali/Nusra Barat/Nusra Timur, Tahun 1959, 1960* (Denpasar).

[67] See "Pengumuman no. 12/1961, Gubernur Suteja," *Suara Indonesia* (Denpasar), 4 April 1961.

[68] According to Wedastera Suyasa, in an interview on 25 February 1986 in Denpasar, a number of the anti-PKI figures in the police and the Army were also transferred at this time.

[69] Brig. Gen. Sjafiuddin was replaced as Pangdam XVI/Udayana in June 1966. It is not clear whether he was implicated in the October 1965 coup or simply was considered to be insufficiently anti-Sukarno.

[70] See "Kalau Perlu Kaum Buruh Dan Tani Dipersendjatai," *Fadjar* (Denpasar), 8 May 1965.

[71] Gerwani = Gerakan Wanita Indonesia, Indonesian Women's Movement.

SK.[72] According to some sources, within the units active in Bali were members of the former Battalion 715 and participants in the 1948 Madiun uprising.[73] Some local units were later alleged to have been involved in the 1965 coup attempt, including the Cakrabirawa unit at the presidential residence in Tampaksiring; a Mobile Brigade company stationed at Baturiti; Company "A" of Battalion 741 in Kuta; a unit from the education and training center (DODIK VIII) in Kediri; and the military police unit of Region XVI/Udayana.[74] Although it is difficult to judge the truth of these allegations, it is clear that by October 1965 serious political rifts existed within the military in Bali, which in the context of an attempted coup and countercoup created an atmosphere of mutual suspicion and a near total breakdown in the normal line of command.

Yet for all the tension and suspicion, Bali did not immediately explode into a state of civil war. As we shall see, with Suteja still in power, the PKI not yet officially banned, and a rough balance of military forces, an uneasy calm prevailed through October and most of November 1965. Widespread political violence began only after Suteja's removal to Jakarta on Sukarno's order in mid-November and the subsequent decision by local military leaders, including Sjafiuddin, to move firmly against the PKI later the same month. The balance shifted even more dramatically in favor of anti-PKI forces with the arrival of troops from Java in early December 1965.

As in other parts of the country, the armed forces played a critical political role in Bali in the years 1950 to 1965. Rather than encouraging a regional or ethnically based consciousness among Balinese—as was the case in parts of Sulawesi and Sumatra in the 1950s—military and police involvement in Bali tended to exacerbate political divisions among Balinese. The number of Balinese absorbed into the regular armed forces was relatively small, and of that number only a few were ever stationed in Bali. Under these circumstances, the political agenda of troops and commanders brought from other parts of the country reinforced local conflicts—between Republicans and collaborators, among pemuda, and between the followers of different political parties—rather than subduing these differences beneath an ethnic or regional solidarity. Moreover, the infusion of military force into the local political equation affected the balance and increased the likelihood that conflicts would be resolved through violence.

The mixed political composition of military and police forces stationed in Bali helped spread political violence between Republicans and former "collaborators." The appointment of a new military commander in late 1950

---

[72] LVRI-SK = Legiun Veteran Republik Indonesia–Sunda Kecil, Veterans' Legion of the Republic of Indonesia–Sunda Kecil.

[73] Interviews with Wija Kusuma, 22 March 1986, Denpasar, and Iwan Stambul, 14 January 1987, Jakarta. Also see *Komando Daerah Militer XVI*, p. 189.

[74] *Komando Daerah Militer XVI*, p. 192.

and the preponderance of Republican military forces in Bali thereafter shifted the political balance decidedly in favor of the Republic. Still, the central government's policy toward Bali's guerrilla forces worsened tensions in the Republican camp.

Between 1951 and 1956, political competition frequently took the form of violent gang activity, sometimes sponsored by political leaders with links to the police and the military forces. The lack of political unity within the local military apparatus had two important consequences. First, it led to a strategy of "contracting out" the task of maintaining order to "civilian" local defense organizations. This policy actually spawned further local violence and created the precedent and model for the vigilante politics of 1965–66. Second, it meant that the security situation in Bali was more dependent on outside military forces, and therefore more vulnerable to changes, structural and political, occurring at the center. Both of these factors contributed to the chronic violence of the 1950s and, as we shall see, to the mass killings of 1965–66.

10 A Political Economy
of Violence

SURVEYS OF MODERN BALINESE HISTORY are curiously silent on the dramatic economic changes between 1950 and 1965.[1] They provide virtually no detailed description or analysis of the poverty, hunger, and spiraling inflation that gripped Bali during these years. Moreover, in contrast to the scholarly energy devoted to such issues in Java, we do not yet have any meaningful analysis of changing rural relations of production in Bali, the dynamics of land reform, or their implications for political conflict there.[2] The gap in our knowledge is in part the result of the continued dominance of a tradition that emphasizes the significance of culturally specific bases of affiliation in Bali rather than those of class. This approach has, I think, helped to obscure the nature of political conflict in this period, and has seriously impaired attempts to understand the internecine violence of 1965–66.

This chapter counters the common assumption that economic factors and class have *not* been important in Bali's politics. It does so by focusing, first, on the relationship between economic conditions and patterns of political mobilization, describing how the hyperinflation of the early 1960s, together

[1] Virtually the only systematic treatment of Bali's economy during these years is Raka, *Monografi Pulau Bali.* More recent economic surveys of Bali pay scant attention to the early postindependence period. See, for example, I. K. G. Bendesa and I. M. Sukarsa, "An Economic Survey of Bali," *Bulletin of Indonesian Economic Studies* 16 (July 1980): 31–53; R. Daroesman, "An Economic Survey of Bali," *Bulletin of Indonesian Economic Studies* 9 (November 1973): 28–61; and Mark Poffenberger and Mary S. Zurbuchen, "The Economics of Village Bali: Three Perspectives," *Economic Development and Cultural Change* 29 (October 1981): 91–133. Of the small number of general works that deal with the period, most refer only in passing to economic issues. An exception is Hanna, *Bali Profile.*

[2] On rural class relations in Java see, for example, W. F. Wertheim, "From Aliran to Class Struggle in the Countryside of Java," *Pacific Viewpoint* 10 (1969): 1–17; Rex Mortimer, "Class, Social Cleavage and Indonesian Communism," *Indonesia* 8 (October 1969): 1–20, and *The Indonesian Communist Party and Land Reform, 1959–1965* (Clayton, Victoria: Centre for Southeast Asian Studies, Monash University, 1972).

236 | *The Dark Side of Paradise*

with a series of natural catastrophes, helped to shift political attitudes and to accelerate political conflict in the final years of the Old Order. Second, it analyzes the role of the local state and political party networks in shaping Bali's economy and thereby also in structuring political relations in Bali. Local state and party involvement in the distribution of economic resources from the center, the creation of a Balinese capitalist class, and the implementation of land reform encouraged political conflict among Balinese, and increasingly along class lines. Finally, returning to a theme touched upon in chapter 8, this chapter makes explicit the relative significance of class and other sociocultural groupings as bases of political affiliation and conflict. I argue that class became increasingly salient in Bali after 1963, when the PKI began to pursue a more militant class-based strategy in the implementation of land reform.

Scarcity and Inflation

In a political report of July 1950 the Dutch Bali expert Ch. J. Grader argued that heightened expectations generated by the Revolution had made economic development one of the most pressing political issues facing the new government in Bali.[3] Great expectations, however, could scarcely be met in the first years of independence. Serious crop failures in 1949–50, shortages of imported basic necessities, and a lack of confidence in the Republic's paper currency during the Revolution had contributed to spiraling inflation.[4] In June 1950 the price of rice in Singaraja was Rp. 1.75 per kilogram, already higher than in other parts of the country.[5] By January 1952 the price had jumped to Rp. 3.50, while the average wage for a laborer in the town remained at Rp. 1.50 per day.[6] Particularly for those without land of their own and for wage employees in the towns, necessities became increasingly difficult to obtain.[7]

It was hardly surprising, under these conditions, that thefts of basic foodstuffs and other economic crimes increased dramatically. The connection was not lost on contemporary observers. A newspaper article commented, "In these times the people of Bali are distraught on account of the increas-

---

[3] Ch. J. Grader, "Bali, Tournee-Aantekeningen, Juli 1950," Collectie Korn, OR 435-23, KITLV.

[4] Ch. J. Grader, "Persatuan Tenun Indonesia" and "Credietbehoefte ten Plattelande," Collectie Korn, ibid.

[5] Grader to Korn, 18 June 1950, ibid., OR 435-59.

[6] "Bali Gontjang Karena Beras," *Suara Rakjat*, 8 January 1952; *Sin Po*, 14, 17 February 1950. This was the public sector wage. In the private sector, the average wage was Rp. 2 a day. For further information on wage rates at this time, see Made Netja, *Pemeriksaan Agronomi Dalam Distrik Tedjakula 1949–1950* (Singaraja, 1951). For wage rates in Bali's coffee-growing regions see Propinsi Bali, Kantor Tjabang Inspeksi Koperasi Buleleng, *Lapuran Mengenai Daerah Kopi di Banjuatis, Munduk, Gobleg, Gesing, dan Umedjero*, by Komang Tjawi (Singaraja, 1952).

[7] "Bali Kekurangan Makanan," *Suara Rakjat*, 4 February 1952.

ingly brazen acts of banditry and theft. The disruption of the peace is related primarily to the increase in the cost of food. Not simply rice, but other foods as well have all increased in price."[8] The shortages were reportedly worst in Buleleng—which traditionally relied for much of its rice on Tabanan—and it was in Buleleng that the robberies and the banditry were most serious.

Economic difficulties also led to a quickening of political mobilization in Buleleng, which already had a relatively large and militant body of migrant agricultural laborers—employed principally in coffee plantations—and unionized urban workers. Singaraja was in fact the site of Bali's first modern industrial action, in 1950. Harbor workers of the transport company ESSER stayed out on strike in Buleleng for nearly two months, demanding wage hikes in line with inflation. The company refused to raise wages above those set for Surabaya, where the cost of living was considerably lower. These conditions helped leftist political parties and organizations, such as IRMI and Partai Buruh Indonesia (Indonesian Workers' Party), develop an early following in Buleleng.[9]

The prices of essential goods were held in check by local government controls through the mid-1950s, but the problems of inflation and the shortage of basic necessities surfaced once again after 1956 (see Table 8). In 1957, for example, a combination of poor local harvests, bottlenecks in the distribution of imported stocks, and speculation gave rise to sudden price increases for rice, from a normal rate of Rp. 3.50 per kilo to Rp. 7.50. It was only in the 1960s, however, that inflation reached crisis proportions and began to have clear social and political ramifications throughout the island. Between 1957 and mid-1962 the price of rice in Bali increased fourfold, and thereafter even more dramatically, reaching Rp. 130 a kilo by 1964. Even when massive infusions of rice from the center temporarily leveled out rice prices in 1964, the cost of other basic necessities continued to rise.[10]

Hyperinflation affected both the urban and rural populations, though in slightly different ways. Workers on fixed wages or salaries, such as teachers and factory workers, suffered a constant and disastrous decline in real earnings.[11] In 1962, for example, the average monthly salary for an elementary school teacher in Bali was Rp. 500, while a month's worth of rice cost roughly Rp. 1,000.[12] The official minimum wage in the local canning factory

[8] *Sin Po,* 14 February 1950.

[9] IRMI = Ikatan Rakyat Murba Indonesia (Indonesian Murba People's Union). For further details on unionization in Bali up to 1957, see Reksodihardjo, *Memorie Penjerahan,* p. 198, and Grader to Korn, 7 September 1950, Collectie Korn, OR 435-59, KITLV.

[10] "Menutup Tahun 1964," *Suara Indonesia* (Denpasar), 1 January 1965.

[11] Propinsi Nusa Tenggara, Kantor Penempatan Tenaga Daerah Nuteng Barat, *Tindjauan Pasar Kerdja Daerah Nusa Tenggara Barat Tahun 1956* (Denpasar, 1957), pp. 81–82. The same report painted a pessimistic picture of local economic prospects: "Rapid population growth and growing pressure on agricultural land without any real development in the fields of trade, finance, and industry will most certainly lead to greater poverty in the coming years" (p. 41).

[12] See "6 Guru S. R. Tinggalkan Tugas Karena Gadji Tak Tjukup," *Suara Indonesia* (Denpasar), 5 December 1962.

Table 8. Rice prices in Bali, 1950–1964 (rupiahs per kg)

Date	Price	Date	Price
1950	1.75	1960	12.00
1951	2.35	1961	18.00
1952	3.50	July 1962	27.00
1953	3.50	December 1962	30.00
1954	3.50	April 1963	40.00
1955	3.50	June 1963	60.00
1956	3.50	October 1963	85.00
1957	7.50	November 1963	125.00
1958	8.00	1964	130.00
1959	11.00		

Sources: "Harga Pasar," *Suara Indonesia* (Denpasar), 1962, 1963; "Menutup Tahun 1964," ibid., 1 January 1964; "Orientasi Beras," ibid., 23 October 1963; "Bali Gontjang Karena Beras," *Suara Rakjat,* 8 January 1952.

was Rp. 8.50 a day, or enough to purchase just over a quarter of a kilo of rice.[13] Though no reliable figures are available, it is safe to say that wages for part-time day labor were considerably lower. In rural areas, rapid inflation —and the diminishing value of cash and savings it implied—meant that real assets, such as agricultural land and produce, became even more valuable than usual. This probably helped landowning peasants and those who produced a surplus to pay off old debts, but rural families who were net *consumers* were hard hit. As the cost of basic daily needs and agricultural inputs—food, fertilizer, tools—soared, marginal peasants with no surplus to sell, and therefore limited cash income, must have fallen increasingly into debt. Landless agricultural laborers, like wage laborers in urban areas, also suffered a decline in real earnings with inflation.[14]

The political problem of inflation was exacerbated by the central government's policy on rice distribution. Substantial infusions of rice were intended, it was said, to act as a brake against inflation, but the mechanism used did not benefit all Balinese equally. "Injection rice"—that is, subsidized rice from the central government—was sold to civil servants and military personnel at far below market prices. In 1962, for example, when the average price for a kilo of rice in Bali was Rp. 30, civil servants were able

[13] Indonesia, Departemen Perindustrian dan Pertambangan, *Monografi Daswati I Bali 1961* (Jakarta, 1962), pp. 60–61.

[14] Ina Slamet, who shared responsibility for organizing a series of village studies conducted by PKI cadres in Java and Bali in early 1965, writes that in Bali "living conditions were seriously deteriorating at the time through inflation (steeply rising prices for necessities that had to be bought, including food for marginal peasants and agricultural laborers), rat plague and drought." The findings of the various village studies and Slamet's analysis of the information can be found in her as yet unpublished work "Views and Strategies of the Indonesian Peasant Movement on the Eve of Its Annihilation in 1965–1966" (1988).

to purchase it for just Rp. 5. At the same time, Bali's producers were required (until 1963) to sell a proportion of their rice to the government at the
artificially low price of Rp. 6 a kilo, but they were not able to purchase rice
for consumption at the subsidized rate.[15] The government's system favored a
segment of the town-dwelling consumers at the expense of rural producers
and laborers, and signified an effort to avoid the political difficulties that
might arise from an alienated urban sector.[16]

A local newspaper report in 1963 noted that "in the villages people are
increasingly having to mix their rice with banana and coconut pulp and
papaya leaves, at a ratio of about 1:3 or 1:4. Indeed, many are at the point
where they are eating only banana pulp and leaves, with no rice whatsoever."[17] Even in villages that produced a surplus of rice, poor peasants
were eating little or none of it.[18] Reports of death from starvation and
widespread malnutrition became increasingly common in the local press
after 1963, though such reports in the national media were limited by the
wish to preserve the image of "fertile," harmonious Bali.[19]

The grave economic conditions of the early 1960s were compounded by a
succession of rat and mouse plagues, insect infestations, and crop failures
between 1962 and 1965, and by the eruption of Gunung Agung in early
1963.[20] Eruptions on 17 March and 16 May claimed an estimated 1,500
lives and took more than 62,000 hectares of land out of production, resulting in severe malnutrition for more than 10,000 people, and the exodus of as
many as 75,000 to neighboring principalities.[21] The most seriously affected

---

[15] *Suara Indonesia* (Denpasar), 4 December 1962.

[16] In 1956 there were an estimated 2,500 civil servants in Bali, not including teachers, of
which there were 2,208. See *Tindjauan Pasar Kerdja*, pp. 32–34.

[17] "Harga Beras Semakin Menggila," *Suara Indonesia* (Denpasar), 22 October 1963.

[18] Slamet cites the example of the village of Singakerta in Gianyar, which in 1965 produced a
surplus of rice but whose poorer peasants ate a 5:1 cassava-rice mixture: "Views and Strategies." Also see "Rakjat Mulai Makan Ketela Melulu: Panen Gagal, Tikus Mengganas," *Suara
Indonesia* (Denpasar), 18 September 1962.

[19] See the stories in *Suara Indonesia* (Denpasar): "Nusa Penida Kering—30,578 Orang
Terantjam Bahaja Kelaparan," 2 August 1963: "22 Orang Penderita Busung Lapar Meninggal,
460 Orang Dirawat," 14 August 1963; and "Saat2 Mendjelang Hari Raja Galungan," 11 May
1964.

[20] On the plagues and infestations, see "Gerakan Masaal Membasmi Tikus," *Suara Indonesia* (Denpasar), 29 January 1963; and "Daging Tikus Tidak Membahajakan," ibid., 31
January 1963.

[21] On the eruption, see Windsor P. Booth and Samuel Mathews, "Disaster in Paradise,"
National Geographic, September 1963, pp. 436–58; and Anna Matthews, *The Night of Purnama* (Kuala Lumpur: Oxford University Press, 1983). All figures are from a report (dated 3
May 1963) by the head of the Protestant Church of Bali, K. Suweca. Casualty estimates were
made by local Red Cross teams and by Dr. Made Jelantik. The estimates of the local KoOGA—
the government organization with responsibility for handling the disaster—were considerably
higher. In October 1963 it reported 98,792 internal refugees, 15,595 suffering severe malnutrition, and 122,743 in serious danger of malnutrition. See *Suara Indonesia* (Denpasar), 21
October 1963. Governor Suteja estimated that 25,000 hectares of land had been permanently
ruined and that 100,000 hectares would be unproductive for many years to come. In April 1963
he said: "We have to feed 85,000 refugees and we simply have not the food to do it": quoted in
Booth and Mathews, "Disaster in Paradise," pp. 454–55.

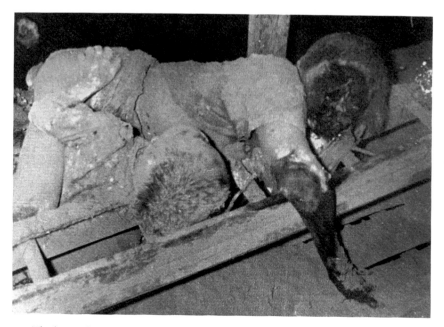

16. The burned corpses of a mother and child, two of an estimated 1,500 people who died during the eruption of Gunung Agung in early 1963. (*Indonesia, Department of Information, Denpasar*)

areas were those in the eastern part of the island: Karangasem, Klungkung, Bangli, and Gianyar. Refugees from these areas crowded into the larger towns of Denpasar and Singaraja, where, together with the urban poor, they formed an underclass ripe for mobilization by the increasingly active mass organizations.

According to official statistics, the number of urban wage laborers in Bali was minuscule; in 1956, only 5,445 persons were employed in businesses with more than ten employees.[22] The actual number who relied on wage labor in the towns and the rural areas, however, was probably several times larger. Even in relatively prosperous times tens of thousands of migrant laborers were employed each year for the coffee harvest in Buleleng, Tabanan, and Bangli. Untold numbers worked seasonally or part-time on construction projects, such as harbor workers and those who worked for businesses with fewer than ten employees; none of these people appeared in official statistics. In view of the fact that pay failed to keep pace with inflation, the number of poor wage earners in the early 1960s must already have been quite substantial. After Gunung Agung erupted, the ranks of urban

[22] See Indonesia, Departemen Perindustrian dan Pertambangan, *Monografi Daswati I Bali 1961*, p. 8.

17. Refugees from the eruption of Gunung Agung gather for a meeting with Balinese government officials in Karangasem, 1963. The eruption left an estimated 75,000 people homeless. (*Indonesia, Department of Information, Denpasar*)

poor and unemployed swelled astronomically. A newspaper report in October 1963 observed that "the number of beggars in the towns is increasing every day. They are leaving their home villages, which are suffering economic shortages, and coming to the towns to beg."[23]

The massive movement of internal refugees—delicately termed "urbanization" in government documents—contributed to serious social and economic problems in the towns—unemployment, rising crime rates, prostitution.[24] The 1963 annual report of the Bali office of the Department of Labor estimated that roughly 30 percent of Bali's adult labor force was unemployed in that year, compared to an estimated rate of 14 percent in 1956.[25] Though no precise figures on criminality are available, reports of theft and unruly behavior were increasingly common after 1960, both in the media and in

[23] "Harga Beras Semakin Menggila," *Suara Indonesia* (Denpasar), 22 October 1963.

[24] Even before the eruption of Gunung Agung, rapid population growth was causing pressure on agricultural land. In 1961 the average population density in Bali was 358 persons per square kilometer. See Indonesia, Departemen Perindustrian dan Pertambangan, *Monografi Daswati I Bali 1961*, p. 6.

[25] Propinsi Bali, *Laporan Tahunan Djawatan Tenaga Kerja, 1963* (Denpasar, 1963). A 1956 government report estimated that roughly 200,000 of a total labor force (men and women aged 14 to 60) of about 1.4 million were unemployed. The most serious unemployment problem was in the towns of Singaraja, Denpasar, and Tabanan. Propinsi Nusa Tenggara, Kantor Penempatan Tenaga Daerah Nuteng Barat, *Tindjauan Pasar Kerdja*, pp. 35–39.

18. A farmer, assuming a posture of respect to people of higher status, registers with officials of the Ministry of Social Affairs in April 1963, after the eruption of Gunung Agung. (*Indonesia, Department of Information, Denpasar*)

government reports.[26] Moreover, anti-Chinese activity rose—a common manifestation of economic and social discontent in Bali, as in other parts of Indonesia.[27]

Economic crisis and concomitant social changes after 1963 appear to have contributed also to the popularity of parties of the left, such as the PKI, Partindo, IRMI, and Partai Buruh. In Denpasar and Singaraja, for example, hamlets with strong PKI bases—such as Suci, Kerenceng, Titih, and Ubung in Denpasar, and Banjar Java in Singaraja—had sizable populations of migrants and workers. Already the third most popular party in Bali in 1955, the PKI and its various mass organizations, by all accounts, experienced a second major wave of expansion in Bali after 1963.[28] The uprooted and the dispossessed—or more precisely, wage earners, migrants, and unemployed

[26] See, for example, "Komplotan Perampok di Jemberana Terbongkar," *Suara Indonesia* (Denpasar), 16 March 1964.

[27] See, for example, *Suara Indonesia* (Denpasar): "Tjegah Tindakan Gedjala2 Rasial di Bali," 19 June 1963; and "Pelakat2 dan Surat2 Kaleng," 15 June 1963.

[28] There were no comprehensive elections during this period, but scattered results from local elections for perbekel indicate strong support for the PKI and Partindo. One such result was the election of a PKI perbekel in the former Republican base area of Sukasada, Buleleng. Moreover, press reports of the creation of new PKI-affiliated ormas branches show a similar pattern of rapid expansion after 1963.

—both in the towns and in rural areas, constituted a significant proportion of the population of Bali by the end of 1963, and they provided fertile soil for ormas, which became increasingly militant at precisely this time.[29]

Economic Dependence

Well known for the fertility of its soils and the sophistication of its system of wet-rice agriculture, Bali nonetheless relied heavily on imports in the postindependence period. Local rice production fell so far short of local requirements that by 1962 Bali was relying on monthly "injections" of 300 tons of rice from the central government.[30] In the same year, the provincial legislature sent a delegation to Jakarta to request that the government rice-purchase target for Bali be reduced by 50 percent, and it called for further increases in "injection rice" from the center. After Gunung Agung erupted, the shortage became so serious that Bali was granted full exemption from obligations under the government rice-purchase system.[31]

Bali's reliance on infusions of basic goods was part of a more general pattern of financial dependence on the center. That dependence became acute after 1956, when national inflationary trends combined with mounting local government expenditures to produce a growing deficit (see Table 9). The problem of revenue dependence was partly the result of the 1951 land-tax exemption, one of the first pieces of legislation enacted by Bali's new Republican-dominated legislature. Apparently in an effort to win broad popular support for the new Republican government, the law exempted a large number of Bali's peasants from the payment of land tax. At the same time, however, it deprived the local state of what in colonial times had been its largest single source of revenue after opium. Between 1951 and 1957, locally generated revenues remained roughly constant, while expenditures rose from Rp. 17,727 to Rp. 104,424, producing a deficit of Rp. 88,927 in

[29] Political polarization and militancy at the national level were accelerated by the nationalization of Dutch plantations beginning in 1957 and the land reform of the early 1960s. Military control of plantations after 1957 placed disputes over wages and working conditions in sharper relief, providing the groundwork for political conflict between the military and agricultural laborers. More significant for Bali, however, was the national legislation that called for redistribution of land and mandated dramatic changes in harvest-sharing arrangements. This legislation is discussed in detail below.

[30] Even this amount was considered insufficient to meet actual needs. In September 1962 Governor Suteja requested a further 200 tons per month, for a total of 500 tons a month, or 6,000 tons a year: *Suara Indonesia* (Denpasar), 27 September 1962. In 1961 at least four of the eight kabupaten in Bali—Klungkung, Karangasem, Bangli, and Buleleng—were rice-deficit areas. The government report that cites these statistics acknowledges that they overestimate the actual availability of rice in Bali, and suggests that even as early as 1961 the entire island was a deficit area, with the possible exception of Tabanan. See Indonesia, Departemen Perindustrian dan Pertambangan, *Monografi Daswati I Bali 1961*, p. 29.

[31] *Suara Indonesia* (Denpasar), 14 September 1962, 2 June 1963.

Table 9. Bali's budgets and central government subsidies, 1951–1961 (in thousands of rupiahs)

Year	Revenues	Expenditures	Deficit	Subsidies
1951	10,174	17,727	7,553	8,126
1952	13,978	21,978	8,000	11,792
1953	15,401	24,641	9,240	7,856
1954	12,160	46,282	34,122	9,358
1955	15,149	50,496	35,347	9,960
1956	12,663	63,246	50,613	19,124
1957	15,487	104,424	88,927	29,750
1960	—	—	100,635	—
1961	—	—	110,896	—

Sources: Sarimin Reksodihardjo, *Memorie Penjerahan Gubernur, Kepala Daerah Propinsi Nusa Tenggara, 1/4/52–30/3/57* (Singaraja), p. 56; Propinsi Nusa Tenggara, Bagian Desentralisasi, *Ichtisar Keuangan Daerah Bali, Lombok, Sumba, Sumbawa, Flores dan Timor, Tahun Dinas 1951–1957* (Singaraja, 1958); *Suara Indonesia (Denpasar),* 14 April 1961.

1957. That deficit was met principally by subsidies from the central government. The situation worsened dramatically with the decline of the island's economy in the early 1960s, so that by 1964 the central government's contributions constituted nearly 90 percent of Bali's total revenues.[32]

Acute financial dependence on the central government distinguished Bali from other areas outside of Java—notably parts of Sulawesi and Sumatra—which were able to generate substantial local revenues through exports and smuggling. This difference was arguably the principal reason for the weakness of regionalist sentiment among Bali's political and economic elite. One of the underlying causes of the discontent in Sulawesi, leading to the Permesta rebellion, was the skimming by the central government of substantial local revenues. This effect was most pronounced in North Sulawesi, where support for Permesta was strongest. By contrast, in South Sulawesi, which relied much more heavily on subsidies from the central government, support for Permesta had substantially dried up by the end of 1957. Bali was an even more extreme case. So great was the local government's economic dependence on the center that there was no incentive to demand greater autonomy. On the contrary, the only hope seemed to be to press the central government for greater outlays. As economic dependence increased, the distribution and control of economic goods became the main political issue in Bali.

[32] From 1960 to 1962, the value of exports from Bali (in constant rupiah) declined by about 50%, from Rp. 50 million to Rp. 27 million: ibid., 31 December 1962. Bali's total estimated revenues for 1964 were Rp. 1,201,554,459, of which Rp. 1,048,308,000 was to come from the central government: Propinsi Bali, *Rantjangan Anggaran Keuangan Daerah Tk I Bali, Tahun Dinas 1964* (Singaraja, 1964). Also see "Daerah [Bali] Bergantung Pada Belas Kasihan Pusat," *Suara Indonesia* (Denpasar), 15 October 1964.

Bali's "National" Capitalists

A "nationalist" economic policy, involving efforts by the local state to wrest control of trade and other commerce from the Chinese, encouraged the growth of a small Balinese capitalist class in the 1950s. As early as 1951, Ch. J. Grader observed:

> While previously importing and a good part of retail trade were in the hands of European firms and Chinese, now the Balinese interest in these fields has grown considerably. Particularly among the younger generation, there is a trend toward cooperative endeavors. These efforts receive the full attention and support of the local government.[33]

This trend was spurred by the strongly interventionist economic policies pursued nationally and locally after 1953. By the late 1950s Balinese firms, with government assistance, apparently had managed to squeeze Chinese and other "foreign" businesses out of a number of key sectors, including transport, import-exporting, construction, and, increasingly, tourism.[34] A government report of 1961 noted, for example, that "there are no foreign exporters in Bali; all are national companies that over the last fifteen years have been designated to replace the foreign businesses."[35] The same pattern was evident in the construction sector, which once had been monopolized by Chinese and Europeans. By the late 1950s twenty-one of the twenty-six construction firms in Bali were owned by Balinese.[36] Significantly, these were the sectors over which the local state had substantial authority to grant licenses, enact protective legislation, and bestow contracts.

Clifford Geertz has identified the small group of capitalists who emerged in postindependence Tabanan as aristocrats who had been politically displaced by the transformations accompanying independence. Arguing that "the dynamism of Tabanan's nobles [came] from a perceived threat to their political dominance," Geertz undertakes to show how the growth of modern firms after 1950 depended on the "traditional patterns of organization and loyalty" they were able to mobilize. Yet his own observations suggest a different conclusion. He writes, for example, that in almost every case, "the success of Tabanan's noble entrepreneurs has partly derived from their ability to gain or demand support from the local wing of the national govern-

---

[33] Ch. J. Grader, "GIEB-I" [1950], Collectie Korn, OR 435-23, KITLV.

[34] See Geertz, *Peddlers and Princes*, pp. 22–23.

[35] Indonesia, Departemen Perindustrian dan Pertambangan, *Monografi Daswati I Bali 1961*, p. 110. In 1961 there were 176 licensed private sector exporters and 154 cooperatives engaged in export activities. In the same year Bali exported 14,730 head of cattle and 106,020 pigs: ibid., pp. 32, 111–12.

[36] For more details on the emergence of the local capitalist class, see Reksodihardjo, *Memorie Penjerahan*, pp. 109–25.

ment, and indeed, they have realized to a notable degree their aim of maintaining through economic means the substance of their local authority."
This suggests that what distinguished the first Balinese capitalists was not
their aristocratic origins per se or their political "displacement" but rather
their close political and personal links to a protectionist local state. Far from
being politically displaced, Tabanan's entrepreneur-aristocrats had managed
to maintain their ties to the local state, and to turn them to good advantage
after independence. As Geertz himself notes, "the emergence, in Tabanan at
least, of a unified elite of top civil servants and entrepreneurs, mainly under
the aegis of the Nationalist Party [PNI], is fairly clear."[37] Elsewhere in Bali,
aristocrats had similar access to the state, but they had to share the limelight
with former pemuda and civil servants of nonaristocratic background.[38]

The experiences of one of the most successful Balinese companies in the
import-export sector, GIEB, are illustrative of the state's role in nurturing
Bali's "national" capitalists during this period.[39] The company was founded
in December 1948, with the assistance of the Dutch-sponsored governments
of Bali and the NIT. In the words of a former Dutch official involved in the
early stages of its formation, the company was established to help the tiny
nascent Balinese bourgeoisie "break the Chinese monopoly on trade."[40]
The founder of GIEB was I Ketut Bagiada, until 1948 a high-ranking employee in the Department of Economic Development in Bali. The company's
initial working capital of Rp. 100,000 increased to Rp. 2 million by mid-
1950, and the firm continued to prosper through the 1950s, with the assistance of the "nationalist" local state and the PNI in Bali. In fact, by 1956
GIEB had secured a monopoly position in the import sector by government
order. *All* local distributors of major commodity imports (petrol, cloth,
sugar, etc.) at that time were supplied by GIEB.[41]

Links with the local state also allowed many pemuda to move easily into
the role of businessman-politician in the early 1950s. A case in point was the
former pemuda Dewa Made Dhana, who owned roughly 50 hectares of

[37] Geertz, *Peddlers and Princes*, pp. 25–26, 106–20, 132. Geertz acknowledges in a foot-
note that "the nobility still dominates the civil service almost everywhere else in Bali. Even in
Tabanan they have not been wholly displaced . . . and their economic efforts are in part supple-
mentary to a continuing governmental role rather than entirely replacing political activity" (p.
132).
[38] Grader wrote in 1950 that "the rise of Indonesian commerce in Bali during this period
was in large part thanks to the enthusiasm and perseverance of a certain group of young men
who emerged during the course of the revolution": "GIEB-III," Collectie Korn, OR 435-23,
KITLV.
[39] GIEB = Gabungan Impor dan Expor Bali (Import and Export Association of Bali). Apart
from GIEB, the more prominent Balinese export-import companies included Bali Baru and the
Madjopahit Trading Co.
[40] The official quoted is P. L. Dronkers, who had worked as a Controleur in Bali since 1946
and in 1949 was serving as adviser on economic affairs: personal communication, 9 February
1988. For further information on the origins of GIEB, see Ch. J. Grader, "Gabungan Impor dan
Expor Bali" [1950], Collectie Korn, OR 435-23, KITLV.
[41] Reksodihardjo, *Memorie Penjerahan*, p. 123.

coffee land near Pupuan, in the highlands of western Buleleng. Shortly after independence he established a coffee-exporting "cooperative" and became a leading figure in the coffee-growing and export community.[42] At the same time, he continued to be politically active in the PNI and served as vice-head of the Buleleng legislature (DPRD-Buleleng) from 1961 to 1966.[43] According to Dewa Made Dhana himself, his personal friendship with the bupati of Buleleng, his pemuda status, and his close ties with officials at the Bank Rakyat ensured that he had no difficulty obtaining licenses, permits, and capital. His case was not exceptional. Two former leaders of the DPRI guerrilla group were among a number of one-time pemuda who established successful trading companies and cooperatives after independence.[44] And as Bali's Republicans gained control of some key local government offices through the 1950s, pemuda access to state resources continued to improve. In many cases, the local political and economic elite were the same people, or at any rate so closely linked by birth or friendship as to make no difference.

The close ties between the local state and Bali's new capitalist class had telling political implications. The overlapping of political and economic elites meant that for much of this period the local state was strongly influenced by the interests of this new element of the middle class, represented principally by the PNI and in some areas by the PSI. This appears to have contributed to dissatisfaction and resentment among less advantaged groups, including urban laborers and peasants, and eventually to a political backlash in the form of support for the PKI and other parties of the left.[45] As the dominance of the PNI and the PSI within the local state apparatus began to be challenged by Suteja and the parties of the left in the early 1960s, however, the position of capitalists associated with the PNI and the PSI was increasingly threatened. This contributed to the dynamic of political conflict leading up to and after the October 1965 coup.

Patronage and Political Conflict

Dependence on the local state and party structures made Bali's new capitalists strong defenders of the principle of state intervention. Yet, despite

---

[42] See Propinsi Bali, Kantor Tjabang Inspeksi Koperasi Buleleng, *Lapuran Kopi di Pulau Bali 1958*, by Komang Tjawi (Singaraja, 1958).

[43] Interview with Dewa Made Dhana, 10 October 1986, Singaraja.

[44] Interviews with Wija Kusuma, 3 April 1986, Denpasar; I Ketut Wijana, 29 September 1986, Singaraja; and Putu Dhana, 28 September 1986, Singaraja.

[45] Commenting on the political implications of the emergence of a high-caste capitalist class in Tabanan in the late 1950s, Geertz writes: "Many of the more articulate and educated commoners do regard [it] . . . as a genuinely ominous and discouraging occurrence and as a betrayal of the promises of the Revolution. . . . it is upon such resentment that communism, just beginning to appear in Bali, feeds": *Peddlers and Princes*, p. 133.

this common interest, Bali's capitalists were not united politically. Their constant jockeying for local-state patronage inevitably resulted in a system of payoffs to key state officials and to accusations of favoritism and corruption. Moreover, because of their diverse political backgrounds—some had worked with the colonial state, some had been revolutionaries, and some were displaced aristocrats—and because political control of the local state remained fluid through most of the period 1950–65, Bali's capitalists became involved with a variety of political parties. In the immediate postindependence period, the majority of Bali's emerging capitalists were affiliated with the PNI, which, particularly from 1952 to 1955, dominated the key economic branches of the national and local bureaucracies. In later years, however, there were also "national" capitalists with links to the PSI and, still later, to the PKI and Partindo. Through their ties to the local state and political parties, the "national" capitalists affiliated with the major parties were able, with varying degrees of success, to secure subsidies, licenses, and contracts from the local state.

The competition for such favors, therefore, also took on a political dimension. The wealth and social prominence of some of Bali's new capitalists and their influence with the political parties gave their personal views and interests much broader political import than might otherwise have been the case. Those who felt excluded from the state's economic patronage, for example, or who felt that their access was threatened by others, often construed their concerns in political language. This was evident in the late 1950s and early 1960s, when Balinese capitalists affiliated with the PNI joined eagerly in the national policy to expel Chinese from Indonesia—a policy resisted by Suteja and the PKI. Later they seized the opportunity provided by the 1965 coup to remove competitors and to establish a dominant position in the local economy.

The interventionist economic policies and the regulatory structures encouraged political manipulation and corruption locally. The procedure for granting export licenses in Bali, for example, provided ample opportunity for political favors and bribery. Prospective exporters were required to undergo a screening process twice every year by a local government coordinating body until 1961; thereafter, screening was done once a year. According to an official government publication:

> Before being designated as a bona fide exporter . . . every business must make an official request to the local government, which includes all of the required letters and documentation. . . . After hearing the considerations and opinions of the coordinating body, as well as the views of the heads of those departments that have some concern with export matters or the products being exported, the local government issues a decision regarding (a) the acceptance or rejection of the new requests for an export license and (b) the extension or cancellation of the licenses of existing exporters.[46]

[46] Indonesia, Departemen Perindustrian dan Pertambangan, *Monografi Daswati I Bali 1961*, pp. 109–10.

The opportunities for graft and political favoritism were enhanced by the system of export quotas. Cattle exporters, for example, were grouped into one of five quota categories, by executive government decision. Those in the lowest category were permitted to export only two animals a month, while those in the highest could export as many as fifty. Similar opportunities were available in the construction sector, as public works projects—bridges, roads, schools, hotels—constituted the largest single category of the local state's expenditure, after public sector wages, in every budget between 1951 and 1965.

The imposition of martial law in 1957 altered the channels if not the basic mechanisms of state patronage. Under martial law, the Regional War Administrator, Lt. Col. Minggu, became the central economic decision-making authority. In 1959 alone he issued several dozen executive orders pertaining to every aspect of economic life: licensing of businesses, contracts, prices, wage scales, directorships.[47] In the same year the Bali Regional Trading Pool, headed by Maj. Iwan Stambul (commander of KODAM XVI Sector–1/Bali), became the omnipotent clearinghouse for economic affairs in Bali.[48] Each new rule provided an additional potential source of illegal revenue for those charged with enforcing it. At the same time, the position of Bali's "national" capitalists came increasingly to depend on the local military apparatus.

For a few years, then, military authorities rather than the civilian bureaucracy or the political parties became the main channels for state patronage. However, the position of the military in Bali differed in one striking respect from that of the military in Java. Whereas in Java it had gained control of large tracts of land with the nationalization of foreign plantations, in Bali there were virtually no foreign plantations.[49] Thus, while the military played a central role as dispenser of state patronage in Bali, it did not quickly amass *landed* wealth, as the military units in Java did. Thus there was less immediate economic reason for local military hostility to land reform and to leftist mobilization in the countryside. Because their economic interests were based on control of the systems of trade and distribution, the military in Bali was ultimately much more concerned with maintaining its position of power within the state apparatus. It could afford to cooperate with virtually any

[47] The official orders and decisions of Lt. Col. Minggu are compiled in Angkatan Darat Republik Indonesia, Komando Daerah Militer Nusa Tenggara, *Himpunan Keputusan, Perintah, Instruksi, Penetapan, Peraturan, Pengumuman Dari Penguasa Perang Daerah Untuk Daerah Tk I Bali/Nusra Barat/Nusra Timur, Tahun 1959–1960* (Denpasar).

[48] The structure and function of this regulatory agency are outlined in Angkatan Darat Republik Indonesia, Komando Daerah Militer Nusa Tenggara, *Pool Perdagangan Daerah Bali* (Singaraja, 1959).

[49] In 1950, for example, there were only two foreign-owned coffee plantations in Bali/Lombok; together they covered a mere 74 hectares and produced only 28 tons of coffee. In East Java, by contrast, there were in the same year 101 Dutch-owned coffee plantations, covering 27,058 hectares and producing 9,698 tons of coffee per year. In total (exclusive of smallholder production), Indonesia produced 11,078 tons of coffee in 1950 on plantations covering 45,065 hectares. See Departemen Pertanian, *Almanak Pertanian 1953* (Jakarta, 1953), p. 359.

political party or grouping, left or right, as long as that position was not fundamentally challenged. Of course, in the absence of landed wealth, the economic base of the military in Bali was much more vulnerable to political change.

That vulnerability was compounded in 1961, when Sukarno decided to bestow the powerful post of Pepelrada on Governor Suteja rather than on the military commander. Stripped of its role as supreme state economic authority, the military in Bali ceased to have an autonomous economic base and so became substantially less independent politically than the military authorities in Java. In the short term this loss appears to have encouraged military cooperation with Suteja. Still, such a pragmatic alliance did not preclude a move against the governor when he became politically vulnerable after the October 1965 coup.

As governor and Pepelrada, Suteja was in a position to manage the flow of economic patronage from 1961 to 1965. And as political relations between the parties grew increasingly antagonistic, charges were heard that he was dispensing favors to political allies in the PKI and Partindo. The most notorious case of alleged patronage involved the lucrative contracts for the construction and staffing of the Bali Beach Hotel.[50] The brainchild of President Sukarno, it was the first luxury hotel on the island. Although it is difficult to assess the verity of the charges, in 1965 PNI-affiliated organizations and businessmen claimed that Suteja had granted the contracts—those for staff training and management as well as the actual construction of roads and the multistory hotel—to PKI/Partindo-affiliated companies, unions, and individuals. And in the aftermath of the October coup came persistent calls for the "retooling" and "freezing" of Bali Beach Hotel contractors, managers, and training staff.[51] To what extent this uproar was merely sour grapes on the part of people who were denied lucrative contracts is difficult to determine. But it was indicative of the way the economic interests of Bali's capitalists influenced and found expression in anti-PKI political campaigns of the postcoup period.

In spite of the allegations against Suteja, it is not at all clear that his decisions on economic policy always followed party lines. It is known, for example, that he had close contact with at least one prominent PNI businessman, who reportedly felt so greatly indebted to Suteja that he intervened to prevent his murder at the hands of the PNI in late 1965. What does seem clear is that in a place as small as Bali, with minuscule and overlapping economic and political elites, personal favors, corruption, and payoffs were an unavoidable part of the system. Bali's new capitalists, whatever their nominal political orientation, remained dependent on state and party pa-

[50] Control of the tourist industry was hotly contested at this time. See "Status NITOUR Bali Office Ditanjakan," *Suara Indonesia* (Denpasar), 5 September 1964.

[51] See, for example, "Bersihkan Bali Beach Hotel Dari Unsur G-30-S," ibid., 11 November 1965.

tronage, and were therefore prepared to work within virtually any state system. It is not surprising, therefore, that some wealthy businessmen became affiliated with the PKI and Partindo in the final years of the Old Order.[52] When it became clear that Suteja had lost control of the state apparatus that effectively determined their livelihood as a class, these businessmen did not find much difficulty in shifting allegiance to the PNI and disavowing any previous connection with the PKI or Partindo. Moreover, they took advantage of the purge politics after the October coup to attack both their Chinese and other Balinese competitors.

Land Reform

Access to agricultural land was one of the burning political issues of the early postindependence years in Bali, prompting local efforts at land reform. As the sense of economic crisis grew through the early 1960s and as inflation accelerated, land, already scarce and always an object of dispute, became virtually the only guarantee of livelihood, so that agrarian reform became an even more pressing priority. The implementation of national land-reform legislation in the early 1960s, therefore, had a singular significance for Balinese politics. Unlike the "confrontation" campaign against Malaysia or the struggle for West Irian, the reform had immediate importance for virtually every Balinese; most stood clearly to gain or to lose in the event of a straightforward interpretation of the laws.

Land reform lay at the core of the sudden expansion of the PKI and the BTI in the early 1960s, and triggered a significant realignment of political forces. Whereas the revolutionary movement and the political party mobilization of the early postindependence years had been based on a coalition of various classes, and had in some cases relied on the resources and autonomy of the more prosperous elements within the coalition, the politics of land encouraged a pattern of division based more clearly on class. Even former Republicans and pemuda, once more or less united by their common struggle, increasingly found themselves in opposite camps.

Control over land was already a contentious issue in the early 1950s because in 1950 at least 3,000 Balinese pemuda had suddenly been returned to "society."[53] In the course of the Revolution, the families of many pemuda had been forced to sell or pawn their land, and still others had lost legal title to their holdings as a consequence of their "illegal" guerrilla activity. Those

---

[52] One of the wealthiest businessmen with links to the PKI was L. L. T., who, according to Soe Hok Gie, "financed the PKI in Bali": "Mass Killings in Bali," p. 257. A report from October 1965 has L. L. T. donating an entire school building to the government of Buleleng. In the aftermath of the coup, he appears to have escaped unscathed by virtue of his friendship with an influential PNI leader and former pemuda.

[53] The figure of 3,000 comes from *Sin Po*, 25 October 1950.

who had taken over these holdings during the Revolution with the blessing of the village assembly or of local officials were not inclined now to return them to their original owners or renters. Together with a general antipathy toward things "feudal," these developments pushed land reform to the center of the pemuda agenda.

One of the first acts of Bali's legislature was the establishment, in March 1951, of a legal minimum harvest share of 50 percent for tenants.[54] The legislation also forbade *melaisin* and other systems of prepayment in cash for the right to farm a tract of land, and placed limits on the right of landlords to evict tenants without due notice or sufficient cause. The new government in Bali also made changes in taxation. Perhaps the most important was the land-tax exemption that was granted to those with holdings smaller than three hectares, and effectively freed more than 80 percent of landowners from taxation.

Though on paper these were encouraging signs for the antifeudal pemuda and for the vast majority of peasants, it soon became clear that the local legislation on landlord-tenant relations was essentially unenforceable. Tenants were unwilling to risk alienating a landlord who happened also to be an important local patron. Moreover, in many areas traditional bonds of loyalty to members of the local puri and other aristocratic families inhibited tenants from seeking strict enforcement of the law. Most still tended to accept the terms set by the landlord. In the early 1950s, moreover, peasant organizations were weakest and Republican state capacity least effective in precisely those areas—primarily the four eastern principalities—where the terms of tenancy were most unfair. Though the local state was in a good position to enact progressive legislation, it was more or less incapable of enforcing it.[55]

The national legislation of the early 1960s which mandated the redistribution of agricultural land and changes in the terms of harvest-sharing arrangements differed substantially from the local agrarian legislation of the 1950s in its political implications in Bali.[56] The changed economic and political environment in which the national legislation was introduced made it far more contentious and more volatile politically. Initiated by the PNI and Sukarno, and later supported by the PKI, the laws appear to have been

[54] This was the Peraturan Penjakap Daerah Bali tgl 30 Maret 1951, no. 5/DPRD. Subsequent local land-reform regulations included the Peraturan Penjakap Penguasa Perang Daerah Nusa Tenggara, tgl. 17 April, 1958, no. P.R.T.R. W/009/P.P.D./1958.

[55] See Ida Bagus Gde Putra, "Pelaksanaan Landreform dan Keresahan Masyarakat di Kabupaten Karangasem (1960–1965)," thesis, Universitas Udayana, Denpasar, 1986.

[56] The national land-reform legislation was a composite of several basic laws and dozens of regulations covering various aspects of land rights. The basic laws were Undang-Undang no. 5 Tahun 1960 Tentang Peraturan Dasar Pokok-Pokok Agraria (24 September 1960); Undang-Undang no. 56 PRP Tahun 1960 Tentang Penetapan Luas Tanah Pertanian (29 December 1960); Undang-Undang no. 2 Tahun 1960 Tentang Perjanjian Bagi-Hasil (Tanah Pertanian) (7 January 1960); and Peraturan Pemerintah no. 224 Tahun 1961 Tentang Pelaksanaan Pembagian Tanah dan Pemberian Ganti Rugi.

intended as least as much to stimulate an increase in agricultural production by small independent producers as to guarantee equitable relations of production in the countryside. Yet whatever their original objective, the laws held a strong appeal for marginal tenant farmers and agricultural laborers, particularly at a time of rampant inflation.

The law on land redistribution allowed a maximum of five hectares per household on wet rice land (sawah) and six hectares on dryland in the most densely populated areas (more than 400 persons per square kilometer), with greater holdings allowed in less densely populated regions.[57] Holdings in excess of these limits were to be redistributed by the state, with priority given to the people who were actually cultivating the plot in question. A separate regulation outlawed ownership of land by absentee landlords, and provided for redistribution of such holdings by the state.[58] Where landholding was not heavily concentrated, these regulations directly affected a small percentage of rural landowners, while effectively exempting many whose extensive holdings were distributed in small packages among relatives and clients. Nevertheless, because so many rural households owned little or no land, the new laws created at least the potential for significant gains by a very large number of people. Optimism was fueled by the stipulation in the land-reform laws of an ideal *minimum* holding of two hectares per household.

Even more dramatic in its implications was the law on harvest sharing.[59] The law acknowledged that local conditions would have to be taken into account in determining the precise division of the harvest between tenant and landowner, but it established as an ideal a division of half to the tenant and half to the owner on sawah and a two-thirds–one-third division on drylands. It also required certain production costs to be borne by the landowner. The terms of the harvest-sharing law were less radical than those earlier proposed by the PKI and BTI and demanded again by some of their members after 1963.[60] Nevertheless, even as it stood, the law promised a significant change from the practice in many parts of Java and Bali, where the customary division of the harvest was heavily balanced in favor of the landowner. Moreover, because it left the final determination of the harvest

---

[57] Maximum holdings in the most sparsely populated areas (fewer than 50 persons per square kilometer) were set at 15 hectares for sawah and 20 hectares for drylands. For further details, see art. 1(2) of Undang-Undang no. 56 PRP Tahun 1960 Tentang Penetapan Luas Tanah Pertanian (29 December 1960).

[58] The regulation governing the redistribution of the holdings of absentee landlords was Peraturan Pemerintah no. 224 Tahun 1961 Tentang Pelaksanaan Pembagian Tanah dan Pemberian Ganti Rugi.

[59] The basic law on harvest sharing was Undang-Undang no. 2 Tahun 1960 Tentang Perjanjian Bagi-Hasil (Tanah Pertanian) (7 January 1960). The ideal division of harvest arrangements were outlined in a clarification of art. 7 of the law.

[60] The PKI had earlier proposed a division of six-tenths to the tiller of the land, two-tenths to the owner, and two-tenths to the state: Slamet, "Views and Strategies," p. 10. In parts of Bali, after 1963, the PKI and BTI demanded a two-thirds–one-third division in favor of the tenant on sawah.

Table 10. Landholdings in Bali, 1963, by number of hectares

Kabupaten	Holdings <0.5 ha. (percent)	Holdings >2.0 ha. (percent)	Average farm size (ha.)	Total farmland (ha.)
Badung	62	5	0.73	37,908
Bangli	43	19	1.25	19,251
Buleleng	44	17	1.38	35,140
Jembrana	22	36	1.48	13,926
Gianyar	70	3	0.56	37,380
Karangasem	68	3	0.55	27,180
Klungkung	66	4	0.78	17,358
Tabanan	44	15	1.13	46,530
All Bali	54	11	0.95	234,673
Java-Madura	52	6	—	—

Source: Propinsi Bali, Kantor Sensus dan Statistik, *Himpunan Hasil2 Sensus Dan Survey 1961–1967* (Singaraja, 1968).

share in each area to the bupati, the law opened opportunities for significant political conflict.

The conditions prevailing in the Balinese countryside during this period gave these laws a unique political significance. By 1950, roughly 85 percent of all agricultural land in Bali was privately owned, but the average size of landholdings was small, and declining in the face of rapid population growth.[61] Fully 89 percent of all holdings in Bali were smaller than 2 hectares, and more than half were smaller than 0.5 hectares, a greater proportion than in Java-Madura (see Table 10). In some areas the proportion of holdings smaller than half a hectare was between 60 and 70 percent. The eruption of Gunung Agung in 1963, which destroyed tens of thousands of hectares of productive land, made the shortage of land even more acute in the final years of the Old Order. One can see here the basis for a very substantial degree of support for a policy of land reform that proposed a *minimum* of two hectares of sawah for each farm household.

While this minimum target was clearly impossible to achieve in Bali— there simply was not enough land to go around—the prospect of getting *any* amount of land was met with great enthusiasm. Moreover, because the average size of landholdings in Bali was so small, more stood to gain than to lose. This factor was central to the success of the PKI and the BTI in Bali.[62]

[61] According to the 1963 agricultural census, the average farm size in Bali was 0.95 hectare, and in some areas, such as Gianyar, Karangasem, Klungkung, and Badung, it was significantly smaller. See Propinsi Bali, Kantor Sensus dan Statistik, *Himpunan Hasil2 Sensus dan Survey 1961–1967 Bali* (Singaraja, 1968).

[62] Interviews with I Gusti Putu Yasa Arimbawa (former head of Petani, Tabanan), 20 December 1986, Banjar Bongan Tengah, Tabanan, and Ida Bagus Indera (former punggawa of Sawan, 1955–60; of Tejakula, 1961–65; and of Kubutambahan, 1966–67), 17 December 1986, Singaraja.

19. An elderly woman with a basket of dried cassava near Gunung Agung, shortly after it erupted in 1963. The eruption destroyed 62,000 hectares of farmland and resulted in widespread malnutrition. Coinciding with the aggressive campaign to implement new land-reform legislation, the destruction of productive land may have contributed to rising militancy and violent confrontations in the countryside. (*Indonesia, Department of Information, Denpasar*)

Though the continued dependence of tenants on their landlords discouraged some from taking action, the issue of land reform brought class differences into sharper focus and encouraged some migration across party lines.

Though there were some large landlords in Bali, landed wealth was generally speaking not heavily concentrated. Holdings of more than two hectares accounted for only 11 percent of the total agricultural land in 1963. The number of holdings that exceeded the legal limit of five hectares of sawah and six of dryland was even smaller.[63] Thus a surprisingly small number of landlords were actually in any immediate danger of losing part of their land. Table 11 indicates that in four kabupaten—Tabanan, Badung, Karangasem, and Gianyar—the total number of owners potentially affected was only about 1,500.

Yet, if the number of owners was relatively small in these areas and throughout the island, their social and political influence was not. They included members of leading puri and other households that remained so-

[63] In accordance with the regulations linking the legal limits to population density, the maximum size of landholdings permitted were even higher in much of Bali. In Karangasem, for example, where the population density was judged to be "quite dense," the limits were 7.5 hectares of sawah and 9 hectares of dryland.

Table 11. Land redistribution in Tabanan, Karangasem, Gianyar, and Badung, 1964

Kabupaten	Total hectares to be redistributed	Area not yet redistributed		Landowners affected	Average holding of affected landowners (hectares)
		ha.	%		
Tabanan	2,257	1,664	74	849	2.65
Karangasem	1,629	351	21	127	10.07
Gianyar	1,525	1,082	71	144	10.59
Badung	1,153	400	35	383	3.01
All Kabupaten	6,564	3,497	53	1,503	4.36

Source: Suara Indonesia (Denpasar), 17 May 1964; Putra, "Pelaksanaan Landreform," pp. 81, 87.

cially and politically influential in their respective communities. Indeed, according to figures compiled in 1949, among the largest landowners in Bali were, in order of the size of their holdings, the former rajas of Karangasem, Gianyar, Bangli, Buleleng, and Badung.[64] The figures for Badung and Buleleng represent the total holdings of the whole family, but the others represent only that portion of the royal family's landed assets that were held by the raja himself. Thus, for example, an uncle of the former raja of Karangasem also had extensive landholdings—92 hectares of sawah and 317 hectares of dryland—so that together the two members of the family owned about 5 percent of the sawah in Karangasem. As leading local patrons, these men wielded substantial influence over the political choices and economic opportunities of other members of the community.

Perhaps more far-reaching in their impact than the redistribution of land, and equally contentious, were the laws governing landlord-tenant relations. Available statistics indicate that 36 percent of farms in Bali were cultivated under some tenancy arrangement, or only slightly less than the figure for Central Java.[65] Conditions of tenancy varied widely from region to region. By far the worst terms for the tenant were found in the eastern kingdoms of Karangasem, Klungkung, Gianyar, and Bangli, where tenants kept as little as one-fifth of the harvest, and where they were often required to pay advances to the landlord in cash or kind for the right to cultivate the land (see Map 5).[66] A 1965 study of a village in western Gianyar, for example,

[64] These figures were compiled by the head of the Bali Land Tax Office in April 1949 at the request of George McT. Kahin, who kindly made them available to me. For details, see chapter 5, Table 2.

[65] See Propinsi Bali, Kantor Sensus dan Statistik, *Himpunan Hasil2 Sensus dan Survey 1961–1967 Bali;* and Raka, *Monografi Pulau Bali,* p. 34.

[66] Raka, *Monografi Pulau Bali,* pp. 33–34. The terms of harvest sharing depended on several factors, including the type of land (sawah or dryland) and the type of crop. Thus in Karangesem, for example, a tenant who cultivated sawah would customarily receive two-fifths the crop, while a tenant on dryland with coconut trees or some other long-term crop would receive only a fifth of the produce. See Putra, "Pelaksanaan Landreform," p. 97.

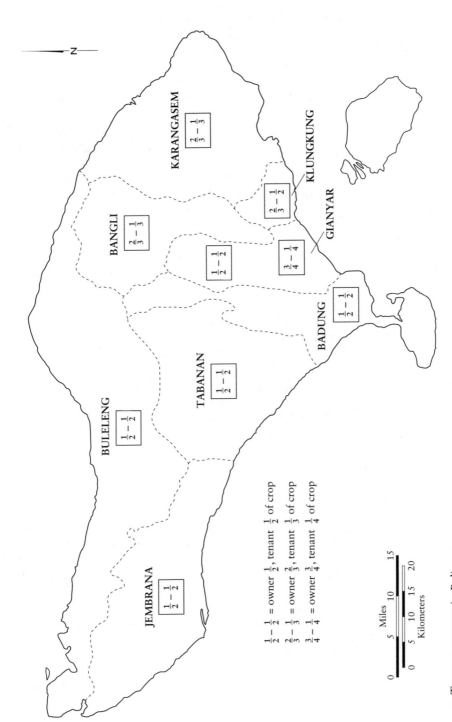

N

BULELENG
$\frac{1}{2} - \frac{1}{2}$

JEMBRANA
$\frac{1}{2} - \frac{1}{2}$

KARANGASEM
$\frac{2}{3} - \frac{1}{3}$

BANGLI
$\frac{2}{3} - \frac{1}{3}$

TABANAN
$\frac{1}{2} - \frac{1}{2}$

$\frac{1}{2} - \frac{1}{2}$

$\frac{3}{4} - \frac{1}{4}$

KLUNGKUNG
$\frac{2}{3} - \frac{1}{3}$

GIANYAR

BADUNG
$\frac{1}{2} - \frac{1}{2}$

$\frac{1}{2} - \frac{1}{2}$ = owner $\frac{1}{2}$, tenant $\frac{1}{2}$ of crop
$\frac{2}{3} - \frac{1}{3}$ = owner $\frac{2}{3}$, tenant $\frac{1}{3}$ of crop
$\frac{3}{4} - \frac{1}{4}$ = owner $\frac{3}{4}$, tenant $\frac{1}{4}$ of crop

Miles
0   5   10   15

Kilometers
0   5   10   15   20

5. Tenancy systems in Bali

recorded the case of a sharecropper who "surrendered his son to the land-lord to work for him for fear of being ousted from his land, and after he had to take back his son because he needed him too much himself, he replaced him with the boy's younger sister."[67]

In the central kingdoms of Badung, Tabanan, and Buleleng—the base areas of the Republican resistance during the Revolution—the conditions were somewhat better for the tenant, the crop generally being divided equal-ly between landowner and tenant.[68] Yet while tenants in these central re-gions were relatively well off from the viewpoint of tenancy arrangements, it would be misleading to characterize them as a uniformly prosperous class. Important differences remained between the prosperous landowning peas-ants and those with little or no land, whose situation deteriorated with the inflation of the mid-1960s. Conditions were probably most disadvantageous for landless agricultural laborers, many of whom worked in the coffee-growing areas of Buleleng and Tabanan. In a coffee-growing village in Bule-leng, for example, a 1965 report noted that "any sharecropper or annual laborer could be ousted at will if his performance or attitude . . . displeased his employers. The landlords would not shrink from destroying the laborers' crops or even razing their huts with the help of hired bandits."[69]

In short, rural relations of production in Bali were such that tenants and agricultural laborers stood to gain in at least two ways under the terms of the national land-reform legislation. They might receive a portion of the land they were actively farming which was deemed to exceed the maximum limits or to be owned by an absentee landowner; or they could hope for the enforcement of certain legal restrictions on the terms of tenancy, such as the distribution of the harvest and production costs.

Class, Culture, and Mass Politics

One of the most tenacious bits of conventional wisdom about Balinese politics under the Old Order is that political parties relied principally on individuals of high caste with "traditional" constituencies to establish and broaden their mass bases. Carol Warren refers to this pattern of mobilization as a "vertical alliance" strategy—implying a political alliance that crossed or transcended class lines.[70] Essentially two arguments—or rather, bits of

---

[67] Slamet, "Views and Strategies," p. 119.

[68] Terms of tenancy varied locally, of course, and according to the kind of crop cultivated. The crop-sharing arrangements mentioned here refer specifically to the main rice crop (*padi kertamasa*) on irrigated fields. There were also variations in the respective burden of owner and tenant with regard to the provision of seed and other inputs.

[69] Slamet, "Views and Strategies," pp. 125–26.

[70] Carol Warren, "Balinese Political Culture and the Rhetoric of National Development," in P. Alexander, ed., *Creating Indonesian Cultures* (Sydney: Oceania Ethnographies, 1989), pp. 39–54.

evidence—have been advanced as proof that class was politically unimportant in Bali; both pertain specifically to the case of the PKI.[71] They deserve closer examination.

The first argument arises from the fact that the PKI in Bali had leaders and members of the three highest castes (triwangsa). This is generally taken as evidence that the PKI was not genuinely a party of workers and peasants. Triwangsa with PKI sympathies or leadership positions included, for example, Governor Suteja (Satria), A.A.G.A. (Satria), A.A.A.D. (Satria), members of the Geria P. (Brahmana), and I.B.D. (Brahmana). The fact of a triwangsa presence in the PKI-Bali is beyond dispute, but if it is advanced as a claim about the party's *class* character, it is misleading. The categories of caste and class in Bali are not interchangeable; that is to say, the caste status of an individual is not a reliable guide to his or her economic, political, and ideological position.

Yet even if we were to accept the premise that a particular caste implies a particular class—for to some degree the two categories do overlap—a serious problem remains. The presence of triwangsa in the PKI organization cannot, in fairness, be taken as an indication of the overall class character of the party and its social base. Evidence, discussed later, shows that by the early 1960s the PKI and BTI had begun to develop a strong mass base among the poorest farmers and towndwellers, and that at the local level, party and mass-organization cadres were not predominantly men and women of high caste. Even at the provincial level, some of the most influential PKI leaders and sympathizers were commoners; including, for example, the head of the PKI Provincial Committee, K.K., and the former pemuda G.P., widely acknowledged to be Suteja's right-hand man. It is not clear, then, why we should accept the existence of a clutch of triwangsa as indicative of the general class composition or character of the PKI in Bali. Similarly, the fact that the PNI and the postcoup killers included, in the words of the PNI-Bali member Ernst Utrecht, "ordinary people" and "small farmers" does not constitute compelling evidence of the fundamental class character of the PNI.[72] To speak of the class character of any party is to speak of a general or essential pattern, both sociologically and ideologically. It is not an empirical claim that *all* members belong to a single narrowly defined socioeconomic stratum.

The second argument advanced to demonstrate the ostensible political insignificance of class as the basis for PKI support in Bali is the patently false claim that class differences did not yet exist in Bali. Utrecht writes: "Sociologically speaking, there was no reason to establish a branch of the PKI in

---

[71] These arguments are articulated most clearly by Ernst Utrecht, a former PNI official in Bali, but similar ones have found their way into much that has been written about Balinese politics in this period. See Utrecht, "Het bloedbad op Bali," *Groene Amsterdammer,* 14 January 1967.

[72] Quotations in this and the following paragraphs are from ibid.

Bali, because the social conditions for it did not exist there." According to this logic, the PKI in Bali was nothing more than a vehicle for a mixed bag of political opportunists and power grabbers, "people and groups who for one reason or another had an axe to grind with members of the PNI." The mobilization of the rural population by the BTI likewise is portrayed as the irresponsible provocation of an otherwise harmonious and happy peasant community.

In order to make this position stick, Utrecht paints a picture of Balinese social harmony and economic well-being reminiscent of prewar travel fantasies. He writes, for example, that "in the Balinese *banjar* [hamlets] . . . there is little difference between rich and poor, and there is no unemployment." The tradition of mutual assistance, he assures us, is still strong and forms the basis of all social interaction in the countryside. Consequently, "no one goes hungry, and there is no real rural proletariat." In the towns "none are left to their fate by the community," so "there is no real urban proletariat" either. The evidence provided in this chapter leaves little doubt that this portrayal is substantially untrue.

The available evidence suggests that it was the poorest and the most land-hungry farmers and agricultural laborers who became members of the BTI in Bali after 1963. This pattern makes intuitive sense and it accords better with the facts of BTI militancy than do existing portrayals of the PKI and BTI organization in Bali as a superficial mask for "traditional" social groupings. It was, moreover, a pattern deliberately fostered by BTI tactics, which included the distribution of clothing, food, and promises of land to the poorest and the most vulnerable.[73] The membership of the PNI peasant organization, Petani, was more heterogenous in class terms, perhaps reflecting the continued use of vertical mobilization strategies by the PNI. Petani members included relatively prosperous landowning peasants, but also poorer tenant farmers who remained socially and economically dependent on landlords affiliated to the PNI.

The differences between the BTI and Petani in Bali were accentuated during the land-reform campaign. While Petani and the BTI both officially supported the reform, there were clear differences in the seriousness and the militancy of their efforts and in the social classes to which they appealed. While the BTI openly advocated a policy of "land to the tiller," for example, Petani emphasized prosperity, security, unity, and upholding Pancasila. A few examples from different parts of the island demonstrate the different patterns of BTI and Petani membership and mobilization during the land-reform campaign.

In Tejakula, Buleleng, a poor district with a high rate of tenancy and a large number of migrant laborers from neighboring Karangasem, the PKI

---

[73] Putra, "Pelaksanaan Landreform," pp. 58–59.

and BTI became very popular with the "little people" in the early 1960s. According to the punggawa at that time, himself a PNI man, the PNI came to be seen there as a party of the landlords, and suffered a serious loss in membership to the PKI after 1963.[74] The decline of the PNI created an opportunity for some PNI-affiliated peasants to migrate to the PKI and the BTI. The more prosperous peasants, however, tended to remain with Petani. Similarly, in Karangasem, the popularity of the PKI and the BTI with migrant laborers and small tenant farmers reportedly increased dramatically after the forceful seizures of land under the *aksi sepihak* campaign in 1963.[75]

Within a given village, the hamlets with the largest BTI memberships appear to have been those with the greatest number of agricultural laborers and poor peasants and the fewest middle and rich peasants.[76] In a village in west Buleleng, for example, the BTI branch was organized and led by a landless agricultural laborer early in 1965, and all of its members were either poor peasants or agricultural laborers. In Mengwi, the two poorest hamlets were almost entirely PKI and BTI, while the other hamlets in the village were more or less equally divided politically between the PNI/Petani and the PKI/BTI.[77] Finally, in Tabanan, according to the former regional head of Petani, the BTI was strongest in those areas with the largest numbers of landless peasants and agricultural laborers, while Petani's strength was in the relatively prosperous areas.[78]

A closer look at relations of production in Tabanan provides some additional clues to the source of Petani's strength there, and to the relative weakness of the BTI. In 1963 the proportion of very small holdings in Tabanan was 44 percent, or less than the average for Bali (54 percent); in other words, this was an area where the average farm size was relatively large. To be sure, Tabanan had its share of landless tenant farmers who stood to gain from the land reform, many of whom gravitated to the PKI and BTI. However, it had a much greater number—in absolute and percentage terms—of prosperous landowning peasants and landlords, in a position to lose as a consequence of the reform. It had then the highest percentage of owner-operated farms (73 percent) and the lowest level of tenancy anywhere in Bali.[79] And of the total of 384,925 landowners registered in Bali as a

[74] Interview with Ida Bagus Indera, 17 December 1986, Singaraja. The district of Kubutambahan, in Buleleng, was also a PKI stronghold, but here the social base of the party was less clear. According to Indera, who was punggawa there in 1966–67, many people joined the PKI on the suggestion of the influential Gde Ngurah Intaran, a punggawa during the colonial period, who had not joined the Revolution.

[75] Putra, "Pelaksanaan Landreform," p. 104.

[76] Slamet, "Views and Strategies," pp. 127, 190.

[77] Personal communication: Henk Schulte Nordholt, 2 May 1987.

[78] Interview with I Gusti Putu Yasa Arimbawa, 20 December 1986, Banjar Bongan Tengah, Tabanan.

[79] Propinsi Bali, Kantor Sensus dan Statistik, *Himpunan Hasil2 Sensus dan Survey 1961–1967 Bali.*

whole in 1956, 81,537 (or more than 20 percent) were in Tabanan.[80] This large group of relatively prosperous landowning peasants and small proprietors very likely formed the core of Petani's strength in Tabanan.[81] The split between the BTI and Petani, then, was not simply between "tenants" and the largest "landlords," but reflected a more subtle gradation of class difference between, on the one hand, poor and landless tenants and, on the other, relatively prosperous, landowning peasants, which was accentuated by the land-reform campaign after 1963.

The implementation of the land reform appears also to have influenced the caste character of the BTI and PKI leadership, such that commoners became increasingly prominent after 1963. A rough survey of the names of hamlet and village PKI and BTI cadres mentioned in press reports and other accounts from 1964 and 1965 reveals that very few indeed were triwangsa. Although caste status cannot be taken as an indication of class position, the small number of triwangsa does suggest that in these years the PKI and BTI in Bali were not relying heavily on "vertical alliance" strategies of mobilization. The PKI and BTI cadres were undoubtedly influential men and women, but on the whole they were not influential as a consequence of their caste status or their wealth. The emergence of such low-caste leaders at the local level may help to account for the radicalism and militancy of the BTI after 1963.

The evidence from Karangasem is revealing. In a place where feudal traditions remained strong, one might reasonably have expected to find the PKI employing a "vertical alliance" strategy. Yet in three areas with substantial PKI memberships in Karangasem (Sidemen, Ababi, and Antiga) the majority of PKI and BTI activists were commoners. The only exception was in Sidemen, where some, though by no means all, of the PKI cadres were of the Satria caste. Like many of the pemuda leaders during the National Revolution, the popularity and credibility of PKI and BTI leaders in these areas appear to have depended far more on their ability as orators and organizers, their intelligence, their skill in martial arts, and their reputation for spiritual or magical powers than on traditional prestige deriving from caste or aristocratic lineage.[82]

---

[80] Tabanan was followed by Badung with 75,004 landowners and Gianyar with 62,811: Propinsi Nusa Tenggara, Kantor Penempatan Tenaga Daerah Nuteng Barat, *Tindjauan Pasar Kerdja*, p. 35.

[81] The strength of this group may also help to explain the stiff resistance to land reform encountered there. Table 11 shows that of the three areas with the worst record of land redistribution as of mid-1964 (Tabanan, Gianyar, and Badung), Tabanan had the largest absolute number of affected landowners, the largest area of land slated for redistribution, and the lowest level of redistributed land (26% of the area slated for redistribution).

[82] Putra, "Pelaksanaan Landreform," pp. 124–26, 51–52. In addition, many of the local PKI and BTI leaders about whom we have information were either teachers or community leaders, such as hamlet heads (*klian banjar*) or village heads (*kepala desa*). The klian banjar appear to have been especially important in mass mobilization. While klian could be very-

Despite this similarity with the revolutionary period, the politics and the economic conditions of postrevolutionary Indonesia had transformed the bases of political loyalty and party allegiance in Bali in the direction of greater class polarization. Thus, in two leading areas of the Revolution—Badung and Tabanan—where one might have anticipated stronger leftist tendencies, opposition to land reform and to the PKI was powerful. We can resolve the paradox by recalling the configurations of social forces that supported the Revolution and the land reform. The social base of the Revolution encompassed a plurality of class positions. As a whole, therefore, it was not a natural base for the PKI, particularly as the party took an increasingly militant stand on land and economic issues. The alliance of social forces that had provided the backbone of the Revolution in the central regions—a relatively prosperous and autonomous peasantry, "progressive" elements of the aristocracy, a small indigenous capitalist class, an educated nationalist middle class, and a mixed bag of pemuda—could hardly have been expected to become the vanguard of a genuine social or agrarian revolution.

Yet, while class appears to have been significant in transforming political affiliation and the character of political conflict in Bali, its political salience should not be overstated. In many instances, strong bonds of loyalty or close religious or familial ties between landlords and tenants did inhibit class-based consciousness and action. Furthermore, because landowners who were immediately threatened by land reform often had substantial followings of clients and tenants, the effective size of the community that felt aggrieved by the reform was actually far larger than just the number of landlords who faced expropriation. This was particularly the case in the eastern kingdoms, where feudal relations remained deeply entrenched and very high rates of tenancy continued to prevail in the 1960s.

Thus a poor peasant who had for years cultivated a plot belonging to the local puri may well have felt threatened by the redistribution of the puri's land, because he could not be sure that the new owner would permit him to remain on the land. Others may have felt that it was wrong or inappropriate to seize the land of one's lord.[83] These kinds of influence tended to work to the advantage of the PNI and Petani in preventing mass defection to the PKI and BTI along class lines. They also help to explain how bitter conflict could erupt not just between the wealthiest landlords and the most marginal tenants but also among relatively poor peasants themselves.

---

influential within their community, their social and political position did not necessarily militate against radicalism. See ibid., pp. 58–59, 125.

[83] In one such case, reported from Sidemen, Karangasem, a peasant (I Wayan Pugleg) refused to join the BTI at a public meeting, despite a promise that as a member he would get to own the puri-owned land that he cultivated. According to others who attended the meeting, Pugleg refused on the grounds that it would "not be fitting to oppose the royal family since he himself had long been a dependent of the puri": Putra, "Pelaksanaan Landreform," p. 112.

Political Conflict over Land

In general treatments of Indonesia's land reform, Bali is mentioned only parenthetically. Rex Mortimer shows how conflict over land in Java was accelerated by and found expression in bitter antagonism between *santri* (committed Muslim) and *abangan* (nominal Muslim) villagers, but he provides no satisfactory parallel explanation of the logic of the conflict in Bali.[84] Those who favored the land reform in Bali he refers to casually as *abangan*, but in Bali's very different religious and cultural environment such a designation is of questionable value. The result is that the violent political conflict of the mid-1960s continues to be seen either as a foregone conclusion— because Balinese politics are understood simply to have reflected developments in Java—or as some sort of mystery, decipherable only in terms of "traditional" Balinese culture. What is needed, clearly, is an explanation of the political conflict over land in Bali that takes account of both the cultural specificities of the island and the broader political and structural forces with which they interacted. The following analysis pays particular attention to the latter because they have been less frequently treated in works on Bali.

The PKI decision in 1963 to implement land reform through an aggressive rural mobilization campaign marked a departure from the party's united front strategy.[85] The decision was made at least in part to increase the political leverage of the party at the center. It also apparently emerged out of an awareness that the party needed to do more than it had done until then to defend the interests of workers and peasants at a time of economic crisis. Once set in motion, however, the reform campaign appears to have taken on its own momentum, and local PKI and BTI cadres began to make demands that exceeded the changes stipulated in the laws. In some areas local activists also went beyond what was considered desirable by the party leadership in Jakarta.[86] The unilateral and sometimes forceful seizures of land known as aksi sepihak were a case in point. Originally supported by the PKI leadership and by President Sukarno as a legitimate means to ensure the implementation of the land reform, the aksi sepihak were officially disavowed by Sukarno and the national leaderships of the PNI and the PKI in a joint

---

[84] Mortimer, "Class, Social Cleavage, and Indonesian Communism," p. 18.

[85] Mortimer writes that by late 1963 the PKI "judged the time ripe for a class offensive in the villages, the first decisive turn to a struggle hinged on class cleavages": ibid., p. 18. For a description of the PKI's strategy and an analysis of the historical and political considerations that shaped it, see ibid., pp. 8–12. Slamet describes the PKI decision as part of a plan to "initiate a real class struggle aiming at a more basic transformation of agrarian relations": "Views and Strategies," p. 18.

[86] Benjamin White writes that on the question of land reform, the BTI was more militant than the PKI leadership, which "often showed an ambivalent attitude towards these more radical campaigns": "Rural Resistance," p. 10. The BTI, which emerged during the Revolution, had not always been associated with the PKI. An institutional and ideological basis therefore existed for the BTI to take a position that diverged from that of the national PKI leadership, particularly on the issue of land reform.

statement issued in December 1964.[87] Nevertheless, the land seizures and acts of intimidation and violence by both PKI and PNI supporters continued into 1965. Indeed, PKI cadres conducting research in villages in Java, Bali, and Sumatra in early 1965 judged some BTI members to be "too leftist, ready to throw themselves on the devils, longing for a quick reversal of the situation and not believing in any peaceful means to break the power of the multifaced devils who control[led] their lives."[88]

The aggressiveness of the PKI and BTI in pushing land reform contributed to the increasing popularity of both organizations after 1963, particularly in the plantation sector but also where average landholdings were small and the terms of tenancy skewed against tenants. Peasant militancy—as evidenced in the aksi sepihak—constituted a real threat to landowners and to the military, who had come to have a strong stake in the economic status quo after the imposition of martial law in 1957. It was in part in retaliation against the successes of the left during this time that the military and its conservative rural allies struck back with such violence at the PKI and BTI after the 1965 coup.

In Bali the implementation of the land-reform legislation began officially on 1 January 1961. The first phase of the process involved the formation of land-reform committees, land registration committees, and working bodies at the kabupaten, kecamatan, and village level. The committees were first to oversee the registration of excess land and then to make the politically sensitive decisions about what land was to be redistributed and to whom. The composition of the committees ensured that government officials played a preponderant role in these controversial decisions.[89] Particularly powerful were the bupati, who served as chairmen of the kabupaten-level land-reform committees and oversaw the formation of the committees at lower levels.[90] Representatives of the farmers' organizations and other mass organizations also served on the committees and working bodies, though they were less numerous and initially less powerful.

These arrangements worked to the advantage of the PNI (and former PSI) members who still held dominant positions in most of the kabupaten-level bureaucracies in Bali. One consequence was that, as in Java, land reform proceeded very slowly for at least two years. By mid-1963, for example, not a single formal harvest-sharing agreement had been completed in accordance with the provisions of the 1960 law. The process of land registration

[87] The statement, issued on 12 December 1964, was known as the Bogor Declaration. Mortimer argues that the PKI was relieved to see a compromise on the issue, because the aksi sepihak campaign had ceased to have any positive benefit for the party at the national level: "Class, Social Cleavage, and Indonesian Communism," pp. 19–20.

[88] Slamet, "Views and Strategies," p. 34.

[89] For details of the composition of the committees at the kabupaten level, see Putra, "Pelaksanaan Landreform," pp. 68–69.

[90] Among their other powers, the bupati were given the authority to determine the precise terms for the division of harvest within their region.

was also proceeding at a snail's pace, with the result that very little land had been redistributed by mid-1963. The situation changed dramatically in the latter half of 1963, when the land-reform legislation became the focus of the PKI's rural mass mobilization campaign and won the backing of Sukarno and key elements in Bali's state apparatus. With this shift, the land reform was implemented far more vigorously, and as a consequence it came to represent a genuine threat to landed interests and to their backers in the PNI.

Governor Suteja's support for land reform was crucial. Shortly after the PKI leadership declared its mass mobilization plans, Suteja began to issue executive orders calling for the rapid completion of land redistribution.[91] In August 1963 he initiated competitions for the implementation of the law on harvest sharing to encourage tenants to take full advantage of their rights. And in 1964 he threatened legal action against land-reform committees that continued to drag their feet.[92] In the provincial administration Suteja worked to ensure that key positions were filled by people who supported radical land reform. His chief agricultural inspector for Bali, Sumbadi, for example, was known to be sympathetic. Suteja was also instrumental in overcoming local-level resistance by the PNI and landlords who dominated many of the kabupaten- and kecamatan-level land-reform and land registration committees, and who were on the whole far less enthusiastic than the national PNI leadership.[93]

Because excess land was to be taken by state authorities and then redistributed, the land-reform system depended critically on the belief that the authorities would act impartially both in expropriation and in distribution. Yet by 1963 the political divisions in Bali's state apparatus were so clear that there was legitimate concern about its impartiality. Governor Suteja's support for radical reform, while it was effective in some areas, therefore also fueled polarization and violence at the local level. By failing to order police intervention in the event of aksi sepihak confrontations, for example, Suteja appeared to lend his support to the PKI. His inaction in turn encouraged activists of the PNI and its peasant organization, Petani, to take direct action rather than rely on the "state" to intervene. In 1986 the former Petani leader in Tabanan recalled the logic of such direct action:

None of the police had the courage to act unless they had the go-ahead from Suteja. If Suteja said nothing, they did nothing. And so we had no choice but to

[91] For a sense of Suteja's stance on land reform, see *Suara Indonesia* (Denpasar): "Titik Tolak Giatkan Pelaksanaan UUP Agraria Selesaikan Revolusi," 25 September 1962, and "Pd. Gub. Bali—Pengakuan Lebih Tegas Thd. Tani dan Buruh Sbg. Soko-gurunja Revolusi," 25 September 1964.
[92] See, for example, "Bali Harus Mampu Menjelesaikan Landreform Belum September Ini," ibid., 17 May 1964.
[93] Eliseo Rocamora writes that in Bali, "PNI control over local administration proved of no avail with a Governor apt to cancel the decisions of pro-PNI local administrators. By late 1964, the confrontation between the two parties over the land problem was so intense that armed clashes had become a frequent occurrence": "Nationalism in Search of an Ideology," p. 530.

fight it out right there. One time the BTI leader said to me, "Why don't we sit down and negotiate?" I said, "Forget it! Denpasar is the place for negotiations. Here we fight to see who wins!"[94]

The PKI and BTI militancy was similarly stimulated by the obstructive behavior of PNI and landlord-dominated committees.

In accordance with their political and economic interests, party and government officials took advantage of bureaucratic contacts either to obstruct or to promote the distribution of land. The pace of land reform therefore varied from one kabupaten to the next, depending in part on the political complexion of the executive in each area. In Jembrana and Buleleng, which had relatively high proportions and absolute numbers of large landowners, one might have expected stiff opposition to land reform (see Table 10). Yet the redistribution of land was almost complete there by the time of the October 1965 coup. The success of land reform in these two kabupaten was attributable in large measure to the existence of pro-PKI/Partindo people in the local administration, such as the bupati I.B.M. in Buleleng and the bupati I.B.D. in Jembrana.[95] In areas such as Badung and Gianyar, by contrast, the position of anti-land-reform forces was, at least until the end of 1964, bolstered by the existence of long-standing PNI (and former PSI) kabupaten administrations (see Table 12). The result was determined and powerful opposition to land redistribution within the state itself.[96]

In the course of implementation, then, there was a good deal of leeway for political meddling by bodies that ostensibly were organs of the state, for example: in the process of land registration; in the determination of which holdings were in excess of the legal maximum and which landlords were considered absentee owners; and in the selection of recipients of redistributed land.[97] A February 1964 report to the provincial legislature specifically mentioned the kabupaten-level land-reform committees and land registration committees and the Agrarian Affairs Inspectorate as loci of political manipulation.

Local committees cooperated with landlords by underreporting actual

---

[94] Interview with I Gusti Putu Yasa Arimbawa (former head of Petani-Tabanan), 20 December 1986, Banjar Bongan Tengah, Tabanan.

[95] The bupati of Buleleng was widely believed to be sympathetic to Partindo. Like Sukarno and Suteja, however, he claimed to be nonparty, and in 1964 he explicitly denied affiliation with Partindo. See "Bupati M: Saja Bukan Partindo," *Suara Indonesia* (Denpasar), 19 May 1964.

[96] The political balance changed in late 1964, when pro-PKI bupati were appointed in both Badung and Gianyar for brief periods. In 1965 Gianyar had a PKI bupati, I.M.S., but his base in the local administration was not well established. He was removed from office on 8 November 1965, only a few days after the "freezing" of the PKI in Bali.

[97] Instances of cheating and foot-dragging were reported frequently in the local press, particularly in 1964, when most of the actual transfers took place. See, for example, the following articles in *Suara Indonesia* (Denpasar): "Petani Ketjil Jang Dirugikan," 6 March 1964; "Selesaikan Landreform Setjara Djudjur," 20 March 1964; "Banjak Faktor-Faktor Negatif Jang Menghambat Djalannja Landreform di Bali," 10 June 1964; and "Feodal Keraton Tuan Tanah Kepala Batu," 2 October 1964.

Table 12. Political affiliations of bupati of Bali, 1964–1965

Kabupaten	Bupati	Party affiliation
Buleleng	I.B.M.	Partindo
Jembrana	I.B.D.	PKI
Tabanan	Ida Bagus Puja	PNI
Badung	I.G.N.A. Pacung (to November 1964)	PSI
	A.A.G.A. (early 1965)	PKI
	I Wayan Dhana (late 1965)	PNI
Gianyar	Cokorda Ngurah (to November 1964)	PSI
	I.M.S. (to November 1965)	PKI
Bangli	Ida Bagus M. Sutha	PNI
Klungkung	Cokorda Anom Putra	PNI
Karangasem	Cokorda Lanang Rai	PNI

holdings or by warning them ahead of time to adjust the records of their holdings. A common tactic for avoiding the confiscation of one's land was to divide it up among kin or loyal allies, thereby bringing each individual holding within the legal maximum.[98] The committees seldom went to the field to verify the information provided by landowners, so that landowners were free to misreport the exact size or location of their holdings. Some also lied about the identity of the tenant, so that when their land was redistributed, it would go to a close friend or relative rather than to the tenant farmer entitled to it by law.[99]

Other tactics for subverting the reform included the falsification of deeds and titles and deliberate foot-dragging in carrying out the formalities involved in the transfer of ownership. The following situation was reported from Singakerta, Gianyar:

> One aristocratic family had formally divided up the land among kin, sharecropping going on as usual; other plots had been illegally sold to the village head, who then sharecropped them out to farmers, instead of the plots being surrendered to the original sharecroppers. Some sharecroppers had indeed received in ownership the land they tilled after paying off the compensation sum, but official certificates were withheld by the village head, or anyway no efforts were made by him to obtain an official confirmation of the transaction from the Ministry.[100]

Landlords also used the court system to challenge the decisions of the land-reform committees and to hold up the actual transfer of their land.[101] These

[98] Interview with Ida Bagus Indera, 30 September 1986, Singaraja.
[99] Putra, "Pelaksanaan Landreform," pp. 89–90.
[100] Slamet, "Views and Strategies," p. 92.
[101] Putra recounts the case of I Serimadi and his relatives, who owned land in Karangasem but had resided in Buleleng for several years. The land-reform committee in their kabupaten judged them to be absentee landlords, but the family took the case to court and won: "Pelaksanaan Landreform," pp. 91–94.

tactics had long-term consequences. When charges were filed in the courts and legal transactions left uncompleted, land transfers remained unresolved and therefore open to dispute. When the political balance shifted against the PKI and BTI in late 1965, the process of reclaiming lost land was therefore relatively simple.

The existence of party-affiliated peasant organizations in virtually all villages and hamlets on the island contributed to the dynamic of conflict in rural areas. Although the vast majority of BTI branches developed in late 1964 and 1965, the organization quickly gained a reputation for unusual militancy and radicalism, emphasizing the principle of "land to the tiller." Like their counterparts in Java, BTI activists in Bali appear to have gone well beyond a strict interpretation of the land-reform laws, thereby stirring up conflict. In Karangasem, for example, some BTI members reportedly demanded two-thirds of the harvest for tenants on sawah, with some proportion of that share to go to the PKI. Apparently BTI activists promised this kind of harvest-sharing arrangement at public meetings in several villages throughout Karangasem, and very likely in other parts of Bali as well.[102]

Mass political action in Bali took a variety of forms, of which the most notorious were the aksi sepihak.[103] Also known as *pendobrakan* in Bali, such actions are known to have occurred throughout Karangasem, Badung, Tabanan, Buleleng, and Jembrana, and probably took place in other areas as well.[104] Though the ultimate target of the aksi sepihak was usually the land of the largest landowners—and quite often that of the local puri—the immediate victim of the action was not infrequently a tenant farmer who cultivated the plot. In one case reported from Karangasem, a group of about forty BTI supporters from Desa Rendang marched with flags and banners to seize a piece of sawah in Desa Sangkan Gunung owned by the Puri Karangasem. The tenant farming the land in question, one I Wayan Kenggo, was in his field when the group arrived, and reportedly died resisting their attempt to seize the land. In a similar case in Yang Taluh, Sidemen, the land in question was also owned by the Puri Karangasem, but the tenant, I Wayan Madra, was supported by other PNI farmers and was not killed.[105]

Whether anyone died or not, such incidents inevitably generated even greater conflict in the countryside and sent people to one party or another, at least in part for protection and revenge. And although BTI members were

---

[102] Putra mentions BTI rallies along these lines in four villages in Karangasem—Padangbai, Sangkan Gunung, Bunutan, and Ababi: ibid., pp. 102–3.

[103] For specific instances of aksi sepihak see the following reports in *Suara Indonesia* (Denpasar): "Jang Bertindak Diluar Ketentuan Agar Ditindak," 18 September 1964; "Demonstrasi Sarbupri-BTI di Perkebunan JKP Sendang," 16 October 1964; and "Aksi Sepihak Kita Ganjang Dengan Aksi Bersama," 4 November 1964.

[104] More details are available for Karangasem than for other areas. Putra identifies several villages as sites of aksi sepihak, including Sideman, Ababi, Tanah Ampo, Gegelang, Ulakan, Sangkan Gunung, Yang Taluh, Bug, and Nyuhtebel. According to Putra, many of the aksi sepihak were directed against land owned by the puri Karangasem: "Pelaksanaan Landreform," pp. 109, 112.

[105] Ibid., pp. 110, 116.

often motivated by a common class interest, one's "class enemies" might include other poor farmers or tenants who appeared to collaborate too closely with their landlords. Thus the groundwork was laid for deep bitterness to develop not only between landlords and tenants but also among Bali's poorest tenant farmers.

A variety of other forms of mass action were employed by the BTI and Petani. Both PKI/BTI and PNI/Petani organizers deliberately held rallies and marches in "enemy" territory, carrying banners and flags, shouting slogans, and singing songs. A marching song sung by PKI/BTI members in Sideman, Karangasem, went like this:

> We swear an oath of equality
> Poverty will surely end
> Farmers and workers will all have work
> A new world will surely come
> Come, come take action now
> Freedom is already ours
> Our flag is red
> And red is the color of the blood of the people
> Red is the color of the blood of the people. . . .[106]

On occasion hundreds of members of each organization joined in mass heckling matches. The BTI members would shout, for example, "Destroy the landlords!" and Petani supporters would respond with cries of "Marhaen! Marhaen!" President Sukarno used the name Marhaen to signify the average poor Indonesian. The term and the ideology of Marhaenism were commonly used by the PNI and Petani. Activists burned government offices, stoned the houses of political opponents, and disrupted religious ceremonies or community meetings. Physical scuffles and armed attacks resulting in death were not uncommon.[107]

Particularly acrid confrontations developed over BTI occupations of temple (*pura*) lands and land attached to one of the more powerful puri. Unilateral BTI seizures of such lands were construed by their opponents as sacrilege, as challenges to the Bali-Hindu religion, and as disruptive of the cosmic order. Also considered offensive and sacrilegious were the refusal by some PKI and BTI members to abide by linguistic etiquette in dealings with their "superiors," and their failure to perform customary ritual obligations. Such interpretations were powerfully reinforced by natural calamities, such as the eruption of Gunung Agung in 1963 and the plagues of rats and other pests that swept the island, which many people viewed as supernatural

---

[106] Ibid., p. 105.

[107] Estimates of the numbers killed in such conflicts range from 100 to 500. A limited survey of precoup clashes in Bali can be found in Universitas Gajah Mada, Pusat Penelitian dan Studi Pedesaan dan Kawasan, *Keresahan Pedesaan Pada Tahun 1960-an* (Yogyakarta, 1982), pp. 93–95.

confirmation of a cosmological imbalance and spiritual impurity. And because these natural disasters coincided with the most militant and aggressively class-based PKI and BTI actions, it seemed plausible to argue that these actions were responsible for the imbalance.

As in parts of Java, then, the manner in which class interests dovetailed with cultural sensibilities may help to explain the intensity of political conflict in Bali. If in East Java the significant cultural division was between santri and abangan, in Bali, where the vast majority were Hindu, the relevant cultural distinction was, broadly speaking, between those who wished strongly to preserve existing social relations (including caste prerogatives) and religious institutions and those who wished to see significant changes in both, in the direction of greater democracy, meritocracy, and egalitarianism. And just as the cultural conflict between santri and abangan in East Java overlapped with a class-based conflict between landlords and poor peasants, so in Bali the conflict between cultural conservatives and iconoclasts was, to some extent, isomorphic with conflict based on class interests.

Whereas in the 1950s political party followings were amorphous cross-class affairs, by 1965 the two major parties (the PNI and the PKI) had each developed a more distinctive class character. In addition to economic scarcity and runaway inflation, the rise of a significant pool of poor wage earners and unemployed in the towns, the development of a political consciousness among Bali's land-hungry tenant farmers, and the emergence of a small but influential group of Balinese entrepreneurs added a new dimension to political relations. As class lines hardened in the early 1960s, the PNI came to be seen as the party of the local "national" capitalist class, civil servants, large landlords, relatively prosperous peasant landholders, a still influential aristocracy, and dependent peasants. The constituency of the PKI and the Partindo included landless and tenant farmers, the urban underclass, schoolteachers, a proportion of the educated middle class, and some progressive members of the old aristocracy.

Despite its financial dependence on the center, Bali's local government powerfully influenced class formation, political party alignment, and conflict. Through granting of licenses and contracts to selected entrepreneurs, the local state encouraged the formation of a class of Balinese capitalists. Their dependence on the patronage of the local state and the PNI gave them reason to be worried when political control of the state moved steadily to the left and out of PNI hands in the early 1960s. In alliance with the PNI the new capitalists sought to recoup their losses in the aftermath of the 1965 coup.

Strong intervention on behalf of radical land reform by key national and local figures after 1963 constituted a genuine threat to the interests of landowners and the political parties that supported them. This fact lay behind the intransigence of the largest landlords and the PNI. Those threatened by the land reform or unlikely to benefit from it also included a substantial number of relatively prosperous landowning peasants, concentrated in the chief rice-growing regions of Tabanan and Badung. Using their still considerable power in Bali's legislative and executive bodies, these forces together offered strong resistance to agrarian reform, contributing to political conflict along class lines in the countryside.

Political polarization was accelerated by the mobilization of mass peasant organizations affiliated with the two major parties. In some areas the strength of economic and cultural ties between landlords and tenants slowed the process of class polarization, so that conflict developed not only between landlords and tenants but also among poor peasants and tenants. Once it had begun, however, the competition between the BTI and Petani members appeared to take on its own momentum, leading to violence. The overlapping effect of class interests and cultural sensibilities fueled the conflict and helped to lay the basis for the mass killings of 1965–66. In fact, the severity of the postcoup violence appears to have been in direct proportion to the radicalism and success of the land-reform campaigns in 1963–65. In Jembrana and Buleleng, for example, where the reform was nearly complete by 1965, the postcoup violence was extreme. Similarly, in Karangasem, where the BTI had been especially aggressive and land reform had led to very serious disputes in 1964 and 1965, the killing was widespread.

The emphasis on economic and class issues provided in this chapter has been intended, in part, as an antidote to conventional wisdom. I do not mean that the political struggles and violence of the 1960s in Bali can be understood simply as a matter of "class war," or that class consciousness superseded all other cultural or religious attachments. That is clearly not the case. But the time has surely come to look more seriously at how class interests and economic issues helped to transform Balinese political consciousness under the Old Order and laid the basis for the violence of 1965–66.

It is important to remember that the still widely accepted arguments regarding the "insignificance" of class in Bali come straight from the PNI manual. The denial of the political salience of class, the claim that the PKI had no real mass base, the effort to depict PKI leaders as mere political opportunists, the view that Balinese were more interested in maintaining harmonious community relations than in fighting for class interests—all were part of the ideological and political arsenal of the PNI in Bali in the mid-1960s. As such, they ought not to be accepted uncritically as good history or good sociology. My sense is that much of what has been written about politics in Bali under the Old Order has been based on precisely these sorts of unexamined arguments. In other words, we have come to know and to believe only the victor's version of history.

I I *The Massacre*

THE MILITARY COUP OF 1 OCTOBER 1965 in Indonesia was the prelude to one of the largest massacres of this century. In less than a year, somewhere between 500,000 and one million people—most of them alleged members of the PKI or one of its affiliated organizations—were killed.[1] The worst of the killing occurred in the provinces of Central Java, East Java, and Bali. In terms of the proportion of the population killed, however, Bali was arguably the province hardest hit. There, between December 1965 and early 1966, an estimated 80,000 people—or roughly 5 percent of the population of under 2 million—were shot, knifed, hacked, or clubbed to death.[2]

In percentage terms, these figures are comparable to losses suffered in Cambodia over a much longer time period under the regime of Pol Pot. Yet, in contrast to the scholarly and popular attention paid to the atrocities of the Khmer Rouge—and to those of other notoriously repressive regimes in this century—the postcoup massacre in Bali has been all but ignored by the academic community and, after a flurry of media attention in 1966 and

---

[1] No one really knows for sure how many died in the massacres. Estimates range from 100,000 to about one million. For a review of the estimates, see Robert Cribb, ed., *The Indonesian Killings of 1965–1966: Studies from Java and Bali*, Monash Papers on Southeast Asia, no. 21 (Clayton, Victoria, 1990), p. 12.

[2] Estimates of the numbers killed in Bali range from a low of 40,000 to a high of about 100,000. Soe Hok Gie cites 80,000 dead as "the most conservative estimate." See "The Mass Killings in Bali," in Cribb, *Indonesian Killings*. W. F. Wertheim refers to police records from Bali that indicate that at least 100,000 died: "De dood van de communisten," *Groene Amsterdammer*, 8 October 1966. An official Army history, which almost certainly underreports the level of killing, gives a figure of 40,000. See Angkatan Bersenjata Republik Indonesia, Dinas Sejarah KODAM XVI/Udayana, *Komando Daerah Militer XVI/Udayana Dalam Lintasan Sejarah* (Denpasar, 1982). Some Balinese with access to military and provincial government records at that time consider the figure of 50,000 dead as "obviously far too low" and 100,000 as "possible": interview with I Dewa Made Dhana (vice-head of DPRD-Buleleng, 1961–1966), 10 October 1986, Singaraja.

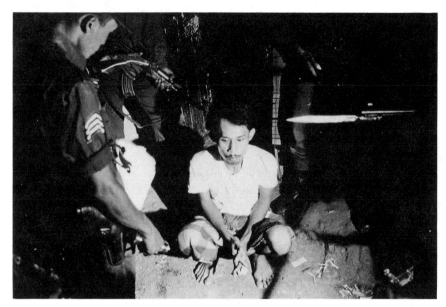

20. Soldiers detain a man found at large after curfew in the wake of the October 1965 coup. Up to a million people, most of them suspected members of the Communist Party, were arbitrarily arrested after the coup, and some of them remained in prison thirty years later. Between 500,000 and 1 million people were killed, most of them in Central Java, East Java, and Bali. An estimated 80,000 Balinese—roughly 5 percent of the island's population of under 2 million—were shot, knifed, hacked, or clubbed to death in less than a year. (*Rory Dell, Camera Press*)

1967, it has ceased to be a subject of popular interest.[3] Indeed, far from stimulating a serious reconsideration of the prevailing image of Bali as a worldly paradise, the massacre has been construed either as evidence of Bali's presumed exoticism or as an unfortunate anomaly, a historical aberration. We still have no adequate factual account of the killings, and very few serious attempts have been made to answer even the most basic questions: Why was there a massacre at all on Bali? Why did it occur when it did? Who was responsible for the killings? Who were the victims and how did they die?

This chapter attempts to provide preliminary answers to these questions and to fill some of the more conspicuous gaps in our factual knowledge

[3] A handful of brief articles touching on the massacre in Bali appeared in the press in 1966 and 1967. The killings are also mentioned, though usually only in passing, in more general works about the coup and the massacre. Recent works on the issue include R. A. F. Paul Webb, "The Sickle and the Cross: Christians and Communists in Bali, Flores, Sumba, and Timor, 1965–67," *Journal of Southeast Asian Studies* 17 (March 1986): 94–112; and the "Editor's Introduction" in Cribb, *Indonesian Killings*, pp. 241–58.

about the postcoup violence in Bali. It begins with a critical discussion of existing accounts of the massacre in Bali and suggests a more satisfactory explanation. In contrast to standard interpretations—which focus on certain presumed features of Balinese character and culture to explain the massacre—this account stresses the interaction of political and historical processes at the local, national, and international levels, paying special attention to the role of military and political authorities in encouraging and accelerating the dynamic of enmity and mass violence against the PKI. I do not mean that cultural forces in Bali were unimportant in generating mass violence, but that their significance was shaped and circumscribed by the broader political and historical context.

Before the coup, very serious economic, social, and political conflicts—some of them with deep historical roots—had already emerged among Balinese. We have seen how bitter conflict had developed over control of the state apparatus, land reform, and questions of "feudal" privilege and caste relations. We have also seen how these conflicts formed the basis for the highly polarized and chronically violent politics in Bali in the final years of the Old Order. These local conflicts unquestionably lay at the heart of the massacre in Bali. To understand why and how such political conflicts led to a massacre after the coup, however, we need to look in detail at historical and political developments in and beyond Bali in the immediate postcoup period. As in other parts of Indonesia, it was the particular convergence of local, national, and international motivations and actions that seems to account for the timing and the intensity of the massacre in Bali.

Massacre as Culture

Most Balinese have been afraid to talk or write about the coup and its bloody aftermath, for to do so honestly is to risk severe retribution from the regime of President Suharto. The contemporary accounts of Western journalists are therefore among the few sources available about the massacre in Bali. The information they provide about particular incidents of murder, patterns of violence, and the attitudes of Balinese are valuable, particularly when they can be corroborated by other sources. Still, these accounts offer only very partial and sometimes very misleading explanations of the causes and nature of the massacre. Most suggest—for none provides a fully developed argument—that the massacre can best be understood in terms of certain essential features of Balinese "character," culture, and religion. At the same time they tend to ignore or to misconstrue the significance of the political and historical context of the killing. Despite these shortcomings, the accounts of Western journalists still form the core of the conventional wisdom about the massacre on Bali and the basis for the very small number of scholarly works that touch on it.[4] Thus, while their descriptions provide useful information about the killings, a reassessment of the explanations they offer is long overdue.

A common theme in existing accounts of postcoup Bali (and Java) is that the extreme violence against the PKI was a reaction to the party's disruption of the ostensible harmony, order, and equilibrium of Balinese culture and religion. Answering the question why "these people of grace and charm" had embarked upon "so frenzied a massacre," for example, John Hughes wrote in 1967: "Obviously the catalyst was the sudden boiling over of resentment toward the Communists, who had been busy beneath the placid surface of Bali but had made the serious mistake of deriding and attempting to undermine not only the island's religious values but its deep-seated cultural traditions as well."[5]

The same theme recurs, with reference to both Bali and Java, in a number of studies by U.S. scholars and officials published since 1966. Buttressed by selective references to the ideas of reputable Indonesia experts, these studies accept uncritically, even enthusiastically, the dubious premise that harmony and order are the core values of Javanese and Balinese village life. Moreover, they assert that these cultural values exercised such powerful influence in Java and Bali in 1965–66 that people were led to commit acts of the most extraordinary collective violence. A 1968 article by Guy Pauker of the Rand Corporation is a case in point. Drawing on the work of Clifford Geertz, he claims that the "local custom" in Java—and, he implies, in Bali too—is to "do all things quietly, subtly, politely, and communally—even starve." By acting in "stark contrast with local custom," he argues, the PKI and BTI in Java and Bali

> made themselves not just enemies of the more prosperous elements in the village . . . but enemies of the community as a whole, whose ancient ways they were disrupting. These considerations, more than genuinely ideological controversies, may have been the decisive factor behind the killings, which were as widespread in Bali . . . as in East and Central Java.[6]

In a memoir published in 1990 the U.S. Ambassador to Indonesia at the time of the coup, Marshall Green, has made virtually the same argument. Summarizing most of the familiar myths about the "harmonious" nature of

---

[4] Cribb notes that John Hughes's account (*Indonesian Upheaval* [New York: David McKay, 1967], chap. 15) "outlines a story repeated by many later authorities": *Indonesian Killings*, pp. 241–43.

[5] Hughes, *Indonesian Upheaval*, p. 175. In a similar effort to reconcile the facts of the massacre with the conventional picture of an idyllic Bali, Donald Kirk concluded that "Communism" had "upset the equilibrium of Balinese society": "Bali Exorcises an Evil Spirit," *Reporter*, 15 December 1966, p. 43.

[6] Guy Pauker, "Political Consequences of Rural Development Programs in Indonesia," *Pacific Affairs* 41 (Fall 1968): 390.

both Javanese and Balinese society, Green manages, like Pauker, to lay responsibility for the massacre squarely upon those who were killed and imprisoned. "In the last analysis," he writes,

> the bloodbath visited on Indonesia can be largely attributed to the fact that communism, with its atheism and talk of class warfare, was abhorrent to the way of life of rural Indonesia, especially in Java and Bali, whose cultures place great stress on tolerance, social harmony, mutual assistance . . . , and resolving controversy through talking issues out in order to achieve an acceptable consensus solution.[7]

There are several problems with this analysis. First, it does not explain why, within a society that ostensibly prizes harmony, tolerance, and consensus, the sanction applied to those accused of breaking the rules of social conduct should necessarily be massive violence. The logical connection between the infringement of "local custom" and violent retribution appears to rest solely on an unstated assumption that Balinese (and Javanese) are prone to behave in wild and irrational ways if they are pushed beyond certain unspecified limits. This is far from an adequate explanation of the massacre.

A second problem is that the historical evidence simply does not support the image of harmonious village life and cultural values on which it rests. It is abundantly clear that, at least in the past century, Balinese society has *not* been characterized by equilibrium, and that not all Balinese (or Javanese) have valued harmony and order above all else. The strength of support for the militant and combative PKI and BTI, the prolonged and bitter fighting among Balinese during the National Revolution, and the evidence of caste conflict even before the war, all suggest that these ideals of harmony were not unquestioningly shared by all Balinese. Rather, the historical evidence I have outlined suggests that there has been ample room for—and possibly even a robust tradition of—disagreement and conflict in Balinese society. What has been portrayed as a "traditional" belief in harmony shared by all Balinese appears instead to represent a social ideal espoused by a particular segment of the population—and by their supporters at home and abroad— in the name of the collectivity.

Third, this sort of analysis cannot explain the timing of the bloodshed. Why did the mass killing begin in early December, a full two months after the Untung coup? If a desire for retribution against the PKI for disrupting village harmony really was the "catalyst" for the massacre, why did it not have effect immediately after the coup? The simple answer, as we shall see, is that the political and military circumstances were not yet conducive to a campaign of mass violence in Bali until early December 1965.

Another argument commonly found in accounts of the slaughter in Bali is

---

[7] Marshall Green, *Indonesia: Crisis and Transformation, 1965–1968* (Washington, D.C.: Compass Press, 1990), pp. 59–60.

that the violence against the PKI was motivated by deep and mysterious religiocultural passions and, more specifically, that the killing was carried out in a spirit of religious "exorcism" or "purification."[8] In a passage typical of the genre, Don Moser writes: "From the very beginning the political upheaval had an air of irrationality about it, a touch of madness even. Nowhere but on these weird and lovely islands . . . could affairs have erupted so unpredictably, so violently, tinged not only with fanaticism but with blood-lust and something like witch-craft."[9] Overcome by their religious passion, this argument has it, Balinese erupted spontaneously into a wild and "frenzied" purge of "Communists." Stressing the alleged unpredictability of the violence—and conveying the impression that it sprang spontaneously from within the mysterious collective psyche of the Balinese— Hughes writes, for example, that Bali "continued its way of life" until December 1965, when suddenly it "erupted in a frenzy of savagery worse than Java's."[10]

There is just enough truth in this sort of interpretation to make it seem plausible. Undoubtedly many Balinese did perceive the campaign against the PKI in terms of the need to exorcise the island of evil or purge it of atheists. Furthermore, as anthropologists have noted since colonial times, "frenzied" behavior does occur in Balinese culture, particularly during trance. Reliable firsthand accounts of incidents of murder in the postcoup period suggest that this behavior played some role in the dynamic of mass killing. Drinking the blood of victims was not unheard of as a sort of guarantee against subsequent guilt or madness.[11] And, according to some Balinese who survived encounters with them, anti-PKI vigilantes appeared to be in a trancelike state, eyes glazed, bodies taut, and evidently unconcerned about the niceties of normal Balinese social interaction.[12]

Yet there is also much that is misleading in this view. For if the religious and cultural passion of Balinese can help us to understand the intensity of the violence once it had begun, it cannot plausibly explain how the idea of annihilating the PKI developed, how the mass violence started, and why it started when it did. Arguments about religious passion and "frenzy" give the impression that the causes of the violence are as exotic and mysterious as

---

[8] Hughes writes, for example, that "the action against the Communists may have been a mass self-purification for the island" and cites an unidentified Balinese as saying that the massacre was "a kind of purging of the land from evil": *Indonesian Upheaval*, pp. 177, 182.

[9] Don Moser, "Where the Rivers Ran Crimson from Butchery," *Life*, 1 July 1966, pp. 26–27.

[10] Hughes, *Indonesian Upheaval*, p. 175. This unpredictable and irrational passion, often described as "frenzy," is invoked repeatedly to explain the killings. See Moser, "Where the Rivers Ran Crimson," p. 28; and Brian May, *The Indonesian Tragedy* (London: Routledge & Kegan Paul, 1978), p. 123.

[11] Interview with Ida Bagus Rama (lecturer in History, Udayana University, Denpasar), 6 March 1986, Denpasar.

[12] Interviews with Dr. Made Djelantik, 4 September 1986, Denpasar, and Jan Mancia, 24 September 1986, Denpasar.

the people of Bali are reputed to be, and that these causes are simply not decipherable or amenable to rational explanation. Yet the weight of historical evidence suggests that such factors were important in accelerating the violence principally to the extent that they converged with and were reinforced by political and military developments in Bali, in Indonesia, and beyond.

Military, party, and religious authorities in Bali actively shaped and encouraged a popular discourse of violent anticommunism based on existing religious ideas and cultural analogies. The fact that massive violence could somehow be justified or plausibly portrayed in terms of Balinese religious beliefs or cultural analogues undoubtedly contributed to the dynamic of killing. But this should not be permitted to obscure the fact that the victimization and the physical annihilation of the PKI were *not* simply or even primarily the consequences of a spontaneous or natural religious impulse, but the products of political and historical processes in which human agency played a central part.

The deep religious belief of Balinese has also been used to explain the alleged willingness and calm resignation with which many Balinese faced death in 1965–66. According to this view, many of Bali's communists allowed themselves to be killed without a fight because they accepted that "the gods" had so willed it, and because they recognized their own guilt. Citing unidentified "Balinese intellectuals," Hughes writes, for example, that many Balinese "faced death calmly, even submissively," and asserts that "party members, knowing their fate, dressed in white ceremonial burial robes and marched calmly with policemen or village officials to their places of execution." Hughes suggests further that in taking this approach, PKI members were seeking to "cleanse both themselves and the island."[13] This image of Balinese facing death with dignity and serenity in ceremonial white robes has been easily incorporated into both popular and scholarly forms of the Bali myth.[14] Placed alongside the royal *puputan* mounted against the Dutch in 1906 and 1908—which Hughes sees as expressions of a "mass joyful death-wish"—the image fits well with that of an exotic and romantic culture. Unfortunately, it does not square with the historical evidence.

It is simply untrue that most Balinese went gently to their deaths dressed in ceremonial costume and in accordance with cultural and religious custom. The vast majority were rounded up without warning from field and home, often in the middle of the night, transported to execution centers, and unceremoniously shot, stabbed, or decapitated, sometimes after being badly mutilated. Few received a proper burial and cremation in accordance with

---

[13] Hughes, *Indonesian Upheaval*, p. 181.

[14] Commenting on the "meekness with which PKI members are often believed to have gone to the slaughter" in Indonesia as a whole, Cribb writes: "Perhaps the strongest image we have of the massacre is of PKI members in Bali lining up, dressed in their white funeral clothes, to be executed methodically": *Indonesian Killings*, p. 20.

Balinese traditions. The corpses of tens of thousands of Balinese were thrown into mass graves or dumped unceremoniously into the sea or rivers. Nor is it true that Balinese did not resist death. As we shall see, some PKI members put up quite a fight, while others fled or hid from the death squads. Finally, it is far from clear that those who did face death with resignation did so out of religion-based fatalism or from a sense of guilt. Many of those arrested in rural areas in October and November—some of whom were later killed—apparently did not fully anticipate the dire consequences they faced for belonging to groups such as the BTI, which had, after all, been legal organizations only a few weeks earlier. And by December 1965, real or alleged communists faced an almost unfathomable political, military, and psychological impasse. Many must have felt that it would be futile to resist.

In short, existing accounts of the massacre divert attention from broader political and historical processes, thereby distorting rather than enhancing our understanding of what happened. Most important, they obscure the critical role of military, political, and religious leaders in fomenting animosity toward the PKI and consciously encouraging massive violence. By diminishing or obscuring the importance of human agency and political manipulation, such accounts serve not only to absolve the regime of President Suharto of direct responsibility for the massacre but also exonerate foreign governments, including the United States, from complicity and acquiescence.

The National and International Setting

The "coup" of 1 October 1965 is better understood as two coups: the Untung coup, later called the G-30-S, and the Suharto countercoup.[15] The first, led by Lieutenant Colonel Untung, involved the execution of six generals of the Army High Command and the formation of a "Revolutionary Council." The second, spearheaded by Major General (later President) Suharto—commander of the Army Strategic Reserve Command, KOSTRAD—crushed the Untung action and established the dominance of anticommunist military officers under Suharto's leadership. Although the Untung coup appears to have had its roots in intramilitary conflict, the Suharto forces soon began to portray it as a treacherous plot against the nation, led by the PKI.[16] This contention became the basis and the justification for the subsequent campaign to destroy the Communist party. It also lies at the heart of the Suharto regime's claim to political legitimacy.

---

[15] G-30-S = Gerakan Tiga-puluh September (Thirtieth of September Movement), the name given to the unsuccessful Untung coup attempt.

[16] A good sense of the genesis of the Army's interpretation of the coup can be gleaned from the Army-controlled press of the postcoup period. Especially revealing are *Angkatan Bersendjata, Duta Masjarakat,* and *Api Pancasila.*

Military forces loyal to Suharto played a leading role in the annihilation of the PKI, both through direct military action and through a variety of political maneuvers in the immediate postcoup period. Starting in October, troops of the West Java–based Siliwangi Division and of the Army Paracommando Regiment (RPKAD) were deployed through Central and East Java with the explicit objective of helping to wipe out the PKI.[17] By the end of November they had killed or had incited civilians to kill several tens of thousands of alleged PKI members and had overseen the arbitrary arrest of at least that many more. In early December 1965, RPKAD troops, together with units of the East Java–based Brawijaya Division, landed in Bali to continue the task. The campaign was accelerated by a well-coordinated nationwide propaganda blitz, depicting PKI members as traitors, barbarians, and atheists and explicitly inciting acts of violence against them.[18] The Army also encouraged religious groups, students' organizations, and an assortment of vigilante-style "action commands" to take a hand in the massacres. With the close cooperation of anticommunist political parties, mass organizations, and religious leaders, the military swiftly turned the tide against the PKI while more gradually undermining the authority of President Sukarno.[19]

Much of the debate concerning the 1 October coup has focused on the question of PKI complicity.[20] Without plunging too deeply into the waters of this debate, I must point out that there is little evidence that the PKI orchestrated the Untung coup attempt. If the party was involved, it was most likely as a relatively minor actor; only a very few PKI officials, let alone members, seem to have known anything about it. There is good reason to believe that the Untung coup was more or less that its leaders claimed it to be: a move by middle-ranking Sukarnoist officers and their allies to save the president and "the Revolution" from a rumored coup by a corrupt, CIA-backed "Council of Generals." The evidence of PKI responsibility for the coup, in

---

[17] RPKAD = Resimen Para Komando Angkatan Darat.

[18] After 1 October 1965, the press was thick with references to the "holy" task of the Army and its civilian allies in destroying the PKI. On 14 October 1965, for example, the army newspaper *Angkatan Bersendjata* editorialized: "God is with us because we are on the path that is right and that He has set for us." On 8 October the same paper seemed to be calling for a "holy war": "The sword cannot be met by the Koran . . . but must be met by the sword. The Koran itself says that whoever opposes you should be opposed as they oppose you."

[19] For a good description of this period of transition, see May, *Indonesian Tragedy*, chap. 4.

[20] Among the most important contributions to this debate are Benedict R. O'G. Anderson and Ruth McVey, *A Preliminary Analysis of the October 1, 1965, Coup in Indonesia* (Ithaca: Cornell Modern Indonesia Project, 1971); W. F. Wertheim, "Suharto and the Untung Coup—The Missing Link," *Journal of Contemporary Asia* 1 (Winter 1970): 50–57; Daniel S. Lev, "Indonesia 1965: The Year of the Coup," *Asian Survey* 6 (February 1966), 103–10; Mortimer, *Indonesian Communism;* Crouch, *Army and Politics in Indonesia*, chap. 4. The official Indonesian version of the coup, *Gerakan 30 September: Pemberontakan Partai Komunis Indonesia*, was finally published by the State Secretariat in 1994. The Central Intelligence Agency has also published an account of the October coup, titled *The Coup That Backfired*, Intelligence Report, December 1968.

other words, appears to have been fabricated or deliberately inflated to justify military reprisals against the party. Even more disturbing is the persuasive evidence that Suharto himself had foreknowledge of the Untung coup plans and that he allowed it to go ahead, presumably so that he might then intervene to crush it.

U.S. Complicity?

The allegations of PKI responsibility for the Untung coup have served to legitimize the violent means by which the Suharto regime came to power. They have also deflected attention from the possible complicity of the government of the United States. It is easy to speculate about foreign covert intervention but difficult to prove it. Yet, in view of the well-established record of U.S. covert intervention in the affairs of foreign states—particularly those with leftist or anti-American inclinations—and of the U.S. government's attempt in the late 1950s to topple the Sukarno government and destroy the PKI, the possibility of U.S. involvement in the coup and the massacre must be taken seriously. If the United States was complicit in the Suharto coup and the anti-PKI campaign that followed, it also shares responsibility for the murderous consequences in 1965–66.

Even if it is not possible to establish definitively the extent of U.S. complicity, it can be demonstrated that U.S. policy contributed substantially to the seizure of power by the military under Suharto and to the massacre that ensued.[21] U.S. foreign policy in Indonesia both inadvertently and consciously influenced domestic Indonesian politics in ways that made a military coup much more likely. At least as early as 1957, U.S. policy deliberately exploited and encouraged internal political cleavages in Indonesia with the intention of bringing down the established government. In the late 1950s, this effort took the form of support for the rebellions in Sulawesi (Permesta) and Sumatra (PRRI). Later the United States supported a variety of anticommunist and anti-Sukarnoist elements in the high command of the armed forces as well as the national-level political parties. By 1965 there were strong domestic forces, both military and political, whose interests were congruent with those of the United States. Evidence in declassified government documents makes it clear that the United States and some of its allies did what they could to provide such forces a convenient opportunity to

---

[21] Geoffrey Robinson, "Some Arguments Concerning U.S. Influence and Complicity in the Indonesian 'Coup' of October 1, 1965," unpublished manuscript, 1984. Peter Dale Scott makes a strong case for U.S. complicity in "The United States and the Overthrow of Sukarno, 1965–1967," *Pacific Affairs* 58 (Summer 1985): 239–64. The opposite case is put by H. W. Brands in "The Limits of Manipulation: How the United States Didn't Topple Sukarno," *Journal of American History* 76 (December 1989): 785–808.

act against the PKI and Sukarno in 1965, and with assurances that they might do so with impunity.

The United States also played a critical role in the consolidation of the Suharto regime and in the annihilation of the PKI after 1 October 1965. Its contributions took essentially three forms: (1) almost immediate de facto recognition of Suharto, disguised by a policy of silence and nonintervention with respect to the countercoup and the massacre; (2) token—but politically and psychologically important—covert military and economic aid carefully designed to bolster the new regime while undermining Sukarno and the PKI; and (3) propaganda and information assistance in support of the anticommunist campaign after 1 October.

In the weeks and months after the coup, though Sukarno officially remained president, the United States increasingly bent its ear to the concerns and demands of Suharto and the Army. This support gave Suharto an advantage in a time of political flux and encouraged the massacre of alleged PKI members in Java, Bali, and elsewhere to continue unabated. U.S. government agencies, including the Central Intelligence Agency (CIA), made every effort to assure Suharto and the Army that America applauded their actions. After receiving private word of U.S. support early in October, an aide of Army Chief of Staff General Nasution reportedly told U.S. embassy officials: "This was just what was needed by way of assurances that we [the Army] weren't going to be hit from all angles as we moved to straighten things out here."[22] There were even occasional expressions of U.S. concern that the Army might not go far enough in its efforts to destroy the PKI.[23]

High U.S. officials were fully aware of the violent methods being used against the PKI within days of the coup. On 5 October the CIA in Jakarta reported to the White House that troops of the Siliwangi Division, under Major General Adjie, had already killed about 150 alleged PKI members.[24] A few days later the CIA told the White House about a 5 October meeting of Army generals, organized by Suharto and Nasution, at which it had been agreed to "implement plans to crush the PKI."[25] As the killing accelerated in the following weeks, U.S. officials in Jakarta were undoubtedly kept informed by their contacts in the Indonesian Army. President Lyndon Johnson's administration also knew early on about Army plans to incite civilians to violence against PKI members. On 9 October, for example, the U.S. embassy in Jakarta reported to the State Department that, on instructions

[22] U.S. Embassy Jakarta to Department of State, cable, 14 October 1965.
[23] Just days after the coup, the CIA in Jakarta telegraphed to the White House: "The Army must act quickly if it is to exploit its opportunity to move against the PKI": CIA Report no. 14 to the White House, 5 October 1965. Two days later the CIA cabled the White House: "The U.S. Embassy comments that there is danger the Army may settle for action against those directly involved in the murder of the Generals."
[24] CIA Report no. 14 to White House, 5 October 1965.
[25] CIA Report no. 22 to White House, 8 October 1965.

from Nasution and Suharto, the Army was "encouraging religious groups to take political actions which Army will support."[26] Early in November the information about Army tactics was even more explicit:

> In Central Java, Army (RPKAD) is training Moslem Youth and supplying them with weapons and will keep them out in front against the PKI. Army will try to avoid as much as it can safely do so, direct confrontation with the PKI. . . . Army is letting groups other than Army discredit them [the PKI] and demand their punishment.[27]

U.S. officials, then, fully aware that the Army was inciting popular violence against the PKI in Java, had good reason to suppose that the same tactics would be employed in Bali, with similar results. They had two months to prevent a full-scale massacre in Bali, but made no effort to do so.

The Johnson administration—though it could scarcely contain its delight at the "break" in political developments—put on a public show of tolerant noninterference in Indonesia's "internal affairs." Yet, as the U.S. embassy in Jakarta noted in a cable to the Department of State in early November, U.S. officials "made clear [to the Army] that Embassy and US G[overnment is] generally sympathetic with and admiring of what Army doing."[28] In private, behind the noble guise of noninterference, then, the United States did not conceal its support for the Army's increasingly vicious campaign to crush the PKI until the worst of the massacre was over. The United States' allies, too, sat back and watched as the grotesque and avoidable tragedy unfolded.

Given the still powerful anti-Americanism in Indonesia at that time, the United States had an interest in "refraining from any *apparent* interference in events taking place" there.[29] Similarly, any association with the United States was considered a serious political danger for Suharto and the Indonesian Army. For these reasons, economic and other assistance to the Suharto junta had to flow through covert channels. A 1966 document from the Department of State explained that "until late March 1966, our major policy on developments in Indonesia was silence." It noted, however, that "while continuing this public position we have throughout made it privately clear that we were ready, at the right time, to begin making limited material contributions to help the new leaders get established."[30] While we do not have a clear picture of its full extent, there is no question that some such aid was provided (including textiles and tens of thousands of tons of rice) and that its objective was explicitly political.[31]

[26] U.S. Embassy Jakarta to Department of State, cable, 9 October 1965.
[27] Ibid., 4 November 1965.
[28] Ibid.
[29] Ibid., 21 December 1965.
[30] Department of State, "Post Mortem on the 1965 Coup" [1966].
[31] For some early discussions of economic assistance and its political purposes, see U.S. Embassy Jakarta to Secretary of State, cables, 9 October and 14 October 1965.

In November the U.S. embassy in Jakarta cabled the State Department that the Indonesian military had requested 200,000 tons of rice and discussed ways of supplying this amount without drawing undue attention to U.S. involvement. The "availability of additional rice," the cable explained, "could be crucially important in . . . maintaining position of those seeking to bring New Order to Indonesia."[32] On 3 December 1965, just as RPKAD troops wound up their campaign of terror in East Java and prepared to land in Bali, the embassy recommended increases in covert economic assistance to the Army in order to "tip the balance" in favor of Suharto's anticommunist forces.[33] A few days later the State Department cabled the embassy in Jakarta regarding a proposal for $10 million in aid, noting that such aid would have to be designed to benefit the Army and not Sukarno.[34] In addition to this short-term aid, the United States began to meet with technocrats engaged by the Army to plot Indonesia's economic recovery. These talks covered plans for debt rescheduling, increased commitments of food aid, long-term economic and military assistance, and the relaxation of restrictions on foreign investment.[35]

Though difficult to prove, there are also indications of U.S. involvement in the coordinated anticommunist media blitz in the immediate postcoup period. At least since 1960, U.S. plans for defeating the PKI suggested the tactic of discrediting the party politically before resorting to a naked show of force. In a letter to President John Kennedy in that year, the executive secretary of the National Security Council, James Lay, wrote that the United States should

> give priority treatment to programs which offer opportunities to isolate the PKI, to drive it into positions of open confrontation with the Indonesian Government, thereby creating the grounds for repressive measures, politically justifiable in terms of the Indonesian national interest.[36]

The emergence of the extraordinarily sensationalistic newspaper *Api Pancasila* only days after the coup and its sudden disappearance after the population had been worked into a sufficient frenzy to permit or cause the slaughter of over half a million souls has raised questions of U.S. involvement in the campaign.[37] So has the peculiar editorial published on 2 October 1965 in *Harian Rakjat*, the PKI daily, which became the single piece of

[32] Ibid., 28 November 1965.
[33] Ibid., 3 December 1965.
[34] Department of State to U.S. Embassy Jakarta, cable, 8 December 1965.
[35] U.S. Embassy Jakarta to Department of State, cables, 6 July 1966.
[36] National Security Council, "US Policy on Indonesia," 19 December 1960. For further evidence see Robinson, "Some Arguments."
[37] Benedict Anderson has argued that the sophistication of the media campaign was beyond the capabilities of a disorganized Army editorial board: personal communication, October 1983.

documentary evidence available to the Army to implicate the PKI in the coup.[38] Finally there is the public admission of a U.S. embassy official that he supplied lists of PKI members to the Army in the weeks after the coup.[39] Indonesian Army intelligence hardly needed them, so the real significance of such assistance, together with the other initiatives just outlined, was to demonstrate unequivocal U.S. support for the Army's violent campaign against the PKI.

Bali after the October Coup

The coup and countercoup of 1 October and the subsequent campaign against the PKI had a profound impact on the balance of political forces in Bali. While the transformation of political relations at the national level did not lead immediately to widespread political violence in Bali, it did produce an important realignment of political forces by the end of November. Renewed cooperation between the local military command and the PNI put Governor Suteja, the PKI, and other parties of the left on the defensive for the first time in several years. This change was one of the structural preconditions for the massacre that began in December, but it was insufficient to give rise to widespread killing. Indeed, before the arrival of crack troops from Java, political violence in Bali was still constrained to some extent by a tense stalemate between competing political forces at the local level.

In the first few days after the Suharto countercoup, when its full political implications remained unclear, all groups in Bali cautiously announced that they remained loyal to Sukarno and to "the Revolution," a safe term that by now meant everything and nothing. But whereas the joint statement of Governor Suteja, the PKI and National Front leader K.K., and Regional Military Commander Sjafiuddin issued on 3 October called on Balinese to

[38] A key passage of the editorial, titled "In Support of the 30 September Movement," ran as follows: ". . . we who are conscious of politics and of the duties of the revolution are convinced of the validity of the action carried out by the 30th of September Movement to safeguard the revolution and the people. The support and the hearts of the people are certainly on the side of the 30th September Movement": *Harian Rakjat*, 2 October 1965; translation from *US-JPRS Translations on Southeast Asia*, no. 105. Whether this editorial constitutes evidence of PKI *initiative* in the coup is questionable, but there is also doubt about whether PKI editors wrote and published the piece at all. It seems odd that, on the day after the obvious failure of the Untung coup and after the Army's seizure of all of Jakarta's newspapers, the official organ of the PKI should have been permitted to publish this one last self-incriminating article. The suggestion that the *Harian Rakjat* editorial was a fabrication, prepared with the assistance of the CIA, cannot be ruled out. See Anderson and McVey, *Preliminary Analysis*.

[39] The journalist Kathy Kadane writes: "As many as 5,000 names were furnished over a period of months to the Army there, and the Americans later checked off the names of those who had been killed or captured": "US Officials' Lists Aided Indonesian Bloodbath in '60s," *Washington Post*, 21 May 1990. For skeptical evaluations of Kadane's story, see Michael Vatikiotis and Mike Fonte, "Rustle of Ghosts," *Far Eastern Economic Review*, 2 August 1990; and Michael Wines, "CIA Tie Asserted in Indonesia Purge," *New York Times*, 12 July 1990. Kadane's rebuttal of Wines's critique—including transcripts of her interviews with U.S. officials—has been published in *Indonesia News Service*, no. 300–303, 22 June 1991.

await further instructions from *Sukarno,* an announcement by the PNI-Bali on 1 October explicitly awaited instructions from the national PNI leadership.[40] This discrepancy indicated that key political groups in Bali were already taking their signals from different elements at the center; in the next few weeks, this became an increasingly significant determinant of political developments on Bali.

Political party organizations in Bali responded to initiatives taken by their national party leaderships, either ignoring or superseding instructions from the local executive and military apparatus. As early as 5 October, statements by the PNI and the modernist Muslim organization Muhammadiyah made increasingly aggressive references to the task of "restoring order" and "crushing the G-30-S traitors," although local military authorities had not yet requested such action.[41] Within a few days the political parties had mobilized armed patrols to "maintain order and vigilance." They were active in hamlets around the town of Gianyar, and no doubt elsewhere, as early as 8 October.[42] As news of possible PKI complicity in the attempted coup began to filter through from Java, along with press reports about events there, Bali's party organizations fell into step and demanded the immediate banning of the PKI and its various mass organizations.[43]

Despite these pressures, the armed forces in Bali did little in the way of rounding up suspected G-30-S "traitors" through October. Some efforts were made, in fact, to limit the activities of the emerging anticommunist vigilante groups. In an instruction dated 13 October, the Second Assistant of the civilian auxiliary defense force, Sumarno, prohibited patrols by armed gangs linked with the mass organizations.[44] In a subsequent public statement Sumarno stressed the fight against Malaysia and neocolonialism and downplayed the importance of the G-30-S. Similarly, the attitude of the regional police commander remained ambiguous until the end of October, while Sjafiuddin maintained an almost complete silence throughout October, fueling suspicion that he had secretly supported the G-30-S.[45] His inaction became conspicuous after several neighboring Regional Military Commanders issued orders banning or "freezing" the PKI and its mass

[40] See the PNI-Bali instructions and the announcement from Suteja et al. in *Suara Indonesia* (Denpasar), 3 October 1965.

[41] See, for example, the statement by Muhammadiyah-Bali, ibid., 6 October 1965: "Assist all military forces in guarding public order and peace." A PNI announcement of the same sort appeared the following day, and on 12 October the PNI-affiliated GSNI (Gerakan Siswa Nasional Indonesia—Indonesian National School Pupils' Movement) called on all members to "work together with ABRI, and provide concrete assistance to ABRI in annihilating the G-30-S."

[42] See "Bandjar2 Dikota Gianyar Dan Sekitarnja Adakan Pendjagaan," ibid., 9 October 1965.

[43] The first clear mention of PKI complicity in the local press was ibid., 7 October 1965. The article described the demand by NU in Java that the PKI be banned.

[44] See "Instruksi Pengamanan Dan Penertiban di Daerah2 Serta Patroli/Kegiatan2 Jang Dilakukan Patroli2 Ormas/Orpol Bersendjata Tadjam," ibid., 18 October 1965.

[45] It was alleged that Sjafiuddin's wife was a Gerwani activist, and though he had never declared open sympathy for the PKI, it was rumored that Sjafiuddin too was sympathetic to the party.

organizations.[46] In late October, moreover, when there were reports that even PKI leaders had admitted their own complicity in the coup, and that PKI and ormas branches had begun to dissolve "voluntarily" in many parts of Java and Sumatra, Sjafiuddin still had not moved. It was only in early November, when it was absolutely clear which way the wind was blowing, and after he had been appointed as regional Kopkamtib commander by Suharto, that Sjafiuddin publicly condemned the PKI and issued instructions to mobilize the action to wipe it out.[47]

Similarly, Governor Suteja made virtually no public statements and appeared only rarely at public ceremonies and gatherings during October. In an apparent effort to create some political breathing space, he imposed a ban on local media coverage of G-30-S-related developments on Bali.[48] Suteja's opponents took his silence and his efforts to limit public debate on the issue as signs of his complicity in the G-30-S and as an attempt to muzzle the PNI, especially since the major newspaper in Bali, *Suara Indonesia* (Denpasar), was PNI-affiliated. In the final week of October, Suteja was summoned to Jakarta by Sukarno who was evidently aware of the governor's increasingly precarious position.[49]

Taking advantage of Suteja's absence in Jakarta, the PNI demanded action against the PKI and for the first time openly expressed the suspicion that Suteja and Sjafiuddin were deliberately dragging their feet. The PNI organizations dominated the October 28 Youth Day rally in Denpasar, which was attended by an estimated 15,000 people.[50] In the keynote speech the PNI leader (and later governor) I Gusti Putu Merta called on President Sukarno to order Suteja to "cleanse" the local government of all G-30-S elements. Why was it, Merta asked rhetorically, that while the rest of the country had begun to take decisive action against the PKI, in Bali this effort had still not been undertaken? Let us hope, he went on, that the authorities in Bali will not continue to act as though Bali were a separate country.[51]

[46] The banning orders reported in the local media included those issued by Pangdam XIV (Makassar), 21 October; Pangdam VII/Diponegoro (Central Java), 25 October; and Pangdam Brawijaya (East Java), 22 October: *Suara Indonesia* (Denpasar), 21, 22, 25 October 1965.
[47] Kopkamtib = Komandan Operasi Pemulihan Keamanan dan Ketertiban (Operational Command for the Restoration of Security and Order). Sjafiuddin was appointed Kopkamtib commander for KODAM XVI on or about 1 November 1965. The commander of KOREM 163 was appointed by Sjafiuddin as Kopkamtib commander for Bali on 29 November 1965. See "Instruksi Pangdam XVI Kepada Segenap Agg. ABRI dan Massa Rakjat Progrev," ibid., 30 November 1965.
[48] The instruction, issued 13 October 1965, ordered that "newspapers published in Bali and Radio Republik Indonesia may not print/broadcast statements or information of any kind pertaining to the G-30-S Affair in Bali": ibid., 13 October 1965.
[49] According to Sjafiuddin's account of this meeting, the president asked Suteja if he had the courage to return to Bali, and Suteja replied emphatically, "I have the courage, sir." See "Hantjur Leburkan Kemampuan dan Kemauan G-30-S," ibid., 4 December 1965.
[50] For an account of the rally and the various speeches given, see "Bali Seolah-olah Negara Sendiri Jang Terpisah dari Pusat," ibid., 29 October 1965.
[51] On 31 October, at a rally in Kesiman Timur, outside of Denpasar, Merta again complained that Bali was far behind the rest of Indonesia in taking action against the PKI. See ibid., 2 November 1965.

Immediately after his return from Jakarta, on 29 October 1965, Suteja met Sjafiuddin, presumably to discuss the most recent developments in Jakarta and to relay Sukarno's advice. On 1 November he issued an order "freezing" a limited number of PKI-affiliated mass organizations. The order emphasized that "freezing" did *not* mean killing or even arresting members, only that the normal activities of the affected organizations should temporarily cease.[52] Only on 3 November did Suteja finally "freeze" the PKI and its major mass organizations. In the same instruction the leaders of affected organizations at all levels were ordered to report to the police.[53]

In a second instruction on 1 November, Suteja ordered the establishment of an "inspection team" to investigate G-30-S involvement in Bali. It was led by the head of the Judicial Inspectorate for the Regional Military Command (KODAM XVI), I Gusti Putu Raka, who was to work closely with the chief of Police Intelligence, R. Sujono, and the regional chief of Military Police, Major R. Susilotomo.[54] The instruction stressed, however, that local authorities and political organizations should take no a priori action against G-30-S suspects, and that all should await a political solution from Sukarno. A priori action, however, was precisely what PNI-affiliated groups had in mind.

While the position of the police and the Army had remained unclear through much of October, a public statement by Bali's police commander, Major Ismono Ismakoen, on 28 October, indicated that the local command was now contemplating the use of violence against the PKI: "If there are still waverers in the economic, political, cultural, and social spheres, the police will not hesitate to take strong measures against them and, if necessary, to shoot them."[55] Sjafiuddin, too, now signaled that he was finally ready to move against the PKI. On 1 November he revealed that there had been considerable support for the Untung coup within the Regional Military Command, and further that a high-ranking officer had tried to persuade him to join the rebels.[56] Now, exactly one month after the coup, Sjafiuddin was establishing an internal inspection team of his own with the aim of "cleansing" the Regional Military Command of "traitors."[57] Significantly, the general supervisor of the team was the chief of Army Intelligence for KODAM

[52] The text of this decision was published ibid., 4 November 1965. It is possible that this partial freeze was announced in an effort to alert other PKI-affiliated organizations to the danger that awaited them, and to give them an opportunity to take refuge.

[53] See "PKI dan Ormas2nja Dibekukan Pepelrada Bali," ibid., 4 November 1965. On the same day, two newspapers said to have PKI and/or Partindo affiliation, *Fadjar* and *Bali Dwipa,* were banned: ibid., 5 November 1965.

[54] The text of the instruction and the full list of inspection team members was published ibid., 4 November 1965.

[55] "Tidak Ragu-Ragu, Ambil Tindakan Tegas," ibid., 29 October 1965.

[56] It was later alleged that this had been Captain Trenggono of the Cakrabirawa unit, the presidential guard, which had been implicated in the coup and which had units stationed at the president's retreat in Tampaksiring, Bali. See "Hantjur Leburkan Kemampuan dan Kemauan G-30-S," ibid., 2 December 1965.

[57] See "KODAM XVI/Udayana Bersihkan Diri Dari Oknum2 Kontrev G-30-S" and "Pangdam XVI/Udayana: G-30-S di Bali Digagalkan," ibid., 2 and 5 November 1965.

XVI, Alex Soetadji.[58] It was rumored that Soetadji had been active in organizing an informal PKI network in KODAM XVI, and that he had been sympathetic to the Untung coup.[59] If these rumors were true, his appointment as general supervisor may have been part of an effort to cover the trail of PKI sympathizers, or at least pro-Untung rebels, in KODAM XVI.[60]

On 11 November 1965 Governor Suteja again left Bali for Jakarta to meet the president. Four days later, on Sukarno's order, he was replaced as Pepelrada by Sjafiuddin.[61] Suteja officially continued as governor until 8 December, but after mid-November he effectively ceased to exercise any authority.[62] With Suteja out of the way and the local military shifting its support from Sukarno to Suharto, two important preconditions had been met for the joint mobilization of forces against the PKI, by the military and political party leaders. The title of a *Suara Indonesia* (Denpasar) editorial— "Now It Is Clear Who Is Friend and Who Is Foe"—ominously presaged the conflict that was about to begin.

Political Violence before the Massacre

Despite serious political tension, the anti-PKI campaign did not result in widespread killing in Bali through October and most of November. Indeed, what is most striking about the pattern of political conflict in Bali to the end of November is that, in spite of the obvious potential for confrontation, and in marked contrast with the situation in Central and East Java, it did not degenerate rapidly into indiscriminate mass murder. The massacre itself did not begin until December, after the alignment of political and military forces at both national and local levels had shifted more decisively against the PKI.

[58] The inspection team was nominally headed by the Regional Military Police commander (*Ka PomDam XVI/Udayana*), Major Soesilotomo.

[59] In 1965 Soetadji had been Assistant I (Intelligence) in KODAM XVI for more than three years. The rumor that he was a PKI sympathizer was reportedly current among Bali's political elite and was related to me by a former PSI-Bali leader, who wished to remain anonymous.

[60] When the dust had settled, both Sjafiuddin and Soetadji had been removed from their posts. Soetadji was relieved as Assistant I on 7 August 1967. In October 1967 he was summoned to Jakarta and discharged from military service for his role in the G-30-S plot. Sjafiuddin was replaced as Pangdam by Brig. Gen. Sukartyo in June 1966, after which there is no further record of him in military command positions. Lesser military authorities are alleged to have taken similar actions. The commander of the KODIM in Singaraja, for example, was suspected of encouraging anti-PKI and anti-Partindo actions until December 1966. Interview with I Dewa Made Dhana (vice-head, DPRD-Buleleng, 1961–66), 10 October 1986, Singaraja.

[61] "Pepelrada Bali Berangkat ke Djakarta," *Suara Indonesia* (Denpasar), 12 November 1965; and "Kekuasaan Pepelrada Bali Dipegang Pangdam XVI/Ud," ibid., 18 November 1965.

[62] "Gubernur Kdh. Bali Sutedja Dibebaskan Dari Djabatan," ibid., 17 December 1965. In the last two weeks of November, Suteja was openly accused of supporting the PKI and the coup. Almost every major political organization and all eight of Bali's bupati joined in calling for his ouster as governor and as head of the provincial National Front and of the provincial assembly. See "Pernjataan 5 Parpol di Bali: Bubarkan PKI dan Ormas2nja . . . Petjat Gubernur Kdh, Bali, Sutedja Karena Dukung G-30-S," ibid., 21 November 1965.

Through October and the first half of November, the assault on the PKI in Bali commonly took the form of political purges in government offices, universities, and political organizations.[63] Apart from losing their jobs, the victims of these purges were required to report to the military authorities with the possibility of detention without formal charge or trial. Those who reported were also required to bring lists of other PKI and mass organization members, thus providing the means for a more systematic purging of the organization at a later date. A limited number of direct, sometimes violent attacks against PKI members in Bali began in early November. According to Sjafiuddin's own account, "police actions" (*aksi-aksi polisionil*) began on 6 November 1965. The houses of people accused of affiliation with the PKI were burned, their possessions stolen, and their families intimidated. Chinese were similarly targeted, particularly if they had been associated with the pro-PKI, ethnically Chinese political party Baperki. Yet according to available reports, remarkably few people had been killed by the end of November.

Some of the November violence took the form of armed clashes between various mass organizations, resulting in a few casualties on both sides and some arrests. In the village of Gerokgak, western Buleleng, for example, a confrontation on 11 November 1965 between Pemuda Rakyat, Ansor (a youth organization affiliated with the Muslim party NU), and PNI supporters, left four members of Pemuda Rakyat, two of Ansor and one of PNI dead and several others wounded.[64] Local police and military units were involved in some of these clashes but apparently did not initiate or encourage them. Nor were the police and military organized at this stage to deploy overwhelming force against the PKI. In fact, accounts of political confrontations in November do not differ substantially from reports of violent clashes in the two years *before* the coup.

On 12 November 1965, for example, there were reports from Desa Bungkulan, eastern Buleleng, of two armed confrontations between PKI and PNI "masses" which bore many similarities to precoup conflicts. In one of these incidents a PKI band of about forty reportedly surrounded the home of a PNI member with the intention of burning it. The head of the Sawan District PNI branch responded by mobilizing local PNI mass organizations and calling the police. In short order a force of two police squads and more than 500 PNI members gathered to confront the PKI group. Apparently expecting support from surrounding hamlets, where alarm drums were sounding to

[63] Udayana University, for example, summarily fired staff belonging to some twenty organizations deemed to be PKI-linked. The language of the "revolution" was almost always used to justify such purges. For example: "as a tool of the revolution, Udayana University must cleanse itself of all counter-revolutionary elements." See "UNUD Bersihkan Diri," ibid., 6 November 1965.

[64] "Bentrokan Physik di Gerokgak," ibid., 15 November 1965. The BTI in Gerokgak had a reputation for militancy because it had initiated several aksi sepihak in the precoup period.

indicate the arrival of police and PNI forces, the PKI band stayed and fought. Earlier in the day, police patrolling in Banjar Kubu Kelod, in the same village, were reportedly confronted by a PKI band armed with bamboo spears and knives. The newspaper report of the clash stated that the band of about forty men had attacked, and "because it was still dark and they were far outnumbered by the PKI gang, the police were forced to fire. . . . After the arrival of reinforcements, the police continued to fire while surrounding the village. Eventually the entire gang surrendered and was taken to Bung-kulan to be interrogated."[65]

Clearly, serious political tension evoked some political violence through November, but it did not approach the scale and intensity of events beginning in December. Indeed, the scattered evidence indicates that in some areas PKI members were still acting from a position of strength and confidence, and not in any sense being slaughtered or led without complaint to their graves.[66] As late as mid-November, a sufficient balance of local political forces still obtained in Bali to prevent powerful political tensions from being transformed into mass murder.

Cultivating Violence

The political and military situation in Bali began to change dramatically in the latter half of November. Local military forces, under pressure to act in line with developments on Java—and perhaps eager to disguise their own complicity in the Untung coup attempt—assumed an increasingly aggressive posture toward the alleged perpetrators of the coup, particularly the PKI. With Governor Suteja out of the way, it was much easier for them to do so. Local military initiatives in November included (1) the compilation of lists and other documentation to "prove" the complicity of the PKI in the G-30-S coup; (2) the deliberate portrayal of PKI members as morally depraved and antireligious; and (3) the use of psychological warfare techniques designed to force ordinary people to choose between the enemy and the state authorities. In different circumstances, these actions might not have contributed significantly to mass violence. In postcoup Bali, however, they converged with and served to exacerbate long-standing political and social tensions, thereby creating another of the essential preconditions for a massacre.

In November, military and police authorities in Bali began to resort to the techniques and the language developed by national military and political party propagandists to inflame passions against the PKI. Following the ex-

---

[65] "AKRI Tumpas Gerombolan PKI Bersenjata Di Sawan Buleleng," ibid., 21 November 1965.

[66] In Banjar Loloan Barat, in the town of Negara, PKI activists were said to have painted the words "Live" and "Die" on houses of allies and enemies, respectively: interview with family of I Wayan Reken, 4 October 1986, Negara.

ample set in Java, they claimed to have discovered documents proving PKI-Bali plans to stage a local G-30-S coup, and indicating a sizable unofficial PKI organization in the Regional Military Command.[67] A list of some seventy-five names of Army men—all of low to middle rank—involved in this underground PKI was said to have been found at the home of a certain Pujo Prasetio, who was named as the principal G-30-S organizer in the command.[68]

Along with a "hit list" of prominent local government and military figures, the documents included details of alleged PKI plans to commit a variety of depraved acts. Leading political leaders, for example, were to be humiliated by being undressed before a mass rally to be held on 2 October 1965.[69] Later investigations purportedly revealed that Gerwani members in Bali had been instructed to "sell" themselves to ABRI men in order to obtain weapons for the PKI, and having done so, to murder and castrate the soldiers they had seduced. Like the fabricated stories about Gerwani women performing a naked dance while castrating and gouging the eyes of the captured generals in Jakarta on 1 October, these revelations served to make PKI members appear not merely as simple political traitors but as immoral, debauched, and inhuman. This tactic made the delegitimation of the party and the murder of alleged members very much easier than they otherwise might have been.[70]

A campaign was launched under Kopkamtib auspices to make it impossible for ordinary people to remain politically neutral—a technique of psychological warfare later employed by Indonesian forces in Aceh and East Timor. Beginning in mid-November, propaganda teams toured rural areas propagating the deadly logic of non-neutrality: "It was stressed that there are only two possible alternatives; to be on the side of the G-30-S or to stand behind the government in crushing the G-30-S. There is no such thing as a neutral position."[71] If one was not unequivocally against the G-30-S, one was necessarily for it. To escape arrest or death, all Balinese, especially

[67] Those familiar with the style of Indonesian Army Intelligence operations treat these "discoveries" of documentary evidence with circumspection.

[68] Interview with a former PSI-Bali leader, 30 July 1986. At the end of November, the Army reported that seventy-six men from KODAM XVI had been arrested for suspected involvement in the coup plot. See "Rumah Djl Kambodja D 60 Sarang G-30-S," *Suara Indonesia* (Denpasar), 28 November 1965. Pujo Prasetio was tried and sentenced to life imprisonment for subversion. He remained in jail in Denpasar in 1995.

[69] *Suara Indonesia* (Denpasar), 5 November 1965.

[70] The local newspaper commented: "It is clear from these revelations how base and depraved PKI plans were. After scraping as much profit as possible from their shameless sexual activities, Gerwani members were supposed to murder and at the same time cut off the genitals of their victims": "Pengakuan Seorang Ketua Gerwani. Diperintahkan Mendjual Diri Kepada Anggota2 ABRI," ibid., 21 November 1965; and "Serahkan Kehormatan Untuk Dapatkan Sendjata/Mesiu," ibid., 30 November 1965.

[71] "Orpol/Ormas PKI Bujar, Pagi, Kekridan, Patjung dan Senganan Lempar Badju," ibid., 18 November 1965. The propaganda teams were known as Team Penerangan Operasi Mental (Operation Mental Information Teams).

former PKI members, had to show that they fully rejected the party, that they condemned the treacherous G-30-S, and that they would cooperate fully in whatever official plan was initiated to destroy it.

At first a written declaration renouncing involvement in or support for the PKI and the G-30-S seemed to be sufficient. The first such declarations, from the workers at the Balitex textile factory outside of Denpasar, appeared in *Suara Indonesia* on 11 November 1965. By December, however, the classified advertisement section of the paper was crowded with similar statements from all over the island. Yet disavowal and self-criticism after the fact turned out to be no guarantee of safety, because the attack on the party was based not on the presumption of actual complicity but on the logic of *associative* guilt and the need for collective retribution.[72]

By late November it was clear that more definitive evidence of political reliability was required. At an official ceremony marking the banning of the PKI in Kerambitan, Tabanan, the District Military Commander, Capt. S. Paidi, stressed that he wanted "concrete proof of ex-PKI members' loyalty to the Republic of Indonesia and to Pancasila, because making a written statement is very easy; what matters most is real proof."[73]

Similar language began to appear in the speeches and pronouncements of political leaders about this time. In mid-November, two days after the removal of Gianyar's pro-PKI bupati, the acting bupati, Made Kembar Kerepun, minced no words in addressing a Heroes' Day rally. Drawing heavily on the rhetoric developed by military and political party authorities at the national level, he told a crowd estimated at 100,000 that "those who are not prepared to repent and who remain obstinate must be cut down to the very roots."[74] The most effective way of proving one's rejection of the PKI—and so of saving one's skin—was to take an active role in the campaign to obliterate the party politically and physically.[75] The logic of non-neutrality, together with the impulse for self-preservation, compelled not only the genuinely neutral but even former PKI members to join in the attack on the PKI.[76] It was a time to go with the flow.

The concerted anti-PKI offensive that began in early December built on the rhetoric and the deep animosity cultivated earlier. By the end of Novem-

[72] This logic apparently penetrated rather deep into the political consciousness of Balinese. A night-market vendor in Kintamani (Bangli) was killed after the coup on the evidence that once, during a power outage, he had provided a storm lantern to allow a PKI rally to continue. His murder was justified not on the grounds that he personally had done anything wrong but rather that he was associated with an organization that had.

[73] "Kerambitan Bersih Dari PKI," *Suara Indonesia* (Denpasar), 1 December 1965.

[74] *Suara Indonesia* (Denpasar), 11 November 1965.

[75] Soe Hok Gie, writing in 1967, noted: "Survival is a very strong motive for action. To succeed, one has to cover one's tracks and leave no traces. Killing is the easiest and safest way to do this, because dead people do not speak": "Mass Killings in Bali," p. 255.

[76] The increasingly aggressive campaign by local military commanders to punish the PKI in connection with the coup may have been an effort to deflect attention from support for the Untung coup within the local military command.

ber, PKI members stood completely alone against the combined military power of the Army, the police, and the anticommunist mass organizations and their vigilante shock troops. Not only was Suteja gone, but influential local leaders had fled or been arrested.[77] Demoralized by the repeated allegations of PKI wrongdoing, abandoned by their leaders, hopelessly overpowered, and unable to live safely even in their own communities, ordinary PKI members must have sensed that resistance would be quite pointless. The stage was finally set for wholesale massacre.

Organizing Violence

The incident that is said to have sparked the massacre in Bali was the killing of an Army officer and two Ansor youths by PKI members in Desa Tegalbadeng, Jembrana, on 30 November.[78] According to the conventional wisdom, anti-PKI violence spread spontaneously throughout the island after this incident, rapidly becoming so "frenzied" that when troops of the RPKAD and the Brawijaya Division arrived from Java on 7–8 December, their main task was "to stop it before irreparable damage was done to the social structure."[79] Very little evidence supports this view. Indeed, virtually all evidence indicates that military forces, both local and Java-based, together with political party authorities, orchestrated and incited the violence in Bali, as they did in Java.[80] It is probably no coincidence that several high-ranking generals, including Suharto, visited Bali on the day after the RPKAD landing.[81] Before we examine the pattern of the killing in more detail, it is important first to deal with the role of the military.

The notion that Java-based troops helped to put a stop to the massacre on Bali is based principally on the often-quoted remarks of the RPKAD commander, Colonel Sarwo Edhie. Speaking to journalists sometime in December 1965, he is *reported* to have said: "In Java we had to egg the people on to kill Communists. In Bali we have to restrain them."[82] These remarks do imply, correctly, that political tensions were already severe in Bali, and that

[77] The PKI bupati of Gianyar I.M.S., for example, was removed from office on 8 November. Early in November the head of Pemuda Rakyat in Jembrana, A.A.N.D., was arrested in Banyuwangi.

[78] See "Rapat Gelap Gestapu di Tegalbadeng Digagalkan," *Suara Indonesia* (Denpasar), 10 December 1965.

[79] May, *Indonesian Tragedy,* p. 123.

[80] Cribb has also expressed some skepticism about the conventional wisdom. He notes that "a number of stories make it clear that it was the arrival of army units with death lists which played a key role in prompting the killings in many cases": *Indonesian Killings,* p. 247.

[81] Others in the group were Brigadier Generals Soemitro, Dharsono, Hartono, Wahju Hargono, and Soedirgo. Although the precise purpose of the visit is not clear, it may have been intended to ensure the full cooperation of the local military authorities—particularly Sjafiuddin—who were still not regarded as politically reliable. See "Djendral2 Ke Bali—Masalah Bali Dapat Perhatian Penuh," *Suara Indonesia* (Denpasar), 10 December 1965.

[82] Quoted in Hughes, *Indonesian Upheaval,* p. 181.

violent political conflict had begun in some form by the time RPKAD troops arrived there. Yet the implication that the worst of the violence was over before RPKAD troops arrived, or that the principle role of the troops was to put an end to it, deserves to be treated with skepticism for at least three reasons.[83]

First, it is unlikely that several tens of thousands of people could have been killed in the seven days between the 30 November incident in Jembrana and the arrival of Java-based troops on 7–8 December. Killing may indeed have begun immediately after 30 November, but a great deal more must necessarily have occurred *after* the troops arrived from Java, and in all probability took place under their supervision.

Second, it is doubtful that the 30 November incident, on its own, could have sparked killings on such a massive scale. Several previous clashes of precisely the same kind had resulted in casualties on both sides, but none had led to widespread anti-PKI violence even remotely comparable to that which began in December. Under the circumstances, it is difficult to believe that the popular reaction to the Jembrana incident was wholly spontaneous. And if the incident itself did not bring about the dramatic and fundamental change in the nature of the political violence after 30 November, it seems reasonable to suggest that the RPKAD—arriving so soon afterward—had some part in doing so.

Third, there is doubt as to whether Col. Sarwo Edhie actually spoke the words so often attributed to him. The probable source for his reported remarks is a December 1965 interview conducted by a journalist of the Armed Forces Information Service and published in 1966.[84] The remarks usually attributed to the RPKAD commander, however, resemble more closely the comments made by the journalist (or possibly the author of the book) in his introduction to the transcript of the interview.[85] Col. Sarwo Edhie's own remarks, as published in the transcript, are considerably more ambiguous:

> The situation in Bali is different from the situation in Central Java. Whereas in Central Java I was concerned to encourage the people to crush the Gestapu, [in Bali] on the other hand, the people were already eager to crush the Gestapu to its roots. The important thing was not to let that enthusiasm be misused by certain people, leading to anarchy. That is what we had to prevent.[86]

[83] Hughes claims that "the worst was over" before the paracommandos arrived: ibid.

[84] The interview was published under the title "Kegagalan Gestapu/PKI Terletak Pada Rentjananja Jang Serba Wishfulthinking," in Dharmawan Tjondronegoro, *Ledakan Fitnah Subversi G-30-S* (Jakarta: Matoa, 1966).

[85] The relevant passage in the introduction reads: ". . . while in Central Java the spirit of the people had to be raised to fight the Gestapu, according to Colonel Sarwo, in Bali their spirit was already overflowing, so it only had to be controlled to keep it from being misused by a certain group:" ibid., p. 158.

[86] Ibid., p. 165.

This comment, along with that of another RPKAD officer, Major Djasmin, can be read to mean that the RPKAD was less concerned to bring an end to the anti-PKI violence than to bring it under the Army's control and direction. According to a local press account, Major Djasmin said that

> the actions to annihilate the G-30-S are at present extremely confused, with the result that it is difficult to distinguish which is the movement of the revolutionary masses and which is the G-30-S. For this reason . . . the annihilation of the G-30-S must be carefully led and channeled in order to prevent an eruption of chaos and violence that have no limits.[87]

These remarks suggest that, in the view of the officers from Java, the campaign against the PKI on Bali was not yet being properly conducted. They may well have suspected that local military forces, while claiming to take anti-PKI actions, were mainly trying to cover their tracks. They may also have been concerned that the violence was not overwhelmingly one-sided, but still involved armed clashes between pro- and anti-PKI forces, so that a good number of noncommunist lives were threatened.

"Leading" and "channeling" the destruction of the PKI, then, meant not that communists were no longer to be killed but that the killing was thereafter to be done in a more orderly fashion, with the military controlling the action.[88] Thus an official Army history of this period notes that in Bali, "after 1 January 1966 the actions to destroy the members of the G-30-S no longer involved mass actions. By that time, ABRI officers had brought a degree of order to the methods used."[89] Bringing "order" to the campaign meant ensuring that only PKI forces were killed, and that they were killed systematically.

The Logistics of Mass Murder

One way in which the military controlled and facilitated the execution of suspected communists was through the provision of critical logistical support—weapons, ammunition, trucks, communications, and detention facilities. In some cases, mass execution could not possibly have been carried out without such support. In Negara, Jembrana, for example, where the Java-based troops first landed in early December, eyewitnesses have reported that dozens of Army trucks, loaded with alleged communists picked up from surrounding villages, formed a slow and orderly procession down the main

[87] "Tindakan ABRI—Massa Rakjat Harus Searah," *Suara Indonesia* (Denpasar), 12 December 1965. Also see "Djangan Bertindak Sendiri2," ibid., 24 December 1965; "Perhatikan Sila Kemanusiaan," ibid., 29 December 1965.
[88] Hughes, *Indonesian Upheaval*, p. 181.
[89] Angkatan Bersenjata Republik Indonesia, Dinas Sejarah KODAM XVI/Udayana, *Komando Daerah Militer XVI/Udayana Dalam Lintasan Sejarah*, p. 192.

street for several days. At a large warehouse the prisoners were unloaded one by one, hands bound, and taken inside, where they were shot with automatic weapons. Describing the operation, a local historian, the late I Wayan Reken, wrote: "Through the month of December, the Army with angry people of the Front Pancasila destroyed the communists in the most horrible massacre. It was a river of blood in which several thousands were killed in Jembrana alone, a tragic summary of the history of Jembrana."[90] In the course of three days in December, an estimated 6,000 were killed.[91] Most of the corpses were dumped either into the sea or into mass graves.

Logistical support provided by the military was of considerable importance in the annihilation of the PKI in other parts of Bali as well. An article in the Denpasar newspaper the second week of December 1965 declared that "they don't even need to see the red beret [of the RPKAD], it is enough simply to hear the roar of a truck, and the hearts of the big-shot G-30-S types begin to beat wildly with fear."[92] A woman who lived near one of the detention camps in the southern part of the town recalls the endless roar of military truck engines, the unloading of their human cargo, which she observed from a window, and the constant popping of automatic weapons fire.[93] A Dutch journalist who visited Bali in 1966 also recorded military and police assistance in western Gianyar:

> Riding in police trucks, the militant Balinese entered villages where communists lived. The communists were rounded up and taken by truck to another village where they were slaughtered with knives [*klewang*] or shot dead in police prisons. To prevent later acts of revenge, in most cases the entire family or even the extended family were killed.[94]

As these observations suggest, the killing was also facilitated by a strong element of "civil-military cooperation." John Hughes writes that after the troops had arrived from Java, "the military and police got together with civilian authorities and made sure the right people were being executed. People were . . . arrested and, usually, shot by the soldiers."[95] In other cases, military authorities instructed village communities to carry out the executions:

> Sometimes villages were specifically assigned to purge themselves of their Communists. Then took place communal executions as the village gathered its Communists together and clubbed or knifed them to death. Sometimes the army

[90] I Wayan Reken, "A History of Djembrana from the 18th Century," Manuscript.
[91] Interview with an anonymous eyewitness, 4 October 1986, Negara.
[92] "Kontrev G-30-S Takut RPKAD," *Suara Indonesia* (Denpasar), 9 December 1965.
[93] Interview with an anonymous eyewitness, 24 September 1986, Denpasar.
[94] Paul van 't Veer, "Bali zuivert zich zelf na gruwelijke moordgolf," *Vrij Uit*, 17 December 1966.
[95] Hughes incongruously concludes this passage by saying: "But the mayhem in the villages was at an end": *Indonesian Upheaval*, p. 181.

handed back to a village Communist Party members it had already arrested. The village as a whole was instructed to execute them.[96]

The massacre was accelerated by the manipulation of institutions of community obligation. Some community leaders simply ordered people to kill. In one reported case, a number of young boys—temple attendants at Pura Besakih—apparently killed three local PKI members near the temple. When asked why they had done so, one of the boys reportedly replied: "Some authorities just came by one day and said to get rid of them . . . and so we did."[97] Some village and hamlet authorities exploited the "traditional" institutions of communal responsibility and labor in carrying out the annihilation of the PKI: "One man would stab a victim while another would hit him on the head with a rock. 'I couldn't believe it,' a foreigner who witnessed the blood bath told me. 'One Balinese never killed another alone. It was all community work. The whole village was instructed.' "[98]

Though certainly not all did so, religious authorities, including Brahmana priests (pedanda), lay priests (pemangku), and soothsayers (balian) were in a position to stoke a sense of outrage against the PKI, contributing to the violence. Their advice was sought on all manner of questions, such as the permissibility of taking a human life or the whereabouts of particular PKI members. Sometimes out of genuine religious conviction but often for narrowly political reasons, religious leaders justified the killing of communists on the grounds that the PKI was "antireligious." Donald Kirk quotes a "priest" as saying: "Our religion teaches us not to kill or hurt . . . but we felt we had to crush whoever tried to disgrace God."[99]

As they had done in Java, the military authorities encouraged the PNI and other parties to destroy the PKI.[100] Political party figures proved to be willing accomplices, inciting and organizing violence against alleged PKI members. Some individuals were deliberately singled out for execution by the PNI. One of those targeted was the former pemuda leader G.P., Suteja's close associate. According to reports that are difficult to confirm, G.P. was tortured and dismembered by his captors before being killed. One such report claims that pieces of his flesh were sliced from his body while he was still alive.[101] Another target of PNI wrath was the extended family of Gover-

[96] Ibid., p. 180.
[97] Moser, "Where the Rivers Ran Crimson," p. 28.
[98] Kirk, "Bali Exorcises an Evil Spirit," p. 42.
[99] Ibid.
[100] Ibid.
[101] Dismemberment and decapitation figure prominently in reports about killings in Bali. According to Don Moser, one of Bali's bupati was detained by the military and executed in custody. Later the same day, one of the soldiers involved was seen with a paper parcel containing the ears and fingers of the dead bupati. Describing the murder of a BTI official by his friend on a beach in Klungkung, Moser writes: "Then Ali took his *parang*—a short swordlike knife used for chopping in the fields—and cut off his friend's left ear, then his right ear, then his nose. Finally he raised his *parang* high and chopped his friend's head off": "Where the Rivers Ran Crimson," p. 26.

nor Suteja. The royal puri in Jembrana was burned to the ground and family members were either killed or taken prisoner.

The military also encouraged armed anti-PKI vigilante gangs. The most prominent and most feared were the PNI-backed Tameng Marhaenis, bands of eight or ten men who roamed about dressed in black, armed with knives, spears, and firearms.[102] In Buleleng, where the killing continued until December 1966, there were reports of slightly larger gangs (fifteen or twenty men) armed with modern automatic weapons, in all probability supplied by the military.[103] Also active in some parts of Bali were the NU-affiliated Ansor youth groups. As in Java, Ansor gangs, backed by the military, took part in arrest and execution operations.[104] Like their predecessors in the Revolution and the 1950s, the vigilantes of 1965–66 were primarily young men eager to demonstrate their "courage" and their sense of "revolutionary" commitment. Many, too, were martial arts adepts, something that gave them special status and added to their aura of power. It was military officers and party leaders, however, who identified their political targets and gave them license to kill.

The parties, in particular the PNI, also fostered the idea that the campaign against the PKI was a "holy war," masking the powerful element of political opportunism and revenge that motivated many of its leaders and members. Writing in 1967, the PNI member Ernst Utrecht claimed that "the killing of PKI members and sympathizers was not seen by the killers themselves as a criminal deed or a political act. If one asks a Balinese what made him join in the killing, the answer will always be the same: the fulfillment of a *religious* obligation to purify the land."[105]

According to Soe Hok Gie, however, PNI leaders in Bali "incited people to violence by saying that God approved of the killing of PKI people, and that the law would not condemn those who did this."[106] In a public address Ida Bagus Oka made precisely this case, saying that truly religious Balinese Hindus should be in the vanguard of the movement to wipe out the G-30-S traitors. "There can be no doubt" he said, that "the enemies of our revolution are also the cruelest enemies of religion, and must be eliminated and destroyed down to the roots.[107]

A clear example of the way enemies of the PKI manipulated religious and

[102] Interviews with Dr. Made Jelantik, 4 September 1986, Denpasar, and I Gusti Putu Yasa Arimbawa, 20 December 1986, Banjar Bongan Tengah, Tabanan. Hughes and Cribb refer to them as "Tamin," but local newspaper reports and informants used "Tameng," which means shield.

[103] Interview with Dewa Made Dhana, 7 October 1986, Singaraja. Dhana's own house was surrounded by such gangs on several occasions.

[104] Jan Pluvier, among others, suggests that some of the killings in the western part of Bali were actually carried out by Ansor gangs that had come across the Bali Strait from Banyuwangi: *Indonesie, kolonialisme, onafhankelijkheid, neokolonialisme: Een politieke geschiedenis van 1940 tot heden* (Nijmegen: Socialistische Uitgeverij, 1978), p. 270.

[105] Utrecht, "Bloedbad op Bali."

[106] Gie, "Mass Killings in Bali."

[107] "Musuh Revolusi Adalah Musuh Agama Jang Paling Garang," *Suara Indonesia* (Denpasar), 7 October 1965.

cultural precepts was the conscious encouragement of the practice of *nyupat,* or what amounted to voluntary execution. Utrecht notes that in conversation the new PNI bupati of Gianyar said, "One should speak not of murder but rather of nyupat—that is, the shortening of someone's life in order to free them from their suffering, and to give them a chance to be reincarnated as a better person, just as in the Barong the witch Rangda, symbol of evil, asks Sudewa to end her life."[108] Balinese eyewitnesses confirm that victims were sometimes given a choice before execution—to die willingly (to nyupat) or simply to be shot. Nyupat, it was said, signified repentance and provided a guarantee against a hellish afterlife or rebirth. The man in charge of the executions—usually a military officer—would shout: "Who wants to nyupat?" After that, however, there was not much to distinguish nyupat from murder. Those who came forward were sent to a different part of the execution area, where they were either shot, beheaded, or stabbed like the others.[109] Few received a proper burial or cremation according to Balinese custom.[110]

The PNI was also responsible for spreading the story that Governor Suteja had chosen to nyupat, ostensibly in recognition of his personal responsibility for the cosmic imbalance in Bali.[111] By stressing the religious and cultural dimensions of Suteja's death, the PNI was able to obscure the overtly political objectives of his murder. And by virtue of presiding over this symbolic cleansing, the PNI enhanced its claim to moral as well as political authority in postcoup Bali.

The manipulation of cultural and religious symbols was crucial to the dynamic of the massacre. For while the PKI was in some respects iconoclastic, it was not self-evidently atheistic, nor was it obviously responsible for the island's economic and social problems or for the apparent cosmic imbalance. These ideas about the PKI's nature and culpability had to be, and were, nourished as the foundation for collective action. Likewise, the idea that the problem of cosmic imbalance or impurity would best be resolved by mass murder did not emerge naturally from precepts of Balinese Hinduism but

[108] Utrecht, "Bloedbad op Bali."

[109] Execution spots were located either within military encampments or in hamlets with a solid and militant PNI or NU base. One of the more notorious killing centers was the village of Kapal, on the road between Denpasar and Tabanan. There is no way of knowing how many died at Kapal, but it appears that operations continued there for at least two months.

[110] Bodies were dumped in a variety of places, including beaches, rivers, and mass graves. Moser mentions a beach in Klungkung where 1,500 were said to be buried: "Where the Rivers Ran Crimson," p. 29. Hughes notes that in Jembrana corpses were buried in mass graves or were dumped at sea: *Indonesian Upheaval,* p. 180.

[111] According to this story, a PNI delegation went to Jakarta some time in December 1965 to dispose of Suteja. After a brief meeting, he reportedly expressed his wish to nyupat in the hope that this gesture would bring an end to the mass violence in Bali. Then, dressed in white, he was reportedly taken to a nearby wood or plantation and killed with a *keris.* PNI officials consulted a balian somewhere near Singaraja in early 1966 to confirm that Suteja had indeed been killed. Suteja's image was said to have appeared at a seance organized by the balian. According to one of the PNI officials in attendance, he was dressed in white garments that were marked with small circles of blood, presumably where he had been stabbed: interview with Wedastera Suyasa, 25 February 1986, Denpasar.

21. President Suharto, in Balinese attire, worships at a religious site in Bali, November 1967. After the 1965 coup attempt, General Suharto, then commander of the Army Strategic Reserve Command (KOSTRAD), spearheaded the military and political campaign to destroy the PKI. After gradually undermining President Sukarno's power, Suharto was finally named president, and he remained in power three decades later. (*Indonesia, Department of Information, Denpasar*)

originated rather with the Indonesian military leadership. All of these ideas were consciously disseminated with the assistance of political party and religious leaders eager to see the demise of the PKI at any cost.

The consequences of the coup and countercoup of 1 October 1965 made clear the extent to which Balinese politics responded to signals from the center. Just as the absence of a strong and cohesive central state in the revolutionary period (1945–49) had contributed to political turmoil, so in

1965 the disintegration and conflict at the center led ultimately to political chaos in Bali. But the slaughter that started in December was not simply the result of a political "vacuum" in which antagonistic social and political forces ran wild. Rather, the massacre started after and because elements of the state itself—particularly the local and national military commands—in alliance with powerful civilian political forces and with the support of key international actors, consciously sanctioned and encouraged the annihilation of a substantial segment of the population.

In October, with the continuing confidence of Sukarno in Jakarta, and with as yet no serious challenge by local military or police authorities, Suteja and the PKI were still in a position to resist the demands of the local PNI and other political parties. In November, however, the balance began to change rapidly. As Sukarno's position weakened nationally, Suteja's authority in Bali became increasingly tenuous. And as Suharto's forces consolidated their power in Java, the military command in Bali began to shift its allegiance from Suteja (and Sukarno) toward Suharto and the anticommunist forces under his command. With the removal of Suteja to Jakarta in late November, the stage was set for the violent attacks on the PKI.

However, the massive, organized killing of alleged PKI members did not begin in earnest until early December, when troops arrived from Java to bring "order" to the campaign against the G-30-S and the PKI. Contrary to the received wisdom, the massacre that began in early December, then, was not an unavoidable tragedy caused by a spontaneous outpouring of religious fervor, a shared desire to preserve the balance and harmony of village life, or a cultural predilection for slipping into trance and running amok. It was largely the result of deliberate efforts by military and civilian authorities to destroy the PKI.

These efforts had two related dimensions, physical and rhetorical. Providing logistical support to local vigilante groups and mass organizations, the military ensured that the task of destroying the PKI, begun in Java in October, would be carried to a successful conclusion in Bali. The idea of killing members of the PKI, however, did not emerge spontaneously in Bali, but was deliberately cultivated and made to appear both natural and morally acceptable. The rhetoric articulated nationally and locally helped to create an atmosphere in which the killing of one's enemy appeared not only morally justifiable but a patriotic and religious obligation. In this context of cultivated anticommunist hysteria, the fuses of Bali's historical conflicts over land, politics, religion, and culture were easily ignited.

Without the conscious and well-orchestrated campaigns to cast the PKI as evil, and without the conscious encouragement, both in principle and in practice, of its physical annihilation, it is unlikely that any of Bali's long-standing political and economic tensions, or any predisposition toward revenge or violence that may have existed in Balinese culture, would ever have given rise to a massacre of such staggering brutality.

12 *Myth and Reality in Bali*

THE POSTCOUP MASSACRE IN BALI should have come as no surprise. Though killing on such a scale was unprecedented, political violence was hardly a novelty for Balinese, and the political preconditions that triggered the killings were not in any way mysterious. In fact, viewed in the stark light of history, the massacre made perfect sense. That it should have defied reasonable explanation for so many years is attributable largely to the pervasive image of Balinese as harmonious, apolitical, and peaceable, and to the poverty of scholarship on Bali's modern political history. My principal aims in writing this book were to lay bare the specious nature of that image of Bali and to provide a reasonable account of the massacre and of Balinese politics in the twentieth century. It remains now to draw together the main threads of the argument and to suggest some of their broader implications. Let me begin with a few remarks on the significance of the prevailing discourse about Bali before discussing the roots of political conflict and violence there.

The Bali Myth

The "traditional" Bali so admired by travelers and scholars alike is a historical fiction, a product of political calculation and conservative political objectives. The popular image of "traditional" Bali as a "last paradise" has been perpetuated and exploited by a series of governments, both Dutch and Indonesian, and by political parties and leaders with an interest in preserving the status quo, or in creating an entirely new "tradition" more suitable to their personal, political, or class interests. The image has been given an added boost by a multimillion-dollar tourist industry that has found in Balinese "tradition" a highly profitable scheme. These powerful actors have had little interest in publicizing Bali's violent political history, except insofar

22. The Bali myth. A studio image by the Dutch photographer Thilly Weissenborn, this photograph was used in official tourist brochures of the 1920s and 1930s. Images like these, and the elaborate mythology of which they form a part, were an artifact of colonial rule but have profoundly influenced popular attitudes, scholarly studies, and official policy toward Bali ever since. (*Photo and print collection of the Koninklijk Instituut voor Taal-, Land- en Volkenkunde, Leiden*)

as it can be woven into the fabric of Balinese exotica. Even the postcoup massacre has somehow been incorporated into the Bali myth.

The strength of the exotic image has been reflected not only in popular and official perceptions but also in the prevailing scholarly discourse about Bali. Academics have appeared to accept the notion that Bali does not have a political history to speak of and that any manifestations of political conflict and violence are best understood by reference to certain unique features of Balinese temper, character, culture, or "tradition." They have, moreover, tended to accept uncritically the views of politically interested groups and individuals, and to portray them as representative of the "Balinese" world-view. We have seen, for example, how scholars both before World War II and after have either ignored or misconstrued evidence of class and caste conflict while emphasizing the view, espoused by local political elites, that Balinese are more interested in maintaining harmonious community relations and preserving their "culture" than in fighting for political, economic, or class interests.

One consequence of this consensus has been that critical themes and issues—including political violence, the role of the state, caste relations, and class conflict—simply have not been addressed, and analytical approaches deployed with sophistication in efforts to understand other political communities have scarcely begun to be considered with respect to Bali. In this way, academics have obscured or distorted the historical record, leaving us misinformed about issues that have intrinsic political and moral ramifications. For historians and other scholars, these are serious problems that demand a serious reply.

Yet this is more than an academic problem, because the Bali myth—and the ideology of "tradition" it has spawned—has had, and will continue to have, real political consequences for real people. Over many years now, such misleading discourse about Balinese "tradition" has served to justify policies and political actions that have led to pauperization, economic disparity, conflict, and violence among Balinese. We have seen, for example, how during the colonial period the twin Dutch objectives of maintaining political order and maximizing tax revenues were justified by reference to Balinese "tradition," and how these policies in turn brought increasing rural poverty and landlessness. In the revolutionary period, too, Dutch perceptions of an imaginary apolitical Bali gave rise to, or at least helped to justify, military and political strategies that exacerbated political violence among Balinese.

The seeds of historical manipulation of "tradition" again bore bitter fruit in 1965 when a real or pretended concern for the preservation of Balinese culture served to excuse not just the destruction of a legal political party (the PKI) with an agenda that appealed to many ordinary Balinese but the murder or imprisonment of tens of thousands who could not possibly be held accountable for that party's alleged wrongdoings. The pattern has continued under Indonesia's New Order government. Once again the restoration and preservation of an imagined Balinese "tradition" has disguised deeply conservative political objectives while simultaneously preventing the rehabilitation or financial compensation of the victims of 1965. Thousands of families of alleged PKI members lost property seized by the military; some PKI members remain in prison more than a quarter of a century after the coup; thousands of others and their families continue to face onerous restrictions on their civil and political rights. In other words, the Bali myth has helped to falsify history in a way that has served the people in power while silencing those who have suffered injustice.

The Roots of Conflict and Violence

In writing about Bali's political history, I have been guided by three questions. How can we account for the dramatic variations in the pattern of political conflict in Bali, from apparent harmony to open political conflict? What explains the historical tendency for political conflict in Bali to follow class, caste, and ideological lines, and to override the sense of Balinese solidarity based on an awareness of ethnic, religious, or regional community? And finally, what were the historical and structural causes of political violence in Bali? I have not attempted to provide tidy or theoretically airtight answers to these questions, but the arguments and evidence I have assembled may have a broader significance.

At the outset, I suggested that the variation between the political violence and apparent harmony in Bali's modern history and the absence of any powerful regionalist movement might best be explained by reference to changes in the character of the modern states under whose authority Balinese have lived over the past century. I noted that changes in the relative strength and cohesiveness of those central states appeared to be closely associated with broad shifts in the pattern of Balinese politics. Under the Dutch and the Japanese, for example, Balinese politics was characterized by a high degree of political order and apparent harmony; on the other hand, when central states were weak or divided, as in the precolonial period, during the Revolution, and under the Old Order, Bali experienced political turmoil. That much seems beyond dispute.

Yet, if variations in the strength of central states appear to coincide with broad shifts in the patterns of political relations in Bali, they do not, on their own, explain why Balinese politics was characterized by chronic internal conflict, why that conflict was manifested in the ways it was, and why, in particular, it turned to mass violence at certain times. Not surprisingly, the historical forces at work were enormously complex, involving the interplay of different sorts of states at the international, national, and local levels and a wide range of social, economic, and cultural factors. At the risk of oversimplifying, I will try to outline the main patterns discernible from the historical evidence.

It is clear that we need to know a good deal more about central states than whether they were "strong" or "weak." Other factors were just as significant: their military capacity; which social groups or classes they favored; their fiscal, administrative, and judicial policies; and the ideological preoccupations and attitudes that underpinned them. Viewed from this perspective, the Dutch and Japanese colonial states shared certain characteristics that distinguished them both from the precolonial systems and from the various central states of 1945 to 1965. These characteristics gave rise to broadly similar patterns of superficial political order, masking worsening economic and political tensions among Balinese.

At their height, both the Dutch and the Japanese had a clear monopoly over military and police power in Bali. Thus they were able to put down incipient unrest swiftly and decisively, contributing to an overall impression of peace and order. Yet when the Dutch and Japanese lost that monopoly, in 1942 and 1945 respectively, opportunities appeared for open conflict; to the extent that the parties to such conflict had managed to secure arms, political violence inevitably increased.

Through very similar systems of indirect rule, both the Japanese and the Dutch were able to co-opt influential political and social groups, notably members of the landowning aristocracy and the political elite. That strategy undermined the possibilities for the development of cross-class alliances that might have posed a challenge to the state. Thus it ensured a superficial harmony, but also contributed to a dynamic of enmity and conflict among Balinese. By fostering an alliance with leading political figures in Bali, the Dutch state shifted the locus and the nature of political authority there. The resuscitation of traditional Balinese elites, beginning in the 1920s, did more than restore them to their precolonial status; it actually enhanced their power vis-à-vis the local population and their erstwhile local rivals. Paradoxically, a good proportion of Bali's aristocracy came to rely on Dutch power, and therefore also became defenders of colonial rule. A similar dynamic was evident under the Japanese, though the beneficiaries of Japanese rule included people of lower caste and a greater number of the young and educated.

Both the Japanese and the Dutch established regularized, even if exploitive, systems of revenue and labor extraction. This strategy allowed them to expand the state bureaucracy and to maintain the loyalty of key groups through political patronage. Because they relied so heavily on the collaboration of Balinese officials, however, these systems also exacerbated tensions among Balinese, providing the basis for open political conflict once central state power had collapsed. Because the Japanese systems of forced production and labor were more clearly exploitive, they seem to have given rise to a somewhat deeper antagonism between Balinese beneficiaries and victims.

Finally, both the Dutch and the Japanese developed more or less plausible pretexts to justify the political systems they had established and the role of the central state within them. There were significant differences in the governing myths and policies of the Dutch and Japanese regimes, yet paradoxically, both resulted in profound changes in political consciousness and terms of political discourse among Balinese. The Dutch preoccupation with the preservation of Balinese culture through the policy of Baliseering stimu lated consciousness of educational and cultural issues among Bali's educated sudra, while Dutch judicial policy increased awareness of caste issues and led to caste disputes. Together these policies ensured that caste prerogative, culture, and education became central political issues from the late colonial period onward. Japan's efforts to mobilize the Balinese population in support of its wartime objectives led to dramatic and irreversible changes in political consciousness and forms of organization, particularly among the young, who learned a powerful anti-Western nationalism and the idea that any obstacle might be overcome through struggle and spiritual power.

In short, these states shaped Balinese political and social relations and brought about critical changes in political consciousness. Despite marked differences between the two, through their policies, practice, and structure both tended to reinforce enmity among Balinese rather than foster a sense of Balinese unity against the state. Thus, while they maintained a superficial peace and order, these states laid the groundwork for later political conflict among Balinese.

The strong Dutch and Japanese states were not unique in bringing about significant realignments of political consciousness and affiliation and in stimulating open conflict among Balinese. Weak or divided states—during the precolonial era, in the revolutionary period, and under the Old Order—also created the preconditions for political conflict and violence. Where a number of states competed for the political loyalty of a single population, as was the case during the revolutionary period, different groups and classes looked to the various centers for their political signals, thereby increasing the likelihood of conflict among Balinese. Naturally, the impact of splits and divisions at the center depended on the way they overlapped with and reinforced preexisting local conflicts. During the National Revolution, for example, the shifting balance of power between the Republic, the State of East Indonesia (NIT), and the Dutch government affected not only the relative strength of Bali's Republicans and loyalists but also relations within the Republican camp.

Significantly, the weakness of the central state after 1945 did not simply permit the free expression of long-standing social and economic grievances. It also created an opening for the emergence of new political contenders in Bali, people who espoused fundamentally new ideas about political authority and justice and engaged in new forms of political organization and mobilization. Open competition for local power, which began in mid-1945 and continued for the next two decades, was a major cause of violence. The struggles that developed during the Revolution, both between Republicans and loyalists and among Republicans, continued to form the basis of political conflict and violence well into the postindependence period. They quickly found expression in the rapid development of the major national political parties in Bali immediately after independence. In itself, this was not a problem. As the first national elections approached, however, party competition took an increasingly violent turn. And as the parties engaged in ever more vigorous mass mobilization in the late 1950s and 1960s, ordinary people were inevitably drawn into the dynamic of violence.

Political violence intensified with the involvement in the political process of the regular armed forces and a range of paramilitary groups. Because the central state was weak in the revolutionary and postindependence periods, control of the military and police was not unified, and branches of the armed forces took opposite sides on virtually all political questions, even allying with different political parties. The availability of weapons on both sides of every political equation from 1945 to 1965 inevitably increased the chances that political differences would find expression in violence. That tendency was exacerbated by the decision of political and military leaders throughout this period to recruit civilians to take part in security operations against alleged political opponents. The strategy of "civil-military cooperation" was used, to tragic and divisive effect, by the Dutch from 1946 to 1949, and later by Indonesian authorities seeking to combat gang activity in the 1950s. It reached its gruesome climax in 1965–66 with the deployment of armed vigilantes, such as the Tameng Marhaenis, to arrest and slay alleged members of the PKI.

The weakness of Sukarno's Old Order presented its enemies, domestic and foreign, with unusual opportunities to bring about its downfall. Their efforts to do so directly affected the balance of political forces in Bali and fueled mass political violence there. Had the United States and its allies not supported the Suharto countercoup of October 1965 and approved of its use of violence against the PKI, it is unlikely that there would ever have been a massacre in Bali or, for that matter, in Java. Yet it is unlikely that the U.S. influence would have been so decisive had there not already been deep rifts within the Indonesian military command and between key figures in the high command and President Sukarno.

The weakness of the central state in this period was reflected in the relative ineffectiveness of its bureaucratic apparatus and the greater influence of individual actors with charismatic authority. In these circumstances, dramatic changes occurred in political consciousness, in modes of political organization, and in the balance of political forces. During the early revolutionary period, for example, such leaders as Bung Tomo and Sjahrir provided inspiration for Bali's young Republican activists, while the organizations they had developed on Java offered models that were quickly appropriated by Bali's pemuda. Sukarno, too, captured the imagination of many Balinese, and his personal interventions—in political appointments, religion, and land reform—changed the balance of political forces on Bali and moved the political focal point increasingly leftward.

As I postulated at the outset, political relations in Bali were also affected by the strength and character of local states there and by their position within the larger political environment. Throughout the period under consideration, states encompassing the whole of Bali were very weak, if they existed at all. That weakness stemmed in part from the absence of historical institutions for governing the island as a whole, but it was also the result of the policies of successive central states that undermined Bali's development of statelike institutions. One consequence was that impulses from outside had a somewhat more powerful effect on local politics than might otherwise have been the case, often accentuating intra-Balinese conflict. It was not that Bali's local state had no influence on politics, but that that influence was conditioned by its dependent position within the national system.

Bali's reliance on the central government as the main source of revenue from 1950 to 1965, for example, shaped local political relations in two ways. It circumscribed the autonomy of the local state and therefore made less likely and certainly less plausible any political movement toward regionalism. It also gave the local state special significance as a distributive authority, responsible for allocating the funds made available from the center. That function in turn contributed to a system of patronage and to political bickering among Bali's emerging "national" capitalists.

Elsewhere in Indonesia—in Sumatra and Sulawesi, for example—local states and power structures with greater potential economic and military autonomy and with more lasting grievances against the central state articulated political goals that openly challenged the center or deflected its demands and intrusions. These regions tended to develop patterns of conflict that expressed regional solidarity vis-à-vis the center, while at the same time underplaying internal conflicts. Such patterns emerged not principally because these areas had distinctive local cultures, unique languages, or other "primordial" attributes that forged them into a political community, but rather because they had a relatively cohesive and autonomous local state apparatus.

Bali's lack of military and political autonomy was a crucial precondition for the eruption of political violence after the coup. It is fair to say that the massacre could not have happened without the active participation of elements of the local executive and security forces. Through the 1950s and 1960s, conflict between the main political parties had been encouraged, but in some sense also contained, by their links with state authorities. However, the sudden severance of the link between the PKI and the local state executive about November 1965, together with the bolstering of the alliance between the PNI and the local and central military, changed the nature of conflict in Bali. It was no longer a struggle between roughly equal groups, each with a grip on some component of the state; now the struggle was between two groups with entirely unequal access to the power—particularly the coercive power—of the state.

The weakness of the Bali-wide state, together with the absence of a cohesive central state between 1945 and 1965, lent weight to the smaller statelike structures in Bali. In the revolutionary period, wide variations in the personal prestige, political acumen, and resources of the individual rajas, as well as differences in the strength of the tradition of royal rule from one kingdom to the next, influenced the fortunes of the Republican movement and the level of open conflict in each. After independence, the political affiliation of local executives at the kabupaten and kecamatan levels resulted in significant variations in patterns of political conflict and violence. Their influence was particularly strongly felt in the course of the land-reform campaign of the early 1960s, since local executives had considerable authority to promote or to impede the full implementation of the laws.

As these examples suggest, the precise pattern of political conflict in Bali depended on the local configuration of socioeconomic and cultural forces, and the way these forces interacted with impulses from outside. Despite Bali's reputation for social and political harmony, a wide range of potential sources of conflict existed there throughout the twentieth century, including rivalries between noble houses, caste disputes, class conflict, ideological differences over cultural and political matters, and anger arising from real or perceived economic injustices. The political significance of such conflicts depended in part on the sort of class alliances they implied or permitted and the political resources the alliances were able to bring to bear. For example, we saw how the configuration of social and economic forces in western Bali during the Revolution allowed the formation of a cross-class alliance prepared to support the Republic and with sufficient resources to do so; meanwhile in the eastern kingdoms, where a similar coalition of forces was objectively not possible, the Republican movement was weak and a conservative political order was more easily maintained. These differences were accentuated by cultural and historical differences between the western and eastern kingdoms, and especially by the greater strength of the royal tradition and feudal relations of production in the east. The political significance of such configurations also depended critically on the way they dovetailed with other political issues. We have seen, for example, how in 1945–46 the long-standing puri rivalries came to reflect and to be expressed in the idiom of the political conflict between Republicans and loyalists.

However, contrary to the widely accepted notion that Balinese politics has simply reflected a range of "traditional" divisions and cleavages repackaged in a variety of forms, the lines of political affiliation and loyalty in Bali have undergone significant transformation over the years. In part these shifts have reflected changes in basic social and economic conditions in Bali—such as poverty, landlessness, inflation, unemployment—but they have also come about as a result of interventions by states and other powerful political actors at critical historical junctures. Though there were significant class divisions in Bali even during colonial times, for example, they did not become politically salient until the early 1960s, when the PKI and the BTI began to pursue a more militant class-based strategy in the implementation of land reform, with the clear support of Governor Suteja and other key actors in the local and national states. This strategy contributed to a realignment of party affiliation along class lines in the final years of the Old Order and provided one of the long political fuses that were ignited after the coup. The cross-class coalitions that had supported and opposed the Republic during the Revolution were replaced by a substantially new pattern of alliances in the 1960s. As a consequence, the "winners" and "losers" after the coup represented fairly distinct class positions, reflecting twenty years of intense political conflict and not simply a repackaging of "traditional" groupings from an imaginary apolitical past.

Any light we can shed on Bali's past—and especially on its dark history of violence—may help us to understand its current and future politics. On the surface, Bali now appears to be a model of political restraint and order. Yet if history tells us anything, it is that such political quiescence should not be understood as a return to "traditional" norms of harmony and order, any more than the condition of rust en orde under Dutch rule should be viewed as the natural condition of Balinese society. Rather it must be recognized as at least in part a symptom of the weakness of the local Balinese state in a new authoritarian political order. My sense is that old conflicts dating from the Revolution and from the postcoup massacre continue to simmer beneath the placid surface, while new ones, stimulated by aggressive government development projects and perhaps also by increased awareness of basic human rights, are growing apace. The implications for Indonesian politics in the coming years are worth considering. Because to the extent that Indonesia's military-bureaucratic state has been successful in undermining local state structures, in Bali as elsewhere, turmoil or collapse at the center may well imply widespread political violence in the hinterland.

The evidence from Bali may also help us to understand political conflict and violence farther afield. If I am correct in locating the sources of political conflict and violence in certain structural features of the broader political environment—including the weakness of central and local states, divisions within the military, the existence of civilian vigilante forces, and foreign covert intervention—rather than in the character, temper, or cultural make-up of a given political community, then it may be possible to explain or even predict eruptions of political violence among other populations with reputations for political quiescence and social harmony.

More broadly still, Bali's experience over the twentieth century may help to explain how, in different historical periods and in different societies, the categories of class, caste, ethnicity, region, and nation become foci of political community, solidarity, organization, and conflict. The case of Bali indicates clearly that the foundations of political community are neither preordained nor immutable, but the outcome of historical process and human agency. In other words, the roots of loyalty, conflict, and violence in any political community are unlikely to be located in primordial givens or in patterns of "traditional" rivalry, but rather in the dialectical interplay of historical forces.

Selected Bibliography

ARCHIVAL SOURCES

Algemeen Rijksarchief (ARA), The Hague

Algemeen Secretarie te Batavia, Eerste Zending (Alg. Sec. I)

Letter: Lt. Gov. Gen. H. J. van Mook to Hr. CLG, 22 February 1946. Kist XXII, no. 19.

"Lijst van personen waarmede de propagandist Soekardani in aanraking is gekomen." Kist XXII, no. 19.

MBU-DPRI. "Sifat Perdjuangan Kita di Bali Pada Saat Ini." In "Politiek Verslag van de Residentie Bali en Lombok, 2e h. March 1948." Kist IV, no. 48.

Memorandum: Charles O. van der Plas, "Data about Bali [from Schlager]," 8 December 1945. Kist XXII, no. 19.

"Nota herbezetting Bali." [November 1945.] Kist XXII, no. 19.

"Overzicht Politieke Ontwikkeling Oost-Indonesia, Mei 1948." Kist V, no. 34.

"Politiek Verslag van de Residentie Bali en Lombok." [January to May 1948; title varies.] Kist IV, No. 48.

"Punten uit de mededeelingen van Dr. Djelantik." [N.d.]. Kist XXII, No. 19.

"Rapport Bali." [April 1946]. Kist XXII, no. 19.

"Report on the situation on Bali and Lombok, compiled from the notebooks of the Republican propagandist Soekardani." Kist XXII, no. 19.

Ministerie van Kolonien na 1900 (MvK)

"Dagboek van den Controleur van Klungkung over het tijdvak tot en met 9 Feb. 1916." Mailrapport 1071/1916.

"Herstel van zelfbesturen op Bali." June 1935. Mailrapport 655 geh./35 [Verbaal, 16 June 1937, no. 4].

"Herziening Heerendienst Ordonnantie." Mailrapport 26/1938.

"Kort verslag der Residentie Bali en Lombok over Juni 1916." Mailrapport 1655/1916.

"Kort verslag der Residentie Bali en Lombok over Mei 1917." Report by Hove Kamp, 3 July 1917. Mailrapport 1451/1917.

Letters:
Adviseur voor Bestuurszaken der Buitenbezittingen to Directeur van Binnenlands-Bestuur, 24 August 1916. Mailrapport 2126/1916.

H. T. Damsté, Resident of Bali and Lombok, to Governor General, 16 May 1921. Mailrapport 514/1921.

F. A. E. Drossaers, Directeur van Binnenlands-Bestuur, to Governor General, 31 October 1936. Mailrapport 1089 geh/1936 [Verbaal, 15 July 1938, no. 14].

F. A. E. Drossaers, Directeur van Binnenlands-Bestuur, to Governor General, 7 December 1937. Mailrapport 12/1937 [Verbaal, 15 July 1938, no. 14].

G. A. W. Ch. de Haze Winkelman, Resident of Bali/Lombok, to Governor General, 20 July 1936. Mailrapport 739 geh./1936 [Verbaal, 15 July 1938, no. 14].

H. J. E. Moll, Resident of Bali and Lombok, to Governor General, 25 April 1938 (on "Civiele lijsten der Zelfbestuurders op Bali"). Mailrapport 636 geh/1938.

Memorandum from V. E. Korn, noted in the Memorie van Overgave of H. T. Damsté, Resident of Bali and Lombok (1919–23).

Note by L. van Stenis, Resident of Bali and Lombok, appended to "Politieke Verslag," by A. M. Ballot, Controleur of Karangasem, 24 June 1916. Mailrapport 1703/1916.

"Politieke Verslag." A political report by the Controleur of Karangasem, A. M. Ballot, 24 June 1916. Mailrapport 1703/1916.

"Rapport omtrent het verzet in Gianyar door een 136 tal veroordeelden op Zondag, den 27sten Mei 1917," with covering letter from L. van Stenis, Resident of Bali and Lombok, to Governor General, 9 June 1917. Mailrapport 1281/1917.

"Rapport Zuid-Bali," from Adviseur voor Bestuurszaken der Buitenbezittingen to Directeur van Binnenlands-Bestuur, 1 September 1916. Mailrapport 2430/1916.

Telegrams from L. van Stenis, Resident of Bali and Lombok, to Governor General, 28 May 1917, and to Minister of Colonies, 29 May 1917. Mailrapport 1104/1917.

"Vervolg op het rapport omtrent het verzet in Gianjar op Zondag, 27 Mei 1917." A report by J. F. Mirandolle, Controleur of Gianyar, 3 June 1917. Mailrapport 1201/1917.

"Verzoekschrift" by the Rajas of Bali, n.d. Mailrapport 655 geh./1935 [Verbaal, 15 July 1938, no. 14].

Rapportage Indonesie

"Djaminan keselamatan bagi pemuda2 jang menjerahkan diri." Letter from Capt. G. H. Gaade to MBU-DPRI, 3 February 1948. Appendix to OOT/BL, no. 36 (6–20 May 1948). Inv. no. 741.

"Geheim Militaire Overzicht—Nefis," no. 5, 22 March 1946. Inv. no. 151.

MBU-DPRI. "Instructie Istimewa," 25 May 1948. Appendix to OOT/BL, no. 36 (6–20 May 1948). Inv. no. 741.

——. "Minimum Program." Appendix to OOT/BL, no. 19 (11–25 September 1947). Inv. no. 740.

——. "The New Struggle Program." Appendix 6 to OOT/BL, no. 19 (11–25 September 1947). Inv. no. 740.

Meulen, Lt. Col. F. H. ter. "Commandementsorder no. 1," 8 April 1946. Inv. no. 737.

"Overzicht en Ontwikkeling van de Toestand Troepenco Bali/Lombok" [OOT/BL]: no. 16 (24 July–7 August 1947); no. 19 (11–25 September 1947); no. 21 (9–23 October 1947); no. 33 (25 March–8 April 1947). Inv. nos. 740–41.

"Politieke Notitie nr. IV," 6–15 December, 1946. Inv. no. 727.
"Politiek Verslag, Bali/Lombok le h. Mei 1948." Inv. no. 734.
"Politiek Verslag, Bali/Lombok, August 1949." Inv. no. 738.
Secret Report on Badung, by Secretary of State for Home Affairs H. van der Wal, 15 December 1948. Inv. no. 737/12.
Sujana, Kompiang. "Tournee Verslag, April 17–25, 1947." [Dutch translation of original.] Appendix 4 to OOT/BL, no. 19 (11–25 September, 1947). Inv. no. 737.
"Wekelijksch (Militaire) Inlichtingenrapport" [WIR]. Inv. no. 740.

Centraal Archievendepot, Ministerie van Defensie (MvD/CAD), The Hague

"Gevechtsrapport van de actie op 20-11-46" and "Bevel voor de actie op 20-11-46," by Troepen-Comandant Bali/Lombok Capt. J. B. Th. Konig. Inv. no. 20/2, GG 28-5.
KNIL-CMI Makassar. "14-daags Politiek Verslag over de periode 18/2 t/m 3/3, 1949." Inv. no. 32/1, GG 64, 8604.
KNIL/KL Stafkwartier Oost-Indonesie. Wekelijkse (Militaire) Inlichtingen Rapport [WMIR/OI]: no. 3 (5 May 1949); no. 10 (23 June 1949); no. 17 (11 August 1949); no. 21 (8 September 1949); no. 23 (22 September 1949); no. 25 (6 October 1949); no. 26 (13 October 1949); no. 27 (20 October 1949); no. 28 (27 October 1949); no. 30 (10 November 1949); no. 32 (24 November 1949); no. 34 (8 December 1949); no. 35 (15 December 1949); no. 37 (29 December 1950). Inv. no. 32/1, GG 65, 12032.
Letters:
KNIL Army Commander to Lt. Gov. Gen. H. J. van Mook, 24 September 1947. Inv. no. 30/3, Doos 7, Bundel 107.
Maj. Gen. Buurman van Vreeden to KNIL Army Commander, 20 September 1947. Inv. no. 30/3, Doos 7, Bundel 107.
Cokorda Gde Raka Sukawati to Lt. Gov. Gen. H. J. van Mook (copied to van Vreeden), 14 February 1948. Inv. no. 30/3, Doos 2, Bundel 12.
"Overzicht en Ontwikkeling van de Toestand, Bali/Lombok" [OOT/BL], nos. 18–26 (28 August 1947–1 January 1948). Inv. no. 32/2, AA37-1-1947.
"Overzicht en Ontwikkeling van de Toestand, Oost Indonesia" [OOT/OI], nos. 6–8 (24 July–4 September 1947). Inv. no. 32/2, AA37-1-1947.
"Rapport B-25 Actie, Troepencommando Bali/Lombok," 11 May 1946. Inv. no. 32/1, GG 8, Bundel 1.2.3.4, d.
Telegram: Cokorda Gde Raka Sukawati to The Hague, 15 September 1947. Inv. no. 30/3, Doos 7, Bundel 107.
Van Beuge, J. A. "Report on Situation in Tabanan." Inv. No. 32/1, GG 8, Bundel 1.2.3.4, d.

Collectie Korn, Koninklijk Instituut voor
Taal-, Land-, en Volkenkunde (KITLV), Leiden

Grader, Ch. J. "Bali: Tournee-Aantekeningen Juli 1950—Dewan Pemerintah Daerah Bali." OR 435-23.
——. "Gabungan Impor dan Expor Bali (GIEB)." [1950] OR 435-23.
——. "GIEB-I." [1950] OR 435-23.
——. "GIEB-III." [1950] OR 435-23.
——. "Persatuan Tenun Indonesia," and "Credietbehoefte ten Plattelande." OR 435-23.

Letters:

Ch. J. Grader to V. E. Korn, 3 March 1950. OR 435-59.
Ch. J. Grader to V. E. Korn, 18 June 1950. OR 435-59.
Ch. J. Grader to V. E. Korn, 7 August 1950. OR 435-59.
Ch. J. Grader to V. E. Korn, 7 September 1950. OR 435-59.
Ch. J. Grader to V. E. Korn, 7 November 1950. OR 435-59.
Roelof Goris to J. Ph. Vogel, 3 October 1950. OR 435-59.

Archief Sectie Militaire Geschiedenis (SMG), The Hague

"Appreciation of the Dutch Reoccupation of Bali," 26 January 1946. Collectie de Vries, Bundel X, box 0519.
"De geschiedenis van het XIIe Bat. Inf. v/h Terr. Tv. Tropenco Bali/Lombok." Bundel "Korpsgeschiedenis," box 0110/b.
"Details about Bali." Appendix 1-a to "Operational Instruction for the Occupation of Bali and Lombok," 4 January 1946, top-secret report prepared by an officer of the KNIL General Staff, Collectie de Vries, Bundel X, box 0511.
"Geschiedenis van het XI Batalyon Infanterie." Bundel "Korpsgeschiedenis," box 0110/b.
Konig, Capt. J. B. T. "Mededeeling gegevens Bali—bestemd voor 8 R[egiment] S[toottroepen] by aankomst te Singaraja op 22 Juli 1946." Bundel "Ned. Indie 1945–1950, 1e en 2e Pol. Actie—Regiment Stoottroepen VIII, Bali, Zuid Sumatra," box 0141.
"Korpsgeschiedenis van het Xe Batalyon Infanterie." Bundel "Korpsgeschiedenis," box 0110/b.
"Memorandum betreffende de vorming der 'Y' Brigade—t/m 31 July 1946." Bundel "Korpsgeschiedenis," box 0110/b.
Meulen, Lt. Col. F. H. ter. "Aanwijzing voor het Militaire optreden op Bali," 17 January 1946. Collectie de Vries, Bundel X, box 0518.
——. "Force Operation Order no. 2-B, 22 Febr. '46." Bundel "Bali/Lombok Force," box 0226/3.
——. "Summary of Landing," 15 January 1946. Bundel "Bezetting Bali," box 0231/3.
"Nefis overzicht gegevens betreffende Bali," 2 January 1946. Bundel "Bezetting Bali," box 0231/4.
"Operational Instruction for the Occupation of Bali and Lombok." Top secret report prepared by an officer of the KNIL General Staff, 4 January 1946. Collectie de Vries, Bundel X, box 0511.
"Overzicht omtrent VIII R.S. tot 31 December 1946." Bundel "Korpsgeschiedenis," box 0110/b.
"Report on Bali Island" [an F2 report], 7 December 1945. Bundel "Bezetting Bali (Inhoud: Operatieve instructies bezetting Bali, 1946)," box 0231/4.
"Toestand op Bali op 11.11.1945." Telegram from CRN to BSO tk MCA, no. 1584, received through the Signal Office of the Royal Netherlands Navy [November 1945]. Bundel "Bezetting Bali," box 0231/4.

Private Collections

Archive Boon (Dr. Marinus Boon), Amsterdam

"Bestuur over Bali en Lombok tijdens de Japanse bezetting en daarna." [Anonymous, 1946.]

"[British Army] Recce Report." October 1945.

"De Gebeurtenissen in Kloengkoeng op Maart 4, 1946."

Ellerbeck, A. W. A. A. "Personalia—Tabanan." [1946.]

——. "Politiek Overzicht Over het Landschap Tabanan," 16 September 1946.

"Instructies voor het Amacab—Detachement Bali," 1 March 1946.

KNI-Bali "Makloemat no. 01-1-20," signed by Governor I Gusti Ketut Puja and Ida Bagus Putra Manuaba [January 1946].

Letters:

    Anak Agung Gde Agung to all Residents in NIT, 7 July 1947.

    Dewa Agung of Klungkung to Resident of Bali/Lombok, 6 December 1948.

    Lt. Gov. Gen. H. J. van Mook to Charles O. van der Plas, 13 November 1945.

Memorandum: Cokorda Gde Raka Sukawati to Lt. Gov. Gen. H. J. van Mook, "Toepassing Standrecht voor Bali," 16 October 1947.

Meulen, Lt. Col. F. H. ter. "Detachementsorde No. 22," 17 March 1946.

——. "Nota Betreffende Bali," 16 March 1946.

"Nefis Overzicht Gegevens Over Bali" [1946].

"Nota Herbezetting Bali," November 1945.

"Overzicht Politiek Situatie," May 1946.

"Politiek Overzicht" [April 1946].

"Politiek Overzicht Over het Landschap Tabanan," 16 September 1946.

Plas, Charles van der. "Verdere gegevens over Bali van Schlager," 6 December 1945.

Post, R. J. F. "Nopens Zelfbestuurder Bangli," 29 December 1947.

Archive Cilik (I Nengah Wirta Tamu), Denpasar

Cilik. "Kehadliran YKP di Bali." [Manuscript, n.d.]

——. "P.D.R.I." [Manuscript, n.d.]

Letter: Ketut Wijana to "Saudara-ku Ketjil tertjinta," 8 October 1949.

Archive Dronkers (Pieter L. Dronkers), Eindhoven

MBU-DPRI. "Bimbingan Untuk Propaganda Rabaan Dalam Artian Naskah Renville," 20 March 1948.

Oldenborgh, Capt. L. C. "Eenige Gegevens omtrent het Eiland Bali." Manuscript, 1946.

Archive Franken (H. J. Franken), Leiden

Ledang, Wayan. "Lapoeran Singkat tentang peroendingan dua hari anggauta MBO-DPRI Soenda Ketjil, Sdr2: Noerai dan Widjana, pada tanggal 14 Mei 1948 di Moendoek." [Unsigned copy.]

Letter: Nurai and Ketut Wijana to punggawa of Singaraja, 20 May 1948.

Archive Tisna (Anak Agung Nyoman Panji Tisna), Singaraja

"Lapoeran kwartalan tentang economi rajat II 2602," by I. Goesti Gde Djlantik, Poenggawa Sukasada [3 July 1942]. Singaraja.

"Notulen Sangkepan Pangreh Pradja Keradjaan Boeleleng," 2 August 1947.

"Tjatatan dari Pembitjaraan Waktoe Sangkepan Para Poenggawa." Monthly reports from February 1944 to August 1945 [titles vary slightly].
"Tjatatan harian dari Sjutjo Boeleleng dalam boelam San-Gatsu," 3 February 1944.

GOVERNMENT DOCUMENTS AND STATEMENTS

Indonesia

Angkatan Bersenjata Republik Indonesia, Dinas Sejarah KODAM XVI/Udayana. *Komando Daerah Militer XVI/Udayana Dalam Lintasan Sejarah*. Denpasar, 1982.
———. "Lembaran Sejarah; Ex-Komandan Res. Inf. 26/VII." Edisi no. 1, Jarahdam XVI/Udayana. Denpasar, 1974.
Angkatan Darat Republik Indonesia, Komando Daerah Militer Nusa Tenggara. *Himpunan Keputusan, Perintah, Instruksi, Penetapan, Peraturan, Pengumuman Dari Penguasa Perang Daerah Untuk Daerah Tk.I Bali/Nusra Barat/Nusra Timur, Tahun 1959–1960*. [Denpasar.]
———. *Pool Perdagangan Daerah Bali*. Introduction by R. Moch. Iwan Stamboel, Pelaksana Kuasa Perang Sektor I, Ketua Pool Perdagangan Daerah Bali. Singaraja, 1959.
Indonesia, Departemen Pendidikan dan Kebudayaan. *Sejarah Perlawanan Terhadap Imperialisme dan Kolonialisme Di Daerah Bali*. Proyek Inventarisasi dan Dokumentasi Sejarah Nasional. Jakarta, 1983.
———, ———. *Kolonel TNI Anumerta I Gusti Ngurah Rai*. Jakarta, 1976.
———, Departemen Perindustrian dan Pertambangan. *Monografi Daswati I Bali 1961*. Jakarta, 1962.
———, Departemen Pertahanan dan Keamanan, Lembaga Sedjarah. *I Gusti Ngurah Rai, Pahlawan Dari Pulau Dewata*, by Zainabun Harahap. Jakarta, 1968.
———, ———. Pusat Sejarah ABRI. *Operasi Lintas Laut Banyuwangi-Bali*. Jakarta, 1982.
———, Departemen Pertanian. *Almanak Pertanian 1953*. Jakarta, 1953.
———, [Kementerian Dalam Negeri]. *Konperensi Para Gubernur Se-Indonesia Dilangsungkan di Djakarta, 19-21 Mei 1952*. Jakarta, 1952.
———, Kementerian Penerangan. *Bali, Atlas Kebudayaan*, by Roelof Goris and P. L. Dronkers. Jakarta, n.d.
———, ———. *Tjalon-Tjalon Dewan Perwakilan Rakjat Untuk Pemilihan Umum I, 1955*. Jakarta, 1955.
———, ———. *Daftar Tjalon Tetap Anggota Konstituante Tahun 1954*. Jakarta, 1955.
———, ———. *Kepartaian di Indonesia*. Jakarta, 1951.
———, ———. *Lukisan Revolusi Indonesia 1945–1950: Dari Negara Kesatuan Ke Negara Kesatuan*. Jakarta, 1954.
———, ———. *Republik Indonesia: Propinsi Sunda Ketjil*. Jakarta, 1953.
Negara Indonesia Timur, Kementerian Penerangan. *Bali: Membuat Sejarah Baru, 1938–1948*. Makassar: Drukkerij Makassar, 1948.
———. *Pidato Anak Agung Gde Agung, Menteri Dalam Negeri, Badan Perwakilan Sementara Indonesia Timur*. Makassar, April 1947.
Pemerintah Daerah Bali. *Peraturan Tentang Penjakap no. 1/1951*. 7 July 1951.
———, Sekretariat DPRD-Bali. *Peringatan Satu Tahun Dewan Perwakilan Rakjat Daerah Bali*. Denpasar, 1951.

Propinsi Bali. *Laporan Tahunan Djawatan Tenaga Kerja, 1963.* Denpasar, 1963.
——. *Rantjangan Anggaran Keuangan Daerah Tk I Bali, Tahun Dinas 1964.* Singaraja, 1964.
——, Kantor Gubernur Kepala Daerah, Biro Hukum. *Himpunan Peraturan Perundangan Mengenai Pemerintahan Daerah I Bali.* Denpasar, 1974.
——, Kantor Gubernur Kepala Daerah, Panitia Penulisan Sejarah Pemerintahan Daerah Bali. *Sejarah Pemerintahan Daerah Bali.* Denpasar, 1977.
——, Kantor Sensus dan Statistik. *Himpunan Hasil2 Sensus dan Survey 1961–1967 Bali.* Singaraja [1968?]
——, Kantor Tjabang Inspeksi Koperasi Buleleng. *Lapuran Kopi di Pulau Bali 1958,* by Komang Tjawi. Singaraja, 1958.
——, ——. *Lapuran Mengenai Daerah Kopi di Banjuatis, Munduk, Gobleg, Gesing, dan Umedjero,* by Komang Tjawi. Singaraja, 1952.
[Propinsi Nusa Tenggara]. *Pengoemoeman Resmi Gaboengan Keradjaan-Keradjaan Bali dan Angka-Angka Perbandingan Anggaran Belandja Daerah Bali Tahun-Tahun 1953–1958.* [Singaraja, 1959?]
——, Bagian Desentralisasi. *Ichtisar Keuangan Daerah Bali, Lombok, Sumba, Sumbawa, Flores dan Timor, Tahun Dinas 1951–1957.* Singaraja, 1958.
——, Dewan Perwakilan Rakjat Daerah Bali. *Peringatan 1 Tahun Dewan Perwakilan Rakjat Daerah Bali.* Denpasar, 1951.
——, Dinas Pertanian Rakjat. *Beberapa Tjatatan Tentang Daerah Bali,* by Soekardjo Sastrodihardjo. [Singaraja], 1958.
——, Djawatan Pertanian. *Laporan Tahunan Djawatan Pertanian Rakjat,* by R. Sukardjo, Inspektur Pertanian Propinsi Nusa Tenggara. Singaraja, various years.
——, Kantor Penempatan Tenaga Daerah Nuteng Barat. *Tindjauan Pasar Kerdja Daerah Nusa Tenggara Barat Tahun 1956.* Denpasar, 1957.

Netherlands Indies

Algemeen Regeeringscommissariat voor Borneo en de Grote Oost. *De Conferentie te Denpasar, 7–24 December 1946.* Batavia: G. Kolff, 1947.
Commissie voor het Landrenteonderzoek op Bali en Lombok. *Landrente monographie, Klungkung.* [1935?]
——. *Monographie der Onderafdeeling Karangasem.* Denpasar, 1926.
——. *Monographie van de Onderafdeeling Boeleleng.* [1926?]
Department van Economische Zaken. Centraal Kantoor voor de Statistiek. *Jaaroverzicht van den in- en uitvoer van Nederlandsch-Indie gedurende het jaar [various], Deel II, Buitengewesten.*
——. *Mededeeling van het Centraal Kantoor voor de Statistiek,* nos. 67/1927, 98/1930, 105/1931, 114/1932, 121/1933, 129/1934.
Department van Landbouw, Nijverheid en Handel, Centraal Kantoor voor de Statistiek in Nederlandsch Indie. *Statistisch Jaar Overzicht van Nederlandsch Indie.* Various isues to 1932.
Regeerings Voorlichtingsdienst. *Denpasar Bouwt een Huis,* by W. A. Goudoever. Batavia, 1947.
Regerings Commissaris voor de Bestuurshervorming in de Groote Oost [Government Commission for Government Reform in the Great East]. "Nota van Toelichtingen betreffende het in te stellen Zelfbesturend Landschap Badoeng," by H. J. Hoekstra. Typescript. [1938?] Gedung Kirtya Liefrinck, Singaraja.

——. "Nota van Toelichtingen betreffende het in te stellen Zelfbesturend Landschap Bangli," by W. F. van der Kaaden, Controleur Bangli. Typescript. [1938?] Gedung Kirtya Liefrinck, Singaraja.

——. "Nota van Toelichtingen betreffende het in te stellen Zelfbesturend Landschap Boeleleng," by C. J. Grader, Controleur t.b. van den Resident van Bali en Lombok. Typescript. [1938?] Gedung Kirtya Liefrinck, Singaraja.

——. "Nota van Toelichtingen betreffende het in te stellen Zelfbesturend Landschap Djembrana," by C. J. Grader, Controleur t.b. van den Resident van Bali en Lombok. Typescript. [1938?] Gedung Kirtya Liefrinck, Singaraja.

——. "Nota van Toelichtingen betreffende het in te stellen Zelfbesturend Landschap Karangasem," by H. J. Hoekstra, Assistant Resident t.b. voor den Regerings Commissaris. Typescript. [1938?] Gedung Kirtya Liefrinck, Singaraja.

——. "Nota van Toelichtingenbetreffende het in te stellen Zelfbesturend Landschap Klungkung," by W. F. van der Kaaden. Typescript. [1938?] Gedung Kirtya Liefrinck, Singaraja.

——. "Nota van Toelichtingenbetreffende het in te stellen Zelfbesturend Landschap Tabanan," by H. J. Hoekstra. Typescript. [1938?]. Gedung Kirtya Liefrinck, Singaraja.

Verslag betreffende de Opium en Zoutregie en de Zoutwinning over het Jaar 1935. Batavia: Landsdrukkerij, 1936.

Verslag van den belastingdruk op de Inlandsche bevolking in de buitengewesten. Weltevreden: Landsdrukkerij, 1929.

United States (Declassified Documents)

Cables:
Department of State to U.S. Embassy Jakarta, 8 December 1965.
U.S. Embassy Jakarta to Department of State, 9 and 14 October, 4 and 28 November, 3 and 21 December 1965; 6 July 1966.
CIA Reports to White House: no. 14, 5 October 1965; [no. 18?], 7 October 1965; no. 22, 8 October 1965.
Department of State. "Post Mortem on the 1965 Coup." [1966.]
National Security Council. "U.S. Policy on Indonesia." 19 December 1960.

SECONDARY SOURCES

Adnyani, Ni Ketut Putri. "Perkumpulan Bali Dharma Laksana di Bali Th. 1936 sampai Th. 1942." Thesis, Universitas Udayana Denpasar, 1982.

Agung, Anak Agung Gde. *Bali Pada Abad XIX: Perjuangan Rakyat dan Raja-Raja Menentang Kolonialisme Belanda 1808–1908.* Yogyakarta: UGM Press, 1989.

——. *Dari Negara Indonesia Timur ke Republik Indonesia Serikat.* Yogyakarta: UGM Press, 1986.

Agung, Anak Agung Gde Putra. "Lahirnya Idee-idee Pembaharuan Dalam Organisasi Sosial di Bali." *Basis* 21, (March 1972): 183–89.

——. "Masalah Perdagangan Budak Bali (Abad 17–19)." *Basis* (November 1971): 38–48.

——. *Sejarah Revolusi Kemerdekaan (1945–1949) Daerah Bali.* Proyek Inventarisasi dan Dokumentasi Kebudayaan Daerah Bali. Denpasar: Departemen Pendidikan dan Kebudayaan, 1979.

"Akan meradja lelahkah bahaja merah di poelau Bali dan Lombok?" *Bali Adnyana* 16 (June 1926): 4–5.

Anandakusuma, I Gusti Ngurah. *Pergolakan Hindu Dharma II.* Denpasar: Pustaka Balimas, 1966.

Anderson, Benedict R. O'G. "Japan: 'The Light of Asia.'" In *Southeast Asia in World War II: Four Essays,* ed. Josef Silverstein, pp. 13–50. Southeast Asia Studies, Monograph Series no. 7. New Haven: Yale University Press, 1966.

——. *Java in a Time of Revolution: Occupation and Resistance, 1944–1946.* Ithaca: Cornell University Press, 1972.

——. "Old State, New Society." *Journal of Asian Studies* 42 (May 1983): 477–96.

——. "Some Aspects of Indonesian Politics under the Japanese Occupation, 1944–45." Interim Report Series no. 29. Ithaca: Cornell Modern Indonesia Project, 1961.

Anderson, Benedict R. O'G., and Audrey Kahin, eds. *Interpreting Indonesian Politics: Thirteen Contributions to the Debate.* Interim Report Series no. 62. Ithaca: Cornell Modern Indonesia Project, 1982.

Anderson, Benedict R. O'G., and Ruth McVey. *A Preliminary Analysis of the October 1, 1965, Coup in Indonesia.* Ithaca: Cornell Modern Indonesia Project, 1971.

Astina, Ida Bagus Ketut. "Sistem Kepemimpinan Dalam Revolusi Fisik di Bali, 1945–1950." Thesis, Universitas Udayana Denpasar, 1985.

Baal, J. van. "Uit de nadagen van het Nederlands bestuur over Bali en Lombok." *Bijdragen tot de Taal- Land- en Volkenkunde* 138 (1982): 211–31.

Bagus, I Gusti Ngurah. "Pertentangan Kasta Dalam Bentuk Baru Pada Masjarakat Bali." Denpasar, 1969.

"Bahasa." *Bali Adnyana* 16 (June 1926): 1–2.

Bakker, J. B. "Goederenbalans en belastingdruk van de afdeeling Zuid-Bali." *Koloniaal Tijdschrift* 26 (1937): 287–94.

——. "Landbouw in de afdeeling Zuid-Bali." *Koloniaal Tijdschrift* 26 (1937): 63–73.

Bateson, Gregory. "Bali: The Value System of a Steady State." In *Traditional Balinese Culture,* ed. Jane Belo, pp. 384–402. New York: Columbia University Press, 1970.

Bateson, Gregory, and Margaret Mead. *Balinese Character: A Photographic Analysis.* New York: New York Academy of Sciences, 1942.

Belo, Jane. *Bali: Rangda and Barong.* Monographs of the American Ethnological Society, ed. Marian W. Smith, vol. 16. New York: J. J. Augustin, 1949.

——. "The Balinese Temper." In *Traditional Balinese Culture.* New York: Columbia University Press, 1970.

——. *Trance in Bali.* New York: Columbia University Press, 1960.

——, ed. *Traditional Balinese Culture.* New York: Columbia University Press, 1970.

Bendesa, I. K. G., and I. M. Sukarsa. "An Economic Survey of Bali." *Bulletin of Indonesian Economic Studies* 16 (July 1980): 31–53.

Bigalke, Terance W. "Social History of Tana Toraja, 1870–1965." Ph.D. diss., Cornell University, 1981.

Boon, James A. *The Anthropological Romance of Bali, 1597–1972: Dynamic Perspectives in Marriage and Caste, Politics and Religion,* Cambridge: Cambridge University Press, 1977.

——. "The Birth of the Idea of Bali." In *Interpreting Indonesian Politics: Thirteen Contributions to the Debate,* ed. Benedict R. O'G. Anderson and Audrey Kahin, pp. 1–12. Interim Report Series no. 62. Ithaca: Cornell Modern Indonesia Project, 1982.

Booth, Anne. "The Burden of Taxation in Colonial Indonesia in the 20th Century." *Journal of Southeast Asian Studies* 11 (March 1980): 99–109.

Booth, Windsor P., and Samuel Mathews. "Disaster in Paradise." *National Geographic*, September 1963, pp. 436–58.

Brands, H. W. "The Limits of Manipulation: How the United States Didn't Topple Sukarno." *Journal of American History* 76 (December 1989): 785–808.

Bruyn Kops, G. F. de. "Het evolutie tijdperk op Bali, 1906–1909." *Koloniaal Tijdschrift* 4 (1915): 459–79.

——. "Uit de rechtspractijk van een Binnenlands-Bestuur ambtenaar." *Koloniaal Tijdschrift* 23 (1934): 472ff.

Bunnel, Frederick, P. "The Central Intelligence Agency—Deputy Directorate for Plans 1961 Secret Memorandum on Indonesia: A Study in the Politics of Policy Formulation in the Kennedy Administration." *Indonesia* 22 (October 1976): 131–69.

Burger, D. H. *De ontsluiting van Java's binnenland voor het wereldverkeer.* Wageningen: H. Veenman, 1939.

Central Intelligence Agency. *The Coup That Backfired.* Intelligence Report, December 1968.

Cheong, Yong Mun. *H. J. van Mook and Indonesian Independence: A Study of His Role in Dutch-Indonesian Relations, 1945–48.* The Hague: Nijhoff, 1982.

Connor, Linda H. "Corpse Abuse and Trance in Bali: The Cultural Mediation of Aggression." *Mankind* 12 (December 1979): 104–18.

——. "In Darkness and Light: A Study of Peasant Intellectuals in Bali." Ph.D. diss., University of Sydney, 1982.

Covarrubias, Miguel. *Island of Bali.* New York: Knopf, 1938.

Crawfurd, J. "On the Existence of the Hindu Religion in the Island of Bali." *Asiatick Researches* 13 (1820): 128–70.

Cribb, Robert, ed. *The Indonesian Killings, 1965–1966: Studies from Java and Bali.* Monash Papers on Southeast Asia, no. 21. Clayton, Victoria, 1990.

Crouch, Harold. *The Army and Politics in Indonesia.* Ithaca: Cornell University Press, 1978.

"Damai? Damai?" *Surya Kanta* 9/10 (September/October 1926): 132–34.

Damsté, H. T. "Balische Splinters—Nang Moekanis, de wonderdokter." *Koloniaal Tijdschrift* 13 (1924): 650–57.

——. "Balische Splinters—Zending." *Koloniaal Tijdschrift* 13 (1924): 532–44.

Daroesman, Ruth. "An Economic Survey of Bali." *Bulletin of Indonesian Economic Studies* 9 (November 1973): 28–61.

"Dengan siapakah Bali akan dikawinkan?" *Surya Kanta* 5 (May 1927): 49–54.

Donnison, Frank Siegfried Vernon. *British Military Administration in the Far East, 1943–1946.* History of the Second World War, United Kingdom Military Series. London: H.M. Stationery Office, 1956.

Doulton, A. J. F. *The Fighting Cock: Being the History of the 23rd Indian Division, 1942–1947.* Aldershot: Gale & Polden, 1951.

Dubois, Fritz. "Huit jours dans l'ile de Bali." *Revue des Deux Mondes* [1890?], pp. 571–601.

Dunia, I. Wayan. "Pemberontakan Cokorde Oka Negara di Gianyar, Tahun 1884–1890." Denpasar: Universitas Udayana, 1984.

Eiseman, Fred B. Jr. *Bali: Sekala & Niskala.* Vol. 1: *Essays on Religion, Ritual, and Art.* Berkeley, Calif.: Periplus, 1989.

Fasseur, C. "De weg naar het paradijs: Nederland en Bali." *Spiegel Historiael* 20 (December 1987): 535–42.

——. *The Politics of Colonial Exploitation: Java, the Dutch and the Cultivation System*. Trans. R. E. Elson and Ary Kral. Ithaca: Cornell Studies on Southeast Asia, 1992.

Feith, Herbert. *The Decline of Constitutional Democracy in Indonesia*. Ithaca: Cornell University Press, 1962.

——. *The 1955 National Election in Indonesia*. Ithaca: Cornell Modern Indonesia Project, 1960.

Finch, Susan, and Daniel Lev. *Republic of Indonesia Cabinets, 1945–1965*. Interim Report Series no. 38. Ithaca: Cornell Modern Indonesia Project, 1965.

Flierhaar, H. ter. "De aanpassing van het inlandsch onderwijs op Bali aan de eigen sfeer." *Koloniale Studien* 25 (March 1941): 135–59.

Franken, H. J. "The Festival of Jayaprana at Kalianget." In *Bali: Studies in Life, Thought and Ritual*, ed. W. F. Wertheim, pp. 233–66. Dordrecht: Foris, 1984.

Friederich, Rudolf Th. A. *The Civilization and Culture of Bali*. Calcutta: Susil Gupta, 1959.

Furnivall, J. S. *Netherlands India: A Study of Plural Economy*. Cambridge: Cambridge University Press, 1944.

Geertz, Clifford. *Negara: The Theater State in Nineteenth-Century Bali*. Princeton: Princeton University Press, 1980.

——. *Peddlers and Princes: Social Development and Economic Change in Two Indonesian Towns*. Chicago: University of Chicago Press, 1963.

Geertz, Hildred. "The Balinese Village." In *Local, Ethnic, and National Loyalties in Village Indonesia: A Symposium*, ed. G. William Skinner, pp. 24–33. New Haven: Yale University Cultural Report Series, 1959.

——. "Ritual and Entertainment: An Analysis of a Topeng Performance." Paper presented at Workshop on Balinese State and Society, KITLV, Leiden, 20–25 April 1986 (photocopy).

——. "A Theatre of Cruelty: The Contexts of a Topeng Performance." In *State and Society in Bali*, ed. H. Geertz, pp. 165–98. Leiden: KITLV Press, 1991.

——, ed. *State and Society in Bali: Historical, Textual and Anthropological Approaches*. Leiden: KITLV Press, 1991.

Geertz, Hildred, and Clifford Geertz. *Kinship in Bali*. Chicago: University of Chicago Press, 1975.

Geunsz, M. van. *Een en ander over Bali en zijne bewoners*. N.P., n.d. Reprinted from *Soerabajasch Handelsblad*, 24, 27, and 29 November and 1, 4, 6, 11, 14, and 17 December 1906.

Gie, Soe Hok. "The Mass Killings in Bali." In *The Indonesian Killings of 1965–1966: Studies From Java and Bali*, ed. Robert Cribb, pp. 252–58. Monash Papers on Southeast Asia, no. 21. Clayton, Victoria, 1990.

Goris, Roelof. *"De strijd over Bali en de zending": De waarde van Dr. Kraemer's boek*. Batavia: Minerva, 1933.

Green, Marshall. *Indonesia: Crisis and Transformation, 1965–1968*. Washington, D.C.: Compass Press, 1990.

Grosvenor, Donna K., and Gilbert Grosvenor. "Bali by the Back Roads." *National Geographic*, November 1969, pp. 667–70.

Hanna, Willard, A. *Bali Profile: People, Events, Circumstances (1001–1976)*. New York: American Universities Field Staff, 1976.

Harvey, Barbara S. *Permesta: Half a Rebellion.* Monograph Series no. 57. Ithaca: Cornell Modern Indonesia Project, 1977.

——. "Tradition, Islam and Rebellion: South Sulawesi, 1950–1965." Ph.D. diss., Cornell University, 1974.

Headquarters of the 16th Army, Java. *Explanations Regarding All Kinds of Armed Bodies.* Nishijima Collection, no. JV.45, Materials on the Japanese Military Administration in Indonesia, Institute of Social Sciences, Waseda University, Tokyo.

Hilbery, Rosemary. *A Balinese Journal, 1971–72.* Southeast Asian Studies Program. Honolulu: University of Hawaii, 1975.

——. *Reminiscences of a Balinese Prince, Tjokorda Gde Agung Sukawati.* Southeast Asia Paper Series no. 14. Honolulu: University of Hawaii, 1979.

Hindley, Donald. *The Communist Party of Indonesia, 1951–1963.* Berkeley: University of California Press, 1964.

Hobart Mark. "Orators and Patrons: Two Types of Political Leader in Balinese Village Society." In *Political Language and Oratory in Traditional Society,* ed. Maurice Block, pp. 65–92. New York: Academic Press, 1975.

——. "Thinker, Thespian, Soldier, Slave? Assumptions about Human Nature in the Study of Balinese Society." In *Context, Meaning, and Power in Southeast Asia,* ed. Mark Hobart and Robert H. Taylor, pp. 131–56. Ithaca: Cornell SEAP Studies on Southeast Asia, 1986.

Hobart, Mark, and Robert H. Taylor, eds. *Context, Meaning, and Power in Southeast Asia.* Ithaca: Cornell SEAP Studies on Southeast Asia, 1986.

Hobsbawm, Eric J. "Peasant Land Occupations." *Past and Present* 62 (February 1974): 120–52.

——. *Social Bandits and Primitive Rebels.* Glencoe, Ill.: Free Press, 1959.

Hobsbawm, Eric J., and T. E. Ranger. *The Invention of Tradition.* Cambridge: Cambridge University Press, 1983.

Hooykas, C. *Religion in Bali.* Leiden: E. J. Brill, 1973.

Hughes, John. *Indonesian Upheaval.* New York: David McKay, 1967.

Hunger, F. W. T. "Adat-desa's en Gouvernements-desa's in Zuid-Bali." *Koloniaal Studien* 26 (1932): 603–16.

——. "Balische deelbouwcontracten gewijzigd also gevolg der huidige crisis." *Koloniale Studien* 27 (April 1933): 174–82.

Ikranegara, M. "G-30-N di Bali." *Suara Muhammadijah* 38, no. 3 (1966): 9–10.

Indisch Genootschap: Jaarvergadering van 28 Mei 1923 [Minutes of the Annual Meeting of the Indisch Genootschap], 23 May 1923, with a speech by H. T. Damsté.

Jacobs, Dr. Julius. *Eenigen tijd onder de Baliers. Eene reisbeschrijving met aanteekeningen betreffende Hygiene, Land en Volkenkunde van de eilanden Bali en Lombok.* Batavia: G. Kolff, 1883.

Java Instituut. *Verslag van het Bali Congres, 18–23 October 1937.* Djokjakarta: Kolff-Buning, 1937.

Junianti. "Peranan Budi Welas Asih Dalam Merintis Ide Nasionalisme di Tabanan, 1937–1942." Thesis, Universitas Udayana, Denpasar, 1982.

Kaaden, W. F. van der. "Geschiedenis van de Bestuursvoering over Bali en Lombok van 1898–1938." *Tropische Nedrland* 11 (1938–39): 203–8, 219–24, 234–40, 253–56, 265–72.

Kadane, Kathy. "US Officials' Lists Aided Indonesian Bloodbath in '60s." *Washington Post,* 21 May 1990.

Kahin, Audrey, ed. *Regional Dynamics of the Indonesian Revolution: Unity from Diversity*. Honolulu: University of Hawaii Press, 1985.

Kahin, George McT. *Nationalism and Revolution in Indonesia*. Ithaca: Cornell University Press, 1970.

Kartodirdjo, Sartono. *Agrarian Unrest and Peasant Mobilization on Java in the 1960s: A Study of Configurations and Conditions*. Institute of Rural and Regional Studies, Occasional Paper Series, no. 8. Yogyakarta: Gadjah Mada University, 1977.

[Kartodirdjo], Soejatno. "Revolution and Social Tensions in Surakarta 1945–1950." Trans. Benedict O'G. Anderson. *Indonesia* 17 (April 1974): 99–112.

Kat Angelino, P. de. "De ambtsvelden en petjatoe-pengajah in Gianjar." *Koloniaal Tijdschrift* 10 (1921): 225–65.

——. "De hygiene, de ziekten en de geneeskunst der Baliers." *Tijdschrift Bataafsche Genootschap* 59 (1920): 209–48.

"Keperloean Onderwijs." *Surya Kanta* 5 (May 1926): 68–69.

Kirk, Donald. "Bali Exorcises an Evil Spirit." *Reporter*, 15 December 1966, pp. 42–53.

Kol, H. H. van. *Driemaal dwars door Sumatra en zwerftochten door Bali*. Rotterdam: W. L. & J. Brusse, 1914.

Korn, V. E. *Het Adatrecht van Bali*. 2d ed. The Hague: G. Naeff, 1932.

Kraan, Alfons van der. "Bali: Slavery and the Slave Trade." In *Slavery, Bondage and Dependency in Southeast Asia*, ed. Anthony Reid, pp. 315–40. Brisbane: University of Queensland Press, 1983.

——. *Lombok: Conquest, Colonization and Underdevelopment, 1870–1940*. Singapore: Heinemann Educational Books (Asia), 1980.

Kraemer, Hendrik. *De strijd over Bali en de zending*. Amsterdam: H. J. Paris, 1933.

——. "Het eenig-toelaatbaar experiment. Bali en de zending." *De Stuw* 3 (1932): 219–23.

Kwantes, R. C., ed. *De ontwikkeling van de nationalistische beweging in Nederlandsche-Indie (1923–1928)*. 12 vols. Groningen: Wolters-Noordhoff, 1978.

Lane, Max, "Wedastera Suyasa in Balinese Politics, 1962–72: From Charismatic Politics to Socio-Educational Activities." B.A. thesis, Sydney University, 1972.

Last, Jef. *Bali in de Kentering*. Amsterdam: De Bezige Bij, 1955.

Legge, J. D. *Sukarno: A Political Biography*. Sydney: Allen & Unwin, 1990.

Legiun Veteran Republik Indonesia, Markas Cabang Gianyar. *Patah Tumbuh Hilang Berganti: Kumpulan Riwayat Hidup Pahlawan P.K.R.I. Gianyar*. Denpasar: Percetakan Bali, 1979.

Legiun Veteran Republik Indonesia, Markas Cabang Tabanan. *Geguritan Wiracarita Puputan Margarana*. Tabanan, 1977.

Lekkerkerker, C. "De tegenwoordige economische toestand van het geweest Bali en Lombok." *Koloniaal Tijdschrift* 12 (1923): 153–210.

——. "Dreieerlei visie op het Balische zendings vraagstuk." *Koloniaal Tijdschrift* 22 (1933): 343–58.

Lev, Daniel S. "Indonesia 1965: The Year of the Coup." *Asian Survey* 6 (February 1966): 103–10.

——. *The Transition to Guided Democracy: Indonesian Politics, 1957–1959*. Ithaca: Cornell Modern Indonesia Project, 1966.

Liefrinck, F. A. *Bali en Lombok*. Amsterdam: J. H. de Bussy, 1927.

Liefrinck, F. A., and H. J. E. F. Schwartz. "Dagverhaal van eene reis van den Resident van Bali en Lombok vergezeld van den Controleur voor de Politieke Aanrakingen en de Poenggawa's Ida Bagoes Gelgel en Goesti Ktoet Djlantik naar Tabanan en Badoeng van 17 Juli t/m 5 Augustus 1899." *Tijdschrift voor Taal-, Land- en Volkenkunde* 43 (1901): 132–58.

Mackie, J. A. C. *Problems of the Indonesian Inflation.* Interim Report Series no. 42. Ithaca: Cornell Modern Indonesia Project, 1967.

Mathews, Anna. *The Night of Purnama.* Kuala Lumpur: Oxford University Press, 1983.

May, Brian. *The Indonesian Tragedy.* London: Routledge & Kegan Paul, 1978.

McMahon, Robert J. *Colonialism and Cold War: The United States and the Struggle for Indonesian Independence, 1945–1949.* Ithaca: Cornell University Press, 1981.

McPhee, Colin. *A House in Bali.* New York: Oxford University Press, 1985.

McVey, Ruth. "The Post-Revolutionary Transformation of the Indonesian Army." Pts. 1 and 2. *Indonesia* 11 (April 1971): 157–76; 13 (April 1972): 147–82.

——, ed. *Southeast Asian Transitions: Approaches through Social History.* New Haven: Yale University Press, 1978.

Mead, Margaret. "The Arts in Bali." In *Traditional Balinese Culture,* ed. Jane Belo, pp. 331–40. New York: Columbia University Press, 1970.

——. "Community Drama, Bali and America." In *Traditional Balinese Culture,* ed. Jane Belo, pp. 341–49. New York: Columbia University Press, 1970.

[Medhurst, Dr.]. *Journal of a Tour along the Coast of Java and Bali and with a Short Account of the Island of Bali, Particularly Bali Baliling.* Singapore: Mission Press, 1830.

Mellor, Bridget. "Political Killings in Indonesia." *New Statesman,* 5 August 1966.

Mortimer, Rex. "Class, Social Cleavage and Indonesian Communism." *Indonesia* 8 (October 1969): 1–20.

——. *Indonesian Communism under Sukarno: Ideology and Politics, 1959–1965.* Ithaca: Cornell University Press, 1974.

——. *The Indonesian Communist Party and Land Reform, 1959–1965.* Clayton, Victoria: Centre for Southeast Asian Studies, Monash University, 1972.

Moser, Don. "Where the Rivers Ran Crimson from Butchery." *Life,* 1 July 1966.

Mountbatten of Burma, Vice-Admiral the Earl. *Post-Surrender Tasks: Section E of the Report to the Combined Chiefs of Staff by the Supreme Commander, Southeast Asia, 1943–1945.* London: H.M. Stationery Office, 1969.

Netja, Made. *Pemeriksaan Agronomi Dalam Distrik Tedjakula 1949–1950.* Singaraja, 1951.

"Ngaben di Bali." *Surya Kanta* 9/10 (September/October 1926): 141–42.

Nieuwenkamp, W. O. J. *Leven en Werken, Bouwen & Zwerven van de Kunstenaar W. O. J. Nieuwenkamp.* Utrecht: A. W. Bruna, n.d.

Notosusanto, Nugroho, and Ismail Saleh. *The Coup Attempt of the "September 30 Movement" in Indonesia.* Jakarta, 1968.

O.S.S. Research and Analysis Branch. *Programs of the Japanese Government in Java and Bali.* Honolulu, 1945.

Padmawati, Ni Putu. "Pertumbuhan Perkoempoelan Shanti di Singaraja Antara Tahun 1921–1924." Thesis, Universitas Udayana, Denpasar, 1982.

Paerels, B. H. "Bevolkings koffie cultuur." In *De Landbouw in de Indische Archipel* vol. 2B, ed. Dr. C. J. J. van Hall and C. van de Koppel, pp. 89–119. The Hague: van Hoeve, 1946.

Palmier, Leslie. *Communists in Indonesia, Power Pursued in Vain.* New York: Doubleday, 1973.

Pancarwati, Ni Made. "Bali Pada Masa Zelfbestuur." Thesis, Universitas Udayana, Denpasar, 1984.

Partai Nasionalis Indonesia [PNI], Dewan Daerah Bali. *Ketegangan Kegawatan Kekatjauan Akibat: Ketiadaan Kepimpinan Gubernur Kepala Daerah Bali, A.A. Bagus Suteja.* N.p., March 1965.

Pauker, Guy. "Political Consequences of Rural Development Programs in Indonesia." *Pacific Affairs* 41 (Fall 1968): 386–402.

"Pemoeda-pemoeda Bali jang akan mendjadi bibit di tanah itoe dengan Osvia." *Surya Kanta* 3/4 (March/April 1927): 33–34.

Pendit, Njoman S. *Bali Berdjuang.* Denpasar: Jajasan Kebaktian Pedjuang, 1954.

———. *Bali Berjuang.* 2d ed. Jakarta: Gunung Agung, 1979.

"Pengadilan." *Surya Kanta* 3/4 (March/April 1927): 26–27.

"Perhatikanlah." *Bali Adnyana* 16 (June 1926): 5–6.

Pindha, I Gusti Ngurah. *Kirikumi Besar2an Terhadap Kota Denpasar.* Serie Gempilan Perjuangan Physic di Bali, no. 1. [Denpasar], 1973.

Pluvier, Jan. *Indonesie, kolonialisme, onafhankelijkheid, neokolonialisme: Een politieke geschiedenis van 1940 tot heden,* Nijmegen: Socialistische Uitgeverij, 1978.

"Poelau Bali Akan Kombali Mendjadi Bali." *Bali Adnyana* 19 (August 1929): 1–2.

Poeze, Harry A. *Politieke-politionele overzichten van Nederlandsch-Indie,* vol. 2. The Hague: Nijhoff, 1982.

Poffenberger, Mark, and Mary S. Zurbuchen. "The Economics of Village Bali: Three Perspectives." *Economic Development and Cultural Change* 29 (October 1981): 91–103.

Pollmann, Tessel. "Margaret Mead's Balinese: The Fitting Symbols of the American Dream." *Indonesia* 49 (April 1990): 1–36.

Powell, Hickman. *Bali: The Last Paradise.* New York: Dodd, Mead, 1930.

Putra, Ida Bagus Gde. "Pelaksanaan Landreform dan Keresahan Masyarakat di Kabupaten Karangasem (1960–1965)." Thesis, Universitas Udayana, Denpasar, 1986.

Putra, I Gusti Ngurah. "Masa Pendudukan Jepang di Bali." Thesis, Universitas Udayana, Denpasar, 1977.

Raffles, Thomas Stamford. *The History of Java.* 2 vols. London: Black, Parbury & Allen, 1817.

Rai, I Gusti Ngurah. "Pengaruh Pendidikan Pada Masa Pendudukan Jepang di Singaraja Tahun 1942 Sampai Tahun 1945." Thesis, Universitas Udayana, Denpasar, 1982.

Raka, I Gusti Gde. *Monografi Pulau Bali.* Jakarta: Jawatan Pertanian Rakyat, 1955.

Reid, Anthony J. S., ed. *Slavery, Bondage, and Dependency in Southeast Asia.* Brisbane: University of Queensland Press, 1983.

Reid, Anthony, and Lance Castles, eds. *Pre-colonial State Systems in Southeast Asia: The Malay Peninsula, Sumatra, Bali-Lombok, South Celebes.* Monographs of the Malaysian Branch of the Royal Asiatic Society no. 6. Kuala Lumpur, 1975.

Reken, I Wayan. "A History of Djembrana from the 18th Century." Manuscript.

Reksodihardjo, Sarimin. *Memorie Penjerahan Gubernur Kepala Daerah Propinsi Nusa Tenggara (1 April 52–30 March 1957).* 2 vols. [Singaraja], 1957.

Robinson, Geoffrey. "The Economic Foundations of Political Conflict in Bali, 1950–1965." *Indonesia* 54 (October 1992): 59–93.

———. "Some Arguments Concerning U.S. Influence and Complicity in the Indonesian 'Coup' of October 1, 1965." Manuscript, 1984.

——. "State, Society and Political Conflict in Bali, 1945–1946." *Indonesia* 45 (April 1988): 1–48.

Rocamora, J. Eliseo. "Nationalism in Search of an Ideology: Indonesia's Nationalist Party, 1946–1965." Ph.D. diss., Cornell University, 1974.

——. *PNI 1963–1965, Menyingkap Kehidupan Sebuah Partai Politik di Indonesia.* Yogyakarta: C. V. Kaliwangi, 1985.

Sarwa, I Nyoman. "Pergolakan Sosial-Politik di Bali Sejak Pemilihan Umum, 1955–1965." Thesis, Universitas Udayana, Denpasar, 1985.

Schiller, A. Arthur. *The Formation of Federal Indonesia, 1945–1949.* The Hague: van Hoeve, 1955.

Schulte Nordholt, H. *Bali: Colonial Conceptions and Political Change 1700–1940. From Shifting Hierarchies to "Fixed Order."* Comparative Asian Studies Program (CASP) Paper no. 15. Rotterdam, 1986.

——. "Een Balische Dynastie: Hierarchie en Conflict in de Negara Mengwi, 1700–1940." Ph.D. diss., Vrij Universiteit te Amsterdam, 1988.

——. *Macht, mensen en middelen: Patronen van dynamiek in de Balische politiek, 1700–1840.* Amsterdam, 1980.

——. "Paradox, Contradictie, Crisis: Koloniale beeldvorming en politiek conflict in Bali." Typescript, August 1985.

Schwartz, H. J. E. F. "Aanteekening omtrent het landschap Gianjar." *Tijdschrift voor het Binnenlands Bestuur* 19, no. 3 (1900): 166–89.

——. "Dagverhaal van eene reis van den Resident van Bali en Lombok, vergezeld van den Controleur voor de Politieke Aangelegenheden en de Poenggawa's Ida Njoman Bandjar en Goesti Njoman Raka naar Karangasem en Kloengkoeng van 11 t/m 26 April 1898." *Tijdschrift voor Indische Taal-, Land- en Volkenkunde* 43 (1901): 108–23.

——. "Rapport van de reis van den Controleur Schwartz naar Bangli." Singaraja, 1899.

Scott, Peter Dale. "The United States and the Overthrow of Sukarno, 1965–1967." *Pacific Affairs* 58 (Summer 1985): 239–64.

Simpen, I. Wayan. *Sejarah Bali.* Denpasar: Balimas, 1958.

Sjahrir, Soetan. *Out of Exile.* Trans. Charles Wolf, Jr. New York: John Day, 1949.

Slamet, Ina. "Views and Strategies of the Indonesian Peasant Movement on the Eve of Its Annihilation in 1965–1966." Manuscript, 1988.

"Statistics on Bali and Lombok." Nishijima Collection, Materials on the Japanese Military Administration in Indonesia, Institute of Social Sciences, Waseda University, Tokyo.

Stein Callenfels, P. V. van "De rechten der vorsten op Bali." *Indonesie* 1 (1947–48): 193–208.

Stevens, J. A. *Vrij: Een verzameling foto's uit Indie van den foto-journalist van den Marine-Voorlichtingsdienst.* Deventer: R. Borst, n.d.

Stuart-Fox, David J. "Pura Besakih: Changes in Temple-State Relations from Pre-Colonial to Modern Times." Paper presented at Workshop on Balinese State and Society, KITLV, Leiden, 21–24 April 1986.

Suarma, I Made. "Peranan Djembrana Dalam Revolusi Phisik." Thesis, Universitas Udayana, Denpasar, 1971.

Sudirdjo, Radik Utojo, ed. *Album Perang Kemerdekaan 1945–50.* Jakarta: Badan Penerbit Almanak Indonesia, 1981.

Sukarniti, Ni Luh Ketut. "Perkembangan Parindra di Bali, 1938–1942." Thesis, Universitas Udayana, Denpasar, 1985.

"Surya Kanta Pengroesak Keamanan Tjatoerwangsa." *Bali Adnyana* 7 (March 1928): 1.

Swellengrebel, J. L. *Kerk en tempel op Bali.* The Hague: van Hoeve, 1948.

Teitler, G., and P. M. H. Groen, eds. *De Politionele Acties.* 2d ed. Amsterdam: De Bataafsche Leeuw, 1988.

Tekeja, I Wayan. "Revolusi Physik di Kabupaten Badung, 1945–1949." Thesis, Universitas Udayana, Denpasar, 1973.

Tjondronegoro, Dharmawan. *Ledakan Fitnah Subversi G-30-S.* Jakarta: Matoa, 1966.

Universitas Gajah Mada, Pusat Penelitian den Studi Pedesaan dan Kawasan. *Keresahan Pedesaan Pada Tahun 1960-an.* Yogyakarta, 1982.

Utrecht, Ernst. "Het bloedbad op Bali." *De Groene Amsterdammer,* 14 January 1967.

———. "Land Reform in Indonesia." *Bulletin of Indonesian Economic Studies* 3 (November 1969): 71–88.

———. "Massamoord in het paradijs." *De Groene Amsterdammer,* 1 January 1967.

———. *Sejarah Hukum Internasional di Bali dan Lombok.* Bandung: Penerbitan Sumur Bandung, 1962.

UUPA dan Landreform: Beberapa Undang Undang Dan Peraturan Hukum Tanah. Surabaya: Karya Bhakti, 1984.

Vatikiotis, Michael, and Mike Fonte. "Rustle of Ghosts." *Far Eastern Economic Review,* 2 August 1990.

Veer, Paul van 't. "Bali zuivert zich zelf na gruwelijke moordgolf." *Vrijuit* (weekend ed. of *Het Vrijevolk*), 17 December 1966.

Vickers, Adrian. *Bali: A Paradise Created.* Victoria: Penguin, 1989.

Vink, G. J. "Over de koffiecultuur der Baliers." *Tijdschrift Landbouw* 5 (1929–30): 1–75.

Visman, F. H. "Herstel van zelfbesturen." *Koloniale Studien* 12 (1928): 103–36.

Vlijman, B. R. F. van. *Bali 1868: Eene bladzijde der Indische krijgsgeschiedenis.* Amsterdam: J. C. Loman Jr., 1875.

Wal, S. L. van der (with P. J. Drooglever and M. J. B. Schouten), ed. *Officiële Bescheiden Betreffende de Nederlands-Indonesische Betrekkingen, 1945–1950.* 12 vols. The Hague: Nijhoff, 1971–84.

Warren, Carol. "Adat and Dinas: Village and State in Contemporary Bali." In *State and Society in Bali,* ed. Hildred Geertz, pp. 213–50. Leiden: KITLV Press, 1991.

———. "Balinese Political Culture and the Rhetoric of National Development." In *Creating Indonesian Cultures,* ed. Paul Alexander, pp. 39–54. Sydney: Oceania Ethnographies, 1989.

Wartama, I Ketut. "Sedjarah Perkembangan Djembrana Sampai Timbulnya Daerah Kabupaten." Thesis, Universitas Udayana, Denpasar, 1972.

Webb, Paul. "The Sickle and the Cross: Christians and Communists in Bali, Flores, Sumba, and Timor, 1965–67." *Journal of Southeast Asia Studies* 17 (March 1986): 94–112.

Wehl, David. *The Birth of Indonesia.* London: Allen & Unwin, 1948.

Weitzel, Kapt. A. W. P. *De derde militaire expeditie naar het eiland Bali in 1849.* Gorinchem: J. Noorduyn, 1859.

Wertheim, W. F. "Bloed zonder tranen." *De Groene Amsterdammer,* 1 October 1966.

———. "De dood van de communisten." *De Groene Amsterdammer,* 8 October 1966.

——. "From Aliran Towards Class Struggle in the Countryside of Java." *Pacific Viewpoint* 10 (1969): 1–17.

——. "Klassenstrijd op het kapmes." *De Groene Amsterdammer,* 15 October 1966.

——. "Suharto and the Untung Coup—The Missing Link," *Journal of Contemporary Asia* 1 (Winter 1970): 50–57.

——, ed. *Bali: Studies in Life, Thought and Ritual.* KITLV Reprints on Indonesia. Dordrecht: Foris, 1984.

Wija Kusuma, Made, Ketut Wijana, and Ida Bagus Indera. "Laporan Mengenai Penurunan MBO DPRI Sunda Kecil Tanggal 24 Mei 1948." Typescript. Denpasar, February 1987.

Wines, Michael. "CIA Tie Asserted in Indonesia Purge." *New York Times,* 12 July 1990.

Wirata, I Gusti Putu. "Pergerakan Taman Siswa di Bali, Tahun 1933 Sampai Tahun 1943." Thesis, Universitas Udayana, Denpasar, 1971.

Wirata, I. Ketut. "Revolusi Phisik Daerah Kabupaten Buleleng." Thesis, Universitas Udayana Denpasar, 1972.

Yayasan Kebaktian Proklamasi [Bali]. "Daftar Pahlawan Pejuang Kemerdekaan R.I. Daerah Tingkat I Propinsi Bali, Gugur Antara Tahun 1945 s/d 1950." Photocopy, n.d.

Index

Muhammadiyah, 287
Murjani, 47–48
Muzakkar, Lt. Col. Kahar, 222, 224

Nasakom, 208, 211, 230
Nasution, Gen. A. H., 230, 283–84
Nationalism, Indonesian:
  Dutch response to, 36–42
  under Dutch rule, 47–50, 99, 113n
  under Japanese rule, 85–90
  Islam and, 39–42
  See also National Revolution; Republican
  movement
Nationalist party. *See* PNI
National Revolution (1945–49), 95–128,
  147–80
  and caste issues, 107–10, 172n
  casualties in, 15, 96, 136, 156
  character of states and, 114–28, 147–48,
  178–80
  as civil war, 97, 137–42, 146, 178
  cultural politics during, 142–46
  and Dutch military strategy, 7, 15, 132–
  37, 145–46
  nature and roots of, 15, 95–97, 99–114
  and postindependence political struggles,
  189–95, 216
  puri rivalries and, 99–107
  scholarly study of, 3, 15–16
  See also MBU-DPRI; Military, Dutch;
  Military, Indonesian; Nationalism,
  Indonesian; Republican movement
Natural disasters, 18, 239–41, 254
Nefis (Netherlands Forces Intelligence
  Service), 95, 129, 131, 220
NICA (Netherlands Indies Civil
  Administration), 119n, 169, 181
NIT (Negara Indonesia Timor):
  collapse of (1949–50), 183
  establishment of, 148, 151–52
  and "family government" in Bali, 169–80
  after Renville Agreement, 156–60
  and "surrender" of May 1948, 162–63
  See also Agung, Anak Agung Gde
Nurai, 158, 162, 163n, 165, 225n

Oka, Anak Agung Gde, 171n, 172–73,
  177, 192, 204, 222. *See also* Council of
  Rajas; Puri Agung Gianyar; Raja of
  Gianyar
Oka, Ida Bagus, 300
Oka, I Gusti Bagus, 116n, 151n, 153n
Opium, 25, 54

PADI (Partai Demokrat Indonesia), 165
Paramilitary bodies:
  anti-Republican (1945–49), 101, 103–4,
  123n, 124, 151, 171–72
  under Japanese, 87–92

and postcoup massacre, 219, 234, 278,
  281, 287, 300, 310
postindependence, 219, 224–29, 234,
  278, 281, 287, 300, 310
See also LOGIS; Peta
Parindra (Partij Indonesia Raya), 47–49, 91
Parrindo (Partai Rakyat Indonesia), 152–53,
  165, 192n
Partai Buruh Indonesia, 237, 242
Partindo (Partai Indonesia), 211, 214–16,
  248
Paruman Agung, 73–74, 121–22, 152, 159,
  174, 191–93
Paruman Negara, 121n, 152
Pauker, Guy, 276
PDRI (Pemerintah Daururat Republik
  Indonesia), 157–58, 195, 220, 222–24,
  226
Pegeg, Nyoman, 90n, 101n, 108, 171n,
  201n, 202n
Pemuda:
  under Japanese rule, 85, 87, 90–94
  in National Revolution, 110, 114–18,
  120–21, 144, 150, 153, 169
  and politics (1950–65), 174, 189–91,
  193, 195, 199–200, 210–11
  See also MBU-DPRI; PDRI
Pencak silat, 48, 87, 91, 166
Pendit, Nyoman, 72n, 154, 181
Permesta rebellion, 182, 230–31, 244
Pesindo (Pemuda Sosialis Indonesia), 93,
  108, 110, 115, 149
Peta (Pembela Tanah Air), 87–92
Petani (Petani Nasionalis Indonesia). *See*
  Land reform; PNI
PGSI (Pasukan Gerilya Seluruh Indonesia),
  224–25
Pidada, Ida Bagus, 104n, 153n, 201n
PKI (Partai Komunis Indonesia), 209–11
  class and caste character of, 259–63, 271
  election results of, 8, 194, 196, 214–16,
  242
  and land reform, 16–18, 253–55, 262–
  63, 264–71
  military opposition to, 230
  and police, 226–27
  position of, in local state, 212–13
  and postcoup massacre, 275–86,
  292–303
  and Sukarno, 209–10
  and religion, 18, 211
PNI (Partai Nasionalis Indonesia), 205–9
  and capitalist class, 247–48
  class character of, 259–63, 271
  election results of, 8, 194, 196, 214–16
  and land reform, 265–71
  and military and police, 206, 226, 232
  and postcoup massacre, 287–88, 291,
  294, 299–302

Asia East by South

A series published under the auspices of
the Southeast Asia Program, Cornell University

Cambodian Culture since 1975: Homeland and Exile
edited by May M. Ebihara, Carol A. Mortland, and Judy Ledgerwood

Southeast Asia in the Early Modern Era: Trade, Power, and Belief
edited by Anthony Reid

The Dark Side of Paradise: Political Violence in Bali
by Geoffrey Robinson

*Opium to Java: Revenue Farming and Chinese Enterprise in Colonial
Indonesia, 1860–1910*
by James R. Rush

An Age in Motion: Popular Radicalism in Java, 1912–1926
by Takashi Shiraishi

Opium and Empire: Chinese Society in Colonial Singapore, 1800–1910
by Carl A. Trocki